Firms, Markets, and Hierarchies

FIRMS, MARKETS, AND HIERARCHIES

The Transaction Cost Economics Perspective

edited by

Glenn R. Carroll and David J. Teece

New York   Oxford
Oxford University Press
1999

Oxford University Press

Oxford   New York

Athens   Auckland   Bangkok   Bogotá   Buenos Aires   Calcutta
Cape Town   Chennai   Dar es Salaam   Delhi   Florence   Hong Kong   Istanbul
Karachi   Kuala Lumpur   Madrid   Melbourne   Mexico City   Mumbai
Nairobi   Paris   São Paulo   Singapore   Taipei   Tokyo   Toronto   Warsaw

and associated companies in
Berlin   Ibadan

Library of Congress Cataloging-in-Publication Data

Firms, markets, and hierarchies : the transaction cost economics
perspective / edited by Glenn R. Carroll and David J. Teece.
p.   cm.
"This book represents the outgrowth of a conference organized for
the Haas School of Business and the Institute of Management,
Innovation and Organization at the
University of California, Berkeley"—Pref.
Includes index.
ISBN 0-19-511951-7
1. Industrial organization (Economic theory)—Congresses.
2. Industrial management—Congresses.   3. Trusts, Industrial—
Congresses.   4. Institutional economics—Congresses.
5. Williamson, Oliver E. Markets and hierarchies, analysis and
antitrust implications—Congresses.   I. Carroll, Glenn.
II. Teece, David J.
HD2326.F548   1998
338.7—dc21   98-11411

Coventry University

1 3 5 7 9 8 6 4 2

Printed in the United States of America
on acid-free paper

To Olly,
with admiration and affection

Foreword

An increasing theme of modern economics, on which a large number of the variations have been composed by Oliver Williamson, is the role of nonmarket mechanisms in the operation of the market. It is not merely that many transactions take place without the intervention of the market mechanism: love, gifts, taxes, transfers, and regulation. It is more that the nonmarket mechanisms are essential to the workings of the market. Any standard economic theory, not only the neoclassical, starts from the existence of firms. Usually, the firm is a point or at any rate a black box. There are inputs and outputs, a production possibility set, and a motive—maximization of profits (possibly in some sophisticated form that takes account of uncertainty and the future).

But firms are palpably not points. They have internal structure. This internal structure must arise for some reason. Within the firm, there is necessarily a greater or lesser degree of decentralization of decision making, which must be regulated for efficiency in the same sense that prices regulate efficiency in competitive markets. The allocation within firms is not based on anything like markets (with the mild exception of transfer prices, which have as much to do with tax minimization as they do with achieving internal efficiency). Rather the within-firm allocation is authoritative and hierarchical, as Williamson puts it. It is very much a form of politics, not a form of economic behavior as portrayed in standard textbook theory. (Perhaps I shouldn't refer so assuredly to textbooks; by now much of the New Institutional Economics has penetrated even that backward corner of learning.) It may be based on rational considerations, but the opportunity and need for some bounded rationality are even more prominent than they are in a perfectly competitive market, where the consequences of decisions are measured by apparently simple formulas.

Why the firm finds a hierarchical structure preferable to market transactions, say by breaking up into parts, is too long a story to be referred to here. The analysis was adumbrated by Ronald Coase and developed with rich detail and application by Oliver Williamson and, more recently, Paul Milgrom and John Roberts. But one of the consequences of the study has been to shift the emphasis in economic research. Where the standard paradigm emphasizes resource allocation and perhaps degree of utilization of factors, the newer analysis asks different questions, though it also discusses the old ones. Why did economic institutions (firms and other organizations) evolve the way they did? What is the detailed structure (the "nanoeconomics," one level more detailed than conventional microeconomics) of firms and other institutions and how has it responded to external stimuli? To some extent, indeed, the New Institutional Economics, like the old institutional economics of Thorstein Veblen, John R. Commons, and Wesley Mitchell, merges into economic history, but an economic history with a strong analytic bent, as in the work of Douglass North.

This volume contains many studies built around the institutional paradigm — in particular, the book by Oliver Williamson, *Markets and Hierarchies*, now twenty years old. The present volume shows the vitality of the field and the breadth of its interests. It is an appropriate tribute to Williamson's innovative scholarship and intellectual leadership, as well as a mark of how warm the feelings about him are.

Kenneth J. Arrow

Preface

This book represents the outgrowth of a conference we organized for the Haas School of Business and the Institute of Management, Innovation and Organization at the University of California at Berkeley. The conference was designed to accomplish three major goals. First, we wished to celebrate the twentieth anniversary of the publication of Oliver Williamson's book, *Markets and Hierarchies: Analysis and Antitrust Implications.* This landmark contribution laid out a way of thinking—transaction cost reasoning—that spurred much new and important research in a wide variety of social science areas; it deserved another round of applause, in our view. Second, we wanted to assess the state of organizational studies as an interdisciplinary field, especially as it has developed between economics and sociology. This goal was closely connected to the first because, despite its pervasive influence, *Markets and Hierarchies* was, above all, about organization. It also was largely responsible for the interdisciplinary dialogue that has developed and flourished between certain economists and sociologists. Third, we hoped that the papers written for the conference would constitute, in and of themselves, important new contributions to theory and research on organizations and other institutional phenomena. We did not want simple review papers that covered old ground; we wanted papers that used, developed, and criticized the transaction cost approach, as well as some that showed new possibilities by drawing on compatible work from other areas. Accordingly, we chose the same title for the conference as for this book because we felt that much of the more interesting work in this area dealt specifically with business firms—with their strategies, structures, behavior, and performance.

We were gratified by the overwhelmingly positive response we received from those social scientists we invited to write papers and to attend the conference. It seemed that our desire to recognize *Markets and Hierarchies* and to reckon with its aftermath struck a resonant chord among even the most distinguished social scientists in the various disciplines. It was also obvious that there was no shortage of goodwill in the social science community for Oliver Williamson, a man who had clearly won both the intellectual and personal respect of his colleagues around the world.

The conference was a rousing success. The papers presented there were published in a special issue of the journal *Industrial and Corporate Change* (vol. 5, no. 2, 1996). Many (but not all) of them are presented here. At the suggestion of Oxford University Press reviewers, this volume was designed to have greater focus on Williamson's work and the transaction cost approach. That meant making it a condensed intellectual history lesson where the point is not so much the facts of the history (which are recounted in other places) but an understanding of how we got to where we are now intellectually and some hints as to where we might best try to go next in order to advance the research enterprise. Such a lesson should contain praise for past achievements, but it should also not be afraid to criticize, to modify, and to search in totally new directions.

Our efforts to compile this lesson as a book consisted of first assembling a core set of background materials for Williamson's version of transaction cost economics. With help from Oxford's reviewers, we then selected and organized thematically those conference papers that fit most squarely into our lesson plan (and, unfortunately, in a process known well by all instructors, we were also forced to omit other excellent papers that did not fit so neatly). Finally, we solicited some new material in order to fill the gaps and round out the lesson into a coherent whole.

Of course, readers will judge for themselves whether our lesson is effective. The book cannot be faulted, however, for a lack of diversity or intellectual talent. The various chapters include contributions by leading figures on a wide range of social science topics including organizations, regulations and law, institutions, strategic management, game theory, entrepreneurship, innovation, finance, and technical information. The interdisciplinary nature of these chapters is evidenced by their combined reference lists, which span the literatures of economics and sociology, as well as political science, strategic management, and organizational behavior. More important, many of the chapters reflect the serious and respectful exchange across disciplines on topics about organizations and institutions that has often developed since publication of *Markets and Hierarchies.*

Above all, we wish to thank the chapter authors for their contributions because without them there would be no book. We are also grateful to the conference discussants and participants, whose questions and comments helped the authors improve the final versions of their chapters. Major funding came from the Institute of Management, Innovation and Organization at Berkeley, as well as the Mitsubishi Bank Chair of International Business and Finance. Dean William Hasler of the Haas School provided supplemental financial assistance that allowed us to do things right, both at the conference and later in the publication process. Patricia Murphy and her able staff at the Institute of Management, Innovation and Organization put together all the many events, activities, and papers in a flawless demonstration of organizational competence. Giovanni Dosi aided us enormously in the editorial process. Josef Chytry, managing editor of *Industrial and Corporate Change*, gave us terrific and timely assistance in the publication efforts. Kyle Mayer assisted with the publication process. And Herb Addison of Oxford University Press supported the project from its inception and guided us as we attempted to make our history lesson plan a reality. Thanks to all!

Berkeley, California   G. R. C.
November 1997   D. J. T.

Contents

PART II   Conceptual Uses

PART III   Industrial Applications

PART IV Microanalytics

Contributors

Kenneth J. Arrow, Stanford University

James N. Baron, Stanford University

M. Diane Burton, Harvard University

Glenn R. Carroll, University of California at Berkeley

John M. de Figueiredo, Massachusetts Institute of Technology

Avner Greif, Stanford University

Michael T. Hannan, Stanford University

Bengt Holmström, Massachusetts Institute of Technology

Paul L. Joskow, Massachusetts Institute of Technology

Peter G. Klein, University of Georgia

David M. Kreps, Stanford University

Scott E. Masten, University of Michigan

Roberta Romano, Yale University

Howard A. Shelanski, University of California at Berkeley

Pablo T. Spiller, University of California at Berkeley

David J. Teece, University of California at Berkeley

Albert C. Y. Teo, National University of Singapore

Oliver E. Williamson, University of California at Berkeley

Firms, Markets, and Hierarchies

CHAPTER ONE

Firms, Markets, and Hierarchies
Introduction and Overview

GLENN R. CARROLL AND DAVID J. TEECE

This book is about transaction cost analysis, a major theoretical perspective of the social sciences. Transaction cost analysis originated in economics with several seminal articles by Ronald Coase, for which he was awarded the Nobel Prize. The perspective has since broadened its base and now envelops all the social sciences and addresses a variety of research questions not previously considered the purview of economic theory. It is perhaps the single most influential theory found in the social sciences.

A great deal of the responsibility for the widespread influence and popularity of transaction cost economics lies with Oliver E. Williamson.[1] His 1975 book, *Markets and Hierarchies: Analysis and Antitrust Implications*, gave new life to the theory and attracted enormous interest among all kinds of social scientists. As a result of this book, transaction cost analysis suddenly seemed relevant and compelling for addressing a whole host of research questions and policy issues ranging from organizational design to law to the international normative order. Williamson's subsequent efforts, represented in numerous articles as well as the books *The Economic Institutions of Capitalism* and *The Mechanisms of Governance*, developed the perspective to a fuller extent and demonstrated its continued applicability to a wide range of phenomena. Informed criticism has also helped to make transaction cost economics a huge success story for the social sciences.

Success in science is often short-lived. What are new and exciting ideas at one point in time become received wisdom at a later point. Periodic stock-taking gives scientists a chance to look beyond their current study or next study, to see where they have been, to gauge where they are headed, and to make readjustments when appropriate. This book represents a stocktaking exercise around transaction cost economics—its general conceptual orientation, its specific theoretical propositions, its applications to policy and practice, and its use in systematic empirical research.

---

[1] Citation counts give a good indication of a scientist's influence in a field. Using the Social Science Citation Index, we found 5,393 citations to Williamson's work in the period from 1991 to September 1996.

We chose to review and contemplate transaction cost economics because it has reached a milestone in that *Markets and Hierarchies* was published just over twenty years ago. In the interim, economics and the other social sciences have changed considerably. Have these changes, some of them prompted by transaction cost economics, rendered the theory less compelling? Conversely, can transaction cost theory and research be strengthened by drawing on insights and developments that were not present in its foundation period? These are the kinds of questions that we believe are appropriate at this point.

Given the range and breadth of transaction cost analysis, very few social scientists would be capable of making such an assessment single-handedly. Our alternative strategy involved two tacks. First, we sought to assemble a set of important papers from and about transaction cost theory and research. These involved classic original texts, as well as reflective reviews and commentaries. Second, we asked a group of highly renowned experts to write new papers about transaction cost economics and related matters. We did not seek simple review papers but rather papers that used, developed, and criticized the transaction cost approach, as well as some that hinted at potential new developments by relying on compatible work from other areas.

The book is organized into parts, defined by the types of articles each contains. Part I contains background chapters that describe and review the origins and development of transaction cost economics. Part II is devoted to conceptual uses of the perspective. Part III contains industrial applications of transaction cost theory. Part IV is about microanalytics.

1. *Background*

The five chapters in Part I provide a broad overview of contemporary theory and research on transaction cost economics. As a set, the chapters are intended to be informative about the specific accomplishments of those theorists and researchers working within the transaction cost perspective. Part I is also intended to give a sense of the enormous impact the perspective has had—both directly and indirectly—on relevant social science areas.

"The Vertical Integration of Production: Market Failure Considerations" by Oliver Williamson was originally published in 1971 in the *American Economic Review* and is now rightfully regarded as a classic. It was the first extended use of transaction cost reasoning by Williamson, and it started development of the theory using what was to become a touchstone problem—the relative efficiency advantages of internal production over the market under certain specified conditions. According to Masten in Chapter 4, Williamson in this article "previewed many of the arguments later to become cornerstones of the comparative institutional framework." It is indeed interesting to see now how much of later developments is presaged in this early article.

The short retrospective commentary, "Some Reflections," was written by Williamson recently when we asked him to reflect on the 1971 article. Williamson notes the origins of his thinking about vertical integration in both the academic (through exposure to Ronald Coase's work in graduate school) and policy worlds (through his own position at the U.S. Department of Justice's Antitrust Division). Noting his frustration with the prevailing theories and the lack of appealing alternatives, he tells us that it was only later, when he returned to university teaching, that he saw a new way to conceptualize the problem. This new way took form initially in the 1971 article, where Williamson says that he posed the question as, When and in what ways does internal organization serve to mitigate contractual hazards that would otherwise be posed by market procurement? The commentary lists some of the many insights that this viewpoint yielded.

"About Oliver E. Williamson" is a review and analysis by Scott E. Masten of the influence and contributions of Williamson to economic theory and economics generally. As Masten notes, "no one has more consistently and steadfastly pursued . . . inquiry [of New Institutional Economics] than Oliver Williamson." The "crowning professional achievement" of Williamson is the development of transaction costs economics. Although this theory was initially advanced by Ronald Coase, it was Williamson—Masten recounts—who rescued it from obscurity and irrelevance by operationalizing the theory and "giving . . . [it] predictive content." Masten traces the intellectual history of the theory's development and makes incisive analytical observations along the way. His review covers the foundations of the theory, the impact on the theory of the firm, the theory's applications and extensions, and its reception and influence in economics and elsewhere in the social sciences.

"Transaction Cost Economics: Its Influence on Organizational Theory, Strategic Management, and Political Economy" by Glenn Carroll, Pablo Spiller, and David Teece is best seen as a complement to the Masten review. This article reviews the influence of Williamson and transaction cost economics on three important areas outside the discipline of economics. As the authors note, these three areas are home to some of the most exciting social science developments over the last twenty years. Transaction cost theory has played a major role in each area, sometimes by providing a general orientation to theory and research and sometimes by advancing specific theoretical claims. The net effect of transaction cost theory's influence has been to make the areas more unified than they were previously.

Howard A. Shelanski and Peter G. Klein's "Empirical Research in Transaction Cost Economics: A Review and Assessment" should forever put an end to the ill-founded criticism that transaction cost theory lacks sufficient empirical support. In all, Shelanski and Klein find well over one hundred scientific studies reporting tests of some specific transaction cost prediction. The studies cover a range of topics including organizational form and ownership issues. The bulk of studies, however, address questions of comparative contracting that lay at the heart of transaction cost theory. Despite the occasional discrepant finding, Shelanski and Klein conclude that the tests generally support the theory. Indeed, they claim that empirical support for transaction cost theory is greater than it is for many economic theories, including those of competing theories of industrial organization.

2. *Conceptual Uses*

The four chapters in Part II make conceptual use of the transaction cost framework or major theoretical or methodological elements within it (such as bounded rationality). The chapters all contain some interesting theoretical propositions, but for the most part, the goals of each are more ambitious than simply developing new hypotheses. Each chapter examines a specific field, area, or research program and attempts to fashion at least the beginnings of a new way of thinking about research questions. There is no doubt that each chapter is inspired in large part by the accomplishments of transaction cost economics—either directly through the borrowing of concepts or indirectly through an appreciation of the potential theoretical power of incorporating more realistic behavioral assumptions into analysis.

"Markets and Hierarchies and (Mathematical) Economic Theory" by David M. Kreps compares and analyzes developments in institutional approaches to transaction cost economics (as exemplified by *Markets and Hierarchies*) to those of game-theoretic approaches. The comparison is of great interest because, as Kreps notes, many economists and other social scientists believe that the rigorous game-theoretical analyses of several common research problems have superseded and possibly made obsolete institutional efforts. Despite his status as a major contributor to game theory, and despite his belief that game theory has made great progress on many problems, Kreps believes that this opinion is wrong. According to him, "mathematics-based theory still lacks the language needed to capture essential ideas of bounded rationality, which are central to Williamson's concepts of transaction costs and contractual form." The chapter illustrates this point by delving at length into issues of employment contracting and organizational inertia using "more life-like models of individuals." Kreps urges other game theorists to adopt similar theoretical strategies. For transaction cost analysts, Kreps advises a similar adjustment—among other things, he suggests that these more realistic models of individuals might help to clarify when and how strongly the routinely used economizing assumption should be invoked.

"Technical Information and Industrial Structure" by Nobel Laureate Kenneth J. Arrow notes that major advances in institutional analysis, including many of those of transaction cost analysis, have been made through analysis of "the strategic implications of asymmetric information among economic agents." He goes on to describe a number of the special characteristics of information as an economic commodity. These include (1) its generation of increasing returns, requiring it to enter into the production function differently than other goods; and (2) the difficulty of making it into property, thereby making it a kind of fugitive resource. Arrow notes that economic theory has been successful in dealing with the effects of a given information structure but has been much less successful in considering information as a choice variable. He suggests some ways to conceptualize the firm as an information base and hints at the implications. He also emphasizes that "in an economy in which information is important for both cost and utility, competition between firms is conducted under large fixed costs" but that "the two standard paradigms [of economics] . . . are both inadequate to model this competition."

"Financing of Investment in Eastern Europe: A Theoretical Perspective" by Bengt Holmström notes how the field of corporate finance assumes that adequate capital simply arrives whenever there is a project with positive net present value. Holmström points out that this is hardly the case with real investments and so his goal in the chapter is to help us think "about investments in a more realistic way." Achieving the goal involves understanding and analyzing the contractual problems of investment that must be overcome for firms to obtain appropriate levels and forms of investment. These problems occur as a result of an information gap between those with ideas and those with money. The vehicles for overcoming the problems include collateral and intermediation, which Holmström analyzes extensively. The chapter follows earlier work by Williamson on asset characteristics and firm capital structure in that it challenges many long-held notions about corporate finance and proposes a new conceptual strategy.

In "Revisiting Legal Realism: The Law, Economics, and Organization Perspective," Oliver E. Williamson examines the moribund scholarship tradition known as Legal Realism and asks why it failed to fulfill its promise. Legal Realism, Williamson notes, was concerned with the limitations of orthodox legal formalism, which held that law could be "reduced to a set of well-categorized rules and principles" (Kalman, 1986:11; quoted in Williamson's chapter). Its heyday was the early part of the twentieth century, when it attracted such intellectual leaders as Karl Llewellyn and prominent jurists such as William O. Douglas. Williamson recognizes Legal Realism's similarities to transaction cost economics, including (1) an opposition to orthodox views; (2) a willingness to draw from other social science disciplines; (3) a focus on institutions; and (4) a concern with empirical reality, not just prescription (positivism). A major difference between the two, though, Williamson argues, is that transaction cost economics has a more coherent intellectual framework—a logic of organization, refutable implications, and an empirical research agenda (it also helps, he claims, that transaction cost economics' view is not overly clouded by zealous practitioners with revolutionary aspirations, as was Legal Realism). He suggests that the compelling questions of Legal Realism, which have gone unanswered for the most part, might be productively re-examined from a transaction cost perspective. The chapter illustrates this claim by discussing rationality, remediableness, and corporate finance, among other topics.

3. *Industrial Applications*

Part III contains four chapters that describe applications of transaction cost theory to industrial settings. The industries addressed range from utilities, to telecommunications, to laser printing, to early international trade. Each chapter uses transaction cost theory to understand the chosen setting but also attempts to use the setting to refine elements of the theory or its typical mode of application.

In "Introducing Competition into Regulated Industries: From Hierarchies to Markets in Electricity," Paul L. Joskow examines the governance structures of electric power companies around the world. As he notes, in recent years in many countries these companies have experienced great change in ownership forms and regulatory structures. Joskow's main concern here is with the shift from horizontally and vertically integrated governance structures to decentralized ones, a core problem of transaction cost economics and *Markets and Hierarchies*. Joskow believes that policy makers often advocate decentralization without appreciating that its effectiveness "assumes either that there are no economies of vertical integration or that the efficiencies associated with vertical integration can be replicated with simple 'access rules' and a simple set of 'bottleneck' service prices." The chapter explains why these assumptions may be problematic in some contexts. In a well-informed institutional analysis, Joskow describes the economics of power generation and transmission, as well as the organizational and regulatory structures commonly found in this industry. Joskow sees the key to efficient restructuring of these industries as "properly defining the role of the network operator, recognizing that a variety of network functions have natural monopoly attributes and/or are potential sources of market failure, and creating a system that yields appropriate price signals, linking generators with the network operator, and defining appropriate network operating protocols when prices cannot be expected to allocate resources efficiently."

Pablo T. Spiller also addresses questions that involve utilities industries in the chapter "Institutions and Commitment." Spiller's primary concern is with the design of regulatory structures—in particular, how to design these structures to limit potential problems of opportunism by the government. Such constraints must be credible to ensure efficient investment—otherwise investors will worry that large sunk investments might be expropriated. The threat of expropriation might lead to underinvestment or to investments that are poorly maintained, of lower quality, or perversely priced. Designing credible regulatory systems, Spiller claims, is not easy. It involves two parts, a first concerning regulatory governance and a second about regulatory incentives. The chapter discusses these aspects of various regulatory systems around the world, using illustrations from the telecommunications and other utility industries.

In "Mitigating Procurement Hazards in the Context of Innovation," John M. de Figueiredo and David J. Teece discuss some problems found in many high-technology industries. They are concerned with contractual hazards in technical innovation and ways to mitigate them. The specific context de Figueiredo and Teece address is that of a firm buying component products from its vertically integrated upstream competitor. The hazards that are likely to arise in this context include those associated with an inability to maintain proper technological pacing, a loss of control over core knowledge, and possible "technological foreclosure." De Figueiredo and Teece develop a set of prescriptive strategies to overcome these hazards, using transaction cost economics as a basis. The prescriptive theory they develop will be strengthened by future systematic empirical research, but it already shows promise for bringing dynamic considerations into transaction cost analysis.

In "The Study of Organizations and Evolving Organizational Forms through History: Reflections from the Late Medieval Firm," Avner Greif combines ideas and methods from game theory, organizational theory, comparative institutional analysis, and history to examine the emergence of the late medieval family firm form of organization. He briefly compares the Italian family firm with the Maghribi of the Muslim world. This is insightful because while the Italians introduced and used the family firm for international trade in the thirteenth century, the Maghribi did not do so even though they were engaged in similar long-distance trade. The comparison shows that common explanations that suggest the family firm solved potential generic problems of agency and servicing in long-distance trade are not sufficient. Instead, Greif argues, its emergence in Italy rather than in the Muslim world "may reflect different incentives with respect to the agglomeration of capital brought about by the distinct manner in which agency relations were mitigated." His analysis also suggests that the structure of Italian family firms was the result of learning by observing organizational processes of evolutionary selection.

4. *Microanalytics*

Part IV contains four chapters that analyze the organizational and other structures of firms. The efforts are decidedly microanalytical as the analysts delve into the structures and behaviors of very specific aspects of firms and organizations—boards of directors, equity structures, employment models, human resource policies and practices, technology strategies, and innovation events. The many theoretical and methodological concerns of the chapters include assessment of transaction alignment, discussion of which outcome variables are appropriate, consideration of what level of analysis makes most sense, and analysis of what time frame should be employed. These important concerns suggest the likely directions for future developments of transaction cost economics.

"Corporate Law and Corporate Governance" by Roberta Romano discusses how these two topics are "flip sides of the same coin" because "the fundamental task of corporate law is to provide a framework of governance institutions that mitigate the agency problem arising from the separation of ownership and control in the modern corporation." Developments in both literatures draw heavily from the transaction cost economics perspective, and Romano's chapter reviews and analyzes this linkage in depth. Romano focuses on three specific governance issues: (1) the composition of corporate boards of directors; (2) the idea of relational investing by large corporate shareholders; and (3) the competition among states in the United States for corporate charters. For each issue Romano discusses relevant theory, practice, and empirical research. She points precisely to the relevant insights from transaction cost theory and reviews how they square with corporate practice and extant empirical evidence. Her concern throughout the chapter is with the effects of governance structures on corporate performance.

"The Road Taken: Origins and Evolution of Employment Systems in Emerging Companies" by James N. Baron, M. Diane Burton, and Michael T. Hannan addresses questions about the design of employment systems in firms. Although this topic has been of long-standing interest to transaction cost analysts, little by way of in-depth systematic empirical research has been conducted. Moreover, as Baron, Burton, and Hannan point out, even basic descriptive information about how employment and human resource systems evolve as firms develop over time is lacking. The chapter begins to fill the gap. It describes initial findings from the Stanford Project on Emerging Companies (SPEC), a longitudinal exploratory study of newly founded high-technology firms focused on the design of human resource systems. Baron et al. find four generic pure-types of employment systems in these firms: (1) a *star* model "that involves challenging work, autonomy and professional control, and selection of elite personnel based on long-term potential"; (2) an *engineering* model that entails "a focus on challenging work, peer group control, and selection based on specific task abilities"; (3) a *commitment* model that relies "on emotional/familial attachments of employees to the organization, selection based on cultural fit, and peer group control"; and (4) a *factory* model that is based "on purely monetary motivations, control and coordination through formal organization and close managerial oversight, and selection of employees to perform pre-specified tasks." They find that a founder's initial choice of employment system affects the rate at which many human resource policies and practices are adopted, including the establishment of a human resource manager position. Although Baron et al. do not explicitly examine any transaction cost predictions about the design of employment systems, they explain that their basic finding of general firmwide consistencies in the elements of firms' human resource strategy is important for transaction cost economics. This is so because it implies greater complementarity in the various parts of the firm (and their various types of employees) than transaction cost analysis typically recognizes. Baron et al. suggest that the question of transaction alignment and firm coherency deserve more consideration. Among other things, such analysis might go a long way in assisting in interpretation of the kinds of inconsistent findings in firm-level empirical studies reviewed by Romano.

"Inertia and Change in the Early Years: Employment Relations in Young High-Technology Firms" is by the same set of authors (although with Michael T. Hannan as the first author) and also reports empirical findings from SPEC. The central topics of this chapter concern alignment between the employment model of a firm and the firm's basic business strategy. Hannan et al. investigate the patterns of initial alignment (at founding) as well as their change (or inertia) over time. They identify five basic business strategies among these high-technology firms: (1) a technological leadership strategy whereby "firms seek to gain first-mover advantages by winning a technology race"; (2) a strategy based on enhancing existing technology by introducing "some general modification to the technology to gain competitive advantage"; (3) a strategy based on superior marketing or customer service; (4) a hybrid strategy involving advantages of both technology and marketing; and (5) a cost-minimization strategy whereby firms "seek cost advantages through superior production techniques, economies of scale, and the like." In assessing alignment with the employment model, they find some strong associations at founding, most notably: Technological strategies often lead to star or engineering employment models; marketing-service strategies generate commitment and engineering models; and cost-based strategies are associated with factory models of employment. Surprisingly, they find that these associations weaken over time, although there is great inertia in the firms' employment models. They suggest that the weaker association occurs because "with growth in the scale, complexity, and heterogeneity of their tasks and employees, transaction cost economizing in a firm's employment system may occur at ever-lower levels of aggregation, rather than at the level of the organization as a whole or major subunits with it." The paired findings of inertia and loose association also have important implications for the time frame within which it is reasonable to expect transaction cost alignments to obtain and to hold. The extent of inertia, in turn, contains strong implications for which mechanisms of organizational change most accurately depict the industrial world.

"Creative Self-Destruction among Organizations: An Empirical Study of Technical Innovation and Organizational Failure in the American Automobile Industry, 1885–1981" by Glenn R. Carroll and Albert C. Y. Teo addresses directly some of the questions of organizational change raised by Hannan et al. It asks the general question of whether firms change mainly by the adaptation of individual organizations or by the selective founding and replacement of organizational forms (because individual organizations are rigid or inertial). Transaction cost minimization could operate through either mechanism, but the often implicit assumption of most transaction cost theory and research is that adaptation dominates. Carroll and Teo review briefly the debate over adaptation and selection. They note that the organizational change of perhaps greatest economic importance—technical innovation within an industry—has not been studied. They argue that even with the beneficial effects of innovation, the costs and risks associated with organizational change per se may impede adaptation. The chapter then proceeds to model the impact of technical change on organizational mortality in the U.S. automobile industry. Carroll and Teo find that technical innovations generate primarily beneficial effects for the firms that spawn them and primarily detrimental effects for their competitors. However, they also find that in large firms the risks of innovation may on occasion outweigh benefits. Carroll and Teo propose a general reconciliation of the different positions on organizational inertia found in the research literature. The implication for transaction cost economics is to relax the almost universal assumption of adaptation and to consider other possible processes of organizational change that might lead to transaction cost alignments.

5. Conclusion

The only way for a theoretical perspective to avoid becoming stale with acceptance is for it to continue evolving, to deal with the criticisms it receives, and to branch out into new and unexpected territory. We believe that this book demonstrates that transaction cost economics is capable of such growth and renewal.

PART I

Background

CHAPTER TWO

The Vertical Integration of Production
Market Failure Considerations

OLIVER E. WILLIAMSON

The study of vertical integration has presented difficulties at both theoretical and policy levels of analysis. That vertical integration has never enjoyed a secure place in value theory is attributable to the fact that, under conventional assumptions, it is an anomaly: if the costs of operating competitive markets are zero, "as is usually assumed in our theoretical analysis" (Arrow, 1969, p. 48), why integrate?

Policy interest in vertical integration has been concerned mainly with the possibility that integration can be used strategically to achieve anticompetitive effects. In the absence of a more substantial theoretical foundation, vertical integration, as a public policy matter, is typically regarded as having dubious if not outright antisocial properties. Technological interdependencies or, possibly, observational economies constitute the principal exceptions.

The technological interdependency argument is both the most familiar and the most straightforward: successive processes which, naturally, follow immediately in time and place dictate certain efficient manufacturing configurations; these, in turn, are believed to have common ownership implications. Such technical complementarity is probably more important in flow process operations (chemicals, metals, etc.) than in separable component manufacture. The standard example is the integration of iron- and steelmaking, where thermal economies are said to be available through integration. It is commonly held that where "integration does not have this physical or technical aspect—as it does not, for example, in integrating the production of assorted components with the assembly of those components—the case for cost savings from integration is generally much less clear" (Bain, 1968, p. 381).

Reprinted with permission from the *American Economic Review* 6(1971):112–123.

Research on this essay has been supported by a grant from the Brookings Institution. It is part of the larger study referred to in note 1. Helpful comments from Noel Edelson, Stefano Fenoaltea, Julius Margolis, and Almarin Phillips are gratefully acknowledged.

There is, nevertheless, a distinct unease over the argument. This is attributable, probably, to a suspicion that the firm is more than a simple efficiency instrument, in the usual scale economies and least-cost factor proportions senses of the term, but also possesses coordinating potential that sometimes transcends that of the market. It is the burden of the present argument that this suspicion is warranted. In more numerous respects than are commonly appreciated, the substitution of internal organization for market exchange is attractive less on account of technological economies associated with production but because of what may be referred to broadly as "transactional failures" in the operation of markets for intermediate goods. This substitution of internal organization for market exchange will be referred to as "internalization."

The two principal prior contributions on which the argument relies are Coase's seminal discussion on "The Nature of the Firm" (1937) and Arrow's more recent review of market versus nonmarket allocation (1969). As will be evident, I agree with Malmgren (1961) that the analysis of transaction costs is uninteresting under fully stationary conditions and that only when the need to make unprogrammed adaptations is introduced does the market versus internal organization issue become engaging.

But while Malmgren finds that the advantage of the firm inheres in its capacity to control information and achieve plan consistency among interdependent activities, which may be regarded as an information processing advantage, I mainly emphasize the differential incentive and control properties of firms in relation to markets. This is not to suggest that information processing considerations are unimportant, but rather that these incompletely characterize the distinctive properties of firms that favor internal organization as a market substitute.

1. *Internal Organization: Affirmative Aspects*

A complete treatment of vertical integration requires that the limits as well as the powers of internal organization be assessed. As the frictions associated with administrative coordination become progressively more severe, recourse to market exchange becomes more attractive, *ceteris paribus*. It is beyond the scope of this essay, however, to examine the organizational failure aspect of the vertical integration question.[1] Rather it is simply asserted that, mainly on account of bounded rationality and greater confidence in the objectivity of market exchange in comparison with bureaucratic processes, market interme-

---

[1] I discuss the organizational failure dimension of this issue in *Aspects of Monopoly Theory and Policy* (forthcoming). Policy implications of the argument are also examined there.

diation is generally to be preferred over internal supply in circumstances in which markets may be said to "work well."[2]

The properties of the firm that commend internal organization as a market substitute would appear to fall into three categories: incentives, controls, and what may be referred to broadly as "inherent structural advantages." In an incentive sense, internal organization attenuates the aggressive advocacy that epitomizes arm's length bargaining. Interests, if not perfectly harmonized, are at least free of representations of a narrowly opportunistic sort; in any viable group, of which the firm is one, the range of admissible intraorganizational behavior is bounded by considerations of alienation. In circumstances, therefore, where protracted bargaining between independent parties to a transaction can reasonably be anticipated, internalization becomes attractive.[3]

Perhaps the most distinctive advantage of the firm, however, is the wider variety and greater sensitivity of control instruments that are available for enforcing intrafirm in comparison with interfirm activities (Williamson, 1970). Not only does the firm have the constitutional authority and low-cost access to the requisite data which permit it to perform more precise own-performance evaluations (of both a contemporaneous and *ex post* variety) than can a buyer, but its reward and penalty instruments (which include selective use of employment, promotion, remuneration, and internal resource allocation processes) are more refined.

Especially relevant in this connection is that, when conflicts develop, the firm possesses a comparatively efficient conflict resolution machinery. To illustrate, fiat is frequently a more efficient way to settle minor conflicts (say differences of interpretation) than is haggling or litigation. *Inter*organizational conflict can be settled by fiat only rarely, if at all. For one thing, it would require the parties to agree on an impartial arbitrator, which agreement itself may be costly to secure. It would also require that rules of evidence and procedure be established. If, moreover, the occasion for such interorganizational settlements were to be common, the form of organization converges in effect to vertical integration, with the arbiter becoming a manager in fact if not in name. By contrast, *intra*organizational settlements by fiat are common (Whinston, 1964, pp. 410–414).

---

[2] An intermediate market will be said to work well if, both presently and prospectively, prices are nonmonopolistic and reflect an acceptable risk premium, and if market exchange experiences low transaction costs and permits the realization of essential economies. To the extent that the stipulated conditions do not hold, internal supply becomes relatively more attractive, *ceteris paribus*.

[3] Common ownership by itself, of course, does not guarantee goal consistency. A holding company form of organization in which purchaser and supplier are independent divisions, each maximizing individual profits, is no solution. Moreover, merely to stipulate joint profit maximization is not by itself apt to be sufficient. The goal needs to be operationalized, which involves both rulemaking (with respect, for example, to transfer pricing) and the design of efficacious internal incentives. For a discussion, see Williamson (1970).

    The firm may also resort to internalization on account of economies of in-
formation exchange. Some of these may be due to structural differences between firms and markets. Others, however, reduce ultimately to incentive and
control differences between internal and market organization. It is widely accepted, for example, that communication with respect to complex matters is
facilitated by a common training and experience and if a compact code has
developed in the process. Repeated interpersonal interactions may permit even
further economies of communication; subtle nuances may come through in
familiar circumstances which in an unfamiliar relationship could be achieved
only with great effort. Still, the drawing of an organizational boundary need
not, by itself, prevent intensely familiar relations from developing between organizations. Put differently, but for the goal and control differences described
above, the informational advantages of internal over market organization are
not, in this respect, apparent. Claims of informational economies thus should
distinguish between economies that are attributable to information flows *per
se* (structure) and those which obtain on account of differential veracity effects (see "Information Processing Effects" in the following Section 2).

2. *Market Failure Considerations*

What are referred to here as market failures are failures only in the limited
sense that they involve transaction costs that can be attenuated by substituting internal organization for market exchange. The argument proceeds in five
stages. The first three are concerned with characterizing a successively more
complex bargaining environment in which small numbers relations obtain.
The last two deal with the special structural advantages which, either naturally
or because of prevailing institutional rules, the firm enjoys in relation to the
market.

Static Markets

Consider an industry that produces a multicomponent product, assume that
some of these components are specialized (industry specific), and assume further that among these there are components for which the economies of scale
in production are large in relation to the market. The market, then, will support only a few efficient sized producers for certain components.
    A monopolistic excess of price over cost under market procurement is com-
monly anticipated in these circumstances—although, as Demsetz (1968) has
noted, this need not obtain if there are large numbers of suppliers willing and
able to bid at the initial contract award stage. Assume, however, that large
numbers bidding is not feasible. The postulated conditions then afford an "ap-

parent" incentive for assemblers to integrate backward or suppliers to integrate forward. Two different cases can be distinguished: bilateral monopoly (oligopoly) and competitive assembly with monopolistic supply. The former is considered here; the latter is treated in the following "Strategic Misrepresentation Risk."

Bilateral monopoly requires that both price and quantity be negotiated. Both parties stand to benefit, naturally, by operating on rather than off the contract curve—which here corresponds to the joint profit maximizing quantity (Fellner, 1947). But this merely establishes the amount to be exchanged. The terms at which this quantity will be traded still need to be determined. Any price consistent with nonnegative profits to both parties is feasible. Bargaining can be expected to ensue. Haggling will presumably continue until the marginal private net benefits are perceived by one of the parties to be zero. Although this haggling is jointly (and socially) unproductive, it constitutes a source of private pecuniary gain. Being, nevertheless, a joint profit drain, an incentive to avoid these costs, if somehow this could be arranged, is set up.

One possible adaptation is to internalize the transaction through vertical integration; but a once-for-all contract might also be negotiated. In a perfectly static environment (one that is free of disturbances of all kinds), these may be regarded with indifference: the former involves settlement on component supply price while merger requires agreement on asset valuation. Bargaining skills will presumably be equally important in each instance (indeed, a component price can be interpreted in asset valuation terms and conversely). Thus, although vertical integration may occur under these conditions, there is nothing in the nature of the problem that requires such an outcome.

A similar argument in these circumstances also applies to adaptation against externalities: joint profit considerations dictate that the affected parties reach an accommodation, but integration holds no advantage over once-for-all contracts in a perfectly static environment.

Transforming the relationship from one of bilateral monopoly to one of bilateral oligopoly broadens the range of bargaining alternatives, but the case for negotiating a merger agreement in relation to a once-for-all contract is not differentially affected on this account. The static characterization of the problem, apparently, will have to be relaxed if a different result is to be reached.

Contractual Incompleteness

Let the above conditions be enriched to include the stipulation that the product in question is technically complex and that periodic redesign and/or volume changes are made in response to changing environmental conditions.

Also relax the assumption that large numbers bidding at the initial contract award stage is infeasible. Three alternative supply arrangements can be considered: a once-for-all contract, a series of short-term contracts, and vertical integration.

The dilemma posed by once-for-all contracts is this: lest independent parties interpret contractual ambiguities to their own advantage, which differences can be resolved only by haggling or, ultimately, litigation, contingent supply relations ought exhaustively to be stipulated. But exhaustive stipulation, assuming that it is feasible, is itself costly. Thus although, if production functions were known, appropriate responses to final demand or factor price changes might be deduced, the very costliness of specifying the functions and securing agreement discourages the effort. The problem is made even more severe where a changing technology poses product redesign issues. Here it is doubtful that, despite great effort and expense, contractual efforts reasonably to comprehend the range of possible outcomes will be successful. An adaptive, sequential decision process is thus indicated. If, however, contractual revisions or amendments are regarded as an occasion to bargain opportunistically, which predictably they will be, the purchaser will defer and accumulate adaptations, if by packaging them in complex combinations their true value can better be disguised; some adaptations may be foregone altogether. The optimal sequential decision-making process can in these respects be distorted.

Short-term contracts, which would facilitate adaptive, sequential decision-making, might therefore be preferred. These pose problems, however, if either (1) efficient supply requires investment in special-purpose, long-life equipment or (2) the winner of the original contract acquires a cost advantage, say by reason of "first mover" advantages (such as unique location or learning, including the acquisition of undisclosed or proprietary technical and managerial procedures and task-specific labor skills).

The problem with condition (1) is that optimal investment considerations favor the award of a long-term contract so as to permit the supplier confidently to amortize his investment. But, as indicated, long-term contracts pose adaptive, sequential decision-making problems. Thus optimal investment and optimal sequential adaptation processes are in conflict in this instance.

It might be argued that condition (2) poses no problems since initial bidders will fully reflect in their original bids all relevant factors. Thus, although anticipated downstream cost advantages (where downstream is used both here and subsequently in the sense of time rather than place) will give rise to small numbers competition for downstream supply, competition at the initial award stage is sufficient to assure that only competitive returns will be realized over the entire supply interval. One might expect, therefore, that the low bidder would come in at a price below cost in the first period, set price at the level of alternative supply price in later periods, and earn normal returns over-all. Appropriate changes can be introduced easily at the recontracting interval.

A number of potential problems are posed, however. For one thing, unless the total supply requirements are stipulated, "buying in" strategies are risky. Also, and related, the alternative supply price is not independent of the terms that the buyer may subsequently offer to rivals. Moreover, alternative supply price is merely an upper bound; an aggressive buyer may attempt to obtain a price at the level of current costs on each round. Haggling could be expected to ensue. Short-term contracts thus experience what may be serious limitations in circumstances where nontrivial first-mover advantages obtain.

In consideration, therefore, of the problems that both long- and short-term contracts are subject to, vertical integration may well be indicated. The conflict between efficient investment and efficient sequential decision-making is thereby avoided. Sequential adaptations become an occasion for cooperative adjustment rather than opportunistic bargaining; risks may be attenuated; differences between successive stages can be resolved more easily by the internal control machinery.

It is relevant to note that the technological interdependency condition involving flow process economies between otherwise separable stages of production is really a special case of the contractual incompleteness argument. The contractual dilemma is this: On the one hand, it may be prohibitively costly, if not infeasible, to specify contractually the full range of contingencies and stipulate appropriate responses between stages. On the other hand, if the contract is seriously incomplete in these respects but, once the original negotiations are settled, the contracting parties are locked into a bilateral exchange, the divergent interests between the parties will predictably lead to individually opportunistic behavior and joint losses. The advantages of integration thus are not that technological (flow process) economies are unavailable to nonintegrated firms, but that integration harmonizes interests (or reconciles differences, often by fiat) and permits an efficient (adaptive, sequential) decision process to be utilized. More generally, arguments favorable to integration that turn on "supply reliability" considerations commonly reduce to the contractual incompleteness issue.[4]

---

[4] It is sometimes suggested that breach of contract risk affords an additional reason for integration: the small supplier of a critical component whose assets are insufficient to cover a total damage claim leaves the purchaser vulnerable. But this is an argument against small suppliers, not contracting quite generally; the large, diversified supplier might well have superior risk pooling capability to that of the integrated firm. The risks of contractual incompleteness, however, remain and may discourage purchasing from large, diversified organizations. For a discussion of "ideal" contracts in this connection, see Arrow (1965, pp. 52–53).

Strategic Misrepresentation Risk

Contractual incompleteness problems develop where there is *ex ante* but not necessarily *ex post* uncertainty. Strategic misrepresentation risks are serious where there is uncertainty in both respects. Not only is the future uncertain but it may not be possible, except at great cost, for an outside agency to establish accurately what has transpired after the fact. The advantages of internalization reside in the fact that the firm's *ex post* access to the relevant data is superior, it attenuates the incentives to exploit uncertainty opportunistically, and the control machinery that the firm is able to activate is more selective.

1. AFFIRMATIVE OCCASIONS FOR INTEGRATION. Three affirmative occasions to integrate on account of strategic misrepresentation risk and two potentially anticompetitive consequences of integration can be identified.

(a) *Moral Hazard.* The problem here arises because of the conjoining of inharmonious incentives with uncertainty—or, as Arrow puts it (1969, p. 55), it is due to the "confounding of risks and decisions." To illustrate, consider the problem of contracting for an item the final cost and/or performance of which is subject to uncertainty. One possibility is for the supplier to bear the uncertainty. But he will undertake a fixed price contract to deliver a specific result the costs of which are highly uncertain only after attaching a risk premium to the price. Assume that the buyer regards this premium as excessive and is prepared on this account to bear the risk himself. The risk can easily be shifted by offering a cost-plus contract. But this impairs the incentives of the supplier to achieve least-cost performance; the supplier may reallocate his assets in such a way as to favor other work to the disadvantage of the cost-plus contract.

Thus, although, if commitments were self-enforcing, it might often be institutionally most efficient to divide the functions of risk bearing and contract execution (that is, cost-plus contracts would have ideal properties), specialization is discouraged by interest disparities. At a minimum, the buyer may insist on monitoring the supplier's work. In contrast therefore to a fixed-price contract, where it is sufficient to evaluate end-product performance, cost-plus contracts, because they expose the buyer to risks of inefficient (high cost) contract execution, require that *both* inputs and outputs be evaluated.

Internalization does not eliminate the need for input evaluation. Rather, the advantage of internalization, for input monitoring purposes, resides in the differential ease with which controls are exercised. An external agency, by design, lacks recourse to the internal control machinery: proposed remedies require the consent of the contractor and then are highly circumscribed; unrestricted access by the buyer to the contractor's internal control machinery (including selective use of employment, promotion, remuneration, and internal resource allocation processes) is apt to be denied. In consideration of the costs and limitations of input monitoring by outsiders, the buyer may choose instead to bear the risk and perform the work himself. The buyer thus internalizes, through backward vertical integration, a transaction which, but for uncertainty, would move through the market. A cost-type contract for *internal procurement* is arranged.

(b) *Externalities/Imputation*. The externality issue can be examined in two parts. First, has a secure, unambiguous, and "appropriate" assignment of property rights been made? Second, are the accounting costs of imputing costs and benefits substantial? If answers to these questions are affirmative and negative respectively, appropriability problems will not become an occasion for vertical integration. Where these conditions are not satisfied, however, integration may be indicated.

The assignment aspect of this matter is considered in the following "Institutional Adaptations." Here it is assumed that an efficacious assignment of property rights has been made and that only the expense of imputing costs and benefits is at issue. But indeed this is apt often to be the more serious problem. High imputation expenses which discourage accurate metering introduce ambiguity into transactions. Did party A affect party B and if so in what degree? In the absence of objective, low cost standards, opposed interests can be expected to evaluate these effects differently. Internalization, which permits protracted (and costly) disputes over these issues to be avoided, may on this account be indicated.

(c) *Variable Proportions Distortions*. Consider the case where the assembly stage will support large numbers; fewness appears only in component supply. Whether monopolistic supply prices provide an occasion for vertical integration in these circumstances depends both on production technology and on policing expense. Variable proportions at the assembly stage afford opportunities for nonintegrated assemblers to adapt against monopolistically priced components by substituting competitively priced factors (McKenzie, 1951). Although conceivably the monopolistic component supplier could stipulate, as a condition of sale, that fixed proportions in assembly should prevail, the effectiveness of such stipulations is to be questioned—since, ordinarily, the implied enforcement costs will be great. Where substitution occurs, inefficient factor proportions, with consequent welfare losses, will result. The private (and social) incentives to integrate so as to reduce total costs by restoring efficient factor combinations are evident.

2. ANTICOMPETITIVE CONSEQUENCES. Anticompetitive effects of two types are commonly attributed to integration: price discrimination and barriers to entry (cf. Stigler, 1968, p. 303).

(a) *Price Discrimination.* The problem here is first to discover differential demand elasticities, and secondly to arrange for sale in such a way as to preclude reselling. Users with highly elastic demands which purchase the item at a low price must not be able to service inelastic demand customers by acting as a middleman; all sales must be final. Although vertical integration may facilitate the discovery of differential elasticities, it is mainly with respect to the non-resale condition that it is regarded as especially efficacious.

Integration, nevertheless, is a relatively extreme response. Moreover, price discrimination is clearly practiced in some commodities without recourse to vertical integration (witness electricity and telephone service). What are the distinguishing factors? Legality considerations aside, presumably it is the cost of enforcing (policing) terms of the contract that are at issue. Some commodities apparently have self-enforcing properties — which may obtain on account of high storage and repacking costs or because reselling cannot be arranged inconspicuously. The absence of self-enforcing (policing) properties is what makes vertical integration attractive as a means of accomplishing discrimination.

(b) *Entry Barrier Effects.* That the vertical integration of production might be used effectively to bar entry is widely disputed. Bork (1969, p. 148) argues that "in general, if greater than competitive profits are to be made in an industry, entry should occur whether the entrant has to come in at both levels at once or not. I know of no theory of imperfections in the capital market which would lead suppliers of capital to avoid areas of higher return to seek areas of lower return." But the issue is not one of profit avoidance but rather involves cost incidence. If borrowers are confronted by increasingly adverse rates as they increase their finance requirements, which Hirshleifer suggests is a distinct possibility (1970, pp. 200–201), cost may not be independent of vertical structure.

Assuming that vertical integration has the effect of increasing capital requirements, the critical issues are to what extent and for what reasons the supply curve of finance behaves in the way postulated. The following conjecture is offered as a partial explanation: unable to monitor the performance of *large, complex* organizations in any but the crudest way or to effect management displacement easily except on evidence of seriously discreditable error, investors demand larger returns as finance requirements become progressively greater, *ceteris paribus.* Thus the costs of policing against the contingency that managers will operate a rival enterprise opportunistically are, on this argument, at least partly responsible for the reputed behavior of the supply curve of capital. In consideration of this state of affairs, established firms may use vertical integration strategically to increase finance requirements and thereby to discourage entry if potential entrants feel compelled, as a condition of successful entry, to adopt the prevailing structure—as they may if the industry is highly concentrated.

Information Processing Effects

As indicated in the preceding Section 1, one of the advantages of the firm is that it realizes economies of information exchange. These may manifest themselves as information impactedness, observational economies, or what Malmgren (1961) refers to as the "convergence of expectations."

1. INFORMATION IMPACTEDNESS. Richardson illustrates the problems of information impactedness by reference to an entrepreneur who was willing to offer long-term contracts (at normal rates of return, presumably) but which contracts others were unprepared to accept because they were not convinced that he had "the ability, as well as the will, to fulfill them. He may have information sufficient to convince himself that this is the case, but others may not" (Richardson, 1960, p. 83). He goes on to observe that the perceived risks of the two parties may be such as to make it difficult to negotiate a contract that offers commensurate returns to each; objective risks are augmented by contractual risks in these circumstances. Integration undertaken for this reason is akin to self-insurance by individuals who know themselves to be good risks but are priced out of the insurance market because of their inability, at low cost, to "reveal" this condition to insurers.

2. OBSERVATIONAL ECONOMIES. As Radner indicates, "the acquisition of information often involves a 'set-up cost'; i.e., the resources needed to obtain the information may be independent of the scale of the production process in which the information is used" (Radner, 1970, p. 457). Although Radner apparently had horizontal firm size implications in mind, the argument also has relevance for vertical integration. If a single set of observations can be made that is of relevance to a related series of production stages, vertical integration may be efficient.

Still, the question might be raised, why common ownership? Why not an independent observational agency that sells information to all comers? Or, if the needed information is highly specialized, why not a joint venture? Alternatively, what inhibits efficient information exchange between successive stages of production according to contract? In relation, certainly, to the range of intermediate options potentially available, common ownership appears to be an extreme response. What are the factors which favor this outcome?

One of the problems with contracts is that of specifying terms. But even if terms could be reached, there is still a problem of policing the agreement. To illustrate, suppose that the common information collection responsibilities are assigned by contract to one of the parties. The purchasing party then runs *a veracity risk*: information may be filtered and possibly distorted to the advantage of the firm that has assumed the information collection responsibility. If checks are costly and proof of contractual violation difficult, contractual sharing arrangements manifestly experience short-run limitations. If, in addition, small numbers prevail so that options are restricted, contractual sharing is subject to long-run risks as well. On this argument, observational economies are mainly to be attributed to strategic misrepresentation risks rather than to indivisibilities.

3. CONVERGENCE OF EXPECTATIONS. The issue to which the convergence of expectations argument is addressed is that, if there is a high degree of interdependence among successive stages of production and if occasions for adaptation are unpredictable yet common, coordinated responses may be difficult to secure if the separate stages are operated independently. March and Simon (1958, p. 159) characterize the problem in the following terms:

> Interdependence by itself does not cause difficulty if the pattern of interdependence is stable and fixed. For, in this case, each subprogram can be designed to take account of all the subprograms with which it interacts. Difficulties arise only if program execution rests on contingencies that cannot be predicted perfectly in advance. In this case, coordinating activity is required to secure agreement about the estimates that will be used as the basis for action, or to provide information to each subprogram unit about the activities of the others.

This reduces, in some respects, to a contractual incompleteness argument. Were it feasible exhaustively to stipulate the appropriate conditional responses, coordination could proceed by contract. This is ambitious, however; in the face of a highly variable and uncertain environment, the attempt to program responses is apt to be inefficient. To the extent that an unprogrammed (adaptive, sequential) decision process is employed instead, and in consideration of the severe incentive and control limitations that long-term contracts experience in these circumstances (See preceding "Contractual Incompleteness"), vertical integration may be indicated.

But what of the possibility of short-term contracts? It is here that the convergence of expectations argument is of special importance. Thus assume that short-term contracts are not defective on account either of investment disincentives or of first-mover advantages. It is Malmgren's (1961) contention that such contracts may nevertheless be vitiated by the absence of structural constraints. The costs of negotiations and the time required to bring the system into adjustment by exclusive reliance on market (price) signals are apt to be great in relation to that which would obtain if successive states were integrated and administrative processes employed as well or instead.

Institutional Adaptations

Institutional adaptations of two types are distinguished: simple economic and extra-economic.

1. SIMPLE ECONOMIC. As has been noted by others, vertical integration may be a device by which sales taxes on intermediate products are avoided, or a means by which to circumvent quota schemes and price controls (Coase, 1937, pp. 338–339; Stigler, 1968, pp. 136–137). But vertical integration may also be undertaken because of the defective specification of property rights.

Although the appropriate assignment of property rights is a complex question, it reduces (equity considerations aside) to a simple criterion: What assignment yields maximum total product (Coase, 1960, p. 34)? This depends jointly on imputation and negotiation expenses and on the incentives of the compensated party. So as to focus on the negotiation expense aspect, assume that imputation expenses are negligible and set the incentive question aside for the moment.[5] An "appropriate" assignment of property rights will here be defined as one which automatically yields compensation in the amount of the external benefit or cost involved, while an "inappropriate" assignment is one that requires bargaining to bring the parties into adjustment. Thus if A and B are two parties and A's activity imposes costs on B, the appropriate assignment of property rights is to require A to compensate B. If instead property rights were defined such that A is not required to compensate B, and assuming that the externality holds at the margin, efficient adaptation would occur only if B were to bribe A to bring his activity into adjustment—which entails bargaining. Only if the costs of such bargaining are neglected can the alternative specifications of property rights be said to be equivalent. For similar reasons, if A's activity generates benefits for B, the appropriate specification of property rights will be to require B fully to compensate A. Harmonizing the otherwise divergent interests of the two parties by internalizing the transaction through vertical merger promises to overcome the haggling costs which result when property rights are left either undefined or inappropriately specified.

---

5 As Coase has emphasized (1960, pp. 32–33, 41), compensation can impair the incentives of the compensated party that experiences an external cost to take appropriate protective measures. Parties that are assured of compensation will be content to conduct business as usual. Such a practice easily contributes to greater social cost than would obtain were compensation denied. A sensitivity to what, in a broad sense, might be regarded as contributory negligence is thus required if the system is to be brought fully into adjustment. Clairvoyance with respect to contributory negligence would of course permit the courts to supply those who experience the external cost with requisite incentives to adapt appropriately. Since, however, such clairvoyance (or even unbiasedness) cannot routinely be presumed, internalizing the transaction through vertical integration may be indicated for this reason as well. (Interestingly, a symmetrical problem is not faced where the externality is a benefit. Stipulating that compensation shall be paid induces Meade's [1952] orchard grower not merely to extend his production appropriately, but also to shift from apples to peaches if this is socially advantageous.)

2. OTHER. Risk aversion refers to the degree of concavity in the utility valuation of pecuniary outcomes. Decision-makers who are risk averse will be concerned not merely with the expected value, but also with the dispersion in outcomes associated with alternative proposals: the greater the dispersion, the lower the utility valuation. *Ceteris paribus*, decision-makers who are the less risk averse will presumably assume the risk-bearing function. Even, however, if attitudes toward risk were identical—in the sense that every individual (for any given set of initial endowments) would evaluate a proposal similarly—differing initial asset positions among the members of a population could warrant a specialization of the risk-bearing function, with possible firm and market structure effects (Knight, 1965).

Arrow calls attention to norms of social behavior, including ethical and moral codes. He observes in this connection that "it is useful for individuals to have some trust in each other's word. In the absence of trust, it would become very costly to arrange for alternative sanctions and guarantees, and many opportunities for mutually beneficial cooperation would have to be foregone" (1969, p. 62). One would expect, accordingly, that vertical integration would be more complete in a low-trust than a high-trust culture, *ceteris paribus.*

3. *Conclusions*

That product markets have remarkable coordinating properties is, among economists at least, a secure proposition. That product markets are subject to failure in various respects and that internal organization may be substituted against the market in these circumstances is, if somewhat less familiar, scarcely novel. A systematic treatment of market failure as it bears on vertical integration, however, has not emerged.

Partly this is attributable to inattention to internal organization: the remarkable properties of firms that distinguish internal from market coordination have been neglected. But the fragmented nature of the market failure literature as it bears on vertical integration has also contributed to this condition; the extensive variety of circumstances in which internalization is attractive tends not to be fully appreciated.

The present effort attempts both to address the internal organization issue and to organize the market failure literature as it relates to vertical integration in a systematic way. The argument, however, by no means exhausts the issues that vertical integration raises. For one thing, the discussion of market failures may be incomplete in certain respects. For another, a parallel treatment of the sources and consequences of the failures of internal organization as they relate to vertical integration is needed. Third, the argument applies strictly to the vertical integration of production; although much of it may have equal relevance to backward vertical integration into raw materials and forward integration into distribution, it may have to be delimited in significant respects. Fourth, game theoretic considerations, which may permit the indicated indeterminacy of small numbers bargaining situations to be bounded, have been neglected. Finally, nothing in the present analysis establishes that observed degrees of vertical integration are not, from a social welfare standpoint, excessive. It should nevertheless be apparent that a broader a priori case for the vertical integration of production exists than is commonly acknowledged.

References

Kenneth J. Arrow (1965), *Aspects of the Theory of Risk-Bearing*. Helsinki: Yrjo Jahnssonin Saato.

———(1969), 'The Organization of Economic Activity: Issues Pertinent to the Choice of Market versus Nonmarket Allocation,' in *The Analysis and Evaluation of Public Expenditures: The PPB System*, Vol. 1. Washington, D.C.: U.S. Joint Economic Committee, 47–64.

Joe S. Bain (1968), *Industrial Organization*. New York: John Wiley.

Robert H. Bork (1969), 'Vertical Integration and Competitive Processes,' in J. Fred Weston and Sam Peltzman, eds., *Public Policy toward Mergers*, Pacific Palisades, Calif.: Goodyear Publishing, 139–149.

Ronald H. Coase (1937), 'The Nature of the Firm,' *Economica*, **4**, 386–405; reprinted in George J. Stigler and Kenneth E. Boulding, eds., *Readings in Price Theory* (Homewood, Ill.: Richard D. Irwin. 1952), 331–351.

———(1960), 'The Problem of Social Cost,' *Journal of Law and Economics*, **3**, 1–44.

Harold Demsetz (1968), 'Why Regulate Utilities?' *Journal of Law and Economics*, **11**, 55–66.

William Fellner (1947), 'Prices and Wages under Bilateral Oligopoly,' *Quarterly Journal of Economics*, **61**, 503–532.

J. Hirshleifer (1970), *Investment, Interest and Capital*. Englewood Cliffs, N.J.: Prentice-Hall.

Frank H. Knight (1965), *Risk, Uncertainty and Profit*. New York: Harper & Row.

Lionel McKenzie (1951), 'Ideal Output and the Interdependence of Firms,' *Economic Journal*, **61**, 785–803.

H. B. Malmgren (1961), 'Information, Expectations and the Theory of the Firm,' *Quarterly Journal of Economics*, **75**, 399–421.

James G. March and Herbert A. Simon (1958), *Organizations*. New York: John Wiley.

James E. Meade (1952), 'External Economies and Diseconomies in a Competitive Situation,' *Economic Journal*, **62**, 54–67.

Roy Radner (1970), 'Problems in the Theory of Markets under Uncertainty,' *American Economic Review*, **60**, 454–460.

G. B. Richardson (1960), *Information and Investment*. London: Oxford University Press.

George J. Stigler (1968), *The Organization of Industry*. Homewood, Ill.: Richard D. Irwin.

Andrew Whinston (1964), 'Price Guides in Decentralized Organizations,' in W. W. Cooper, H. J. Leavitt, and M. W. Shelly II (eds.) *New Perspectives in Organization Research*. New York: John Wiley, 405–448.

Oliver E. Williamson (1970), *Corporate Control and Business Behavior*. Englewood Cliffs, N.J.: Prentice-Hall.

CHAPTER THREE

Some Reflections

OLIVER E. WILLIAMSON

Easy choices are always gratifying. The suggestion that I select an early transaction cost article for inclusion in this book presented an easy choice: "The Vertical Integration of Production: Market Failure Considerations" (*American Economic Review*, 1971) was the obvious candidate. Not only was this my first effort to use transaction costs to explain a puzzling economic condition, but also the essay employed and/or introduced many of the key ideas that would figure prominently as transaction cost economics played out in the years ahead.

Vertical integration is central to the theory of the firm, and my interests in the latter reach back to my graduate student days, when I was first exposed to Ronald Coase's classic article, "The Nature of the Firm" (1937). Vertical integration is also central to the field of industrial organization, and I had been teaching IO at Berkeley and at the University of Pennsylvania. My assignment as special economic assistant to the head of the Antitrust Division of the U.S. Department of Justice during the academic year 1965–1966 was also important to my choice of this topic. Issues of vertical integration (especially in relation to the Vertical Merger Guidelines [1968]) and vertical market restrictions (especially in connection with the Schwinn [1966] case) were matters on which I was asked to advise. It was my sense that the prevailing orthodoxies— barriers to entry (Harvard) and price discrimination (Chicago)—dealt with only a fraction of the relevant issues. However, because I did not have an alternative story, I was unable to dissuade Donald Turner (head of the Antitrust Division) and Richard Posner (in the Solicitor General's Office) from arguing the Schwinn case on grounds that I thought to be mistaken (see Williamson, 1985, pp. 183–185).

The lack of an alternative theory notwithstanding, I was intrigued by the puzzles of vertical integration and was unwilling to set them aside. When given the opportunity, therefore, to offer a graduate seminar on a topic of my choice when I returned to the University of Pennsylvania, I chose vertical integration. The students and I worked our way through the literature and confirmed my suspicion: the literature was preoccupied with narrow and sometimes contrived concerns (of a barriers to entry kind) or was dealing with second order effects (such as efficient factor proportions and price discrimination). Albeit pertinent to a complete catalog of factors that bear on the vertical integration, too many observations did not fit. The main action had to reside elsewhere.

It was not until several years later, however, when I was teaching a course on organization theory in which the market failure literature figured prominently that I saw a way to reconceptualize the problem. The aforementioned article by Coase was one of the three legs on which my analysis rested. I was also convinced that market failures had transaction cost origins, which Kenneth Arrow's article "The Organization of Economic Activity: Issues Pertinent to the Choice of Market versus Nonmarket Allocation" (1969) confirmed in a decisive way: "Market failure is not absolute; it is better to consider a broader category, that of transaction costs, which in general impede and in particular cases completely block the formation of markets" (p. 48). The third leg of the stool was my Ph.D. training at Carnegie Tech (now Carnegie-Mellon), in which the economics of organization was informed by both economics and organization theory.

Coase, I think, had put the issues exactly right: Firm and market are alternative modes of organization, whence the boundary of the firm needs to be derived rather than taken as given by technology. Considering the wide range of transactions across which a firm can either produce to its own needs or purchase the good or service in question, when should it make, when should it buy, and why? Although strategic entry considerations and possible factor price distortions are pertinent, tails do not wag dogs.

Viewing vertical integration as a choice between alternative modes of contracting—market and hierarchy—shifted attention to transactions and the differential contractual hazards that accrue thereto. When and in what ways does internal organization serve to mitigate contractual hazards that would otherwise be posed by market procurement? That at least was the viewpoint that I attempted to develop in my 1971 article.

Among the key ideas that were featured in this short article of twelve pages [see Chapter 2] and which have figured prominently in the subsequent development of transaction cost economics are as follows:

1. The firm is more than a production function; it is also a governance structure. Thus, I aver that the firm "possesses coordinating potential that sometimes transcends that of the market" and that "the properties of the firm that commend internal organization as a market substitute . . . fall into three categories: incentives, controls, and . . . 'inherent structural advantages'." The firm, for example, has differential access to fiat for purposes of dispute resolution and to exercise command and control more generally.

2. I also argue that problems of contracting under fully stationary conditions are uninteresting: "Only when the need to make unprogrammed adaptations is introduced does the market versus internal organization issue become engaging." Specifically, it is when incomplete contracts are confronted by unanticipated disturbances that an interesting choice among alternative modes of contracting (especially in terms of their comparative efficacy for implementing adaptive, sequential decision making) is posed.

3. I further observe that the differential propensity to behave opportunistically in outside procurement varies with the attributes of investment and has an intertemporal aspect. That is because outside procurement can "pose problems . . . if either (1) efficient supply requires investment in special-purpose, long-life equipment, or (2) the winner of the original contract acquires a cost advantage, say by reason of 'first mover' advantages (such as unique location or learning, including the acquisition of undisclosed or proprietary technical and managerial procedures and task-specific labor skills)." Plainly, issues of asset specificity and what was to become known as the fundamental transformation were contemplated.

4. Although issues of lock-in are introduced, I deal with lock-in as it bears on adaptation/maladaptation to disturbances. That is very different from much of the literature on "hold-up," which merely requires asset specificity and can arise on a whimsy, whereas maladaptation requires asset specificity plus unanticipated disturbances which push the parties off the contract curve. My position, then and now, is that simple hold-up is rare and that the central problem of economic organization is adaptation (of both autonomous and cooperative kinds).

5. Express reference is made to opportunism and opportunistic bargaining. Relatedly, I discuss the limits of contract as promise and the problems that beset information discovery and disclosure by reason of information impactedness. Choice of organization form is very much a product of the behavioral attributes of human actors.[1]

6. Because firms supplant markets selectively rather than comprehensively, there is a need to ascertain the limits of firms. I ascribe these limits to bureaucracy, which places a differential burden on hierarchy. Also, the attributes of transactions that support self-enforcing contracts, hence operate to the advantage of markets, need to be worked up. More generally, the need is to work out the trade-offs that characterize firm and market organization, as these vary with the attributes of transactions. (Operationalization took a decade and more and the combined efforts of many scholars.)

[1] Although I made numerous references to incomplete contracts; costs of information; the need for adaptive, sequential decision making; the absence of clairvoyance; and the like, I did not make express reference to bounded rationality in my 1971 article, there being other and better occasions to wave a red flag before a bull. Things have changed a good deal since, and economics is much the better for it (Conlisk, 1996).

7. I expressly eschew comparison with hypothetical ideals in favor of comparisons with feasible alternatives, all of which are flawed: "What are referred to here as market failures are failures only in the limited sense that they involve transaction costs that can be attenuated by substituting internal organization for market exchange." This relates to arguments made earlier by Coase (1964) and Harold Demsetz (1969) and prefigured the remediableness criterion.

Many of the pieces for a different economic rationale for vertical integration had thus been sketched. Arguably, a more veridical theory of vertical integration was taking shape. The key ideas nevertheless needed to be more fully explicated and delimited, and the mechanisms of governance needed to be worked out.

Interestingly, vertical integration turns out to be a paradigm problem: Once vertical integration has been worked through in comparative contractual terms, a number of other phenomena could be recognized as variations on a few key themes. Applications to the employment relation, regulation (and deregulation), vertical market restrictions, the organization of labor, corporate governance, the modern corporation, hybrid forms of organization, corporate finance, economic development and reform, and transaction cost politics were all to come. Furthermore, all of these applications have invited follow-on empirical analysis.

Conceptual work of a transaction cost economics kind, moreover, is "not yet done." Inasmuch as any problem that arises as or can be posed as a contracting problem can be examined to advantage in transaction cost economizing terms, a huge number of phenomena qualify. Extant applications, moreover, can be refined, and additional empirical tests should be conducted. Thus, although transaction cost economics is an empirical success story—for which the people who have collected the requisite microanalytic data and performed the statistical tests deserve enormous credit—more and better empirical work is needed.

Also, additional efforts to formalize transaction cost economics (Grossman and Hart, 1986; Hart, 1995) are needed. That is not easy: "Mathematics-based theory still lacks the language needed to capture essential ideas of bounded rationality" (Kreps, 1996, p. 562). The growing interest in incomplete contracting (Magill and Quinzii, 1996) nevertheless speaks to the importance now accorded to bounds on rationality (Conlisk, 1996). A healthy give-and-take between formal modeling and institutional economics, moreover, has been taking shape. Although others might take exception with David Kreps's contention that "game theory . . . has more to learn from transaction-cost economics than it has to give, at least initially" (1996, p. 562), it suffices for my purposes to observe that game theory and transaction cost economics have already learned much from each other.

The 1971 article had only one purpose: to unpack the puzzles of vertical integration. The focus was on specific mechanisms, as against a general theory, which emphasis is consonant with Jon Elster's dictum that "explanations in the social sciences should be organized around (partial) *mechanisms* rather than (general) *theories*" (1994, p. 75; emphasis in original). This focus on the microanalytics of transactions and governance has continued since. As a consequence, transaction cost economics has taken shape piecemeal—in a "modest, slow, molecular, definitive" way, which is Peguy's prescription for progress (and is one to which I and many others subscribe). That is very different from the prevailing orthodoxy in 1971, which was preoccupied with prices and output and held that "organization" was uninteresting and unimportant.

References

Arrow, Kenneth (1969), 'The Organization of Economic Activity: Issues Pertinent to the Choice of Market versus Nonmarket Allocation," in *The Analysis and Evaluation of Public Expenditure: The PPB System*, Vol. 1, U.S. Joint Economic Committee, 91st Congress, 1st Session. Washington, DC: U.S. Government Printing Office, pp. 47–64.

Coase, Ronald (1937), 'The Nature of the Firm,' *Economica*, 4 (November): 386–405.

Coase, Ronald (1964), 'The Regulated Industries: Discussion,' *American Economic Review*, 54 (May), 194–197.

Conlisk, John (1996), 'Why Bounded Rationality?' *Journal of Economic Literature*, 34 (June), 669–700.

Demsetz, Harold (1969), 'Information and Efficiency: Another Viewpoint,' *Journal of the Law and Economics*, 12 (April), 1–22.

Elster, Jon (1994), 'Arguing and Bargaining in Two Constituent Assemblies,' unpublished manuscript, University of California, Berkeley.

Grossman, Sanford J., and Oliver D. Hart (1986), 'The Costs and Benefits of Ownership: A Theory of Vertical Integration,' *Journal of Political Economy*, 94 (August), 691–719.

Hart, Oliver (1995), *Firms, Contracts, and Financial Structure*. New York: Oxford University Press.

Kreps, David (1996), 'Markets and Hierarchies and (Mathematical) Economic Theory,' *Industrial and Corporate Change*, 5, No. 2, 561–596.

Magill, Michael, and Martine Quinzii (1996), *The Theory of Incomplete Markets*. Cambridge, MA: MIT Press.

Williamson, Oliver E. (1985), *The Economic Institutions of Capitalism*. New York: Free Press.

CHAPTER FOUR

About Oliver E. Williamson

Scott E. Masten

There is perhaps a little want of the historical spirit which sees the perpetual struggle of mankind to improve institutions so as to confine self interest more and more closely within beneficent channels.
—Edwin Cannan (1913, p. 333)

In the history of economic thought, there has been perhaps more than a little want of the spirit of which Cannan spoke. Although a wide variety of institutions and organizational forms influence economic activity, economists have preoccupied themselves primarily with the performance and limitations of markets and, particularly, the role of prices in coordinating production and exchange. The operation and limitations of non-market institutions and, correspondingly, the issue of when one institutional arrangement will—or should—be substituted for another had, until quite recently, elicited relatively little systematic attention. Over the last twenty or so years, however, a new science of organization has been emerging in which the determinants and implications of alternative organizational forms are the central concern. Where traditional price theory assumed the institutional structure under which parties exchange — typically individuals transacting with for-profit firms across a market interface—the economics of organization attempts to answer questions like why are some transactions administered within firms rather than mediated through the market, why are there nonprofit organizations, what are the merits of franchise bidding as an alternative to rate-of-return regulation, and what determines the duration and structure of contractual agreements?

Although a number of economists have contributed to the development of the New Institutional Economics, no one has more consistently and steadfastly pursued that inquiry than Oliver Williamson. The approach that Williamson advocates, and with which he has become eponymous, begins with the observation that all organizational forms have drawbacks and that de-

Reprinted with permission from *American Economists of the Late Twentieth Century*, Warren J. Samuels (ed.), Edward Elgar, 1996.

cisions regarding organizational form thus involve choices among variously faulty alternatives. The task then, becomes one of (i) identifying the features that distinguish governance alternatives, (ii) assessing the differential capacities and hazards of those alternatives, and (iii) matching transactions with governance structures so as to economize on the cost of carrying out the transaction. Williamson's research and prodigious writings over the past two decades have been devoted almost exclusively to making this broad analytical blueprint operational and to refining and applying it to an ever-wider range of governance problems. Those efforts have altered irreversibly the way in which economists perceive and analyze the problem of economic organization.

1. *Transaction-Cost Economics*

Williamson's contributions to economics and public policy over the course of his career have been many and diverse, but his crowning professional achievement has been the development of the economics of transaction costs. At the heart of the transaction-cost approach is the proposition, due originally to Ronald Coase (1960), that all potential gains from trade would be realized but for the costs of reaching and enforcing agreements. Hence, in comparing alternative institutional arrangements, the focus of attention becomes the nature and size of the barriers preventing transactors from securing those gains.

Although Coase's insight firmly established the centrality of transaction costs in assessing the merits of organizational alternatives, his original formulation of the theory lacked a basis for determining which institution was preferred other than through the direct comparison of the costs of transacting under each. Because the costs of transacting can, at best, only be observed for institutions actually chosen, claims that observed institutional arrangements minimized transaction costs were easy to make and impossible to refute, a weakness that led economists to disparage early transaction-cost arguments as tautological. In the words of Stanley Fisher, 'Transaction costs have a well-deserved bad name as a theoretical device . . . [partly] because there is a suspicion that almost anything can be rationalized by invoking suitably specified transaction costs' (1977, p. 322, as quoted in Williamson 1979b, p. 233).

Williamson rescued transaction-cost reasoning from this state by giving the theory predictive content. The key to operationalizing the theory, Williamson reasoned, was (i) to identify the behavioral traits responsible for the emergence of transactional frictions and (ii) to relate the incidence of those frictions to institutional structures and observable attributes of transactions in a discriminating way, that is, in a way that would permit hypotheses about organizational form to be formulated and tested. Even if transaction costs could not be compared directly, refutable propositions could nevertheless be derived by showing how the details of transactions affected the *differential* efficiency of organizational alternatives.

Setting out to implement this strategy for operationalizing transaction-cost reasoning, Williamson soon discovered that conventional economic assumptions regarding human behavior and the economic environment were not conducive to analyzing questions of organizational form. In particular, the high levels of rationality and efficacious enforcement of promises routinely assumed in economic models were incompatible with the existence of organizational failures: interesting institutional choice problems simply do not arise where omniscient administration and comprehensive contracting are feasible options. On the contrary, Williamson argued, organizational form matters only to the extent that individuals are limited in their foresight and cognition and are willing and able to renege on promises. These conditions, encapsulated in the concepts *bounded rationality* and *opportunism*, thus became the critical behavioral attributes to which all organizational arrangements must be responsive. In Williamson's conception, self-interest seeking remains the underlying assumption regarding human motivation, but special emphasis is placed on the limitations of human rationality and on the willingness of individuals to conceal or misrepresent facts, skirt rules, exploit loopholes, or otherwise capitalize on strategic advantages. Compared to their neoclassical counterparts, individuals are, on the one hand, less competent optimizers and, on the other, better liars, cheaters and shirkers. (Lest this seem too cynical a view of human nature, Williamson is careful to note that not everyone need be so unprincipled but that bounded rationality makes it difficult to distinguish the trustworthy from the unscrupulous.) Because efforts to control opportunism invariably place additional demands on bounded rationality, the goal of economic organization becomes to '. . . *organize transactions so as to economize on bounded rationality while simultaneously safeguarding them against the hazards of opportunism*' (1985a, p. 32; emphasis in original).

Having identified the human factors responsible for organizational failures, it remained to show how the incidence of those failures related to features of the economic environment. Central to this task was Williamson's recognition that even bounded rationality and opportunism pose few organizational problems in a static world. 'Transactions conducted under certainty are relatively uninteresting. Except as they differ in the time required to reach an equilibrium exchange configuration, any governance structure will do' (1979b, pp. 253–254). In the presence of change and uncertainty, however, transactors need to plan, monitor and continually adjust their behavior, activities that demand attention and often cooperation. Thus, for Williamson, as for Hayek, *change* is the pivotal feature of the economic environment and *adaptation* to unfolding events the central problem of economic organization (1975a, p. 5; 1991a, pp. 277–278).

Economic institutions represent alternative ways of governing the process of adaptation and differ both in their capacities to effect adaptations and in the costs associated with doing so. Discrete market transactions, for instance, provide transactors considerable autonomy and flexibility in the periods both leading up to and following the actual transaction (1979b; 1991a). In such transactions, parties are generally free to bargain or not bargain as they please and, once the transaction is consummated, have relatively few ongoing obligations. The latitude afforded transactors in simple market transactions provides them both the incentive and the ability to adjust their behavior to unfolding events. But it also furnishes a variety of tactics through which transactors may seek to elicit a more favorable distribution of the gains from trade. Parties to a simple exchange may haggle, stall, or walk away from a deal altogether in hopes of extracting more of the rents accruing to exchange.

Such opportunistic tendencies matter little where the identity of traders is unimportant; the scope for opportunism is limited where transactors can easily turn to alternative trading partners if one seeks to gain at the expense of the other. But realization of cost economies or design benefits often requires investments in relationship-specific assets that isolate the transactors from market alternatives. Relationship-specific investments can take at least four forms: (i) physical-asset specificity, which involves investments in equipment such as tooling or dies specially designed to serve a particular customer; (ii) site or location specificity, which occurs when a buyer or seller locates his or her facilities next to the other to economize on transportation costs; (iii) human-asset specificity, which arises when one or both parties develop skills or knowledge valuable only when dealing with the other; and (iv) dedicated assets, which are investments made to support exchange with a particular customer that, though not specific to that customer, would result in substantial excess capacity were the customer to discontinue purchases (Williamson 1983a, p. 526). Once the die is cast and physical or human capital has been specially designed or located for a particular use or user, continuity in trading relationships becomes important.

This 'Fundamental Transformation' from a situation of *ex ante* competition to small numbers bargaining when relationship-specific investments are made is the dominant force motivating the adoption of specialized governance structures (Williamson 1985a, pp. 61–63). Without some form of safeguard against appropriation, parties will be reluctant to invest in relationship-specific assets, despite the gains from doing so, for fear those gains will be dissipated in subsequent contention over their distribution. Securing the terms of trade at the outset through a long-term contract is one such safeguard. But contracting increases the demands on bounded rationality and only imperfectly limits opportunism. To accommodate uncertainty, contractors must either anticipate and devise responses to a large number of contingencies or prescribe a process through which adaptations can be executed. They must do so, moreover, in terms that courts can be expected to understand and implement at reasonable cost. The difficulty of anticipating and defining contractual obligations that avoid the prospect of costly adjudication means that contracts will, on the one hand, tend to be inflexible and, on the other, leave considerable opportunity to cheat on the agreement or otherwise seek to evade performance (1983a, pp. 526–527; 1985a, p. 21).

As transactions become more complex and the environment more uncertain, the limitations of contracting as a safeguard against opportunism grow, increasing the attraction of other institutional arrangements that better support adaptive, sequential decision making while circumscribing or redirecting opportunistic tendencies. Naturally, such arrangements also come at a cost. Structures that constrain opportunism inevitably sacrifice some of the high-powered incentives that distinguish market transactions and, consequently, demand greater investments in monitoring and administration (1985a, ch. 6; 1991a).

By relating the advantages and liabilities of alternative organizational arrangements to features of the transaction in a discriminating way, Williamson demonstrated that a transaction-cost orientation could indeed generate refutable implications. In doing so, moreover, he provided a systematic conception of the problem of economic organization in which all organizational forms are recognized to be subject to the same fundamental limitations. The aim of transaction-cost economics, as Williamson describes it, is to 'assign transactions (which differ in their attributes) to governance structures (the adaptive capacities and associated costs of which differ) in a discriminating (mainly transaction cost economizing) way' (1989, p. 136).

2. *The Theory of the Firm*

Williamson first conceived and applied this framework for analyzing economic organization in the context of the problem that had also originally led Coase to focus on transaction costs, namely, the nature and boundaries of the firm. The orthodox portrayal of the firm as a production function that combines inputs purchased from individuals and other firms into outputs that it in turn sells on the market had proved useful for the analysis of market equilibrium. But this abstraction failed to illuminate the purpose or consequences of the vast array of economic activity organized administratively within firms.

In the absence of an efficiency rationale, integration of production tended to be seen either as technologically determined or as serving monopoly purposes.

Transaction-cost economics recast the firm as a governance structure, one among several alternative ways in which production and exchange might be organized. By integrating a transaction, transactors alter the rules and processes through which disputes are resolved and adjustments effected. But though a firm-as-governance-structure orientation was a significant step, a complete theory of the firm awaited resolution of three great puzzles. First, what are the properties that distinguish organization within the firm from market exchange? Second, what determines which transactions get integrated? And third, what limits firm size or, as Coase (1991 [1937], p. 23) put it, 'Why is not all production carried out in one big firm?'

Williamson's initial assault on the boundaries of the firm issue, 'The Vertical Integration of Production: Market Failure Considerations' (1971), previewed many of the arguments later to become cornerstones of the comparative institutional framework. In particular, Williamson (i) described the advantages of markets in incentive and bounded-rationality economizing respects; (ii) portrayed the infeasibility of long-term, complete contingent claims contracts; and (iii) identified the hazards of short-term contracting 'if either (1) efficient supply requires investment in special-purpose, long-life equipment, or (2) the winner of the original contract acquires a cost advantage, say by reason of "first mover" advantages (such as unique location or learning, including the acquisition of undisclosed or proprietary technical and managerial procedures and task-specific labor skills)' (1971, p. 116). 'In circumstances where protracted bargaining between independent parties to a transaction can reasonably be anticipated,' internalization offered 'a wider variety and sensitivity of control instruments' that included 'low-cost access to the requisite data' and 'a comparatively efficient conflict resolution machinery' (1971, p. 113).

It was not until the publication of *Markets and Hierarchies* in 1975, however, that the importance and scope of Williamson's analysis of organization began to be fully appreciated. In this path-breaking book, Williamson organized the components of his earlier analysis into a unified and systematic framework for analyzing the problem of economic organization in comparative terms. Among other things, he categorized the behavioral and environmental attributes responsible for organizational failures, described the distinctive features of market and hierarchical organization, and analyzed the differential effects of idiosyncratic investments and uncertainty on the costs of governing intermediate product transactions internally versus externally. The problems posed by incomplete or 'impacted' information—which Williamson traced to their rudiments in bounded rationality and complexity—also played a central role (1975a, pp. 31–37). The publication of *Markets and Hierarchies* was a landmark in the development of transaction-cost reasoning that opened the door to the investigation of a host of organizational problems that had previously resisted economic analysis.

Williamson continued the refinement and extension of transaction-cost reasoning and his analysis of the governance of intermediate product transactions in a series of subsequent articles, the most influential of which has been 'Transaction-Cost Economics: The Governance of Contractual Relations' (1979b). This article offered a refined statement of the logic of matching governance modes with transactions and identified parallels between governance modes and contract law regimes. Williamson also related the choice among governance arrangements to three critical dimensions of transactions: uncertainty, frequency of exchange, and the degree to which investments are transaction specific, the last of which was taking on an increasingly prominent role.

Through his efforts to operationalize transaction-cost theory, Williamson had provided by this point an answer to the question, what determines which transactions get integrated? He had, moreover, as part of that analysis, also described some of the properties that distinguish internal organization from markets (1975a, pp. 29–30) and the limits to internal organization (1975a, ch. 7). But the basis for the superior auditing and dispute resolution properties Williamson and others ascribed to internal organization remained a matter of controversy. Where does the authority of management to direct production or settle disputes come from, and why are employees less able to hide or distort information than independent contractors? As Alchian and Demsetz had earlier protested, employers have no authority or disciplining power beyond that available in any ordinary contractual relationship; all an employer can do is 'fire or sue' (1972, p. 777). A fully satisfactory accounting of the source of internal organization's distinctive properties and the limits to firm size remained elusive.

Williamson supplied the last two pieces of the integration puzzle with the notions of 'forbearance law' and 'the impossibility of selective intervention.' Building on his earlier association of governance modes and contract regimes (1979b), Williamson proposed that the distinctive feature of the law governing internal organization is forbearance: 'whereas courts routinely grant standing to firms should there be disputes over prices, the damages to be ascribed to delays, failures of quality, and the like, courts will refuse to hear disputes between one internal division and another over identical technical issues' (1991a, p. 274). The decision to make rather than buy thus has substantive implications: while parties to a contract can resort to courts to resolve disputes, top management exercises ultimate authority in disputes between divisions; it is its own court of last resort. Ultimately, termination and legal action are, as Alchian and Demsetz maintained, the only options available, but *when* you can fire and *what* you can sue for depend on the mode of organization adopted. The refusal of courts to intervene in internal disputes affords management flexibility to conduct business and adapt operations as they deem appropriate and thus provides a basis for the control and adaptability advantages of internal organization (1991a).

But if internal organization possesses superior control and adaptation properties, why are not all transactions organized with the firm? In principle, a newly integrated firm should be able to operate at least as efficiently as the two independent firms from which it was formed simply by allowing each division of the combined firm to operate independently as it had before and only intervening where net benefits were likely to be realized. As long as managers intervened selectively, combined operations would always dominate independent ones (1985a, pp. 131–135).

Williamson's answer to the question 'what limits firm size?' lay in the impossibility of selective intervention (1985a, ch. 6). Unable to use the courts to enforce promises to intervene selectively, management would be drawn to intervening even where joint benefits are not realized. Without effective assurances that owners will not appropriate performance enhancements, the incentives of division managers to innovate, maintain assets, acquire and utilize information, and otherwise invest in the efficient operation of the division are ineluctably compromised. In their place, the firm is forced to substitute weaker, indirect incentives dependent on managerial oversight. The loss of incentive intensity combined with the limited capacity of management to administer additional transactions—which manifest themselves in a variety of bureaucratic inefficiencies—ultimately undermines the efficacy of internal organization and thereby limit firm size.

With the last pieces of the puzzle in place, the tradeoffs between market and internal organization came into still sharper focus. Although the high-powered incentives attainable with market exchange economize on bounded rationality, the dissociation of effort and compensation and resulting loss in incentive intensity resulting from integration is not always to be lamented: high-powered incentives motivate efforts to redistribute as well as increase rents. Where asset specificity is great and uncertainty high—hence the gains to ongoing exchange large and flexibility highly valued—flatter, low-powered incentives supported by enhanced monitoring are likely to be preferred (1988b; 1991a).

3. *A Fundamental Transformation*

Although his name has become synonymous with transaction-cost reasoning, Williamson's approach to analyzing organization was itself the result of a fundamental transformation. Like his work on transaction-cost economics, his early research was marked by brilliance and innovation. But the orientation and methods he brought to this research were more conventional in nature. Entering the doctoral program at Carnegie in 1960 as a transfer from the Ph.D. program in business administration at Stanford, Williamson was attracted to the issues being addressed by the behavioral group led by Herbert Simon, Richard Cyert and James March, but he favored the methods employed by the economists, which included John Muth, Merton Miller and Allan Meltzer. His dissertation combined those interests by addressing the issue of managerial discretion in terms of constrained maximization. In a prelude to later agency treatments, Williamson argued that managers have preferences over such things as staff and emoluments and that costs of detecting and policing managers actions prevented owners from effectively overseeing managers. Modeling the tradeoff between profits and other managerial objectives, he derived a set of testable hypotheses distinguishing profit-maximization and managerial-discretion assumptions and showed, using data from field studies, that observed managerial behavior was consistent with the latter. This research, which was awarded a Ford Foundation Dissertation Prize in 1963 and published as *The Economics of Discretionary Behavior* (1964), introduced the first consistent and economically sound model of firm behavior based explicitly on utility maximization rather than profit maximization and opened for the first time the black box of the firm to the tools of modern economics.

Williamson went on to make a number of important contributions to economics and public policy, including original and influential papers on peak-load pricing (1966), social choice (1967), and the dynamics of interfirm behavior (1965), as well as a pair of articles on barriers to entry, 'Selling Expense as a Barrier to Entry' (1962) and 'Wage Rates as a Barrier to Entry: The Pennington Case in Perspective' (1968b), that were the first to treat entry barriers as a strategic decision and were forerunners to the strategic barriers literature of the 1980s. His primary interest, however, remained issues of organization, and he continued to develop and refine his analysis of the relation between the internal structure and behavior of the firm (1967; 1970).

The transformation of Williamson's perspective and approach appears to have begun during a year at the Justice Department (1966–67) in which he served as special economic assistant to the head of the Antitrust Division. During this experience, Williamson began to suspect that many of the practices antitrust authorities then regarded with hostility actually had efficiency motivations. A prudent antitrust policy, he reasoned, should recognize those motives and distinguish practices that, on net, enhanced efficiency from those that were detrimental to social welfare.

Williamson's concern with the tradeoffs inherent in antitrust policy was first revealed in 'Economies as an Antitrust Defense' (1968a), in which he demonstrated that potential cost economies from horizontal mergers could easily outweigh the dead-weight losses from increased market power and advocated that antitrust policy be modified to recognize demonstrable cost economies as a valid defense in merger cases. The potential for antitrust policy to impede efficient behavior was also evident in his efforts to develop a practical rule for distinguishing competitive from predatory behavior (1977). The resulting quantity-based rule both exhibited superior welfare properties and was easier to implement than previously proposed rules based on the comparison of prices and costs.

Williamson's analyses of horizontal mergers and predatory pricing contributed importantly to the debate over the formulation of a more discriminating antitrust policy. But while both were topics to which existing economic models could be adapted, the same could not be said for the analysis of vertical mergers and restrictions. Among the cases Williamson observed firsthand while in Washington was the Justice Department's successful challenge before the Supreme Court of the Schwinn bicycle company's contractual restraints with its dealers. Williamson was uncomfortable with the Justice Department's position that vertical restrictions had no redeeming features and served only to enhance market power. A conceptual apparatus to support his conjecture that vertical restraints could enhance efficiency had yet to be developed, however.

With antitrust policy as an impetus, Williamson's research began to tilt away from behavior and organization within firms to the structure of relations between them. The first products of those efforts were his 1971 article on vertical integration, which he motivated with references to antitrust policy (1971, p. 112), and *Markets and Hierarchies*, which he subtitled *Analysis and Antitrust Implications*. The necessary apparatus now in place, Williamson returned to the merits of the *Schwinn* decision with an analysis of vertical restrictions in transaction-cost terms (1979b). The economizing orientation of transaction-cost economics as a counter to monopoly and strategic arguments has since been a recurring theme (1985a, chs. 1 and 14; 1991c; 1992).

4. *Applications and Extensions*

In the meantime, Williamson was discovering the power and generality of the framework he had developed. Indeed, it appeared that any issue that would be posed as a contracting problem could be usefully examined in transaction-cost terms. Two early applications were to the organization of labor and the governance of public utility transactions. In 'Understanding the Employment Relation: The Analysis of Idiosyncratic Exchange' (1975b), Williamson (with Michael Wachter and Jeffrey Harris) assessed the role of internal labor markets as solutions to the problems of bounded rationality and opportunism where workers had developed firm-specific skills and, in so doing, developed an efficiency rationale for the promotion ladders and grievance procedures that were common elements of collective labor agreements.

The debate over the prospects for franchise bidding as an alternative to rate-of-return regulation provided another arena in which to demonstrate the value of a transaction-cost orientation. The conventional wisdom in the late 1960s was that public utility regulation was a necessary response to natural monopoly cost conditions. Harold Demsetz (1968) exposed the fallacy in that reasoning by noting that public utility services could be efficiently procured — even where cost conditions dictated a single supplier — simply by awarding a franchise to the firm that offered to serve the market at lowest price. Williamson, who had served on Mayor John Lindsay's task force on cable television in 1969–1970, perceived parallels to the theory of vertical integration on which he had been working. In particular, because the supply of public utility services typically requires large, durable investments in production and distribution facilities that are specialized to a particular market, efficient franchise agreements would have to take the form of long-term contracts to avoid repeated haggling over the terms of trade once those investments were in place. But uncertainty about cost and demand conditions over such long horizons and the complexity of public utility services would leave long-term contracts for public utility services perilously incomplete. To accommodate that uncertainty, franchise contracts would have to employ contract terms and administrative machinery — cost-plus price adjustment, auditing procedures, elaborate and formal dispute resolution processes — that mirrored both in character and in costs the administrative apparatus traditionally associated with rate-of-return regulation (Williamson 1976). While Demsetz had revealed the potential for the efficient supply of public utility services using market arrangements if 'irrelevant complications' were ignored (1968, p. 57), Williamson had shown that it was precisely such complications that underlay the choice between regulation and franchise bidding and that the complications that impeded effective regulation were likely to frustrate franchise bidding solutions as well.

Williamson also showed how the transaction-cost paradigm could be used to provide a fresh perspective on firms' financing decisions (1988a). According to Williamson, debt and equity represent alternative governance structures for the procurement of financial capital analogous to contracting and internal organization for the procurement of intermediate products. For projects involving standardized, redeployable assets, debt, which offers contractual protections for investors, is the low-cost governance arrangement. As asset specificity increases, however, the residual value of the assets and, hence, the value of debtholders' preemptive claims declines. The willingness to supply capital in such cases will be enhanced if management offers investors a safeguard against appropriation or misuse of their investments in the form of a body (the board of directors) that can monitor the use of investors' capital and has the authority to oversee, compensate and replace management. Like internal procurement of intermediate goods and unlike debt, which affords investors the power to intervene only under a set of relatively extreme events (such as bankruptcy), equity financing provides a mechanism for regularized interventions. In contrast to traditional agency treatments, transaction-cost economics 'regards debt and equity principally as governance structures rather than as financial instruments' (1988a, p. 579).

Although the *choice* among organizational forms has been the primary focus of transaction-cost analyses, the *design* of market and firm relations has been another major theme of Williamson's research. Williamson's earliest exploration of organizational design was his analysis of the internal structure of firms. Intrigued by Alfred Chandler's description of the advent of the multidivisional corporation, Williamson set out to analyze how growth in the size and complexity of a firm affected the way tasks and responsibilities are divided within the organization (1970; 1975a). Comparing unitary, or U-form, organization, in which operations are grouped along functional lines (sales, finance, manufacturing, and so forth), with multidivisional, or M-form, organization, in which decision-making responsibility was assigned to quasi-autonomous operating divisions organized along product, brand or geographic lines, Williamson argued that the strains on management inherent in large organizations favored M-form organization, which, appropriately administered, had the properties of a miniature internal capital market. The analysis resulted in the M-form hypothesis: 'The organization and operation of the large enterprise along the lines of the M-form favors goal pursuit and least-cost behavior more nearly associated with the neoclassical profit maximization hypothesis than does the U-form organizational alternative' (1970, p. 134).

Williamson turned to the design of contractual relations with 'Credible Commitments: Using Hostages to Support Exchange' (1983a). Rejecting at the outset the assumption 'common to both law and economics, that the legal system enforces promises in a knowledgeable, sophisticated, and low-cost way' (1983a, p. 519), Williamson argued that the cost and imperfections inherent in court enforcement will lead contracting parties to seek out devices that foster cooperative adaptation to change without the need for recourse to the court system. One such device is the use of economic hostages. As in the days when kings extended their daughters as collateral against breach of their commitments to other monarchs, modern commercial transactors might find it advantageous to make relationship-specific investments whose value would be sacrificed if they failed to perform as promised. Although a unilateral investment in relationship-specific assets exposes the transaction to appropriation hazards, a reciprocal investment by a trading partner that balances the parties' exposure to such hazards may strengthen the integrity of a trading relationship. A range of otherwise enigmatic practices, such as reciprocal dealing and aspects of franchise contracts, can thereby be seen to have efficiency motivations (1983a).

5. *Reception and Influence*

Widely revered for his keen judgement and generous advice, Williamson has been known to summarize his overall assessment of the prospects of a student's research with a statement either that 'I don't see where this is going' or 'I think there might be something there,' the latter being understood by all as a signal of approval and encouragement.

Initial reaction of much of the mainstream of the economics profession to Williamson's early writings on the theory of the firm might similarly be described as 'I think there might be something there.' Clearly, Williamson was addressing fundamental questions about the operation of the economic system that had yet to receive a satisfactory treatment. But the analysis developed in *Markets and Hierarchies* involved a significant departure from orthodox assumptions and an investment both in some unfamiliar concepts and in new terminology. To some in a profession increasingly enamored of mathematics and predisposed to skepticism regarding transaction-cost reasoning, Williamson's 'preformal' presentation of the theory seemed vague and unproven. Still, the logic was compelling, and the approach soon developed adherents. Besides Williamson, Victor Goldberg (e.g., 1976a; 1976b) and Benjamin Klein, Robert Crawford and Armen Alchian (1978), among others, began making headway in the development and application of transaction-cost reasoning. Empirical research and formal modeling following soon thereafter fostered further acceptance. By the mid-1980s, *Markets and Hierarchies* rivaled Adam Smith's *The Wealth of Nations* and Keynes's *General Theory* in terms of citations according to the *Social Science Citation Index*. By 1992, *Markets and Hierarchies* and *The Economic Institutions of Capitalism* had surpassed Marx's *Capital* to become the most frequently cited books in the social sciences.

The first empirical studies offering econometric tests of transaction-cost propositions began to appear in the early 1980s. Although Williamsonian transaction-cost economics, unlike earlier transaction-cost arguments, offered a set of testable implications, testing those hypotheses was not without its difficulties. The level of detail at which the theory operates made acquisition of appropriate data difficult; objective measures for factors like asset specificity and uncertainty are hard to devise and, even though variables representing organizational form pose fewer measurement problems, transaction-level data on organization form and contract terms are often not readily accessible. Nevertheless, these impediments gradually gave way to persistent efforts, and the result is a substantial body of evidence supporting the importance of asset specificity and transaction costs more generally in the choice among organizational forms and in the design and duration of contractual relationships (see Joskow 1988; Shelanski 1991; and Crocker and Masten 1994, for recent surveys).

Progress modeling transaction-cost arguments began shortly thereafter. Although economic theorists had developed an enormous body of theoretical work on contracting by the mid-1980s, most of those developments had occurred in the context of agency and asymmetric information models. Gradually, however, awareness was growing that the complete contracts and costless enforcement assumed in these models were inconsistent with contracting as it was observed in practice and did little to explain the variety of terms and duration of contractual agreements (see, e.g., Hart and Holmstrom 1987, pp. 131–133, 147–148). In response, contract theorists began to shift their attention to models of incomplete contracts that permitted, among other things, more rigorous investigation of the tradeoffs involved in the integration decision (see, for instance, Grossman and Hart 1986; Riordan 1990; and the survey by Holmstrom and Tirole 1989).[1] The extent to which Williamson's arguments have held up under these formalizations and their influence on formal theorists is reflected in the extensive and favorable treatments transaction-cost arguments have received in recent textbooks by theorists David Kreps (1990) and Paul Milgrom and John Roberts (1992).

Williamson's influence has also extended beyond economics to law, political science, business strategy and sociology. No doubt, the accessibility of Williamson's analysis to scholars in fields less reliant than economics on formal modeling has contributed to its dissemination. But the more important factors in the adoption and influence of Williamson's ideas have been their immediate relevance to the concerns of scholars in these fields and Williamson's willingness to engage these scholars on their own territory. Williamson has, through his writings on contract, become one of the leading figures in the 're-

---

[1] Williamson (with Michael Riordan) also published an early model of the integration decision in which the level of investment in specific assets was treated as endogenous (1985b).

lational contracting' school of legal scholarship. At the same time, Williamson has been a vocal critic of 'legal centralism,' the widely held view among legal scholars that governments, and particularly the legal system, represent indispensable and efficacious dispute resolution forums. Instead, Williamson emphasizes the efforts of contracting parties to '"contract out of and away from" the governance structures of the state by devising private orderings' (1983a, p. 520). Recognition of the ubiquity of bounded rationality and opportunism has important implications for the way courts interpret and enforce contracts and for the design of the legal system more broadly, and has begun to be incorporated in analyses of political institutions as well (see, for instance, Weingast and Marshall, 1988, and the special issue of the *Journal of Law, Economics, and Organization*, 1990).

That transaction-cost economics has become one of the dominant paradigms in strategic management research should not be surprising given the strategic management field's abiding interest in questions of organizational form. By providing a systematic way of analyzing the relative merits of alternative governance arrangements and a set of testable propositions relating those merits to attributes of transactions and the surrounding environment, transaction-cost economics offers strategy a set of normative rules for choosing among alternative organizational arrangements. But where the business strategy literature had been primarily concerned with *strategizing*, that is, efforts to acquire and exploit market power, Williamson advocates an orientation that emphasizes *economizing* (1991c). Not only is economizing more fundamental, according to Williamson, but 'emphasis on economizing restores manufacturing and merchandising to a place of importance within the business firm and on the academic research agenda' (1991c, p. 76).

More so than most economists, Williamson has also endeavored to both draw on and contribute to the sociology of organizations. In articles and essays addressed directly to sociologists, Williamson has sought to expand the dialogue between sociologists and economists by laying out the common ground and describing the advantages a transaction-cost economizing orientation offers for analyzing phenomena of long-standing concern to organization theorists (1981; 1990; 1993a; 1993c). At the same time, Williamson has demonstrated an uncommon receptivity to and appreciation of sociological concerns, as is evident from his discussions of the costs of bureaucracy, which trace bureaucratic inefficiencies to sociological phenomena such as the propensities of individuals to manage and forgive (1985a, pp. 148–151) and in his references to concepts such as atmosphere and dignity with which economists have yet to come to terms (1985a, ch. 10). More broadly, Williamson has repeatedly made the case that economists have potentially a lot to learn from sociologists regarding such matters as the role of process and the di-

mensions and implications of bounded rationality. This openness notwithstanding, Williamson has been critical of much of the sociological research
on organizations, challenging those who would explain organizational structure in terms of power and trust relations to define and operationalize those
concepts in a way that allows testable predictions (1990, p. 123; 1993a;
1993c).

Despite the substantial measure of respect and acceptance afforded
Williamson's approach by legal scholars, sociologists, and strategic management and organization theorists, transaction-cost reasoning has nevertheless
generated its share of disputes and controversies.[2] An example is the debate
engendered by Williamson's 1980 article on the organization of work. Williamson's analysis corroborated radical economist Stephen Marglin's verdict
that technology alone was not enough to explain hierarchical relations but disputed his claim that the failure of neoclassical economics to supply an efficiency justification for hierarchy supported the Marxian interpretation of
hierarchy as a device to exploit workers. Williamson's rejection of both tech-
nology- and power-based explanations of the evolution of work organization
in favor of an interpretation based on transaction-cost economies prompted
a series of replies, to which Williamson offered gracious yet compelling re-
joinders (e.g., Williamson 1983b; 1988c).

Through debates of this nature substantive disagreements are aired, mistakes uncovered, arguments clarified, and knowledge ultimately advanced. But
transaction-cost economics has occasionally been the target of less construc-
tive criticism as well. Richard Posner's assessment of the contributions of
Coase and Williamson at the annual conference on the New Institutional Economics held in Saarbrucken, Germany, in June 1992, is an example of the latter (see Posner 1993 and the responses by Williamson 1993d and Coase
1993). Posner praised Williamson for helping to correct 'collectivist deforma-
tions of theory' (1993, p. 85) and for having invited 'economists' attention to
a host of underexplored problems and [for] contributing to their solution by
exploring the ways in which businessmen overcome transaction costs by a variety of devices and in a variety of settings' (1993, p. 81). Posner went on,
however, to question the novelty of the framework Williamson developed and
its contribution to our understanding of the problem of economic organization. The distinctions between transaction-cost economics and other economic analyses of institutional arrangements are, as far as Posner was concerned, mainly terminological, whatever substantive insights transaction-cost
economics may once have offered long since superseded by developments else-

---

[2] See Zald (1987) for a review of Williamson's *Economic Institutions of Capitalism* from a sociologist's perspective and a summary of the reaction of sociologists to Williamson's work.

where in economics and particularly in information and game theory (1993, pp. 80–81).

Does transaction-cost economics represent a distinct approach to problems of economic organization? Certainly, parallels can be drawn between the concepts and concerns of transaction-cost economics and those found in neoclassical treatments. Concerns with the effects of bounded rationality, opportunism and asset specificity in transaction-cost economics overlap more mainstream concerns with information asymmetries, moral hazard and bilateral monopoly. Indeed, given that meaningful institutional choice problems simply do not arise in the absence of bounded rationality and opportunism, it would have been surprising had the critical dimensions underlying the problem of economic organization gone completely unappreciated except by transaction-cost economists.

But to characterize transaction-cost economics solely in terms of a set of isolated concepts and a particular terminology misses the critical features that distinguish a transaction-cost orientation (see Williamson 1993d). First, whereas conventional analyses are content to treat information, bargaining and contracting costs as parameters, transaction-cost economics regards these as consequences of human cognitive limitations and behavior. It is true, for instance, that the complications introduced by bounded rationality can be captured in models of utility maximization constrained by imperfect information. But, without disparaging the contributions of that approach, it is also true that the results of asymmetric information models are extremely sensitive to the particular constraints assumed. Moreover, despite occasional acknowledgements that the roots of market failures lay in transaction costs (Arrow 1969), neoclassical treatments have kept transactional frictions largely hidden in the background, their presence or absence implicit in the behavioral and institutional options assumed available to economic actors. Little effort is made to analyze their determinants and dimensions systematically or to assure that assumptions were employed consistently. By invoking (prohibitive) search and information costs selectively, the literature on asymmetric information risks exposing itself to the sorts of charges of *ex post* rationalization leveled at early transaction-cost arguments.

Transaction-cost economics, by contrast, traces the origins of information costs to bounded rationality, which is omnipresent, and seeks to relate the incidence of information costs to characteristics of transactions and to the informational demands placed on decision makers under alternative organizational forms. Thus, modern transaction-cost economics regards information and other transaction costs as something to be explained rather than assumed, a difference that accounts in large measure for why transaction-cost economics, unlike information and game theories, has generated a substantial body of empirical work using real-world data.

Second, transaction-cost economics contemplates a wider range of behavior than conventional analyses (Williamson 1993b, pp. 100–101). Although both moral hazard and opportunism are motivated by self-interest, moral hazard describes actions taken in response to price signals contained in the contract and thus consists of efforts to effect a de facto adjustment of the distribution of surpluses *within the existing terms of an agreement.* The concept of opportunism, in contrast, encompasses actions designed to force a renegotiation of those terms and thereby to effect a *de jure* modification in the distribution of the gains from trade. Opportunism in contractual settings includes making false claims of dissatisfaction, suing for trivial deviations, and interfering with the other party's performance in hope of inducing a breach of contract (Williamson 1983a, pp. 526–527). Such behavior does not benefit an actor directly but is undertaken solely to impose costs on a trading partner in hope of eliciting concessions, the goal being to make the status quo so disagreeable that your partner finds it less costly to accede to a renegotiation than to insist on the current terms. Compared to the types of behavior contemplated in conventional analyses, opportunism is more ingenious, active and likely to provoke strategic responses by other parties.

These differences in the characterization of human behavior, in turn, affect perceptions about the role of contracts. In standard agency models of contract, the primary concern is with aligning incentives to discourage shirking and other forms of moral hazard (Williamson 1985a, ch. 1; 1988b). Transaction-cost economics, in contrast, views contracts as means of establishing procedures for adapting exchange and resolving disputes rather than purely as incentive mechanisms. Thus, whereas conventional analyses emphasize the efficiency of *outcomes*, transaction-cost economics focuses on the *processes* through which agreements are reached, modified and implemented (Williamson 1988b). What varies as transactions are relocated from one organizational form to another are the duties, procedures and sanctions available to transactors and, hence, the tactics they can employ and the processes through which adaptations are realized. Since it is the legal system that establishes and supports those distinctions, studying the practical operation and limitations of the legal system becomes an essential element of research on organization.

Most important, while conventional analyses continue to assess the efficiency of organizational arrangements relative to the absolute standard of Pareto optimality, transaction-cost economics is relentlessly comparative, maintaining that the merits of particular organizational arrangements can *only* be assessed relative to the performance of the relevant alternatives constrained by the same human frailties and propensities, technology and information (Williamson 1985a; 1993d). A transaction-cost orientation fosters an appreciation that problems ascribed to markets, contracts or regulation often inhere in the circumstances. Given the powerful motives to find and adopt organizational forms that increase the available surplus, prudence requires consideration of the remediability of a problem before condemning the performance of a particular arrangement.

6. *Concluding Remarks*

The collapse of central planning and the subsequent problems encountered attempting to establish market economies have contributed to a growing appreciation of the importance of institutions and organization to economic performance. While traditional macroeconomic policy concerns such as fiscal budgets, price-level stabilization and currency convertibility are important to providing an environment conducive to growth, the roots of a successful free-enterprise economy rest in individual competence, sound business organization and the maintenance of a range of supporting institutions to define and protect property rights, facilitate trade and settle disputes (Williamson 1991b).

Simultaneously, awareness has been growing that understanding the economic institutions of capitalism requires an appreciation of the sources and consequences of transaction costs. The two most illustrious figures in the development of transaction-cost reasoning have been Ronald Coase and Oliver Williamson. Coase's contribution, for which he was honored with the 1991 Nobel Prize in Economics, was to show that, in the absence of transaction costs, efficiency could be achieved under any number of institutional arrangements and, hence, that the choice among alternative institutional arrangements, including the choice between firm and market organization, turned on a comparison of the costs of transacting under each. By demonstrating how systematic variations in the incidence of transaction costs across organizational forms and transaction types could be used to explain observed patterns of organization, Williamson elevated Coase's insight from a tautology to a predictive theory, an accomplishment that Coase himself has acknowledged. In a series of lectures celebrating the 50th anniversary of the publication of 'The Nature of the Firm,' Coase observed that his 1937 article on the nature of the firm 'had little or no influence for thirty of forty years after it was published' (Coase 1988, p. 33). Referring to Williamson's explanation that this lack of influence resulted from a failure to operationalize the theory, Coase concluded, 'I think it is largely correct' (1988, p. 38; also 1992, p. 718).

On the surface, the operationalization of organizational choice problems might have appeared a natural and straightforward extension of neoclassical methods, the choice among governance arrangements being simply part of an individual's overall optimization problem. But Williamson's efforts to identify and enumerate the factors that lead one transaction to be integrated and another left to market mediation revealed that conventional assumptions regarding human behavior and the economic environment were not conducive to analyzing questions of organizational form. What emerged as a result of those efforts was not merely another extension of price theory and a handful of new insights regarding the decision to integrate but a whole new paradigm for analyzing the structures that govern economic activity. Through his extensive research and prolific writings, Williamson has demonstrated that the issues posed and the factors emphasized in the transaction-cost paradigm are pervasive and, from the point of view of both individual economic actors and society as a whole, of considerable economic importance. In Williamson's words, 'Any attempt to deal seriously with the study of economic organization must come to terms with the *combined* ramifications of bounded rationality and opportunism in conjunction with a condition of asset specificity' (1985a, p. 42).

Emphasis on the transaction as the basic unit of analysis is not without its costs, of course. Concentration on individual transactions involves some sacrifice of attention to interactions in the general economy. Moreover, the fact that investments are durable so that the profitability of a current investment is contingent on preceding investment decisions—and recursively, therefore, on all preceding decisions—underscores the need for an evolutionary orientation (or 'historical spirit' as Cannan put it). Nevertheless, Williamson's contributions represent by far the most comprehensive treatment of the issues of economic organization and institutions in the economic literature to date and, given their scope and quality, are likely to remain so for the foreseeable future.

Williamson's Major Writings

Williamson, Oliver E. (1962), 'Selling Expense as a Barrier to Entry,' *Quarterly Journal of Economics*, **77**, 112–128.

(1964), *The Economics of Discretionary Behavior: Managerial Objectives in a Theory of the Firm*. Englewood Cliffs, NJ: Prentice-Hall.

(1966), 'Peak Load Pricing and Optimal Capacity under Indivisibility Constraints,' *American Economic Review*, **56**, 810–827.

(1967a), 'Hierarchical Control and Optimum Firm Size,' *Journal of Political Economy*, **76**, 123–138.

(1967b), (with Thomas Sargent), 'Social Choice: A Probabilistic Approach,' *Economic Journal*, **27**, 797–813.

(1968a), 'Economics as an Antitrust Defense: The Welfare Tradeoffs,' *American Economic Review*, **58**, 18–35.

(1968b), 'Wage Rates as a Barrier to Entry: The Pennington Case in Perspective,' *Quarterly Journal of Economics*, **82**, 85–116.

(1970), *Corporate Control and Business Behavior*, Englewood Cliffs, NJ: Prentice-Hall.

(1971), 'The Vertical Integration of Production: Market Failure Considerations,' *American Economic Review*, **61**, 112–123.

(1975a), *Markets and Hierarchies: Analysis and Antitrust Implications*. New York: Free Press.

(1975b), (with Michael Wachter and Jeffrey Harris), 'Understanding the Employment Relation: The Analysis of Idiosyncratic Exchange,' *Bell Journal of Economics*, **6**, 250–278.

(1976), 'Franchise Bidding for Natural Monopolies—in General and with Respect to CATV,' *Bell Journal of Economics*, **7**, 73–104.

√(1977), 'Predatory Pricing: A Strategic and Welfare Analysis,' *Yale Law Journal*, **87**, 284–340.

(1979a), 'Assessing Vertical Market Restrictions,' *University of Pennsylvania Law Review*, **127**, 953–993.

√(1979b), 'Transaction-Cost Economics: The Governance of Contractual Relations,' *Journal of Law and Economics*, **22**, 233–261.

√(1980), 'The Organization of Work,' *Journal of Economic Behavior and Organization*, **1**, 5–38.

√(1981), 'The Economics of Organization: The Transaction Cost Approach,' *American Journal of Sociology*, **87**, 548–577.

(1983a), 'Credible Commitments: Using Hostages to Support Exchange,' *American Economic Review*, **73**, 519–540.

(1983b), 'Technology and the Organization of Work: A Rejoinder,' *Journal of Economic Behavior and Organization*, **4**, 67–68.

(1985a), *The Economic Institutions of Capitalism*, New York: Free Press.

√(1985b), (with Michael Riordan), 'Asset Specificity and Economic Organization,' *International Journal of Industrial Organization*, **3**, 365–378.

(1988a), 'Corporate Finance and Corporate Governance,' *Journal of Finance*, **43**, 567–591.

√(1988b), 'The Logic of Economic Organization,' *Journal of Law, Economics, and Organization*, **4**, 65–93. Repr. In O. E. Williamson and S. G. Winter (1991), *The Nature of the Firm: Origins, Evolution, and Development* (New York: Oxford University Press), 90–116.

(1988c), 'Technology and Transaction Cost Economics: A Reply,' *Journal of Economic Behavior and Organization*, **10**, 355–364.

(1989), 'Transaction Cost Economics,' in Richard Schmalensee and Robert Willig, eds., *Handbook of Industrial Organization*. New York: North-Holland, 135–182.

(1990), 'Interview with Oliver E. Williamson,' in Richard Swedberg, ed., *Economics and Sociology*, Princeton, NJ: Princeton University Press, 115–129.

(1991a), 'Comparative Economic Organization: The Analysis of Discrete Structural Alternatives,' *Administrative Science Quarterly*, **36**, 269–296.

(1991b), 'Institutional Aspects of Economic Reform: The Transaction Cost Economics Perspective' (mimeo).

(1991c), 'Strategizing, Economizing, and Economic Organization,' *Strategic Management Journal*, **12**, 75–94.

(1992), 'Antitrust Lenses and the Uses of Transaction Cost Economics Reasoning,' in Thomas Jorde and David Teece, eds., *Antitrust, Innovation, and Competitiveness*. New York: Oxford, 137–164.

(1993a), 'Calculativeness, Trust, and Economic Organization,' *Journal of Law and Economics*, **36**, 453–486.

√(1993b), 'Opportunism and Its Critics,' *Managerial and Decision Economics*, **14**, 97–107.

(1993c), 'Transaction Cost Economics and Organization Theory,' *Industrial and Corporate Change*, **2**, 107–156.

(1993d), 'Transaction Cost Economics Meet Posnerian Law and Economics,' *Journal of Institutional and Theoretical Economics*, **149**, 99–118.

Other References

Alchian, Armen and Harold Demsetz (1972), 'Production, Information Costs, and Economic Organization,' *American Economic Review*, **62**, 777–795.

Arrow, Kenneth J. (1969), 'The Organization of Economic Activity: Issues Pertinent to the Choice of Market vs. Non-Market Allocation,' in *The Analysis and Education of Public Expenditure: The PPB System*, Joint Economic Committee, 91st Congress, 1st Session. Washington, DC: U.S. Government Printing Office, 59–73.

√Cannan, Edwin (1913), 'Review of N. G. Pierson's *Principles of Economics*,' *Economic Review*, **23**, 331–333.

Coase, Ronald (1937), 'The Nature of the Firm,' *Economica n.s.*, **4**, 386–405. Repr. In O. E. Williamson and S. G. Winter (1991), *The Nature of the Firm: Origins, Evolution, and Development* (New York: Oxford University Press), 18–33.

√Coase, Ronald (1960), 'The Problem of Social Cost,' *Journal of Law and Economics*, **3**, 1–44.

√Coase, Ronald (1988), 'The Nature of the Firm: Origin, Meaning, Influence,' *Journal of Law, Economics, and Organization*, **4**, 3–47. Repr. In O. E. Williamson and S. G. Winter (1991), *The Nature of the Firm: Origins, Evolution, and Development* (New York: Oxford University Press).

√Coase, Ronald (1992), 'The Institutional Structure of Production,' Alfred Nobel Memorial Prize Lecture in Economic Sciences. Repr. in *American Economic Review*, **82** (1992), 713–719.

Coase, Ronald (1993), 'Coase on Posner on Coase,' *Journal of Institutional and Theoretical Economics*, **149**, 96–98.

Crocker, Keith J. and Scott E. Masten (forthcoming), 'Regulation and Administered Contracts Revisited: Lessons from Transaction-Cost Economics for Public Utility Regulation,' *Journal of Regulatory Economics*.

Demsetz, Harold (1968), 'Why Regulate Utilities?' *Journal of Law and Economics*, **11**, 55–66.

Fisher, Stanley (1977), 'Long-Term Contracting, Sticky Prices, and Monetary Policy: Comment,' *Journal of Monetary Economics*, **3**, 317–324.

Goldberg, Victor P. (1976a), 'Regulation and Administered Contracts,' *Bell Journal of Economics*, **7**, 426–448.

Goldberg, Victor P. (1976b), 'Toward an Expanded Economic Theory of Contract,' *Journal of Economic Issues*, **10**, 45–61.

Grossman, Sanford J. And Oliver D. Hart (1986), 'The Costs and Benefits of Ownership: A Theory of Vertical and Lateral Integration,' *Journal of Political Economy*, **94**, 691–719.

Hart, Oliver and Bengt Holmstrom (1987), 'The Theory of Contracts,' in Truman Bewley, ed., *Advances in Economic Theory: Fifth World Congress*. Cambridge: Cambridge University Press, 71–155.

Holmstrom, Bengt and Jean Tirole (1989), 'The Theory of the Firm,' in Richard Schmalensee and Robert Willig, eds., *Handbook of Industrial Organization*. New York: North Holland, 61–133.

Joskow, Paul L. (1988), 'Asset Specificity and the Structure of Vertical Relationships: Empirical Evidence,' *Journal of Law, Economics, and Organization*, **4**, 95–117.

Klein, Benjamin, Robert Crawford and Armen Alchian (1978), 'Vertical Integration, Appropriable Rents, and the Competitive Contracting Process,' *Journal of Law and Economics*, **21**, 297–326.

Kreps, David M. (1990), *A Course in Microeconomic Theory*. Princeton: Princeton University Press.

Marglin, Stephen A. (1974), 'What Do Bosses Do? The Origins and Functions of Hierarchy in Capitalist Production,' *Review of Radical Political Economics*, **6**, 33–60.

Masten, Scott E. (1986), 'The Economic Institutions of Capitalism: A Review Article,' *Journal of Institutional and Theoretical Economics*, **142**, 445–451.

Milgrom, Paul and John Roberts (1992), *Economics, Organization, and Management*. Englewood Cliffs, NJ: Prentice-Hall.

Posner, Richard A. (1993), 'The New Institutional Economics Meets Law and Economics,' *Journal of Institutional and Theoretical Economics*, **149**, 73–87.

Riordan, Michael (1990), 'What Is Vertical Integration?' in Mashiko Aoki, Bo Gustafsson and Oliver Williamson, eds., *The Firm as a Nexus of Treaties*. London: Sage Publications, 94–111.

Shelanski, Howard (1991), 'Empirical Research in Transaction Cost Economics: A Survey and Assessment,' University of California, Department of Economics (mimeo).

Weingast, Barry and William Marshall (1988), 'The Industrial Organization of Congress; or, Why Legislatures, Life Firms, Are Not Organized as Markets,' *Journal of Political Economy*, **96,** 132–163.

Zald, Mayer N. (1987), 'Review Essay: The New Institutional Economics,' *American Journal of Sociology*, **93,** 701–718.

CHAPTER FIVE

Transaction Cost Economics

Its Influence on Organizational Theory, Strategic Management, and Political Economy

GLENN R. CARROLL, PABLO T. SPILLER,
AND DAVID J. TEECE

1. *Introduction*

The social sciences develop over time in a variety of ways. Core theoretical areas in each of the disciplines progress as scientists pick up and work on established and well-defined research problems. New areas of inquiry emerge and become increasingly important as discoveries are made. Often, these new areas are not so new at all but are instead fields rejuvenated by different ways of defining research problems, theorizing about existing problems, or collecting and examining empirical evidence. When such rejuvenation occurs, there is a collective sense of excitement in the discipline and development often proceeds rapidly.

Many social scientists would agree that three areas where exciting scientific progress has occurred in the last 20 years are organization theory, strategic management, and political economy. While it would be too strong to claim that transaction cost economics has spawned these rejuvenations, it has clearly played major roles in their development and direction to date. In fact, the influence of transaction cost economics has been so great that it is difficult to imagine any of these areas today without its presence.

This chapter reviews the recent intellectual histories of each of these three areas and traces the influence of transaction cost economics. In doing so, it shows the broad range of social science topics and disciplines to which transaction cost reasoning usefully applies. Organizational theory has roots in sociology and political science, strategic management theory in business, and political economy in political science. Few, if any, social science theories have appeal of this kind to analysts working in areas with such disparate origins.

For comments on an earlier draft of parts of this chapter, we appreciate the efforts of Lyda Bigelow, Michael Hannan, Jackson Nickerson, and Oliver Williamson. We also appreciate the assistance of Patrick Moreton.

The chapter begins with organizational theory, then turns to strategic management, and finally takes up political analysis. Our review covers developments in each area, as well as widely agreed upon points of intersection with transaction cost economics. At certain points, we also offer opinions as to the likely direction of future developments.

2. *Transaction Cost Economics and Organizational Theory*

Until 1975 very few economists thought seriously about formal organizations. As a result, organizational theorists operated pretty much without direct influence from economics. Organizational theory was situated exclusively in the disciplines of sociology and political science. Building on the work of Robert Michels and especially Max Weber, sociologists and political scientists in the post–World War II period steadily developed theories and conducted empirical studies of life in formal organizations. Most notable in this effort were sociologist Robert K. Merton and political scientist Herbert A. Simon. Merton's students Philip Selznick, Alvin Gouldner, Peter Blau, Seymour Martin Lipset, Martin Trow, and James Coleman researched and wrote important theses that became the modern classics of organizational theory (Scott, 1992). Simon's analytical work on organizations, along with those of Carnegie colleagues James March and Richard Cyert, drew on insights from psychology and political science to redefine simple rational models of decision making and organizational behavior.

Organizational theory progressed rapidly with such distinguished leadership. Theory and research moved from an emphasis on rational internal factors, to a consideration of institutional behaviors, to a pronounced focus on the environment as the source of structure and performance differentials (see Scott, 1992). The resulting synthesis in the late 1960s and early 1970s led to a dominant concern with the contingent factors of size, technology, and environment (Thompson, 1967). The prevailing view then held that organizations were the superior way to control and coordinate work but that the best structure for achieving control and coordination depended on the organization's size, technology, and environment. Empirical research tended to examine large samples of diverse organizations and to search for associations between the contingent factors and structural features of organizations such as level of formalization. The approach, known as contingency theory, formed the basis for much knowledge on organizational design that is still widely found in textbooks today. Contingency theory, however, quickly ran up against its own limitations: There was only so much to learn about the universal relationships between these variables; the theory did not provide much guidance about how to decompose further the relationships; and there

appeared to be limited useful applicability of these ideas to other social science problems.

A paradigmatic revolution struck organizational theory in the mid-1970s.
Contingency theory was swept aside by the nearly simultaneous appearance of
four seminal theoretical statements that defined new issues in the analysis of
and approaches to understanding organizations. The four were: Jeffrey Pfeffer
and Gerald Salancik's (1978) book *The External Control of Organizations*,
which defined the resource dependence approach to organizations; John
Meyer and Brian P. Rowan's (1977) article on institutionalized organizations,
which laid out a new institutional theory of organizations; Michael T. Hannan and John Freeman's (1977) article on the population ecology of organizations, which made a compelling case for studying environmental selection
processes; and Oliver E. Williamson's (1975) book *Markets and Hierarchies*,
which advanced the transaction cost approach to organizations. Each of these
statements proposed a new and intriguing theoretical perspective on organizations; each involved the definition of new research problems or the redefi-
nition of old ones; each presented new concepts and theories; and each implied new research agendas, sometimes with different methods.

The transaction cost approach was unique among the new perspectives in
that it originated in economics while the others, radical as they may have
been, developed out of known lines of thought within sociology and political science. Undoubtedly, *Markets and Hierarchies* was the first serious economic analysis read by many organizational theorists for professional reasons
in a long time. Because of this, the overall general impact of *Markets and Hierarchies* on organization theory was enormous. Beyond its specific contributions, the book increased the familiarity and understanding of economics by
organizational theorists, initiated a useful and persisting conversation across
the social science disciplines involved in organizational analysis, and spurred
along the nascent subdisciplines of organizational economics and economic
sociology. For all these reasons, Williamson is perhaps the most cited figure in
organizational theory today (Pfeffer, 1996); he is also one of the few economists regularly cited by sociologists (Baron and Hannan, 1994).

Why was *Markets and Hierarchies* so popular among organizational theorists? First, the book dealt squarely with organizational issues that were the
theorists' home turf (for example, bounded rationality, the divisionalized corporation, and employment). This was not a tangential analysis that simply
used the organizations label. Second, it dealt seriously with the received literatures and research of the field. *Market and Hierarchies* was not an attempt to
supplant the behavioral tradition but an effort to build directly on it. It also
likely helped that Williamson was from the Carnegie school of Simon, Cyert,
and March and recognized 'that the behavioral assumptions are the ones we

ought to be keenly aware of' (Williamson, 1990, p. 125). Third, the book was accessible. It was not beyond the ordinary technical competence of many organization theorists, as was much mathematical economics. Fourth, Williamson himself made efforts to reach out (in talks, seminars, conferences, etc.) and engage the behavioralists. Few other economists of his caliber could be found at conferences and meetings populated by organizational theorists and sociologists. Even fewer published articles in journals such as the *American Journal of Sociology* (Williamson, 1981) and the *Administrative Science Quarterly* (Williamson, 1991a), the top outlets for organizational theory.

But, most important, the specific arguments found in *Markets and Hierarchies* resonated well with many organizational theorists. Like the other new perspectives, *Markets and Hierarchies* proposed to broaden the scope of organizational analysis. Unlike the other perspectives, it proposed to do this through looking at markets and hierarchies as alternative modes for conducting the very same transactions. Organizational theorists were not unaware of markets at the time; they commonly thought of organizations as actors competing against each other in product and consumer markets, and empirical research often attempted to measure competition. However, the existence of organizations was readily assumed and was not compared to market alternatives until *Markets and Hierarchies*.

Above all, *Markets and Hierarchies* heightened awareness of efficiency considerations within organizational theory. In the prior search for effective organizational structures, contingency theory researchers had been motivated by an underlying, implicit concern with efficiency. *Markets and Hierarchies* showed researchers how to think about efficiency in a more explicit and analytical way (see Williamson's [1981, pp. 568–569] comparison of his work with Thompson's). It also offered an attractive programmatic research agenda.

The efficiency orientation brought many long-standing research problems into new relief. One of the more prominent dealt with the divisionalized corporation (called the M-form by Williamson). Organizational theorists had long recognized the importance of this organizational form, and numerous analyses compared it to other prevalent organizational forms such as the functional and matrix forms. The result, found in most textbooks, was a laundry list of advantages and disadvantages of the divisional form relative to others. *Markets and Hierarchies* did not challenge many of these observations so much as it proposed a prioritization. The divisionalized corporation, it said, prevailed primarily because its structure 'served to economize on bounded rationality and attenuate opportunism' (Williamson, 1975, p. 137). This is because resolving operating decisions at the divisional level 'relieved the communication load,' while reserving strategic decisions for the central headquarters 'reduced partisan political input into the resource allocation process'

(Williamson, 1975, p. 137–138). Information impactedness in the division could be overcome by the 'internal auditing and control techniques' available to the central office.

A second long-standing issue brought into new focus by *Markets and Hierarchies* concerned organizational boundaries. Although organizational theorists had long been fascinated with questions about boundaries, the interest often lacked analytical focus: At various times, researchers asked where the true boundaries of organizations actually existed, how permeable various types of boundaries were, and whether different types of boundaries coincided with each other. *Markets and Hierarchies* staggered into this epistemological discussion and showed that a centrally important question about boundaries had to do with the formal boundaries of the organization, those defined by legal ownership and implying administrative control. The compelling part of the case explained why efficient boundaries are determined by the alignment of governance structures with transaction attributes. The argument was to be the subject of much subsequent research (see the review chapter by Shelanski and Klein in this book). Other questions about boundaries of individual organizations thereafter seemed trivial in comparison and pretty much died from neglect.

In almost prescient fashion, the *Markets and Hierarchies* framework and its efficiency orientation equipped organizational theory with the tools for analyzing some coming major organizational trends. Joint ventures and then all forms of strategic alliances would be the order of the day for the corporate landscape in the late 1970s and 1980s. So, too, would corporate downsizing and the retrenchment of large diversified corporations back to activities related to the core business. Transaction cost economics provided explanations for the rise and spread of these phenomena; their increased prevalence in turn helped spur development of the theory to hybrid organizational forms as well as to underscore the theory's relevance.

How does transaction cost economics compare with the other three perspectives within organizational theory? A complete assessment would require a book-length treatment (for a start, see Scott, 1992). However, it is instructive to note here a few points of intersection and departure between the various major theoretical perspectives and transaction cost economics. Of the three, greatest conceptual affinity clearly lies with the resource dependence perspective developed by Pfeffer and Salancik (1978) and Burt (1992).

Resource Dependence Theory

Resource dependence theory holds that 'organizations will (and should) respond more to the demands of those organizations or groups in the environment that control critical resources' (Pfeffer, 1982, p. 193). These resource dependencies shape the distribution of intraorganizational power, which in turn affects many unrelated activities. The organization is not passive, however: 'Managers and administrators attempt to manage their external dependencies, both to ensure the autonomy of the organization and to acquire, if possible, more autonomy and freedom from external constraint' (p. 193). These attempts are envisioned to include co-optation, joint agreements, formal alliances, joint venture, and merger by acquisition.

Obviously, asset specificity in transaction cost economics bears strong resemblance to resource dependency in this theory. Indeed, the two theories typically yield similar basic explanations for issues such as hybrid organizational form, mergers, and vertical integration. Williamson (1990, p. 123) acknowledges this similarity but also contends that 'a real difference between resource dependency and the transaction cost economics is that the latter approaches the study of contracting from the standpoint of . . . "contracting in its entirety"—that is, it looks at the whole transaction including the original negotiations. Resource dependency, on the other hand, neglects the original negotiations. It simply looks at the outcomes and says, "Oh, my God! We've got a resource dependency outcome".'

Williamson has also been very critical of resource dependence theorists' usage of the concept of power. He critiques many usages of power for ambiguity (1990). Most important, Williamson insists that power and control emanate from economic factors. A primary focus on power, he holds, 'is a pied piper whose enticements are better resisted in favor of more mundane efficiency considerations' (1981, p. 573). He concludes that 'many dependency issues can be addressed in efficiency terms, whereupon power considerations largely vanish' (1996, p. 39). At best, he claims, 'perhaps power theory can sometimes add detail' (1981, p. 573).

Pfeffer (1996, p. 33) retorts that economic models of organization, including transaction cost economics, present 'a very benign view of social organization.' He claims that 'by stressing markets and the operation of voluntary exchange, power, coercion and exploitation are left out.' His argument, held by many organizational theorists, holds that while power and control may emanate from economic concerns in many contexts, this need not necessarily be the case. Extreme versions of the argument hold that ability to gain political control is a virtually separate process and that such control determines economic outcomes (Fligstein, 1990).

Some of the difficulty here arises because advocates of both camps often try to explain very similar sets of facts and the theories do not discriminate among them. Specifically, cross-sectional observations of bilateral exchanges with asset specificity usually show that the actor possessing the specific assets holds 'power' over the other party in the exchange. Both efficiency and power offer plausible explanations of this situation; both also make fairly similar suggestions about how the other actor might overcome this dependence. However, if the observations are made over time and begin before the process has had the opportunity to reach equilibrium, then perhaps causal primacy can be detected. (This possibility may be why Burt [1992] describes resource dependence theory and transaction cost economics as possessing a 'powerful complementarity'.)

Likewise, the most interesting part of the power argument in resource dependence theory concerns the ability of actors and units to influence organizational activities clearly *outside* the specific exchanges which determine power. Following Thompson (1967), resource dependence theorists hold that certain exchanges are of critical importance to the overall survival of the organization. Examining whether power that emanates from these critical resource dependencies transcends its 'source' exchanges, including into activities for which transaction cost economics would likely offer other context-dependent explanations, might ascertain the explanatory value added by resource dependence theory.

Williamson's objections about this theory's failure to address the original intentions and negotiations of dependent exchange relationships ('contracting in its entirety') strike a deeper, more fundamental chord. Resource dependence theory holds, like all three sociological perspectives under discussion, that individual level intentions and actions do not necessarily coincide with consequences of social structures arising from the interactions of many actors. This difference separates much of economics and sociology. Baron and Hannan (1994, p. 1114) explain: 'Economics, at least in its neoclassical variants, relies on a highly simplified model of individual action (rational choice) and a simple mechanism to aggregate individual actions to derive system-level implications. Most sociology uses complicated models of individual behavior (including effects of values, prior experience, commitments, location in the social network and context) and complicated mechanisms to aggregate interests and actions.' According to the sociologist's view, complex action and aggregation almost certainly imply a disconnection between micro and macro levels of analysis, lead to what would likely be viewed as unanticipated outcomes, and thus require analytical separation (Barnett and Carroll, 1993).

Freedom from the constraint of working only with macro structures that can be understood through individual action has often allowed sociologists to examine what might be called 'organizations in their entirety.' For resource dependence theory, this freedom leads to a focus on all the exchange relationships experienced by an organization, not just one or several dyadic relations. As Burt (1992) has suggested, formal network models provide enormous analytical power in summarizing these relationships and in converting them into a common metric capable of being associated with firm-level outcomes. Although Williamson (1985, p. 570) concedes 'that triadic or higher order analysis is sometimes indicated' by the phenomenon, transaction cost economics remains more microanalytical because 'dyadic exchange is very powerful and less delimiting than some suggest.'

Institutional Theory

Organizational theory's variant of institutional theory holds that organizational structures derive from institutionalized societal structures. The theory posits that organizational structures arise and are adopted because there is normative consensus about what is the appropriate way to organize for a particular activity. Although the normatively favored form is assumed by participants and observers to be technically and economically rational, the central claim of the theory is that this need not be the case and, indeed, frequently is not. Instead, 'institutionalized products, services, techniques, policies, and programs function as powerful myths, and many organizations adopt them ceremonially' (Meyer and Rowan, 1977, p. 340). These myths legitimate particular bureaucratic structures as rational, designation of which transforms them into socially accepted or taken-for-granted building blocks of organizations. The structure is often formal and functions mainly for external symbolism; internally, the organization's activities are only loosely coupled to this structure. The processes theorized to generate such structures include coercion, imitation, and normative sanctioning by authoritative bodies (DiMaggio and Powell, 1983). Contexts held to be especially prone to such structures include those where tangible outcomes of organizational effectiveness do not exist or are difficult to evaluate.

Obviously, institutional theory and transaction cost economics display some fundamental differences. Unless norms also serve an efficiency rationale, then the two theories yield contradictory explanations about most phenomena. Although institutional theory does not deny the potential coincidence of rationality and norms, these are not the unique aspects of the theory and they are not the ones typically emphasized by its advocates. Indeed, the economic irrationality of such norms is usually the flash point for institutionalists (see Meyer and Rowan, 1977; DiMaggio and Powell, 1991).

Williamson, for his part, has apparently not commented directly on this theory. However, his treatment of the concept of trust (1996, pp. 274–275), a central component in many theories of institutionalism, suggests that he disagrees with much of what institutional theory offers. For Williamson, trust is frequently misused in the social science literature; it should be reserved for

'noncalculative personal relations.' What is often called trust in economic exchanges can be, in his view, explained by resort to 'a farsighted approach to
contracting (in which credible commitments, or the lack thereof, play a key
role).' Institutionalists would disagree. Although trust might arise when credible commitments are present, these are not the only spawning grounds in
their views—prior personal relations, social status, and norms might generate strong personal confidence in economic relations as well. Moreover, institutionalists would argue that once trust relations are established (for whatever
reason), they are likely to be enduring when conditions change and determinative of the exchange outcome (Uzzi, 1996). The issue shows many parallels
with the disagreement between Williamson and resource dependence theorists
over power.

Despite these basic major differences, the two theoretical perspectives have
more in common than might seem possible. Both view organizations as highly
adaptive. Both also show a deep appreciation for the authority of the state and
its influence as an environmental force. In transaction cost economics, this
arises from analysis of specific rights (for example, property) and regulations
(for example, antitrust) and the state's ability to enforce them (Williamson,
1991a). In institutional theory, it arises from analysis of specific legislative acts
and executive orders and the organizational forms promulgated in response
(Edelman, 1990). Common ground can also be seen in the empirical research
of institutional theory, much of which uses a logic of resource dependence.
That is, researchers typically find that normative prescriptions about organizational forms follow resource flows from the state and other agencies.

Organizational Ecology

Organizational ecology constitutes the third other major theoretical perspective on organizations (Hannan and Freeman, 1984). This perspective holds
that organizational structures are highly inertial and resistant to change. Because of strong inertia, ecologists claim that most organizational change occurs through the selective replacement of one organizational form by another
rather than by adaptive efforts of individual organizations. Ecologists study
the life histories of organizations that compose unitary populations over long
periods of time. They attempt to identify selection processes through empirical research that focuses primarily on organizational founding and failure
rates and relates these to environmental characteristics and population dynamics (see Singh and Lumsden, 1994). Organizational change and its consequences is another popular topic of ecological research (Haveman, 1992;
Amburgey, Kelly, and Barnett, 1993).

As Williamson (1981, p. 568) has noted, much of the distinctiveness of or-

ganizational ecology resides at a high level of abstraction—in its metatheo-
retical orientation and its methodological framework. So, many of the differences between organizational ecology and transaction cost economics have to
do with general orientation rather than specific theoretical predictions. One
of the more fundamental of these concerns involves the adaptiveness of individual organizations, with transaction cost theory assuming that organizations
are rationally adaptive and organizational ecology holding that such occurrences are rare (see Barnett and Carroll, 1995). Transaction cost economics
also assumes that organizations adjust to environments fairly quickly, as least
fast enough to assume that organizational systems in mature industries are in
temporal equilibrium. This assumption justifies the cross-sectional approach
to empirical research found in much transaction cost work; it also allows researchers to justify ignoring performance-related outcome variables and looking only at organizational structures. Organizational ecology strongly rejects
this assumption; it assumes that organizational systems have trouble adjusting
quickly to environmental changes. As a result, organizational ecology requires
longitudinal analysis and outcome variables other than the simple existence or
prevalance of a structure. Finally, transaction cost economics is more microanalytical. Clearly, many social scientists see this as a virtue. But for many ecologists the microscopic focus of transaction cost analysis carries with it an inability (or unwillingness) to deal with problems of aggregation in generating
firm-level predictions related to overall performance. By contrast, organizational ecologists (like other organizational theorists) prefer to work with 'organizations in their entirety.' In this case, that orientation implies explaining
organizational-level outcomes such as structural transformation and failure,
often through the explicit modeling of competition (Barnett and Carroll,
1995).

Despite these differences in current formulations, it should be noted that
there is nothing inherent in the two theories that precludes a synthesis. Although several specific ecological theories that match organizational form and
environmental characteristics exist (for example, Carroll, 1985; Hannan and
Carroll, 1992), similar predictions derived from other theories are potentially
compatible with the ecological framework. So, as long as transaction cost economics theorists are willing to claim that, say, a particular governance structure alignment might affect the survival of the entire firm, then transaction
cost economics could be used to develop specific predictions about organizational failure rates and these could be applied to data on populations of organizations (see Silverman, Nickerson, and Freeman, 1996). Such syntheses
seem a natural direction for future research because they allow not only testing of particular theories but also examination of the more general mechanisms of organizational change, adaptation, and selection (see Boone and

Witteloostuijn, 1995, for other ideas that combine ecology and economics). One potentially plausible resolution of organizational ecology and transaction cost economics that could result from such efforts would be a finding that although populations of organizations move toward the organizational form predicted by transaction cost economics, they do so fairly slowly and via selection rather than adaptation (Ohanin, 1994).

Despite Williamson's enormous influence and the demonstrated power of transaction cost theory, advocates of all three other perspectives—and, indeed, most social scientists other than economists who study organizations—are still unwilling to accept the whole of the rational action approach and the strong efficiency orientation. For instance, ecologists Hannan and Freeman (1984, p. 339), frequently seen within organizational theory as strong believers in the power of markets and competitive processes, state clearly that 'although . . . considerations of efficiency have powerful consequences for many kinds of organizations, . . . they do not obviously override institutional and political considerations.' Meanwhile, Williamson and transaction cost economics seem to many to be going in the other direction, tightening the anchoring assumptions of economic rationality and efficiency. This movement is seen most clearly in Williamson's recent ruminations on remediableness (1996).

Why the resistance to efficiency analysis? Objections vary by researcher. For some, the bizarre occurrences observable regularly in organizations suggest that much life simply cannot be explained in this way. For others, the powers of efficiency processes are not denied, but they are seen as subordinate to political, institutional, and cultural considerations. For others still, the issue is not efficiency per se but the process by which it is held to obtain and the likelihood of organizational systems existing in equilibrium. For even others, the issue is the underlying basic conception of man as opportunistic and calculative. For yet another set, the problem is with the tight connection between theoretical models of individual and collective action.

In Williamson's view, however, the obstacle is that many social scientists have yet to come to terms with one of the basic tricks in the economist's bag: examination of incomplete contracts "in their entirety." The idea is that parties to recurrent contracts look ahead, perceive hazards, and fold these back into ex ante and ex post structures of contract, thereby mitigating hazards.

The implications of these differences in 'behavioral' and economic approaches to organizations are potentially profound (March and Olsen, 1989; Carroll and Harrison, 1994). Some economists may raise their hands in dismay, but others will find these views refreshing and stimulating (see, for example, David M. Kreps's chapter in this book). As Williamson has recently noted (1996, p. 219): 'The evolving science of organizations . . . has benefited from the variety of insights that are revealed by the use of different lenses.' Because of this, 'economic and sociological approaches have reached a state of healthy tension' (p. 219). This state of affairs ensures that organizational theory will remain an interesting and fertile area for cross-discipline exchange and debate.

3. *Transaction Cost Economics and Strategic Management*

Transaction cost economics has also had a powerful impact on the field of strategic management.[1] This ought not be surprising, as transaction cost economics was invented in the first place to help explain the existence and organization of firms, and of economic institutions more generally, and these are central issues in the field of strategic management.

Indeed, of all the developed new subfields of economics, transaction cost economics has the greatest affinity with strategic management. Within strategic management, transaction cost economics is the ground where economic thinking, business strategy, and organization theory meet. Because of its focus on institutional detail, rather than mathematical display, it has a broader audience among noneconomists than other branches of organizational economics. The affinity derives in part from common domains of inquiry. They also derive from a common intellectual style, which encourages inquiry into the reasons for specific institutional details. Not surprisingly, the clinical studies conducted by strategy researchers and business historians also have helped shape the development of transaction cost economics.

Transaction cost economics seeks to explain why a contract has a particular structure and has particular features, and this microanalytical specificity holds great appeal for strategic management scholars, who have a definite taste for disaggregation. Moreover, the transaction cost economics framework is explicitly comparative and enables one to say something about the efficiency properties of different organizational forms and structures. Transaction cost researchers have also looked at questions of internal structure and the manner in which specific decisions and actions are taken. Transaction cost economics thus carries considerable normative import and is therefore of great value to the field of strategic management, which yearns to be prescriptive.

Upon analysis, one can find at least three principal classes of contributions that Oliver Williamson and transactions cost economics have made to management theory and to strategic management in particular. The first is Williamson's early work on the M-form organization. The second is his work on vertical integration and the boundaries of the firm more generally, and the third is his

---

[1] Parts of this section draw from Rumelt, Schendel, and Teece (1994).

general organizing framework, especially his emphasis on economizing. Each area will be briefly reviewed.[2]

The Multidivisional Corporation

One of the fundamental issues in strategy, as noted elsewhere, is proper characterization of the function of the headquarters unit in a multibusiness firm (Rumelt, Schendel, and Teece, 1994). Building on Alfred Chandler's (1966) historical work, Williamson developed the theoretical basis for the multidivisional corporation, which he labeled the M-form. Williamson argued that the M-form improved capital allocation by exploiting the informational advantages that internal processes had over external market processes.[3] In *Markets and Hierarchies*, Williamson (1975) argued that the firm's internal capital market, by being able to utilize the firm's own internal audit structures, could gather information cheaper and better than could bankers and other financial institutions. The central insight is that managerial discretion could be checked not merely by competition in both the product market and capital market but also by management itself through the use of organizational form. This was a powerful insight of great relevance to managers, investors, and public policy analysts.

While our understanding of the headquarters function is now somewhat more advanced, Williamson's early development of the M-form hypothesis stimulated a series of empirical inquiries that helped put the M-form in a new light and helped established new methodological standards for empirical research in industrial organization theory. Williamson also was one of the first to emphasize that new organizational structures were themselves innovative and of great importance to society. The empirical studies in the United States and the United Kingdom showed that the financial impacts were substantial, although these benefits were quickly competed away (Armour and Teece, 1978; Cable and Steer, 1978; Teece, 1981b), thereby demonstrating that the M-form was relatively easy to copy (Teece, 1980a). Still, the results showed that at least transitory competitive advantage can flow from this generic organizational form. This fact had been suspected (even assumed routinely) but never statistically demonstrated until the studies which Williamson stimulated were completed. Moreover, this work made it transparent that organizational form could itself constitute an innovation and provide the basis of competi-

---

[2] Here there is no attempt whatsoever at completeness; we are content simply to flag the main contributions and cite some of the relevant literature. The emphasis will be mainly on the early impact of transaction cost economics, as this is easier to trace.

[3] Williamson's analysis predates the rapid growth of venture capital; with hindsight the framework appears a bit remiss in not analyzing the role of venture capital.

tive advantage for at least a period of time. This insight was itself important to subsequent developments in the field of strategic management, where organizational structure and process, along with technology, came to be seen as a potential sources of competitive advantage.

Boundaries of the Firm

The largest contribution made by Williamson and the transaction cost approach has been in analyzing the boundaries of the firm—that is, addressing issues of where the firm should give way to the market and vice versa. Boundary questions are absolutely central to the field of strategic management: Vertical integration, outsourcing, diversification, joint ventures, and divestiture are all fundamentally boundary issues; and their analysis is the lifeblood of many leading management consulting firms. Yet before development of transaction cost economics, there were almost no analytic frameworks in the field of strategic management that addressed these issues coherently. This is where transaction cost economics first began to impact business practice. Williamson had a coherent theory of integration. Not only did the theory have explanatory power with respect to describing the organization of firms (see Monteverde and Teece, 1982a; 1982b for initial evidence), but it had normative power as well. There is now a very large 'boundaries' literature in the field of strategic management that uses transaction cost economics or some variant of it. Examples are as follows.

Vertical integration and the virtual corporation. There are a plethora of studies in both industrial organizational and strategic management that draw on transaction cost economics to help explain integration questions in particular industrial contexts; Klein, Crawford, and Alchian (1978) sharpened the transaction cost economics framework and can lay some claim to helping popularize the approach, but the key ideas are all in Williamson (1975). The very first explicit applications of transaction cost reasoning to vertical integration in a specific industrial context were in the petroleum industry (Teece, 1976; 1978), followed by automobile manufacturing (Monteverde and Teece, 1982a; 1982b) and aerospace (Masten, 1984). Other early applications included forward integration into selling (Anderson and Schmittlein, 1984). These initial applications illustrated the power of the framework and stimulated a considerable research program and literature (see Shelanski and Klein, 1995, reprinted in this book).

While the applications developed in the academic literature are sometimes two steps removed from what managers and consultants find readily digestible, there have been many successful efforts to present the framework in ways useful to managers. For instance, a very faithful rendering of the framework, in clear, un-cluttered managerial language, can be found in Stuckey and White (1993).

In recent years, efforts have been made to look at the virtual corporation and explore the limits of firms, rather than the limits of markets.[4] Transaction cost economics has much to say (as do some other approaches, too) about out-sourcing. Illustrative efforts are: Chesbrough and Teece (1996) and Mowery, Oxley, and Silverman (1996).

Diversification and the multinational firm. An equally expansive literature has emerged, driven by transactions cost economics, around the question of di-versification. While not explicitly addressed by Williamson early on, the trans-action cost economics framework can be used to explain lateral diversification, particularly if explicit attention could be given to knowledge assets. The first efforts to show purchase to the transaction cost economics framework in the context of the diversification were Teece (1980b; 1982). These papers sparked a series of related papers, showing not only the opportunities but also the lim-its of diversification. Indeed, the beauty of the transaction cost economics ap-proach is that it was discriminating: Integration and diversification were ap-plicable in some circumstances, but not in others. Prior to transaction cost economics, there was no discriminating framework in the field of strategic management. Moreover, transaction cost economics has been extended to em-brace know-how/intellectual assets and the role of complements. Empirical tests in the transaction cost economics spirit that statistically explain diversi-fication activities include Helfat (1997).

The theory of the multinational enterprise has likewise borrowed heavily from transaction cost economics. The concept of internalization, as developed by Ronald Coase (1937), has become a major synthesizing and unifying con-cept in the theory of multinational enterprises. Applied in a pure Coasian way, the concept can become tautological: Firms internalize imperfect mar-kets until the costs of further internalization outweighs the benefits. Buckley and Casson (1976) were the first to lay out the internalization argument in the context of multinational enterprise, self-consciously employing transac-tion cost economics. Teece (1981a; 1982; 1985) attempted to juxtapose the efficiency framework against the monopoly framework and endeavored to provide a discriminating framework. Foreign direct investment was presented as just a special case of vertical integration, or horizontal expansion to exploit difficult to trade knowledge assets.

---

[4] The earlier concentration involved focusing more on market factors, not organizational factors. However, an excellent treatment of organizational factors can be found in Williamson's (1975) discussion of the limits of vertical integration.

Alliances and cooperation. Hybrid firms of economic organization, especially strategic alliances, have generated tremendous interest in recent years. This is in part because of the ubiquity of the phenomena, at least since the late 1970s. Early efforts to employ transaction cost economics to explain alliances include Teece (1986a), Pisano, Russo, and Teece (1988), Pisano, Shan, and Teece (1988), and Pisano and Teece (1989). The drivers of alliance formation were seen to be (at least in the context of innovation) transaction costs, appropriability, and access/location issues. The literature has employed transaction cost economics to examine equity and nonequity issues (Williamson, 1988). Williamson (1991a) has subsequently expanded the markets and hierarchies dichotomy to include hybrid forms of organization—long-term contracts, franchises, alliances, and so forth.

There is no doubt that transaction cost economics is a useful element for the study of alliances and hybrid forms. However, asset specificity can only go so far in explaining the nature and structure of alliances. An important strand in the alliances literature looks at the central role of innovation and the need for cooperation to assist firms to not only develop but also to commercialize innovation. Ownership of the right complementary assets is also seen as significantly affecting the distribution of the rents from innovation. Hence, internalization is not only a mechanism to protect specific assets from recontracting hazards. It is also a way to benefit from asset appreciation.

As mentioned, asset specificity, standing alone, does not carry the day, especially when innovation is at issue. Williamson recognizes this, explicitly noting that 'the introduction of innovation plainly complicates the earlier described assignments of transactions to markets or hierarchies based entirely on an examination of their asset specificity qualities' (1985, p. 143). Indeed, Shuen (1994) shows that firms often knowingly enter into asymmetric dependency relations with suppliers where the 'exchange of hostages' is anything but complete; de Figueriedo and Teece (1996) show how asymmetric dependence in one contract can be balanced by an offsetting asymmetric dependence in other contracts. In short, protecting specific assets is only one part of the story and, in high-technology markets, arguably a rather small part.

General Organizing Framework

The influence of transaction cost economics documented thus far relates to particular narrow but important questions in strategic management. While it would be too strong, at least based on this brief survey, to characterize the use of transaction cost economics as representing a 'school of thought' in strategic management, an effort by Williamson (1991b) to put forward a distinctive worldview for strategy is contained in the *Strategic Management Journal* article 'Strategizing, Economizing, and Economic Organization'. The article is an important one in that it sees competitive advantage as flowing primarily from efficient systems of production and methods of organization. As he puts it, 'all the clever plays and positioning, aye, all the king's horses, all the king's men, will rarely save a project that is seriously flawed in first order economizing respects' (1991b, p. 75). This is not simply advancing Michael E. Porter's (1980) 'low cost strategy' as the dominant strategy. Rather, Williamson emphasizes adaptation, proper incentive design, the right choice of contractual and market modes, and the creation of an efficient system of corporate governance. There is an implicit recognition that privileged market positions, if somehow attained, will quickly wither if not supported by organizational arrangements which are properly designed and astutely implemented. In short, absent a relentless focus on efficiency, firms will fail to achieve superior performance.

We believe that there is considerable sympathy in the field of strategic management to the basic tenants of transaction cost economics. Indeed, there have been some efforts to craft a theory of strategy around a contract theory of the firm (e.g., Reve, 1988). But in our view, transaction economics, powerful as it is, is best viewed as a set of important concepts which assist greatly in understanding organization design questions. What is missing for strategic management theory, so far at least, is an appreciation of the entrepreneurial side of strategy. Sensing and seizing opportunities is critical in the global economy today. The particular alignment of incentives, skills, and organization structures which facilitates this is not well developed in transaction cost economics. Nor is the role of knowledge and knowledge accumulation.

One way forward for transaction cost economics may be systematic analysis of the market for know-how. By analyzing the comparative economics of technology transfer within the firm and across markets, transaction cost economics can be readily extended to embrace many of the emerging issues of the knowledge economy. In addition, our understanding of complex organization can undoubtedly be assisted by a fusion of transaction cost economics and what might be called the competencies/capabilities theory of the firm (Teece, Pisano, and Shuen, 1997). The competencies/capabilities theory introduces notions of strategic coordination, entrepreneurship, and transformation. Chester Barnard's notion that the central problem of organization is that of adaptation is embraced by transaction cost economics. Of special interest to transaction cost economics is how parties engaged in long-term contracts can adapt efficiently to disturbances. The design of contractual structures in which parties can have mutual confidence in support of cooperative adaptation is well established by the framework (Teece, 1992).

Juxtaposed against adaptive coordination is entrepreneurial coordination—

the selection and piecing together of new value chains to build competitive advantage. In the global economy today, innovation may be so radical that organizational adaptation does not suffice. Transformation may be the imperative.

As Kaldor (1934) pointed out over half a century ago, coordination is also the essence of entrepreneurship. But the coordination required for entrepreneurship is not merely adaptive. Entrepreneurial coordination involves sensing and seizing opportunities. This type of coordination is rather different from that implicitly embedded in the Barnard/Williamson framework. In a static world—and transaction cost economics is inclined to assume a rather static world where there are orderly changes—dynamic capabilities are valueless.[5] However, as external shocks become the norm because of changes in demand or technology (now amplified by more open markets), the importance of dynamic capabilities is amplified. A strategy flawed in first-order economizing sense may yet win, at least for a while, if a firm's dynamic capabilities enable it to get to the right market at the right time with the right products. Virtual corporations can be virtuous if they possess dynamic capabilities and if markets are fast changing. In the early stages of the evolution of an industry—what has been called elsewhere the pre-paradigmatic phase (Teece, 1986a)—the premium to dynamic capabilities/entrepreneurship may sometimes exceed the premium to first-order economizing.

In a way, aspects of transaction cost economics seem most apt for industries which show limited turbulence and incremental innovation that requires adaptation, not transformation. Since all industries go through life cycles, knowing just when and where to appeal to transaction cost economics is in itself an art—an art that we believe few have mastered. The frustration that some may have experienced with the framework in our view (see, for example, Kay, 1997, chap. 3) often stems from either a lack of deep understanding of what transaction cost economics is all about or the limited ability to gauge when, where, and how to apply it. Like most theories in economics, transaction cost economics was not self-consciously developed with the needs of managers in mind. Accordingly, there is plenty of work left to hone the framework so that it can be readily applied by managers and their advisers.

In our view, the research agenda of transaction cost economics is by no means spent and has much more to contribute to strategic management. Further progress will undoubtedly benefit from artful integration with other theories and ideas.

---

[5] The fundamental transformation of Williamson (1985: 61), which is discussed in the following pages in the context of political organizations, is a dynamic, process-based concept. In our view, however, it is often a drift phenomenon and is relatively slow, at least in product markets. Yet high-technology markets are often exposed to rapid and continuous change.

4. *Transaction Cost Economics and the Theory of Political Organizations*

The insights of transaction cost economics have been directly applied to the organization of government agencies and legislatures.[6] The most important insights of transaction cost economics for the organization of regulatory agencies are Williamson's analysis of the 'fundamental transformation' (1975) and his treatment of 'credible commitments' (1983). The fundamental transformation refers to when 'a large numbers bidding condition at the outset [of a particular transaction] is effectively transformed into one of bilateral supply thereafter' because the transaction partner makes or somehow obtains transaction-specific assets (Williamson, 1985, p. 61). This transformation occurs in regulatory settings because once a legislature delegates to an agency, the latter has informational advantages that allow it to depart from the objectives of those that created the agency. This fact of bureaucratic life raises two basic questions for positive political theory: Why do legislatures delegate to agencies? And what implications does this transformation have for the organization of agencies?

The main insight of transaction cost economics into the organization of legislatures is the need to organize them in ways that facilitate both cooperation among the legislators and the pursuit of common objectives. Credible contracting issues are posed.

The Organization of Regulatory Agencies

Agencies are not created in a political vacuum. Instead, they are created and given a mandate following a particular political bargain. McCubbins, Noll, and Weingast (1987; 1989) emphasize the implications for the organization and control of regulatory agencies of the fact that those interests involved in the agency's creation also want to see that the agency will promote the goals of the political bargain. Sophisticated politicians know that, following the creation of the agency, the agency will have an incentive to deviate from the original mandate, whether it was explicit or implicit. First, other interests will attempt to move the agency in their own directions. Second, the agency will attempt to implement its own view of the world rather than that of the initial bargain. And third, legislators will attempt to move the agency toward their own view of the world (Macey, 1992; Shepsle, 1992).

To limit the extent of agency discretion, legislators will strategically design the agency's structure and organization (Gilligan, Marshall, and Weingast,

---

[6] Parts of this section appear in Spiller (forthcoming).

1989), its administrative procedures for decision making (McCubbins, Noll, and Weingast, 1989; Spiller and Tiller, 1997), its budgetary allocation (Spiller and Tiller, 1997), and the nature of judicial review. The nature of these procedures, the nature of the organizational structure of the agency, and the extent to which they may actually limit agency discretion depend on the institutional environment (Spiller, 1997). In the United States, for example, limits to agency decision making are based on the regulation of the various forms of rule making, the participation of interested parties in the regulatory process, the extensive use of public hearings, and an active judicial review. In the United Kingdom, in contrast, limits to regulatory decision making are either very few or, as in the case of utilities, based on the procedures for license modification (Levy and Spiller, 1994; Spiller and Vogelsang, 1997). The difference between the two regulatory styles can be traced back to the difference in the institutional environment (Spiller, 1997). On the one hand, the United Kingdom has traditionally had a parliamentary system that systematically has brought about unified governments without the need for coalition building. On the other hand, the U.S. electoral system assures the development of divided governments, with the president seldom having full control over the legislative process (Jacobson, 1990). As a consequence, legislators in the United States will tend not to delegate to the executive too much regulatory discretion, and instead they will tend to impose on the executive branch much stronger procedural burdens as a way to limit the executive's ability to deviate from legislators' interests. Conversely, in the United Kingdom, as in other Westminster countries, the government controls the legislative process (Cain, Ferejohn, and Fiorina, 1987; Cox, 1987; Shugart and Carey, 1992; Taagepera and Shugart, 1993). Procedural restrictions on regulatory decision making, then, will seldom be introduced as they may not be needed to assure consistency between legislative interests and executive action (Spiller and Vogelsang, 1997). In the case of utilities, however, companies will not invest in highly specific sunk assets without either very high up-front rents or assurances that once invested regulatory rules will not be changed to expropriate those assets via the administrative process. Thus, regulating the license amendment process provides such assurance to the companies (Spiller and Vogelsang, 1997).

Interest group participation in the regulatory process.   Interest groups play a particularly important role in the administrative process in the United States (McCubbins and Schwartz, 1984). Indeed, the Administrative Procedure Act, as well as most of the enacting legislation of regulatory agencies, sets a series of procedural requirements that provides for ample participation of interest groups in the regulatory process. Regulatory agencies must provide notice, must inform about proposed rule makings, must make their decisions taking into account the submissions of interested parties, and cannot rush or make decisions in the dark. In this setting, interest groups play two important roles: First, they provide information to the regulatory agency about the state of the world; and second, they provide information about their own preferences. Both are important for the agency. On the one hand, agencies are resource-constrained and hence information about the state of the world is always beneficial. On the other hand, information about interest groups' preferences is important as it allows the agency to forecast potential political problems they may encounter at the legislature. The procedural restrictions on decision making also provide the opportunity for interest groups to attempt to block agency decision making through lobbying their politicians. In a particularly important article, McCubbins and Schwartz (1984) claim that the participation by interest groups makes the regulatory process work like a "fire alarm." Interest group participation allows legislators to supervise the agency without having to be actively involved in the regulatory process and hence limiting the time that legislators have to expend in regulating regulators. The information revealed through the lobbying of each interest group, though, even if truthful is naturally biased (Spiller and Urbiztondo, 1991; Lupia and McCubbins, 1994). Interest groups will not reveal information that will bring about a regulatory outcome that is worse than if they had not revealed the information. As a consequence, politicians who base their decisions exclusively on the information provided by a single interest group, even if that group is a natural ally, will find the legislative outcome to be biased. Thus, the incentive for politicians to allow for the participation of multiple interest groups, preferably with conflicting interests (Spiller and Urbiztondo, 1991). Indeed, under some conditions, open participation by multiple interest groups cancels out whatever information advantage each interest group may have vis-à-vis the politicians (Spiller and Urbiztondo, 1991).

Why delegation to independent agencies?   Given that agencies will naturally deviate from the will of the enacting Congress, a basic question is why in such an environment legislatures choose to delegate to agencies and the courts the interpretation of their statues. This question needs to be broken in two parts: First, is there such a thing as independent agencies and, second, why will Congress delegate to independent agencies? Spiller and Urbiztondo (1994) answer the first question in the following way: The probability of observing independent agencies is higher in systems characterized by divided government. They show that in systems characterized by unified governments control over the bureaucracy will be stronger, with a much smaller proportion of political appointees, than in systems characterized by divided governments. The use of political appointees (including independent agencies), it is claimed, arises from the fact that in divided governments' systems the executive has a much smaller control over the professional bureaucracy, as the latter will naturally tend to be aligned with the legislature, a political institution that tends to be longer-lasting than the executive. Spiller and Urbiztondo (1994) find that such characterization of divided and unified governments hold both across countries and across cities in the United States.

In an important article, Weingast and Moran (1983) raised the Congressional Dominance Hypothesis. This hypothesis, presented in a different form by McCubbins and Schwartz's (1984) (fire alarm) framework, suggests that independent agencies are not truly independent, as they are subject to continuous—although not active—congressional oversight. Active congressional reversal is not necessary; all that is needed is the threat of legislative action. Spiller (1992) shows that independent administrative agencies' discretion in a system of division of powers depends, among other things, on the composition of the legislature and the executive (determining the threat of congressional reversal) and also on the organization and budget of the judiciary (determining the threat of judicial reversal). In a system of division of powers, however, Congressional Dominance is a corner solution. Spiller (1990) shows that congressional budgetary decisions of agencies reflect an internal rather than a corner solution. Thus, agencies do not fully respond to congressional desires. If this is the case, then, a basic question is why Congress delegates to agencies that are not fully aligned with it.

Schwartz, Spiller, and Urbiztondo (1993) developed a framework to understand the congressional choice between specific and vague legislation. Specific legislation is that where substantive administrative actions are specified in great detail (for example, the Federal Communications Commission [FCC] is to hold auctions for the allocation of the spectrum or the Environmental Protection Agency [EPA] is to organize markets for pollution rights granting utilities specific allowances), whereas vague legislation is that where Congress just specifies the general principles to be interpreted by the agency and the courts (for example, the FCC is to implement policies in telecommunications promoting the welfare of the U.S. citizens). They show that the choice of legislative specificity is a strategic one in a system characterized by division of powers and informational asymmetries. The rationale is that in such a system the current Congress cannot trust either the agencies or the courts in implementing what it actually wants. Informational issues are important. In the absence of informational asymmetries, Gely and Spiller (1990) show that legislative intent plays no role as the initial legislative act has no consequence on the final equilibrium. There are, however, several informational problems that may have implications for the choice. First, agencies and courts may not fully know congressional preferences on particular issues. Schwartz, Spiller, and Ur-biztondo (1993) differentiate between uncertainty on legislators' most desired policies and their intensity over policies. Most desired policies relate to an individual's ideal point. Intensity is related to how such individual's utility falls as the policy moves away from his or her ideal point. The higher the degree of uncertainty on preferences, the greater the chance that agencies and courts will err in their actions and that Congress will then have to spend resources in reversing agencies and courts. In a separating equilibrium, then, specific legislation provides a signal about congressional preferences, in particular, that Congress cares much about this particular issue. Second, agencies and courts may be uncertain about Congress' costs of reversing their decisions (Spiller, 1992). In a separating equilibrium, then, specific legislation provides a signal that the enabling Congress believes it will have low reversal costs in the future. If the enabling Congress believed that its future reversal costs would be high, then there would be no point in drafting specific legislation as courts and agencies could then deviate and the future Congress would not be able to reverse it. A major result from the analysis of Schwartz, Spiller, and Urbiztondo (1993) is that legislative vagueness and agency and judicial activism are, in equilibrium, correlated. But the correlation does not arise because of courts or agencies wanting to follow the intent of Congress, but rather because legislative vagueness is correlated with high reversal costs and low saliency issues, environments in which agencies and courts have more discretion.

Thus, delegation to independent agencies requires a system of division of powers. In this environment, legislative specificity will most probably not be the norm, as legislative costs will be high and preference homogeneity among the members of Congress will most probably be low, increasing the costs of reversing agencies and courts. Under those circumstances, it is where we can expect agency independence. But it is also here where we should expect judicial independence that, to some extent, counterbalances and limits the independence of agencies.

The Organization of Legislatures

A basic dual problem of legislatures is the need to gather information so as to develop relevant policy alternatives and to protect the enacted policies from political opportunism and from the effect of transitory electoral changes. In a series of articles, Shepsle, Weingast, and collaborators[7] brought forth the hypothesis that the organization of the U.S. legislature was designed so as to

---

[7] See, in particular, Ferejohn (1974), Shepsle (1978), Shepsle and Weingast (1987), and Weingast and Marshall (1988).

maximize the rents that legislators may extract from the political process. This approach has been called the 'demand side,' in opposition to the 'supply side' view, mostly brought forth by Krehbiel and others,[8] that the way legislators organize their actions is the result of attempts to improve information gathering and processing.

The 'demand side' view of legislatures is more closely aligned with the transaction cost approach to organizations. The problem legislators face is not dissimilar from the problem economic agents face in undertaking a particular transaction. Legislators' objectives are electoral, and hence their efforts will be to gather political and economic support so as to improve the lot of their constituencies. The gathering of political, and economic support can be seen as a series of highly specialized transactions. The exchange of economic and political support is subject to several hazards: First, usually the exchange of support will involve noncontemporaneous benefits, exposing the party with delayed benefit realization to the opportunistic termination of the transaction prior to the realization of the complete stream of benefits. Second, legislators' identity changes over time, again exposing the party to early termination of the transaction. Third, these transactions must also deal with unanticipated events, like changes in electoral preferences, that require the renegotiation of the transaction. As a consequence, if long-term programs are to be developed, institutions have to be created that facilitate these transactions (Weingast and Marshall, 1988). As Shepsle and Weingast (1996, p. 11) say, 'a spot market for exchanging support will not do.' Thus, the demand side approach to legislative organization emphasizes the role of committees as agenda controllers and gate keepers (providing security that programs created cannot be eliminated too rapidly); and the role of seniority as assuring legislators that as long as they are reelected they will be able to protect the programs of their choice (Weingast and Marshall, 1988).

The demand side approach to legislative organization, however, assumes away an essential problem of legislators: making decisions with limited information. The informational theories of congressional organization, as developed by Krehbiel and collaborators,[9] emphasize the collective objectives of legislators, not just their distributional interests. The core of Krehbiel's (1991) approach, as developed at great length in his *Information and Legislative Organization,* is the Majoritarian Principle. This principle says that congressional institutional features are not exogenously given but, rather, endogenous. Indeed, they are "selected by majorities, are subject to change by majorities and therefore presumably serve the interests of majorities" (Shepsle

---

[8] See, in particular, Gilligan and Krehbiel (1989) and Krehbiel (1991).
[9] See Krehbiel (1991) and references therein.

and Weingast, 1996, p. 14). Thus, institutional features, like committees, seniority, and leadership organization, cannot serve particularistic interests but, rather, must serve majoritarian objectives. Otherwise, these features will be unraveled by the majority. The main majoritarian objective is informational efficiency. That is, legislators need to gather information. This requires specialization, but specialization provides informational advantages. Thus, organizations must arise to limit the ability of legislators to exploit too much these informational advantages. Thus, the organization of committees, the role of conference committees, and the way legislators vote on bills and other congressional norms and institutions will be influenced by the need to provide incentives, on the one hand, to legislators to gather information and, on the other hand, at the same time, to limit their ability to exploit their informational advantages.

5. *Summary and Conclusion*

By examining recent progress in organizational theory, strategic management, and political economy, this chapter shows clearly the wide range of transaction cost economics. It also illustrates the broad influence of transaction cost economics on developments in sociology, business, and political science. The potential implications of this influence should not be overlooked. Transaction cost economics shows that it is possible to have greater unification in the social sciences than many scientists believe possible. The extent to which this unification is achieved depends, in turn, on the continued adaptability and flexibility of the theory.

References

Amburgey, Terry L., Dawn Kelly and William P. Barnett (1993), 'Resetting the Clock: The Dynamics of Organizational Change and Failure,' *Administrative Science Quarterly*, **38**, 51–73.

Anderson, E. and D. Schmittlein (1984), 'Integration of the Sales Force: An Empirical Examination,' *Rand Journal of Economics*, **15**, 385–395.

Armour, Henry and David Teece (1978), 'Organizational Structure and Economic Performance,' *Bell Journal of Economics*, **9**, 106–122.

Barnett, William P. and Glenn R. Carroll (1993), 'How Institutional Constraints Affected the Organization of Early Telephony,' *Journal of Law, Economics and Organization*, **9**, 98–126.

Barnett, William P. and Glenn R. Carroll (1995), 'Modelling Internal Organizational Change,' *Annual Review of Sociology*, **21**, 217–236.

Baron, James N. and Michael T. Hannan (1994), 'The Impact of Economics on Contemporary Sociology,' *Journal of Economic Literature*, **32**, 1111–1146.

Boone, Christophe and Arjen van Witteloostuijn (1995), 'Industrial Organization and Organizational Ecology,' *Organization Studies*, **16**, 265–298.

Buckley, P. S. and M. C. Casson (1976), *The Future of the Multinational Enterprise*. London: Macmillan.

Burt, Ronald S. (1992), *Structural Holes: The Social Structure of Competition*. Cambridge, MA: Harvard University Press.

Cable, J. and W. Steer (1978), 'Internal Organization and Profit: An Empirical Analysis of Large U.K. Companies,' *Journal of Industrial Economics*, **27**, 13–30.

Cain, Bruce, John Ferejohn and Morris Fiorina (1987), *The Personal Vote*. Cambridge, MA: Harvard University Press.

Carroll, Glenn R. (1985), 'Concentration and Specialization: Dynamics of Niche Width in Populations of Organizations,' *American Journal of Sociology*, **90**, 1262–1283.

Carroll, Glenn R. and J. Richard Harrison (1994), 'On the Historical Efficiency of Competition between Populations of Organizations,' *American Journal of Sociology*, **100**, 720–749.

Chandler, A. D., Jr (1966), *Strategy and Structure*. New York: Doubleday, Anchor Books Edition.

Chesbrough, H. W. and D. J. Teece (1996), 'When Is Virtual Virtuous? Organizing for Innovation,' *Harvard Business Review*, January–February, 65–73.

Coase, R. H. (1937), 'The Nature of the Firm,' *Economica*, **4**, 386–405.

Cox, Gary (1987), *The Efficient Secret*. New York: Cambridge University Press.

de Figueiredo, J. M. and D. J. Teece (1996), 'Mitigating Procurement Hazards in the Context of Innovation,' *Industrial and Corporate Change*, **5**, 537–559.

DiMaggio, Paul J. and Walter W. Powell (1983), 'The Iron Cage Revisited: Institutional Isomorphism and Collective Rationality in Organizational Fields,' *American Sociological Review*, **48**, 147–160.

DiMaggio, Paul J. and Walter W. Powell (1991), 'Introduction,' in W. W. Powell and P. J. DiMaggio, eds., *The New Institutionalism in Organizational Analysis*. Chicago: University of Chicago Press, pp. 1–38.

Edelman, Lauren B. (1990), 'Legal Environments and Organizational Governance: The Expansion of Due Process in the American Workplace,' *American Journal of Sociology*, **95**, 1401–1440.

Ferejohn, John (1974), *Pork Barrel Politics*. Stanford: Stanford University Press.

Fligstein, Neil (1990), *The Transformation of Corporate Control*. Cambridge, MA: Harvard University Press.

Gely, Rafael and Pablo T. Spiller (1990), 'A Rational Choice Theory of Supreme Court Statutory Decisions, with Applications to the *State Farm* and *Grove City* Cases,' *Journal of Law, Economics, and Organization*, **6**, 263–301.

Gilligan, Thomas and Keith Krehbiel (1989), 'Asymmetric Information and Legislative Rules with Heterogeneous Committee,' *American Journal of Political Science*, **33**, 459–490.

Gilligan, Tom, William Marshall and Barry Weingast (1989), 'Regulation and the Theory of Legislative Choice: The Interstate Commerce Act of 1887,' *Journal of Law and Economics*, **32**, 35–61.

Hannan, Michael T. and Glenn R. Carroll (1992), *Dynamics of Organizational Populations*. New York: Oxford University Press.

Hannan, Michael T. and John Freeman (1977), 'The Population Ecology of Organizations,' *American Journal of Sociology*, **82**, 929–964.

Hannan, Michael T. and John Freeman (1984), *Organizational Ecology*. Cambridge, MA: Harvard University Press.

Haveman, Heather (1992), 'Between a Rock and a Hard Place: Organizational Change and Performance under Conditions of Fundamental Environmental Performance,' *Administrative Science Quarterly*, **37**, 48–75.

Helfat, C. (1997), 'Know-how and Asset Complementary and Dynamic Capability Accumulation: The Use of R and D,' *Strategic Management Journal*, **18**, 339–360.

Jacobson, Gary C. (1990), *The Electoral Origins of Divided Government: Competition in the House Elections, 1946–1988*. Boulder, CO: Westview Press.

Kaldor, N. (1934), 'The Equilibrium of Firms,' *Economic Journal*, **44**, 60–76.

Kay, N. (1997), *Pattern in Corporate Evolution*. New York: Oxford University Press.

Klein, B., R. Crawford and A. Alchian (1978), 'Vertical Integration, Appropriable Rents, and the Competitive Contracting Process,' *Journal of Law and Economics*, **21**, 297–326.

Krehbiel, Keith (1991), *Information and Legislative Organization*, Ann Arbor: The University of Michigan Press.

Levy, Brian and Pablo T. Spiller (1994), 'The Institutional Foundations of Regulatory Commitment: A Comparative Analysis of Telecommunications Regulation,' *Journal of Law, Economics, and Organization*, **10**, 201–246.

Lupia, Skip and Matthew D. McCubbins (1994), 'Learning from Oversight: Fire Alarms and Police Patrols Reconstructed,' *Journal of Law, Economics, and Organization*, **10**, 96–125.

Macey, Jon (1992), 'Organizational Design and Political Control of Administrative Agencies,' *Journal of Law, Economics, and Organization*, **8**, 93–110.

March, James G. and Johan Olsen (1989), *Rediscovering Institutions: The Organizational Basis of Politics*. New York: Free Press.

Masten, Scott (1984), 'The Organization of Production: Evidence from the Aerospace Industry,' *Journal of Law and Economics*, **27**, 403–417.

McCubbins, Matthew D., Roger G. Noll, and Barry R. Weingast (1987), 'Administrative Procedures as Instruments of Political Control,' *Journal of Law, Economics, and Organization*, **3**, 243–277.

McCubbins, Matthew D., Roger G. Noll, and Barry R. Weingast (1989), 'Structure and Process, Politics and Policy: Administrative Arrangements and the Political Control of Agencies,' *Virginia Law Review*, **75**, 431–482.

McCubbins, Matthew D. and Thomas Schwartz (1984), 'Congressional Oversight Overlooked: Police Patrol vs. Fire Alarms,' *American Journal of Political Science*, **28**, 165–179.

Meyer, John and Brian P. Rowan (1977), 'Institutionalized Organizations: Formal Structure as Myth and Ceremony,' *American Journal of Sociology*, **83**, 340–363.

Monteverde, K. and D. J. Teece (1982a), 'Supplier Switching Costs and Vertical Integration in the Automobile Industry,' *Bell Journal of Economics*, **13**, 206–213.

Monteverde, K. and D. J. Teece (1982b), 'Appropriable Rents and Quasi-Vertical Integration,' *Journal of Law and Economics*, **25**, 321–328.

Mowery, E., J. Oxley and B. Silverman (1996), 'Strategic Alliances and Interfirm Knowledge Transfer,' *Strategic Management Journal*, **17**, 77–91.

Ohanian, Nancy Kane (1994), 'Vertical Integration in the U.S. Pulp and Paper Industry, 1900–1940,' *Review of Economics and Statistics*, **76**, 202–207.

Pfeffer, Jeffrey (1982), *Organizations and Organization Theory*. Boston: Pitman.

Pfeffer, Jeffrey (1996), 'Understanding Organizations: Concepts and Controversies,' forthcoming in Daniel Gilbert, Susan Fiske, and Gardner Lindzey, eds., *Handbook of Social Psychology* (4th ed.). New York: McGraw–Hill.

Pfeffer, Jeffrey and Gerald Salancik (1978), *The External Control of Organizations*. New York: Harper and Row.

Pisano, G., M. Russo and D. J. Teece (1988), 'Joint Ventures and Collaborative Arrangements in the Telecommunications Equipment Industry,' in David Mowery, ed., *International Collaborative Ventures in U.S. Manufacturing*. Cambridge, MA: Ballinger, pp. 23–70.

Pisano, G., S. Shan and D. J. Teece (1988), 'Joint Ventures and Collaboration in the Biotechnology Industry,' in David Mowery, ed., *International Collaborative Ventures in U.S. Manufacturing*. Cambridge, MA: Ballinger, pp. 183–222.

Pisano, G. and D. J. Teece (1989), 'Collaborative Arrangements and Global Technology Strategy: Some Evidence from the Telecommunications Equipment Industry,' in Robert A. Burgelman and Richard S. Rosenbloom, eds., *Research on Technological Innovation, Management and Policy*, Vol. 4. Greenwich, CT: JAI, pp. 227–256.

Porter, Michael (1980), *Competitive Strategy: Techniques for Analyzing Industries and Competitors*. New York: Free Press.

Reve, T. (1988), 'Toward a Theory of Strategic Management,' unpublished manuscript, Norwegian School of Business Administration, July.

Rumelt, Richard P., Dan Schendel and David J. Teece (1994), *Fundamental Issues in Strategy*. Cambridge, MA: Harvard Business School Press.

Schwartz, Edward, Pablo T. Spiller and Santiago Urbiztondo (1993), 'A Positive Theory of Legislative Intent,' *Law and Contemporary Problems*, **57,** 51–74.

Scott, W. Richard (1992), *Organizations: Rational, Natural and Open Systems* (3rd ed.). Englewood Cliffs, NJ: Prentice-Hall.

Shelanski, H. A. and P. Klein (1995), 'Empirical Research in Transaction Cost Economics: A Review and Assessment,' *Journal of Law, Economics and Organization*, **11,** 335–361.

Shepsle, Kenneth A. (1978), *The Giant Jigsaw Puzzle*. Chicago: University of Chicago Press.

Shepsle, Kenneth A. (1992), 'Bureaucratic Drift, Coalitional Drift, and Time Inconsistency—a Comment,' *Journal of Law, Economics and Organization*, **8,** 111–118.

Shepsle, Kenneth A. and Barry R. Weingast, eds. (1996), *Positive Theories of Congressional Institutions*. Ann Arbor: University of Michigan Press.

Shepsle, Kenneth A. and Barry R. Weingast (1987), 'The Institutional Foundations of Committee Power,' *American Political Science Review*, **81,** 85–104.

Shuen, Amy (1994), 'Technology Sourcing and Learning Strategies in the Semiconductor Industry,' unpublished Ph.D. dissertation, University of California, Berkeley.

Shugart, Matthew S. and J. M. Carey (1992), *Presidents and Assemblies*. New York, NY: Cambridge University Press.

Silverman, Brian, Jackson Nickerson and John Freeman (1996), 'Profitability, Transactional Alignment and Organizational Mortality in the U.S. Trucking Industry,' unpublished manuscript, University of California, Berkeley.

Singh, Jitendra V. and Charles J. Lumsden (1990), 'Theory and Research in Organizational Ecology,' *Annual Review of Sociology*, **16,** 161–195.

Spiller, Pablo T. (1990), 'Politicians, Interest Groups and Regulators: A Multiple Principals Agency Theory of Regulation, (or Let Them Be Bribed),' *Journal of Law and Economics*, **33,** 65–101.

Spiller, Pablo T. (1992), 'Agency Discretion under Judicial Review,' *Mathematical and Computer Modelling*, **16,** 185–200.

Spiller, Pablo T. (1997), 'Institutions and Commitment,' *Industrial and Corporate Change*, **5,** 421–452.

Spiller, Pablo T. (forthcoming), 'Agency Discretion and Accountability in Regulation,' in P. Newman, ed., *The Palgrave Dictionary of Economics and the Law*.

Spiller, Pablo T. and Emerson H. Tiller (1997), 'Decision Costs and the Strategic Design of Administrative Process and Judicial Review,' *Journal of Legal Studies*, **26,** 347–370.

Spiller, Pablo T. and Santiago Urbiztondo (1991), 'Interest Groups and the Control of the Bureaucracy: An Agency Perspective on the Administrative Procedure Act,' unpublished manuscript, Urbana, IL: University of Illinois.

Spiller, Pablo T. and Santiago Urbiztondo (1994), 'Political Appointees vs. Career Civil Servants: A Multiple-Principals Theory of Political Institutions,' *European Journal of Political Economy*, **10,** 465–497.

Spiller, Pablo T. and Ingo Vogelsang (1997), 'The Institutional Foundations of Regulatory Commitment in the UK: The Case of Telecommunications,' *Journal of Institutional and Theoretical Economics*, forthcoming.

Stuckey, J. and D. White (1993), 'When and When Not to Vertically Integrate,' *McKinsey Quarterly*, No. 3, 3–27.

Taagepera, R. and M. Shugart (1993), 'Predicting the Number of Parties: A Quantitative Model of Duverger Mechanical Effect,' *American Political Science Review*, **87,** 455–464.

Teece, D. J. (1976), *Vertical Integration and Vertical Divestiture in the U.S. Oil Industry*. Stanford: Stanford University Institute for Energy Studies.

Teece, D. J. (1978), 'Vertical Integration in the U.S. Oil Industry,' in E. Mitchell, ed., *Vertical Integration in the Oil Industry*. Washington, DC: American Enterprise Institute, pp. 105–189.

Teece, D. J. (1980a), 'The Diffusion of an Administrative Innovation,' *Management Science*, **26**, 464–470.

Teece, D. J. (1980b), 'Economies of Scope and the Scope of an Enterprise,' *Journal of Economic Behavior and Organization*, **1**, 223–247.

Teece, D. J. (1981a), 'The Market for Know-how and the Efficient International Transfer of Technology,' *Annals of the Academy of Political and Social Science*, **458**, 81–96.

Teece, D. J. (1981b), 'The Multinational Enterprise: Market Failure and Market Power Considerations,' *Sloan Management Review*, **22**, 3–17.

Teece, D. J. (1982), 'Towards an Economic Theory of the Multiproduct Firm,' *Journal of Economic Behavior and Organization*, **3**, 39–63.

Teece, D. J. (1985), 'Multinational Enterprise, Internal Governance, and Industrial Organization,' *American Economic Review*, **75**, 233–238.

Teece, D. J. (1986a), 'Profiting from Technological Innovation: Implications for Integration, Collaboration, Licensing and Public Policy,' *Research Policy*, **15**, 285–305.

Teece, D. J. (1986b), 'Transactions Cost Economics and the Multinational Enterprise: An Assessment,' *Journal of Economic Behavior and Organization*, **7**, 21–45.

Teece, D. J. (1992), 'Competition, Cooperation, and Innovation: Organization Arrangements for Regimes of Rapid Technological Progress,' *Journal of Economic Behavior and Organization*, **18**, 1–25.

Teece, D. J. and H. Armour (1978), 'Organizational Structure and Economic Performance: A Test of the Multidivisional Hypothesis,' *Bell Journal of Economics*, **9**, 106–122.

Teece, D. J., Gary Pisano and Amy Shuen (1997), 'Dynamic Capabilities and Strategic Management,' *Strategic Management Journal*, **18**, 509–533.

Teece, D. J., R. Rumelt, G. Dosi and S. Winter (1994), 'Understanding Corporate Coherence: Theory and Evidence,' *Industrial and Corporate Change*, **2**, 317–350.

Thompson, James D. (1967), *Organizations in Action*. New York: McGraw-Hill.

Uzzi, Brian (forthcoming), 'The Sources and Consequences of Embeddedness for the Economic Performance of Organizations: The Network Effect,' *American Sociological Review*.

Weingast, Barry R. and William Marshall (1988), 'The Industrial Organization of Congress,' *Journal of Political Economy*, **96**, 132–163.

Weingast, Barry R. and Mark J. Moran (1983), 'Bureaucratic Discretion or Congressional Control? Regulatory Policymaking by the Federal Trade Commission,' *Journal of Political Economy*, **91**, 765–800.

Williamson, Oliver E. (1975), *Markets and Hierarchies: Analysis and Antitrust Implications*. New York: Free Press.

Williamson, Oliver E. (1981), 'The Economics of Organization: The Transaction Cost Approach,' *American Journal of Sociology*, **87**, 548–577.

Williamson, Oliver E. (1983), 'Credible Commitments: Using Hostages to Support Exchange,' *American Economic Review*, **73**, 519–540.

Williamson, Oliver E. (1985), *The Economic Institutions of Capitalism*. New York: Free Press.

Williamson, Oliver E. (1988), 'Corporate Finance and Corporate Governance,' *Journal of Finance*, **43**, 567–591.

Williamson, Oliver E. (1990), 'Interview,' in R. Swedberg (ed.), *Economics and Sociology*. Princeton, NJ: Princeton University Press, pp. 115–129.

Williamson, Oliver E. (1991a), 'Comparative Economic Organization: The Analysis of Discrete Structural Alternatives,' *Administrative Science Quarterly*, **36**, 269–296.

Williamson, Oliver E. (1991b), 'Strategizing, Economizing, and Economic Organization,' *Strategic Management Journal*, **12**, 75–94.

Williamson, Oliver E. (1996), *The Mechanisms of Governance*. New York: Oxford University Press.

CHAPTER SIX

Empirical Research in Transaction Cost Economics

A Review and Assessment

HOWARD A. SHELANSKI AND PETER G. KLEIN

This article summarizes and assesses the growing body of empirical research in transaction cost economics (TCE). Originally an explanation for the scale and scope of the firm, TCE is now used to study a variety of economic relationships, ranging from vertical and lateral integration to transfer pricing, corporate finance, marketing, the organization of work, long-term commercial contracting, franchising, regulation, the multinational corporation, company towns, and many other contractual relationships. The main insights and predictions of TCE—in particular, the importance of governing transactions—are becoming increasingly accepted. The empirical support for these claims, however, is much less known. We believe the empirical literature, on the whole, is remarkably consistent with the predictions of TCE—more so than is typically the case in economics. After presenting an overview of the theory and a discussion of some theoretical and methodological preliminaries, we summarize the major findings and discuss their implications, particularly the potential applications to public policy. In an appendix we provide a more comprehensive list of articles, arranged by type of study, as a reference aid for researchers.

1. Introduction

> *[The new institutional economics] suggests a whole agenda of microeconomic empirical work that must be performed . . . Until that work has been carried out . . . the new institutional economics and related approaches are acts of faith, or perhaps of piety.*
> —Herbert Simon (1991, p. 27)

Transaction cost theories of exchange, part of what has been termed the "New Institutional Economics," have been the subject of growing interest in recent years. Originally an explanation for the scale and scope of the firm, transac-

We are grateful to Nicholas Argyres, Paul Joskow, Vai-Lam Mui, Joanne Oxley, Pablo Spiller, Oliver Williamson, and an anonymous referee for very helpful comments and for correcting numerous errors, and to the Center for Research in Management, University of California, Berkeley, for financial support.

tion cost economics (TCE) is now used to study a variety of economic phenomena, ranging from vertical and lateral integration to transfer pricing, corporate finance, marketing, the organization of work, long-term commercial contracting, franchising, regulation, the multinational corporation, company towns, and other contractual relationships, both formal and informal. The basic insight of transaction cost economics—that transactions must be *governed* as well as designed and carried out, and that certain institutional arrangements effect this governance better than others—is now increasingly accepted. The purpose of this article is to outline this empirical literature and to offer a preliminary assessment of its impact on the development of TCE theory and related fields. We make no effort to examine all the existing empirical work in the TCE tradition; such a project would require several essays. Instead, we focus on several key empirical issues or phenomena on which we think TCE has enabled researchers to make substantial progress. We find that, on balance, a remarkable amount of the empirical work we have examined is consistent with TCE predictions—much more so, perhaps, than is the case with most of industrial organization.[1]

The article is organized as follows. Section 2 presents a brief overview of TCE, and Section 3 discusses some theoretical and methodological issues related to the testing of TCE hypotheses. In Section 4 we summarize the relevant empirical research, organized by topic; Section 5 covers the public policy implications of this evidence. We summarize and conclude in Section 6. The appendix provides a comprehensive list of articles, arranged by type of study, as a reference aid for researchers.

2. *Transaction Cost Economics: An Overview*

Transaction cost economics studies how trading partners protect themselves from the hazards associated with exchange relationships. As developed by Williamson (1975; 1985; 1995), Klein, Crawford, and Alchian (1978), and more formally by Grossman and Hart (1986) and Hart and Moore (1990), TCE maintains that in a complex world, contracts are typically incomplete.[2] Because of this incompleteness, parties who invest in relationship-specific assets expose themselves to a hazard: If circumstances change, their trading partners may try to expropriate the rents accruing to the specific assets. One way to safeguard those rents is through integration, where the parties merge and

---

[1] Compare Joskow (1991, p. 47). For another example of the tension between theoretical and empirical work in industrial organization, see Peltzman's (1991) highly critical review of the *Handbook of Industrial Organization*.

[2] This may be because agents are boundedly rational, or because certain quantities or outcomes are unobservable (or not verifiable to third parties, such as the courts), in which case contracts cannot be made contingent on these variables or outcomes.

eliminate adversarial interests. Less extreme options include reciprocal buying arrangements, in which each party exposes itself to form a mutual exchange of "hostages," and partial ownership agreements. In general, a variety of such "governance structures" may be employed; the appropriate one depends on the particular characteristics of the relationship. In this way, TCE may be considered the *study of alternative institutions of governance.* Its working hypothesis, as expressed by Williamson (1991, p. 79), is that economic organization is really an effort to "align transactions, which differ in their attributes, with governance structures, which differ in their costs and competencies, in a discriminating (mainly, transaction cost economizing) way." Simply put, TCE tries to explain how trading partners choose, from the set of feasible institutional alternatives, the arrangement that offers protection for their relationship-specific investments at the lowest total cost.

Transactions differ in a variety of ways: the degree to which relationship-specific assets are involved, the amount of uncertainty about the future and about other parties' actions, the complexity of the trading arrangement, and the frequency with which the transaction occurs. Each matters in determining the preferred institution of governance, although the first—asset specificity—is held to be particularly important.[3] Williamson (1985, p. 55) defines asset specificity as "durable investments that are undertaken in support of particular transactions, the opportunity cost of which investments is much lower in best alternative uses or by alternative users should the original transaction be prematurely terminated." This could describe a variety of relationship-specific investments, including both specialized physical and human capital, along with intangibles such as R&D and firm-specific knowledge or "capabilities."

Governance structures can be described along a spectrum. At one end lies the pure, anonymous spot market, which suffices for simple transactions such as basic commodity sales. Market prices provide powerful incentives for the exploitation of profit opportunities, and market participants are quick to adapt to changing circumstances as information is revealed through prices. When specialized assets are at stake, however, and when product or input markets are thin, bilateral coordination of investment decisions may be desirable, and combined ownership may be efficient. At the other end of the spectrum from the simple, anonymous spot market thus lies the fully integrated firm, where trading parties are under unified ownership and control. TCE posits that such hierarchies offer greater protection for specific investments and provide relatively efficient mechanisms for responding to change

---

[3] Indeed, TCE (associated mainly with Williamson) is sometimes described as the "governance" branch of the New Institutional Economics, as opposed to the "measurement or asset, specificity" or agency-theoretic branch (associated with Alchian and Demsetz, 1972).

where coordinated adaptation is necessary. Compared to decentralized structures, however, hierarchies provide managers weaker incentives to maximize profits and normally incur additional bureaucratic costs.[4] Between the two poles of market and hierarchy are a variety of "hybrid" modes, such as complex contracts and partial ownership arrangements. The movement from market to hierarchy thus entails a trade-off between the high-powered incentives and adaptive properties of the market, and the safeguards and central coordinating properties of the firm.[5]

Implicit in TCE is a notion that market forces work to bring about an "efficient sort" between transactions and governance structures, so that exchange relationships observed in practice can be explained in terms of transaction cost economizing. The existence of this selection mechanism is usually assumed rather than explained, though, and thus TCE is subject to some of the same criticisms that evolutionary economists (Nelson and Winter, 1982, for example) have made of standard microeconomic theory. Some students of business organization have also charged TCE with having a too narrowly "economic" or efficiency-oriented view of individual and firm behavior. To be sure, TCE usually abstracts away from issues of market power, resource dependence, social embeddedness, and the like; the bulk of the empirical literature inspired by TCE takes as given an economizing framework. The basic framework is applicable to a wide range of phenomena. While vertical and lateral integration are perhaps the best-known examples, there are many others.

3. *Some Theoretical and Methodological Preliminaries*

Much of the empirical work in TCE can be considered a variation of the following basic model. The efficient form of organization for a given economic relationship—and, therefore, the likelihood of observing a particular organizational form or governance structure—is a function of certain properties of the underlying transaction or transactions: asset specificity, uncertainty, complexity, and frequency. Organizational form is the dependent variable, while asset specificity, uncertainty, complexity, and frequency are independent variables. Specifically, the probability of observing a more integrated governance structure depends positively on the amount or value of the relationship-specific assets involved and, for significant levels of asset speci-

---

[4] An example of these bureaucratic costs would be the "influence costs" studied by Milgrom and Roberts (1990).

[5] The general theoretical framework of TCE is now sufficiently accepted to have been incorporated in a number of textbook treatments. See, for example, Kreps (1990, p. 744–90), Baye and Beil (1994), Milgrom and Roberts (1992), and Rubin (1990).

ficity, on the degree of uncertainty about the future of the relationship, on the complexity of the transaction, and on the frequency of trade.

Organizational form is often modeled as a binary variable—"make" or "buy," for example—though it can sometimes be paramaterized by a continuous variable. Of the independent variables, asset specificity is the most difficult to measure. Among the common proxies are component "complexity," qualitatively coded from survey data, as a proxy for physical asset specificity (Masten, 1984); worker-specific knowledge, again coded from survey data, as a proxy for human asset specificity (Monteverde and Teece, 1982b); physical proximity of contracting firms, as a proxy for site specificity (Joskow, 1985, 1987, 1988b, 1990; Spiller, 1985); and R&D expenditure, as a proxy for physical asset specificity. Other proxies, such as fixed costs or "capital intensity," have more obvious limitations and are rarely used.

The empirical work in TCE uses a variety of econometric and historical methods. In general, these studies fall into one of three categories: qualitative case studies, quantitative case studies, and cross-sectional econometric analyses. Williamson's (1976) study of cable TV franchising in Oakland, California, is an example of the first category, while Masten's (1984) investigation of contracting practices in a large aerospace corporation is an example of the second, and Levy's (1985) study of vertical integration across industries is an example of the third. The bulk of the empirical literature in TCE consists of case analyses of various kinds. This is primarily because the main variables of interest to transaction cost economists—asset specificity, uncertainty, frequency—are difficult to measure consistently across firms and industries. Typically, these characteristics are estimated based on surveys or interviews: for example, a manager might be asked to rate on a Likert-type scale of 1 to 7 the degree to which an investment has value in outside uses. Such data are of course subject to the general limits of survey data; namely, that they are based on the respondents' stated beliefs, rather than on their beliefs or valuations as revealed through choice. More important, since these measurements are based on ordinal rankings, it is hard to compare them from industry to industry. What is ranked as a relatively specialized asset in one firm may be rated differently in another firm or industry. Similarly, what one firm considers a comparatively uncertain production process may be the standard operating environment in another. Multi-industry studies therefore may contain variables that are labeled the same thing but are really incommensurable or, conversely, may contain variables that are identical but labeled differently.

Besides these measurement difficulties, empirical research in TCE is often hampered by confusion about the definitions, and therefore the empirical parameterizations, of key variables. The primary conceptual problem that we have found lies in the treatment of uncertainty as a factor that raises transaction costs and increases the probability of integration. This confusion may explain some seemingly contradictory results on the effects of sales volume uncertainty on the vertical integration decision.

Uncertainty about future events is of course a common feature of many trading relationships; sales volume uncertainty due to volatile market conditions is an obvious example. Empirical studies sometimes treat this kind of uncertainty as an independent variable, regressing the choice of organizational form on the variance of sales or another variable, but without including any measure of asset specificity in the model. Absent fixed investments, however, TCE does not predict that uncertainty would itself lead to hierarchical governance. Changes in circumstances allow for expropriation only when there are quasi-rents at risk; that is, when one side's investment is exposed. When there are no relationship-specific investments at stake, it may be less costly for a firm to contract on the market for goods and services in an uncertain environment than to assume the risk of producing them internally. In this way, the effect of uncertainty depends on competitive conditions. If there is no asset specificity and thus there are many potential suppliers of a component for which future demand is uncertain, it may be cheaper to buy the component than to make it internally.

The effect of uncertainty on governance structure thus hinges on asset specificity and the consequent bilateral dependency. The failure of some studies to take this into account may explain a few conflicting results on the effects of uncertainty. Hence, Harrigan's (1986) finding that uncertainty reduced the probability of integration in a large, cross-sectional sample may be reconciled with opposite results by Levy (1985) and Macmillan, Hambrick, and Pennings (1986), as Harrigan abstracts from asset specificity in her study. In Walker and Weber's (1987) study of automobile parts procurement, they test the interactive effects of uncertainty and competition by dividing the sample according to the level of supplier-market competition for that component, and then testing the role of uncertainty on each part of the sample separately. They find that sales volume uncertainty, as expected, increases the probability of a "make" rather than "buy" decision, for those components produced in thin markets.[6]

Asset specificity has been more successfully treated in the empirical litera-

---

[6] There may also be situations where uncertainty is so great that efficient governance structures cannot be crafted at all, in which case trade may fail to materialize. While there is a considerable stream of theoretical literature, following Akerlof (1970), on the possibility that markets might break down due to private information, there is relatively little theoretical or empirical work on nonmarket exchange under these conditions. An exception is Wiggins and Libecap's (1985) study of unitization agreements in oil production. Under such an agreement, producers designate a single firm to develop a given field, with the net returns shared among all producers. This reduces recovery costs and improves oil yields by eliminating the negative externalities associated with concurrent independent development of a single field. Yet very few oil fields are unitized. Wiggins and Libecap argue that asymmetric information encourages opportunistic holdout strategies that usually have prevented the agreements from being signed.

ture than has uncertainty. Relationship-specific physical, site, and human capital investments have all been studied, both independently and comparatively. Further refinement and analysis need to be done here, however, particularly in the area of measurement. Proxies such as capital intensity or fixed costs are very imperfect, and may not capture whether an investment has alternative value outside the transaction for which it was initially made. Another concern is that asset-specificity effects may be confused with market power. While specific investment may lead to bilateral monopoly, the existence of a small-numbers bargaining situation is not by itself evidence of relationship-specific investment.

Besides the difficulties of measurement and definition that are unique to TCE, empirical TCE is also subject to the problems found in empirical work more generally: namely, alternate hypotheses that could also fit the data are rarely stated and compared. Usually, the data are only found consistent or inconsistent with the hypothesis at hand. We believe there is a need and opportunity for studies that explicitly compare competing, observationally distinct, hypotheses about contractual relationships, because rival theories commonly posit mutually exclusive outcomes. One example is Spiller's (1985) comparison of asset-specificity and market-power explanations of vertical merger, explanations that have rival predictions about the size of the gains from merger under various competitive conditions. Another prototype for such a project might be MacDonald's (1985) cross-sectional study of vertical integration, which incorporated elements of both TCE and Stigler's theory of the vertical "life-cycle" of the firm (though it did not attempt to distinguish between them). Further studies of this kind are essential to a better understanding of the predictive power of the transaction cost model.

4. *Comparative Contracting: A Sampling of the Evidence*

The goal of transaction cost economics is to explain contracting arrangements observed in practice. Where possible, TCE tries to explain these phenomena on efficiency grounds. We consider below five major categories of empirical phenomena explained by TCE: vertical integration, "hybrid" contracting modes, long-term commercial contracts, informal agreements, and franchise contracting. We believe that TCE has added to our understanding of each of these practices.

Because asset specificity is usually the main variable of interest in these studies, we should keep in mind Williamson's (1983) distinction between four distinct types of asset specificity. The first is *site specificity*, in which parties are in a "cheek-by-jowl" relationship to minimize transportation and inventory costs, and assets are highly immobile once in place. The second is *physical asset specificity*, referring to relationship-specific equipment and machinery. The third is *human asset specificity*, describing transaction-specific knowledge or human capital, achieved through specialized training or learning-by-doing. The fourth is *dedicated assets*, referring to substantial, general-purpose investments that would not have been made outside a particular transaction, the commitment of which is necessary to serve a large customer.

We now consider some main findings of the empirical literature.

Vertical Integration

Vertical integration, or the "make-or-buy" decision, has been described as the "paradigm problem" of TCE. Much of the earliest empirical work addresses this topic.[7] Monteverde and Teece (1982b) made one of the first systematic efforts to test a contractual interpretation of vertical integration. They examine the effects of asset specificity, defined here as worker-specific knowledge or "applications engineering effort," on the decision to produce components in-house or to obtain them from outside suppliers. Starting with a list of 133 automobile components, each coded as either made or bought, the authors enlisted an automobile design engineer to develop an index measuring the degree of applications engineering effort involved in the production of each component. Their thesis is that "[t]he greater is the applications engineering effort associated with the development of any given automobile component, the higher are the expected appropriable quasi-rents and, therefore, the greater is the likelihood of vertical integration of production for that component" (207).

Monteverde and Teece test a probit model of the component sample, regressing "make" or "buy" on the degree of applications engineering effort. They also include proxies for whether the component is specific to the manufacturer or generic, and a proxy for the specific company involved (Ford or G.M., to pick up any idiosyncratic firm-specific effects). They find applications engineering effort to be a statistically significant determinant of backward integration. The results are consistent with an earlier finding by Globerman (1980) on firm-specific technical knowledge and integration in the Canadian telecommunications industry. Globerman studied evidence from public hearings and found a tendency toward common ownership of telephone lines and equipment as the research and development demands of a carrier on its equipment suppliers become more complex and uncertain and require more relationship-specific investments.[8]

---

[7] For more on these early efforts, see the discussions in Williamson (1985, pp. 103–30) and Joskow (1988a, pp. 107–11).

[8] In a related study, Monteverde and Teece (1982a) look at "quasi-integration" in the auto industry, where quasi-integration refers to assembler ownership of tooling equipment. They find a significant, positive relationship between appropriable rents and quasi-integration, although the proposed explanation accounts for only a small proportion of the total variation in integration patterns.

Other studies of component procurement in the auto industry find similar support for transactional explanations of vertical relationships. Two studies by Walker and Weber (1984, 1987) focus on uncertainty as a determinant of vertical integration. Like Monteverde and Teece, they work with a list of automobile components, coded as made or bought, as the dependent variable. They find that greater uncertainty about production volume raises the probability that a component is made in-house, but that "technological uncertainty," measured as the frequency of changes in product specification and the probability of technological improvements, has little effect. Their second study (1987) includes measures of market competition, testing the interactive effects of both uncertainty in production and competition among suppliers, and adds the qualification that volume uncertainty matters only when supply markets are thin.

In a further refinement, Masten, Meehan, and Snyder (1989) attempt to distinguish among types of specific assets, comparing the relative importance of relationship-specific human and physical capital. They also study automobile component production, finding that engineering effort, as a proxy for human asset specificity, appears to affect the integration decision more than physical or site specificity. Klein (1988), in a discussion of the G.M.-Fisher Body case, also suggests that specific human capital in the form of technical knowledge was a major determinant of G.M.'s decision to buy out Fisher.[9] Other studies have documented a similar link between integration and research and development (R&D), which usually involves specific human capital (Armour and Teece, 1980; Globerman, 1980; Joskow, 1985; Pisano, 1990).

Asset specificity, then, appears to be an important determinant of vertical integration, particularly when examined together with uncertainty and product complexity. Site specificity, dedicated assets, and the need for specifically tailored products or production facilities have been shown to increase vertical integration in a variety of industries, including electricity generation (Joskow, 1985), aerospace (Masten, 1984), aluminum (Stuckey, 1983; Hennart, 1988), forestry (Globerman and Schwindt, 1986), chemicals (Lieberman, 1991), and offshore oil gathering (Hallwood, 1991).

Spiller (1985) examines site specificity in an attempt to distinguish between TCE and market-power explanations for vertical mergers. While TCE predicts that the gains from merger should be increasing in the degree of asset

---

[9] The relationship between G.M. and Fisher Body in the 1920s is a frequently discussed application of TCE. Both Klein, Crawford, and Alchian (1978) and Williamson (1985, pp. 114–115) explain G.M.'s buyout of Fisher in terms of the specific physical assets that accompanied the switch from wooden- to metal-bodied cars. The account in Klein (1988) is somewhat different, emphasizing specific human capital. Langlois and Robertson (1989) also criticize the earlier TCE account of the G.M.-Fisher relationship, arguing that systemic uncertainty, rather than asset specificity, accounted for the failure of long-term contracting there.

specificity, market-power considerations suggest that the gains will be increasing in the degree of supplier-market concentration. Using site specificity, defined as the proximity of the merging firms, to represent asset specificity, Spiller studies the gains from merger according to unexpected changes in the firms' stock prices at the announcement of the merger. He finds the total gain from merger to be smaller the greater the distance between the merging firms (the lower the site specificity), whereas the industry concentration ratio has no significant effect. This appears to support the asset-specificity explanation over the market-power explanation.

Except for Spiller (1985), all the papers cited above are case studies of particular industries or production processes. As such, they avoid the problems discussed in Section 2 of inconsistent measurement across industries. Indeed, the limits of interindustry studies in industrial organization more generally have been recognized for some time (Joskow, 1988a: 111). These case studies have measurement difficulties of their own, however. The classification of dichotomous variables like "make-or-buy," for example, typically is based on survey data and may require the researcher to exercise a certain amount of discretion or intuitive judgment. Nonetheless, most of the empirical work in TCE on vertical integration has been of this type. While it is of course difficult to generalize the results, the cumulative evidence from different studies and industries is quite consistent with the basic theory.

Also, there do exist some cross-sectional studies on transactional determinants of vertical integration using multi-industry data. An early effort by Levy (1985) uses the ratio of value-added to sales as a cross-industry measure of vertical integration, the number of firms and amount of R&D spending as measures of asset specificity, and the variance of sales as a measure of uncertainty. Using data from 69 firms representing 37 industries for the years 1958, 1963, 1967, and 1972, he finds each of the independent variables to have a statistically significant effect on the likelihood of vertical integration. Macmillan, Hambrick, and Pennings (1986) obtain very similar results with a larger sample. Harrigan (1986), by contrast, finds sales variability to result in a lower chance of vertical integration, although she does not include a measure for asset specificity.

Accounting constructs like value-added-to-sales ratios, such as those used by Levy, are highly problematic as measures of vertical integration. Caves and Bradburd (1988) construct a more complicated cross-industry measure of integration based on an input-output matrix of distribution shipments across several industries. They use this metric to compare asset specificity, small-numbers bargaining conditions, and risk as determinants of vertical integration. They find asset specificity and small-numbers situations, but not risk, to be significant. TCE-based hypotheses thus do well in their study as compared to competing approaches. The approach of Caves and Bradburd is promising and warrants further exploration where possible. Unfortunately, their procedures are exceptionally data-intensive and may not be feasible in many cases. Other potentially fruitful approaches use financial data on merging firms' pre- and post-merger performance, either to study the gains from merger as a function of asset specificity (Spiller, 1985) or to examine the likelihood of merger as a function of pre-merger bilateral relationships (Weiss, 1992).

While economists typically think of vertical integration as backward integration into components, materials, or R&D, forward integration into marketing and distribution may be just as important. Several studies of the integration of marketing channels have used TCE as an explanatory framework. Anderson and Schmittlein (1984) consider two marketing alternatives for an electronics component producer: the use of employees as a direct sales force (a form of vertical integration) vs. reliance on independent manufacturers' representatives. This choice is regressed on managers' perceptions of the importance of specific human capital, sales volume uncertainty, and measurement uncertainty (all based on survey data), each of which is predicted to increase the likelihood of a direct sales force. Both specific human capital and measurement uncertainty are statistically significant, though sales uncertainty is not. A second study by Anderson (1985), also on the electronics industry, finds the same basic results, as does work by John and Weitz (1988) using data from a variety of industrial-product industries. Marketing and distribution depend on other factors as well, of course. A recent study of the carbonated beverage industry by Muris, Scheffman, and Spiller (1992) finds that the shift from independent bottlers to captive subsidiaries over the last 20 to 30 years can be explained without reference to changes in asset specificity. Instead, they account for the shift in terms of the emergence of national cola markets, which required greater coordination of advertising and promotional activities. Along with changing technologies in cola production and distribution (namely, falling transportation and communication costs), it was this need for more centralized decision-making—for given levels of asset specificity—that explains the change toward a more vertically integrated industry.

To sum up, the evidence on the transactional determinants of vertical integration seems quite striking. Asset specificity and uncertainty appear to have significant effects on the vertical structure of production. This is especially remarkable when compared with the relative dearth of evidence on market-power explanations for integration, and with the results of rare studies that explicitly compare TCE-based theories with market-power theories (Spiller, 1985).

Complex Contracting and "Hybrid" Modes

Integration, as discussed previously, is an extreme form of internal governance. Intermediate forms also exist: long-term contracts, complex contracts with reciprocity agreements, agreements to provide offsetting specific investments ("hostages"), equity linkages, and so on. These may be adopted because the benefits of full integration are not worth the costs, given the properties of the transaction, or because integration is prohibited by regulation.

A simple example of a hybrid or intermediate form of governance is an exclusive dealing contract. Gallick (1984) examines such contracts in the U.S. tuna industry. Exclusive dealing, he argues, is an efficient means of discouraging opportunism by fishing boat captains. Because most tuna sold in the United States is canned, it is cheaper for tuna processors to buy a boat's output at a price reflecting average quality than to pay for the inspection, sorting, and grading usually found in fresh fish markets. Exclusive dealing arrangements prevent the boat captains from selling the higher quality tuna, ex post, to rival processors at higher prices. Until the mid-1960s, reputation effects were sufficient to enforce the contracts; the practice of frequent, small deliveries prevented the processors from trying to renegotiate the terms of trade after the catches had been made. Interestingly, Gallick reports, when fishing technology changed such that catches could be much larger—increasing the short-term gains to the processor from reneging on an exclusive dealing agreement after the catch—reputation was no longer an efficient enforcement mechanism, and a new institutional practice emerged: co-ownership of fishing vessels by the boat captains and the processors.[10]

In another context, Heide and John (1988) study marketing relationships between manufacturers and sales agencies. To service a particular manufacturer, sales agencies typically make investments specific to that manufacturer—most often, a human-capital investment in developing a sales territory for the manufacturer's product. Because agencies are small relative to manufacturers, they cannot safeguard their investments by backward integration into manufacturing. Similarly, they lack the bargaining power to demand long-term contracts with manufacturers. Instead, they protect their relationship-specific assets by making *other* specific investments, namely in routines or procedures that tie or "bond" them with a manufacturer's customers. These might be the establishment of personal relationships with the customers, the development of an identity separate from the manufacturer's particular prod-

---

[10] On the antitrust implications of such exclusionary practices, see Masten and Snyder's (1993) analysis of *United States v. United Shoe Machinery Corporation*. They interpret United's equipment-leasing provisions as a means of governing the operation and maintenance of complex shoe machines.

uct, or the creation of specialized procedures for ordering, shipping, and servicing the product. In this way they "balance their dependence" on the manufacturer with the customers' dependence on them.

Heide and John use data from 199 manufacturers' agents to test this dependence-balancing hypothesis. The evidence is supportive: agencies with specific assets invested in the agency-manufacturer relationship tended to make more offsetting investments to lessen their dependence on the manufacturer. This suggests quite clearly the importance of asset specificity in determining the governance of marketing channel exchange.

Pisano (1990) asks why firms may rely on equity linkages instead of contracts to support certain transactions. He argues that partial ownership will dominate contractual governance when a relationship involves uncertainty, transaction-specific capital, and other variables. He tests the hypotheses that (i) equity linkages are more likely when R&D is to be performed during collaboration; (ii) equity arrangements are more likely when collaboration encompasses multiple projects; and (iii) equity arrangements are less likely in environments in which there are more potential collaborators. Each of the three hypotheses is supported by tests using data from 195 collaborative arrangements in the biotechnology industry. The study corroborates TCE explanations for the role of equity linkages in governing exchange. Pisano, Russo, and Teece (1988) apply a similar analysis to the telecommunications equipment business and find that the same basic framework can explain the choice between equity linkages and other forms of cooperative ventures (joint ventures, consortiums, or non-equity linkages).

In another hybrid mode case study, Eccles (1981) uses a transaction cost framework to explain the existence of the prime-contractor/subcontractor organizational unit ("quasi-firm") in the home construction business. He argues that the quasi-firm can be explained as an efficient governance structure for the construction industry. Using data from interviews with 38 home-building firms, Eccles finds strong support for the role of governance costs in explaining the quasi-firm structure. Also, he finds that the quasi-firm structure allows market suppliers to be governed like integrated organizational units. If such contractual relations are efficient at high levels of asset specificity, then TCE may assign too much attention to asset specificity for the integration decision. Alternatively, it could be that the observed level of asset specificity is close to a threshold or switchover value, in which case either organizational alternative is efficient. Clearly, more work needs to be done on hybrid modes of organization before the implications of Eccles's results can be fully understood.

Long-term Commercial Contracts

A series of studies by Joskow (1985, 1987, 1988b, 1990) investigates the
effects of asset specificity on contract duration and price adjustment in
agreements between coal suppliers and coal-burning electrical plants. He examines a large sample of coal contracts and finds strong support for the hypothesis that the greater are relationship-specific investments (in this case,
site specificity and dedicated assets), the longer are the periods covered by
the contract. Furthermore, he finds that long-term contracts performed well
despite large fluctuations in the nominal price of coal. This suggests that
long-term contracting can be a feasible alternative to integration when asset
specificity is moderate. Crocker and Masten (1988) found similarly that
contracts in the natural gas industry tended to cover longer terms when specific assets were involved. More generally, they argue that efficient contract
duration depends on the costs of contracting—contract terms become
shorter, for example, as uncertainty increases. Goldberg and Erickson (1987)
analyze 90 contracts for petroleum coke written between 1946 and 1973
and conclude that many provisions of the contracts can best be interpreted
as efforts by the parties to protect themselves against expropriation of specialized investments.[11]

Decanio and Frech (1993) tried to measure more precisely the efficiency
gains from long-term contracts in natural gas. Relationship-specific investments are critical for transactions between wellhead owners and pipelines. For
that reason, "take-or-pay" contracts, in which the buyer is required to pay for
some minimum quantity even if delivery is not taken, are often used to safeguard against buyer (pipeline) opportunism.[12] In 1987, the Federal Energy
Regulatory Commission (FERC) eliminated such long-term agreements. The
authors use data from before and after the FERC order to test its effect on spot
gas prices and prices at the wellhead. They find that FERC's interference with
parties' ability to craft long-term governance mechanisms raised natural gas
prices between 21 and 31 percent in the year following FERC's order. The results support TCE explanations for the relative efficiency of long-term contracts where asset specificity is required, while representing an effort to quan-
tify that efficiency gain.

Pirrong (1993) has recently argued that long-term contracts (and sometimes vertical integration) can be efficient in the presence of smaller contracting hazards—even when obvious physical, human, and site asset speci-

---

[11] Other relevant studies on natural gas contracts include Crocker and Masten (1991) and Hubbard and
Weiner (1986, 1991).

[12] Mulherin (1986) and Masten and Crocker (1985) also examine "take-or-pay" contracts.

ficities are absent. In a study of bulk shipping, he finds that more integrated governance structures can dominate spot trading in the presence of what Masten, Meehan, and Snyder (1991) call "temporal specificities." When a processing or refinery plant contracts with a particular bulk carrier, for example, both plant and carrier capacities suddenly become specific assets. Small delays in delivery can then result in large losses of quasi-rents for the plant, just as the plant's refusal to take full delivery can impose substantial losses on the carrier. Hence, Pirrong concludes, "spatial/temporal proximity is a form of relationship-specific capital" (1993, p. 943), at least when markets are thin. To avoid costly strategic bargaining, then, these parties will choose a complex, long-term agreement.

A key feature of long-term contracts is their *incompleteness*. Indeed, TCE holds that all complex contracts are necessarily incomplete; otherwise, why would specialized governance arrangements be necessary? Yet the degree of incompleteness of a contract need not be exogenous. If there are degrees of incompleteness—the extent to which renegotiation procedures are specified, for example—it then becomes important to study how complete a contract should be. In a recent study of Air Force engine procurement, Crocker and Reynolds (1993) tested the relationship between contractual incompleteness and the likelihood of opportunistic behavior. Using a sample of procurement agreements from the 1970s and 1980s, they assigned each contract a measure of incompleteness and regressed this on variables representing the contractor's history of litigiousness and a dummy for dual sourcing (representing the expected degree of ex post opportunism); the time between contract agreement and delivery, and historical failure rates for the engine type (proxies for environmental uncertainty); and other structural variables.

The results are significant and in the expected directions for a variety of specifications (including ordinary least squares and ordered probit). Contracts are observed to be more complete when the contractor has a history of disputes with purchasers and less complete when there are increases in associated intertemporal or technological uncertainty (increasing the cost of writing more complete contracts). One implication is that federal rules governing military procurement should allow for flexibility in contract design, because the optimal contract will vary from case to case, depending on the attributes of the transaction. Most important, this study shows that the degree of contractual completeness may reasonably be treated as an endogenous variable.

Informal Agreements

TCE pays special attention to the importance of "private ordering" for dispute resolution, in contrast to the older tradition of "legal centralism"

(Williamson, 1985, pp. 20–21).[13] Several studies have investigated whether informal trade arrangements, which are not legally enforceable, may also be motivated by the desire to make exchange more efficient. Important work in this area has been done by Palay (1984, 1985). In two closely related papers, Palay studies the role of informal, legally unenforceable agreements between rail-freight carriers and shippers. He argues that Interstate Commerce Commission regulation of the industry, which prohibits vertical integration of carriers and shippers, was geared to "classical contracting" (Macneil, 1978) but is inappropriate for transactions requiring more complex agreements. Shipment of items like automobile parts and chemicals, for example, requires specially designed rail cars and equipment that cannot be easily redeployed for other uses. Palay's hypothesis is that informal agreements, substituting for combined ownership, would emerge both to encourage and to protect these relationship-specific investments. Furthermore, he argues that the underlying characteristics of a transaction predict whether it will be supported by an informal agreement. Evidence from 51 case studies of shipper–carrier transactions reveals a pattern of informal agreements highly consistent with TCE. Equipment tailored for particular users—custom carrier racks for automobile parts, tank and covered hopper cars for specific volatile chemicals, and so on—was owned by individual shippers. Equipment for more standardized shipments would be owned by rail carriers. The informal agreements also provided handling procedures for unusual circumstances related to shipment. The transactions that did not use informal contracting all involved nonspecialized capital such as standard box cars. All of this suggests the importance of asset specificity for complex contracting.

Two studies of New England fishing industries also examined the role of transaction costs in determining trade agreements and market structure. Wilson (1980) conducted an intensive study of the New England fresh fish market. He found that underlying the smooth functioning of the market was a system of mutual dependence created by the particular trade arrangements there; reputation effects provided an enforcement mechanism. Acheson's (1985) study of the Maine lobster market reached similar conclusions, finding the lobster market to be characterized by long-term, informal relationships between fishermen and lobster-pound operators. Fisherman and pound operators typically crafted agreements designed to reduce the costs of information and the possibility of opportunistic use of informational asymmetries. The agreements were reinforced by reputation considerations and interdependencies arising from the sharing of scarce resources, such as market information,

---

13 The recent work on private law and its evolution by Ellickson (1991) and Benson (1990), for example, is in this same spirit.

boat fuel, and bait. Informal agreements and norms in eighteenth- and nine-teenth-century whaling have been studied similarly by Ellickson (1989) and Gifford (1993).

Finally, in an interesting application of TCE to the context of personal re-lationships, Brinig (1990) employs transaction cost reasoning to explain the sudden increase in the demand for diamond engagement rings in the mid-1930s. The increase, she argues, can be traced to the abolition in several states of the "breach of promise to marry action" around the same time. Before this action was abolished, a broken engagement could trigger a lawsuit, because a woman in this situation faced considerable loss of reputation. Once the cause of action was eliminated, however, another arrangement was needed to ensure the credibility of the marriage commitment. Diamond engagement rings filled that role. In this way, rings may be seen as a governance structure: they safe-guard the future bride's relationship-specific investment—her good reputation.

In general, although none of the agreements in the above studies were legally enforceable, they were not easily broken. The reputation effects and rec-iprocity provisions embodied in these arrangements evidently work well and provide strong safeguards for the parties involved; the short-term gains from opportunism are largely offset by long-term losses from a damaged reputation in the particular industry community. These empirical studies support trans-action cost reasoning not only because they find that observed arrangements can be explained in terms of asset specificity, uncertainty, and the like, but also because they reflect an emphasis on private ordering over resort to the courts.

Franchise Contracting

Williamson's (1976) case study of the Oakland, California, cable TV (CATV) franchise was an early empirical study using transactional reasoning. Re-sponding to the Posner-Demsetz argument that competitive bidding for mo-nopoly franchises would result in competitive prices, Williamson claimed that once idiosyncratic investments are in place, what was a large-numbers bar-gaining situation during the bidding process is transformed into a bilateral monopoly. Because of this, the terms of the original contract may no longer be applicable. Williamson outlined the difficulties faced by the city of Oak-land in the early 1970s over its CATV franchise. The franchise was awarded to the lowest bidder in 1970. After the franchise was awarded, however, the construction process went more slowly than expected, fewer households signed up than predicted, and costs escalated. Consequently, the franchisee re-quested a renegotiation of the contract. A complex dual-source agreement was eventually reached, and the outcome in no way reflected the intent of the ini-tial agreement.

Two later studies of CATV have looked for similar problems, with mixed results. Zupan (1989a) examined a series of public cable franchise agreements, comparing the terms of trade struck during the original franchise agreement with those prevailing at the time of renewal, after relationship-specific investments had been made; he found no significant differences in those terms. Prager (1990), however, found that opportunistic behavior by the franchisee, as perceived by cable customers, was higher for franchises awarded through competitive bidding.[14]

Of course, it is not always the franchisee who is engaged in opportunism; the franchisor may behave in opportunistic fashion as well. Grandy's (1989) examination of 19th-century railroad regulation in New Jersey finds that the railroads in that state were willing to make large specialized investments only when they were protected by "special corporation charters" limiting state action against them. Levy and Spiller's (1994) comparative study of telecommunications regulation in Argentina, Chile, Jamaica, the Philippines, and the United Kingdom shows that private investment is forthcoming only when regulators can commit not to pursue arbitrary administrative actions. Furthermore, many private franchise contracts can also be explained in terms of TCE (Norton, 1989; Dnes, 1992).

Besides the contractual phenomena described above, TCE has been brought to bear on such diverse topics as labor market contracts and regulation (Barker and Chapman, 1989), tie-ins and "block booking" (Kenney and Klein, 1983), international trade and the multinational corporation (Hennart, 1989; Yarbrough and Yarbrough, 1987b; Gatignon and Anderson, 1988; Klein, Frazer, and Roth, 1990), company towns and company stores (Fishback, 1986, 1992), land tenure agreements (Roumasset and Uy, 1980; Alston and Higgs, 1982; Alston, Datta, and Nugent, 1984; Datta, O'Hara, and Nugent, 1986) and even indentured prostitution (Ramseyer, 1991). These and other "nonstandard" contracting practices, when viewed through a transaction cost lens, often turn out to have efficiency properties, particularly in offering safeguards for specific investments.

5. *Public Policy Implications and Influence*

Theoretical and empirical TCE research has strong implications for antitrust, regulation, and other aspects of public policy. The full title of Williamson's 1975 book, after all, is *Markets and Hierarchies: Analysis and Antitrust Implications*. A basic conclusion of TCE is that vertical mergers, even when there

---

[14] Even when successful at curbing opportunism, though, the agreements do not always induce efficient pricing (Zupan, 1989b).

are no obvious gains in technological possibilities, may enhance efficiency by reducing governance costs. Hence Williamson (1985, p. 19) takes issue with what he refers to as the "inhospitality tradition" in antitrust; namely, that firms engaged in nonstandard business practices like vertical integration, customer and territorial restrictions, tie-ins, franchising, and so on, must be seeking monopoly gains. In the 10 years between the celebrated *Schwinn* (1967) and *GTE-Sylvania* (1977) cases, Williamson argues, economists began to incorporate transaction cost considerations into their understanding of vertical restrictions. This change in the intellectual climate was reflected in the Supreme Court's reversal in *GTE-Sylvania* of its earlier position that vertical restraints are necessarily anticompetitive.[15]

However, as Joskow (1991, pp. 79–80) points out, this change may reflect sensitivity to claims that vertical integration and restraints need not reduce competition, rather than to claims that such arrangements provide contractual safeguards. While TCE proponents argued that nonstandard business practices may reduce transaction costs, Chicago school writers like Posner, Peltzman, and Bork were maintaining that such practices do not necessarily result in reduced competition. Therefore it is not certain to what extent TCE, as compared to complementary though distinct developments in industrial organization, has contributed to the observed changes in antitrust enforcement.

Joskow argues, more generally, that much of TCE is problematic for policy purposes:

> The hard problems in antitrust and regulatory economics often involve potential tradeoffs between apparent increases in market power and potential reductions in costs or between regulatory imperfections and organizational or contractual imperfections. To perform such tradeoffs, we need more than an ordinal ranking of the efficiency of different organizational arrangements. We would like to know how much we lose by going from the best to the next best. . . . Unless we can find good ways to quantify the magnitude of the differences in costs of alternative institutional arrangements it will be very difficult to do the necessary tradeoffs even when we convince antitrust authorities or regulators that tradeoffs are appropriate. Unfortunately, it is unlikely that the data econometricians typically rely on, drawn from actual organizational choices, will reflect the ideal natural experiment to perform such computations. (1991, pp. 81–82)

Joskow commends the recent attempt by Masten, Meehan, and Snyder (1991) to measure directly the costs of internal organization (though not the benefits). Their study represents an early effort to estimate actual costs and

---

[15] For a discussion of *Schwinn* and *GTE-Sylvania*, see the recent exchange between Williamson (1993) and Posner (1993).

benefits of alternate institutional arrangements, rather than rank them ordinally by reference to reduced-form estimation. This type of analysis, were it to become more common, could be used in making the comparative judgments to which Joskow refers.

TCE also has direct implications for many other contracting practices and regulations, though it does not yet appear to have had any influence in those areas. Barker and Chapman (1989) argue, for example, that closed-shop agreements in labor markets may serve to protect workers' job-specific training rather than to exploit a monopoly position. They attack New Zealand's "blanket coverage clause," which effectively prohibits the closed shop, supporting their claims with arguments based on TCE. Studies of optimal contract design such as Crocker and Reynolds's (1993) examination of Air Force procurement contracts are also relevant as a guide to public policy toward government purchases of goods and services. Other contracts between government agencies and private firms, such as franchise contracts for the provision of public utilities (like cable TV), can be evaluated using TCE reasoning. TCE also points out how the potential for opportunism by the state affects private incentives to make specific investments (Levy and Spiller, 1994). This is particularly important for economic and political reform in the former communist countries, where the need to provide incentives for private investment is paramount.

Summary and Conclusions

Empirical studies of transaction cost economizing cover a broad range of phenomena. Topics range from problems traditionally within the domain of industrial organization to those more frequently addressed by sociologists, business strategists, or organization theorists. The articles discussed above generally support the TCE predictions. Studies that examine the make-or-buy decision and the structure of long-term contracts, in particular, overwhelmingly confirm transaction cost economic predictions.

In each area, however, there are also results that contradict fundamental and important TCE arguments, and others that provide only weak or tangential support for the framework. The purpose of this article is not to address each of these contradictions or to assess rigorously the validity of individual studies. It suffices to say that researchers in TCE must address empirical challenges to the theory. Taken as a whole, the body of empirical research in TCE shows that a good deal of economic activity aligns with transactions in the manner predicted by the theory. As Joskow concludes, the growing body of empirical work in transaction cost economics is in many ways in "much better shape than much of the empirical work in industrial organization generally" (1991, p. 47). Nonetheless, much remains to be done, both in applying those approaches already developed to additional data and in further refining and developing the methods used to test transaction cost hypotheses.

Appendix

This appendix lists a large sample of empirical studies that either directly test transaction cost economic hypotheses or have important implications for TCE. While the list is not exhaustive, we believe it is reasonably comprehensive. The arrangement is by topic and, within that, mainly by type of study. Clearly, some articles could easily fit within more than one category, while others fit only uneasily into any category at all. Our purpose is simply to provide a picture of the scale and scope of empirical TCE research, and to provide readers with a general road map through the literature. Full citations for each article are in the references.

A.1 Comparative Contracting

This section, which contains the bulk of the empirical work on TCE, focuses on the choice between internal and external procurement of components and supplies and between internal and external distribution and marketing of final products.

A.1.1 Vertical integration. Tests of the effects of transaction costs on vertical integration cover a broad spectrum of industries and methods. They also focus on different sources of transaction costs. Some studies focus on asset specificity, some on uncertainty or small-numbers exchange conditions, and some on a combination of these variables. Much of the work listed below consists of focused single-industry studies, though several studies test TCE hypotheses using multi-industry data.

Focused single-industry studies. Globerman (1980); Globerman and Schwindt (1986); Hennart (1988); Joskow (1985); Lieberman (1991); Masten (1984); Masten, Meehan, and Snyder (1989, 1991); Monteverde and Teece (1982a, 1982b); Pisano (1990); Stuckey (1983); Walker and Weber (1984, 1987).
Studies using multi-industry data. Butler and Carney (1983); Caves and Bradburd (1988); Harrigan (1986); Levy (1985); MacDonald (1985); Macmillan, Hambrick, and Pennings (1986); Mahoney (1992); Weiss (1992).
Forward integration into marketing and distribution. Anderson (1985); Anderson and Schmittlein (1984); John and Weitz (1988); Lilien (1979); Muris, Scheffman, and Spiller (1992); Noordewier, John, and Nevin (1990).
Company towns and company stores. Fishback (1986, 1992).

A.1.2   Complex contracting and "hybrid modes."   For a large class of transactions, simple market exchange is not feasible, yet the transactions are not vertically integrated. The decision not to integrate may be due to regulatory restrictions, or to the fact that relatively efficient arrangements short of unified ownership can be set up to govern the transaction. Examples include complex contracts with reciprocity agreements, offsetting specific investments, or other safeguards. Another type of arrangement, closer to integration along the market-hierarchy continuum, is equity linkage between firms. This section lists research into how transaction costs determine the structure of exchange relations that lie between market and hierarchy ("hybrid modes"). Included are studies of both formal contracts and informal agreements.

Long-term commercial contracts. Crocker and Masten (1988); Crocker and Reynolds (1993); DeCanio and Frech (1993); Eccles (1981); Heide and John (1988); Joskow (1985, 1987); Leffler and Rucker (1991); Masten and Crocker (1985); Mulherin (1986); Pirrong (1993); Pisano (1990); Pittman (1991); Walker and Poppo (1991).

Franchising and franchise bidding. Dnes (1992); Kaufmann and Lafontaine (1994); Lafontaine (1993); Norton (1989); Prager (1990); Williamson (1976); Zupan (1989a, 1989b).

Exclusive dealing, tie-ins, and specific leases. Gallick (1984); Kenney and Klein (1983); Masten and Snyder (1993).

Land tenure agreements. Alston, Datta, and Nugent (1984); Alston and Higgs (1982); Datta, O'Hara, and Nugent (1986); Roumasset and Uy (1980).

Informal exchange relations. Acheson (1985); Brinig (1990); Ellickson (1989); Gifford (1993); Jones and Pustay (1988); Palay (1984, 1985); Wilson (1980).

Labor market contracts. Barker and Chapman (1989).

Auctions. Hallwood (1991).

A.1.3.   Price adjustment in long-term contracts.   TCE predicts that long-term contracts should be designed to protect fixed investments and to limit the extent to which either side can benefit from market changes not anticipated at the time of bargaining. These articles examine more carefully the adjustment mechanisms for price and/or quantity in long-term contracts: Crocker and Masten (1991); Crocker and Reynolds (1993); Goldberg and Erickson (1987); Hubbard and Weiner (1986, 1991); Joskow (1988b, 1990).

A.1.4.   Multinational corporations and the structure of foreign trade.   The complexities of transacting across national boundaries include ownership restrictions, government participation, and a variety of political factors. Exchange agreements often take apparently peculiar forms. These studies use transaction cost analysis to explain the structure of multinational corporations and foreign trade agreements: Anderson and Coughlan (1987); Davidson and McFetridge (1984, 1985); Gatignon and Anderson (1988); Hallwood (1990); Hennart (1989); Klein, Frazer, and Roth (1990); Murtha (1993); Teece (1977); Yarbrough and Yarbrough (1987a).

A.2. Effects of Organizational Form

The internal structure of firms, and the effects of internal organization on firm performance, have been subject to relatively few empirical TCE studies. One possible reason is that data for internal transactions are difficult to obtain. Another may be that the internal workings of a firm comprise a complex system, in which social, managerial, economic, and technological forces all operate. Nonetheless, several important studies have been carried out.

A.2.1. Effects of vertical integration. This section lists research into the effects of vertical integration on several types of firm performance. The range of work includes transaction cost analyses of governance cost savings, of changes in activities that the firm can undertake, and of changes in capital costs due to vertical integration.

Performance effects of vertical integration: Anderson (1988); Armour and Teece (1980); Balakrishnan and Wernerfelt (1986); Eccles and White (1988); John (1984); Klein (1988); Mitchell (1989); Teece (1980).
Financial market effects of vertical integration: Helfat and Teece (1987); Spiller (1985); Weiss (1992).

A.2.2. Comparative studies of organizational form. The comparative performance of firms adopting different methods of internal organization has received considerable attention. Most often, this consists of attempts to test the "M-form hypothesis" associated with Chandler and Williamson. This hypothesis states that firms adopting a particular internal governance structure—namely, the multidivisional or M-form structure—will outperform firms organized either as traditional unitary (U-form) structures or as holding companies (H-form). The evidence on relative M-form performance is decidedly mixed, especially when comparing results from the United States and the United Kingdom. These comparative studies include: Armour and Teece (1978); Blackwell, Brickley, and Weisbach (1994); Burton and Obel (1988); Butler (1983); Cable and Dirrheimer (1983); Cable and Yasuki (1985); Dwyer and Oh (1988); Harris (1983); Hill (1988); Hill and Pickering (1986); Jones (1987); Shelanski (1993); Steer and Cable (1978); Teece (1981); Thompson (1981); Williamson (1981).

A.2.3. Firm ownership and governance.   The application of transaction cost principles to corporate governance and ownership has led to several theoretical predictions (Williamson, 1985, chap. 12). These theories so far have received limited, but increasing, empirical attention. Such studies include: Balakrishnan and Fox (1993); Baysinger and Butler (1985); Baysinger and Zardkoohi (1986); Brickley and James (1987); Romano (1985).

References

Acheson, James A. (1985), 'The Main Lobster Market: Between Market and Hierarchy,' *Journal of Law, Economics, and Organization*, **1**, 385–398.

Akerlof, George A. (1970), 'The Market for "Lemons": Qualitative Uncertainty and the Market Mechanism,' *Quarterly Journal of Economics*, **84**, 488–500.

Alchian, Armen A. and Harold Demsetz (1972), 'Production, Information Costs, and Economic Organization,' *American Economic Review*, **62**, 777–795.

Alston, Lee J., Samar K. Datta and Jeffrey B. Nugent (1984), 'Tenancy Choice in a Competitive Framework with Transaction Costs,' *Journal of Political Economy*, **92**, 1121–1133.

Alston, Lee J. and Robert Higgs (1982), 'Contractual Mix in Southern Agriculture since the Civil War: Facts, Hypotheses, and Tests,' *Journal of Economic History*, **42**, 327–353.

Anderson, Erin (1985), 'The Salesperson as Outside Agent or Employee: A Transaction Cost Analysis,' *Marketing Science*, **4**, 234–254.

Anderson, Erin (1988), 'Transaction Costs as Determinants of Opportunism in Integrated and Independent Sales Forces,' *Journal of Economic Behavior and Organization*, **9**, 247–264.

Anderson, Erin and A. T. Coughlan (1987), 'International Market Entry and Expansion via Independent or Integrated Channels of Distribution,' *Journal of Marketing*, **51**, 71–82.

Anderson, Erin and David C. Schmittlein (1984), 'Integration of the Sales Force: An Empirical Examination,' *RAND Journal of Economics*, **15**, 385–395.

Armour, Henry O. and David J. Teece (1978), 'Organizational Structure and Economic Performance: A Test of the Multidivisional Hypothesis,' *Bell Journal of Economics*, **9**, 106–122.

Anderson, Erin and David C. Schmittlein (1980), 'Vertical Integration and Technological Innovation,' *Review of Economics and Statistics*, **62**, 470–474.

Balakrishnan, Srinivasan and Isaac Fox (1993), 'Asset Specificity, Firm Heterogeneity, and Capital Structure,' *Strategic Management Journal*, **14**, 3–16.

Balakrishnan, Srinivasan and Birger Wernerfelt. (1986), 'Technical Change, Competition and Vertical Integration,' *Strategic Management Journal*, **7**, 347–359.

Barker, George R. and Ralph B. Chapman (1989), 'Evaluating Labor Market Contracting and Regulation: A Transaction Costs Perspective with Particular Reference to New Zealand,' *Journal of Institutional and Theoretical Economics*, **145**, 317–342.

Baye, Michael and Richard Beil (1994), *Managerial Economics and Business Strategy*. Irwin: Burr Ridge, IL.

Baysinger, Barry D. And Henry N. Butler (1985), 'The Role of Corporation Law in the Theory of the Firm,' *Journal of Law and Economics*, **28**, 179–191.

Baysinger, D. Barry and Asghar Zardkoohi (1986), 'Technology, Residual Claimants, and Corporate Control,' *Journal of Law, Economics, & Organization*, **2**, 339–349.

Benson, Bruce L. (1990), *The Enterprise of Law: Justice Without the State*. Pacific Research Institute for Public Policy: San Francisco, CA.

Blackwell, D., J. Brickley and M. Weisbach (1994), 'Accounting Information and Internal Performance Evaluation: Evidence from Texas Banks,' *Journal of Accounting and Economics*, **17**, 331–358.

Brickley, James A. and Christopher M. James (1987), 'The Takeover Market, Corporate Board Compensation, and Ownership Structure: The Case of Banking,' *Journal of Law and Economics*, **30**, 161–180.

Brinig, Margaret (1990), 'Rings and Promises,' *Journal of Law, Economics, & Organization*, **6**, 203–215.

Burton, Richard M. and Borge Obel (1988), 'Opportunism, Incentives, and the M-Form Hypothesis,' *Journal of Economic Behavior and Organization*, **10**, 99–119.

Butler, Richard V. (1983), 'Control of Workflow in Organizations: Perspectives from Markets, Hierarchies and Collectives,' *Human Relations*, **36**, 421.

Butler, Richard V. and M. G. Carney (1983), 'Managing Markets: Implications for the Make-Buy Decision,' *Journal of Management Studies*, **20**, 213–231.

Cable, John and M. Dirrheimer (1983), 'Hierarchies and Markets: An Empirical Test of the Multidivisional Hypothesis in West Germany,' *International Journal of Industrial Organization*, **1**, 43–62.

Cable, John and Hirohiko Yasuki (1985), 'Internal Organization, Business Groups, and Corporate Performance: An Empirical Test of the Multidivisional Hypothesis in Japan,' *International Journal of Industrial Organization*, **3**, 421–438.

Caves, Richard E. and Ralph E. Bradburd (1988), 'The Empirical Determinants of Vertical Integration,' *Journal of Economic Behavior and Organization*, **9**, 265–279.

Crocker, Keith J. and Scott E. Masten (1988), 'Mitigating Contractual Hazards: Unilateral Options and Contract Length,' *RAND Journal of Economics*, **19**, 327–343.

Crocker, Keith J. and Scott E. Masten (1991), 'Pretia Ex Machina? Prices and Process in Long-Term Contracts,' *Journal of Law and Economics*, **24**, 69–99.

Crocker, Keith J. and Kenneth J. Reynolds (1993), 'The Efficiency of Incomplete Contracts: An Empirical Analysis of Air Force Engine Procurement,' *RAND Journal of Economics*, **24**, 126–146.

Datta, Samar K., Donald J. O'Hara and Jeffrey B. Nugent (1986), 'Choice of Agricultural Tenancy in the presence of Transaction Costs,' *Land Economics*, **62**, 145–158.

Davidson, W. H. and Donald G. McFetridge (1984), 'International Technology Transactions and the Theory of the Firm,' *Journal of Industrial Economics*, **32**, 253–264.

Davidson, W. H. and Donald G. McFetridge (1985), 'Key Characteristics in the Choice of International Technology Transfer Mode,' *Journal of International Business Studies*, **16**, 5–21.

DeCanio, Stephen J. and H. E. Frech (1993), 'Vertical Contracts: A Natural Experiment in Natural Gas Pipeline Regulation,' *Journal of Institutional and Theoretical Economics*, **149**, 370–392.

Dnes, Anthony W. (1992), '"Unfair" Contractual Practices and Hostages in Franchise Contracts,' *Journal of Institutional and Theoretical Economics*, **148**, 484–504.

Dwyer, F. Robert and Sejo Oh (1988), 'A Transaction Cost Perspective on Vertical Contractual Structure and Interchannel Competitive Strategies,' *Journal of Marketing*, **52**, 21–34.

Eccles, Robert G. (1981), 'The Quasifirm in the Construction Industry,' *Journal of Economic Behavior and Organization*, **2**, 335–357.

Eccles, Robert G. and Harrison C. White (1988), 'Price and Authority in Inter–Profit Center Transactions,' *American Journal of Sociology*, **94** (supplement), s17–s51.

Ellickson, Robert C. (1989), 'A Hypothesis of Wealth-Maximizing Norms: Evidence from the Whaling Industry,' *Journal of Law, Economics, & Organization*, **5**, 83–97.

Ellickson, Robert C. (1991), *Order Without Law: How Neighbors Settle Disputes*. Harvard University Press, Cambridge, MA.

Fishback, Price V. (1986), 'Did Coal Miners "Owe Their Souls to the Company Store?" Theory and Evidence from the early 1900s,' *Journal of Economic History*, **46**, 1011–1029.

Fishback, Price V. (1992), 'The Economics of Company Housing: Historical Perspectives from the Coal Fields,' *Journal of Law, Economics, & Organization*, **8**, 346–365.

Gallick, Edward C. (1984), *Exclusive Dealing and Vertical Integration: The Efficiency of Contracts in the Tuna Industry* (Federal Trade Commission Bureau of Economics Staff Report). Federal Trade Commission: Washington, DC.

Gatignon, Hubert and Erin Anderson (1988), 'The Multinational Corporation's Degree of Control Over Foreign Subsidiaries: An Empirical Test of a Transaction Cost Explanation,' *Journal of Law, Economics, & Organization*, **4**, 305–336.

Gifford, Adam, Jr. (1993), 'The Economic Organization of 17th- through mid-19th-Century Whaling and Shipping,' *Journal of Economic Behavior and Organization*, **20**, 137–150.

Globerman, Steven (1980), 'Markets, Hierarchies, and Innovation,' *Journal of Economic Issues*, **14**, 977–998.

Globerman, Steven and Richard Schwindt (1986), 'The Organization of Vertically Related Transactions in the Canadian Forest Products Industries,' *Journal of Economic Behavior and Organization*, **7**, 199–212.

Goldberg, Victor and John R. Erickson (1987), 'Quantity and Price Adjustment in Long-Term Contracts: A Case Study of Petroleum Coke,' *Journal of Law and Economics*, **30**, 369–398.

Grandy, C. (1989), 'Can Government Be Trusted to Keep Its Part of a Social Contract? New Jersey and the Railroads, 1825–1888,' *Journal of Law, Economics, & Organization*, **5**, 249–269.

Grossman, Sanford J. and Oliver D. Hart (1986), 'The Costs and Benefits of Ownership: A Theory of Vertical and Lateral Integration,' *Journal of Political Economy*, **94**, 691–719.

Hallwood, Paul C. (1990), *Transaction Costs and Trade Between Multinational Corporations*. Unwin Hyman: Boston.

Hallwood, Paul C. (1991), 'On Choosing Organizational Arrangements: The Example of Offshore Oil Gathering,' *Scottish Journal of Political Economy*, **38**, 227–241.

Harrigan, Kathryn Rudie (1986), 'Matching Vertical Integration Strategies to Competitive Conditions,' *Strategic Management Journal*, **7**, 535–555.

Harris, Barry (1983), *Organization: The Effect on Large Corporations*. University of Michigan Press: Ann Arbor.

Hart, Oliver D. and John Moore (1990), 'Property Rights and the Nature of the Firm,' *Journal of Political Economy*, **98**, 1119–1158.

Heide, J. B. and G. John (1988), 'The Role of Dependence Balancing in Safeguarding Transaction-Specific Assets,' *Journal of Marketing*, **52**, 20–35.

Helfat, Constance and David J. Teece (1987), 'Vertical Integration and Risk Reduction,' *Journal of Law, Economics, & Organization*, **3**, 47–67.

Hennart, Jean-Francois (1988), 'Upstream Vertical Integration in the Aluminum and Tin Industries,' *Journal of Economic Behavior and Organization*, **9**, 281–299.

Hennart, Jean-Francois (1989), 'The Transaction Cost Rationale for Countertrade,' *Journal of Law, Economics, & Organization*, **5**, 127–153.

Hill, Charles W. (1988), 'Internal Capital Market Controls and Financial Performance in Multidivisional Firms,' *Journal of Industrial Economics*, **37**, 67–83.

Hill, Charles W. and J. F. Pickering (1986), 'Divisionalization, Decentralization, and Performance of Large United Kingdom Companies,' *Journal of Management Studies*, **23**, 26–50.

Hubbard, R. Glenn and Robert J. Weiner (1986), 'Regulation and Long-Term Contracting in U.S. Natural Gas Markets,' *Journal of Industrial Economics*, **35**, 71–79.

Hubbard, R. Glenn and Robert J. Weiner (1991), 'Efficient Contracting and Market Power: Evidence from the U.S. Natural Gas Industry,' *Journal of Law and Economics*, **34**, 25–67.

John, George (1984), 'An Empirical Investigation of Some Antecedents of Opportunism in a Marketing Channel,' *Journal of Marketing Research*, **21**, 278–289.

John, George and Barton A. Weitz (1988), 'Forward Integration into Distribution: An Empirical Test of Transaction Cost Analysis,' *Journal of Law, Economics, & Organization*, **4**, 337–355.

Jones, G. (1987), 'Organization-Client Transactions and Organizational Governance Structures,' *Academy of Management Journal*, **30**, 197–218.

Jones, G. and M. W. Pustay (1988), 'Interorganizational Coordination in the Airline Industry, 1925–1938: A Transaction Cost Approach,' *Journal of Management*, **14**, 529–546.

Joskow, Paul L. (1985), 'Vertical Integration and Long Term Contracts: The Case of Coal-Burning Electric Generating Plants,' *Journal of Law, Economics, & Organization*, **1**, 33–80.

Joskow, Paul L. (1987), 'Contract Duration and Relationship-Specific Investments: Empirical Evidence,' *American Economic Review*, **77**, 168–185.

Joskow, Paul L. (1988a), 'Asset Specificity and the Structure of Vertical Relationships: Empirical Evidence,' *Journal of Law, Economics, & Organization*, **4**, 95–117.

Joskow, Paul L. (1988b), 'Price Adjustment in Long-Term Contracts: The Case of Coal,' *Journal of Law and Economics*, **31**, 47–83.

Joskow, Paul L. (1990), 'The Performance of Long-Term Contracts: Further Evidence from the Coal Markets,' *RAND Journal of Economics*, **21**, 251–274.

Joskow, Paul L. (1991), 'The Role of Transaction Cost Economics in Antitrust and Public Utility Regulatory Policies,' *Journal of Law, Economics, & Organization*, **7**, 53–83.

Kaufmann, Patrick J. and Francine Lafontaine (1994), 'Costs of Control: The Source of Economic Rents for McDonald's Franchisees,' *Journal of Law and Economics*, **37**, 417–453.

Kenney, Roy W. and Benjamin Klein (1983), 'The Economics of Block Booking,' *Journal of Law and Economics*, **26**, 497–540.

Klein, Benjamin (1988), 'Vertical Integration as Organized Ownership: The Fisher Body–General Motors Relationship Revisited,' *Journal of Law, Economics, & Organization*, **4**, 199–213.

Klein, Benjamin, Robert A. Crawford and Armen A. Alchian (1978), 'Vertical Integration, Appropriable Rents, and the Competitive Contracting Process,' *Journal of Law and Economics*, **21**, 297–326.

Klein, S., G. L. Frazer and V. J. Roth (1990), 'A Transaction Cost Analysis Model of Channel Integration in International Markets,' *Journal of Marketing Research*, **27**, 196–208.

Kreps, David M. (1990), *A Course in Microeconomic Theory*. Princeton University Press: Princeton, NJ.

Lafontaine, Francine (1993), 'Contractual Arrangements as Signaling Devices: Evidence from Franchising,' *Journal of Law, Economics, & Organization*, **9**, 256–289.

Langlois, Richard N. and Paul L. Robertson (1989), 'Explaining Vertical Integration: Lessons from the American Automobile Industry,' *Journal of Economic History*, **49**, 361–375.

Leffler, Keith B. and Randal Rucker (1991), 'Transactions Costs and the Efficient Organization of Production: A Study of Timber-Harvesting Contracts,' *Journal of Political Economy*, **99**, 1060–1087.

Levy, Brian and Pablo T. Spiller (1994), 'The Institutional Foundations of Regulatory Commitment: A Comparative Analysis of Telecommunications Regulation,' *Journal of Law, Economics, & Organization*, **10**, 201–246.

Levy, David (1985), 'The Transaction Cost Approach to Vertical Integration: An Empirical Examination,' *Review of Economics and Statistics*, **67**, 438–445.

Lieberman, Marvin B. (1991), 'Determinants of Vertical Integration: An Empirical Test,' *Journal of Industrial Economics*, **39**, 451–466.

Lilien, Gary L. (1979), 'Advisor 2: Modeling the Marketing Mix Decision for Industrial Products,' *Management Science*, **25**, 191–204.

MacDonald, James M. (1985), 'Market Exchange or Vertical Integration: An Empirical Analysis,' *Review of Economics and Statistics*, **67**, 327–331.

Macmillan, I., D. C. Hambrick and J. M. Pennings (1986), 'Uncertainty Reduction and the Threat of Supplier Retaliation: Two Views of the Backward Integration Decision,' *Organization Studies*, **7**, 263–278.

Macneil, Ian R. (1978), 'Contracts: Adjustrnents of Long-Term Economic Relations under Classical, Neo-classical, and Relational Contract Law,' *Northwestern University Law Review*, **72**, 854–906.

Mahoney, Joseph T. (1992), 'The Choice of Organizational Form: Vertical Financial Ownership versus Other Methods of Vertical Integration,' *Strategic Management Journal*, **13**, 559–584.

Masten, Scott E. (1984), 'The Organization of Production: Evidence from the Aerospace Industry,' *Journal of Law and Economics*, **27**, 403–417.

Masten, Scott E. and Keith J. Crocker (1985), 'Efficient Adaptation in Long-Term Contracts: Take-or-Pay Provisions for Natural Gas,' *American Economic Review*, **75**, 1083–1093.

Masten, Scott E. James W. Meehan and Edward A. Snyder (1989), 'Vertical Integration in the U.S. Auto Industry: A Note on the Influence of Specific Assets,' *Journal of Economic Behavior and Organization*, **12**, 265–273.

Masten, Scott E. James W. Meehan and Edward A. Snyder (1991), 'The Costs of Organization,' *Journal of Law, Economics, & Organization*, **7**, 1–25.

Masten, Scott E. and Edward A. Snyder (1993), '*United States Versus United Shoe Machinery Corporation:* On the Merits,' *Journal of Law and Economics*, **36**, 33–70.

Milgrom, Paul A. and John Roberts (1990), 'Bargaining Costs, Influence Costs, and the Organization of Economic Activity,' in J. E. Alt and K. A. Shepsle, (eds.), *Perspectives on Positive Political Economy*, Cambridge University Press: Cambridge.

Milgrom, Paul A. and John Roberts (1992), *Economics, Organization, and Management*. Prentice-Hall: Englewood Cliffs, N.J.

Mitchell, W. (1989), 'Whether and When? Probability and Timing of Incumbents' Entry into Emerging Industrial Subfields,' *Administrative Science Quarterly*, **34**, 208–230.

Monteverde, Kirk and David J. Teece (1982a), 'Appropriable Rents and Quasi-Vertical Integration,' *Journal of Law and Economics*, **25**, 321–328.

Monteverde, Kirk and David J. Teece (1982b), 'Supplier Switching Costs and Vertical Integration in the Automobile Industry,' *Bell Journal of Economics*, **13**, 206–213.

Mulherin, J. Harold (1986), 'Complexity in Long-Term Contracts: An Analysis of Natural Gas Contractual Provisions,' *Journal of Law, Economics, & Organization*, **2**, 105–117.

Muris, Timothy J., David Scheffman and Pablo T. Spiller (1992), 'Strategy and Transaction Costs: The Organization of Distribution in the Carbonated Soft Drink Industry,' *Journal of Economics and Management Strategy*, **1**, 83–128.

Murtha, Thomas P. (1993), 'Credible Enticements: Can Host Governments Tailor Multinational Firms' Organizations to Suit National Objectives?' *Journal of Economic Behavior and Organization*, **20**, 171–186.

Nelson, Richard R. and Sidney G. Winter (1982), *An Evolutionary Theory of Economic Change*. Harvard University Press: Cambridge, MA.

Noordewier, Thomas G., George John and John R. Nevin (1990), 'Performance Outcomes of Purchasing Arrangements in Industrial Buyer–Vendor Relationships,' *Journal of Marketing*, **54**, 80–93.

Norton, Seth W. (1989), 'Franchising, Labor Productivity, and the New Institutional Economics,' *Journal of Institutional and Theoretical Economics*, **145**, 578–596.

Palay, Thomas M. (1984), 'Comparative Institutional Economics: The Governance of Rail Freight Contracting,' *Journal of Legal Studies*, **13**, 265–287.

Paley, Thomas M. (1985), 'Avoiding Regulatory Constraints: Contracting Safeguards and the Role of Informal Agreements,' *Journal of Law, Economics, & Organization*, **1**, 155–176.

Peltzman, Sam (1991), 'The Handbook of Industrial Organization: A Review Article,' *Journal of Political Economy*, **99**, 201–217.

Pirrong, Stephen Craig (1993), 'Contracting Practices in Bulk Shipping Markets: A Transactions Cost Explanation,' *Journal of Law and Economics*, **36**, 937–976.

Pisano, Gary P. (1990), 'Using Equity Participation to Support Exchange: Evidence from the Biotechnology Industry,' *Journal of Law, Economics, & Organization,* **5,** 109–126.

Pisano, Gary P., Michael V. Russo and David J. Teece (1988), 'Joint Ventures and Collaborative Arrangements in the Telecommunications Equipment Industry,' in D. Mowery, (ed.), *International Collaborative Ventures in U.S. Manufacturing.* Ballinger: Cambridge, MA.

Pittman, Russell (1991), 'Specific Investments, Contracts, and Opportunism: The Evolution of Railroad Sidetrack Agreements,' *Journal of Law and Economics,* **34,** 565–589.

Posner, Richard A. (1993), 'The New Institutional Economics Meets Law and Economics,' *Journal of Institutional and Theoretical Economics,* **149,** 73–87, 119–121.

Prager, Robin A. (1990), 'Firm Behavior in Franchise Monopoly Markets,' *RAND Journal of Economics,* **21,** 211–225.

Ramseyer, J. Mark (1991), 'Indentured Prostitution in Imperial Japan: Credible Commitments in the Commercial Sex Industry,' *Journal of Law, Economics, & Organization,* **7,** 89–116.

Romano, Roberta (1985), 'Law as a Product: Some Pieces of the Incorporation Puzzle,' *Journal of Law, Economics, & Organization,* **1,** 225–284.

Roumasset, James A. and Marilou Uy (1980), 'Piece Rates, Time Rates, and Teams: Explaining Patterns in the Employment Relation,' *Journal of Economic Behavior and Organization,* **1,** 343–360.

Rubin, Paul H. (1990), *Managing Business Transactions: Controlling the Cost of Coordinating, Communicating, and Decision Making.* Macmillan: New York.

Shelanski, Howard A. (1993), 'Transfer Pricing and the Organization of Internal Exchange,' unpublished Ph.D. dissertation, Department of Economics, University of California, Berkeley.

Simon, Herbert A. (1991), 'Organizations and Markets,' *Journal of Economic Perspectives,* **5,** 25–44.

Spiller, Pablo (1985), 'On Vertical Mergers,' *Journal of Law, Economics, & Organization,* **1,** 285–312.

Steer, Peter and John Cable (1978), 'Internal Organization and Profit: An Empirical Analysis of Large U.K. Companies,' *Journal of Industrial Economics,* **27,** 13–30.

Stuckey, John (1983), *Vertical Integration and Joint Ventures in the Aluminum Industry.* Harvard University Press: Cambridge, MA.

Teece, David J. (1977), 'Technology Transfer by Multinational Firms: The Resource Costs of Transferring Technology Knowhow,' *Economic Journal,* **87,** 242–261.

Teece, David J. (1980), 'Economies of Scope and the Scope of the Enterprise,' *Journal of Economic Behavior and Organization,* **1,** 223–247.

Teece, David J. (1981), 'Internal Organization and Economic Performance: An Empirical Analysis of the Profitability of Principal Firms,' *Journal of Industrial Economics,* **30,** 173–199.

Thompson, R. S. (1981), 'Internal Organization and Profit: A Note,' *Journal of Industrial Economics,* **30,** 201–211.

Walker, Gordon and Laura Poppo (1991), 'Profit Centers, Single-Source Suppliers, and Transaction Costs,' *Administrative Science Quarterly,* **36,** 66–87.

Walker, Gordon and David Weber (1984), 'A Transaction Cost Approach to Make-or-Buy Decisions,' *Administrative Science Quarterly,* **29,** 373–391.

Walker, Gordon and David Weber (1987), 'Supplier Competition, Uncertainty and Make-or-Buy Decisions,' *Academy of Management Journal,* **30,** 589–596.

Weiss, Avi (1992), 'The Role of Firm-Specific Capital in Vertical Mergers,' *Journal of Law and Economics,* **35,** 71–88.

Wiggins, Steven N. and Gary D. Libecap (1985), 'Oil Field Unitization: Commercial Failure in the Presence of Imperfect Information,' *American Economic Review,* **75,** 368–385.

Williamson, Oliver E. (1975), *Markets and Hierarchies: Analysis and Antitrust Implications.* Free Press: New York.

Williamson, Oliver E. (1976), 'Franchise Bidding for Natural Monopolies—In General and with Respect to CATV,' *Bell Journal of Economics*, **7**, 73–104.

Williamson, Oliver E. (1981), 'The Modern Corporation: Origins, Evolution, Attributes,' *Journal of Economic Literature*, **19**, 1537–1568.

Williamson, Oliver E. (1983), 'Credible Commitments: Using Hostages to Support Exchange,' *American Economic Review*, **73**, 519–540.

Williamson, Oliver E. (1985), *The Economic Institutions of Capitalism*. Free Press: New York.

Williamson, Oliver E. (1991), 'Strategizing, Economizing, and Economic Organization,' *Strategic Management Journal*, **23**, 75–94.

Williamson, Oliver E. (1993), 'Transaction Cost Economics Meets Posnerian Law and Economics,' *Journal of Institutional and Theoretical Economics*, **149**, 99–118.

Williamson, Oliver E. (1995), *The Mechanisms of Governance*. Oxford University Press: New York.

Wilson, James A. (1980), 'Adaptation to Uncertainty and Small Numbers Exchange: The New England Fresh Fish Market,' *Bell Journal of Economics*, **4**, 491–504.

Yarbrough, Beth V. and Robert M. Yarbrough (1987a), 'Cooperation in the Liberalization of International Trade: After Hegemony, What?' *International Organization*, **41**, 1–26.

Yarbrough, Beth V. and Robert M. Yarbrough (1987b), 'Institutions for the Governance of Opportunism in International Trade,' *Journal of Law, Economics, & Organization*, **3**, 129–139.

Zupan, Mark A. (1989a), 'Cable Franchise Renewals: Do Incumbent Firms Behave Opportunistically?' *RAND Journal of Economics*, **20**, 473–482.

Zupan, Mark A. (1989b), 'The Efficacy of Franchise Bidding Schemes in the Case of Cable Television: Some Systematic Evidence,' *Journal of Law and Economics*, **32**, 401–456.

PART II

Conceptual Uses

CHAPTER SEVEN

Markets and Hierarchies and (Mathematical) Economic Theory

David M. Kreps

Over the past decade transaction-cost economics has been partially translated in the more mathematical language of game theory, and understanding of the costs of transactions has been deepened, refined and extended. But the translation is incomplete: a great deal of human behaviour is missed, and doing game theory with more life-like models of individuals will bring theory closer to phenomena. Transaction-cost economics, particulary the economics of relational contracts, provides a major arena for these developments, since the important issues of bounded rationality and individual behavior are central to the topic.

1. *Introduction*

Consider the following bit of recent history of economic thought: When it appeared in 1975, Oliver Williamson's *Markets and Hierarchies* stood somewhat outside the flow of mainstream economic theory. Initial developments in information economics were around five years old, the revelation principle was nearly contemporaneous, and the widespread embrace of the language of game theory for dealing with dynamics, small numbers, and incomplete information was about five years in the future. Without these tools to work with, it was perhaps inevitable that Williamson's theory would be rendered without the mathematical apparatus of mainstream theory. But as those tools worked their way into the mainstream, it was equally inevitable that the ideas set forth in *Markets and Hierarchies* would be reworked and further developed in symbols. And this has taken place; nowadays courses in contract theory are a mainstay of graduate microeconomics, and eminent symbol manipulators such as Oliver Hart and Jean Tirole choose this subject for their public lectures (Hart, The Clarendon Lectures; Tirole, the Walras-Bowley Lecture). As for the book itself, *Markets and Hierarchies* was a step along the way to a proper (mathematical) theory of contracts and transactions costs, but its place is now in the history of thought; it has been superceded by more precise and nuanced mathematical theories of these things. Notwithstanding the protests of Williamson (1993a), Richard Posner (1993) opines that Williamson's version of transaction-cost economics nowadays adds little more than neologisms to mainstream mathematical theory.[1] Since these neologisms can only serve to confuse students, it is time to consign *Markets and Hierarchies* to a relatively inaccessible shelf.

It is certainly true that important ideas in *Markets and Hierarchies* have been translated into the more mathematical language of non-cooperative game theory. Some of this is recalled below, although I will not give anything like a complete survey; for this, see Hart (1995) and Tirole (1995). But notwithstanding this work, the history given above is inaccurate. If *Markets and Hierarchies* has been translated into game theory using notions from information economics, it is a very poor translation. If some of the central and critical ideas in transaction-cost economics as formulated by Williamson have been captured, others, equally important, have been missed. In particular, mathematics-based theory still lacks the language needed to capture essential ideas of bounded rationality, which are central to Williamson's concepts of transaction costs and contractual form.[2] Anyone who relies on the translations alone misses large and valuable chunks of the original.

The missing pieces of theory are nearly within the grasp of mainstream theorists. To incorporate the missing pieces will take a bit of courage; further compromises with the high paradigm world of general equilibrium will be necessary. But it can be done, and to do it, we must continue to have *Markets and Hierarchies* on our desks; speaking as a tool-fashioner interested in developing tools that better deal with the world-as-it-is, I believe game theory (the tool) has more to learn from transaction-cost economics than it will have to give, at least initially.

But it will give something back. Specifically, regarding the principle of economizing—transactions *tend* to be arranged to maximize their benefits net of transaction costs—we may get a better sense of what bears on the strength of the economizing force; i.e. on how strong (relatively) is the tendency to move from inefficient transactional forms to those more efficient.

These ideas are developed in this paper. Because the hard work of theory development still remains to be done, I cannot claim to have a completely

---

[1] Posner's critique would be unfair even if now correct, since *Markets and Hierarchies* predated and in many ways provided the impetus for subsequent developments by Grossman, Hart, Holmstrom, etc.

[2] Posner (1993) goes on to say that bounded rationality is well handled within mainstream theory by incorporating the cost of information acquisition and processing; I will comment at the end.

convincing story, but I believe that these ideas are worth pursuing and, at least, that the bit of history of thought in the first paragraph is wrong.

Why is this of interest? To tool developers like myself, the interest is clear; *Markets and Hierarchies* provides unreconciled puzzles which help us to produce more robust tools. But what of the much greater number of readers who are interested in the substance of transaction-cost economics? It is incontestable that mathematics-based theory has become the common language of economics (see Debreu, 1990 or Kreps, 1996). Most economists, and especially and most critically, new recruits in the form of graduate students, learn transaction-cost economics as translated and renamed (incomplete) contract theory. I hope it is not taken amiss if I claim that (for the prototypical graduate student) it is harder to read *Markets and Hierarchies* or *The Economic Institutions of Capitalism* than the classics-illustrated versions, written in the comfortable language of middle-brow theory. If the classics-illustrated versions miss subtleties connected with, say, bounded rationality and truly unforeseen contingencies, or they do not give any indication of how social embeddedness or internal consistency/simplicity affects a relational contract, then the consumer of the classics-illustrated editions has missed important pieces of the message. We should be clear on how (in)complete the translations are, to fight misguided tendencies to put *Markets and Hierarchies* away on that semi-accessible shelf.

2. *Game-theoretic versions of Markets and Hierarchies*

Game-theoretic renditions of the transaction-cost economics of *Markets and Hierarchies* have focused on contract incompleteness and *ex post* governance. Starting with the seminal paper Grossman and Hart (1986), in much of the literature the transaction is modeled as stretching over relatively few dates. Parties to a transaction face some well-understood uncertainty, typically bearing on the costs and benefits of the transaction if consummated. The parties to the transaction will make private investment decisions that (eventually) affect the costs and benefits of the transaction. Contracts between them may be written prior to the investment decisions, but it is assumed by fiat (with rationales usually given informally—see below) that contracts explicitly and fully contingent on the uncertain contingencies are impossible. Instead, *ex post* decision rights determine (implicitly) how the contract will be completed, with the *ex post* decision rights determined by aspects of the contract (most prevalently, the residual rights of control conferred by ownership).

For example, in the seminal paper by Grossman and Hart, two parties (A and B) must make four decisions, labelled a_x and q_x for $X = A,B$. Decisions

a_x are *ex ante* investment/maintenance decisions; decision a_x must be taken by party X. Decisions q_x are *ex post* 'implementation' decisions. The right to take decision q_x, while initially belonging to party X, can be assigned to the other party contractually. (Think of q_x as the decision how to employ physical capital; *ex post* ownership of the capital confers the residual decision rights.) The gross outcome for party X is given by a benefit function $B_x(a_x, \phi_x(q_A, q_B))$, where ϕ_x is real-valued and B_x is strictly increasing in ϕ_x; in addition, utility is freely transferable between the parties. Negotiations over decision rights (or ownership) take place, then the private investment decisions a_x are taken, and then the q_x are chosen. Binding *ex ante* contracts involving the levels of the a_x or the gross benefit levels or the levels of the ϕ_x are not feasible. Final implementation decisions (q_A, q_B) are assumed to be chosen efficiently (to maximize the sum of the gross benefits, given the levels of a_A and a_B already chosen), with the benefits above the non-cooperative-equilibrium threat point divided 50-50 through an unmodeled negotiation process.

The question analyzed is, which pattern of ownership (assignment of implementation rights) leads to the most efficient outcome? Suppose that high levels of a_B are most effective given high levels of $\phi_B(q_A, q_B)$, and ϕ_B is very positively responsive to q_B and negatively responsive to q_A. If A is given decision rights to q_B, then A implicitly threatens a relatively low choice of q_B (insofar as ϕ_A depends on q_A and q_B in symmetric fashion). Since the choices of q_A and q_B are assumed to be *ex post* efficient, this threat is not carried out. But the threat determines the division of surplus from moving to efficient (q_A, q_B). Thus B will not fully internalize the benefit from his own investment in a_B (assuming this ownership structure); lack of *ex post* control and the particular negotiation process leads him to underinvest.

The model captures beautifully the idea that ownership-driven *ex post* decision rights can affect *ex ante* private investments decisions, hence the pattern of ownership can affect overall efficiency. Note that this is not driven by any supposed *ex post* inefficiency in residual decisions, but instead through a feedback into *ex ante* investments.

However, some important aspects of the original theory in *Markets in Hierarchies* are missing. Most importantly (for purposes of this paper), the notion of bounded rationality enters in a very peculiar way. Grossman and Hart assume by fiat within their model that binding contracts contingent on the investment levels and the levels of the ϕ_x and B_x are not possible; their verbal explanation for this is that the required contracts would be too complex to write. But within their model, the parties anticipate *ex ante* what decisions will be taken (contingent on observables).

In a subsequent paper, Hart and Moore (1990) write '. . . there is no inconsistency in assuming, on the one hand, that date 0 contingent *statements* are infeasible and, on the other hand, that agents have perfect foresight about the consequences of this lack of feasibility . . .' (emphasis added). Hart (1990), arguing that bounded rationality in the sense of Simon is unnecessary for contract theory, suggests that parties may suffer not from bounded rationality—he points out that per his analysis they must be quite rational and computationally able—but instead from 'bounded *writing* or *communication* skills' (emphasis in the original).

Maskin and Tirole (1995) extend this argument, showing that (even) truly unforeseen contingencies need not compromise the logic of economic (or Nash) equilibrium, if parties can anticipate the payoffs they will subsequently receive as a function of current decisions. To caricature their argument slightly, consider the pair of assertions: you and I correctly anticipate what is the distribution of utility that we will get next year from some joint venture we may enter into; but neither of us have any idea where that utility will come from and what we will be doing (specifically) in a year. As Maskin and Tirole observe, these two assertions are not logically inconsistent. But not everything that is logically consistent is credulous.[3]

Other authors have performed similar analyses, using somewhat different rationales for assumptions that contracts may not involve certain variables. In some instances the rationale is that the uncontractible variables are unobservable.[4] In others, they may be observable but unverifiable in a legal sense, hence not usable in implementable formal contracts. (Hart (1990) argues that unverifiability may stem from an initial inability to write out clearly the relevant clauses.)

Unobservability and unverifiability leads to a vast class of mainstream-theory models; viz., agency theory models, in which contracts are written in terms of signals that are (only) noisy indications of variables that would be used in a first-best (efficient) contract. That is, instead of an outright prohibition against including a variable in a contract, the parties to the transaction are able to contract on 'noisy' indicators of the variable and/or to rely on self-selection (subject, of course, to self-selection constraints). Of course, these analysis are almost always equilibrium analyses in the game-theoretic sense (I would say always, but there may be a part of this vast literature that I have missed).

My point is that although these models capture important aspects of con-

---

[3] I am somewhat wary of this caricature, because it implies that Maskin and Tirole are spouting nonsense. A written version of their paper does not exist yet, but based on comments in Tirole (1994), it is quite likely that they take the position that this result, while formally correct, indicates a modeling weakness of this general approach.

[4] When, say, private investment decisions are unobservable by the other party, some care in the equilibrium conditions is required. But a strength of game theoretic techniques is that it is clear on what care is required for this sort of thing.

tract incompleteness, the sense in which the contracts are incomplete must be borne in mind. The contracts are incomplete in the Arrow-Debreuvian sense that there are contingencies on which *ex ante* efficient contracts would turn that do not turn up in the *ex ante* contract. In the Grossman-Hart model (and others), *ex post* decisions are taken based on ownership rights; these decisions are not contractually specified *ex ante*. Indeed, in Grossman-Hart, and in some pieces of the agency literature, such as Fudenberg and Tirole (1990), *ex post* renegotiation takes place based on 'threat points' determined *ex ante; ex ante* contracts certainly fail to reflect the outcomes of the renegotiations. But the analysis entails an equilibrium in anticipations and actions. Specifically, all participants are assumed able to say, *ex ante*, what will be the eventual 'terms of trade' based on the resolution of any physical uncertainty. (This is not true for Maskin and Tirole (1995), but then the argument that the participants anticipate perfectly the distribution of utility outcomes is particularly incredible.) As Hart (1990) observes, these models miss aspects of bounded rationality that are part of the original story. Are the missing parts important? This question will be discussed later.

Reputation, Reciprocity and Relational Contracts

A second type of model for translating ideas from transaction-cost economics into game-theoretic models concerns relational contracts modeled using (infinitely) repeated games and the Folk Theorem. This part of the theory will be recounted at substantial length, because (I believe) it is less well known than the short-horizon models and it is more important to the ideas I wish to develop.[5]

The seminal reference in this case predates both *Markets and Hierarchies* and most of the developments of the relevant pieces of game theory. Simon's 'A Formal Theory of the Employment Relationship' (1951) lacks some modern terminology and some of the formal polish that the subsequent 40-plus years have given to the topic, but the basic ideas are there.

Simon's model concerns an employment transaction between employer and employee. The employer offers a wage for the labor services of the employee, in return for which the employee agrees to accept the directions of the employer. The employee may retain the right to terminate the relationship whenever he chooses to; in simple language, the employee can always quit.[6] Except for that (in Simon's model), the employer makes all the

---

[5] I am also convinced that long-horizon relational contracts are of underestimated importance in exchange generally, because they form the basis for most of the most important form of incomplete-contract exchange; viz., employment.

[6] But see the footnote following.

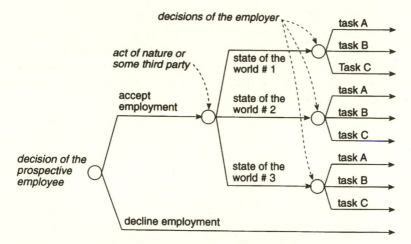

FIGURE 1. Simon's simple model of employment.

subsequent decisions about the nature of the relationship. The relationship is hierarchical, with the employer as the hierarchical superior and the employee as the hierarchical subordinate.

Figure 1 gives a simple example of Simon's model. The employment transaction is a three-stage affair. First, the employee must decide whether to accept employment. Then nature intervenes; uncertainty resolves, which determines the costs and benefits of the various tasks that might be done. Finally, the employer stipulates which task the employee will undertake. We have depicted a choice of three tasks, but in general there will be many more.[7]

Note that the contract is incomplete in that the employer and employee are presumed unable to write an enforceable contingent contract specifying what the employee will do as a function of the state of the world. Governance enters in the presumption that the employer will determine, *ex post*, what task the employee will undertake. The employee faces a simple 'accept employment/reject' decision, where accepting employment obligates the employee to accept the decision of the employer concerning what task must be done. Both presumptions need rationalization, to which we will return after exploring the model as formulated.

Why would the employee accept under these conditions? Simon tells two stories. The first is that the employee may anticipate that the assigned tasks

[7] To keep the analysis simple, we have not given the worker an option to quit after learning what the employer wants. If this option is included, the payoff to the worker of quitting after accepting employment should be less than the payoff if the worker declines employment at the outset; the employee must have something at risk if he accepts employment. The difference between pre- and post-acceptance payoffs could reflect, for example, costs of relocation, or simply the opportunity cost of lost time. On this general point, also see the next footnote.

will not be so onerous on average as to make rejection of employment better than acceptance.

Assume that employer and employee evaluate options using expected pay-offs. We have normalized payoffs so that no employment gives each party a payoff of zero. In Simon's first story, the employee reasons that the employer will demand whatever task makes her (the employer) as well off as possible, given the state of nature. In Figure 2, this means task A in state 1, task B in state 2, and task C in state 3. Although the employee finds task C quite onerous (he would not accept employment if he thought he would be given task C all or even most of the time), if the probability of state 3 is less than 1/11, getting tasks A and B in two states of the world and task C only in the third gives the employee a strictly positive expected payoff, which is better than he gets if he declines employment.

This story comes to grief if either it is in the interest of the employer to demand onerous actions with high probability or if the onerous tasks are exceedingly onerous; in either case the employee's average payoff may make employment worse than unemployment. Consider, for example, changing the example in Figure 2 so that the three states are equally likely. Task C is so onerous that a one-third chance of getting this assignment means a negative expected payoff for employment to the employee; in the unique Nash equilibrium outcome of this game, the employee declines employment.

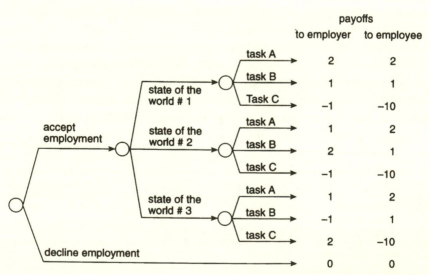

FIGURE 2. Simon's second story. If the employer asks for whichever task is best for her in each contingency, the employee may decline employment, depending on the probability of the three states. But if the employer will never ask for task C, in order to protect her reputation, then the employee will accept employment.

Here Simon's second story comes into play. Imagine the situation is as in Figure 2 with equally likely probabilities for the three states, and also that the employer is engaged in this transaction (or others like it) repeatedly, either with this employee or with other employees.[8] If the situation is repeated indefinitely, and if the employer does not discount payoffs from future situations too severely, then we can construct reputational equilibria in which the employee will accept employment. In one such equilibrium, the employer does not ask for task C; she asks for task A in state 1 and task B in states 2 and 3. (Note that this makes her expected payoff 2/3.) She does not ask for task C in state 3 because asking any employee for task C would brand her as an exploitative employer; this would become generally known among (future) potential employees; and no one would ever work for her again. When and if state 3 arises, the employer must weigh the immediate payoff of 2 that she can get by wrecking her reputation followed by payoffs of zero forever after against absorbing the payoff of -1 this period, preserving her reputation, and an expected payoff of 2/3 in each subsequent period. If the future is not too heavily discounted, preservation of her reputation is more important, and she will refrain from asking for task C. For the employee, then, accepting employment is safe; task C will not be requested because the employer wishes to protect her reputation, and (with the numbers in Figure 2) accepting employment is better than declining no matter what is the state of the world. Simon concludes that workers can accept hierarchical subordination in some instances because they are protected by the employer's desire to safeguard her reputation.

It is fairly obvious (to anyone trained in game theory) where game theory enters into Simon's story.[9] Figures 1 and 2 describe an extensive form game, and Simon's two stories why the employee might trust the employer are no more or less than typical examples of Nash equilibrium analysis of the corresponding games and infinitely repeated versions of these games. Game

---

[8] The payoffs in Figure 2 work for the specification where the employer deals with a sequence of employees. Most of the remarks to follow work equally for the formulation of a long-term relationship with a single employee, but then to be closer to reality the model should be changed as follows: the employee makes an initial decision whether to accept employment and then has a quit option each period, either before or after that period's task assignment by the employer. After the initial decision to accept employment is taken, the utility of quitting is less than the zero-base level of never accepting employment at all, reflecting relocation costs, etc. Indeed, it might be sensible to assume that the costs of relocation (quitting) rise as the relationship matures, reflecting psychic costs of lost friendships, raised costs of moving a family, decreasingly attractive prospects back on the job market, and so on. We could also assume that the value to the employer of the employee rises as the relationship matures and the employee learns more about the employer's specific technology, builds a network within the employer's establishment, and so on. Such considerations add depth to the story that is missing in this very simple first-cut analysis.

[9] Simon wrote at a time where the formal language of game theory was, for his purposes, undeveloped. But anyone trained in game theory will find it hard to read his paper without considering it a piece of applied game theory.

theory adds little or nothing to Simon's first story, but our understanding of the second story, which concerns a reputation construction in a repeated game setting, is enhanced by recalling some more-general analysis of these sorts of games:

(i) **Multiplicity of equilibria.**   In a repeated game setting when reputational equilibria are feasible, there are usually many of them. For the payoffs of Figure 2, our description of the behaviour of the employer—ask for task A in state 1; ask for B in states 2 and 3—and the employee(s)—accept employment as long as the employer has never asked you or any other previous employee to undertake task C—describes a Nash equilibrium of the game when payoffs are discounted from one period to the next, the horizon is infinite, and the discount factor is close enough to one.[10] But in another equilibrium, the employer asks for task A in all contingencies and each employee declines employment if ever the employer asks (previously) for any task except A. Note that this raises the payoff to the employee and lowers the payoff to the employer, but (for discount factors close enough to one) the employer is better off always requesting A than asking for (and getting) B or C once and thereafter having all offers of employment declined; i.e. this is another Nash equilibrium.

The is just the tip of the iceberg. There are equilibria in which the employer asks for task B in every contingency, or where she asks for task A in states 1 and 2 and for B in state 3, and so on. There are equilibria in which the request in period t depends on the state in that period and the value of the tth digit in a decimal expansion of π. In another equilibrium, the employees decline employment at all dates (because the employer would request task C in state 3).

Is there any basis on which to choose among these equilibria? A theory that produces a continuum of possible answers gives weak testable propositions at best and so is not very useful. There are at least two things which can be said in this instance:

● Suppose the employer is simultaneously engaged in this sort of relationship with a large number of employees, each of whom deals with only the single employer but who observe how the employer treats other employees. Or suppose the employer deals sequentially with many employees,

---

[10] I will not be precise about the game theory used in this paper on grounds that for those who know the relevant theory, it is easy to provide the needed precision; while for those who do not, it is fruitless to begin to go into details. But while aficionados will know that I am being sloppy, novices might not, so let me add here that I have not described full strategies for the employer and employee. Enough is described to verify that however we fill out the strategies, we have a Nash equilibrium, but we would need more details to know that the strategy fragments described are pieces of a (subgame) perfect equilibrium.

each of whom deals with the single employer only and each of whom sees how the employer has dealt in the past with earlier employees. Then it can be argued (in a somewhat more complex model) that the employer should have the power of a 'Stackelberg leader' in choosing among the equilibria; i.e. she can choose whichever equilibrium is best for her, subject to a participation constraint by the workers.[11]

- *Ex post* observability can be crucial. Suppose, for example, that the payoff to the employee of task B was -2 and the employer prefers B to A in state 3. Then in the simple model of Figure 2, a reputational equilibrium can be constructed (for high enough discount factors) in which the employer will select task A in states 1 and 2 and task B in state 3. But the enforcement of this equilibrium requires that the employee is able to observe the state of the world. If the employer (only) observes the state of the world, or if the employee observes the state of the world only imperfectly, then the employer might be tempted in state 2 to claim that the state is 3, so that task B is 'appropriate'. If the employee accepts this, and if, in consequence, the employer begins to ask for task B in states 2 and 3 both, the employee will find himself inadequately compensated on average for entering into employment. When employees can observe the state of the world only imperfectly (as best), equilibrium in which task B is sometimes requested can be constructed, but these equilibria are complex.

(ii) Efficient governance forms.   General game-theoretic considerations also give us some leverage for choosing among different forms of governance in long-run relational contracts. Simon's model describes a hierarchical relationship, so called because the employer enjoys the preponderance of authority in determining how contingencies will be met as time passes. The employee retains the right to sunder the relationship—to quit—but (in this classic and extreme form of the employment relationship) that is the only decision left to the employee.

Contrast this with, say, the relationship between a physician and patient. The physician is in a very real sense the employee of the patient, but the distribution of *ex post* decision rights, including the right to specify the level of

---

[11] In the simultaneous-play formulation, we assume the employer is making continuous (or, at least, many) assignment decisions for each employee, who can quit as each decision is rendered. Thus taken separately, the employee and employer are 'symmetric' as regards threats, and we would normally be unable to discriminate among all the Folk-Theorem equilibria. But if the employer's reputation turns on incomplete information as to type, she has this sort of relationship with many employees simultaneously, and there is perfect (or strong) correlation in her 'type' from one relationship to the next, she is strengthened to the position of Stackelberg leader by the spillover effects each has on the others. See Fudenberg and Kreps (1987) for details. The analysis for the sequential-interaction variation is simpler (and stronger) and can be found in Fudenberg and Levine (1989). These two papers give Nash equilibrium analyses. Watson (1993) shows how somewhat weaker non-equilibrium analysis can be used to obtain the same conclusions.

payment (wages), is much more heavily skewed towards the physician/
employee. Patients retain the right to get a second opinion or to decline recommended treatment; hence the physician is not a pure hierarchical superior
in this transaction. But the physician is a lot closer to hierarchical superior
than is his 'employer', the patient, in any practical sense. Why? From a
game theoretic sense, the answer is clear. Insofar as party A is given decision-making authority in a relationship, authority that puts party B in danger of being exploited, party A must (i) have the information needed to take
(relatively) efficient decisions[12] and (ii) be trustworthy; party B must believe
that party A will not abuse her decision-making rights. In standard employment relationships, it is patent that the employer, who coordinates the
efforts of many employees, enjoys the informational advantage. In the physi-
cian-patient relationship, it is equally clear that physician has the
expertise/information requires. As for being trustworthy, for party A's reputation to constrain her effectively, she must have an ongoing interest in
maintaining her reputation (she at least must repeat this or a similar transaction in the relatively near future), her efforts must be general observable to
subsequent potential trading partners, and the stakes for her in any single
transaction must not vary so much that she is enticed into exploitation in a
single instance, if it means forfeiture of her reputation. Employers tend to be
more permanent in location than employees, their behavior tends to be more
observable by potential employees (than is the actions of a given employee
by prospective employers), and their stakes with single employees tend to be
relatively small (while a single employee can sometimes have enormous
incentives to defraud and flee). These factors all reverse in the physician-
patient relationship. Hence, the theory suggests the observed change in governance form.

In many employment relationships (beyond professional services), the
employer does not have a monopoly on information; efficient transactions
require that employees act with discretion. In such cases, we find governance
that is more nearly balanced bilateral, where to support the incentives for
the employee to behave in the transaction, employers will take steps to
lengthen the duration of the employment relationship (e.g. as in Lazear,
1979), and/or to provide employees with increased costs of sundering the
specific relationship.[13]

---

[12] On this point in particular, see Aghion and Tirole (1994).

[13] Note the standard efficiency-or-market-power dilemma: an employer puts a greenfield plant in a
location where it will exercise a great deal of control over employees; e.g. Honda builds an assembly plant
in Marysville, Ohio, instead of in Cleveland. Is this a case of (i) the employer attempting to exploit workers by increasing its (labor) market power, or (ii) an employer who aims to invest heavily in training and
to give workers significant discretion, to make for more efficient labor exchange, but who therefore wishes
to lengthen average employment tenures and to increase the cost to workers of voluntary turnover?

In some cases the employer is insufficiently constrained by its reputation with workers as a class. Worker B101 may not be inclined to withdraw his labor services if worker B2 is mistreated by the employer, especially if the facts of mistreatment are in dispute. Insofar as it is costly to monitor the actions of the firm in its dealings with others, individual workers have little private incentive to expend the necessary resources. But if workers do not act collectively, either because they lack private incentives to act or to monitor, and if the firm's reputation is putatively based on the threat of collective action, the reputation equilibrium falls. A role is established in theory for trilateral governance, in which the workers bind themselves to act collectively, following the directions of a third-party monitor. That is, the theory suggests a role for a shop steward. (Compare with empirical studies of the union productivity effect and voice-based theories of unions. And note that, owing to the multiplicity of reputational equilibria, we have no problem rationalizing non-uniform effects of unionization.)

Trilateral governance is also suggested in cases where 'appropriate actions' are unclear, because of observability problems. Especially where these instances arise infrequently in a specific ongoing relationship, a role arises for an external trilateral authority (that can be trusted because it deals with this sort of issue in many relationships, hence relatively frequently, and derives rents from its reputation as a fair adjudicator in such circumstances). The equilibrium can be, when there is noise in the observables, the dispute is referred externally, and the decision of the external authority is accepted. It is not necessary in this construction that the external authority can penetrate the fog of noise better than either party, but only that by issuing a decision, it provides the two parties with a non-noisy signal of how to adapt. What is necessary is that the external authority is trusted by both sides to be 'fair', given the information it has, and its trustworthiness can arise at least in part by its independence from consequences of the specific decision it offers. (Consider, for example, the role of external auditors.)

In some settings, the momentary incentives for the employer to abuse its workers may on occasion outweigh the costs of lost reputation with those employees. An example of such an instance is a decision to move an entire manufacturing operation offshore. Reputation constructions alone will leave workers unprotected against such actions, and other forms of governance for this class of actions may be necessary, e.g. balanced-bilateral governance with a unanimity rule as in the Works Councils of Germany, or trilateral governance, either contractually provided or with the state as the trilateral authority.

The game theory that lies behind reputation-and reciprocity-based equilibria tells us that the bases of trust in such equilibria are enduring interest in the relationship, *ex post* observability, and single decisions that loom small relative to the overall value of the relationship (which speaks both to frequency and to variability in the immediate stakes). These bases in turn are quite informative about the different forms of governance found in specific relational contracts, when combined with considerations of who holds what information. Of course, this is nothing more than common sense, the theory is not telling us anything profound. Indeed, it cannot be profound, because a reputational equilibrium must, by its very nature, depend on the participants understanding how it works. But it allows us to organize our thinking about relational contracts and forms of governance.

A First-level Critique

Recall the earlier critique of the short-horizon models: contract incompleteness is rationalized by bounded rationality/communication (too hard to specify all the contingencies and the adaptation thereto), but the parties involved are sufficiently rational to anticipate accurately what will transpire in every possible contingency which includes, knowing every possible contingency. As per Maskin and Tirole, less than this is actually needed; parties need only have correct assessments concerning the flow of utility they will derive as a function of decisions taken today. But this is still rather a lot to swallow.

In the long-horizon, reputation/reciprocity models, this problem is if anything worse. Why is it impossible for employer and employee to specify a full contingent contract *ex ante*? The obvious and quite convincing story is that employment relationships can stretch over decades. No one seriously believes the parties involved can anticipate all the possibly relevant contingencies and draft a contract that covers them all. But then how can we convincingly use equilibrium analysis to study these relationships, where we assume that the parties involved understand at the outset what will happen over the course of the relationship as a function of all the contingencies that arise?

Multiplicity of equilibria in these settings compounds the problem. Consider the unrealistic situation in which the two parties literally play the game in Figure 2 repeatedly. Now an explicit contingent contract can be written. Indeed, some contracts are simple to write, such as: Task A in states #1 and #3 (period by period), task B in state #2.[14] Such an explicit contract,

---

[14] To be more exact, I have in mind a situation where the employee always retains the right to quit, although the employer cannot discharge the worker except for cause. Then this 'contract' specifies the path of equilibrium play, with the somewhat more implicit provision that the worker will depart if the firm does not follow the contractually-specified path of play. Of course, with the possibility of relatively cheap court enforcement, especially if sufficient punitive damage awards are possible, such contracts can go beyond the limitations of self-enforcing repeated-game equilibrium paths.

assuming it is self-enforcing, has the advantage of spelling out what the equilibrium is going to be. In this unrealistic setting, if the parties are not explicit *ex ante*, can they implicitly agree on what the arrangement will be? Since repeated games have a continua of equilibria, it is hard to see how they might do so (unless for the reasons given earlier one party has the power of Stackelberg leader or noise-avoidance considerations points toward a particular equilibrium).

Returning to the real world where future contingencies are vague at best, we are unable to specify explicitly what will be the path of play. Hence, we are in a world where the parties must anticipate not only what will happen over time, as (unforeseeable!) contingencies arise, but they must do this foreseeing in a situation where a continua of specifications can give an equilibrium arrangement. Equilibrium analysis presumes, rather incredibly, that (i) they all do this foreseeing and (ii) their prediction coincide and turn out to be factually correct.

The problem of multiplicity arises in many of the short-horizon models as well; at least, in those that conclude the *ex post* renegotiation as, for example, in Grossman and Hart (1986). Grossman and Hart assume that the gains from renegotiation are split equally, where gains are measured relative to the threat point of a non-cooperative (subgame) equilibrium. (In subsequent work to accommodate more than two parties, Hart and Moore have used the Shapley Value.) The threat point is unique, but where does the 50-50 split come from? Many explicit bargaining models suffer from a multiplicity of equilibria. Some others, e.g. the Rubinstein (1982) alternating-offer bargaining model, have a unique subgame-perfect equilibrium. But uniqueness turns on the very delicate application of subgame perfection, and incomplete information as to the bargaining aspirations of the parties can muddy the pristine waters of a unique perfect equilibrium. Economics textbooks have, for quite a while, asserted that the outcome in a situation of bilateral monopoly is unclear—even taking the Panglossian view that efficiency will be attained—and my reading of recent work in bargaining theory is that Rubinstein notwithstanding, that intuition is theoretically supported.[15] Since expectations about the division of rents in the renegotiation stage drives almost completely the initial investment levels, the multiple-equilibria problem arises in the short-horizon models just as soon as we get serious (i.e. do something other than assume the result) about *ex post* renegotiation.

[15] I will also add that the lack of theoretical support for a specific bargaining outcome does not mean that, in controlled bargaining situations, we cannot predict what the outcome will be. We know from experimental work that by manipulating the expectations of subjects and by framing, we can influence the outcome of bargaining situations rather substantially, and somewhat in contradiction to what simple-minded application of game-theoretic ideas would predict for some protocols.

Milton Friedman for the Defense

We can agree, I hope, that traditional game-theoretic models, with their assumptions of perfect (accurate) contingent foresight, do not do justice to boundedly rational behavior. Insofar as contract incompleteness is rationalized primarily by bounded rationality, important pieces are missing from our model.

There are those who will argue with the conclusion of the previous paragraph. Let me propose three lines of argument:

(i)   In a formal sense, it is not necessary (to invoke the predictions of Nash equilibrium) that players have perfect contingent foresight for all contingencies that arise, but only for those that are *relevant* in the technical sense that they can be reached by one deviation from the equilibrium by any one player (Fudenberg and Kreps, 1994, Proposition 4.1). Indeed, for two-player games, perfect contingent foresight is needed only along the path of play (Fudenberg and Kreps, 1995, Proposition 6.1). *Rejoinder*: These technical emendations do not really affect the argument above, insofar as it is hard to imagine that players have a good idea of what contingencies they will meet even assuming they stick to 'the agreement'. The path of play (all events that will be reached with positive probability if there are no deviations) itself is uncharted territory in a world of boundedly rational individuals.

(ii) Following Maskin and Tirole (1995), in short-horizon situations, the parties do not need to describe accurately (in their mind's eye) what contingencies will arise and what actions will be taken given those contingencies. It is enough that they have an accurate feel for the distribution of 'utility' ramifications of the action-contingency pairs. For long-horizon models, we will need more than this; it must be feasible for them to assess *ex post* that their trading partners lived up to the implicit agreement. Justice Stewart's '[Although difficult if not impossible to define *ex ante*], I know [pornography] when I see it' is apposite. To extend the Maskin and Tirole argument to longer horizon models, this becomes: The participants cannot say *ex ante* precisely what is expected of each other in this agreement, but they recognize what it is as contingencies arise, and after the fact each is able to say whether the other fulfilled her obligations. *Rejoinder*: This simply compounds the original Maskin and Tirole assumptions. If they were not credulous before, they are surely less so compounded in this fashion.

(iii) It is not important that our models capture all aspects of the situation, as long as they give us testable predictions about the world that are not rejected by the data. That is, we have Milton Friedman's defense of positive economic theory.

3. *Institutional Inertia*

My rejoinder to argument (iii) is to list real-world phenomena that, I contend, are important and suggestive of boundedly rational behavior. To address these phenomena adequately, we should go beyond standard game theory. In this section and the next, I deal at some length with the first of these phenomena, institutional inertia. Section 5 presents further phenomena of this type.

It is widely held that organizations exhibit substantial inertia in what they do and how they do it (Hannan and Freeman, 1984). In the face of changing external circumstances, organizations adapt poorly or not at all; the economy and/or market evolves as much or more through changes in the population of live organizations than through changes in the organizations that are alive. Moreover, adaptations resemble a piecewise constant function; one sees little or no change and then a sudden discontinuous shift, which (often) involves many practices of the organization.[16] Organizational policies/procedures tend to be derived from the early history of the organization (Stinchcombe, 1965; Hannan and Freeman, 1977) and to be derived from (or at least crystallized out of) specific noteworthy events in the early history of the organization (Schein, 1983).

Standard-theory Rationales

Granting its existence, can the phenomenon of institutional inertia be rationalized using standard economic/game theory? To answer, we first must be clear on how inertia connects to the models of Section 2.

Inertia is manifestly a phenomenon of long-enduring organizations and relationships. Thus, the short-horizon models of Section 2 are ill-suited to speak directly to inertia. The long-horizon models, on the other hand, seem very well suited to the task. (We could consider stacking together a sequence of short-horizon models, i.e. we imagine the two parties A and B engaged in a sequence of investment/employment interactions, but this would move us into the realm of repeated games and the Folk Theorem, in any case.)

---

[16] See, for example, Hannan and Freeman (1984) or Amburgey, Kelly, and Barnett (1993). At the level of the industry ecology, see Stinchcombe (1965). Small continuous changes do take place, and especially after a major jump in practices, there is a period during which new practices can adjust, seeking a new equilibrium. Hence, I use the formulation, adaptations *resemble* a piecewise constant function.

Beginning with the long-horizon model of relational contracting, inertia might be viewed as simple equilibrium selection, which is orthogonal to standard game theory. That is, in the Simon model (specified as a repeated game version of Figure 2), there is a reputational equilibrium in which the employer calls for task A in each period, a second in which she asks for task A in state 1 and task B in states 2 and 3 in each period, and (for example) a third in which her request in period t depends on the period t state and, say, the tth element in a binary expansion of the number π. The first equilibrium certainly seems to be 'inertial', the second probably does, and the third almost certainly does not. But all are equilibria, and standard theory is mute on a selection among them.

The problem here is that inertia refers to the organization's adaptation to a changing environment; in the simple long-horizon model of Section 2, the environment is entirely time homogeneous. So to discuss how standard theory deals (or does not) with inertia, we must elaborate on the simple long-horizon model. The easiest way to do this is to imagine that the payoffs in period t depend on the actions taken by the actors on that date *and* on some random environmental parameter θ_t. We can imagine that the stochastic process $\{\theta_t\}$ is very slow moving (i.e. with high probability, the payoffs at date t as a function of the actions are nearly the same as the payoffs at date $t - 1$) or that it jumps around somewhat. But however we think of this process, inertia then becomes: the employer and employee maintain the 'form' of their relationship for a long time—the employee expects, say, that the employer will ask for task A regardless of the state of nature—despite changes in the environment (in θ_t) that render this relationship fairly inefficient.

Recall from transaction-cost economics the fundamental precept that transactions tend to take the form that maximizes the net benefits of the transaction, net of the costs of the transaction. As a selection device for the game of Figure 2, this would seem to push for the reputational equilibrium in which the employer asks for that action in a given state that maximizes the sum of the payoffs (if utility is transferable), or at least does not ask for an action that is Pareto dominated by some other. As θ_t changes, this would argue for contingent-action requests that shift through time, and inertia would be observed if the actual requests shift markedly less quickly than this.

Can we generate inertia using standard-theory arguments? There are at least three ways to do so:

(i) Suppose first that θ_t is not observable by the employee(s), or is observable only with noise. Insofar as the employer's private interests diverge from the socially efficient choice of contingent action (even if the date-to-date state is fully observable), employee(s) will worry that the employer's modification of the state-contingent action rule is directed not at efficiency-enhancement but at maximizing her own welfare. Thus, fewer changes than are called for by full-observation efficiency would lead to greater efficiency under the informational constraints.

(ii) Suppose (in a more elaborate model) that employees seek employment with employers whose assignments/work conditions match well the tastes of the employee. Some employees seek employers who ask for many hours of work away from home (for premium pay), because these employees are relatively willing to take on such assignments; others seek employers who rigidly adhere to the rule no-more-than-one-day-away-a-month, because of the high personal value they put on being with their families. A particular employer, facing a particular environment, might find that she can live with the second, rigid rule, and still be fairly efficient. Thus, she puts that rule in place and attracts the corresponding work-force. Then her environment shifts, so that it would be more efficient to send employees out on the road much more (and more variably). If she changes her practices for extant employees, she must either compensate those employees, who will otherwise suffer (on average) from the increasing (average) mismatch, or suffer from high levels of turnover, with concomittent recruitment and training costs. Inertia in HR practices would seem to result. But why then should she not adopt better fitting practices for new hires? A complementary story concerning the need for homogeneity among employees will work: suppose (i) a significant portion of an employee's compensation is the psychic benefits of comradeship with other employees and (ii) one gets greater comradeship benefits from people who have similar tastes.

(iii) In Section 2 we relied on the models of reputation construction that depend on infinite horizon arguments. But there is another way to construct reputation equilibria (even with finite horizon models)—models based on incomplete information about the employer's 'type'—and these constructions can give a third standard theory argument for inertia.

In short, incomplete-information-about-type formulations assume that, at the outset, there is some chance that parties will behave in a way to conform to some behavioral type (with small probability, summing over the types) or they will behave in standard, utility-maximizing fashion (with large probability *ex ante*). Each participant knows his/her own type, but this is private information. Then with repeated play for stakes that are low relative to the overall stakes in the game, even a small chance that a participant behaves rigidly in a particular manner can affect equilibria dramatically. If (in equilibrium) the standard utility maximizer is to take some action that distinguishes herself from the pure type, then by mimicking the pure type instead she will be mistaken for the pure type and treated accordingly. (If no one but a paranoid person would hold a handgrenade on a bus, then anyone holding a handgrenade will be perceived as being paranoid and subsequently treated as such.) Hence, the standard utility maximizer must do (nearly) as well in expected payoff as she would do if mistaken for any type—either her behavior distinguishes herself from the pure type, in which case the mimicking argument works, or it does not, in which case she is treated exactly as one treats the pure type.[17]

The connection to inertia is: to be an attractive type to mimic, the type behavior must be predictable by the other side.[18] One can imagine, in theory, a predictable type whose behavior at date t depends on the tth digit of the binary expansion of π, but more plausible predictable types are those that are fairly steady in behavior. Having cultivated a reputation for such behavior, an employer (say) who suddenly 'shifts' loses her reputational asset; and a positive case for equilibrium inertia is made.

Note in passing that in this form of reputation construction, a lot of information about the reputation bearer's type is passed in the first few actions she takes. Hence we have a rationale for the observation that the early actions of the organization can be very influential concerning how it acts later.

4. *Bounded Rationality and Organizational Inertia*

The three standard-theory rationales of organizational inertia just advanced all work, in the sense that they hold together as theoretical constructs. There is probably some truth to them (or, at least, to the first and the second—I find the third rather far fetched). But, at the same time, alternative rationalizations/explanations of inertia can be advanced, using the (so-far) unmodeled concept of bounded rationality. Broadly, the connection between bounded rationality and inertia is something of a variation on the first rationale offered previously. The idea is that employees (in the Simon game)

[17] The formal argument first appears in Kreps and Wilson (1982) and Milgrom and Roberts (1982) and has been refined subsequently. For current purposes, good references are Fudenberg and Kreps (1987), Fudenberg and Levine (1989), and Watson (1993).

[18] In a confrontational setting, this certainly is not true. Someone who is perceived to act irrationally may get very gentle treatment in an otherwise harsh environment. But we are thinking here of contexts in which parties must cooperate to their mutual benefit; i.e. we are applying these ideas to beneficial exchange.

must understand and anticipate what the employer is doing (in the Simon game, to monitor the employer's compliance with the implicit contract they have with her). Thus in the first rationale above, the employer cannot be shifting her demands at will, based on information that the employees lack. But even if the employees had access to this information, their ability to do the requisite equilibrium calculations are probably more limited than standard theory assumes. They forecast the employer's future actions (and check her compliance with the implicit contract) based more on her adherence to a pattern of behavior. If they learn adaptively in this sense, it is in her interests to confirm their adaptively-learned expectations; i.e. to adhere to her pattern or previous behavior even if that pattern is no longer an efficient response to the changing environment.

The first key to building a (mathematical) model of this is to construct the model of individual boundedly rational behavior. There are many alternative models that can be employed here, and it is beyond my abilities to survey them all or even a wide subset. Instead, one class of models of behavior that has been studied extensively, adaptive (co-)learning, will be described followed by a discussion of how this model of individual behavior might connect to inertia.

Adaptive Co-learning in Repeated Games

Imagine that individuals play a game at dates $t = 1,2, \ldots$. At each date t, each player has an assessment concerning the play of her rivals, and she chooses her own action according to some criterion evaluated relative to those assessments. Some of the literature assumes that the choice criterion is precise and myopic; players form assessments of how their rivals will act in the current version of the game, and they then choose actions to maximize their (subjective) immediate payoffs.[19] In other analyses, myopia is assumed but a level of suboptimality is permitted; players can use any (mixed) strategy giving an immediate payoff that is suboptimal (in terms of immediate payoffs) by no more than an exogenously specified amount, an amount that vanishes as the player gains more experience. Other versions assume greater foresight; at the extreme, each player uses a fully specified assessment of how

[19] Myopia is sometimes justified by assuming that interactions come from random matches in a population so large that the rivals of Player X at date $t + k$ are very unlikely to have had any contact, direct or indirect, with rivals of Player X at dates t through $t + k - 1$, for k large enough so that α^k is very close to zero where α is the player's per period discount factor. Note that if each individual interaction involves M players and the total population size is N, the chances that a player will meet someone indirectly connected to one of her rivals from dates t to $t + k - 1$ at date t is bounded above by $(M^{k+1} - M)/(N[M - 1])$, which is vanishingly small for fixed k as M/N converges to zero. For more on this sort of justification of myopia, see Ellison (1993).

her rivals will act for the rest of time (contingent on formation her rivals will receive as time passes), and then solves precisely the infinite horizon dynamic programming problem, Find a strategic response that maximizes (say) discounted expected payoffs.

Myopic decision criteria, whether extreme or an intermediate form, are one expression of bounded rationality in these models. But the main way in which bounded rationality appears is in the players' adaptive assessments. Players begin with some form of prior assessment about the actions of their rivals, and they update based on the history of their rivals' play through time. In some studies, very specific updating rules are used; e.g. players use Bayes' rule on an initially given prior assessment on their rivals' full (infinite-horizon) strategies. This includes as a special case instances where each prior is that the sequence of actions by one's rivals at each date forms an exchangeable sequence, and Bayes' rule is used to update the prior on the limiting frequencies. In others, it is assumed (only) that the updating rules satisfy certain asymptotic properties; an example is asymptotic empiricism, which is that the behavior assessed of rival Y in a given situation converges together with the empirical frequencies of the actions taken by Y in that situation, if the situation recurs infinitely often (or, in other treatments, a non-vanishing fraction of the time).

In some studies, it is assumed that the population of players is large, subject to death and replacement, and the behavior of the population has achieved a steady state, so that players are attempting to learn that steady state. (This justifies asymptotic empiricism, if the priors are sufficiently diffuse.) In others, the model is one of a small group of players interacting repeatedly, each learning and reacting to what the others do. These models involve co-learning; as players learn, they change their actions, hence each is attempting to estimate a moving target.[20]

For the most part, these models have so far been used to study the question, if players in a game are learning and acting in this fashion, will they learn to play a Nash equilibrium of the game?[21]

Inertia

Adaptive behavior would seem to be a ready source for inertia. This does not follow immediately or always; suppose for example that the players in a gen-

---

[20] For these models asymptotic empiricism is quite a leap of faith. However, one can pose statistical tests for the validity of asymptotic empiricism as a maintained hypothesis without greatly affecting the results in this literature; see Fudenberg and Kreps (1995).

[21] The literature concerns both global convergence issues—will play converge at all?, and issues connected to the nature of stable points—if play converges, will it be to a Nash equilibrium, or something stronger or weaker? For a recent survey, see Marimon (1995).

eral repeated game have Cournotian assessments (the prediction what an opponent will do at date t is what he did at date $t-1$). But for many models of adaptive learning, assessments of a rival's behavior at date t reflects that rival's behavior at many previous dates. In the 'extreme' case of fictitious play (or, more generally, asymptotic empiricism), assessments at date t reflect equally the rival's behavior at all previous dates. If adaptation takes this form and behavior settles into a stable state (or, as in Sonsino (1995), a stable pattern of behavior), both assessments and thus behavior will eventually be very difficult to move because of the increasingly large history that must be overcome.[22] Note the self-fulfilling feedback here: if players in the game form assessments adaptively, using data for behavior gathered over an increasing large period of time, it will take an increasingly long time to move their expectations and hence their behavior (if they are myopic or asymptotically myopic). Even a sophisticated individual (top management?) who understands the adaptive behavior of others and who optimizes accordingly will have little incentive to try to move the others from one established equilibrium to another; it will take a while to do so, which will make it unworthwhile at any reasonable discount factor.

Coordination as a game-theoretic metaphor for mutually beneficial exchange will clarify and refine these assertions. Imagine a number of individuals playing the following game.[23] At each date t, each must choose an action from some set A. The payoff to player i at date t is $v_i(\theta_t, a_i, n(a_i),)$, where θ_t is an environmental parameter (chosen by nature), a_i is the action chosen by i, and $n(a_i)$ is the number of players choosing precisely this (same) action. Imagine that v_i is strictly increasing in its third argument and that if $v_i(\theta, a, n) > v_i(\theta, a', n)$ for some n, then this inequality holds for all n. The first assumption is, essentially, that players benefit by coordinating their choices with others (and the more, the better); the second assumption is that a player's interests about where coordination takes place does not change with the level of coordination.[24]

Fix θ_t. Depending on the scale of the benefits of coordination *vis-à-vis* the 'personal preferences' of individuals (measured by the relative values of $v(\theta_t, a, 1)$ for various a), it is evident that the game at θ_t (and at date t) can have a vast number of Nash equilibria of varying efficiencies. To take a very simple example, if there are two actions a and a', even if $v_i(\theta_t, a, 1) > v_i(\theta_t, a', 1)$ for everyone, it is a Nash equilibrium for everyone to coordinate on a' if $v_i(\theta_t, a', 2) \geq v_i(\theta_t, a, 1)$. But if there are decreasing returns to scale in coordination

---

[22] This assumes convergence to strict best responses. Aficionados will recognize the problems that arise when, in the limit, more than one pure strategy is asymptotically a best response.

[23] A game of roughly this form is studied by Farrell and Shapiro (1996) on the topic of the adoption of compatible standards.

[24] This restriction is only to simplify the analysis.

(roughly, if $v_i(\theta_t, a, n + m) - v_i(\theta_t, a, n)$ is decreasing in n for fixed m), then as the total population grows, we can increasingly find equilibria for the θ_t stage game in which players coalesce into several pools; the pressures to coordinate are not sufficient so that everyone necessarily coalesces into a single lump (although a single pool almost anywhere remains a good prospect for an equilibrium).

If we look for Nash equilibria of the repeated game, inertia is not necessarily produced. Any string of single-period Nash equilibria (and more besides) give a equilibrium of the repeated game, including strings where both the actions chosen for coordination and the members of the various pools change dramatically with each date.

But, of course, such equilibria depend on players having hyper-rational expectations about the actions of their fellows. If, as seems more realistic, i's prediction about j's action choice is largely determined by how j chose in the past, then once a stable configuration is reached, it may be very hard to upset. For example, suppose that θ_t is unchanging and players begin with an equal-probability prior on how others will act and are myopic. Then $_i$ will initially choose the action $a_i{}^*$ that maximizes $v_i(a, 1)$ (where I suppress θ_t, since it is momentarily constant). When these choices are noted, each player will increase the probability assessed that j will pick $a_j{}^*$. Perhaps the changed assessments will be insufficient to get anyone to abandon their personal best actions, but then after another round of seeming chaos, each will be more sure about what the others will do. At some point, someone will be moved to abandon her own personal best, to join at the best of someone else (at least, this is so if $v_i(a_i{}^*, 1) < v_i(a_j{}^*, 2)$ for some i and j. Barring a coincidental simultaneous shift, the action of coordination by these two will be self-confirming—the more often they coordinate, the more attractive coordination at this point will look to them. Then, as others become convinced that the two are coordinating there, they will be moved to join, unless they have already formed their own coordinating groups. Groups of various sizes will coalesce. There is no reason to suppose that eventually everyone will coordinate at a single action; whether a player abandons one coordinating group to join another depends on the relative sizes of the groups and the inherent attractiveness of the two actions (measured by $v_i(a, 1)$). But note that if one player drops from a coordinating group, this simultaneously makes the joined group more attractive and the group departed less.

The dynamic system depends on the precise rules for assessing what others will do, the form of myopia that is assumed, and any noise put into the system. This paper is not the place to spell out a very precise formulation and make all this specific, but five points should be clear: (i) Corresponding to the many Nash equilibria of the stage game, the dynamic system will have many stable configurations. Moreover, if we put some noise into the action selection process (noise pertaining, say, to how, to how one chooses among actions that are nearly equally good), the eventual limiting configuration will be random. (ii) Initial coordinating decisions will be very influential on the eventual configuration that emerges. A chance coordination at the outset by two individuals will be reinforcing and will attract others. (iii) Insofar as assessments are not much affected late in the sequence of periods by single individual actions, because there is more and more data to draw upon, once a stable configuration (a Nash equilibrium) is reached it will tend to persist. (iv) A single sophisticated individual participating in this repeated situation may find it impossible to shift the configuration. Even if she can shift it, it will take a great deal of time (spend uncoordinated with others) to do so. (v) The dynamic model has (potentially) two reinforcing sources of inertia: Stable configurations will persist, even if (say) assessments are Cournotian (the prediction of what i will do at date t is i's choice at $t - 1$. If assessments are increasingly rigid as history at a specific configuration builds up—if, say, the assessment of what i will do at date t is some sort of average of what i did at the past $\eta(t)$ dates, where $\lim_t \eta(t) = \infty$ (as in fictitious play models)—then the longer a stable configuration persists, the more persistent it becomes.

Now reintroduce variable θ_t, thinking of θ_t as a slowly evolving environmental variable. With enough variation in the θ_t, stable coalition structures may 'collapse'; player i may at some date t shift from a coalition at action a to one at a', if the ratio of $v_i(\theta_t, a', 1)/v_i(\theta_t, a, 1)$ grows sufficiently. Such a shift may occasion a cascade of further changes; when i abandons action a, everyone else who was choosing a sees less value in the choice (since $n(a)$ is reduced), and further defections may result. This effect will be stronger in small organizations (actions a with low $n(a)$) and in settings with more rapidly decreasing returns to scale in coordination, since the value of being in a larger coalition is less diluted by a single defection.[25] The picture is one of local equilibrium configurations that, once formed, persist for long periods of time, and then perhaps suddenly crumble. A configuration may be relatively efficient at date t and then become increasingly inefficient compared to other configurations that might be formed, while still staying a local equilibrium. Sophisticated individuals, getting to the process early, may strongly influence the configuration that is reached at the outset and after an unfreezing. But a single sophisticated individual may be unable to shift to a better (for her) stable configuration unless she can work directly on the assessments of

---

[25] Note in this formulation each player is concerned only with the number and not the identities of those with whom she coordinates. If player i was anxious to coordinate with a specific player j, then even if that coordination was achieved in a large cluster, it might not be any more stable in consequence.

other individuals, and even if she can do so, it will be very expensive in time and missed coordination opportunities to do so. As a metaphor for descriptions one reads of organizational inertia, this has some appeal.

Of course, this metaphor is only a metaphor; it is far from a serious model of organizations or transactions. The coordination game with conflicting interests that has been suggested is convenient for showing how adaptive expectations can lead to inertia at any of a number of different configurations, with local adaptation but few (if any) jumps to a globally more efficient solution. But unless and until we are ready to accept coordination as an appropriate reduced form for transaction issues, it would be better to build a model of transactions that looks more like the real thing. I have not done this, so I cannot claim for certain that such a model, populated by adaptive decision-makers, will give the sort of inertial behavior the metaphor provides. But I am fairly confident it will,[26] and so the suggestion is that we ought to populate models of transactions (such as the Simon model) not with the hyperrational agents of standard game theory but with the sort of individuals who increasingly populate models of learning in (non-standard) game theory.

Some Missing Aspects of Adaptive Behavior

As we do this, we (game theorists) will need to tune up our models of adaptive behavior. There are a number of aspects of behavior that would be useful for addressing inertia (and the phenomena to be listed in Section 5) and that are currently outside of even the non-standard arsenal. There are four obvious candidates.

First, with one exception of which I am aware (Li Calzi, 1993), the models used presuppose that players are involved in repeated play of a fixed game. Inferences about what a rival will do in situation X are (usually) restricted by the past behavior of the rival in precisely that situation.[27] In real life, situations do not recur precisely as before. Instead, a situation X' may arise that seems very similar to past situations (the same rival is called upon to move, she has roughly the same options, her payoffs are roughly the same), in which case a player may use the evidence of what happened in X to assess what will happen in X'. Note my list of what makes the two situations similar—same player, roughly same options, roughly same playoffs—I have an intuition derived from experience as to what makes

---

[26] Which is to say, I think coordination with conflict will turn out to be a good metaphor for long-horizon transactions.

[27] To be clear about this, it is not typically assumed that behavior in situation X' is completely uninformative about behavior in situation X, but neither is any link presumed to hold.

situations similar. More precisely, one can have many hypotheses as to what makes situations similar—call these hypotheses theories or models—which abstract from a complex real life situation a short/simple list of important attributes; and the theories are subjected through time to empirical testing, to see whether (per the data) things happen roughly the same way in similar situations. Those versed in computer science will recognize basic ideas of pattern recognition here; psychologists will recognize cognitive psychology.

Second, the literature generally assumes that players understand the underlying structure of the game that is being repeated. They know what information their rivals have, what all the options are, and so on. In real life these things are more vague, and learning models should be constructed reflecting this.

Third, players cannot be expected to learn how their rivals act in situations that recur very, very rarely (formally, a finite number of times; see Fudenberg and Levine (1993) and Fudenberg and Kreps (1994). Players, by their own actions, preclude certain observations; put the other way around, to obtain certain data, players sometimes must conduct experiments that are costly in the short-run. How is the decision made whether to experiment? The models in the literature either invoke an incredible level of sophistication (players are presumed to solve non-stationary multi-armed bandit problems precisely) or are silent on the process except to make broad-gauge assumptions such as, every action that can be taken infinitely often is taken infinitely often. Adaptive learning models in general need better models of the process of experimentation by boundedly rational decision makers, especially where the experiments take us to regions of the sort mentioned in the second point above, where the options and payoffs are *ex ante* unclear.

Finally, an important aspect of the equilibrium analysis of long-horizon relational contracts is that players reciprocate, assuming that their trading partners will reciprocate. We lack a good story on learning to reciprocate in a small numbers formulation. In the literature on small numbers interactions, most papers have very myopic decision-makers; they essentially forecast what their rivals will do in the current encounter and, at least asymptotically, choose a stage-game strategy that maximizes their stage-game expected payoff. Kalai and Lehrer (1993) give a small-numbers formulation with more far-sighted players, but their players are incredibly far-sighted and computationally sophisticated; they (each) solve a dynamic programming problem that is at least as hard as a multi-armed bandit problem with non-independent arms. Since we have stories of learning to play extensive form games (e.g. in Fudenberg and Kreps, 1994, 1995), we can imagine learning reciprocation as a general rule; Player A plays a long-horizon game against B, then another against C, then D, and so on, taking what she has learned in each interaction into the next.[28] This may be an interesting story—indeed, it makes reciprocation into something of a social phenomena rather than something internally arising between two individual players—but we would like as well a story about A and B interacting and each learning how each will reciprocate (or not) in their specific relationship.

5. *Other Phenomena*

Inertia is not the only phenomenon which, I believe, can be fruitfully studied with models of individual behavior that go beyond the hyper-rationality of standard economics and game theory. Among the other phenomena of interest are the following.

(1) Consistency/comprehensibility/transparency/simplicity. At least in the domain of employment practices, 'internal consistency' is held to be important. I am unable to give a concise definition of consistency (Potter Stewart is apposite once more); and so I resort to some examples: (i) If the organization promotes cooperation among employees in its compensation practices, it should not simultaneously base promotion on individual (relative) performance. (ii) If workers are exhorted to take risks and be forthcoming with criticisms or ideas, incentive systems should not penalize failure harshly. (iii) An organization whose compensation and promotion practices have the flavor of a competitive marketplace does better with a cafeteria-style benefits plan than with benefits configured to look like gifts.

Another form of consistency that is sometimes recommended is consistency of practices among workers otherwise undistinguished by education or other apparent demographic factors. For example, notwithstanding the obvious transaction-cost advantages, IBM found it difficult to treat differently engineers in its PC division and engineers in other parts of the firm. Firms will use artificial distinctions in some instances, such as job titles, or they will resort to things like geographic separation that prevent communication/cross-observation.

Other aspects of employment practices that are sometimes held to be efficiency-promoting are comprehensibility, transparency, and simplicity. These concepts are even harder to define than is consistency. Indeed most definitions I have formulated are internally referential. But (in the context of

---

[28] Note that this is not quite true, since Fudenberg and Kreps have a small numbers formulation. That is, to cite those papers directly, we would need A and B to play a long-horizon game, then another, and another, etc. where for some reason they are myopic between, but of course not within, each individual 'encounter'. To make up the story suggested, we would need a large numbers formulation of Fudenberg and Kreps. It does not seem difficult, but it has not (to my knowledge) been done formally.

employment practices, at least), employers are enjoined to create HR practices that give positive answers to questions such as: do you (the employee) understand what is expected of you?; and do you understand how your compensation and promotion prospects are determined? I hypothesize that positive answers to parallel questions for other forms of relational exchange are associated with greater efficiency in those exchanges.

(2) Social embeddedness. Employment (and other transactional) practices are embedded within the general milieu of social exchange, and the efficiency of various practices changes with changes in the social milieu (Grannovetter, 1985). Specifically, practices that are generally consistent with norms for general social exchange in the society in which the transaction is embedded tend to do better than those that are at variance with those norms. An employer with assembly plants in the USA and Thailand may find it counterproductive to subject employees in the US plant to daily searches by metal detectors, where such searches promote an aura of distrust (which is then reciprocated), while such practices have lesser adverse consequences in Thailand. A handshake agreement made following joint attendance at a club or at Church may take on greater sanctity than the same agreement made in an airport hotel suite.

(3) Gift exchange. Party A to a long-run transaction provides 'gifts' to party B; extra benefits, above-market wages, free drinks during the work day, and so on. Party B reciprocates with 'gifts' such as working extra hours without compensation, giving consummate effort (Akerlof, 1982).

(4) The psychology of escalating commitment and other dynamic effects. Escalating commitment concerns behavior in which an individual's commitment to a goal or a relationship grows over time (as the goal is pursued or the relationship matures), to the point where the goal/relationship is pursued past the seeming point of 'economic' sense (Staw and Ross, 1986). Sunk-cost illusions are one example; firms that have invested (in a sunk cost fashion) in a venture will continue to invest in the venture even if it is increasingly clear that the return on continued investments is such that the investments would not be undertaken de novo. In terms of long-horizon contracting, party A may continue to transact with party B even if it seems a better (more efficient) trading relation with some party C could take its place. In a more positive aspect, parties A and B may, as their relationship matures, become more willing to trust the other; contracts between them may become less detailed, with greater reliance on either one-party-determined adaptation or adaptation by unanimous consent. In terms of the repeated-game model of long-horizon contracting, it appears that the simple fact that A and B have dealt with each other over time increases the value to each of continuing to deal with each other, beyond the value that seems to arise from the economic exchanges that take place

(5) The managerial risk of forgiveness, and high- and low-powered incentives. As something of a special case of escalating commitment (but more besides), we have one of the reasons given by Williamson that firms cannot attain the high-powered incentives offered by markets; viz., the managerial risk of forgiveness. Markets can and do punish poor performance quite severely, and (thus) provide high-powered incentives to avoid failure. But within an organization, failure by an individual or group of individuals can be and often is forgiven, reducing the incentive to avoid failure. (I would imagine that this effect is stronger the longer the malefactor has been associated with the firm and, especially, his particular boss, assuming the relationship to date has been positive.)

(6) Noncalculative and non-intrusive trust, and atmosphere in general. In response to agency theory, social psychologists and sociologists often cite evidence that close monitoring of individuals and rewards based on extrinsic measures of performance may perversely (for economists, at least) increase slacking and lower effort. For the former, an individual who is closely monitored takes from the very fact the idea that he is not trusted, and thus that trust is not expected (think of common rationales for honor codes). For the latter, extrinsic reward schemes supposedly blunt the (sometimes) very powerful effect of intrinsic rewards. Moreover, the very act of calculation (of personal costs and benefits) may injure trust (Williamson, 1993b).

Each of these phenomena can be rationalized to some extent with standard-theory models. In particular, efficiency-wage theory works well with gift exchange (albeit not with the part of gift-exchange theory that stresses the symbolic importance attached to the form of the gift). But I have selected these phenomena because I believe that they will respond well to non-standard treatments of individual behavior.

First, in the real world, where no situation ever repeats precisely, predictions of how a trading partner will act will be made on the basis of similarities and 'general principles'. Moreover, *ex post* checking on adherence to an implicit contract will be made on the basis of similarly unclear criteria. A rule/principle/similarity will be more or less efficient as a basis for trade according to (i) how easily it is for the trading partners to learn, through experience or communication; (ii) how unambiguous it is to apply *ex ante* and to verify *ex post*; and (ii) how widely and efficiently it applies to contingencies that arise. Clearly these desiderata will conflict: ambiguity is likely to rise with range of applicability; letting a fixed third party arbitrate disputes is widely applicable and relatively unambiguous (follow whatever the third party dictates), but in a world with privately held information this is likely to give less than efficient adaptation to contingencies that arise. Notwithstanding the tradeoffs that must be made, the general desirability for purposes of learnability and unambiguous applications of qualities such as simplicity, comprehensibility, and consistency seems clear. Consistency, moreover, means both internal consistency and consistency of the specific rule/principle with rules/principles found generally in society; it is easier to learn and apply a pattern of behavior that conforms with generally observed patterns of behavior than to learn and apply a pattern that mixes many generally observed forms, so that social embeddedness and the symbolic character of actions play a role. I am uncertain how to model these aspects within (mathematical) economic models of adaptive behavior (see earlier remarks concerning similarities), but there are obvious sources to tap for insights: psychological theories of perception and cognition; sociological theories of norms; computer science theories of pattern recognition.

Second, economic models have (with rare exceptions) left untouched the notion that, putting aside expectations, one's own tastes and preferences change with experience. In particular (and particularly germane for the current context), individuals internalize to greater or lesser extent the welfare of others depending on such factors as kinship, social similarity, and length of (positive or negative) interactions. Models of endogenously evolving tastes that capture these ideas ought to be very helpful refining our understanding of escalating commitment, the managerial risk of forgiveness, and the like. Models where such tastes are influenced by symbolic actions (e.g. non-calculative trust suggests friendship or kinship, which leads to greater internalization of the other's welfare) may help us to understand non-calculative trust or the importance in gift exchange of the symbolic character of the gift.

6. Conclusions

Transaction-cost economics has been partially translated in the more mathematical language of game theory over the past decade, and (I hope and believe) our understanding of the costs of transactions has been deepened, refined and extended in consequence. But the translation is incomplete. There is a lot to human behavior that standard game-theoretic models miss, and undertaking 'game theory' with more life-like models of individuals will get us much closer to phenomena that we (game theorists) currently must ignore or leave unexplained, at least insofar as we stick rigidly to the standard rules of our toolkit. Transaction-cost economics, especially the economics of relational contracts, provides an outstanding arena for these developments, because the important issues of bounded rationality and (more generally) individual behavior are central to the topic. I have suggested models that take off from recent work on adaptive co-learning as a useful starting point, but I do not mean to suggest that these models are exclusively the way to proceed: the models of reinforcement learning that have recently been studied by Erev and Roth (1995) are very attractive (and come with something of a theory of similarities); I have just argued for models with exogenously influenced and endogenously evolving levels of internalization of the welfare of others.

I can imagine responses to this thesis from economists, from social psychologists and sociologists, and from those interested primarily in the economics of transactions. Traditionalist economists will look at Section 5 especially and mark this down as an appeal to ad hockery run amok. Allowing tastes to change with, say, the social millieu, is just assuming the result. Put differently, can the program I am advocating be carried out without losing the things of value that game theory does provide, namely a strongly deductive treatment of the behavior of reasonably rational individuals? I find the position today quite similar to where game theory was in the late 1960s, just before the brilliant technical innovations of Selten (concerning the importance of dynamics in game theory) and Harsanyi (on incomplete information), which substantially increased the reach of game theory as a language for discussing and tool for analyzing economic phenomena. Those innovations, and the way they played out in economic applications, gave modelers the ability to spin a lot of 'stories'. It has been said, with substantial justice, that a lot of the armchair theorizing that went on was uninformed by facts. But deductive theory is language and not a divining rod for empirical truth. It is a high order language that allows us to check for logical consistency of our sentences and paragraphs, and it is a language that allows for fairly precise communication. But a lot of stories can be constructed in this language, only some of which will resemble real-world economic phenomena, and empirical tests are run at the level of particular (one hopes, well-constructed) paragraphs, and not at the level of the language itself. If there is a difference in the current situation, I do not see it. Of course widening what we can say will allow us to say more, and to say more garbage in consequence. But if the language is used sensibly, and the paragraphs are subjected to empirical tests (both in the field and in the lab), we ought to be better off in consequence.

Economists will also ask whether any expansion is necessary. Are not the tools we have already adequate? After all, each of the phenomena I have mentioned can be rationalized to some extent with standard-theory models. And per Posner (1993) and some of my high theory colleagues, I imagine that, at some level, everything having to do with bounded rationality can be reduced to a model of full rationality in a setting of incomplete information and positive costs of computation. But as a practical matter of constructing useful and illuminating models, it seems to me that those who advocate these positions bear the burden of proof; where proof is not a formal proposition to this effect, but instead a set of workable modeling techniques by which (for example) organizational theorists can come fully to grips with organizational inertia, forgiveness, etc.

Sociologists and social psychologists may wonder what is in it for them. I have written this paper as an invitation and challenge to my own (that is, to economists) and have therefore focused on what is missed in standard economic models. It ill behooves me to lecture sociologists and social psychologists on what their models miss (or, to put if more positively, what economic reasoning contributes); in any case, I have not the space left to do so. But notwithstanding comments from colleagues that I seem to be evolving into a sociologist, I reaffirm my faith in models in which individuals maximize (albeit as best they can) and admit that my objective is to convert the heathens to economics by mild cooption.

And for the economics of transactions: Since most of the hard work of modeling and analyzing remains to be done, I do not have any solid returns to offer. But let me suggest a question that the models I propose may help to answer.

A central tenet of *Markets and Hierarchies* and transaction-cost economics more generally is that transactions *tend* to be arranged in a way that economizes on transaction costs or, perhaps more precisely, that maximizes the net benefits of the transaction, net of costs of the transaction. The italicized *tend* in this principle gives some scope for things like organizational inertia; it is an open question (in my mind, at least) how much scope transaction-cost economists mean to allow. Or to put it more sensibly, clearly the degree of this tendency will be influenced by environmental variables; it would be helpful to know when the economizing tendency is strong and when it is relatively weak. Based on the metaphorical model of Section 4, the strength of the tendency will be influenced by: the extent to which expectations are blindly adaptive and/or can be unfrozen by direct and explicit intervention of 'leaders'; the extent to which expectations are increasingly frozen as time passes (i.e. are expectations closer to Cournotian or closer to those suggested by fictitious play?); the extent to which participants can foresee where other stable configurations may be found.

Since the model is a very bare metaphor, these are not conjectures on which I would care to stake my professional reputation. In any event, it is not at all clear (to me) how we could measure these environmental factors empirically; i.e. how we might test these conjectures. But my point for now is not that I have a good answer to the question. Instead, I assert (only) that the question is interesting, and better models of individual behavior is a good place to look for good answers.

Acknowledgements

Prepared originally for presentation at the conference celebrating the 20th anniversary of Williamson's *Markets and Hierarchies*, held in Berkeley, October 1995. My thinking on this subject has been affected by too many colleagues to list here, but I should certainly acknowledge (with gratitude) the time and effort taken by Jim Baron to educate me. The financial assistance of the National Science Foundation (Grant 92-08954) is gratefully acknowledged.

References

Aghion, P. and J. Tirole (1994), 'Formal and Real Authority in Organizations,' mimeo, IDEI and Oxford.

Akerlof, G. A. (1982), 'Labor Contracts as Partial Gift Exchange,' *Quarterly Journal of Economics*, 97, 543–569.

Amburgey, T. L., D. Kelly and W. P. Barnett (1993), 'Resetting the Clock: The Dynamics of Organizational Change and Failure,' *Administrative Science Quarterly*, 38, 51–73.

Debreu, G. (1990), 'The Mathematization of Economic Theory,' *American Economic Review*, 81, 1–7.

Ellison, G. (1993), 'A Little Rationality and Learning from Personal Experience,' mimeo, Harvard University.

Erev, I. and A. E. Roth (1995), 'On the Need for Low Rationality, Cognitive Game Theory: Reinforcement Learning in Experimental Games with Unique, Mixed Strategy Equilibria,' mimeo, University of Pittsburgh.

Farrell, J. and C. Shapiro (1993), 'The Dynamics of Bandwagons,' in J. W. Friedman (ed.), *Problems in Coordination of Economic Activity*, Kluwer: Amsterdam, 149–184.

Fudenberg, D. and D. M. Kreps (1987), 'Reputation in the Simultaneous Play of Multiple Opponents,' *Review of Economic Studies*, 54, 541–568.

Fudenberg, D. and D. M. Kreps (1994), 'Learning in Extensive-Form Games I. Self-Confirming Equilibrium,' *Games and Economic Behavior*, 8, 20–55.

Fudenberg, D. and D. M. Kreps (1995), 'Learning in Extensive-Form Games II. Experimentation and Nash Equilibrium,' mimeo, Stanford University.

Fudenberg, D. and D. Levine (1989), 'Reputation and Equilibrium Selection in Games with a Patient Player,' *Econometrica*, 57, 759–778.

Fudenberg, D. and D. Levine (1993), 'Steady State Learning and Nash Equilibrium,' *Econometrica*, 61, 523–546.

Fudenberg, D. and J. Tirole (1990), 'Moral Hazard and Renegotiation in Agency Contracts,' *Econometrica*, 58, 1279–1320.

Grannovetter, M. (1985), 'Economic Action and Social Structure: The Problem of Embeddedness,' *American Journal of Sociology*, 91, 481–510.

Grossman, S. and O. Hart (1986), 'The Costs and Benefits of Ownership: A Theory of Vertical and Lateral Integration,' *Journal of Political Economy*, 94, 691–719.

Hannan, M. T. and J. Freeman (1977), 'The Population Ecology of Organizations,' *American Journal of Sociology*, 89, 929–964.

Hannan, M. T. and J. Freeman (1984), 'Structural Inertia and Organizational Change,' *American Sociological Review*, 49, 149–164.

Hart, O. (1990), 'Is "Bounded Rationality" and Important Element of a Theory of Institutions?' *Journal of Institutional and Theoretical Economics*, 146, 696–702.

Hart, O. (1995), *Firms, Contracts, and Financial Structure*. Clarendon Press: Oxford.

Hart, O. and M. Moore (1990), 'Property Rights and the Nature of the Firm,' *Journal of Political Economy*, 98, 1119–1158.

Kalai, E. and E. Lehrer (1993), 'Rational Learning Leads to Nash Equilibrium,' *Econometrica*, 61 1019–1045.

Kreps, D. M., R. Wilson (1982), 'Reputation and Imperfect Information,' *Journal of Economic Theory*, 27, 253–79.

Kreps, D. M. (1996), 'Economics—The Current Position,' mimeo, forthcoming in *Daedalus*.

Lazear, E. T. (1979), 'Why Is There Mandatory Retirement?' *Journal of Political Economy*, 87, 1261–1284.

Li Calzi, M. (1993), *Similarities and Learning*, PhD thesis, Stanford.

Marimon, R. (1995), 'Learning from Learning in Economics,' presentation to the Seventh World Congress of the Econometric Society, mimeo, European University Institute, Florence.

Maskin, E. and J. Tirole (1995), 'Dynamic Programming, Unforseen Contingencies, and Incomplete Contracts,' oral presentation at the Seventh World Congress of the Econometric Society, Tokyo.

Milgrom, P. N. and D. J. Roberts (1982), 'Predation, Reputation, and Entry Deterrence,' *Journal of Economic Theory*, 27, 280–312.

Posner, R. A. (1993), 'The New Institutional Economics Meets Law and Economics,' *Journal of Institutional and Theoretical Economics*, 149, 73–87.

Rubinstein, A. (1982), 'Perfect Equilibrium in a Bargaining Model,' *Econometrica*, 50, 97–109.

Schein, E. H. (1983), 'The Role of the Founder in Creating Organizational Culture,' Organizational Dynamics, reprinted in B. M. Staw (ed.), *Psychological Dimensions of Organizational Behavior*, 2nd edition. Prentice-Hall: Englewood Cliffs, NJ, 1995.

Simon, H. (1951), 'A Formal Model of the Employment Relationship,' *Econometrica*, 19, 293–305.

Sonsino, D. (1995), 'Learning to Learn, Pattern Recognition, and Nash Equilibrium,' Ph.D. thesis, Stanford.

Staw, B. M. and J. Ross (1986), 'Understanding Behavior in Escalation Situations,' *Science*, 246, 216–220.

Stinchcombe, A. (1965), 'Social Structure and Organizations,' in J. G. March (ed.) *Handbook of Organizations*. Rand McNally: Chicago, pp. 142–193.

Tirole, J. (1994), 'Incomplete Contracts: Where Do We Stand?,' mimeo, IDEI, Toulouse, (Walras-Bowley Lecture for 1994).

Watson, J. (1993), 'A 'Reputation' Refinement without Equilibrium,' *Econometrica*, 61, 199–206.

Williamson, O. E. (1975), *Markets and Hierarchies*. Free Press: New York.

Williamson, O. E. (1985), *The Economic Institutions of Capitalism*, Free Press: New York.

Williamson, O. E. (1993a), 'Transaction Cost Economics Meets Posnerian Law and Economics,' *Journal of Institutional and Theoretical Economics*, 149, 99–118.

Williamson, O. E. (1993b), 'Calculativeness, Trust, and Economic Organization,' *Journal of Law and Economics*, 36, 453.

CHAPTER EIGHT

Technical Information and Industrial Structure

KENNETH J. ARROW

This paper attempts to relate the role of information in production to the organization of industry, particularly the organization into firms and the competitive behavior of these firms. Its emphasis is technical information or the knowledge needed to produce goods. Information is an economic good but it has many characteristics which differentiate it from the goods usually modeled in economics. In particular, it is surprising to find how poorly current theories apply to the situation of high fixed costs which arises when information acquisition becomes a major part of a firm's activity. The paper concludes by conjecturing an increasing tension between legal relations and fundamental economic determinants. In addition, unresolved problems in the economic theory of pricing and competition arise in an economy in which information is important for both cost and utility, producing conditions of competition between firms that are conducted under large fixed costs. Standard paradigms for modeling this competition are inadequate since they postulate a market price in the sense that buyers can buy at their pleasure at a fixed price. The role of information requires a new approach to the theory of oligopoly.

1. Introduction

This paper is a very preliminary attempt at outlining the interrelationship between two of the basic concepts of economic analysis, the role of information in production and the organization of industry, particularly the organization into firms and the competitive behavior of these firms. The paper builds on an earlier study in this area (1994); I intend to develop these ideas, both theoretically and empirically, in research over the next two years.

The information I will concentrate on is *technical information*, that is the knowledge needed to produce goods. More precisely, it defines the probability distribution of inputs, outputs and product quality. Changing information can take the forms of improved processes or new products (including new qualities of existing products). There are, of course, other kinds of information relevant to the economy, especially marketing information, i.e. information about demand conditions. Much of this can be treated analogously to technical information; some cannot.

Information is an economic good, in the sense that it is costly and valuable; but it has many characteristics which differentiate it from the goods usually modeled in economics, e.g. in competitive equilibrium theory or in its modifications to take account of imperfect competition and monopoly. It is also true that technical information is in ordinary economic analysis a defining characteristic of a firm. Neither of these concepts is novel, but the treatment of neither is fully satisfactory, and their interrelations need much more exploration. In particular, it is surprising to find how poorly current theories apply to the situation of high fixed costs which arises when information acquisition becomes a major part of a firm's activity.

2. *Characteristics of Information as an* Economic Commodity

Economic analysis in the last 30 years has been devoted in good measure to the analysis of the strategic implications of asymmetric information among economic agents. Asymmetric information arises because one party cannot obtain freely (or at all) information available to another. This work has been of the greatest importance. It has explained the existence of many institutions which find no place in standard theory. In particular, the interactions among economic agents take many forms of which the market is only one. Especially important in this context is the study of the internal organization of the firm and the substitution between inter-firm and intra-firm transactions, a study brought to the attention of economists by Ronald Coase (1937) and given rich content and explanatory power by Oliver Williamson (1985) in his classic work.

The literature, especially the formal literature, in this field has largely traced the effects of a given information structure. An agent, for example, is assumed to observe a random variable, while the principal knows only the distribution of that variable. Not enough weight has been given to the possibility that information can be and is daily altered by economic decisions. A firm can buy information in one way or another or it can expend resources in research and development to wrest the information from nature. It is the treatment of information as a variable and its implications for economic behavior that needs further analysis. The current literature on asymmetric information certainly stresses the scarcity of information and this insight must be maintained.

The study of information as a choice variable has been given much more weight by disciplines other than economics, especially mathematical statistics, communications engineering and decision theory. The studies have tended to emphasize particular cases, for, indeed, information tends to become amorphous in the general case. To take the most elementary point, there is no *general* way of defining units for information. What is true in the statistical and communications perspectives is that information is a *signal*, that is, an observed random variable, which may be of no economic interest itself but which is not independent of unobserved variables which affect benefits or costs. This definition does not easily lend itself to measurement in general. In some specific models, particular measures seem to play a leading role. The well-known Shannon measure of information emerges in several models, sometimes as a cost measure, sometimes as a benefit measure. An alternative approach starts with Bayesian normal sampling; it tends to use as its preferred measure of information the *precision* of a distribution, defined as the reciprocal of the variance. These approaches are actually useful, but only on very limited problems. Nevertheless, they give some purchase on the analysis of information as a choice variable.

Economic theory has been less forthcoming in this respect. Mainstream economics from Ricardo through Arrow and Debreu has made virtually no explicit reference to information. There are some important exceptions, and they point to the significant relation between information and increasing returns to scale. Adam Smith had several arguments for the superior efficiency obtained by division of labor; some of them refer to the acquisition of skills, a form of information, by dint of practice. Similarly, Alfred Marshall also alludes to the acquisition and transmission of information as among the causes of a downward-sloping industry supply function.

The reason for this wariness has to do, I would conjecture, with the analytic difficulties which would follow introducing information as an economic variable. Competitive equilibrium is still the central paradigm of economics, and it is viable only if production possibilities are convex sets, that is, do not display increasing returns. This point was first made by A.A. Cournot in 1838. No one read Cournot for many years, but a brief passage shows that John Stuart Mill gave the same argument 10 years later. Marshall sought to reconcile competition with increasing returns, whether due to information or to other causes, by introducing the even more striking doctrine of externalities. Important and even basic as this notion is, it does not in fact adequately resolve the difficulty.

Let us turn more specifically to the special properties of information, including among others those that give to increasing returns. Increasing returns can occur for other reasons than information. But with information, constant returns are impossible. Two tons of steel can be used as an input to produce more than one ton of steel in a given productive activity. But repeating a given piece of information adds nothing. On the other hand, the same piece of information can be used over and over again, by the same or a different producer. This means both that the way information enters the production function is different than the way other goods do and that property rights to information take on a different form. These remarks are obvious enough, but their implications are not.

To elaborate the point, the usual logic of the price system depends on constant returns. For conventional inputs, the buyer can buy more or less at a given price (or at least close to it if there are elements of monopoly). But information is different. Technical information needed for production is used once and for all. The same information is used regardless of the scale of production. Hence, there is an extreme form of increasing returns.

Much of the recent literature on imperfect competition assumes a fixed cost of production with constant marginal costs. The fixed cost can be identified with the cost of technical information. This can be modeled by assuming that technical information is an on-off variable; either the firm acquires it (at some cost) or it does not. In the latter case, the firm does not produce. But the models derived from statistical or communications theory make information a variable with many values, in the limit a continuous variable. It is in fact usually true that there is better or worse information and that better information can be acquired at a higher price. 'Better' here may have several different connotations: more reliable information, production of a given product at lower cost, or ability to produce a higher-quality product. This generalization is very important in applications. It does not, however, contradict the general proposition that the need for information in production leads to increasing returns.

As already indicated, there is a second implication to the ability to use information without destroying it for further use. Once obtained, it can be used by others, even though the original owner still possesses it. It is this fact which makes it difficult to make information into property. It is usually much cheaper (not usually, however, free) to reproduce information than to produce it. The argument lends into the general area of intellectual property rights. Two social innovations, patents and copyrights, are designed to create artificial scarcities where none exists naturally, in order to create incentives for the acquisition of information. They have well-known problems in creating inefficiencies.

Further, they offer only a partial protection. There are many paths by which knowledge is diffused. (i) The interfirm mobility of technical personnel is one. To what extent is knowledge acquired by an individual employee in the course of development at one firm the property of that firm and to what extent is it the property of the employee? This question points up the fact that knowledge to a large extent is inherent in individuals. (ii) The appearance of a product on the market automatically conveys information; if nothing else, the information that the product can be produced. The existence of the product is a signal that the product can be produced. The probability of success in a development is, after all, the product of the probability that success is possible by the conditional probability that the firm will achieve success given that it is possible. If the first probability becomes 1, then the expected return from the development project must rise. (iii) There is, of course, the diffusion that academics are most accustomed to, that through written materials. The motives for written dissemination include royalties, pride and scientific reproduction. (iv) Finally, but very importantly, there is diffusion by informal interpersonal contacts. Indeed, the usual explanation for economies of spatial agglomeration in high technology industries is precisely this factor, since informal contact even in the era of modern communication is facilitated by propinquity.

The ability of information to move cheaply among individuals and firms has analogues with one class of property, so-called *fugitive resources*. Flowing water and underground liquid resources (oil or water) cannot easily be made into property. How does one identify ownership, short of labeling each molecule? With the development of environmental concerns, we recognize that air too is a fugitive resource. It is for this reason that water has always been recognized as creating a special property problem and has been governed by special laws and judicial decisions.

3. *Modeling Information in Firms*

Despite the central role of the firm in both law and economic theory, there is a vagueness about its definition which reflects a fundamental ambiguity. Legally, incorporated firms are defined by the legal control and residual claims of its owners, ordinarily identified with stockholders. But in a world in which information is important, there is a question of what the owners have claims to. In any case, as has long been understood, the management in large limited liability public companies is only weakly responsive to the stockholders. In fact, the management is more nearly the firm than the stockholders, typically investors who trade their holdings with considerable frequency and have no close relation to the firm. Management itself is by no means a simple concept.

In economic theory, the firm is thought to be a locus of information, as embodied in a production possibility set. But where is this information located and in what sense is it characteristic of the firm itself, as opposed to its managers and other employees? No doubt some of the technical information is embodied in written material and a database which might be regarded as owned by the firm like other property (although the low cost of reproduction makes this analogy less than compelling). But much of the most important information is embodied in individuals, not in reproducible form. A specific item of software may be embodied in a program; but the capability of creating similar kinds of software, far more valuable, is embodied in individual minds. Much of the information that is most important is *tacit*, to use the common phrase. Some scholars, such as Hayek, have perhaps exaggerated the role of tacit as opposed to explicit information, but it is nevertheless of great importance. Tacit information can still be transmitted, but that is done by direct personal contacts. New workers learn partly from older workers, as young scholars from professors, and perhaps partly from sources outside the firm.

A firm then has an *information base* but it is typically *distributed*; not everyone in the firm has every piece, and transmission, even within the firm, is costly. As a result, we expect to see specialization of function to economize on the transmission of information.

The distributed nature of information within the firm and the definition of the firm by its information lead to some difficulties in the neoclassical theory of the firm. In the latter, workers are not part of the firm; they are inputs purchased on the market, like raw materials or capital goods. But in fact they carry at least part of the information base which defines the firm, even though they are not permanently attached to it. What then is the knowledge that defines the firm?

It appears that the resolution of the issue has to do with the typical durability of the worker's relation with the firm. Mobility is not zero; indeed, to explain the diffusion of technical knowledge, an essential aspect of economic growth, it cannot be. However, mobility is also not infinitely rapid. The *expected* decay of the firm's information base and the expected gain to other firms due to mobility is moderate.

As a result, the information base of the firm is an asset, perhaps wasting but at a finite rate. The firm, therefore, has a value as a *going concern* which may considerably exceed the value of the firm's physical assets. The information base embedded in workers, managers and technical personnel is an important part of the market's valuation of a firm, though not property in the usual sense.

The extreme case of this phenomenon is the valuation of computer software firms, some of which are worth more than large industrial corporations. Their physical assets are trivial and so is their marginal cost of production. Their expenditures are for acquisition of information, but this information is held essentially in the minds of their employees. Why do not the forces of competition draw away some of these employees and thereby erode profits?

To the extent that the value of information to the firm is explained to some extent by limited mobility, it must itself be explained. One answer is Becket's concept of *firm-specific human capital*, but this is itself a concept in need of a rationalization. Its very existence is a critique of standard value theory.

There is still another question raised by the distributed information base of a firm: the need for internal coordination. Specialization leads to this need in any case, but the matter is made more acute and more difficult to analyze when there are differences of information within the firm. Consider, for example, the choice of research and development projects. Since they require resources, there is a need for choice at some central level, but the level of financial control is apt to be less well-informed than the research and development level.

The problem of finance of new ventures also, of course, arises across firms. A start-up firm requires venture capital; how are the capital-providers going to be informed enough to make good choices? A whole industry has developed devoted to gathering the relevant information and transmitting it in some form to potential investors. No good study on the information flows implicit in venture capital seems to exist currently. The comparison of information flows between internal and external financing remains to be undertaken.

4. *Implications and Applications of Information Considerations*

Let me conclude with some conjectures about the future of industrial structure. Information overlaps from one firm to another, yet the firm has so far seemed sharply defined in terms of legal ownership. I would forecast an increasing tension between legal relations and fundamental economic determinants. Information is the basis of production, production is carried on in discrete legal entities, and yet information is a fugitive resource, with limited property rights. Small symptoms of these tensions are already appearing the legal and economic spheres. There is continual difficulty in defining intellectual property; the US Courts and Congress have come up with some strange definitions. Copyright law has been extended to software, although the analogy with books is hardly compelling. There are emerging problems with mobility of technical personnel; employers are trying to put obstacles in the way of future employment which would in any way use skills and knowledge acquired in their employ. These are still minor matters, but I would surmise that we are just beginning to face the contradictions between the systems of private property and of information acquisition and dissemination.

There are also unresolved problems in the economic theory of pricing and competition. In an economy in which information is important for both cost and utility, competition between firms is conducted under large fixed costs. The two standard paradigms, due to Cournot and Bertrand respectively, are both inadequate to model this competition. In the simplest form of these paradigms, both postulate a market price, in the sense that any buyer can buy as much as he or she pleases at a fixed price. With fixed costs, it is reasonable to expect more complicated pricing schemes, for example, two-part prices or prices depending on how much is purchased. More generally, one might expect the firm to announce a price to a buyer for each amount purchased. There has been very little research on this question. Sanford Grossman [1981] has shown that, under very strong assumptions, the outcome would be the same as under perfect competition. This solution is not, however, even feasible if there are large fixed costs. The role of information would seem to require a new approach to the theory of oligopoly.

References

Arrow, K. J. (1994), 'Information and the Organization of Industry,' *Rivista internazionale di scienze sociali*, 102, 111–116.

Coase, R. H. (1937), 'The Nature of the Firm,' *Economica* N.S., 4, 386–405.

Grossman, S. (1981), 'Nash Equilibrium and the Industrial Organization of Markets with Large Fixed Costs, *Econometrica*, 49, 1149–1172.

Williamson, O.E. (1975). *Markets and Hierarchies: Analysis and Antitrust Implications*. The Free Press: New York.

CHAPTER NINE

Financing of Investment in Eastern Europe
A Theoretical Perspective

BENGT HOLMSTRÖM

Eastern Europe suffers from a worsening capital shortage problem. This paper studies ways to find the needed funds. It is argued that firms need funds in order to transform illiquid ideas into liquid claims, possibly through a chain of intermediaries. It shows that collateral (proven assets) plays the central role in increasing liquidity of liabilities and determining the firm's capacity to fund investments. A model is offered to illustrate how firm growth is limited by the net worth of its marketable assets. The analysis is extended to specialized assets for which the liquidation value is less than the ongoing value. The important second variation of intermediation is also examined. A key feature of the intermediation model is that intermediaries themselves are constrained by their net worth. Some lessons are then drawn regarding the status and future of financing in Eastern Europe. The intermediation model suggests that granted the scarcity of capital, financing of investments will have to be more information-intensive: intermediaries will have to take a more active role in monitoring firms. Capital formation is likely to be a slow process, since the capital base is so small. Private investments will be geared towards smaller, safer and shorter-term projects. The logic of liquidity-constrained growth argues for letting small firms carry the brunt of the responsibility for future prosperity in Eastern Europe.

1. Introduction

In the aftermath of liberalization, Eastern Europe has suffered from a worsening capital shortage problem. The capital stock from the Communist era is outmoded and much of it is obsolete. One can expect unemployment to worsen as the process of privatization progresses and the capital base deteriorates further through shutdowns of plants and enterprises. To alleviate unemployment and set the economies back on a growth path, major investments in new technologies and capacity are required. The key question is

where to find the needed funds. Some funds will be provided through Western subsidies, but for sustained growth, new private sources need to be
mobilized. How will that be accomplished? And what can and should be
done to speed up the process?

The potential for growth is evident. Unlike most developing economies that
suffer from a capital shortage, Eastern Europe has a relatively well-educated
labor force with substantial skills. In addition, most of the countries are
close to the central markets in Europe. This should make Eastern Europe
attractive to Western investors. Yet the pace of investment has remained
sluggish. One reason is the remaining uncertainty about the political future
of Eastern Europe as well as the details of taxation and the general legal
framework in which business can be conducted in these countries. Another
reason is the current European recession, brought on by a stifling monetary
policy that has driven real interest rates up and squeezed credit markets
severely. A third reason, and the one that is the focus of this paper, is the
primitive state of the capital markets in the East. Investment funds are
short, because the institutions needed to channel funds from investors to
firms are missing or function badly. If investment efforts are to be successful,
proper credit mechanisms have to be developed.

This funding problem will be examined at a conceptual level, drawing on
recent theoretical work in corporate finance. It should be noted at the outset
that corporate finance is still in a primitive state. In developed economies,
the task of allocating capital and coordinating real investments is shared
between a large variety of institutions: firms, banks, financing companies,
venture capitalists, stock and bond markets, and many less formal arrangements. It is a complicated network of intermediaries, a network we do not
yet understand well. The various institutions compete with each other in
some respects, and complement each other in other respects. How effective
the overall results have been is hard to gauge. It is notable that countries
with very different institutional choices seem to have been equally successful. The USA and the UK have relied more heavily on external market
finance than have most other economies, including Germany and Japan.
Some would argue that this explains differences in growth, but I think this
is a premature conclusion. The record seems surprisingly similar. That, of
course, does not mean that the choice of financial institutions is a matter of
indifference, but merely that there appear to be several internally consistent
solutions to the problem of allocating funds.

Despite the fact that our current understanding is so limited, it is timely
to discuss the emerging theoretical approach to corporate finance. First, the
theory has advanced far enough to offer a conceptual framework for thinking
about investment problems in a new, more realistic way. Understanding the

underlying reasons why financing is needed, and the contractual problems that must be overcome, helps us to focus on the right set of issues. My experience is that practitioners have found the paradigm useful for interpreting current Western financing schemes, and my hope is that those who have to grapple with the design of financial institutions in Eastern Europe will find the approach similarly illuminating.

The second reason for discussing the new theory somewhat prematurely is that the old theory is so misleading. Finance textbooks commonly give the impression that, since security markets are efficient, these markets automatically solve the problem of allocating funds among competing real investment proposals. Therefore, funding shortages in Eastern Europe should be dealt with by creating well-functioning stock and bond markets. In fact, 'efficient markets' has a particularly narrow meaning in the finance literature. In layman terms it simply says that prices will adjust so speedily to information that only a fair return can be earned on investments into special information. What this has to do with real investment is less clear. The fact that relative prices of existing assets are constantly adjusted to eliminate arbitrage opportunities, provides us with information about the return opportunities and risk preferences in the stock market, but not about the return opportunities and risks in funding real investments. When a person buys a share of IBM, that money does not go to IBM, but to the seller of the share. At the margin, such a trade does not affect any IBM decisions. Taking 'market efficiency' to mean that the funding of real investments is dealt with effectively through asset markets, is one of the great misconceptions of finance. This does not mean that asset markets are unimportant for investment, but the true link between asset markets and real investment remains to be spelled out in a satisfactory way.

At the recent IPR meetings in Prague, it was evident that the representatives of Eastern Europe believed that establishing liquid stock markets is one of the first steps in the direction of improving access to capital. It is sobering to consider Western evidence on this matter. Colin Mayer (1988) has recently studied the financing of real investments empirically, and the results are quite surprising. Looking at the data on flow of funds into and out of the non-financial sectors of various economies, including the USA, the UK, Germany and some other European nations, he finds that approximately 70% of new investment into physical capital is financed by retained earnings, approximately 25% is provided by bank loans and the rest by trade credits, equity issues and bonds issues. In other words, less than 5% of financing comes from asset markets. These calculations apply equally to the Anglo-American economies as to the more bank oriented European economies. The findings sound paradoxical, since it is well known that firms in the USA and the UK have relied more extensively on stock and bond issues than have firms in, for example, Germany or Scandinavia, in which stock and bond markets are less developed. The paradox is resolved by noting that the quoted figures refer to aggregates across all firms over a fifteen year period. If subsets of firms are looked at, for instance small and large ones, there are differences across countries, and the patterns vary over time in any given country. Nevertheless, Mayer's findings are useful in getting into the right frame of mind: an emphasis on stock and bond markets can be misguided, particularly at the early stages of development.

The third reason for theorizing at this early stage is that the only alternative would seem to be imitation. But which financial system is the best one to copy? And how relevant is it in the current situation? It should be keenly remembered that the advanced financing networks that we observe in developed economies have evolved over a long period of time to suit changing needs and to match new opportunities. It may be more appropriate to seek blueprints from historical records than to try to adopt institutions that are not yet ripe for a less developed economy. For instance, in the early days of banking in the Northeastern USA, the investment practices were diametrically opposite to what they are today. The owners of the banks invested the bulk of their funds into their own industrial projects, something that would be considered corrupt today. Yet this history played itself out in a different context, without the benefits of modern information technologies, or the potential support of highly advanced capital markets in neighboring nations. Again, it is hard to draw lessons that are readily applicable to the situation in Eastern Europe. Having a paradigm for thinking about the reasons why institutions developed the way they did, and what the problems were that they tried to solve, ought to be useful for assessing their relevance in today's situation.

The paper proceeds as follows. It begins by asking why firms need funds for investment. This seemingly naive question leads most expediently to the heart of the matter: the need for liquid funds, because of informational problems in evaluating and monitoring projects. Liquid funds are assets about which there is symmetric information. The fundamental problem of real investment, is to match those with money (liquid funds) but no information (ideas), to those with information but no money. All solutions involve transforming illiquid ideas into liquid claims, possibly through a chain of intermediaries. Intermediaries, and this includes firms, bridge the gap by offering liabilities that are more liquid than their assets. Collateral (proven assets) plays the central role in increasing the liquidity of liabilities and in determining the firm's capacity to fund investments. This general perspective is laid out and discussed in Section 2.

Section 3 offers the simplest possible model in which the central role of collateral can be studied (following Hoshi *et al.* (1992)). It illustrates how firm growth is limited by the net worth of its marketable assets. Section 4 extends the analysis to specialized assets for which the liquidation value is less than the on-going value. Section 5 looks at an important second variation, that of intermediation. It shows that firms for which the information gap is large will rely on intermediation, while firms which can bridge the information gap through marketable collateral can do without. The analysis shows why firms may want to use several different sources of funds to minimize the cost of financing and how the mix may change over time from more information intensive financing (intermediation) in the early stages to less information intensive financing (secured debt) at a more mature stage. A key feature of the intermediation model is that intermediaries themselves are constrained by their net worth.

The final section concludes the paper by drawing some lessons from the analysis regarding the status and future of financing in Eastern Europe, albeit that these lessons are illustrative and general. To give specific policy advice would require a much more detailed knowledge of the Eastern European situation. Indeed, the objective is not to influence policy directly but indirectly, through a framework that is believed to be useful for those involved in implementing policy.

2. *Why do Firms Need Financing?*

Modern asset pricing theories are all descendants of the famous Modigliani-Miller propositions. These propositions introduced the powerful logic of arbitrage. When the logic of arbitrage is combined with the assumption that markets are complete, the result is a very elegant theory of the relative prices of assets. There exists a pricing operator for the underlying state-contingent claims and every asset price can be expressed as a suitably weighted average of these primitive claims.

The theory has straightforward implications for investment. It says that at any given moment in time all projects with positive net present value should be undertaken. The identity of the firm that is considering a project makes no difference, only the cash flow matters. Whether the firm is just starting up or already is a large conglomerate or has little debt or much debt, none of these things should influence the decision. Nor does it matter whether the firm has money to finance the project. If it does not it will readily find investors in the capital market willing to provide the needed cash. It does not matter how the cash is raised: equity or debt will do equally well, since how the proceeds from the project are sliced up between investors will not influence the cost of capital. Finally, the identity of the lender is of no relevance. A bank, an insurance company, a finance firm or an individual investor, all will do equally well.

In this 'it doesn't matter' world—or more appropriately, 'only cash flow matters' world—firms are viewed as portfolios of projects with total firm value equalling the sum of its individual parts, each independently priced by the logic of arbitrage. This theory is helpful in understanding the pricing of securities (or mutual funds) in the secondary markets. It is not very helpful for understanding the constraints facing those who have to finance real investment projects.

Perhaps the most striking way of expressing the shortcoming of the standard theory for corporate finance is by asking the simple question: Why do firms need financing? In the world of standard theory the answer is that they do not. The very logic that underlies the Modigliani-Miller proposition about the indifference between equity and debt financing, also implies that firms should not have to ask for money in the first place. They could equally well pay all the needed inputs with claims on the future returns of the project, thereby making the input suppliers the financiers.

To understand funding needs and the distinguishing features of corporate finance compared with asset pricing, it is illuminating to ask why, in practice, firms seek financing for their investments when they do not have money of their own. The answer seems straightforward. Suppose a worker is needed to build a new plant. If the worker were offered a share in the future returns of the plant, it would most likely be the case that the worker could not tell how much such a claim was worth. The resulting adverse selection problem would cause the share of a positive net present value project to be priced at a discount. On many projects no agreement would be reached, because the worker would demand an excessive share. But even in the unlikely case that the worker did know the value of the share and a fair price could be found, the worker, unless he had money of his own, would face a similar adverse selection problem when he tried to pay for his consumption. The grocer would not know how to value a claim on the future returns of an unknown company. Or if she did, what about the next party from whom the grocer bought her inputs?

The problem is evident. The difficulty in valuing the firm's claim makes it an unacceptable means of payment; the claim is illiquid.[1] What the worker wants is a claim that is highly liquid so that he can pay his consumption needs with it. The asset that is most liquid is money. The reason

---

[1] Banerjee and Maskin (1991) use this line of reasoning to develop a formal model of money. The interpretation of illiquidity as an adverse selection problem, is particularly clearly articulated in S. Williamson (1988), who also offers an analysis of intermediation based on this view.

it is the most liquid asset is that it is also the asset about which different individuals in the economy hold the most symmetric information. When the firm offers the worker money, the worker need not worry that the firm is trying to peddle him some asset, which the firm knows is less valuable than the worker thinks. The reason information about money is so symmetric is that it represents a claim on a large portfolio of future assets about which it is unlikely that the firm has private information. Even if it has private information on pieces of the full portfolio, the pieces are so small as to make the potential adverse selection problem trivial.

This logical sequence has been mentioned, not because it holds any surprises, but because it shows how the question, 'Why do firms need financing', directly leads to the heart of the problem, that of asymmetric information. In the traditional theory all assets are fully liquid because there is no asymmetric information (markets are complete). Only if the firm's investments forces it to hold assets that are less than fully liquid, that is, assets about which there is private information, will there be a need for financing.

In the parable above, illiquidity is caused by adverse selection: the worker's inability to evaluate the project. Moral hazard is an alternative reason for illiquidity: the worker may fear that if he were to wait for payment until the project is completed, the firm could take a part of his share or squander it in some other way. The worker would have to spend time monitoring the firm's activities, but rarely knowing whether the actions taken by management represent legitimate or illegitimate decisions, he could be deceived. It is the implications of this line of reasoning that will be modeled. As we will see, moral hazard causes illiquidity, in the sense that some projects with positive net present will not be possible to finance.[2]

3. *The Role of Net Worth*

The purpose of this section is to introduce the simplest model in which the liquidation value of a firm's assets, the firm's current net worth, restricts the amount of investment it can undertake.[3] It is a two-period moral hazard model featuring a risk neutral firm (entrepreneur) and a risk neutral investor.

In the initial period, indexed $t = 0$, there is an opportunity to invest. The investment costs I dollars. The gross payoff from the investment one period later ($t = 1$) is either R (a success) or 0 (a failure). The probability of success depends on an unobserved action taken by the firm. This action can be given

---

[2] Search costs provide a third reason for illiquidity. A model of money based on costly search has been developed recently by Kyotaki and Wright (1990).

[3] The model is taken from Hoshi *et al.* (1992). The seminal paper on credit rationing is Stiglitz and Weiss (1981).

many interpretations. Here, it is interpreted as the firm's choice on how to spend the investment funds I. For simplicity, assume that the money can be spent in one of two ways. It can be spent on an efficient technology H, which consumes all the funds I, or it can be spent on an inefficient technology L, which costs $I-B$ and leaves B dollars for the firm to use for its own consumption. The probability of success is p_H if H is chosen and p_L if L is chosen. Naturally, $p_H > p_L$. The following diagram describes the two return options from investing:

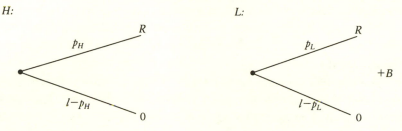

I will assume that the expected return on the investment is negative if the low action is taken and positive if the high action is taken:

$$p_H R - I > 0 > p_L R - I + B. \qquad (1)$$

Thus, it is better not to invest at all, than to invest and have the firm choose the inefficient technology.

The firm currently has assets worth A dollars. It is assumed that this also is the amount of cash that can be obtained if the assets are liquidated in the second period. Some of these assets could be cash, but as we will see shortly, this makes no difference in the basic model, so as a convention, it is assumed that all of A is tied up in fixed assets that are needed for production. The value A thus represents the maximum liability of the firm, that is, the maximum the firm can be forced to pay under liquidation, because the investment I is assumed to have no salvage value. This is inconsequential, since in this simple model a non-contingent salvage value would just reduce the effective investment cost, dollar for dollar.

Because the firm has no cash, it can invest only if it can obtain I dollars from the outside investor. It is assumed the investor can observe whether the investment is a success or a failure. With the liquidation proceeds added to the investment return, the total cash value of the firm is $R+A$ if the investment succeeds and A if it fails. A contract δ divides these proceeds between the investor and the firm in any feasible way, $\delta = \{y_s, y_f\}$, where y_i is the amount of cash that the investor is paid back in state $i = s, f$. Feasibility requires that the payment to the investor does not exceed the cash value of the firm in either state:

$$y_s \leq R+A, y_f \leq A. \tag{2}$$

This limited liability constraint is the source of the firm's liquidity problem. For convenience, assume the opportunity cost of the investor's funds is zero. Then the investor's expected payoff from the contract δ is:

$$E_i(y_s, y_f) = p_j y_s + (1-p_j)y_f - I,$$

where p_j is the probability of success (either p_H or p_L). Let $x_s = R+A-y_s$ denote the firm's residual claim when the investment succeeds, and $x_f = A-y_f$, its residual claim when the investment fails. The firm's payoff then is:

$$E_e(x_s, x_f) = p_j x_s + (1-p_j)x_f + B_j,$$

where $B_H = 0$ and $B_L = B$.

There are two decisions to be made: First, whether to undertake the investment at all and second, what contract δ to use if an investment is made. Since the investment return is negative if the firm does not choose the efficient technology, a necessary condition for investing is that the following incentive compatibility constraint be satisfied:

$$p_H x_s + (1-p_H)x_f \geq p_L x_s + (1-p_L)x_f + B.$$

This constraint can be rewritten in the simpler form

$$x_s - x_f \geq B/\Delta p, \tag{3}$$

where $\Delta p \equiv (p_H - p_L)$. To induce the firm to invest efficiently, the firm must be given a reward that at a minimum covers its opportunity cost of raising the probability of success.

If we can find a feasible contract, satisfying (2), such that the incentive constraint (3) is met, and the investor at least breaks even,

$$p_H y_s + (1-p_H)y_f \geq I, \tag{4}$$

then it is also optimal to undertake the investment. To see this, note that if there exists a contract δ satisfying (2)–(4)—call such a contract *viable*—then there also exists a viable contract δ' satisfying (4) as an equality; simply reduce y_s and y_f by a constant. Since the investor earns zero under δ', the firm receives the total surplus. According to (1), the total surplus is maximized by choosing H.

To see when there exists a viable financing contract, first note that we can restrict attention to contracts that set $x_f = 0$, the smallest feasible value by (2). Any viable contract δ with $x_f > 0$, can be replaced by a viable contract δ' with $x_f = 0$ by lowering the value of x_f and raising the value of x_s in a way that keeps the investor's, and hence the firm's payoff unaltered. Since this change relaxes the incentive constraint (3), δ' is viable.

Given the minimum payment $x_s = B/\Delta p$ that is necessary to keep the firm diligent, is there enough left over for the investor to recoup the investment cost I? Substituting $x_s = B/\Delta p$ and $x_f = 0$ into (4) and rearranging terms shows that this is the case if and only if:

$$A \geqslant \bar{A} \equiv I - p_H(R - B/\Delta p). \tag{5}$$

Condition (5) puts a lower bound $\bar{A}$ on the assets that the firm must have in order to be able to attract funds. Assumption (1) implies that the term in parenthesis is strictly positive and also that $p_H R - I > 0$. Consequently, $\bar{A}$ is always less than I; this is just another way of saying that the firm's assets are equivalent to cash. $\bar{A}$ can be negative, in which case the firm does not need any assets at all to invest. This happens when the minimum payment to keep the firm diligent, $B/\Delta p$, leaves enough of R to cover the full investment cost: $p_H(R - B/\Delta p) > I$. In what follows it will be assumed that this is not the case. Then all firms with $A < \bar{A}$ will be excluded from investing even though they could technologically undertake a project with positive net present value: in other words, these firms are capital constrained.

It is instructive to elaborate on the reason why firms are capital constrained. Rewrite (5) in the form:

$$p_H R - I \geqslant p_H B/\Delta p - A. \tag{5'}$$

The right hand side measures the rent a firm earns if it is paid the minimum viable amount $B/\Delta p$. A firm with $A < p_H B/\Delta p$, earns a strictly positive rent. This rent is taken out of the total surplus, the left hand side of (5'). We see then that the presence of a positive rent will push the hurdle rate for acceptable projects above the opportunity cost of funds. In other words, the net present value of the project, $p_H R - I$, must be strictly positive to cover the rent. The fact that projects with positive net present value get rejected is an allocational distortion, caused by the inability to transfer sufficient surplus from the firm to the investor. In this model, as in most other models with liquidity constraints, total surplus maximization does not define efficiency.

The comparative statics of (5) are straightforward. The cut-off value $\bar{A}$ decreases in p_H, R and I and increases in p_L and B. This simply says that the need for own capital decreases when the efficient H-project becomes more attractive or when the inferior L-project becomes less attractive. The transfer problem, and the consequent allocational distortion, is less severe, the larger is the value differential between the efficient and the inefficient project. Of course, an increase in I also raises $\bar{A}$, since the effective need for funding is $I - A$.

These comparative statics are simple, but useful. They suggest a remedy to the incentive problem that does not rely on financial rewards. Instead, the firm's opportunity cost from choosing the efficient project could be reduced, by making the inferior L-project less attractive. This idea is discussed again in section 5.

Related to this, suppose there are several positive net present value projects (H-projects) which the investor and the firm can jointly choose from (without being able to prevent the firm from choosing L, however). Which projects will be favored, when the incentive costs are taken into account? To look at this, consider a variation in p_H and R that leaves the expected return $p_H R$ unaltered. Specifically, assume p_H goes up and R goes down, that is, we are moving in the direction of safer projects. This decreases $p_H/\Delta p$. It follows from (5) that the minimum level of assets $\bar{A}$ needed to finance the project decreases, or alternatively from (5$'$), that the hurdle rate for accepting the project is reduced. Thus, firms that are capital constrained can be expected to move towards safer projects to get financing, even though the net present value of such projects are lower. The rent that accrues to the firm, $p_H B/\Delta p$, is lower for safer projects, leaving more surplus to be distributed to the investor. This is another manifestation of allocational distortions that arise when transfers are limited, that is, when there are liquidity constraints. It should be noted that this conclusion is distinct from the typical conclusion that a firm with debt will wish to take riskier projects. In this model, it is assumed that the choice between different H-projects is observed by the investor, or in an alternative interpretation, that the investor is choosing between firms of different riskiness.

The main results can be summarized.[4]

Proposition 1. In the model described above:

(i)   A firm for which $A < p_H B/\Delta p$ can only invest if the project has a strictly positive net present value.

(ii) The minimum level of assets required for an investment in a project with $p_H(R - B/\Delta p) < I$ is $\bar{A}$, defined in (5). Firms with $A < \bar{A}$ cannot get funds. $\bar{A}$ decreases in p_H and R and increases in p_L, B and L.

(iii) Capital constrained firms will at the margin invest in safer projects.

Assuming a single positive net present value project (p_H, R, I), the net value of the firm as a function of its own assets A is:

$$V_1(A) = \begin{cases} A & \text{, if } A < \bar{A}, \\ A + p_H R - I, & \text{if } A \geq \bar{A}. \end{cases}$$

There is a discontinuity in $V_1(\bar{A})$, at the minimum level of capital $\bar{A}$, which means that, at the margin, a dollar is worth more inside the firm than out-

---

[4] These results can be generalized to outcomes that are continuous. With a continuous outcome variable z, the optimal contract would look like debt: there would be an outcome level $\bar{z}$, such that the firm pays the investor $\min\{\bar{z}, z\}$; see Innes (1990). For alternative models of debt, see Gale and Hellwig (1985); Lacker (1992); Townsend (1979).

side. With variable investment the internal rate of return is always higher. To illustrate this, suppose that the project can be undertaken at any scale $I > 0$, with the return in case of success proportional to I: $R(I) = R \cdot I$. Also, assume that the funds that the firm can divert to its own use are proportional to I: $B(I) = B \cdot I$. Everything else, including p_H and p_L, is unchanged. In this case, the firm's assets determine the scale of investment. Solving (5) for I, gives the maximum investment level:

$$I(A) = A/\bar{A}(1), \qquad (6)$$

where $\bar{A}(1) = 1 - p_H(R - B/\Delta p)$, represents the level of assets needed for an investment of size $I = 1$ according to (5). Note that $\bar{A}(1) > 0$, because it is assumed that the firm earns a rent, that is, $p_H(R - B/\Delta p) < 1$. The value of the firm in the variable investment scenario is:

$$V_2(A) = ((p_H R - 1)/\bar{A}(1) + 1) \cdot A. \qquad (7)$$

By definition, we have $V_1(\bar{A}) = V_2(\bar{A})$. The two cases are compared in Figure 1.

From (7) we see that the value of each inside dollar exceeds the value of an outside dollar by the amount $p_H R/\bar{A}(1)$. If a dollar is transferred from the market to the firm, this dollar could be used to expand the firm by $1/\bar{A}(1)$ for an added net return of $(p_H R - 1)/\bar{A}(1) > 0$. In other words, the inside dollar is worth a dollar plus the value of the incentive effect. Consequently, the internal cost of capital is higher than the market cost of capital.

Does this mean that the social surplus could be increased by transferring funds from those with money but no projects to those with projects but no money? Total surplus would clearly increase. But the move would not be a Pareto improvement, since there would be no way to compensate those from which the dollar is taken; as noted earlier, this is not a model where Pareto optimality is characterized by total surplus maximization.[5] Put differently, there are no externalities in this model other than those between the investor and the firm, and these are fully internalized by the optimal investment arrangement identified above. The case for subsidizing investment by direct or indirect transfers of funds must rest either on interpersonal comparisons of utility, or on externalities across firms. To address this issue, the case of specialized assets will be looked at next. In addition, this case gets rid of an unattractive feature of the basic model, namely that the optimal contract is not unique. In the model above, the investor could be paid back in many different ways; having the firm receive nothing in case of failure was just the most convenient contract for calculating a minimum asset level.

[5] See Bernanke and Gertler (1990) for a discussion of government redistribution in a similar model with capital shortage. They use total surplus rather than Pareto optimality as a welfare criterion, but that is inappropriate. On the other hand, if one is merely interested in maximizing the rate of growth, then total surplus is the right criterion.

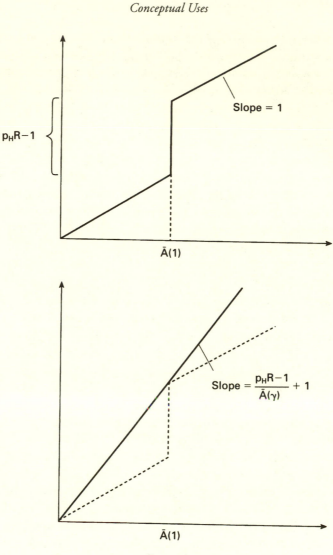

FIGURE 1.

4. *Specialized Assets*[6]

In the basic model firm assets were equivalent to cash; giving the investor a dollar or a dollar's worth of assets (liquidated) made no difference to the firm. In this section it is assumed that assets are specialized in the sense that the liquidation value of the assets is less than their value in continued use by the firm.

[6] A closely related liquidation analysis, based on Townsend's (1979) costly state verification model, can be found in Bolton and Scharfstein (1996). See also Lacker (1992).

Let L be the amount of assets liquidated, measured in the same units as A. Let $(A-L)$ be the firm's valuation of the remaining assets. That the internal value is linear in the amount of assets is merely a normalization; we can always measure assets along a scale that gives linearity. Let $f(L)$ be the market value of the liquidated assets, where f is an increasing function with $f(0) = 0$. Specialization then means that $f(L) < L$, an assumption that will be maintained.

It is convenient to include in the contract the cash to be transferred as well as the amount of assets to be liquidated in the second period as a function of the outcome.[7] Let l_j be the amount of assets, and r_j the amount of cash given to the investor in state $j = s$ or f. A contract is a four-tuple $\delta = \{l_s, l_f, r_s, r_f\}$. The investor's payoff in state j is $y_j = r_j + f(l_j)$. The firm's payoff is $x_j = z_j - r_j + (A - l_j)$, where $z_s = R$ and $z_f = 0$.

An efficient contract, assuming there is one involving investment, solves the following program:

Maximize $p_H x_s + (1 - p_H) x_f$

$$\text{subject to}$$

(IC) $\quad (p_H - p_L)(x_s - x_f) \geqslant B,$

(P) $\quad p_H y_s + (1 - p_H) y_f \geqslant I,$

(Dy) $\quad y_j = r_j + f(l_j), j = s, f$

(Dx) $\quad x_j = z_j - r_j + (A - l_j), j = s, f$

(LL) $\quad l_j \leqslant A, r_s \leqslant R, r_f \leqslant 0.$

The constraints are: incentive compatibility (IC), participation by the investor (P), definition of y_j (Dy), definition of x_j (Dx), and limited liability of the firm (LL).

The solution to the program is easy to see. First, note that there must be some liquidation, unless the maximum cash disbursement to the investor, $r_s = R - B/\Delta p$, is enough to cover the initial investment cost. As before, it will be assumed that this is not the case. Since assets are worth more within the firm than liquidated, it is clear that $l_j > 0$ implies $r_j = z_j$, that is, the firm is left with no cash if any assets have to be liquidated. Also, it cannot be the case that l_s and l_f are both strictly positive, since then the firm would be better off not investing; it gets no cash and loses assets. Finally, since $x_s > x_f$, we cannot have $l_s > 0$, and $l_f = 0$. This leaves as the remaining possibility that $l_s = 0$ and $l_f > 0$, implying that $r_s < R$ and $r_f = R$. This solution has the feature that the firm gets to retain all its assets and some cash, if there is a success, while failure leaves the firm with no cash and forces it to surrender some of its assets.

---

[7] This is not necessary. If the contract asked for more cash than the firm has, the balance would determine the amount of assets that the firm would have to liquidate.

Liquidation raises the amount that the investor can recover from the project both directly and indirectly. Directly, there is $f(l_f)$ more cash in state f that the investor gets. Indirectly, the cash that can be paid in the good state rises. The fact that liquidation lowers the payoff to the firm in the bad state, implies that the firm's payoff can be lowered also in the good state without violating incentive compatibility. From the (IC) constraint, we see that the maximum disbursement to the investor in the good state is $r_s = R - B/\Delta p + l_f$, which is l_f more than without liquidation. In total, the investor's expected payoff can be increased by $p_H l_f + (1-p_H)f(l_f)$. Since the total surplus decreases in l_f, it is optimal to minimize the amount of assets liquidated. The minimum necessary is obtained by satisfying (P) with an equality:

$$p_H(R - B\Delta p + l_f) + (1-p_H)f(l_f) = I. \tag{8}$$

If this cannot be done with $l_f \leq A$, then the project cannot be financed at all.

Proposition 2. Assume $p_H(R - B/\Delta p) < I$. Then the optimal contract is unique and has the following features:

(i)   There will be some liquidation in the bad state (f), but not in the good state (s). The amount to be liquidated, l_f, is given by (8).
(ii) The firm pays out all its cash in the bad state.
(iii) If the functions $f_1(L)$ and $f_2(L)$ describe two different degrees of asset specialization, and $f_1 < f_2$, implying that f_1 represents a higher degree of specialization, then $\bar{A}_1 > \bar{A}_2$: the minimum level of assets required for investment is larger for the more specialized assets.

Parts (i) and (ii) were argued earlier. Part (iii) is obvious from the optimization program. By inspection, if an investment is viable with more specialized assets it is also viable with the less specialized assets (see (8)).

Note that the optimal contract is unique as soon as there is any degree of asset specialization, unlike in Section 3. But with only two outcomes, the optimal contract cannot be associated with debt or equity (or any other common financial instrument), because it can be interpreted in either way. Yet, there is a sense in which specialization shifts the optimal contract in the direction of equity: as the degree of specialization increases, relatively more of the investor's payoff will come from cash in the good state than from liquidation proceeds in the bad state. This suggests that firms with few tangible assets are financed more by equity, which appears empirically true.[8]

---

[8] Williamson (1988) was the first to discuss the connection between asset characteristics and capital structure.

The reader is cautioned that the interpretation of equity versus debt is strained in that it does not take account of the fact that equity and debt holders are typically different investors. In my model there is a single investor and the investor's contract is interpreted as a combination of equity and debt. The next section provides a model in which there are two different groups of investors. For other models that rationalize mixed financing, see Dewatripont and Tirole (1994) and Gorton and Pennacchi (1990).

These observations have several simple, but important implications. First, if there is a choice of scale, as discussed earlier, then the scale will be smaller if assets are specialized, since the firm's liquidation cost is higher. Second, if there is a choice between projects that differ in the degree of specialization as well as return characteristics, then a firm with sufficiently low net worth will be forced to invest in less specialized projects that yield a lower total surplus. A lower total surplus is the price to be paid for the improved transferability of funds inherent in less specialized assets.

The third implication is that specialization entails an externality between firms. The value of the assets on the market, in case assets have to be liquidated, depends on the choices made by other firms, the potential buyers of the liquidated assets. If there are firms that can find ready use for the liquidated assets, then liquidation costs may be modest and the effective degree of specialization low. This is the important point made by Shleifer and Vishny (1992). As they observe, there could be multiple equilibria: one in which no firm specializes, because the market value of liquidated assets is expected to be low, and another in which several firms specialize, because they expect that liquidated assets will find a ready market. In each equilibrium, the expectations are self-fulfilling. This is easy to envision without a formal model. Two firms could be just short of capital, because the liquidation value of their assets is low. But were both to invest, then the market value of the assets would go up and both could afford the investment. This, of course, assumes that when one firm is forced to liquidate, the other firm is in a position to buy the liquidated assets; the outcomes of the firms cannot be perfectly correlated. Industries in which aggregate shocks play an important role will have more difficulties with financing than industries in which outcomes are idiosyncratic. That liquidation values depend on other firms' actions means that there is an externality. This raises the possibility that the government can do something to counteract it, a point which will be returned to in Section 6.

So far, it has been assumed that the internal value of assets is higher than their market value. This may seem like an eminently reasonable assumption, since at a minimum, it will cost something to transfer assets from one firm to another. But there remains the deeper question: if assets are worth more inside the firm, why not leave them there and give the investor a share in the future proceeds? Why liquidate at all? To show that liquidation in fact may be necessary, a multi-period extension will be studied.

Suppose that there are two periods of production instead of one. In each period the production returns either R or 0 dollars per unit of capital employed. The firm's private cost of being diligent is B per unit of capital employed. The initial investment brings the level of capital to A. After the first period outcome l_j units of capital are liquidated, where j indexes the first period outcome. For simplicity, assume that the market value of the liquidated assets is λ dollars per unit, so liquidation brings cash in the amount λl_j. The second period commences with $A_j = A - l_j$ units of capital, which return either $A_j R$ or 0, and cost the firm $A_j B$ to operate diligently. After the second period, capital is worthless (its useful life is exactly two periods).

The contract between the firm and the investor can specify cash payments contingent on the sequence of outcomes as well as the amount to be liquidated, if any. Because the contract is complete in this sense, the second period continuation must be Pareto optimal: the initial contract cannot be rewritten after the first period in a way that improves the welfare of both parties. Let u_j and v_j be the second period continuation utilities of the firm and the investor if the outcome in the first period is j. Let $u_j = F_j(v_j)$ characterize the Pareto frontier in state j, that is, $F_j(v_j)$ is the maximum payoff that can be assured the firm, if the investor is guaranteed v_j. The key step is to describe this frontier.

Let z_j be the outcome in the first period. The decisions before the second period are: how to split the outcome z_j, how much of the assets to liquidate and how to share the proceeds from the second period. As a convention, assume the liquidation proceeds are paid directly to the investor. Let m_j be the additional amount of cash that the firm pays the investor before the second period starts (this could be a negative number, i.e. a payment from the investor to the firm). Since the firm has limited liability, $m_j \leq z_j$. Let x_j be the firm's share per employed unit of asset in the second period and $y_j = R - x_j$ the investor's residual share. In order for the firm to choose H rather than L, it has to be given at least a share $x_j \geq B/\Delta p$, leaving at most the share $y_j = (R - B/\Delta p)$ for the investor. Let $k = p_H(R - B/\Delta p)$. Then the maximum expected return to the investor is kA_f. The continuation utilities are:

$$v_j = m_j + \lambda l_j + p_H y_s A_j \leq \lambda l_j + k(A - l_j),$$
$$u_j = -m_j + p_H x_s A_j \geq B p_H (A - l_j)/\Delta p.$$

Keeping m_j fixed, the firm prefers as little liquidation as possible, since $x_s > 0$. But if $\lambda > k$, the investor prefers to liquidate. Let me argue that this is a relevant case. Suppose $\lambda < k$ and therefore that the investor also prefers no liquidation. The maximum amount the investor can be paid back in this case is $2k$, which is provided by paying the investor the share $(R - B/\Delta p)$ of each successful outcome. If $k < \frac{1}{2}$, the investor cannot be paid back without liquidating assets. If in addition, $\lambda > \frac{1}{2}$, that is, more than half of the asset value can be recovered from liquidation, then the investor prefers liquidation in the second period. Hence the investor can be paid back more by liquidating some of the assets. If the gap between what the investor can be paid without liquidation, $2k$, and the cost of investment, I, is not too large, the investment can be carried out, but not without liquidating some assets. Since the total surplus of investing is positive, and the investor gets a zero expected return, the firm also benefits from investing if the liquidated amount is small enough (by continuity). The exact parameter restrictions for which investment, followed by liquidation, is optimal, are not particularly informative, so I record the discussion in the vague form:

Proposition 3. For some parameter values, the optimal investment contract will specify liquidation after the first period.[9]

This case can be interpreted as one in which the investor requires that the firm is scaled down in response to a reduction in the firm's net value, the sum of its fixed assets and cash. If the net value drops too low, the firm will have too little at stake to take the right action. Assets are liquidated to bring net worth in line with the firm's stake. This is a common response to a financial crisis. As part of restructuring, creditors typically require the firm to sell some of its assets to reduce its debt. In this model, complete contracts have been assumed, so the scaling back can be planned in advance and implemented through contingent contracting rather than through renegotiation, but the basic logic is the same.

It is worth noting that the most liquid assets will be sold first. Above, it is assumed that all assets are sold at the reduced rate λ, but it is obvious from the general logic, as well as from the one period model, that those assets that have the highest resale value will be the most efficient to give up first. In the parlance of the business strategy literature, the firm is required to focus in response to a financial crisis. Focus means that the firm concentrates on the activities it has a comparative advantage at. Giving up assets that have the smallest ratio of internal to external value has precisely this meaning: assets that others can employ as efficiently as the firm and, therefore, have the same external as internal value, are by definition ones that are not part of the firm's particular business knowledge.

Finally, it should be noted that the two period model that has been sketched can be used to look at investment choice, particularly with regard to the timing of investment returns. If there is any liquidation in the first period, then a dollar return in the first period is worth more than an expected dollar return in the second period. The dollar adds to the capital base of the firm in the first period and allows the firm to reduce the amount

---

[9] Note that the logic behind this proposition is different from that provided by Stiglitz and Weiss (1983). In their model termination of financing (which is similar to liquidation) after the first period is merely a first period incentive device. In my model liquidation also affects first period incentives, but more importantly, it is part of an optimal continuation contract.

of assets that get liquidated in case of a failure.[10] One dollar of cash buys back more than one dollar worth of assets, just as it did in the one period model. The conclusion is that capital constrained firms can be expected to engage in projects that are of a shorter duration, at the cost of lower expected returns. This allows them to build up their capital base.[11]

5. *Intermediation*[12]

Let us return to the basic one period model with a fixed level of investment and initial assets A. The notation below assumes that A is cash, with the interpretation that the firm is just starting up. Nothing would materially change if it were assumed that A was the liquidation value of assets in place and this extended interpretation will also be used. To produce, the firm needs to buy fixed assets that cost I. For simplicity, these fixed assets are assumed to be worth zero upon liquidation. It was concluded earlier that the firm needs to have cash in the amount $A > \bar{A}$ to be able to produce (see (5)). With less cash it cannot produce, since the maximum amount of outside capital that it can attract is $\bar{I}_u \equiv I - \bar{A} = p_H(R - B_L/\Delta p)$.

An important variation on this basic model introduces an intermediary who can monitor the firm and thereby reduce the required amount of capital that the firm needs. Monitoring is often thought to involve an evaluation of the expected return of a firm's project. This would require that firms differ either in the probabilities p_H and p_L or in the outcomes R and 0. A simpler, and not unrealistic modelling alternative, is to assume that monitoring reduces the firm's opportunity cost of being diligent. Accordingly, it is assumed that if a firm is monitored, the private benefit B will be reduced to a lower level. Let B_L be the private return of an unmonitored firm that chooses an inefficient project (formerly just B) and let $B_M < B_L$ be the private return of a monitored firm that chooses an inefficient project. One interpretation of this assumption is as follows. The firm has two inefficient projects that it can undertake, M and L, with the associated private benefits described above. In other respects the projects are identical to each other (they both return R with probability p_L and 0 otherwise). If both projects are available to the firm, then evidently the firm will choose L over M, since L has a higher private return and the same financial return. Thus, adding M to the earlier story changes nothing. Now enter monitoring. Monitoring eliminates the L option, but not the M option. We may think of the L option as a more blatant form of misconduct, which with sufficient monitoring can be

---

[10] This assumes that the investment returns something in the bad state as well as the good.

[11] A similar point is made by Thakor (1990).

[12] This section is based on joint work with Jean Tirole, extending the model in Hoshi *et al.* (1992).

detected and prevented. It could also be a covenant, the observance of which requires the intermediary's attention. Or it could literally be an investment that a person, representing the intermediary on the company's board, can veto. Whatever the interpretation, monitoring often involves this kind of enforcement of constraints that reduce the firm's opportunity cost of being diligent.[13]

The benefit of monitoring is that it lowers the share of R that needs to be paid to the firm to keep it from making the wrong project choice. Let B be a generic level of the private benefit. As before, it is optimal to pay the firm nothing in case the project fails. Therefore, the minimum payoff in case of success that the firm has to receive in order to be diligent (choose the H project) is:

$$\underline{R}_e(B) = B/\Delta p.$$

Since $B_M < B_H$, a firm that is monitored can be induced to choose H with a lower payment $\underline{R}_e(B_M) < \underline{R}_e(B_L)$. Consequently, there is a larger residual payoff, $R - \underline{R}_e(B_M)$, that can be offered to outside investors. This raises the amount of outside capital that can be brought in to finance the project. A firm that had too little own money to invest without monitoring ($A < \bar{A}$), may now be able to invest with monitoring.

Before jumping to this conclusion, however, we must consider the costs of monitoring. It will be assumed that it costs the intermediary a private amount c to exclude the L-project from the firm's portfolio. The firm can observe whether the monitor has eliminated the L-project; if it has not, the firm still has the option to choose L. It is further assumed that monitoring cannot be contracted for directly, that is, against a flat fee. Rather, the intermediary must be induced to monitor via a contract that is contingent on the project outcome. Just as in the case of the firm's incentive problem, the optimal way to solve the intermediary's incentive problem, is to pay it zero if the project fails and a positive amount R_m if the project succeeds. The minimum amount the intermediary must be paid in order to monitor is:

$$\underline{R}_m = c/\Delta p.$$

Note that $p_H \underline{R}_m - c > 0$, so the intermediary is earning a rent. This rent can be reduced by asking the intermediary to pay a fixed fee up front. It is natural to interpret this fixed fee as capital invested by the intermediary in return for the payment R_m. If I_m is the invested amount, then the intermediary's rate of return (gross of the private cost c) is $\beta = p_H R_m / I_m$. Since we must have $p_H R_m - c - I_m > 0$ in order for the intermediary to participate, it follows that

---

[13] Of course, restrictions on the firm's ability to invest will often be coarse and, therefore, exclude socially valuable activities as well.

$\beta > 1$. The rate of return β will be the variable that equilibrates the market for intermediary capital.

It is assumed that there are many intermediaries: an unspecified but sufficiently large number so that we can view the intermediary market as competitive. In the aggregate, the intermediaries have capital in the amount K_m. It is assumed that intermediaries have no constraints on the time they can spend monitoring. In principle, a single intermediary could monitor any number of firms. This is the sense in which the intermediary market is competitive. What limits the amount of intermediation in equilibrium is that intermediaries have to invest capital in the firms they monitor. In other words, expert or informed capital is scarce.

A firm that is monitored need not obtain all its capital from an intermediary. A key feature of the model is that firms can ask for additional capital from the uninformed, that is, those who do not monitor. As before, the uninformed are assumed to be satisfied with a unit rate of return on their capital. If R_u is the share of the payoff to the uninformed, they are willing to supply $I_u = p_H R_u$ of capital, leaving them with a zero expected profit.

A firm that is monitored must be paid at least $\underline{R}_e(B_L)$ and the intermediary must be paid at least $\underline{R}_m$, to get the firm to choose H. If the intermediary is paid less, it will not monitor and the firm will be able to choose L. Therefore, there is at most $R_u = R - \underline{R}_e(B_M) - \underline{R}_m$ left over to compensate the uninformed investors. It is assumed that $R_u > 0$, so that there is room for uninformed investors. The maximum amount of uninformed capital that a monitored firm can attract is $\underline{I}_u = p_H R_u = p_H(R - B_M/\Delta p - c/\Delta p)$. To make the problem interesting, it is assumed that $\underline{I}_u < I$, so that all investment cannot be financed with uninformed capital alone.

There is a continuum of firms with a total measure N. Firms differ only in the amount of assets A that they own. The distribution of assets across firms is represented by a cumulative distribution function G. Thus, $G(A)$ is the fraction of firms with assets less than A.

Suppose β is the going rate of return on intermediary funds. What will the demand for intermediary funds be? A firm that demands I_m units of informed capital, will have to offer the intermediary $R_m = \beta I_m/p_H$ if the project succeeds. Since the intermediary will not monitor unless $R_m \geq \underline{R}_m$, the minimum amount of informed capital that will be demanded (if any) is $I_m(\beta) = p_H \underline{R}_m/\beta$. It can be argued that this is also the maximum amount that any firm will demand. One way to see this is to recall that the cost of intermediary capital is $\beta > 1$, while the cost of uninformed capital is only 1. However, note that the amount of uninformed capital that the firm can obtain is limited to I_u, as defined above. Suppose this amount of capital together with the firm's own capital A and the minimum intermediary capital

$I_m(\beta)$ is insufficient to cover the cost of the investment I. That is, suppose $A < \underline{A}(\beta) \equiv I - \underline{L}_m(\beta) - \underline{L}_u$. Could the intermediary supply the missing amount by raising its investment above $\underline{L}_m(\beta)$? The answer is no and the reason is as follows. For every dollar more of informed capital that the firm obtains, it has to offer the intermediary β/p_H dollars more out of the return R. This reduces by the same amount the maximum that can be paid out to the uninformed investors. Hence, the uninformed are now willing to contribute $p_H \beta/p_H = \beta$ dollars less. The net effect is that the firm obtains one dollar from the informed, but loses β dollars from the uninformed.

Since $1 - \beta < 0$, the total amount the firm can obtain decreases rather than expands and so a firm that cannot be financed with a minimum of informed capital cannot be financed at all.

With these preliminaries it is easy to describe the demand for informed capital. The demand can be divided into three categories as a function of the level of firm assets A. First, there are those firms which have enough own assets, $A > \bar{A}$, that they can finance their investment with uninformed capital alone. Since informed capital costs more, they will not want any of it. Second, there are those firms which have so few own assets that they cannot finance the investment with any combination of uninformed or informed capital. These are the firms for which $A < \underline{A}(\beta)$, as discussed above. Note that for some values of β, $\underline{A}(\beta)$ could be negative, implying that this category is empty. However, if $NG(\bar{A})(I - \underline{L}_u) > K_m$, that is, if the total amount of funds needed to finance those firms that cannot invest without informed capital exceeds the available amount of informed capital, then $\underline{A}(\beta)$ must be positive in equilibrium. It is assumed this is the case. Finally, the third category of firms are those with assets A such that $\underline{A}(\beta) \leq A < \bar{A}$. These firms can invest by using a mixture of informed and uninformed capital. As described above, they will ask for the minimum amount $\underline{L}_m(\beta)$ needed to induce the intermediary to monitor.

From this discussion follows that the aggregate demand for informed capital is simply:

$$I_D(\beta) = N[G(\bar{A}) - G(\underline{A}(\beta))]\underline{L}_m(\beta). \tag{9}$$

This demand is decreasing in β, since $\underline{L}_m(\beta)$ is decreasing and therefore $\underline{A}(\beta)$ is increasing. The equilibrium value of β, call it β^*, is achieved when the demand for informed capital equals the supply: $I_D(\beta^*) = K_m$.

There are two loose ends that need to be tied up before considering this an equilibrium. The first is that β^* may be lower than the minimum return required to cover the intermediary's monitoring cost c. Given $\underline{R}_m$, the most the intermediary is willing to invest is $p_H R_m - c$, or else it is better off not participating. Therefore, the minimum value for β is $\underline{\beta} = p_H R_m/(p_H R_m - c)$, which implies $\underline{L}_m(\underline{\beta}) = p_L c/\Delta p$. The expression for $\underline{\beta}$ simplifies to $p_H/p_L > 1$ (curiously, if $c = 0$, then $\underline{\beta} = 1$). If $\beta^* < \underline{\beta}$, then the true equilibrium is $\underline{\beta}$ and the intermediaries will invest their excess funds in the general market (without monitoring). This case can be ruled out by assuming that $N[G(\bar{A}) - G(\underline{A}(p_H/p_L))]p_L c/\Delta p > K_m$, that is, at the minimum return $\underline{\beta}$, the demand for informed capital exceeds the supply.

The second loose end is that $\underline{A}(\underline{\beta})$ may be greater than $\bar{A}$, so that at the minimum acceptable return o the intermediary, the amount of funds it is willing to supply, $\underline{L}_m(\underline{\beta})$, is insufficient to make it possible for a firm with assets $A < \bar{A}$ to invest. In other words, $\bar{A} + \underline{L}_u + \underline{L}_m(\underline{\beta}) < I$, or using the definition of $\bar{A}$, $\bar{I}_u - \underline{L}_u > \underline{L}_m(\underline{\beta})$. The implication in this case is that monitoring is ineffective in furthering investment; firms with assets below $\bar{A}$ are unable to invest even with the help of informed capital and therefore no intermediation will take place. Since $\underline{L}_u = p_H(R - B_M/\Delta p - c/\Delta p)$ and $\bar{I}_u = p_H(R - B_L/\Delta p)$, we have $\bar{I}_u - \underline{L}_u = p_H(B_M - B_L - c)/\Delta p$. There is no basis for making an assumption about the sign of this expression. The existence of an equilibrium with intermediation requires that $p_H(B_M - B_L + c) < p_L c$, which is condition $\bar{I}_u - \underline{L}_u > \underline{L}_m(\underline{\beta})$ written in an alternative form. Note that since $B_M - B_L < 0$, this condition is always met for a small enough c. When the condition does not hold, intermediation is socially too expensive and will not be used.

The preceding discussion is recorded in:

Proposition 4. Suppose monitoring is valuable ($c < p_H(B_L - B_M)/\Delta p$) and the demand for informed capital exceeds the supply at the minimum rate of return $\underline{\beta} = p_H/p_L$; i.e. ($N[G(\bar{A}) - G(\underline{A}(p_H/p_L))]p_L c/\Delta p > K_m$). Then there exists an equilibrium, characterized by a rate of return $\beta^* > \underline{\beta}$ on informed capital and a level of intermediary investment $I^* = \underline{L}_m(\beta^*)$ such that:

(i)   If $A \geqslant \bar{A}$, the firm finances its investment with uninformed capital alone ($I_u = I - A$).

(ii) If $i - \underline{L}_u - I^* \leqslant A < \bar{A}$. the firm finances its investment with I^* of intermediary capital and I_u of uninformed capital.

(iii) If $A < I - \underline{L}_u - I^*$, the firm is unable to invest.

The main prediction is that firms with insufficient capital of their own will either not be able to invest or will have to resort to a more information intensive, and hence more expensive form of financing. This is a central, quite robust idea, that holds up well empirically.[14] Most of the financing of small firms and start-ups comes from private sources: own savings, family, friends, venture capitalists and so called 'angels' (individuals investing in small private enterprises that are unable to get sufficient financing from

[14] See Hoshi *et al.* (1992) for supporting evidence from Japan.

other sources). All these lenders typically have some private information either about the entrepreneur or the line of business he is in. Whether they monitor firms in the exact way assumed in the model is less relevant; the model could have been written so that monitoring involves knowledge about the investment alternatives rather than the ability to exclude some of them (tough venture capitalists certainly keep a tight rein on the firms that they finance).

Another key prediction is that financing may often come from several sources. As part (ii) shows, those firms that use informed capital will do so to the minimum extent possible, relying on the uninformed to supply the balance. In such a package deal, the uninformed come along only on condition that the informed take a large enough stake in the firm; the informed must invest their own capital to certify that the firm does not misuse the invested funds.[15] This arrangement is reminiscent of the deals commonly struck in financing low-grade investments, for instance, leveraged buy-outs. In leveraged buy-outs, informed capital is represented by a combination of equity, junior debt and convertible debt (so called mezzanine financing). The less informed capital is held by institutional investors mostly in the form of senior debt.

Of course, the model is abstract enough to give many alternative interpretations to mixed financing. For example, informed capital could represent bank loans and uninformed capital could be public debt. If one were seriously interested in understanding the use of specific kinds of capital— venture capital, bank loans, public debt, public equity, and so on—the model would have to be expanded substantially. Here, however, the main point is that different sources of finance, representing different levels of monitoring, will be used, and that the degree to which more information intensive (monitoring) capital is used, depends on the amount of own capital that the firm has.

To underscore this point consider briefly an extension in which the informed can monitor at different levels of intensity. In the present set-up there is monitoring only on one level; monitoring reduces the private benefit to B_M. Assume instead that monitoring can be varied so that the private benefit can be set to any level B at a cost $c(B)$.[16] Naturally, $c(B)$ is a decreasing function of B. In this set-up, the informed will provide capital in the

---

[15] Note that the uninformed investor is not interested in the amount of informed capital as such, but rather in the payoff that the informed receive (R_m), since it is this payoff that determines whether the informed actually wish to monitor. An investment is a sunk cost without direct incentive effects. So why would the uninformed investor look at the level of informed investment? Because the level of investment signals that the payoff to the informed (which may well be unobservable to the uninformed) is high enough to induce the informed to monitor.

[16] The example we have in mind is that the firm can abscond funds in varying degrees, measured by B. A given level of monitoring intensity assures that at most B can be absconded.

amount $I_m = p_H c(B)/\beta\Delta p$ and the uninformed will provide $I_u = p_H(R-(B+c(B))/\Delta p)$.[17] It is relatively easy to see that a firm with own capital A will choose to be monitored at the minimum level necessary to attract the balance of funds $I-A$ (some firms may still be unable to attract funds, because at high enough levels of B, the cost of financing becomes prohibitively expensive). This way they can minimize the use of informed capital, which costs more. The upshot is that better capitalized firms will choose less information intensive financing and intermediaries which engage in less intensive monitoring will hold a smaller stake in the firms they monitor.[18] Despite the fact that it is impossible in this abstract model to associate varying degrees of monitoring with different types of intermediation observed in the real world, this result points out an important logical association between a firm's net worth, the information intensity of its financing, and the intermediary's stake in the firm. Whatever the precise forms actual financing takes, this general principle is a useful guide.

While the model above is static, it is not imprudent to speculate on how a dynamic version would play itself out. Firms starting off with little wealth will initially have to depend on more informed capital and more intensive monitoring. As firms mature and accumulate wealth, they can be expected to switch to cheaper forms of financing.[19] Informed capital will exit as the financial condition of the firm improves. Thus, firm financing will have a life cycle in which over time and assuming success, firms shift from using more information intensive to less information intensive capital. This is consistent with the fact that established firms tend to rely more on public debt as well as self-financing. It also fits the typical pattern of venture capital deals, where after a fixed period of time the venture capitalist liquidates his position, usually through an initial public offering. A related phenomenon is observed in financial markets, where arbitrageurs hold their capital tied in investments only as long as they enjoy an informational advantage.[20] In all cases the intuition is the same, namely that expert capital should be used only where its monitoring value warrants the extra cost.

The logic of the static model indicates that in a dynamic extension, inter-

---

[17] The reader can check that even though monitoring intensity varies across firms, the return on informed capital is β, independent of the level of monitoring intensity.

[18] In the original model with just one level of monitoring, firms with assets above $\underline{A}(\beta)$ but below $\bar{A}$, were all forced to take on the same minimum level of informed capital $\underline{I}(\beta)$. Here the level of informed capital varies inversely with the firm's asses.

[19] Diamond (1991) describes a dynamic model in which firms switch from bank lending to bond issues as they acquire a higher reputation. Reputation, of course, is a form of capital, so the idea is very similar.

[20] See Shleifer and Vishny (1990) for a related explanation of the short horizon of arbitrageurs. They do not explain why arbitrageurs have limited capital, a necessary ingredient in explaining their desire to exit.

mediary capital will grow along with firm capital. As firms succeed, not only will firms become better capitalized, but intermediaries will too. As Km increases, the cost of informed capital (β) will be reduced, lowering the minimum level of assets needed for investment ($A(\beta)$) and increasing the demand for uninformed capital. Whether the interaction between intermediary capital growth and firm capital growth will be able to explain the well-known fact that intermediation and credit grow disproportionately with the size of the economy is an open question. The main point here is that the demand for information services depends on the level of capitalization, not just of firms, but also of intermediaries, and that balanced growth requires them to expand in tandem.

Some of these ideas can be illustrated by applying them to the current situation in Finland.[21] In the recent severe Finnish recession banks and firms lost large portions of their own capital. This came about because real interest rates were pushed sky-high by the central bank in an effort to defend the currency (its efforts failed, of course). As a consequence, asset prices experienced a catastrophic drop; real estate values fell by 50% and the stock market by 60% in less than two years. All the major banks had to be bailed out by the government as a large number of firms went bankrupt or were unable to service their debts. This sad episode caused a massive redistribution of funds from the informed (equity holders) to the uninformed (debt holders), putting Finland in a situation of capital shortage that is somewhat reminiscent of that in Eastern Europe. As the principles described above suggest, firms have found it difficult obtaining new funds because banks have been reluctant to lend against insufficient collateral. Small, poorly capitalized firms have suffered the most. They have been bitterly complaining about being left to their own devices (often going bankrupt), because of the banks' stringent collateral requirements. This is precisely what the basic model would predict; when Km and A fall, $A(\beta)$ will go up, squeezing small firms out. A second development is that banks have come to realize that they must shift to more information intensive financing now that firms are capital poor. They are hiring corporate analysts and expanding their corporate departments in order to be able to investigate which risks are worth taking and which are not, recognizing that lending against less collateral will be necessary in the future.[22] This shift in monitoring also accords with the model logic.

A final issue worth discussing is this: what determines the supply of intermediary capital? Why cannot intermediaries raise as much funds as

[21] The description applies also to Sweden.
[22] In addition to commercial banks, investment banks and venture capitalists have also responded to the call for more information intensive financing.

they want from the uninformed market and thereby expand their financing capacity?[23]

In Diamond's (1984) original model on intermediation, intermediaries face no capital constraints. Even if they have no initial capital of their own, they can attract as many deposits as they need to in order to finance all firms in the economy. The reason for this is that intermediaries in his model are assumed to invest in small, stochastically independent projects. By the law of large numbers, diversification overcomes the restrictions placed by limited liability.[24] This sounds like a good model of banking, since banks are indeed highly diversified and attract large amounts of deposits.

But given a second thought the result is problematic. It suggests that a single bank could handle the whole economy and that collateral plays no role in financing investments. Both implications are counterfactual. More troubling still, it does not explain why firms could not diversify themselves and avoid intermediation altogether; or why the whole economy could not be a single firm.[25] There are two possible reasons why reality looks different from Diamond's prediction. One is that different intermediaries specialize in different information, determined by their location (regional banks) or by their expertise in a particular industry (the case with firms). The other is that the diversification argument breaks down if it is assumed that the intermediary can choose to concentrate its investments and not in fact diversify.[26] The two arguments are related. Where firms and banks invest depends on what they are experts on. Firms that develop expertise in a particular industry, will be induced to invest in that industry. Their investments will tend to be correlated, preventing them from taking advantage of diversification (at least fully). By contrast, banks invest in more shallow, but general expertise, allowing them to diversify.[27] Thus, banks and firms divide the tasks of intermediation and information gathering in a way that complements each other.

Nothing of this sort is occurring in the model described. In the model

[23] An alternative interpretation of the model described has the uninformed investing their money indirectly via the intermediary rather than directly in the firm. The amount of uninformed capital that an intermediary can raise is constrained just as before by the intermediary's own capital.

[24] It is easy to see that if the firm in Section 3 could invest in two independent, half-sized projects ($I/2$) rather than in a single full-sized project (I), then the required amount of own capital in (5) will be smaller. As the number of projects grow, the required amount of capital goes to zero.

[25] As Diamond recognizes, a firm is itself an intermediary.

[26] Again, this can be easily verified. In the earlier described case where the firm invests in two half-sized projects, if these half-sized projects are perfectly correlated, then the required amount of own capital rises back to the level in (5). Interestingly, the same is true if the firm can observe the outcome of the first project before it makes its investment decision on the second project.

[27] Bank regulations affect the degree of diversification. Some regulations require that banks do not hold too much of their loan portfolio in risky ventures. Other regulations restrict banks from entering certain segments of the market. These regulations appear to be driven by the presence of deposit insurance and by anti-trust concerns.

intermediaries do not diversify. All their investments are perfectly correlated, which is why they need to put their own capital at risk. Diamond's assumption and ours are equally extreme. It would be important to analyze intermediate cases that would test the consistency of the logic just described, where the tasks of monitoring are divided between intermediaries and firms and the division of tasks is matched by the degree of diversification.

The relevance of this discussion for the subject at hand is that the division of tasks may well be ambiguous. As seems to be the case in reality, there are many viable hierarchies of intermediation, some where banks take a more active role and some where they are more passive. Over time, and across economies, different systems have been used. The important point may not be which choice is made among many, but that whatever choice is made, it is made in a way that recognizes the complementarities between information acquisition, task division and contractual forms used to provide incentives.

6. *Summary and some Lessons for Eastern Europe*

In this final section let us reflect briefly on the funding problems facing Eastern Europe from the viewpoint of the preceding analysis. What lessons might be drawn?

Certainly, the models are not designed to give detailed advice on policy; for that they are far too stark. Instead, they are meant to provide a simple conceptual framework, which can give a sense of the likely direction of developments, can help identify key areas to focus on, and can be used as a general sounding board for judging specific issues. It has been argued that for this, traditional finance theory is inappropriate, or at least insufficient, because it does not appreciate the difference between financing real investments that are illiquid and buying claims in markets that are liquid. The information economic approach, which focuses on the sources of illiquidity, seems to provide a better alternative.

In the information economic view, the fundamental problem of financing is an information gap between those who have more money than ideas and those who have more ideas than money. Indeed, without any information gap, every asset would be as liquid as money and individual imbalances between money and ideas would be inconsequential; there would simply be no need to seek financing.

There are two main vehicles for matching money and ideas: collateral, which serves to secure investor's funds, and intermediation, which helps bridge the information gap between the two. The value of collateral is determined by its liquidity. The more symmetric the information about the future returns of an asset, the more liquid the asset is, and the better it can serve as collateral. There must be better information about the assets that are pledged as collateral than there is about the ideas that seek funding. Capital formation can be envisioned as a process in which firms (with the help of other intermediaries) keep transforming illiquid prospective returns into liquid proven returns, using collateral as the means of transformation. This view accords well with Knight's conception of the nature of the entrepreneurial firm. Knight argued that the entrepreneur's main function is to take uncertainty and transform it into risk. In the modern language of information economics he would have said that the entrepreneur takes asymmetric information and transforms it into symmetric information, that is, transforms illiquid assets into liquid ones.

Given this vision of investment dynamics, the first message is that an economy short of capital (collateralizable assets), will have particular difficulties in funding investments. Low labor costs, and promising projects are not sufficient to attract funds. A project that can be undertaken by a well-capitalized Western firm may be impossible to undertake in a capital poor Eastern European firm, even if labor costs are lower. (Note well: this is not possible according to the traditional theory of finance.) As this example suggests, it is not just the economy wide amount of capital that matters, either. The distribution of capital is equally important. If capital and ideas are poorly matched, growth will be slower. In the transitional economies of eastern Europe, this is a major problem, since much of the capital is still in the hands of government, which presumably has little idea of how to employ it efficiently. Redistributing existing capital by privatizing it is therefore a critical and urgent step.

The question how best to privatize productive assets is too large an issue to discuss here at any depth. But there are a few points worth bringing up. The intermediation model suggests that since capital is so scarce, financing of investments will have to be more information intensive. This means that whichever intermediaries will be involved in channeling funds to firms, they will have to take a more active role in monitoring these firms. To give the intermediaries the proper incentives to do so, one has to make sure that they hold a large enough stake in the firms they invest in. It is essential that managers of the intermediaries be given substantial rewards for doing well. It is also important that these intermediaries are sufficiently well capitalized. Intermediaries that are poorly capitalized will have distorted incentives to monitor and invest. Even banking is likely to involve more personal and closely monitored lending than is observed in the West. Consequently, banks need to be better capitalized than the 8% BIS rule requires. Most importantly, however, their permissible range of lending should be restricted to conform with the responsibility that they have for the investment outcomes. If deposit insurance is provided, as we think it should be to improve liquidity, banks must be constrained by regulation.

A big problem with privatizing assets quickly is that there is little information on who the able managers are. Competitive bidding may not be very effective in getting the assets in the right hands if the most able managers have little capital to offer. Distributing ownership rights widely through vouchers does little to eliminate the problem. In this situation it seems reasonable to rely on many small investment companies rather than a few large ones, since this at least allows experimentation. As the evidence comes in, the successful ones will be able to accumulate more capital, or perhaps even be entitled to additional privatized assets as a direct reward. Of course, small intermediaries will not be able to fund large investments, but that seems worth sacrificing for the benefit of more competition and more experimentation.

The fact that collateral plays such an important role in attracting funds suggests that much can be achieved by developing collateral lending. The first step, a seemingly trivial, but in practice quite demanding one, is to put in place a system that records collateral claims.[28] The second step is to focus on improving the market liquidity of those assets that can best serve as collateral. The most common form of collateral in the West, the dominant form, is real estate. Real estate is a good form of collateral because information about its future returns is quite symmetric. It is one of the most potent sources of wealth for entrepreneurs starting a new business. Privatization of real estate will do a lot to make this market more liquid, but also, taxation that favors real estate transactions and investment could have a significant impact. The same goes for stock and bond markets, though it will probably be much harder and of less significance to raise the liquidity in these markets. Note that a rationale for subsidizing asset transactions is the externality between investments discussed in Section 4.[29]

Since information asymmetries are the basic source of problems, another important objective is to narrow the information gap. Part of the gap comes from uncertainty about the future actions of the government: political and legal uncertainties. This is well recognized and we can only join those who have argued the importance of creating political and institutional stability. Given the central role of wealth in creating opportunities for new investment and growth, the right to accumulate wealth, without fearing confiscation, private or public, is surely priority number one. This includes the taxation of capital gains at predictable and reasonable levels, as well as the creation of a corporate legal code that provides understandable rules of conduct.

---

[28] This was pointed out to me by David Dod.

[29] The question whether to subsidize retained earnings is more subtle. The benefit is that firms will be induced to invest more of their retained earnings. But the cost is that it impedes transfer of funds across firms. If the allocation of capital is bad, retained earnings should not be subsidized.

There are many other ways in which the informational burden on foreign investments can be reduced. One is to provide government guarantees for foreign loans, and intermediaries in particular can benefit from this. It is one of the few ways in which the government can intermediate foreign funds effectively. The reason is not that the government has better information than foreigners about the use of funds, though it may. Rather, guarantees eliminate some of the government induced risk that is of concern to foreigners. It is an action that ties the government's hands. Loan guarantees have been the favored approach in Scandinavian countries during their present financial crisis. Banks have been able to maintain their liquidity by obtaining foreign lines of credit, something that they may have found very difficult, or at least more costly, without guarantees.

Another important source of uncertainty is inflation. Money is the most liquid asset, but only as long as its value is predictable. A monetary policy that keeps inflation within acceptable levels is essential. We mention this not because the recommendation is novel, but because the rationale for such a policy fits with the informational perspective being advertised here.[30] More interestingly, contractual models of this kind can be used to analyze the benefits of an active monetary policy that accommodates real, unexpected shocks. It is easy to see that monetary policy can have an effect if contracts are incomplete (which they surely are). As is evident from the current European crisis, monetary policy has dramatically redistributed wealth, a point that is quite relevant for the current discussion. It is much less clear that an accommodating policy can be used to improve matters systematically. Note, however, that parties may deliberately choose nominal contracts over real contracts to allow a third party (most naturally the government) to make implicit adjustments in their contract in response to major events that they cannot foresee at the time of contracting. This could provide a form of risk-sharing that is otherwise unavailable because of illiquid capital markets. Indeed, one interpretation of the devaluation policies followed by Scandinavian countries since the War is precisely this. The subject deserves further study.

The final, and perhaps most important message of the analysis is that capital formation is likely to be a slow, incremental process, at least in the beginning, because the capital base is so small. Given the small base, private investments will be geared towards smaller, safer and shorter-term projects. Appreciating that this is the natural course of events is essential. It can prevent impatient, ill-considered actions, such as trying to force the rate of growth by way of large, glamorous investments backed up by government and foreign funds. There may be good political and distributional reasons for such actions, but on an efficiency basis, such investments are not ones that

[30] See Banerjee and Maskin (1991) for more on this.

the preceding analysis would support. Estonia seems to be on the right track, with an emphasis on small and medium sized businesses. Subcontracting for foreign firms is growing particularly well. Subcontracting does not have the highest potential returns, but it is an informationally less demanding activity and therefore relatively low in contracting costs; apparently an excellent way to attract foreign capital as well as expertise.

Estonia has complained about the funding it has received from the European Bank for Reconstruction and Development, arguing that these loans have been earmarked for large investments that the country is not in urgent need of. Estonia would have appreciated the help more if the funds could have been used for financing smaller firms. We believe the instinct is right. As dire as the economic situation is, patience with the speed of recovery will pay off. The logic of liquidity constrained growth argues for letting small firms carry the brunt of the responsibility for future prosperity.

Acknowledgements

This paper is partly based on the first of three Yrjo Jahnsson Lectures, which I gave at the University of Helsinki, November 1992. I am grateful to Oliver Hart, Martin Hellwig and David Scharfstein for stimulating discussions on this topic and especially to Jean Tirole, with whom I have collaborated on the model of intermediation described in section 5. Financial support from the Institute for Policy Reform, the Yrjo Jahnsson Foundation and the National Science Foundation is gratefully acknowledged.

References

Banerjee, A. and E. Maskin (1991), 'A Theory of Money,' mimeo, Harvard University.

Banerjee, A. and A. Newman (1991), 'Risk-bearing and the Theory of Income Distribution,' *Review of Economic Studies*, 58(2), 211–35.

Bernanke, B. and M. Gertler (1990), 'Financial Fragility and Economic Performance,' *Quarterly Journal of Economics*, 105(1), 87–114.

Bolton, P. and D. Scharfstein (1996), 'Optimal Debt Structure and the number of Creditors,' *Journal of Political Economy*, 104(1), 1–25.

Dewatripont, M. and J. Tirole (1994), 'A Theory of Debt and Equity: Diversity of Securities and Manager-shareholder Congruence,' *Quarterly Journal of Economics*, 109(4), 1027–54.

Diamond, D. (1984), 'Financial Intermediation and Delegated Monitoring,' *Review of Economic Studies*, 51(3), 393–419.

Diamond, D. (1991), 'Monitoring and Reputation: The Choice Between Bank Loans and Directly Placed Debt,' *Journal of Political Economy*, 97(4), 689–721.

Gale, D. and M. Hellwig (1985), 'Incentive Compatible Debt Contracts: The One-period Problem,' *Review of Economic Studies*, 52(4), 647–663.

Gorton, G. and G. Pennacchi (1990), 'Financial Intermediaries and Liquidity Creation,' *Journal of Finance*, 45(1), 49–71.

Hoshi, T., A. Kashyap and D. Scharfstein (1992), 'The Choice Between Public and Private Debt: An Examination of Post-regulation Corporate Financing in Japan,' working paper, MIT.

Innes, R. (1990), 'Limited Liability and Incentive Contracting with ex ante Action Choices,' *Journal of Economic Theory*, 52(1), 45–67.

Kyotaki, N. and R. Wright (1989), 'On Money as a Medium of Exchange,' *Journal of Political Economy*, 97(4), 927–54.

Lacker, J. (1992), 'Collateralized Debt as the Optimal Contract,' mimeo, Federal Reserve Bank of Richmond.

Mayer, C. (1988), 'New Issues in Corporate Finance,' *European Economic Review*, 32, 1167–1189.

Shleifer, A. and R. Vishny (1990), 'Equilibrium Short Horizons of Investors and Firms,' *American Economic Review*, papers and proceedings. 80(2), 148–53.

Shleifer, A. and R. Vishny (1992), 'Liquidation Values and Debt Capacity: A Market Equilibrium Approach,' *Journal of Finance*, 47(4), 1373–66.

Stiglitz, J. and A. Weiss (1981), 'Credit Rationing in Markets with Imperfect Information,' *American Economic Review*, 71, 393–410.

Stiglitz, J. and A. Weiss (1983) 'Incentive Effects of Terminations: Applications to the Credit and Labor Markets,' *American Economic Review*, 73, 912–927.

Thakor, A. (1990), 'Investment Myopia and the Internal Organization of Capital Allocation Decisions,' *Journal of Law, Economics and Organization*, 6(1), 129–54.

Townsend, R. (1979), 'Optimal Contracts with Costly State Verification,' *Journal of Economic Theory*, 21(2), 265–93.

Williamson, O. (1988), 'Corporate Finance and Corporate Governance,' *Journal of Finance*, 43(3), 567–91.

Williamson, S. (1988), 'Liquidity, Banking and Bank Failures,' *International Economic Review*, 29(1), 25–43.

CHAPTER TEN

Revisiting Legal Realism
The Law, Economics, and Organization Perspective

OLIVER E. WILLIAMSON

Although American Legal Realism fell on hard times, the objections of the Realists with legal formalism had substance earlier in the century and have substance today. As developed in this paper, there are many parallels between Legal Realism and older style institutional economics. Both failed for lack of operationalization.

The New Institutional Economics works out of a law, economics, and organizations perspective and takes operationalization much more seriously. This same approach could be applied to the concerns of Legal Realism, bringing added value in the process.

1. Introduction

The contrast between American Legal Realism, which 'ran itself into the sand' (Schlegel, 1979, p. 459), and the law and economics movement, which is 'perhaps the most important development in legal thought in the last quarter century' (Posner, 1986, p. xix), is dramatic. That one foundered while the other flourished is explained largely by the absence of an intellectual framework for Legal Realism and the use by law and economics of the powerful framework of neoclassical economics.

Although movements that lack a 'coherent intellectual force' (Schlegel, 1979, p. 459) ordinarily collapse, the concerns of Legal Realism do not go away. Some may regard that as stubborn refusal to admit defeat, but many social scientists share the conviction of the Legal Realists that 'announced legal rules may differ from what courts actually do and that embedded presuppositions regarding the law's effects and relevance to social behavior are often quite wrong, and at the very least, worthy of serious testing'

197

(Johnston, 1993, p. 217). I am persuaded that the objections of the Realists
with legal formalism had substance earlier in the century and have substance
today (Kalman, 1986).

Given the perceived limitations of neoclassical economics (Ackerman,
1986, p. 940), Bruce Ackerman counsels that lawyer-economists should
'look to the sciences of culture ... anthropology, sociology, and sociolinguis-
tics' (1986, p. 942) to supply the missing framework. Because, however, the
'economic approach' is very powerful and much broader than neoclassical
economics, my suggestion is to combine law, economics and organization (in
relation to which economics is the first among equals) in a concerted effort
to study 'law as it is'. Such a program is related to, but different from, that
of law and economics. Among the differences is that law and economics is
more of a normative and one-way enterprise (orthodox economics is brought
to bear on the law) whereas the law, economics and organization program is
positive and more thoroughly interactive: economics both informs and is
informed by law and organization.

Law, economics and organization can be variously implemented, depending on the perceived needs. Transaction cost economics is one such effort,
the perceived need being to move beyond the proposition that institutions
matter to show that institutions are also susceptible to analysis (Matthews,
1986, p. 903), which is the project associated with the New Institutional
Economics. The New Institutional Economics come in two branches: the
institutional environment and the institutions of governance (Davis and
North, 1971). The institutions of governance are what mainly concern me in
this paper. For a combined treatment, see Williamson (1993a).

There are many parallels between Legal Realism and older style institutional economics. Conceivably, efforts to deal with the needs and limitations
of older style institutional economics will also have application to Legal
Realism. This paper explores that possibility.[1] Comparisons of two kinds are
set out in Section 2: law and economics is compared with law, economics,
and organization; and older style institutional economics is compared with
Legal Realism. The transaction cost economics project is then sketched in
Section 3. The value added of law, economics, and organization in relation
to law and economics is the subject of Section 4. Legal Realism is revisited
in Section 5. Concluding remarks follow.

---

[1] This paper does not deal with the 'legal process' successors to Legal Realism, as represented especially by Hart and Sachs (1994). For a overview of that project, see Eskridge and Frickey (1994). The
importance attached to private ordering, mechanisms and safeguards by legal process (Eskridge and
Frickey, 1994, pp. xciii-xcv) are plainly ones to which transaction cost economics relates. Operationalizing these good ideas eluded the legal process approach.

2. *Some Background*

Comparing L&E with LEO

Although I mainly focus on the differences between law and economics (L&E) and law, economics and organization (LEO), there are many similarities. Both were inspired by Ronald Coase (1937, 1960, 1992); both have taken shape during the past 30 years; both hold that economics is the key discipline; both have been brought to bear on some of the same problems of public policy; and both are much closer to each other than to other interdisciplinary approaches to legal study, such as feminist jurisprudence, law and literature, and critical legal studies. Indeed, although L&E and LEO are sometimes viewed as rivals, they are often complementary.

There are, however, real differences between pronouncing (normatively) 'This is the law here' and inquiring (positively) 'What's going on here?' (D'Andrade, 1986). The first of these is closer to the L&E project. LEO is much more concerned with figuring out how feasible forms of organization work—glitches, dysfunctions, breakdowns, purported perversities and the like included. As developed later in the paper, the science of organization needs to be apprised of all regularities whatsoever, intended and unintended alike. Not only is Richard Posner, who is the leading spokesperson for L&E (Ellickson, 1989), dismissive of organization theory (Posner, 1993), but other practitioners of L&E, like orthodox economists more generally, make little or no provision for organization theory. In the degree to which organization matters, that misses some of the action, which in turn can be (and has been) the source of avoidable public policy error

Perhaps the simplest way to distinguish L&E from LEO is to observe that the three-way intersection of law, economics, and organization deals with only a subset of the problems with which law and economics is concerned (see Figure 1). Since there is general agreement that law and economics is a success story, and if law and economics has greater scope, where does the value added of LEO reside?[2]

At a general level, L&E is the application of orthodox economics (economics as presented in the microeconomics textbooks) to the law. That is an ambitious undertaking and is what the 'economic analysis of law' is all

---

[2] In a general sense, what LEO brings in is much more self-conscious attention to institutions. Robert Ellickson interprets Figure 1 (in his letter to me of 31 October 1995) as follows:

> As you know, much of law deals with relations among persons who are likely to be strangers. The cores of tort law and criminal law offer examples. An 'organization perspective' ... has little relevance in situations where persons are unlikely or unable to contract with one another.

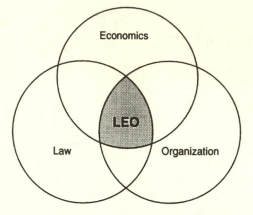

FIGURE 1.   Law, economics and organization.

about.[3] In contrast, LEO works out of an 'economic approach' that is informed by both law and organization. Figure 2 displays the schematic differences.

As shown in (a) in Figure 2, LEO is construed as a one-way enterprise in which orthodox economics is used to interpret and advise the law. In contrast, (b) shows economics as being informed by both law and organization, the three-way product of which is the New Institutional Economics (of which transaction cost economics is a part). The object of the latter is to reshape the way economists and other social scientists think about and investigate the purposes served by economic and political institutions.

Among the ways in which L&E and LEO differ are that the former works predominantly out of a firm-as-production function construction in which contracts are assumed to be complete (or at least comprehensive) and the action is concentrated in *ex ante* incentive alignment whereas the latter works out of a firm-as-governance structure construction in which contracts are assumed to be incomplete and the action is concentrated in the mechanisms of *ex post* governance. David Kreps contrasts the orthodox

---

I do not disagree, although organization can be brought to bear in the following sense: individuals who are aware of differential hazards of accidents and criminality will organize differently (as in protected communities).

In the degree to which *ex ante* incentive alignment (get the relative prices right) solves a problem of law, LEO has little to add. The value added of LEO comes in if and as *ex post* governance is also important (get the institutional supports right).

[3] Richard Posner's famous book, now in its 4th edition, is titled *Economic Analysis of Law.* See also Posner (1993, p. 83). Polinsky's book, (1983) proceeds similarly. Cooter and Ulen likewise apply orthodox economics to the law, although a reverse flow from legal formalism to economics is also contemplated (1988, p. 13).

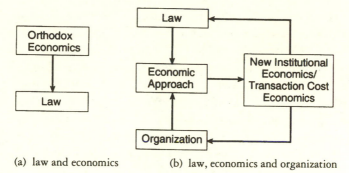

(a) law and economics   (b) law, economics and organization

FIGURE 2.   Comparing law and economics with law, economics and organization.

theory of the firm with that of transaction cost economics as follows (1990, p. 96):

> The [orthodox] firm is like individual agents in textbook economics, which finds its highest expression in general equilibrium theory (see Debreu, 1959; Arrow and Hahn, 1971). The firm transacts with other firms and with individuals in the market. Agents have utility functions, firms have a profit motive; agents have consumption sets, firms have production possibility sets. But in transaction-cost economics, firms are more like markets— both are arenas within which individuals can transact.

Firms and markets are *alternative* modes for mediating transactions under the latter prescription.

Indeed, this move from a technological construction (the firm-as-production function) to an organizational construction (the firm-as-governance structure) is basic to the entire transaction cost economics enterprise. The former holds that the firm is a black box, according to which inputs are transformed into outputs according to the laws of technology; the latter is a comparative institutional construction according to which the mechanisms of governance differ among alternative modes of governance and have real consequences. Organization is ignored and is conceptually irrelevant under the former; organization matters crucially and is susceptible to analysis under the latter.

Among the questions that fall within the LEO intersection are those posed by Coase (1937): Why is there a firm at all? Why is not all production organized in one large firm? What determines the boundaries of the firm? Posing a series of fundamental and related questions for which orthodoxy had no good responses suggested the need for a new outlook. Indeed, that is the way that Coase came to view the project.

Thus, although Coase is deservedly credited with being one of the 'four founders' of the law and economics movement, Coase disclaimed an interest in the economic analysis of the law: 'I have no interest in lawyers or legal education... My interest is in economics, and I was interested in carrying forward the *Journal of Law and Economics* because I thought that it would change what economists did' (Coase, 1983, p. 192). In the degree to which legal institutions come into the analysis—'I do think some knowledge of legal institutions is essential for economists working in certain areas' (Coase, 1983, p. 193)—'it's what [institutions do] to economists that interests me, not what it does to lawyers' (Coase, 1983, p. 193).

Coase's Nobel Prize lecture reaffirms this orientation:[4]

> The time has surely gone in which economists could analyze in great detail two individuals exchanging nuts for berries on the edge of the forest and then feel that their analysis of the process of exchange was complete, illuminating though this analysis may be in certain respects. The process of contracting needs to be studied in a real-world setting. We would then learn of the problems that are encountered and of how they are overcome, and we would certainly become aware of the richness of the institutional alternatives between which we have to choose. (1992, p. 718).

Institutions are plainly where the economics research action resides and the operationalization of a New Institutional Economics is the challenge.

Transaction cost economics is an effort to implement the move from equilibrium analysis (orthodoxy) to comparative institutional analysis. In comparison with the law and economics movement (Figure 2(a)), which has 'no, or at least very few, aspirations to change economic theory' (Posner, 1993, p. 82), transaction cost economics is less deferential to orthodoxy. If institutions are important in ways that are neglected by orthodoxy, then a more thoroughly interdisciplinary treatment (possibly along the lines of Figure 2(b)) may be needed.

---

[4] Whereas his 1937 article on 'The Nature of the Firm,' which inspired the New Institutional Economics, and his 1960 article on 'The Problem of Social Cost,' which inspired law and economics, are given symmetrical treatment by those who prepared Coase's Nobel Prize citation, Coase gives much greater prominence to the first of these in his Nobel Prize lecture. Not only is the lecture titled 'The Institutional Structure of Production,' but it is concerned with the law only as this helps to solve puzzles of firm and market organization, which has been his abiding interest. His famous article on 'Social Cost' is thus introduced with the statement that 'I will not say much about its influence on legal scholarship, which has been immense, but will consider its influence on economics, which has not been immense, although I believe that in time it will be' (Coase, 1992, p. 717). And he indicates that the main importance of the 'Social Cost' article is not in its use of the fiction of zero transaction costs, which is what originally fascinated so many economists and legal scholars (although this is changing), but by placing positive transaction costs (specifically, differential transaction costs) at the center of the economics research agenda.

Parallels Between Legal Realism and Older Style Institutional Economics

Both Legal Realism and older style institutional economics were contemporary movements. Both took exception with formalism (in law and economics, respectively). Neither knew how (or tried hard) to operationalize its program. And both fell on hard times.

Orthodoxy. The orthodoxy that was of concern to Legal Realism was that of legal formalism, while the orthodoxy with which institutional economics took exception was that of neoclassical economics. The principal exponent of legal formalism was Christopher Columbus Langdell, who was dean of Harvard Law School from 1870 to 1895 and 'preached that all law should be reduced to a set of well-categorized rules and principles' (Kalman, 1986, p. 11). Langdell and his associates introduced the 'case method', where students learned the law by studying appellate opinions. Whereas previously lawyers were trained mainly during their apprenticeship, 'Langdell transferred the study of law from the office to the university' (Kalman, 1986, p. 11).

Reservations notwithstanding, legal formalism carried the day. Thus, although Oliver Wendell Holmes 'cursed the casebook and announced that the life of the law was not logic but experience' (Kalman, 1986, p. 13), he nevertheless conceded that the casebook was of 'unequalled value' as a pedagogical device (Kalman, 1986, p. 14). Dissent with legal formalism was nevertheless building and the American Law Institute's Restatement of Law project in 1923 has been described as 'the final effort to realize Langdell's ideal of a science of law' (Kalman, 1986, p. 14).

The economic orthodoxy with which the institutional economists took exception had much earlier origins. Adam Smith's concerns with institutions had given way to a progressively more formal program. Mainly that was the product of efforts to make economic reasoning more rigorous (Ricardo, 1817; Mill, 1848; Marshall, 1890). Efforts to mathematize economics (Cournot, 1838; Walras, 1874; Edgeworth, 1881) were especially neglectful of institutions. Ideas of utility maximization and equilibration at the margin were featured, together with a preoccupation with supply and demand and with prices and output—to the neglect of limits on cognitive competence and with scant attention to evolutionary process considerations or to the economizing purposes served by institutions.

Influential objections to orthodoxy were registered by Thorstein Veblen as early as 1898. John R. Commons's two-volume *Institutional Economics*, published in 1934, was the capstone. Veblen's much quoted description of

'The hedonistic conception of man [as] that of a lightning calculator of pleasures and pains, who oscillates like a homogeneous globule of desire and happiness under the impulse of stimuli that shift him about the arena, but leave him intact' (1898, p. 389) is repeated (with variation) by Commons (1931, p. 650). But Commons went further. He not only described an institution as 'collective action in control, liberation, and expansion of individual action' (Commons, 1931, pp. 647, 651, 654), but he joined this with the idea that the study of transactions involved simultaneous attention to conflict, mutuality, and order (Commons, 1932, p. 4). Evidently something more than equilibration at the margin was going on for which analysis was needed.

Although Commons worked off of the taxonomy of jural opposites and jural correlatives of Wesley Newcomb Hohfeld (1913), this remained a sterile taxonomy and other institutional economists relied little on the Realists. For their part, the Realists appealed to institutional economics for 'a sense of external approval' (Duxbury, 1995, p. 103) and a show of commonality (Kalman, 1986, pp. 16–19; Duxbury, 1995, pp. 97–111), but a productive joinder never materialized. Mainly, these two were separate reactions to the excesses of formalism that each ascribed to its respective form of orthodoxy.

Multidisciplinary.   Legal Realism was unusually eclectic, appealing to economics, sociology, psychology, anthropology, linguistic theory and statistics (Kalman, 1986, pp. 15–20). The object in each case was to bring the law into closer contact with reality. That common purpose aside, however, an overarching unity in the project is not apparent.

Institutional economics also appealed to other disciplines, including in particular psychology and sociology, but also found inspiration in the law. Indeed, the processes of the common law were ones to which Commons expressly related in an article auspiciously titled 'Law and Economics' (1924).

Multidisciplinary, however, is different from interdisciplinary, where the latter aspires to a genuine integration of two or more disciplinary perspectives. Legal Realism never really perceived the project in this fashion, and institutional economics made only limited headway.

Leading minds.   Both movements benefited from the involvement of leading minds. As Kalman observes, Legal Realism at Yale 'had a major impact upon some of the most prominent lawyers and judges of this century, including William O. Douglas, Thurman Arnold, Jerome Frank, and Abe

Fortas' (1986, p. xi). Karl Llewellyn, at Columbia, was the leading intellectual force (Duxbury, 1995, p. 68), but Robert Maynard Hutchins played an important early administrative role at Yale along with his successor as dean, Charles E. Clark (Kalman, 1986). Indeed, the list of prominent names goes on.

Whereas Veblen seems to have been self-inspired (Dorfman, 1947), Commons's interests in institutional economics were clearly stimulated by his teacher (and early luminary in the American Economic Association) Richard T. Ely. Another institutional economist who left a lasting mark on the economics profession through his leadership of the National Bureau of Economic Research was Wesley C. Mitchell, who eschewed theory in favor of meticulous empirical investigation.

Institutions matter. Moreover, both movements were persuaded that institutions mattered and had many good ideas to support that proposition. Veblen emphasized evolutionary considerations and the importance of process. Commons also related to the latter and developed an elaborate taxonomy that was intended to illuminate process but ended in obscurantism. A recurrent theme in Commons is collective action in control of individual action. He argued in this connection that orthodoxy was neglectful of the need for institutionalized rules to constrain individual action because of a presupposed harmony of interests (Rutherford, 1994 pp. 13–14).

An important, but underdeveloped idea in Legal Realism is that the concept of contract-as-legal rules was too legalistic and needed to make way for the purposive idea of contract-as-framework (Llewellyn, 1931). More generally, Legal Realism disputed that judicial opinions were rule-governed and objective but held that they were contextual and rationalized instead (Kalman, 1986):

> The realists preached that law should be studied as part of society; they concentrated their attention on facts rather than concepts; they spent their time studying law's operations and showing that judges made law rather than formulating ethical legal rules or arguing that a higher law guided judges; they believed in objectivity and sometimes in reform as well; and they sought to make the subject of their work relevant to contemporary practitioners (Kalman, 1986, pp. 37–38).

Public policy. Both Legal Realism and institutional economics were enormously influential in public policy, especially during the Great Depression when the felt-needs to reform public policy in a timely way were especially pressing. Initially, in the state of Wisconsin and later in Washington, DC, Commons and his colleagues and students played a large part in shaping public utility and railroad regulation, in labor legislation, in social security, and, more generally, in public policy toward business.

Indeed, the Legal Realists were even more active in their service to the government during the New Deal.[5] 'Berle, Dowling, Arnold, Douglas, Frankfurter, and Frank ... [helped] to shape ... major administrative agencies [and] important systems of rules, such as the Uniform Commercial Code, were crafted by realists' (Fisher, Horwitz, and Reed, 1993, p. xiv). John Henry Schlegel lists:

> ... Douglas's work in securities law, Clark's work on procedural reform that culminated in the adoption of the Federal Rules of Civil Procedure, Llewellyn's work on reforming sales law that ultimately produced the Uniform Commercial Code, Hamilton's work on destroying economic due process, Arnold's work at reviving the antitrust laws, and Borchard's tireless activities on behalf of the Federal Tort Claims Act and the declaratory judgment. What holds these diverse activities together is that at the time they were seen as liberal, reformist projects. One of the characteristics of Realism as a movement was its slightly left of center politics (1979, p. 570, n. 589).

Impatience, non-cumulative, implosion.   Perhaps partly because the policy problems were so pressing, both Legal Realism and institutional economics failed to go beyond good ideas of an informal kind into preformal and semi-formal (to say nothing of fully formal) modes of analysis. Operationalization was never seriously contemplated and a cumulative research tradition replete with refutable implications and empirical testing never developed.

As a consequence, 'As a coherent intellectual force in American legal thought American Legal Realism simply ran itself into the sand' (Schlegel, 1979, p. 459). The schism between the needs of social science research, to do 'modest, slow, molecular, definitive work', and those of progressive reformers, who perceived the need to reshape the study of the law but who put activism ahead of analysis, has been described as follows:

> ... the social scientists found unacceptable the unwillingness of the lawyers interested in empirical research to act in support of the methodological imperatives of the nascent social scientific discipline and would not provide the continuing support for that research. Similarly, the sympathetic legal community, locked in the progressive reform tradition, found empirical legal research that was unrelated to its current reform interests irrelevant and, thus, would not provide continuing support of such research (Schlegel, 1979, p. 544).

---

[5] Neil Duxbury concedes that many of those associated with the Realist movement went to Washington during the New Deal but argues that 'they did not necessarily take their realist ideas with them, ... [whence] realist jurisprudence made a fairly limited impact on American politics in the 1930s' (1995, p. 155).

The early commitment of Legal Realism to empirical social science thus unravelled, it being thought to be unnecessary by some (Schlegel, 1979, p. 512) and a nuisance by others: 'Fact gathering that did not advance an immediate reform objective was scholarship not worth publishing, just as fact gathering that did not fit their model of how the world was structured was an 'irrelevant jumble of figures" (Schlegel, 1979, p. 519). Driven, as some of it plainly was, by 'the right kind of politics' (Duxbury, 1995, p. 4), the quest for an 'interdisciplinary legal science proved futile' (Duxbury, 1995, p. 90).

Criticisms of the old institutional economics by economists have been scathing. Thus, Stigler remarks that 'the school failed in America for a very simple reason. It had nothing in it except a stance of hostility to the standard theoretical tradition. There was no positive agenda of research' (Stigler, 1983, p. 170). Similar views are expressed by R. C. O. Matthews (1986, p. 903) and Coase agrees: the work of American institutionalists 'led to nothing.... Without a theory, they had nothing to pass on' (Coase 1984, p. 230). Sociologists concur: older style institutional economics was largely descriptive, historically specific and non-cumulative (DiMaggio and Powell, 1991, p. 2; Granovetter, 1988, p. 8).

3. *Transaction Cost Economics: A Sketch*

Transaction cost economics is a comparative institutional approach to economic organization in which law, economics and organization are joined. The transaction is made the basic unit of analysis and the object is to align transactions with alternative modes of governance (markets, hybrids, hierarchies, bureaus) so as to effect a transaction cost economizing result. Numerous refutable implications accrue to this framework, in relation to which the data are broadly corroborative. Figure 3, which elaborates upon Figure 2(b), identifies the key features.

Law

The aspect of the law to which transaction cost economics principally appeals is that of contract law. In fact, and as discussed further in Sections 4 and 5, that has a broad reach: 'the seminal and classic subject of American legal education [is contract]' (Rubin, 1995, p. 1). Of special importance to transaction cost economics is Karl Llewellyn's concept of contract as framework (as opposed to the orthodox concept of contract as legal rules).

The Restatement of Contracts defines contract as 'a promise or set of promises for the breach of which the law gives a remedy, or the performance

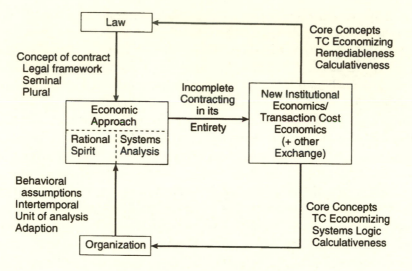

FIGURE 3.   Law, economics and organization.

of which the law in some way recognizes as a duty'. Such a legalistic approach to contract has obvious appeal and 'Law and economics scholars who work in the classical tradition assume that an actor will both know and honor legal rules' (Ellickson, 1989, p. 40). That the legal rules are usually known is probably reasonable for commercial contracting, where contracts are negotiated by experienced managers with the benefit of lawyers. That the rules are efficacious is another thing (see below). That the rules will be honored is an oversimplification.

Many economists understandably concluded that what is good enough for the law is surely good enough for economics. Not only are lawyers the experts, to whom economists defer, but such a legalistic approach to contract permits economists to ignore complex problems of incomplete contract and non-market organization. Albeit a great analytical convenience to purveyors of applied price theory, that came at a high cost to an understanding of both contract and economic organization.

Indeed, there were dissenters. Llewellyn was among the leading Legal Realists who took exception with the prevailing legal rules approach to contract. Llewellyn went beyond mere criticism, moreover, and advanced the rival concept of contract as framework:

> ... the major importance of legal contract is to provide a framework for well-nigh every type of group organization and for well-nigh every type of passing or permanent relation between individuals and groups ... a framework highly adjustable, a framework which almost never accurately indi-

cates real working relations, but which affords a rough indication around which such relations vary, an occasional guide in cases of doubt, and a norm of ultimate appeal when the relations cease in fact to work (1931, pp. 736–737).

If, as Marc Galanter has subsequently argued, the participants to a contract can often 'devise more satisfactory solutions to their disputes than can professionals constrained to apply general rules on the basis of limited knowledge of the dispute' (1981, p. 4), then court ordering is better regarded as a background factor rather than the central forum for dispute resolution. The costliness of courts is also pertinent to the presumed efficacy of common knowledge. If both parties could be presumed to be symmetrically informed, then inefficiency would purportedly be self-correcting because the parties would bargain to an efficient result. That, however, overlooks the possibility that one of the parties could behave strategically, represent the facts falsely, appeal to the formal contract, and ask to have the issues resolved in court. If the courts cannot be costlessly apprised of the true circumstances, then common knowledge between traders will no longer suffice. Absent the extension of common knowledge to the arbiter (which is a much more ambitious prescription), strategizing cannot be disallowed (Williamson, 1975, pp. 31–35).

Thus, although the legal technicalities of contract law remain useful for purposes of ultimate appeal, thereby to delimit threat positions, legal centralism (court ordering) gives way to private ordering as the primary arena. That is also where Hart and Sacks come out: 'private ordering is the primary process of social adjustment' (1994, pp. 161–162). Accordingly, the organization of economic activity, including the offer and acceptance of credible commitments, is where a significant part of the analytical action resides.

Not only is the orthodox preoccupation with price and output supplanted by a more microanalytic examination of transactions and of alternative forms of organization, but the idea of a single, all-purpose concept of contract is supplanted by that of contract laws (plural). Clyde Summers' distinction between black letter law on the one hand and a more circumstantial approach to contract law on the other is pertinent. 'The epitome of abstraction is the *Restatement*, which illustrates its black letter rules by transactions suspended in mid-air, creating the illusion that contract rules can be stated without reference to surrounding circumstances and are therefore generally applicable to all contractual transactions' (Summers, 1969, p. 566). Such a conception does not and cannot provide a 'framework for integrating rules and principles applicable to all contractual transactions' (Summers, 1969, p. 566). A broader conception of contract, with emphasis on the affirmative purposes of the law and effective governance relations, is needed if that is to be realized. Summers conjectured in this connection that 'the principles common to the whole range of contractual transactions are relatively few and of such generality and competing character that they should not be stated as legal rules at all' (1969, p. 527).

Ian Macneil's distinctions between classical, neoclassical, and relational contract law (1974, 1978) are ones to which transaction cost economics easily relates. The proposition that each generic mode of organization is supported by a distinctive form of contract law is an extension of contract laws (plural) reasoning (Williamson, 1991).

Organization

The twin behavioral assumptions out of which transaction cost economics works—bounded rationality and opportunism—have organization theory origins and combine to yield the following heuristic statement of the problem of economic organization: organize so as to economize on the scarce resource of limited rationality while simultaneously safeguarding the transactions in question against the hazards of opportunism.

More important for my purposes here (since I concede that disputes over behavioral assumptions are rarely decisive) are the intertemporal process transformations to which organization theory calls attention. Very broadly, these process transformations are responsible for the proposition that organization, like the law, has a life of its own.

The study of bureaucracy and the intertemporal consequences that accrue to internal organization are important on this account (Williamson, 1990, 1993a). There are two propositions. First, the incipient science of organization needs to be apprised of all significant regularities whatsoever. Second, from an organizational design point of view, all added consequences need to be folded in, whereby unwanted costs can be mitigated and unanticipated benefits can be increased. Although sometimes the firm-as-production function construction may be altogether sufficient to ascertain the relevant consequences, organization theorists are often alert to and have helped to explicate delayed, indirect, and unintended effects.

Examples of where organization theory has deepened our understanding of complex organization are the unintended consequences that accrue to demands for control, the oligarchical propensities that accrue to leadership in organization, the ways and reasons why identity matters (including the atmospherics of organization), and the lessons for comparative economic organization that accrue to bureaucratization (Williamson, 1993a, pp. 117–119). Also, in addition to the benefits of autonomous adaptation that Friedrich Hayek (1945) properly ascribed to markets, the benefits of cooperative adaptation that accrue to hierarchy (Barnard, 1938) also need to be recognized and taken into account.

Orthodox L&E makes little or no provision for organization. Posner, for example, advises that 'organization-theory ... [adds] nothing to economics that the literature on information costs had not added years earlier' (1993, p. 84). That literature, however, has little or nothing to say about all of the matters to which I refer above, the neglect of which is no longer acceptable.

Thus Kreps holds that 'almost any theory of organization that is addressed by game theory will do more for game theory than game theory will do for it' (1992, p. 1). Steven Postrel elaborates as follows:

> The point is that game theory does not, of itself, contain a substantive account of behavior. Game models are extremely sensitive to assumptions about information, the order of moves, constraints on action, and players' beliefs. Yet these assumptions, not game logic itself, are the real substance of a theory of business competition (1991, p. 154; emphasis omitted).

Robert Gibbons likewise advises that economists must come to terms with the internal structure and functioning of firms (1995).

Those conclusions are consonant with the transaction cost economics project. Rather than take the organization of economic activity between firms and markets as given and focus on price and output (equilibration at the margin), transaction cost economics takes the organization of economic activity as something to be derived, treats adaptation as the central problem of economic organization, and examines the differential efficacy of alternative discrete structural modes of governance in relation to the attributes of transactions. New concepts and apparatus needed to be devised in the process.

The Economic Approach

Lon Fuller's definition of 'eunomics' as 'the science, theory or study of good order and workable arrangements' (1954, p. 477) is very much in the spirit of what I refer to as governance. As Fuller subsequently remarks, 'the primary concern of eunomics is with the means aspect of the means-end relation' (1954, p. 478). Governance is also very much an exercise in assessing the efficacy of alternative modes (means) of organization. The object is to effect good order through the mechanisms of governance. A governance structure is the institutional framework within which the integrity of a transaction, or related set of transactions, is decided.

Commons also anticipated much of the conceptual argument in his

insistence that 'the ultimate unit of activity ... must contain in itself the
three principles of conflict, mutuality, and order. This unit is a transaction'
(1932, p. 4). Not only does transaction cost economics concur that the transaction is the basic unit of analysis, but governance is the means by which
order is accomplished in a relation where potential *conflict* threatens to undo
or upset opportunities to realize *mutual* gains.

More generally, transaction cost economics works out of the 'economic
approach', of which the utility maximization that is associated with much of
law and economics (Posner, 1975, 1993; Ellickson, 1989) is a special case.
The economic approach combines a 'rational spirit' with a 'systems
approach' to the study of economic organization.

Although all of the social sciences have a stake in rationality analysis
(Homans, 1958; Simon, 1978), economists push the approach further and
more persistently. As Arrow puts it: 'An economist by training thinks of
himself as the guardian of rationality, the ascriber of rationality to others,
and the prescriber of rationality to the social world. It is this role that I will
play' (1974, p. 16). History records that that has been a productive role, for
Arrow as well as more generally. Rationality is a deep and pervasive condition that manifests itself in many subtle ways.

Note in this connection that the rational spirit approach does not imply
hyper-rationality. Strong form, semi-strong form, and weak form rational
spirits are usefully distinguished. Whereas the strong form contemplates
maximization and/or comprehensive contracting and is associated with
orthodoxy, the latter two work out of bounded rationality. Semi-strong form
analysis joins bounded rationality with farsighted contracting. The weak
form joins bounded rationality with myopic contracting.

Transaction cost economics is a semi-strong form construction. It concedes that comprehensive contracting is not a feasible option (by reason of
bounded rationality), yet maintains that many economic agents have the
capacity to look ahead, perceive hazards, and draw these back into the contractual relation, thereafter to devise responsive institutions. In effect, limited
but intended rationality is translated into incomplete but farsighted contracting, respectively. The concept of contract out of which transaction cost
economics works is therefore that of 'incomplete contracting in its entirety',
which has the appearance of a contradiction in terms. In fact, such a concept
of contract presents healthy tensions to which law, economics and organization theory can productively relate. Systems considerations are posed.

Farsighted, as against myopic, contracting is *the key systems move* that distinguishes economics from the other social sciences. It is also why economics
is so central to the law, economics and organization enterprise. George
Schultz captures the spirit in his statement that:

... training in economics has had a major influence on the way I think about public policy tasks, even when they have no particular relationship to economics. Our discipline makes one think ahead, ask about indirect consequences, take note of variables that may not be directly under consideration (1995, p. 1).

Note that this is very different from the more familiar view that 'What economics has to export ... is ... a very particular and special form of [rationality]—that of the utility maximizer' (Simon, 1978, p. 2)—which is closer to the law and economics perspective. Other social scientists have been understandably wary of such trade. What was once, however, a yawning abyss between economics and the other social sciences has begun to close as non-economists, especially political scientists, have begun to recognize merit in a systems conception of farsighted (but incomplete) contracting.[6]

Ramifications for Law and Organization

Transaction cost economics subscribes to and attempts to implement the conceptual moves described above. Because the operationalization of transaction cost economics is described elsewhere (Williamson, 1985, 1989, 1991, 1996), only three key conceptual features are mentioned here: economizing, the systems logic (with emphasis on remediableness), and calculativeness.

Economizing. Transaction cost economics maintains that economizing is the main case, in relation to which other purposes (monopolizing, strategizing) require that special preconditions be satisfied (and, accordingly, are special cases). The possibility of adventitiousness/history dependence is admitted, but is examined in the context of remediableness (which restores efficiency considerations). The economizing in question is concerned principally with contract and organization (rather than technology), with special emphasis on the mitigation of contractual hazards through governance.

A recognition that hazards can take many forms has taken shape only gradually, as transaction cost economics moved beyond its initial preoccupation with vertical integration (Coase, 1937; Williamson, 1971) to consider related contractual transactions (labor, finance, vertical market restraints and other forms of non-standard contracting, regulation, trust and the like) and to push beyond governance (markets, hybrids, hierarchies, bureaus) to consider the influence of the institutional environment (the political, legal and

---

[6] I do not mean to suggest that L&E does not also appeal to the economic approach. It most certainly does. As described in Section 4, however, L&E emphasizes *ex ante* incentive alignment (which is in the spirit of complete contracting) whereas LEO is more concerned with *ex post* governance (incomplete contracting in its entirety). These are complementary but different exercises.

social rules of the game). Among the hazards with which transaction cost economics is concerned are (i) the aforementioned hazards of bilateral dependency, (ii) those that accrue to weak property rights,[7] (iii) measurement hazards (especially in conjunction with multiple tasks (Holmstrom and Milgrom (1991) and/or oversearching (Barzel, 1982; Kenney and Klein, 1983)), and (iv) intertemporal hazards, where these can take the form of disequilibrium contracting, real-time responsiveness, long latency and strategic abuse. Also, (v) the hazards that accrue to weaknesses in the institutional environment (North and Weingast, 1989; Levy and Spiller, 1994; Weingast, 1995) are important, need to be explicated, and are beginning to be taken into account.

Variety notwithstanding, all of these hazards entail variations on the following themes: (i) all of the hazards would vanish but for the twin conditions of bounded rationality and opportunism; (ii) the action resides in the details of transactions and the mechanisms of governance; and (iii) superior performance is realized by working out of a farsighted but incomplete contracting set-up in which the object is to use institutions as (cost effective) instruments for hazard mitigation. To repeat, the identification, explication, and mitigation of hazards through governance is what transaction cost economics is all about.

Systems Conception

Farsighted (but incomplete) contracting is to be contrasted with the myopic contracting approach that characterizes much of the organization theory literature. The contrast between the resource dependency view of specialized investments and the credible commitment treatment of those same conditions is noteworthy. Given that all complex contracts are incomplete and that promises to behave continuously in a fully cooperative way are not self-enforcing, investments in transaction specific assets pose hazards. Resource dependency theory holds that the dependent party, which varies with the circumstances, is at the mercy of the other. Working, as it does, out of a myopic perspective, the theory holds that dependency is an unwanted and unusually unanticipated condition. The recommended response to a condition of resource dependency is for unwitting victims to attempt, *ex post*, to reduce it.

Transaction cost economics regards dependency very differently because it works out of a farsighted rather than a myopic contracting perspective. Not only is dependency a foreseeable condition but, in the degree to which asset

---

[7] Weak property rights pose contractual hazards for which 'convoluted' forms of organization are sometimes the cost-effective response. For examples of 'inefficiency by design' see Klein and Leffler (1981), Teece (1986), Heide and John (1988) and Moe (1990a, 1990b).

specificity is cost-effective, dependency is (i) deliberately incurred and (ii) supported with safeguards. Therefore, although less dependency is always better than more, ceteris paribus, deliberate recourse to asset specificity will be undertaken in the degree to which net benefits (due allowance having been made for safeguards) can be projected.

Farsighted (but incomplete) contracting is also to be contrasted with frictionless contracting that characterizes much of the economic theory literature. The concept of remediableness arises in this connection.[8] Since all feasible forms of organization are flawed (Coase, 1964), and since choices must be made among feasible forms, a comparative institutional assessment of alternative flawed forms (of which a hypothetical ideal is not one) is needed. The concept of remediableness counsels that an outcome for which no feasible superior alternative can be described and implemented with net gains is presumed to be efficient. That collides with traditional prescriptions in applied welfare economics.

Lapses into ideal, but operationally irrelevant, reasoning will be avoided by (i) recognizing that it is impossible to do better than one's best, (ii) insisting that all of the finalists in an organization form competition meet the test of feasibility, (iii) symmetrically exposing the weaknesses as well as the strengths of all proposed feasible forms, and (iv) describing and costing out the mechanisms of any proposed reorganization. To this list, moreover, there is yet a further consideration: (v) make a place for and be respectful of politics.

This last point has been the most difficult for public policy analysts to concede, but this too is beginning to change. Avinash Dixit's recent treatment of 'transaction cost politics' is pertinent:

> The standard normative approach to policy analysis views this whole process as a social-welfare maximizing black box, exactly as the neoclassical theory of production and supply viewed the firm as a profit-maximizing black box. ... Economists studying business and industrial organization have long recognized the inadequacy of the neoclassical view of the firm, and have developed richer paradigms and models based on the concepts of various kinds of transaction costs. Policy analysis will also benefit by adopting such an approach (1996, p. 9).

Whereas normative economics holds that economics trumps politics, positive analysis places economics in the service of politics. Therefore, rather than describe political choices to which deadweight losses can be ascribed as 'failures,' positive analysis inquires into the political purposes served by indirect and even convoluted mechanisms (Moe, 1990a, 1990b). Absent a showing that these can be supplanted by feasible alternative mechanisms

---

[8] The earlier literature on nirvana economics (Robinson, 1934; Demsetz, 1969) is pertinent.

which will realize expected net gains, such mechanisms are presumed to be efficient (Stigler, 1992; Williamson, 1996, Ch. 8).

Calculativeness.   As indicated, transaction cost economizing is held to be the main case. The concept of governance as a means by which to mitigate conflict and promote mutual gain is central to the exercise and gives the project broad scope. Not only can a wide variety of phenomena be examined in this way, but economizing is an encompassing concept. Accordingly, there is little need—indeed, often, there are real costs—in moving outside of the economizing framework to introduce user-friendly terms such as fairness, justice, trust and the like. That is because the 'missing values' that these terms are intended to convey are already operative within the far-sighted contracting/economizing set-up.

Compare, for example, Frank Michelman's treatment of takings in the context of transaction costs (which take the form of spillover costs, demoralization costs and administrative costs) with the more diffuse notion of 'justice as fairness' (Michelman, 1967; Williamson, 1970). Not only is the latter a vague (and therefore manipulable) criterion for deciding whether or not to compensate, but it is not obvious that adding fairness onto an efficiency assessment adds anything whatsoever.

Or consider the view that 'When we say we trust someone or that someone is trustworthy, we implicitly mean that the probability that he will perform an action that is beneficial or at least not detrimental to us is high enough for us to consider engaging in some form of cooperation with him' (Gambetta, 1988, p. 217). I maintain that the condition in question should be described not as trust but as calculated risk and that to substitute the more user-friendly term (trust) for the more calculative expression (risk) invites confusion (Williamson, 1993b).

Elizabeth Hoffman *et al.* advise similarly with respect to 'reciprocal altruism.' Altruism is a user-friendly word, but it is wholly expendable in most cases where the agents are deciding whether to cooperate in terms of intertemporal reputation effects. If altruism is conditional on the expectation of reciprocation, it scarcely qualifies as altruism at all: 'I am not really being an altruist if my action is based entirely on my expectation of your reciprocation' (1995, p. 17). The exercise being wholly calculative, adding altruism to reciprocity makes a clear concept obscure.

The calculative approach of examining incomplete contracts in their entirety and folding in consequences *is an effort to mitigate hazards and avoid regret.* Thus construed, it is hard-headed but not mean-spirited. As between being calculative and uncovering the deep structure and being user-friendly but superficial, the choice is easy.

Note, moreover, that being relentlessly calculative does not imply that economics trumps either politics or organization. The object is to understand politics and organization, which places comparative institutional analysis in the analytic service of politics and organization.

4. L&E in Relation to LEO: Specific Comparisons

Does the LEO perspective have real consequences? Do the moves described in Figure 3 really matter? Opinions differ on this. Thus, Posner holds that 'When the new institutional economists study long-term contracts and corporate governance and vertical integration and property rights and the like, they are doing the *same thing* that the law and economics scholars do when they study the same subjects' (1993, p. 85; emphasis added). Those who do the same thing should come to the same result. As set out below, real differences are sometimes obtained.

Even, however, where they come out roughly the same, as they do, for the most part, on matters of vertical market restrictions and of strategic anticompetitive behavior, there are still advantages in having the microanalytics of contractual restrictions and strategic behavior worked out. Not only is this interesting in its own right, but more nuanced policy will sometimes result (Williamson, 1979, 1987c; Kenney and Klein, 1983; Masten and Snyder, 1993). Often, moreover, the public policy insights of L&E need to be delimited. The use of franchise bidding to control natural monopoly (Demsetz, 1968; Stigler, 1968; Posner, 1972) is an inspired idea, provided that the requisite preconditions are satisfied. Neglect of those preconditions, however, is fateful. Uncovering and explicating those conditions is an institutional economics exercise in which the attributes of transactions and governance structures are key (Williamson, 1976; Goldberg, 1976; Priest, 1993).

Does, however, the LEO perspective extend beyond antitrust and regulation to offer value-added more generally? I believe that it does. Applications to the study of redistribution, the efficient use of debt and equity, and the study of contract are examined here.

Redistribution

The mechanisms of redistribution out of which politics works are often convoluted and incur large deadweight losses. An oft-cited example is the US sugar program, which has been described by Stigler as follows (1992, p. 459):

> The United States wastes (in ordinary language) perhaps $3 billion per year producing sugar and sugar substitutes at a price two to three times the cost

of importing the sugar. Yet that is the tested way in which the domestic sugar-beet, cane, and high-fructose-corn producers can increase their incomes by perhaps a quarter of the $3 billion—the other three-quarters being deadweight loss. The deadweight loss is the margin by which the domestic costs of sugar production exceed import prices.

The usual interpretation is that such deadweight losses represent inefficiency: 'The Posnerian theory would say that the sugar program is grotesquely inefficient because it fails to maximize national income' (Stigler, 1992, p. 459). A contributing factor, according to efficiency of the law scholarship, is that the sugar program is statute-based (as against common law-based) in origin.

Stigler disagrees. Observing that the sugar program has been renewed for more than 50 years, he declares that the program has 'met the test of time' and should be regarded as efficient (1992, p. 459), where efficiency is judged with reference to its political purposes rather than to an abstract economic ideal, the absence of deadweight loss:

> 'Maximum national income ... is not the only goal of our nation as judged by policies adopted by our government—and government's goals as revealed by actual practice are more authoritative than those pronounced by professors of law and economics' (Stigler, 1992, p. 459).

Transaction cost economics is much closer to Stigler's assessment. Because, however, the test of time comes perilously close to a tautology, efficiency in politics should be treated as a rebuttable presumption. Inefficiency in politics implies either that the overall political process is egregiously defective and needs to be reformed or that particular programs have unacceptable origins or have evolved in unacceptable ways. The mechanisms of politics are therefore where the action resides (Williamson, 1996, Ch. 8), which is very different from conventional deadweight loss analysis. Is the political process in question judged to be well-working (which is a general test)? Is the mechanism through which redistribution is accomplished unacceptably convoluted in a particular case (which is a local test)? Is the condition in question remediable?

This does not deny that the deadweight loss analysis to which L&E appeals is an instructive place to start, but merely to display deadweight losses in relation to a hypothetical ideal is not dispositive. It is elementary that hypothetical ideals are utopian. Since the operational choices are necessarily restricted to feasible alternatives, an extant political outcome for which no feasible superior alternative can be described and implemented with net gains is held to be efficient—unless either of the exceptions referred to above applies.

Debt and Equity

The pure finance theory of debt and equity was set out in the classic paper by Modigliani and Miller, the key result of which is that '*the average cost of capital to any firm is completely independent of its capital structure and is equal to the capitalization rate of a pure equity stream of its class*' (1958, pp. 268–269; emphasis in original). This paper has had a lasting effect on the study of corporate finance and is an elegant, early illustration of the power of farsighted contracting. Because individual investors can engage in home-made diversification of their own portfolios, the cost of capital in a firm is determined entirely by the fundamentals.

Although the strong version of the Modigliani-Miller theorem has since been qualified to make provision for taxes and bankruptcy, financial signaling, resource constraints and bonding, only the last of these introduces governance considerations. Moreover, none of these qualifications regards investment as a transaction for which the discriminating alignment of governance features with the attributes of the transaction would serve to economize on transaction costs. That is because debt and equity are merely financial instruments (rather than governance instruments) under the orthodox set-up.

Frank Easterbrook and Daniel Fischel appeal to Modigliani-Miller (the financial instrument view) for the proposition that 'There is no fundamental difference between debt and equity from an economic perspective' (1986, p. 274, n. 8). Posner likewise invokes the Modigliani-Miller theorem to support the proposition that 'it is unlikely that the value of shareholders' equity can be increased by altering the debt-equity ratio' (1986, p. 411) and elsewhere appeals to differential risk aversion to explain lending by banks (1986, p. 370):

> ... the shareholder is likely to be more risk averse than the bank. Remember that we are talking about how to get individuals to invest money in enterprises. Of course corporations can be shareholders too, but the ultimate investors are individuals, and most individuals, as has been noted many times in this book, are risk averse.

Transaction cost economics holds that organization matters and asks whether debt and equity differ in governance structure respects.[9] In the event that they do, then the possibility that debt and equity align to the

---

[9] See Geoffrey Miller (1995) for a different but complementary treatment of debt and equity in which governance is featured. Also note that Easterbrook and Fischel appear to have moved away from a strict Modigliani-Miller position. Without subscribing to a transaction cost view, they do recognize signaling, monitoring, and managerial incentive aspects of debt (1991, pp. 114, 176, 282). These stop short, however, of treating debt as a governance structure.

attributes of transactions is entertained. Supplanting comprehensive (Modigliani-Miller) contracting by incomplete contracting in its entirety is the key systems move.

Viewing debt and equity as governance structures reveals that debt is the more market-like instrument to which 'rules governance' applies. Equity, by comparison, is a more discretionary instrument and has attributes more akin to hierarchical governance. The predicted alignment is that the market-like instrument (debt) will be used to finance generic projects, whereas equity will be used to finance projects where the assets are more specific and discretionary governance is the source of added value (Williamson, 1988). The argument is a variation on the paradigm problem (vertical integration) out of which transaction cost economics works, according to which generic and specific assets align to markets and hierarchies, respectively. The financial data, moreover, are broadly corroborative and the argument generalizes to asset sales and reorganization (Shleifer and Vishny, 1991).

Contract

As shown in Figure 3, the box within which the New Institutional Economics/Transaction Cost Economics is located includes 'other exchange'. That is intended to signal that transaction cost economics is part of a larger project. As Kohn (1995) interprets recent developments, the basic divide is between the 'theory of value' and the 'theory of exchange', where the former refers to neoclassical economics, especially Walras (with emphasis on costless exchange, technology, equilibrium, relative prices, and Pareto Optimality), and the latter introduces costly exchange (with problems of organization, contract and remediableness).

James Buchanan's distinction between the 'science of choice' and the 'science of contract' (1975, p. 229) is broadly in this spirit. Work of the latter kind divides into that which employs a comprehensive contracting set-up and is very formal, and that in which incomplete contracting is featured. Albeit sometimes in tension,[10] these two are also often very complementary (Edlin and Reichelstein, 1995). Here as elsewhere, my emphasis is on incomplete contracting in its entirety, which is the transaction cost economics project. It bears repeating, however, that the contractual approach to economic organization is much broader than described here and has turned out to be an extraordinarily productive perspective (Werin and Wijkander, 1992).

---

[10] There are fundamental problems with a comprehensive contracting set-up, in that any form of organization ought to be able to replicate any other (Williamson, 1987; Hart, 1990). Some of the tensions are evident in my examination of Fudenberg *et al.* (1990) in Williamson (1991).

Albeit an oversimplification, the L&E and LEO approaches to contract correspond approximately to Llewellyn's distinction between the contract-as-legal rules and contract-as-framework. The first of these is principally an exercise in court ordering in which the competency of the courts is presumed to be great (Tullock, 1996, p. 5). The second works out of private ordering and, the competency of the courts being limited, the courts are reserved for ultimate appeal.

Thus although issues of efficient breach are treated by both L&E and LEO, the legal rules (Barton, 1972; Shavell, 1980) and private ordering (Telser, 1981; Klein and Leffler, 1981; Williamson, 1983) approaches to contract are really very different. Not only is the offer and acceptance of credible commitments—the use of hostages (in various forms) to support exchange; the design of mechanisms to display information, settle disputes, and promote continuity—more in the spirit of the purposive approach to contract (in which legal rules operate in the background), but the legal rules approach is directed principally to the needs of lawyer-economists, whereas private ordering is predominantly concerned with the economics of organization.

Might, however, the purposive approach to contract in which transaction costs are featured be employed more widely by legal scholars? Anthony Kronman's treatment of 'Specific Performance' (1978), which works off of the distinction between property rules and liability rules and the transaction cost differences that accrue thereto (as originally developed by Guido Calabresi and Douglas Melamed,1972), is plainly in this spirit. If, indeed, details which matter to the economics of organization also have ramifications for the law, then more analysis of a Kronman type could be done by working with the microanalytic attributes of transactions and the mechanisms of governance. Asset specificity, in its various forms, is an obvious candidate.

Furthermore, it would be instructive to develop the legal ramifications of differential cognitive competence (bounded rationality) as it relates to the hazards (especially intertemporal hazards) of opportunism. Holding adults to their contracts serves to concentrate the mind, yet adults are merely wiser and more experienced than minors—which is to say that they differ in degree rather than in kind. If, therefore, the attributes of deeply problematic transactions (often due to information impactedness) could be clearly identified, might it be possible to recognize exceptions to literal enforcement for a delimited set of cases to which net benefits can be ascribed? Employment relations involving hazards with long-latency effects (as with asbestos) are an example.

Ian Ayres and Robert Gertner's analysis of 'Filling Gaps in Incomplete Contracts,' which focuses on default rules, is relevant. They not only take exception with majoritarian thinking—'the 'would have wanted' approach to gap filling' (Ayres and Gertner, 1989, p. 98)—because this is needlessly aggregative and fails to make allowance for differences to which some of the contractual parties will be mindful, but they also introduce strategic considerations. Information asymmetries are responsible for the latter and Ayres and Gertner advise that 'The strategic behavior of the parties informing the contract can justify strategic interpretations by the courts' (1989, p. 99). This last needs to be delimited, lest imaginative judges carry the argument to fanciful extremes. Can the circumstances where strategic concerns cross the threshold be described? What are the defining attributes?

Another area to which contractual analysis of a transaction cost economics kind could be applied is to the idea of contract laws (plural). Specifically, if each generic mode of governance is supported by a distinctive form of contract law (Williamson, 1991), then a broad effort (one that goes beyond markets, hybrids, and hierarchies) to investigate this is warranted. What is the (implicit) contract law of bureaus? What about non-profits (Hansmann, 1988)? Where does fiduciary law figure in? The application of transaction cost reasoning to all of these would be instructive.

Plainly, the LEO approach of these and related issues differs from what traditional L&E has been up to. As Richard Craswell and Alan Schwartz put it, 'Most articles in the law-and-economics tradition address the desirability of particular rules of contract law without addressing the more basic question of whether or why promises ought to be binding' (1994, p. 15).

5. *Revisiting Legal Realism*

'Why excavate the writings of the Realists?' William Fisher, Morton Horwitz and Thomas Reed respond to that query by observing that not only was Legal Realism an 'extraordinarily influential movement in American legal history', but the writings of the Realists 'contain many enduring insights' (Fisher *et al.*, 1993, p. xiv). Indeed 'Legal Realism continues to exert an important influence on modern American legal scholarship through its capacity . . . to define the questions that need answering' (Fisher, *et al.*, 1993, p. xiv). Thus, although Fisher, Horwitz and Reed do not dispute that American Legal Realism ran itself into the sand, their position is that American Legal Realism was onto some very important issues for which responsive scholarship is still needed.

Contemporary Legal Scholarship

Transaction cost economics maintains that any issue that arises as or can be posed as a contracting problem can be examined to advantage in transaction cost economizing terms. Many issues, of which the make-or-buy decision (vertical integration) is one, arise directly as contracting problems. Many other issues that originally appear to lack contracting aspects turn out, upon examination, to possess them. (Thus whereas the oligopoly problem is commonly posed in market structure terms, reformulating it as a cartel problem quickly reveals its contracting structure.) The result is that the comparative contractual approach has wide reach and application to economic organization. If contract is really 'the seminal and classic subject of American legal education' (Rubin, 1995, p. 1), possibly it has wide application to the law as well.

Yet Llewellyn's concept of contract-as-framework (supported by private ordering with courts reserved for ultimate appeal) has made only limited headway. American legal scholarship still relates mainly to the legal rules tradition: 'When American legal scholars speak of 'contracts' they typically do not mean contracts at all, but rather judicial decisions ... involving disputes about contracts. Contracts themselves, the transactions that create them, and the business decision to comply with them, renegotiate them, or breach them have rarely surfaced in the academic study of [contract]' (Rubin, 1995, p. 1).

Given the disparity between contract law on the books and contract law in action, it might have been anticipated that 'Law and economics, drawn from a discipline that had no intrinsic affection for judicial decision, should have rapidly redirected the attention of legal scholars to the study of contracts and contractual relations' (Rubin, 1995, p. 3), but that did not materialize. As with tort law, where the law on the books orientation prevailed (Landes and Posner, 1987, p. 312), so too with contract.

Rubin thereupon raises the possibility that transaction cost economics will 'provide a pathway through the thickets where the legal realists and the legal economists got lost' (1995, p. 4). Clearly, transaction cost economics and Legal Realism have overlapping interests in understanding legal purpose and practice. Conceivably the economizing logic and mechanisms out of which transaction cost economics works could be put to the service of Legal Realism.

Such an undertaking is especially important if, as Rubin elsewhere observes, American legal scholarship is:

> ... in a state of disarray. It seems to lack a unified purpose, a coherent methodology, a sense of forward motion, and a secure link to its past traditions. It is bedeviled by a gnawing sense that it should adopt the methods of other disciplines but it is uncertain how the process is to be accomplished (1988, p. 1835).

Might the application of the schema in Figure 2(b), according to which economics both informs and is informed by law and organization, might Figure 2(b) help to relieve this status and recover forward motion?

Recent arguments of a related kind have been advanced by Jason Johnston, George Priest and George Stigler. Thus, Johnston observes that 'close comparative analysis of institutions is home turf for law professors' (1993, p. 216), which is very much in the spirit of law, economics, and organization. Getting beyond the Legal Realists' conviction that announced legal rules may differ from what courts actually do requires linkages with a progressive research program (Johnston, 1993, p. 218).

Related to this, George Priest observes that 'one must abandon the notion that law is a subject that can be usefully studied by persons trained only in the law' (1983, p. 437) and avers that 'the best writing about the legal system *is* interdisciplinary' (1983, p. 440), whereupon he concludes that 'the structure of the law school and its current curriculum must change' (1983, p. 440). If, moreover, 'efficiency of the law' scholarship is too narrow and must make a place for politics and organization (Priest, 1984), then something more akin to Figure 2(b) seems warranted.

George Stigler, if I interpret him correctly, also viewed the economic analysis of law as a worthy but needlessly narrow construction. His provocative essay on 'Law or Economics?' concludes by distinguishing (Stigler, 1992, p. 467):

> ... two fundamentally different roles that [economists] might play in law. The first role is simply to provide expertise on points requested by the lawyers....
>
> A second, more controversial role for economics is in the study of legal institutions and doctrines . . . [Such matters] are not exclusively legal and economic—indeed, they obviously involve the workings of the political system. Understanding the source, structure, and evolution of a legal system is the kind of project that requires skills that are possessed but not monopolized by economists.

Of these two, the second is a more ambitious and more interdisciplinary exercise. It is also more controversial: the law schools may decide that 'Such studies are not necessary and are possibly even disruptive in a discipline whose fundamental task is to train practitioners' (Stigler, 1992, p. 467).

The possible unsuitability of the program described by Stigler (and/or the project that I describe as law, economics and organization) is for others to decide. If, however, the importance of dealing with the law in action (as against the law on the books) persists, then disciplined ways by which to address the concerns of the Legal Realists will be needed. Operationalization is what permitted the New Institutional Economics to succeed where the older style institutional economics had failed. Operationalization is likewise the prescription for a New Legal Realism.

That a New Legal Realism might succeed, where the earlier Legal Realism ran itself into the sand, is favored due to several considerations. First, as Rubin suggests, Legal Realism would find considerable support from the renewal of interest in institutional economics and the evolving programs of research (including transaction cost economics) that are associated therewith. Second, the law schools in the 1990s differ greatly from the 1930s. Not only do many more law school professors have social science training and social science interests today, but the law schools are much more connected (often through joint appointments) with the larger intellectual community in the university. Third, the needs for real-time reform are less pressing than in the 1930s. Finally, the opportunities for lawyers to participate in the 'special multidisciplinary conversation about law, economics, and organization' are numerous and growing:[11]

> The emerging law, economics, and organization literature has already made at least three general contributions: first, it has expanded economic analysis of law to take account of the institutional forms within which legal rules and transactions take place. In so doing it has, in the best tradition of interdisciplinary research, both increased our understanding of law and improved economic theory. Second, this literature has reached out to include the insights of other disciplines (particularly political science, sociology, and psychology) that are concerned with organizational forms and their influence on legal decision-making. Third, this broadened perspective has begun to make interdisciplinary research about law relevant to a broader group of lawyers and legal academics who do not view themselves as being associated directly with law and economics (Mashaw, 1985, p. 4).

The advantages of lawyers (or lawyer-economists), as against economists, for orchestrating a renewal of Legal Realism is that they have deep knowledge about legal phenomena—many of which remain puzzles. What is needed is to join deep knowledge about this subject matter with a productive framework. Employing the economic approach, which includes but goes beyond orthodoxy, and appealing to the New Institutional Economics/ transaction cost economics, if and as institutions figure prominently in the problem, is the strategy proposed here.

Since the comparative analysis of institutions, as Johnston put it, is 'home turf' to law professors, that proposal is congruent with the natural inclinations of many lawyer-economists. A concerted move in this direction nevertheless faces obstacles. For one thing, there is always the lurking hazard that transaction cost reasoning will lapse into *ex post* rationalization. Lawyer-economists need to use and refine these concepts in a disciplined way. For another, it is much easier to see merit in a new framework than it is to work productively out of that framework. History records that legal formalism has

---

[11] The ideas written by Mashaw are ones with which I concurred then and to which I subscribe now.

lasting attractions—not least of all because it is familiar turf over which lawyers have undisputed control.

Be that as it may, the foregoing establishes that (i) American Legal Realism and older style institutional economics in the USA had many similarities, (ii) the transaction cost economics branch of LEO is responsive to some of the key insights of older style institutional economics, and (iii) that the concerns of Legal Realism are enduring. Also, (iv) LEO (I think) relates more closely to the needs of Legal Realism than does L&E. Might some of the lawyer-economists to whom Ackerman (1986) refers—namely, those who are disaffected with L&E yet are not fully persuaded to work through the sciences of culture—find that LEO can breathe operational life into Legal Realism as well? That is my suggestion.

Implementation

Conceptually.   Although both Fuller's interests in the study of 'good order and workable arrangements' and Llewellyn's emphasis on 'contract as framework' have attracted favorable commentary from lawyers (Summers, 1984; Macneil, 1974), neither of these projects have been developed in a sustained way. Especially in combination, these two are potentially very fruitful. The former is an instructive way to think about the purposes of both law and organization. The latter supplants a legalistic view of contract with a purposive one. Taken together, and with the support of apparatus that serves to operationalize these concepts, a positive and predictive theory of contract (more generally, of the law) might be within reach.

If contract is really the unifying subject in the law, it ought to have broad application. It does. Thus, one way to interpret Coase's influential article on 'Social Cost' is that tort law is really a special case of contract law. Because parties will always costlessly contract to an efficient result in a zero transaction cost regime, externalities arise always and only because positive transaction costs make it costly to contract. The upshot is that such comparative contractual reasoning applies quite generally.

Going native.   Transaction cost economics is an effort to apply comparative contractual reasoning to any problem that arises as or can be reformulated as a contracting problem. As Arrow observed, externalities are subsumed by market failures which in turn are subsumed by transaction cost (1969, p. 48). For example, the differential costs of organizing are what prevents consumers from bargaining to an efficient result with a producer cartel (Arrow, 1969, p. 51). Upon observing an 'inefficiency' of any kind, it is useful to pose three questions: What is the contract that would remove the inefficiency? What impediments preclude this contract from being implemented? What are the best feasible contractual alternatives for dealing with this condition?

Transaction cost economics avers that the way to think about issues contractually is in an incomplete but farsighted contracting fashion. That conception of contract is saturated with tension. As between incompleteness and farsightedness, the lawyer-economist is advised to push farsightedness (more generally, the rational spirit/systems approach) to the limit—but not beyond. The object is to discover delayed or indirect consequences, to which organization theory is often attentive, thereafter to work out the ramifications for dealing more knowledgeably and effectively with the phenomena in question by folding these delayed or indirect effects back in. To be sure, looking ahead is what law and economics has been urging right along. What LEO adds, if one buys into transaction cost economics, are: (i) a view of the firm as governance structure (rather than production function); (ii) greater respect for organization and for politics more generally; (ii) greater emphasis on the purposes served by *ex post* governance (as against *ex ante* incentive alignment), (iv) a more microanalytic perspective in which the action resides in the details of transactions and governance; and (v) the remediableness criterion (whereupon failure is not established by a demonstrated deviation from a hypothetical ideal). Transaction cost economics also works out of a generalized 'economic approach' (rather than economic orthodoxy) and appeals to economizing (rather than utility maximization). Furthermore, the new institutional economics/transaction cost economics has been described as 'Politically ... neutral: it has been invoked in support of both market pessimism and market optimism' (Matthews, 1986, p. 907).

The resulting approach nevertheless remains highly calculative, and an obsession with calculativeness is widely thought to be an occupational burden—a trained incapacity—for economists. Indeed, there is a growing chorus of critics—of which Alan Fox (1974) is one of the more thoughtful and Francis Fukuyama (1995) is one of the more recent—who advise that calculativeness is the problem to which fellow-feeling and 'trust' is the solution. Surely lawyers are too wise to fall into the economists' trap.

These issues are outlined earlier in the paper and developed more extensively elsewhere (Williamson, 1993b). It is sufficient to observe here that although calculativeness can be used in a myopic and grasping way, that is not what incomplete contracting in its entirety contemplates. The object of farsighted contracting is to look ahead, recognize potential hazards, and use *ex post* governance (as well as *ex ante* incentive alignment) to reduce hazards and avoid regrets. Those who interpret that as mean-spirited contracting need to explain how they reach that result.

My proposal for implementing the study of good order and workable arrangements is therefore as follows: examine each legal issue through the lens of comparative, farsighted contracting in which transaction cost economizing is featured; be relentlessly calculative; and, because all feasible forms of law and organization are flawed, work through the remediableness criterion.

That is a stringent prescription and some lawyer-economists may prefer greater latitude. Although that is understandable (and perhaps advisable), my recommendation would be to 'go native', which is easier said than done. Thomas Kuhn speaks of the issues:

> To translate a theory or world view into one's own language is not to make it one's own. For that one must go native, discover that one is think-ing and working in, not simply translating out of, a language that was pre-viously foreign, [which can be difficult]. . . . Many who first encountered, say, relativity or quantum mechanics in their middle years . . . [found them-selves] fully persuaded of the new view but nevertheless unable to internal-ize it (1970, p. 204).

The agenda.   An ambitious way to pose the challenge is to take the table of contents in Posner's treatise *Economic Analysis of Law* as the chapter head-ings for a parallel book on *The Analysis of Law, Economics and Organization*. Does LEO add much or little and, where the differences are substantial, why and what do the data support?

6. Conclusions

Legal Realism was examining good issues, had revolutionary pretensions, and faltered for lack of a conceptual framework and scientific commitment. Successors such as 'Bickel, Hart, and Sacks ... co-opted realism and attempted to make it more rational' but lacked revolutionary zeal (Kalman, 1986, p. 231). Even more, they lacked a systematic mode of analysis from which refutable implications could be derived and to which an empirical program of research could be applied.

The program described here as law, economics, and organization also lacks revolutionary purpose but does have a scientific ambition. Conceivably, although this awaits trial, the concerns with which the Realists were grappling can be studied in a 'modest, slow, molecular, definitive' way by adopting (and, as necessary, reshaping) the framework out of which trans-action cost economics operates. (See, for example, Roberta Romano, 1993 and the collection of reprinted articles in Williamson and Masten, 1995).

Acknowledgements

The author is Edgar F. Kaiser Professor of Business Administration, Professor of Economics and Professor of Law at the University of California, Berkeley. This paper has been revised in response to presentations at the Turku School of Economics and Business Administration, Paris I (Sorbonne), Strasbourg University (BETA), the Institutional Analysis Workshop at the University of California, Berkeley, and the European Association of Law and Economics (Gerzensee, Switzerland). Comments by Robert Ellickson, Jason Johnston, Scott Masten, Claude Menard, Richard Posner, Roberta Romano and Edward Rubin are gratefully acknowledged.

References

Ackerman, B. (1986), 'Law, Economics, and the Problem of Legal Culture,' *Duke Law Journal*, 6 (December), 929–947.

Arrow, K. (1969), 'The Organization of Economic Activity: Issues Pertinent to the Choice of Market Versus Nonmarket Allocation,' in *The Analysis and Evaluation of Public Expenditure: The PPB System*, Vol. 1, US Joint Economic Committee, 91st Congress, 1st Session. Washington, DC: US Government Printing Office, pp. 59–73.

Arrow, K. (1974), *The Limits of Organization*. 1st edn. W. W. Norton: New York.

Arrow, K. (1987), 'Reflections on the Essays,' in G. Feiwel (ed.) *Arrow and the Foundations of the Theory of Economic Policy*. NYU Press: New York, pp. 727–734.

Arrow, K. and F. Hahn (1971) *General Competitive Analysis*. Holden-Day: San Francisco, CA.

Ayres, I. and R. Gertner (1989), 'Filling Gaps in Incomplete Contracts: An Economic Theory of Default Rules,' *Yale Law Journal*, 94, 96–114.

Barnard, C. (1938), *The Functions of the Executive*. Harvard University Press: Cambridge, MA (15th printing, 1962).

Barton, J. (1972), 'The Economic Basis for Damages for Breach of Contract,' *Journal of Legal Studies*, 1 (June), 276–304.

Barzel, Yoram. (1982), 'Measurement Cost and the Orbanization of Markets,' *Journal of Law and Economics*, 25 (April): 27–48.

Buchanan, James. (1975), 'A Contractarian Paradigm for Applying Economic Theory,' *American Economic Review*, 65 (May): 225–230.

Calabresi, G. and D. Melamed (1972), 'Property Rules, Liability Rules, and Inalienability: One View of the Cathedral,' *Harvard Law Review*, 85, 1089–1126.

Coase, R. H. (1937), 'The Nature of the Firm,' *Economica N.S.*, 4, 386–405. Reprinted in O. E. Williamson and S. Winter (eds) (1991), *The Nature of the Firm: Origins, Evolution, Development*. Oxford University Press: New York, pp. 18–33.

Coase, R. H. (1960), 'The Problem of Social Cost,' *Journal of Law and Economics*, 3 (October), 1–44.

Coase, R. H. (1964), 'The Regulated Industries: Discussion,' *American Economic Review*, 54 (May), 194–197.

Coase, R. H. (1978), 'Economics and Contiguous Disciplines,' *Journal of Legal Studies*, 7, 201–211.

Coase, R. H. (1983), Remarks appearing in 'The Fire of Truth,' E. Kitch (ed.) *Journal of Law and Economics*, 16, 163–233.

Coase, R. H. (1984), 'The New Institutional Economics,' *Journal of Institutional and Theoretical Economics*, 140 (March), 229–231.

Coase, R. H. (1988), 'The Nature of the Firm: Influence,' *Journal of Law, Economics, and Organization*, 4 (Spring), 33–47.

Coase, R. H. (1992), 'The Institutional Structure of Production,' *American Economic Review*, 82 (September), 713–719.

Coleman, J. (1990), *The Foundations of Social Theory*. Harvard University Press: Cambridge, MA.

Commons, J. R. (1924), 'Law and Economics,' *Yale Law Journal*, 34, 371–382.

Commons, J. R. (1931), 'Institutional Economics,' *American Economic Review*, 71 (December), 648–657.

Commons, J. R. (1932), 'The Problem of Correlating Law, Economics and Ethics,' *Wisconsin Law Review*, 8, 3–26.

Commons, J. R. (1934), *Institutional Economics*. University of Wisconsin Press: Madison, WI.

Cooter, R. and T. Ulen (1988), *Law and Economics*. Scott, Foresman and Co: Glenview, IL.

Cournot, Antoine Augustin. (1838), *Researches into the Mathematical Prinicples of the Theory of Wealth* (W. T. Bacon, tr. 1897). New York: The Macmillan Company.

Craswell, Richard, and Alan Schwartz. (1994), *Foundations of Contract Law*. New York: Oxford University Press.

D'Andrade, Roy. (1986), 'Three Scientific World Views and the Covering Law Model,' in Donald W. Fiske and Richard A. Schweder, eds., *Metatheory in Social Science: Pluralisms and Subjectivities*. Chicago: University of Chicago Press.

Davis, L. and D. C. North (1971), *Institutional Change and American Economic Growth*. Cambridge University Press: Cambridge.

Debreu, G. (1959), *Theory of Value*. Wiley: New York.

Demsetz, Harold. (1968), 'Why Regulate Utilities?' *Journal of Law and Economics*, 11 (April): 55–66.

Demsetz, H. (1968), 'Information and Efficiency: Another Viewpoint,' *Journal of Law and Economics*, 12 (April), 1–22.

DiMaggio, P. and W. Powell (1991), 'Introduction' in W. Powell and P. DiMaggio (eds) *The New Insttutionalism in Organizational Analysis*. University of Chicago Press: Chicago, IL, pp. 1–38.

Dixit, A. (1995), *The Making of Economic Policy: A Transaction Cost Politics Perspective*. (forthcoming).

Donaldson, G. (1981), *Corporate Debt Capacity*. Harvard Business School Press: Boston, MA.

Dorfman, J. (1947), *Thorstein Veblen and His America*. Viking: New York.

Duxbury, N. (1995), *Patterns of American Jurisprudence*. Oxford: New York.

Easterbrook, F. and D. Fischel (1986), 'Close Corporations and Agency Costs,' *Stanford Law Review*, 38 (January), 271–301.

Easterbrook, F. and D. Fischel (1991), *The Economic Structure of Corporate Law*. Harvard University Press: Cambridge, MA.

Eccles, R., and H. White (1988), 'Price and Authority in Inter-Profit Center Transactions,' *American Journal of Sociology* (Supplement), 94, S17–S51.

Edgeworth, F. Y. (1881), *Mathematical Psychics*. Kegan Paul: London.

Edlin, Aaron S., and Stefan Reichelstein. (1995), 'Holdups, Standard Breach Remedies, and Optimal Investment,' *American Economic Review*, 86 (June): 478–501.

Ellickson, R. (1989), 'Bringing Culture and Human Frailty to Rational Actors: A Critique of Classical Law and Economics,' *Chicago-Kent Law Review*, 65, 23–62.

Elster, J. (1994), 'Arguing and Bargaining in Two Constituent Assemblies.' Unpublished manuscript, remarks given at the University of California, Berkeley.

Eskridge, W. and P. Frickey (1994), 'An Historical and Critical Introduction to *The Legal Process*,' in H. Hart and A. Sacks, *The Legal Process*. Foundation Press: Westbury, NY, pp. li-cxxxix.

Fisher, W., M. Horwitz and T. Reed (eds) (1993), *American Legal Realism*. Oxford University Press: New York.

Fox, A. (1974), *Beyond Contract: Work, Power, and Trust Relations*. Faber & Faber: London.

Fudenberg, Drew, Bengt Holmstrom, and Paul Milgrom. (1990), 'Short-Term Contracts and Long-Term Agency Relationships,' *Journal of Economic Theory*, 51 (June): 1–31,

Fukuyama, F. (1995), *Trust: The Social Virtues and Creation of Prosperity*. Free Press: New York.

Fuller, L. (1954), 'American Legal Philosophy at Mid-Century,' *Journal of Legal Education*, 6(4), 457–485.

Galanter, M. (1981) 'Justice in Many Rooms: Courts, Private Ordering, and Indigenous Law,' *Journal of Legal Pluralism*, 19, 1–47.

Gambetta, D. (1988) 'Can We Trust Trust?' in D. Gambetta (ed.), *Trust: Making and Breaking Cooperative Relations*. Basil Blackwell: Oxford, pp. 213–237.

Gibbons, R. (1995), 'Game Theory and Garbage Cans.' Unpublished manuscript. Center for Advanced Study in the Behavioral Sciences, Stanford, CA.

Goldberg, V. (1976) 'Regulation and Administered Contracts,' *Bell Journal of Economics*, 7 (Autumn), 426–452.

Granovetter, M. (1988), 'The Sociological and Economic Approaches to Labor Market Analysis,' in George Farkas and Paula England, eds., *Industries, Firms, and Jobs*. New York: Plenum, pp. 187–218.

Hansmann, H. (1988), 'The Ownership of the Firm,' *Journal of Law, Economics, and Organization*, 4 (Fall): 267–303.

Hart, H. and A. Sacks (1994), *The Legal Process*. Foundation Press: Westbury, NY.

Hart, O. (1990), 'An Economist's Perspective on the Theory of the Firm,' in O. Williamson (ed.) *Organization Theory*. Oxford University Press: New York, pp. 154–171.

Hayek, F. (1945), 'The Use of Knowledge in Society,' *American Economic Review*, 35 (September), 519–530.

Heide, Jan, and George John. (1988), 'The Role of Dependence Balancing in Safeguarding Transaction-Specific Assets in Conventional Channels,' *Journal of Marketing*, 52 (january): 20–35.

Hoffman, E., K. McCabe and V. Smith (1995), 'Behavioral Foundations of Reciprocity: Experimental Economic and Evolutionary Psychology.' Unpublished manuscript.

Hohfeld, W. (1913), 'Some Fundamental Legal Conceptions as Applied in Judicial Reasoning,' *Yale Law Journal*, 23, 16–55.

Holmstrom, Bengt, and Paul Milgrom. (1991), 'Multi-Task Principal-Agent Analysis,' upublished manuscript.

Homans, G. (1958), 'Social Behavior as Exchange,' *American Journal of Sociology*, 62, 597–606.

Johnston, J. (1993), 'The Influence of *The Nature of the Firm* on the Theory of Corporate Law,' *Journal of Corporation Law*, (Winter), 213–244.

Joskow, P. (1988), 'Asset Specificity and the Structure of Vertical Relationships: Empirical Evidence,' *Journal of Law, Economics, and Organization*, 4 (Spring), 95–117.

Kalman, L. (1986), *Legal Realism at Yale, 1927–1960*. University of North Carolina Press: Chapel Hill, NC.

Kenney, Roy, and Benjamin Klein. (1983), 'The Economics of Block Booking,' *Journal of Law and Economics*, 26 (October): 497–540.

Klein, B. (1980),'Transaction Cost Determinants of 'Unfair' Contractual Arrangements,' *American Economic Review*, 70 (May), 356–362.

Klein, Benjamin, and K. B. Leffler. (1981), 'The Role of Market Forces in Assuring Contractual Performance,' *Journal of Political Economy*, 89 (August): 615–641.

Klein, P. and H. Shelanski (1995), 'Empirical Work in Transaction Cost Economics,' *Journal of Law, Economics, and Organization*, 11 (October).

Kohn, Meir. (1995), 'Economics as a Theory of Exchange, unpublished manuscript, Dartmouth College.

Komisar, N. (1994), *Imperfect Alternatives*. University of Chicago Press: Chicago, IL.

Kreps, D. (1990), 'Corporate Culture and Economic Theory,' in J. Alt and K. Shepsle (eds), *Perspectives on Positive Political Economy*. Cambridge University Press: New York, pp. 90–143.

Kreps, David M. (1992), '(How) Can Game Theory Lead to a Unified Theory of Organization?' unpublished manuscript, Stanford University.

Kronman, A. (1978), 'Specific Performance,' *University of Chicago Law Review*, 45, 351–375.

Kuhn, T. (1970), *The Structure of Scientific Revolutions*. University of Chicago Press: Chicago, IL.

Landes, W. and R. Posner (1987), *The Economic Structure of Tort Law*. University of Chicago Press: Chicago, IL.

Levy, B. and P. Spiller (1994), 'The Institutional Foundations of Regulatory Commitment,' *Journal of Law, Economics, and Organization*, 9 (Fall), pp. 201–246.

Llewellyn, K. (1931), 'What Price Contract? An Essay in Perspective,' *Yale Law Journal*, 40 (May), 704–751.

Macaulay, S. (1963), 'Non-Contractual Relations in Business,' *American Sociological Review*, 28, 55–70.

Macneil, I. (1974), 'The Many Futures of Contracts,' *Southern California Law Review*, 47 (May), 691–816.

Macneil, I. (1978), 'Contracts: Adjustments of Long-Term Economic Relations Under Classical, Neoclassical, and Relational Contract Law,' *Northwestern University Law Review*, 72, 854–906.

March, J. and H. Simon (1958), *Organizations*. John Wiley & Sons: New York.

Marshall, A. (1890), *Principles of Economics*. Macmillan: London.

Mashaw, J. (1985), 'Editors' Foreword,' *Journal of Law, Economics, and Organization*, 1 (Spring), 3–4.

Masten, S. (1995), 'Introduction' in O. Williamson and S. Masten (eds), *Transaction Cost Economics*, Vol. II. Edward Elgar: Brookfield, VT, pp. xi–xxii.

Masten, S. and K. Crocker (1985), 'Efficient Adaptation in Long-Term Contracts: Take-or-Pay Provisions for Natural Gas,' *American Economic Review*, 75 (December), 1083–1093.

Masten, S. and E. Snyder (1993), 'United States versus United Shoe Machinery Corporation: On the Merits,' *Journal of Law and Economics*, 36 (April), 33–70.

Matthews, R. C. O. (1986), 'The Economics of Institutions and the Sources of Economic Growth,' *Economic Journal*, 96 (December), 903–918.

Michelman, F. (1967), 'Property, Utility and Fairness: Comments on the Ethical Foundations of 'Just Compensation' Law,' *Harvard Law Review*, 80 (April), 1165–1257.

Mill, J. S. (1848), *Principles of Political Economy*.

Miller, G. (1995), 'Finance and the Firm,' *Journal of Institutional and Theoretical Economics* (forthcoming).

Milton, F. (1962), *Capitalism and Freedom*. University of Chicago Press: Chicago, IL.

Modigliani, F. and M. Miller (1958), 'The Cost of Capital, Corporation Finance, and the Theory of Investment,' *American Economic Review*, 48 (June), 261–297.

Moe, T. (1990a), 'Political Institutions: The Neglected Side of the Story,' *Journal of Law, Economics, and Organization* (Special Issue), 6, 213–253.

Moe, T. (1990b), 'The Politics of Structural Choice: Toward a Theory of Public Bureaucracy,' in O. Williamson (ed), *Organization Theory*. Oxford: New York, pp. 116–153.

Myers, S. (1977) 'Determinants of Corporate Borrowing,' *Journal of Financial Economics*, 5, 147–175.

Nelson, R. (1995), 'Recent Evolutionary Theorizing About Economic Change,' *Journal of Economic Literature*, 33 (March) 48–90.

Polinsky, M. (1983), *An Introduction to Law and Economics*.

Posner, R. (1972), 'The Appropriate Scope of Regulation in the Cable Television Industry,' *The Bell Journal of Economics and Management Science*, 3(1) (Spring), 98–129.

Posner, R. (1975), 'The Economic Approach to Law,' *Texas Law Review*, 53(4) (May), 757–782.

Posner, R. (1986), *Economic Analysis of Law*. 3rd edn. Little-Brown: Boston, MA.

Posner, R. (1993), 'The New Institutional Economics Meets Law and Economics,' *Journal of Institutional and Theoretical Economics*, 149 (March), 73–87.

Postrel, S. (1991), 'Burning Your Britches Behind You: Can Policy Scholars Bank on Game Theory?' *Strategic Management Journal*, 12, 153–155.

Priest, G. (1983), 'Social Science Theory and Legal Education,' *Journal of Legal Education*, 33, 437–441.

Priest, G. (1984), 'Law and Economics and Law Reform,' *Journal of Legal Studies*, 13 (August), 587–592.

Priest, George L. (1993), 'The Origins of Utility Regulation and the "Theories of Regulation" Debate,' *Journal of Law and Economics*, 36 (April): 289–324.

Ricardo, D. (1817), *Principles of Political Economy*.

Robinson, E. A. G. (1934), 'The Problem of Management and the Size of Firms,' *Economic Journal*, 44 (June): 240–254.

Romano, R. (1993), *The Genius of American Corporate Law*. AEI Press: Washington, DC.

Rubin, E. (1988), 'The Practice and Discourse of Legal Scholarship,' *Michigan Law Review*, 86 (August), 1835–1905.

Rubin, E. (1995), 'The Phenomenology of Contract: Complex Contracting in the Entertainment Industry,' *Journal of Institutional and Theoretical Economics* (forthcoming).

Rutherford, Malcomb. (1994), *Institutions in Economics*. New York: Cambridge University Press.

Schlegel, J. H. (1979), 'American Legal Realism and Empirical Social Science: From the Yale Experience,' *Buffalo Law Review*, 28 (Summer), 459–586.

Schlegel, J. H. (1980), 'American Legal Realism and Empirical Social Science: The Singular Case of Underhill Moore,' *Buffalo Law Review*, 29 (Spring), 195–323.

Schultz, G. (1995), 'Economics in Action: Ideas, Institutions, Policies,' *American Economic Review*, 85 (May), 1–8.

Shavell, S. (1980), 'Damage Measures for Breach of Contract,' *Bell Journal of Economics*, 11 (Autumn), 466–490.

Shleiffer, Andrei, and Robert Vishny. (1991), 'Asset Sales and Debt Capacity.' unpublished manuscript.

Simon, H. (1962), 'New Developments in the Theory of the Firm,' *American Economic Review*, 52 (March), 1–15.

Simon, H. (1978),'Rationality as Process and as Product of Thought,' *American Economic Review*, 68 (May), 1–16.

Smith, A. (1776), *The Wealth of Nations*. (1992). J. M. Dent & Sons: London.

Stigler, G. (1968), *The Organization of Industry*. Richard D. Irwin: Homewood, IL.

Stigler, G. (1992), 'Law or Economics?' *Journal of Law and Economics*, 35 (October), 455–468.

Summers, C. (1969), 'Collective Agreements and the Law of Contracts,' *Yale Law Journal*, 78 (March), 537–575.

Summers, R. (1984), *Lon L. Fuller*. Stanford University Press: Stanford.

Teece, David J. (1986), 'Profiting from Technological Innovation,' *Research Policy*, 15 (December): 285–305.

Telser, Lester. (1981), 'A Theory of Self-Enforcing Agreements,' *Journal of Business*, 53 (February): 27–44.

Tullock, Gordon. (1996), 'Legal Heresy,' *Journal of Economic Inquiry* (January): 1–14.

Veblen, T. (1898), 'Why Is Economics Not an Evolutionary Science?' *Quarterly Journal of Economics*, (July), 373–397.

Walras, L. (1874), *Eléments d'Economie Politique Pure*. L. Corbaz: Lausanne.

Weingast, Barry. (1995), 'The Political Foundations of Democracy and the Rule of Law,' unpublished manuscript, Stanford University.

Werin, L and H. Wijkander (1992), *Contract Economics*. Basil Blackwell: Oxford.

Williamson, O. E. (1970), 'Administrative Decision Making and Pricing: Externality and Compensation Analysis Applied,' in Julius Margolis, ed., *The Analysis of Public Output*. New York: National Bureau of Economic Research, Inc., pp. 115–135.

Williamson, O. E. (1971). 'The Vertical Integration of Production: Market Failure Considerations,' *American Economic Review*, 61 (May): 112–123.

Williamson, O. E. (1975), *Markets and Hierarchies: Analysis and Antitrust Implications*. Free Press: New York.

Williamson, O. E. (1976), 'Franchise Bidding for Natural Monopolies—In General and With Respect to CATV,' *Bell Journal of Economics*, 7 (Spring), 73–104.

Williamson, O. E. (1979), 'Assessing Vertical Market Restrictions,' *University of Pennsylvania Law Review*, 127 (April): 953–993.

Williamson, O. E. (1983), 'Credible Commitments: Using Hostages To Support Exchange,' *American Economic Review*, 73 (September), 519–540.

Williamson, O. E. (1985), *The Economic Institutions of Capitalism*. Free Press: New York..

Williamson, O. E. (1987a), *Economic Organization*. New York University Press: New York.

Williamson, O. E. (1987b), 'Kenneth Arrow and the New Institutional Economics,' in G. Feiwel (ed), *Arrow and the Foundations of the Theory of Economic Policy*. New York University Press: New York, pp. 584–599.

Williamson, O. E. (1987c), 'Delimiting Antitrust,' *Georgetown Law Review*, 76, 271–303.

Williamson, O. E. (1988), 'Corporate Finance and Corporate Governance,' *Journal of Finance*, 43 (July): 567–591.

Williamson, O. E. (1989), 'Transaction Cost Economics,' in R. Schmalensee and R. Willig (eds), *Handbook of Industrial Organization*. North Holland: Amsterdam, pp. 135–182.

Williamson, O. E. (1991), 'Comparative Economic Organization: The Analysis of Discrete Structural Alternatives,' *Administrative Science Quarterly*, 36 (June), 269–296.

Williamson, O. E. (1993a), 'Transaction Cost Economics and Organization Theory,' *Institutional and Corporate Change*, 2(2), 107–156.

Williamson, O. E. (1993b), 'Calculativeness, Trust, and Economic Organization,' *Journal of Law and Economics*, 36 (April), 453–486.

Williamson, O. E. (1996), *The Mechanisms of Governance*. Oxford University Press: New York.

Williamson, O. E. and S. E. Masten (eds) (1995), *Transaction Cost Economics*, Vol. I, *Theory and Concepts*; Vol. II, *Policy and Applications*). Edward Elgar: Brookfield, VT.

PART III

Industrial Applications

CHAPTER ELEVEN

Introducing Competition into Regulated Network Industries

From Hierarchies to Markets in Electricity

PAUL L. JOSKOW

This paper examines the technological, economic and organizational attributes of electric power networks and the challenges that must be confronted to expand competition in the supply of generating services from a comparative institutional perspective. The evolution of the governance structures of the electric power sectors around the world, which rely extensively on vertical and horizontal integration and multilateral agreements, can be explained as potentially efficient organizational arrangements for dealing with vertical coordination and network externality problems that are intrinsic to modern AC electricity networks. As a result, the sector evolved with regulated or government-owned monopolies and limited opportunities for competition. The institution of regulated monopoly creates its own cost, however. There is a trade-off between the costs associated with regulated or government-owned monopolies and the benefits of operational and investment coordination within vertically 'and horizontally integrated industrial hierarchies. Around the world countries have come to view the costs of these historical governance structures as exceeding their benefits and are implementing structural and regulatory reforms to promote competition in the supply of generation services while creating new governance structures to maintain efficient short-term coordination relationships between generators and the network, to manage network constraints, and to internalize network externalities. Major issues in designing new governance structures to facilitate efficient competition among generators and reduce the scope of regulation are discussed. Alternative approaches to these challenges in the USA, Europe and other countries are examined.

1. Introduction

During the last decade, dramatic changes have taken place in the industrial structure, ownership forms, and regulatory structures governing the telecommunications, electric power, and natural gas transmission and distribution sectors in many developed and developing countries (Joskow and Noll, 1994; Armstrong *et al.*, 1994). These changes are continuing rapidly in the countries where they began and are spreading quickly to other countries as well. In the USA these sectors account for roughly $400 billion of retail sales each year. The changes taking place in these traditional 'natural monopoly' sectors represent one of the most dramatic government mandated transformations in the last century of vertically and horizontally integrated industrial hierarchies. These hierarchies are being replaced with governance structures that rely much more on unregulated markets, more diffuse vertical and horizontal ownership arrangements and alternative mechanisms for regulating segments that remain 'natural monopolies'.[1]

Discussions of reforms in these sectors focus on three interrelated sets of issues: privatization, restructuring, and regulatory reform. While it is difficult to focus on one set of issues without considering the others, in this paper my plan is to focus on restructuring issues and assume either that the incumbents are regulated private firms or that privatization has accompanied restructuring. My particular interest here is to examine issues associated with alternative 'decentralized' governance structures which may replace operating and investment decisions that were traditionally governed within firms through horizontal and vertical integration. These issues will be examined largely through the lens of the restructuring of electricity supply systems around the world. However, similar issues arise in the telephone, natural gas transportation and railroad sectors as well. These restructuring issues are interesting for at least three reasons.

First, in these industries there generally remains one or more horizontal levels that are natural monopolies and will continue to be subject to regulation or alternative forms of government control. Furthermore, appropriate access to the services provided by these segments is necessary to facilitate competition at other horizontal levels. However, there are often complex operating and cost complementarities between suppliers making investment and operating decisions in the potentially competitive horizontal segments and the operators of one or more of the related regulated monopoly horizontal segments. The natural monopoly segments have 'integrated network' attributes which make some of the services they provide public goods and clear (tradable) property rights difficult to define and enforce, raising free rider and externality problems. In the case of electricity, the physical reliability of the system requires that supply and demand be balanced subject to complex constraints in real time, making it extremely difficult to rely

---

[1] At least some of the issues discussed below relate to railroad sector reforms and to a lesser extent, to reforms in other transportation sectors in some countries. These sectors will not be discussed here.

completely on tradable property rights and spot market transactions to allocate resources efficiently. As these industries evolved, the interactions between horizontal levels were generally handled within organizations through vertical integration. Spacial interdependencies were handled either within organizations through horizontal integration or through multilateral cooperative agreements between interconnected network operators. The natural monopoly at one horizontal level (e.g. transmission) typically led to monopoly at other horizontal levels (e.g. generation) as well once vertical integration became the norm for governing vertical relationships.

Restructuring to promote competition at one or more horizontal levels must necessarily involve at least partial vertical separation of the potentially competitive segments from the natural monopoly segments. This, in turn, necessarily requires careful consideration of the attributes of alternative market and non-market organizational arrangements which decentralize vertical relationships that had previously been governed by internal allocation mechanisms within vertically integrated organizations. Because the natural monopoly segments typically continue to be subject to regulation and provide 'essential services' to support competition in the related competitive sectors, the nature of the associated regulatory environment is of great importance for the performance of the system overall.

Second, because the terms and conditions of access to the natural monopoly segments of these industries affect the behavior and performance of competitors on the competitive levels that rely on them, ownership and control relationships between suppliers in the competitive and complementary monopoly levels have potentially important effects on the intensity of competition in the competitive segments. A firm that owns and controls the regulated monopoly segments and also seeks to participate in the competitive segments that rely on it, may be able profitably to restrict access to or otherwise discriminate against competitors at the competitive levels. It may also be able to cross-subsidize the costs of competitive services by 'hiding' some of these costs in the costs of regulated monopoly services which the regulatory system somehow passes along to consumers without competitive alternatives who continue to take service at regulated rates. How serious such potential problems are in reality will depend upon the nature of the competitive access rules that are applied to regulated monopoly services, the ability of regulators to enforce them, the ability of regulatory rules to separate clearly costs associated with natural monopoly services from those associated with competitive services, and the incentive properties of the regulatory mechanisms used to govern the monopoly segments. These vertical control issues are at the core of the debates about restructuring these industries.

One obvious solution to the vertical control problem is a complete vertical separation of ownership between competitive and monopoly segments. There are two potential problems with this solution. In countries like the USA where the incumbents are largely private, mandatory divestitures are likely to be difficult and time-consuming to achieve. In addition, unless the problems associated with efficiently decentralizing vertical relationships between the competitive and natural monopoly segments have been solved, it may be necessary to rely on the vertically integrated entity to continue to operate the system efficiently, essentially allowing competitors to 'lean' on the integrated operation of vertically integrated network operators.

Third, if one of the aims of reform is to reduce the role of regulation and expand the role of markets that are not subject to price and entry regulation, one would like the competitive segments to exhibit reasonably efficient competitive behavior and performance when regulatory restrictions on prices and entry are removed. If the incumbent supply structure at the competitive level is monopoly or duopoly, the prospects for competitive behavior in the short run may not be very bright. That is, even if we can solve competitive problems associated with vertical control relationships between competitive and regulated monopoly horizontal levels, there still may be horizontal market power problems at the competitive levels that need to be addressed. This raises all of the standard questions regarding how much competition is 'enough', difficulties of imposing mandatory horizontal divestiture on incumbent private firms, the absence of meaningful horizontal divestiture opportunities, and trade-offs between the imperfections of continuing regulation and imperfect competition. For example, when AT&T's interexchange business was separated from its local carriers, AT&T had a very large share of sales in the interexchange markets. However, there was no meaningful way to break up AT&T's interexchange network to create more horizontal competitors.

These restructuring issues are examples of the kinds of governance issues identified by Oliver Williamson in *Markets and Hierarchies*. The focus on electricity here is designed to identify important issues associated with restructuring, deregulation, and regulatory reform of network industries generally as well as to illuminate, through cross-country comparisons, how countries faced with different organizational constraints have developed governance structures to deal with the same set of physical and economic problems. It also identifies trade-offs between the benefits of vertical and horizontal integration and the costs of regulated monopoly. My analysis of these issues applies the comparative institutional approach and the 'remediability' principle (Williamson, 1993; Joskow, 1995a) whose development can be traced back to *Markets and Hierarchies*.

2. *The Standard Prescriptions for Regulated Network Industries*

The standard neoclassical public policy prescription for reforming vertically and horizontally integrated 'natural monopoly' industries is fairly straight-forward. It has been or is being applied, to varying extents, to telecommunications, natural gas, electric power and (more narrowly) to railroads around the world.

The historical 'natural monopoly' industries are typically composed of both *potentially* competitive segments (e.g. long distance telephone service, electricity generation, unbundled natural gas supplies, railroad rolling stock, etc.) and natural monopoly segments (e.g. local telephone exchanges, electricity transmission and distribution networks, unbundled natural has pipeline transportation, railroad track and switching networks). Vertical integration between them, it is argued, has led to an unnecessary expansion of monopoly from one horizontal level to another and has extended inefficient regulation to segments where market forces can and should govern better.

In order for all competitors to compete effectively and for competition to proceed efficiently in the competitive segments, prices charged to customers must be unbundled and competing suppliers of the competitive services must have access to the regulated 'bottleneck' natural monopoly segments based on 'comparable' price and non-price terms and conditions which do not discriminate against any competitive supplier, in particular *de facto* differences in access between suppliers owned by the network operator and independent suppliers.

Vertical integration—that is, common ownership and control—of facilities that provide regulated 'bottleneck' natural monopoly services, access to which is necessary to support competition in the competitive segments, and facilities that provide competitive services, creates potential competitive problems. The problems derive from the incentive and ability owners of the natural monopoly segments have to discriminate in favor of competitive suppliers in which they have a financial interest and against those in which they do not. If vertical integration is to be permitted, then effective rules for ensuring comparable access to the bottleneck facilities must be assured. Developing and enforcing such comparability standards is difficult in both theory and in practice and, absent evidence that there are significant economies from vertical integration, divestiture of assets in the competitive segments by owners of assets in the natural monopoly bottleneck segment is often viewed as the most desirable policy. However, this may not be a practical alternative when the incumbents are private firms, the government must operate subject to constitutional protections against takings without just compensation, and reasonable speed in accomplishing reform is desirable.

Deregulation of the services sold in the competitive sector requires that there be an adequate number of competing suppliers or adequate constraints on prices provided by actual and potential entry of new suppliers to ensure that customers are not burdened by prices significantly above competitive levels. Either horizontal separations or continuing regulation of dominant firms may be required as a transition to an acceptable level of horizontal competition in the competitive sector if the current ownership structure of suppliers is too highly concentrated and entry is not an effective constraint on prices.

Cost separations, regulatory incentive mechanisms, and/or restrictions on entering certain lines of business may be required to guard against distortions caused by cross-subsidization of costs associated with the provision of competitive services by collecting some of the costs of competitive services through prices charged for regulated monopoly services.

Incentive regulation (now increasingly referred to by US regulators as 'Performance Based Regulation') should replace traditional cost of service regulation for the residual natural monopoly services. For example, in the UK, price caps are used to regulate the prices the distribution companies can charge for 'wires' services.

Retail customers should have access to the wholesale markets for competitive services (e.g. natural gas supplies) when direct access to these markets is technologically and economically feasible and should be responsible for arranging for their own supply needs. To do so, they need to see 'unbundled' rates and services from their incumbent vertically integrated or 'bundled' supplier and have access to the network services required to consummate transactions. As Gilbert and Riordan (1995) show, however, unbundling the prices for complementary services *per se* is unlikely to be an attractive strategy unless it is motivated by savings resulting from creating an efficient competitive market in at least one of the sectors that will replace regulation of the associated services. Unbundling itself can increase regulatory distortions. The obligation traditionally placed on public utilities to plan for and to supply all customers located in a designated franchise area with a full bundle of services should wither away as customers can arrange for their own supplies in a competitive market. If utilities continue to be used as vehicles for financing various social programs (e.g. universal service obligations, special low-income rates, subsidies for energy conservation, etc.), the associated costs must be identified clearly and included in non-bypassable access charges paid by all consumers for them to be sustainable in the face of competition (Posner, 1971).

There is nothing inherently wrong with this basic policy prescription. I teach it to my students all the time. However, it glosses over an important set of issues. Perhaps most importantly, it either assumes that there are no economies of vertical integration or that the efficiencies associated with vertical integration can be replicated with simple 'access rules' and a simple set of 'bottleneck' service prices. On the contrary, I would argue that defining the governance structure, prices, and terms and conditions of service that will replace what are now vertically and horizontally integrated organizations relying on internal control mechanisms with an industry structure that relies on multiple competing players at one horizontal level operating through decentralized contractual arrangements with a regulated monopoly network at another level of the vertical chain, is a critical issue in restructuring and deregulation. It is an issue that has attracted too little attention. There is also a view that the gains from replacing competition with regulation in the competitive segments will be very large compared to the costs of imperfect linkages between the competitive sector and the regulated monopoly network on which it depends. This will be discussed later.

The vertical and horizontal structures that we observe for the incumbents did not emerge by accident or solely as a consequence of monopolistic behavior or interest group politics, although these certainly played a role in some countries. Rather, these supply systems have important technological and economic characteristics that can easily explain why these industries have evolved with the vertical and horizontal structures that we observe. In some cases, technological (e.g. computers) and economic changes (e.g. cheap natural gas) may undermine the economic rationale for these governance structures. In other cases, the governance problems have hardly changed at all and the rationale for vertical and horizontal integration, viewed narrowly, has not changed either. In the latter case, however, the efficiencies associated with vertical and horizontal integration may be overwhelmed by the inefficiencies created by the institution of regulated monopoly. We may be willing to sacrifice some of the potential efficiencies associated with vertical and horizontal integration if we can restructure so that we can rely on market allocation in the potentially competitive segments and thereby reduce the costs of imperfect regulation.

3. *Governance Structures in Electricity*

Electric power sectors around the world have many common structural features. These similarities exist largely because the basic physical attributes of modern electric power networks vary little from place to place. Any electricity supply industry structure with good technical performance characteristics must deal with the same set of physical and economic problems. Where industrial structures differ, clearly identifiable governance mechanisms have emerged to deal with the same set of vertical and horizontal coordination problems.

Physical Characteristics

The supply of electricity is generally divided into three separate functions:

(i)   The generation of electricity using falling water, internal combustion engines, steam turbines powered with steam produced with fossil fuels, nuclear fuel, and various renewable fuels, wind driven turbines and photovoltaic technologies.
(ii) The distribution of electricity to residences and businesses at relatively low voltages using wires and transformers along and under streets and other rights of way.
(iii) The transmission of electricity involving the 'transportation' of electricity between generating sites and distribution centers, the interconnection and integration of dispersed generating facilities into a stable synchronized network that maintains a common frequency, the scheduling and dispatching of generating facilities that are connected to the transmission network economically to balance loads and resources in real time, and the management of equipment failures, network constraints, and relationships with other interconnected networks.

The typical separation of electricity supply into three independent functions is, however, somewhat misleading. The generation of electricity and the transmission of electricity are intimately related to one another from both an operating and investment perspective. There are important operating and cost complementarities between generation and transmission. The transmission system is not simply a transportation network, but a more complex 'coordination' system that integrates dispersed generating facilities to provide a reliable flow of electricity within tight voltage and frequency bands (hopefully) economically. Since electricity cannot be stored or otherwise inventoried easily and customers continue to draw power as long as the circuits are closed and they are connected to the network, the generation of electricity and the consumption of electricity must be balanced continuously while maintaining the stability of the network and its physical attributes within narrow ranges that will not damage equipment connected to it or lead to sudden network failures. To do so, both transmission and generating facilities are required to support the operation of the network as well as to provide energy to serve customer loads.

A modern AC transmission network makes it possible to utilize generating facilities dispersed over wide geographic areas efficiently in real time through the substitution of increased production from low marginal cost facilities (say in New Mexico) for production from high marginal cost facilities (say in California). In principle, an efficiently operated network would constantly equate the marginal costs of supplying an additional Kwh of energy at all generating nodes adjusted for marginal losses, thermal and operating constraints throughout the network (Schweppe *et al.*, 1988). It can also economize on reserve capacity required to achieve any given level of reliability (responses to equipment outages and unanticipated swings in demand) by effectively aggregating loads and reserve generating capacity over a wide geographic area and by providing multiple linkages between loads and resources that can provide service continuity when transmission facilities fail. However, to accomplish these tasks, the network must be operated to maintain its frequency and voltage parameters within narrow bands and to respond to changing system conditions on the demand and supply sides, especially unplanned equipment outages. To do so, generating facilities must be called upon almost continuously to provide a variety of network support services in addition to providing energy to run customer appliances and equipment. These services include reactive power, spinning reserves, standby reserves, blackstart capability, automatic generation control, scheduling and dispatch control and others. The physical operation of the network to provide a reliable product and the economically efficient exploitation of the generating and transmission facilities that are part of the network are therefore closely related.

To complicate matters further, a free flowing AC network is an integrated physical machine that follows the laws of physics, not the laws of financial contracting. When a generator turns on and off, it affects system conditions throughout the interconnected network. Large swings in load at one node affects system conditions at other nodes. A failure of a major piece of equipment in one part of the network can affect the stability of the entire system. Moreover, efficient and effective remedial responses to equipment failures can involve coordinated reactions of multiple generators located remotely from the site of the failure. In an AC system there is no meaningful independent direct physical connection between the electricity generated from a particular plant and the load placed on the system by a particular customer or group of customers. We can monitor what goes into the network from a particular generator and we can monitor what is taken out of the network from a customer, but how the customer's load is actually served depends on the physical operation of the entire network.

There are also important cost complementarities associated with investment in generation and transmission capacity. The location of generators may involve trade-offs between generating costs and transmission costs. A generator can be located close to load, where fuel, sites, and air pollution restrictions are costly or further from loads where generating costs are lower, but transmission costs (including the costs of constraints) may be higher. Similarly, investments in transmission capacity to remove network constraints can affect the costs of generating electricity and the value of power produced at various locations on the network.

Not surprisingly, it is not easy to define a full set of tradable property rights that internalize all of the relevant network externalities that would allow us to rely entirely on the 'invisible hand' to allocate the utilization of scarce capacity on a transmission network with many nodes and network constraints that vary widely with rapidly changing system conditions. The capacity of the system to deliver electrical energy to the system and to receive it from the system and the costs of doing so depend on where it is received and where it is delivered and on changing supply and demand conditions that can vary widely from hour to hour over a day and from day to day. While in theory, a full set of contingent delivery and receipt property rights could be defined *ex ante*, in practice it would be both extremely difficult to define them and difficult to monitor their use and provide for appropriate payments to ensure that rights and efforts to exercise those rights do not conflict.[2] Absent property rights, monitoring and payment protocols and decentralization of network operations must confront serious public goods and externality problems. Moreover, in the absence of economical storage, the speed with which network responses must occur creates a challenge for a decentralized price system since complete reliance on prices to guide real time operation of the network would require that prices adjust to changing network conditions *and* that physical responses to these price changes take place almost continuously.

---

[2] Chao and Peck (1995) have developed an interesting mechanism that involves the allocation of transmission capacity rights (see Coase) and a multidimensional settlement rule that prices the use of these rights (see Pigou) to reflect changing system conditions so as to properly price the opportunity cost of using the rights to reflect the impact on their network. The settlement rule is essentially a matrix (potentially a large matrix) of Pigouvian taxes that must be calculated by someone (a computer) other than the invisible hand. This work represents an interesting research program that is aiming at precisely the right targets. Of course, we can always find a set of property rights and taxes that theoretically can replicate what goes on inside an organization. Without additional analysis of transactions, contracting, monitoring, enforcing and information costs, the fact that such rights and shadow prices exist in theory and can be calculated by a computer tells us nothing about whether a fully decentralized market can efficiently replace the organization (Williamson, 1975). In this respect, it is not obvious that the Chao/Peck mechanism, with so many capacity rights, such a complex settlement rule and substantial requirements for bidding information from all traders, is practical to implement or that it would be more attractive than the algorithms that effectively calculate similar shadow prices in Hogan's model. It is also not clear that the mechanism does not distort investment incentives. As with any mechanism that relies on bidding, the attractive properties also depend on the assumption that agents do not have any market power.

In the longer run, investments must be made to expand transmission capacity. Transmission investments are lumpy, are characterized by scale economies, and can have effects on the physical attributes of other portions of the network and the economic value of generators connected to it at various points and the costs of serving load at other points. Moreover, the development of major new transmission lines must confront environmental reviews and public opposition. Assembling the rights of way for a new corridor necessarily involves numerous public agencies and private landowners. It is hard to imagine that the invisible hand will play the primary role in guiding investments to expand the capacity of transmission networks to meet consumer demands reliably.

The difficulty of defining a full set of tradable property rights to allocate network capacity efficiently under all contingencies, the potential incompatibilities between the time-frame within which supply and demand adjustments must be made physically and the operation of an associated set of spot markets and the economic attributes of investments in new transmission capacity have important implications for the efficient structure of this industry and the mechanisms available for facilitating efficient decentralized generation supply decisions on the network. In particular, not only are the physical facilities that compose the transmission network a natural monopoly, but certain operating functions that require service from generators must be under the control of the network operator as well and cannot be ceded to the invisible hand without incurring inefficiencies and reliability problems. The latter include the physical scheduling of generation on the network in response to schedules submitted by generators or determined through an economic dispatch performed by the network operator (or both), dispatch control over adequate amounts of 'swing' generation, procurement of certain ancillary support services, management of network constraints under at least some contingencies, emergency response protocols, etc.

Of course, despite these complexities, the electric power networks in most developed countries operate with very high levels of reliability and, given the short-run operating costs and availability of generators connected to the system, come reasonably close to efficient generator dispatch. The economic efficiency problems in electric power sectors in developed countries have much more to do with poor (evaluated *ex post*) investment decisions, construction cost overruns, excessive fuel prices, too many personnel, low levels of generator reliability, continued operation of plants that should be retired, and regulated price structures that provide poor consumption incentives. That is, once all this is handed over to the operating engineers they do a pretty good job making it all work reliably and economically given the attributes of the equipment that they have been given to operate.

Organizational Arrangements

The structure of the electric power sectors that have emerged around the world have been driven heavily by the operating and investment complementarities between generation and transmission *and* technological advances that have expended the geographic expanse over which integrated AC networks can be controlled reliably to exploit opportunities to trade-off low operating cost generation to displace high operating cost generation and to reduce the cost of reliability. Until recently, virtually all electric power systems were characterized by extensive vertical integration between generation and transmission. Typically, the entity that owns the generating and transmission (G&T) capacity is also the network or 'control area' operator responsible for the physical control of the network, balancing loads and operating resources in real time, dispatching generators based on merit order dispatch protocols and network constraints, scheduling operations with interconnected control areas, identifying investments at both the generation and transmission level and, importantly for private firms, producing revenues sufficient to cover the associated capital and operating costs (either solely from customers or with additional help from government subsidies).

The G&T entity typically transfers the power to one or more distribution entities that are then responsible for distributing electricity to customers in specific geographic areas that they serve exclusively. In some cases, the G&T entities are separate from the distribution entities (as in the old CEGB in England and Wales and TVA in the USA), in which case the G&T entity typically serves the distribution entity on a long-term exclusive basis under tariffs or contracts that are regulated. In other cases, there is also common ownership of both G&T facilities and proximate monopoly distribution franchises (as in most of France, Japan, and for most private utilities in the USA). When the G, T and D functions are under common ownership and control, there is no visible transfer price for services provided by one horizontal level to the other. This is typically the case for retail sales of electricity in the USA, Japan and France for example. Under the old regime in England and Wales, there were no transfer prices between the G and T functions, but the distributors purchased G&T services based on a visible tariff from their sole supplier, the CEGB. Some holding companies in the USA have visible transfer prices between G, T, and D, when the associated assets are held in separate companies within the same corporate entity organized as a holding company. In this case, final consumer prices are regulated based on all of the costs incurred by the vertically integrated firm.

Thus, at first blush, vertical integration between G&T internalizes the operating and investment interrelationships between generation and transmission inside public or private organizations where the potential public goods and externality problems, as well as the challenge of coordinating operations in real time to adapt to changing demand and supply conditions, can be solved with internal operating hierarchies rather than markets. However, vertical integration between the network functions which have natural monopoly characteristics and the generation function effectively turns the supply of generating service into a regulated monopoly as well, even if there are numerous generating plants connected to the network and limited economies of scale associated with generation *per se* in isolation from the coordination functions performed by the network (Joskow and Schmalensee, 1983).

Even if the network or control area operator's job is done perfectly, vertical integration between transmission and generation is not the end of the story, however. Nothing has yet been said about the extent of *horizontal* integration at the transmission network level. Here, institutional arrangements vary quite widely. The old CEGB in England and Wales is a convenient example at one extreme since we are dealing with an area that is physically an island. The old CEGB controlled the entire bulk power network in England and Wales and, aside from small interconnections with Scotland and a DC tie with France, effectively spanned the entire network horizontally. In principle, the CEGB could internalize all of the operating and investment complementarities (vertically) between generation and transmission and (horizontally) across all of the nodes on the network.

Electricité de France (EDF) owns and controls all of the central station generating capacity and the transmission and distribution network in France. The amount of generation controlled by EDF is roughly equivalent to the generating capacity in all of the western states in the USA. EDF performs an integrated dispatch of all of the generating capacity on its network based on its best estimates of marginal running costs, network support requirements and transmission and other operating constraints. However, unlike England and Wales, the French network is synchronized electrically with other networks in Western Europe. To coordinate the operations of synchronized networks, the network operators in the different countries have had to develop operating protocols and compensation arrangements for ensuring that they do not make independent operating decisions that degrade the operations of other interconnected networks or, if they do, pay appropriate compensation for doing so. These arrangements have not always been fully successful in internalizing the network externalities, however.

Responding to Horizontal Network Problems in the USA

Organizational arrangements are even more complicated in the USA. There are roughly 800,000 Mwe of generating capacity (more than Western Europe, Japan and Latin America combined; roughly 200 times more than Chile, and about 40 times more than Argentina). This capacity relies on a diverse mix of fuels (57% coal, 22% nuclear, 8% hydro, 9% gas, 3% oil) and is distributed among thousands of generating plant sites, whose generating capacities vary widely. From a physical perspective, the US system (combined with portions of Canada and northern Mexico) is composed of three synchronized AC systems, the Eastern Interconnection, the Western Interconnection, and the Texas Interconnection. However, there are over 140 separate 'control areas' superimposed on the three networks where individual vertically integrated utilities or groups of utilities are responsible for generator dispatch, network operations, maintaining reliability on specific portions of each of the three physical networks. Thousands of un-integrated or partially integrated municipal and cooperative distribution entities are embedded in an individual control area and rely on its operator to deliver power to them. Typically, the control areas correspond to the portions of the network that a vertically integrate utility (or multistate holding company) owns and operates. In the Northeast, however, control areas have been consolidated over time without horizontal mergers of proximate utilities through the creation of tight power pools. In most other areas of the country there are many control area operators responsible for network control and generator dispatch on portions of the same synchronized system. None of the control areas in the USA is close to the size of EDF or the CEGB and most are much smaller. The Western Interconnection has 35 control areas; California alone has seven.

To harmonize and rationalize the dispersed ownership and control of facilities that are physically interconnected and whose operations have impacts on facilities in remote control areas, the US industry has developed a complex set of operating protocols, bilateral and multilateral agreements designed to maintain reliability, to facilitate coordinated operations, to facilitate trades of power between control areas, and to minimize free riding problems, while maintaining dispersed ownership and control of vertically integrated 'pieces' of the relevant networks. These operating protocols are developed through the National Electric Reliability Council (NERC), nine regional reliability councils, and a larger number of sub-regional reliability organizations. The operating protocols developed by this hierarchy of 'technical' organizations, are essential for the reliable and efficient operation of synchronized networks when there are many hands on the wheel. One might naturally ask why substantial horizontal integration did not take place to respond to these horizontal coordination problems as advances in transmission and network control technology expanded the geographic expanse of synchronized networks. The answer is that the Federal Power Act, the Public Utility Holding Company Act, FERC and SEC interpretation of both, and state laws made mergers very difficult after 1935. In the last few years, legal and regulatory restrictions on mergers have been greatly eased and we have seen substantial merger activity between proximate (and not so proximate) utilities.

These reliability organizations have been reasonably successful in getting control area operators to agree to and adhere to a set of consistent operating rules for three primary reasons. First, this national and regional reliability system does not get into the financial arrangements that accompany the technical operating rules, in particular who pays for what. Rather, utilities enter into separate interconnection and coordination agreements which specify financial arrangements for sharing reserves, providing emergency support, allocating transmission rights, and trading power. These agreements are subject to regulation by the Federal Energy Regulatory Commission (FERC). They also enter into transmission service agreements when power trading 'requires' the use of facilities owned by an intervening utility. This is known as 'wheeling service', something that I will discuss more presently. Thus, power system engineers could write the technical specifications and lawyers and accountants (rarely economists) could argue about who paid for what.

The second reason that this system works reasonably smoothly is that, until recently, the utilities operating the 140+ control areas did not compete with one another to any significant extent. The control area operators were typically vertically integrated utilities serving retail customers pursuant to *de facto* exclusive geographic franchises. They could not compete to serve each other's retail customers. The coordination and trading arrangements generally were to the mutual benefit of interconnected utilities in terms of reliability and economical exploitation of generating capacity. Originally, they relied on interconnections to share reserves and for emergency support and traded energy between them on an hourly, daily, or longer basis to economize on the use of existing capacity. Individual utilities met their generating capacity needs by owning and operating generating facilities, trading energy to reduce costs on the margin (approximating central merit order dispatch). This wholesale market evolved initially as an 'excess energy' market to reduce overall generating costs and active participation in it by all vertically integrated utilities was encouraged by regulators.

Third, the regulation of wholesale transactions provided incentives to enter into obviously beneficial trading arrangements, but did not provide powerful incentives to act in ways that would undermine multilateral agreements regarding network operating protocols, whose primary benefits were perceived to be in the area of reliability. Recovery of the sunk costs of generating and transmission facilities was mediated through the state retail ratemaking process, with the costs and benefits of shorter term wholesale trades treated as a residual with some sharing of the gains from short-term trade with shareholders via regulatory lag or explicit sharing mechanisms. Moreover, although wholesale power transactions are regulated by the FERC, trades between vertically integrated utilities have been accorded significant *de facto* pricing flexibility by FERC.

Competition Strains Traditional Governance Structures in the USA

The situation in the USA began to change in the 1970s. Wholesale trade in electricity expanded rapidly, initially in response to large differences in the short-run marginal cost of coal, oil and natural gas generating units. The potential gains from trade increased significantly when oil and gas prices rose during the 1970s and early 1980s. Moreover, the US industry has been plagued by excess capacity for most of the last two decades. Increasingly, public utility commissions put pressure on utilities to use the wholesale market to make longer-term transactions (e.g. 5 years) with one another to better utilize capacity and to defer the need for new investments. During the 1970s and 1980s, independent municipal and cooperative distribution entities became able to secure their power supplies from suppliers other than the local vertically integrated utility to which they were tied or to vertically integrate themselves through joint ownership of remote generating facilities. These arrangements required that the local vertically integrated utility provide these distribution entities with unbundled transmission service and a variety of network support and residual power supply services. Finally, the Public Utility Regulatory Policy Act of 1978 (PURPA) required utilities to purchase power produced by certain independent 'qualifying facilities' (QFs) when the costs of power produced from these facilities was expected to be less than the costs of utility-owned generation. These entities often required transmission service to get power to utility buyers and, in principle, required other network services as well.

By the 1980s, a set of fairly active *wholesale* electricity markets had emerged (Joskow, 1989). The first set of market transactions involves inter-utility trading of energy within large geographic regions utilizing generating capacity that is temporarily excess to the needs of regulated, vertically integrated utilities to displace production from higher operating higher cost capacity owned by other vertically integrated utilities. A second set of market transactions involves longer-term firm capacity and energy contracts between vertically integrated utilities with excess capacity and unintegrated municipal and cooperative distribution utilities and some vertically integrated utilities under pressure to buy power rather than to build new capacity themselves. A third set of market transactions has evolved involving long-term contracts (20 to 30 years) between vertically integrated utilities on the buying side and QFs on the selling side. These transactions effectively substituting power by long-term contract for some of the new generating capacity that these entities might otherwise have built. In all cases, these are 'utility to utility' wholesale transactions. Retail customers still receive a bundled product from the local monopoly distributor with prices based on the average total cost of generation the distribution utility owns and power purchased under contract from third parties.

A complicated system for accommodating wholesale market transactions among dispersed entities using the same synchronized electrical grid evolved over the last few decades (Joskow and Schmalensee, 1983; Joskow, 1989). It worked reasonably well as long as (i) the bulk of the operation of the network involved 'internal' transactions *within* vertically integrated firms rather than between independent buyers and sellers in the wholesale market; (ii) most wholesale transactions involved short term trades between directly connected vertically integrated utilities with efficient coordination agreements; (iii) desired trades could be accommodated within conservative transfer capacity ratings which did not create significant loop flow or network constraint management problems; (iv) QFs/IPPs did not generally require unbundled transmission, dispatch and network support services; (v) interconnected control area operators were not competing aggressively among one another in wholesale and retail markets and did not try to exploit the many imperfections in this system to their individual benefit; and (vi) the operating rules were viewed as being mutually beneficial to the control area operators.

However, the evolution of wholesale power markets in the USA up to the present has largely side-stepped the difficult vertical and horizontal network coordination issues that were discussed earlier, or dealt with them in ways that relied implicitly on the basic structure of the industry being one that was built *primarily*, but not exclusively, on vertically integrated utilities operating their own control areas. The development of these wholesale markets was essentially accommodated by a long series of minor modifications to the existing system, rather than more fundamental reforms driven by a clear vision for where the expansion of wholesale markets was going. As a result, as wholesale markets expanded to facilitate beneficial electricity trade between utilities, difficulties associated with specifying the relevant network services and setting the right prices for them were largely ignored because the volume of trade that would have been affected was small and the costs associated with supporting these wholesale transactions recovered in cost-based retail rates. Free riding and inefficiencies did emerge, but they were small relative to the overall costs of the system and they too were relatively easily buried in the cost-based regulatory system that was in place to serve retail customers. The cost of these imperfections will grow significantly as competition in generation expands as anticipated, so that they can no longer be ignored without undermining the performance of competitive generation service markets.

4. *Applying the Standard Prescription to Electricity*

The application of the 'standard prescription' to electricity leads to the following general framework for restructuring, regulatory reform and competition in the industry.

First, the generation segment is potentially competitive. Economies of scale in the generation function itself are relatively limited and, ignoring regional network coordination issues, at least some of these economies can be achieved by owning and operating generating facilities in different regions of the USA and in different countries. This is something that is already taking place as an independent generating sector building and operating generating plants under contract for sales to local utilities emerges around the world. In the USA, there are already numerous generating companies in most regions, although they are vertically integrated with transmission ownership and control and are supported financially with exclusive retail service territories and regulated prices.

Second, the 'transmission network' and at least some of its ancillary support functions are natural monopolies and provide the critical platform upon which competition among generators depends. Comparable access to network services to all competing generators, appropriate transmission network and ancillary network support service pricing, and appropriate operating and scheduling protocols are essential to promote efficient behavior and performance of competing generators. From a physical perspective, the networks of relevance in the USA encompass many existing control areas (local networks) operated by vertically integrated utilities. Reliable network operation requires the network operator to schedule all generation, have physical control over at least some dispatchable generation in real time, acquire 'public good' network support services from generating facilities and to deal with other networks to which they are connected. It is uneconomic to build duplicate (overlapping) transmission networks, although there is no particular reason when there cannot be multiple owners of the underlying assets. Because of its natural monopoly attributes, the transmission network and its operation will be subject to continuing regulation and the ability of the regulatory system to guide the network operator to perform whatever tasks are its responsibility reasonably well is an important policy challenge.

Third, new approaches to transmission pricing must be adopted which recognize the physical and economic realities of transmission networks. Transmission pricing arrangements that provide revenues to support efficient investments in transmission capacity, price network constraints to ration scarce network capabilities efficiently in response to changing network constraints and are consistent with least cost dispatch of generators are essential. Precisely how this can be accomplished is still subject to some debate, but substantial progress has been made (Hogan, 1992, 1993; Ruff, 1994; Bushnell and Stoft, 1995; Chao and Peck, 1995).

Fourth, the distribution network also has natural monopoly characteristics and, at the very least, the 'wires' part of the business will continue to be subject to regulation. Some electricity restructuring models (Alberta, France's 'single buyer' model, and the model embodied in the US Energy Policy Act of 1992), anticipate distributors continuing to supply a bundled product to retail customers that they serve exclusively in a geographic area. This is referred to as a 'wholesale competition model' or 'portfolio model' in which the distribution company arranges for a portfolio of generation supply resources through ownership or contract with third parties to provide service for retail customers it serves exclusively. This is similar to the way the natural gas industry used to be structured in the USA. Gas transmission companies arranged for gas supplies with independent producers under long-term contracts. They delivered a bundled product (gas supplies plus transportation, storage, backup service, etc.) to local distribution companies, which added a distribution charge and sold gas to customers in their franchise areas. Now larger customers can buy their own gas in the field and arrange for unbundled pipeline and distribution service.

Alternatively, retail customers would only buy limited 'wires' services from the local distributor and arrange for their own power supplies directly with generators or with competing 'retailing' intermediaries who would arrange power supplies on their behalf. This is referred to as a retail competition model and is the one that is being introduced (in phases) in England and Wales, Chile, Norway, Argentina, New Zealand and elsewhere. Customers must have real time metering to participate directly in such a market in order to keep track of contractual commitments and to settle imbalances. This is necessary because a generator cannot supply physically identifiable electrons to a particular customer over the network, and spot energy prices can vary significantly from hour to hour. Furthermore, without significant expense (telemetering and load control equipment) specific generators cannot be moved up and down to match perfectly with specific customer loads with which they have contracts in real time. It is possible to implement direct access for customers without real time metering by assigning 'deemed' monthly load shapes to all customers in a particular class and then 'squeezing' the monthly Kwh readings into the appropriate load shape. This is, of course, the way retail rate designs are determined now using class specific load shapes. However, this system must be accompanied by a detailed credible accounting and settlements system in which all buyers and sellers agree to abide by the deemed load shapes for both retail billing purposes and for defining supply obligations and energy imbalances. We should also anticipate significant adverse selection as customers with 'good' load shapes opt out of the class by acquiring real time meters. The load factor of the remaining customers will deteriorate and their average generation cost will go up.

A modern AC network with a large number of links frees us from the costs of operating in this fashion, and any 'bilateral contracts' model that endeavors to defeat the network to create the illusion of a direct physical relationship in this way would be very inefficient. When the network is used effectively, if a generator produces more than its contract customers actually take, the network will receive the energy, but must back down other generators to balance supply and demand in real time (a physical necessity without storage) until changes in prices and associated scheduling adjustments can work to rebalance. The residual electricity supplied to the network by the generator in the interim will then actually supply someone else's customers. Similarly, if a generator fails to deliver enough energy to the network to meet customer demands, energy will still be consumed by these customers from the network. The network operator will have to draw it from other generators that are available and, of course, they will have to be paid for what they supply. Thus, both a physical process for dealing with imbalances between contract loads and contractual supply obligations and a financial settlements process for getting everyone paid for what they actually supply and consume is an essential part of any credible retail competition model.

Another factor to consider in the framework is that there are potential problems associated with abusive self-dealing, cross-subsidization and discriminatory access to and pricing of network services when there is common ownership and control of competitive assets (e.g. generation) and regulated monopoly assets (e.g. transmission) that competitive suppliers must have access to. There are a variety of 'fixes' for this problem that are generally considered.

The first approach, involves complete *structural separation* of generation, transmission and distribution by creating separate companies through vertical divestiture. In a country with a structure like that in the USA, this might be accompanied by horizontal integration of the pieces of the transmission network presently under separate ownership, combining what are now separate control areas. The separate companies would not be permitted to own assets in the other vertical segments in the same geographic area. Most importantly, the network operator would have no financial interest in either the generation suppliers nor in the sales to particular wholesale and retail customers.

The second approach involves *functional separation* of generation, transmission, and distribution (costs separations and certain operational separations between competitive and regulated segments) within existing vertically integrated firms combined with open access and pricing rules for use of the transmission and distribution networks applicable to all competing suppliers of generation without regard to ownership. This approach requires the incumbent vertically integrated firms to unbundle the services they supply, post visible prices for these services, and apply them to their own transactions as well as to transactions involving third parties using their network to reach customers. In addition, regulatory reforms are necessary to remove incentives for cross-subsidization of competitive services by regulated monopoly services and for uneconomic purchases of generation supplies from generating facilities that are owned by the network or distribution system owner.

A third approach is a sort of halfway house between the other two. Vertically integrated utilities in a region would turn the *operation* of their transmission system and associated provision of ancillary network support services over to an independent system operator (ISO) who would be responsible for all network functions over a geographic expanse that more closely matches the physical characteristics of a synchronized AC system, effectively consolidating control areas. The pools in the Northeast already have some of these attributes. The existing owners of transmission would effectively lease their systems to the ISO. The ISO would then in turn be responsible for operating the integrated network, purchasing network support services from competing generation suppliers, settling imbalances, and providing the information necessary to operate a financial settlements system. This latter approach is attracting much interest in the USA.

Finally, the competitive segments, in particular generation, may have to be restructured horizontally through divestiture to create a generation market in which there is 'enough' competition so that horizontal market power is not a significant problem. Alternatively, continuing regulation of the generation market will be required.[3] If regulation is required, 'light handed' alternatives to cost of service regulation, such as price cap regulation is typically the favored alternative. The hope is that as entry takes place, the market will become sufficiently competitive so that regulatory constraints can be removed.

In all of the various models for creating new competitive market structures in electricity, the roles of the network operator are of fundamental importance in scheduling and dispatching generation, arranging for and pricing of transmission and network support services provided to generators and distributors, and arrangements to expand transmission capacity to relieve constraints. The economic integration, coordination and reliability functions now performed within vertically and horizontally integrated firms and through a hierarchy of multilateral operating agreements must now be much more decentralized. The structure and behavior of the network operator with regard to physical operations, identification of imbalances, and the support for a credible financial settlements system must act as an effective substitute for vertical integration while supporting competition among generators. Even where the reform policy focuses on functional unbundling rather than vertical separation through divestiture or the creation of an ISO, the associated requirement for unbundling generation, transmission, network support, distribution and retailing services (depending on the model, wholesale or retail competition), visible internal transfer prices, and comparable services and charges applicable to owned and independent competing generation suppliers implicitly require vertically integrated firms to behave as if they were not really vertically integrated! In this case, it is natural to ask whether there are any residual benefits to vertical integration once such operating rules are imposed.

5. *Alternative Approaches to Resolve Vertical and Horizontal Coordination Problems*

A variety of different approaches have been used to harmonize the physical and economic roles of the transmission network operator with the desire to promote competition among generators to supply energy to serve load (wholesale or retail) reasonably efficiently.

The FERC Open Access Initiative

In March 1995, the Federal Energy Regulatory Commission (FERC) issued a Notice of Proposed Rulemaking (NOPR)[4] to provide 'open and comparable

---

[3] This is not the place to ask how much competition is 'enough' and what the appropriate market structure is to achieve it. See Joskow, 1995b and Joskow and Schmalensee, 1983.

[4] 70 FERC 61,357, 29 March 1995.

access' to the transmission systems of all investor-owned utilities (IOUs) to support *wholesale* transactions.[5] The FERC NOPR relies on a partial functional unbundling framework. Vertically integrated utilities must provide comparable access to third parties who want to use their transmission systems (i.e. their individual control areas) to consummate wholesale transactions. They must post tariffs for transmission service and ancillary network support services, including dispatching services, to support these transactions. When a vertically integrated control area operator buys or sells generation service at wholesale it must 'charge itself' the same tariffed prices as it charges to third parties. So, for example, if it sells energy to a neighboring utility for 2.5 cents/kWh and the applicable price for transmission service is 0.5 cents/kWh cents, then the net price it receives for generation service is deemed to be 2 cents/kWh regardless of what the actual cost is of the transmission services provided. The idea is that if the latter price does not cover the utility's generation supply costs, the utility will either not make the sale or (theoretically) lose money on it. However, for internal transfers within a vertically integrated company that does not have separate G, T, and D subsidiaries, this is just an accounting convention that has no direct economic significance. How a vertically integrated firm actually behaves and what the financial implications are of this behavior depends largely on how the state regulators treat the associated costs and revenues for retail price regulation purposes, something over which FERC has no control.

In developing a generic pricing approach for transmission service pricing in its NOPR, FERC essentially has adopted the old contract path model and associated average cost prices which evolved in a world with limited competition and is widely recognized to have serious flaws. It effectively treats each control area as if it were an isolated network on its own. It ignores interdependencies between the transmission facilities operated by control area operators that are part of the same network and associated loop flow problems. Nor does it provide an economically rational method for allocating transfer rights when there are network constraints. FERC does recognize that transmission and generation cannot be neatly separated because the network requires a variety of network support services from generators to operate reliably and efficiently. However, the proposed rules establish extremely crude methods for defining the prices for these services. Furthermore, because there is no economic mechanism specified to ration scarce network

---

[5] FERC also has asserted jurisdiction over the interstate transmission component of retail transactions. However, FERC is barred by Federal law from authorizing retail wheeling. Issues of franchise exclusivity and direct access to generation markets for retail customers is a state decision. However, if a state authorized retail access, then FERC's transmission access and ancillary service pricing rules would govern. Precisely where interstate transmission ends and intrastate distribution begins remains to be resolved. The March 1995 NOPR proposed a method for drawing a bright line between the two.

transfer capacity, and because it retains the existing control area structure, the rules retain the firm/non-firm transaction paradigm, and specify a set of new administrative priorities for allocating scarce network capacity. Finally, since FERC has no control over the *purchasing* decisions of distribution utilities, whether or not they take advantage of the opportunity to buy at wholesale from competing suppliers (rather than building their own generation) depends entirely on state regulatory rules.

This is clearly a fairly modest proposal. It provides mandatory open access to the transmission systems of vertically integrated utilities to support wholesale transactions, but does so with the wrong prices and in the absence of a network model that matches the physical attributes of interconnected AC networks. It builds on many of the contractual fictions about how electricity flows on a network that have grown up over the last few decades to accommodate wholesale competition by placing bandaids on the existing structure. Since the network operator, as a vertically integrated utility, will also typically control large amounts of generation connected to the network, regulators will have to monitor carefully the comparability and non-discrimination provisions.

England and Wales

Prior to 1990, the electric power sector in England and Wales was composed of a government-owned generation and transmission company (the CEGB) which owned and operated all generating and transmission capacity in the area. There were also 12 government-owned distribution entities (the Area Boards) which served retail customers in exclusive franchise areas with bundled service. The Area Boards purchased all of their power from the CEGB on a bulk supply tariff. When the government decided to privatize the electricity sector it also chose to restructure it more or less along the lines of the 'standard prescription'. Three generating companies were established, two with fossil-fueled generation which were privatized and one with all of the nuclear capacity which remained in the hands of the state. An independent grid company was created with responsibilities for the transmission network, and the Area Boards (distribution) were privatized. Large retail customers were given the option of arranging for their own electricity supplies (retail wheeling or direct access) and this option is being phased in over time for all retail customers. These customers can obtain unbundled 'wires' service from their local distributors and deal with an independent retail electricity supplier to make financial arrangements for their power supplies.

A key feature of this restructuring is the creation of a spot energy 'pool' and its interaction with the grid company. The pool runs a day ahead auction in which generators bid to supply electricity (energy to serve load, start-up and ramping services, spinning reserves, standby reserves, and other network support services) for each of 48 half-hours during the following day. A uniform market clearing price is determined for each half-hour based on the highest bid that brings forth enough supply to clear projected demand for each half-hour in the following day. All generators are paid (approximately) this *ex ante* market clearing price for each half hour if they are run. Financial settlements are actually based on the *ex post* realizations of demand and the actual dispatch of generators to supply it. The bid prices are also used to develop a merit order dispatch schedule for each half-hour for the following day. The network dispatcher controls all generators connected to the network and dispatches them from lowest to highest according to the generators' bids so as to balance aggregate supply and demand and to maintain system frequency and voltage in real time. It also calls generators to be dispatched out of merit order when this is necessary to deal with network constraints or to support network reliability requirements. The pool, combined with the real time controls by the grid operator based on bid price information, essentially performs the same functions as does a control area operator in a vertically integrated system. It retains physical control of the network and the generators connected to it in the sense that if they are available, it can call on them to increase or decrease production to respond to fluctuating supply and demand conditions and network constraints. However, the pool/grid does not own the generators[6] on the system and they must compete to obtain a place in the dispatch based on their bids. Unlike a vertically integrated system, however, the pool/grid relies on decentralized bids, clearing prices, and competitive procurement mechanisms to guide the bulk of its operations.

Although all purchases and sales must physically be scheduled through the pool and the pool prices are used as the default mechanism for financial settlements, generators, retailers and retail customers routinely enter into financial contracts with one another written against the pool price (contracts for differences). The bulk of the electricity sold at wholesale or retail is supported with such hedging contracts. Indeed, a typical retail customer need have nothing to do with the mechanics of the grid or pool. It signs up with a retailer who agrees to provide for the customer's needs at a set price (e.g. 5p/kWh). The retailer then handles all of the underlying physical arrangements and financial settlements with the grid, the distribution company, the

---

[6] It actually owns some pumped storage hydro capacity which was originally viewed as a source of regulating margin for the network (variations between half-hour schedules). These facilities were in the process of being sold off in late 1995.

pool and any generators with which it has financial contracts. The customer's takes from the pool create a liability for the retailer with the pool based on the quantities taken and the pool price at that time. The customer in turn pays the retailer an agreed price for the power he consumes. The retailer may in turn hedge the pool price by signing a contract with a generator where the generator commits to sell a certain quantity at a set price, e.g. 4p/kWh. The retailer's takes are then (effectively) matched with the supplies from the generator with which he contracts. If less is supplied by the generator than is sold by the retailer, the generator owes the pool for the difference with the associated settlement based on pool prices. These funds in turn flow back to other generators who supplied the energy to balance supply and demand at the relevant times.

I believe that the market structure adopted in England and Wales is a very clever solution to the problems associated with harmonizing the operation of an integrated AC network while at the same time relying on independent dispersed generators both to compete to make sales to serve load and to provide required network support services. There are, however, a number of problems that have emerged with regard to network coordination, vertical control and market power issues in the new system in England and Wales.

The theory that underlies this model assumes that the generating sector is perfectly competitive in the sense that the price that clears the market will equal the marginal cost of an additional unit of production, that all generators bid all their available generation into the pool, and that they bid their marginal cost for each generator. Since the bid prices are then supposed to equal the marginal cost of running each generator, they act as a substitute price signal for central economic dispatch in a vertically integrated system where the dispatcher uses its internal computations of marginal cost to perform the dispatch. However, it is quite clear that the generators have at least some market power (Green and Newbery, 1992; Armstrong *et al.*, 1994; Green 1995; Newbery, 1995), that some bid prices and the market clearing price exceed the relevant marginal cost, and that the resulting dispatch based on bid prices is also inefficient (Fehr and Harbord, 1992). Although there are several competing suppliers (PowerGen, National Power, Nuclear Electric, EDF, Scotland, and new entrants operated gas CCGT technology), the pool price is set by the bids of National Power or PowerGen, which control virtually all of the swing generating capacity, 90% of the time. Customers buying in the pool pay prices higher than they would have been had there been more competition. Wolfram (1995a) shows that the prices are not nearly as high as they would be if the generators colluded are played a simple Cournot quantity game, or the more complex bidding game modeled by Green and Newbery (1992). The fact that customers pay high prices is not an inherent failure of the pool-based framework, but rather a consequence of having too few generators with 'swing' or mid-merit order generating capacity that sets the pool prices in the auction.[7]

The system deals poorly with transmission and other network constraints. Ideally, one would like to perform an integrated least cost dispatch of the generators based on their marginal supply costs *and* network constraints simultaneously. This is because a generator that is chosen to run in an unconstrained dispatch based on bid prices may not be able to be run once network constraints are taken into account in real time operations. So, a unit that must be constrained off because there is too much generation scheduled to be run given network constraints has a lower market value with the constraint than without these constraints. Similarly, network support requirements to maintain frequency, voltage, to respond quickly to contingencies, or even to serve load in areas that have inadequate import capacity may make it necessary to run certain generators regardless (almost) of what they bid. The England/Wales system currently handles these situations poorly and creates opportunities for gaming the system and exploiting local market power. It is important to recognize that the information structure in a system like this is such that all of the generators know a lot about each other's costs and the operating attributes of the network. Generators probably know that they are not likely to be run, even if they are selected for the merit order dispatch, due to network constraints. They can bid a generator into the merit order dispatch knowing that it will not be called to run and be 'constrained off.' When they are constrained off, however, they are paid based on their bid price. Other generators may know that they will be run for reliability reasons even if their bid is far too high to be included in the merit order dispatch. They can bid very high, not be scheduled for dispatch and then be run anyway because of network reliability constraints. They too are paid their bid price. These 'out-of-merit' generation costs are the costs of network constraints and are passed on through an uniform 'uplift charge' that includes these and other network support costs. The constrained off problem can be handled with an appropriate nodal pricing mechanism. The constrained on problem is one of local market power and can only be fixed through a regulatory or *ex ante* contractual mechanism or by making network investments that relieve the constraint. This kind of local market power problem is inherent in the configuration of the grid (at least in the short run) and the geographical distribution of generators and has nothing

---

[7] It is not at all clear to me that a zero profit equilibrium where prices exactly equal short-run marginal cost in all hours is even feasible. This is because there are fixed operating costs associated with a generator that is capable of operating and these are largely unaffected by how much it actually generates.

in particular to do with the pooling model adopted in England and Wales.

The system provides poor locational incentives and poor incentives for grid expansion. In a competitive system there should be locational price differences to reflect losses and network constraints. Precisely what these price differences should be and how they can best be determined in a decentralized system is complicated and controversial (Schweppe *et al.*, 1988; Hogan, 1992, 1993; Chao and Peck, 1995; Oren *et al.*, 1995). Absent these price incentives, however, generators do not see the full impact of their locational decisions on the overall costs of the network. The treatment of constrained off plant may exacerbate this problem. Furthermore, the grid company does not have good incentives to make efficient transmission investments. It operates on a price cap mechanism that is geared to the cost of transmission service. But keeping the cost of transmission service low may increase the overall costs of power by creating bottlenecks that increase the costs of power supply in some areas. Since the costs of constrained on and constrained off plant are passed through to wholesale and retail customers dollar for dollar, there is no incentive for the grid company to make the right economic decisions about transmission investment.[8]

The California Proposals

In April 1994, the California Public Utilities Commission (CPUC) issued a report (the 'Blue Book') proposing a dramatic restructuring of the (private) electric power industry [9] in California to promote competition at wholesale and retail in the supply of generation services and to reform regulation of transmission and distribution. The reform proposals were motivated by some of the highest electric rates in the country, and a deep recession that made the price of electricity an important political issue. There was a large gap between the cost of generation reflected in retail tariffs and the market value of generation in the wholesale market, and the widespread perception that California's regulatory system had become so burdensome and politicized that if it was not reformed it would collapse under its own weight.

---

[8] One other problem has emerged in the England/Wales system, although it has nothing directly to do with network coordination or vertical integration issues. The regional distribution companies are regulated using a price cap (RPI-X+Z) plus a set of service quality standards and associated penalties for failing to meet them. The productivity improvement norms were set too low (X was too low —actually it was negative) from a rent extraction perspective. The regional electricity suppliers were able to reap substantial profits from efficiency improvements and (apparently) holding back on reinforcing their systems as had been assumed in the original X calculation. This has created much public dissatisfaction with the system, no doubt reinforced by the fact that the compensation of the REC's CEOs tripled in the two years after privatization (Wolfram, 1995b).

[9] There is a large municipal utility sector in California serving cities such as Los Angeles, Sacramento, Pasadena and Anaheim which is not regulated by the CPUC and is not directly affected by its restructuring and competition rulings.

The electricity supply sector in California (including both private and public power entities) is approximately the size of the sector in England and Wales and has a large amount of operating independent generating (QF) capacity under contract to utilities. Unlike England and Wales, California is not an electrical island. The network in California is fully integrated with the Western grid and large amounts of power flows between utilities throughout the western USA and Canada, supported by a wide array of short and medium-term bilateral wholesale power contracts and multilateral agreements that define protocols for harmonious operation of the 35 control areas in the WSCC, the allocation of transmission rights, and rationing protocols that go into effect when the rights conflict due to network constraints.[10]

Since April 1994, a large number of interest groups have participated in extensive administrative proceedings aimed at defining how the concepts outlined in the Blue Book will actually be implemented and when. Much of the debate over the restructuring options has focused on the vertical and horizontal structure of the market and, in particular, the role of the network operator and its relationships with upstream and downstream suppliers and customers. Although this debate has taken place in terms of technical attributes of a so-called 'Poolco Model' and an alternative 'Bilateral Contracts Model', in fact the political economy surrounding this debate largely reflects disputes over the allocation of sunk costs that might not be recoverable in a fully competitive market or shifted from one group of customers to another, the hope that some interests have that alternatives will provide them with transmission rights at favorable prices, and the desire of brokers and some utilities to create a market structure with high transactions and information costs which they will be able to exploit to their advantage.

In May, 1995, the CPUC issued two more refined restructuring proposals, one a majority proposal and one a dissenting proposal.[11] The majority's Proposed Policy Decision envisioned an Independent System Operator (ISO) which would (i) run an hourly uniform price sealed bid auction open to all generators in the WSCC to supply energy to meet projected demand a day ahead, use the bids and information about network constraints to determine a constrained economic merit order dispatch and associated day ahead schedules, and calculate market clearing prices for each hour based on the competitive bids and network constraints; (ii) physically schedule and dispatch generators to balance loads and resources using the network in real time based on the lowest bids obtained in the auction *and* transmission and

---

[10] In addition, there is the Western Systems Power Pool (WSPP), which involves utilities from all over the WSCC. The WSPP agreement allows the participants to negotiate prices for short-term power and transmission service under a price cap. It is not a traditional dispatch pool like NEPOOL or PJM.

[11] A final restructuring decision was due to be issued on 6 December 1995, but was delayed until 20 December, after the draft of this paper was completed.

other network constraints to achieve the least cost utilization of available generation and transmission facilities; (iii) competitively acquire through bids or contracts certain ancillary network support services required to maintain reliability and to facilitate efficient operation of generators capable of supplying energy to customers using the transmission facilities operated by the ISO; (iv) physically operate the transmission network facilities over which it has physical control to maintain reliability, including responses to unplanned outages of transmission and generation equipment and other emergencies, and to manage network constraints in an economically efficient manner; (e) coordinate operations with interconnected control areas to facilitate competitive sales and purchases of energy and to maintain reliability; (v) provide information to the public regarding the market clearing spot prices on an hourly or half-hourly basis, including locational price differences resulting from network constraints; and (vi) establish a financial settlements system to ensure that suppliers are properly paid for the energy they deliver to the network, buyers are properly charged for energy they take from the network, and charges for transmission and network support services are properly billed and paid for by all of the sellers and buyers responsible for them.

The majority's Proposed Policy Decision envisioned that the ISO would be responsible for operating the high voltage transmission facilities of the three investor-owned utilities in California, as well as the facilities of other entities, in particular municipal utilities with high voltage transmission facilities, which might choose voluntarily to turn over the operation of their transmission facilities to the ISO so that they could be operated in an integrated fashion with the IOU's transmission facilities. Any generator seeking access to the transmission facilities operated by the ISO would have open and comparable access to the ISO's network based on the same terms and conditions. These terms and conditions would be specified in transmission tariffs and interconnection agreements subject to FERC regulation. The majority's Proposed Policy Decision provided that the purchasers of electricity in this market would initially be distribution utilities rather than retail customers. However, rates would be redesigned to give customers with appropriate meters 'virtual direct access' at the same time, and opportunities for parties to enter into unregulated bilateral financial contracts to hedge variations in the spot price in the wholesale market were anticipated to emerge. Under the majority's Proposed Policy Decision, direct access—in the form of 'physical bilateral contracts'— to the wholesale market by retail customers would be deferred until these wholesale market institutions are established and refined and a variety of jurisdictional and public policy issues resolved.

The POOLCO model proposed by the majority in May 1995 shares many common features with the system in England and Wales, although its proponents anticipate implementing a much more sophisticated method for pricing network constraints and integrating these constraints into generator dispatch and for determining the net price of power at each generation and consumption node.

In September 1995, Southern California Edison Company and groups representing its industrial customers and independent power suppliers in California entered into a settlement agreement and signed a Memorandum of Understanding (MOU) that deals with various aspects of the restructuring program including the market structure and, in particular, the coordination of the generators and the network. As I read the MOU, particularly the market structure discussion included in its 'Attachment A', it appears to retain much of what was envisioned in the Majority's Proposed Policy Decision. It also incorporates a number of suggestions included in Commissioner Knight's Proposed Policy Decision. There are three major changes from the market structure envisioned in the majority's Proposed Policy Decisions.

First, under the MOU, an hourly bid-price energy pool and an associated economic merit order dispatch for generators scheduled through this auction process would be determined by a separate entity called the 'Power Exchange' rather than by the ISO. The Power Exchange would take day-ahead bids from generators to meet the projected demand for service by loads served through the ISO net of demands that have been specified as being served under bilateral contracts (see below). The Power Exchange then passes its merit order dispatch and associated economic information to the ISO which integrates it with preferred schedules that have been submitted to generators with bilateral contract commitments.

Second, all generators submitting schedules to the ISO will not be required to bid their supplies into the Power Exchange and be scheduled based on the economic merit order dispatch determined by it. Instead, generators may choose to submit 'bilateral' schedules directly to the ISO and be scheduled by the ISO based on the preferred scheduled and associated scheduling and economic information they submit directly to it. It is expected, however, that at least initially, California's three major investor-owned utilities will bid the bulk of their generation into the Power Exchange. The ISO will still be responsible for integrating the schedules received from the Power Exchange with the bilateral schedules, constraint resolution, reliability management, real time load balancing and defining protocols for identifying energy imbalances and for associated financial settlements.

Finally, direct 'physical' access for retail customers would become available, based on a phased in schedule, at the same time that the Power

Exchange and ISO go into operation. The MOU provides that the new market structure, including the first tranche of direct access, will be operational no later than 1 January 1998. This is a year later than the schedule established for the wholesale power exchange/ISO envisioned in the majority's Proposed Policy Decision.

On 20 December 1995, the CPUC voted out a final decision on industry restructuring (on a 3 to 2 vote). Although many of the details remain unclear as this is written, it appears to adopt almost all of the principles included in the MOU. Most importantly, there is an ISO, a separate Power Exchange (the day ahead spot energy pool), opportunities for bilateral schedules outside of the Exchange, a phased in schedule for direct access for retail customers beginning in 1998, and constraint management protocols that involve congestion pricing based on the difference in the marginal bid prices (or related constraint reservation prices supplied by bilateral schedules) as determined by a *de facto* constrained economic dispatch of Power Exchange and bilateral preferred schedules to resolve conflicts between preferred schedules and transmission capacity. The primary difference between the final decision and the MOU, is that the MOU specified general principles for transmission pricing—to rely on mechanisms that transmission constraints in an economically efficient manner, leaving the details to later negotiation. The final decision steers the parties toward the nodal pricing mechanism proposed by Hogan. The final decision preserves all of the important features of the original 'wholesale only' POOLCO proposal while providing more transparency, more options for suppliers and customers, and direct access sooner than the original did. The decision has a very rapid implementation schedule aimed at having the ISO, Power Exchange, direct access and incentive regulation protocols for remaining regulated monopoly functions in operation by 1 January 1998.

I believe that the market structure envisioned in the CPUC's final decision makes very good sense, although there are several important implementation details that need to be worked out. In particular, it deals very well with the network attributes discussed earlier and the associated vertical and horizontal control issues, free rider and externality problems that any good governance structure must deal with. Most importantly, it does so in a way that makes it easy for generators to compete to make both physical sales and to enter into bilateral financial contracts of any kind. It ensures that all users of the grid pay for transmission and network support costs, that schedules are harmonized reasonably efficiently when constraints cause scheduling conflicts, that energy imbalances are properly settled, and (assuming that the auction markets are efficient) that there will be economic dispatch of generators. These arrangements are characterized by low transaction costs for both buyers and sellers and very easy access to information about market prices. The changes made in the MOU, in particular the separation of the ISO and the Power Exchange, may create some information transfer costs, but if the provisions are implemented properly the MOU reforms should work reasonably well. The MOU structure has some advantages. It provides for direct access to the wholesale market for retail customers sooner than the May 1995 Majority Proposal, it provides more transparency in pricing, and it gives generators the option of self-scheduling if they perceive that the ISO is not properly dispatching generators. At the same time it does not allow generators to use self-scheduling rights to grab rights to scarce transmission capacity at attractive prices or to bypass responsibility for network support or congestion costs.

Other Countries

A number of other countries have implemented structural and regulatory reforms to promote competition in generation and to reform regulation in the electricity sector. These efforts provide useful case studies, but their relevance to the USA, Western Europe, Japan and other countries is limited. Much has been made of the system in Chile, for example. However, the Chilean system is tiny (only 5,700 Mw), has a simple linear transmission network, is characterized by collusive behavior in a number of dimensions, and involves more *de facto* administrative regulation than first meets the eye. Endesa, the dominant supplier of generation services in Chile, controls 60% of the generating capacity and has various cross-holding with other electricity and gas suppliers. New Zealand's system is also quite small (8,000 Mw) and the restructuring in New Zealand left the owner of virtually all of the generating capacity intact, creating a virtual monopoly over generation (it is now being broken up). Argentina's system is more interesting, both because it is larger (18,000 Mw) and because it has a more diverse resource mix and more interesting grid structure. The Norwegian system (27,000 Mw) is also interesting, although it is virtually a 100% hydro system and the national and municipal governments own the bulk of the generation (85%), the transmission grid and the distribution entities. Privatization did not accompany restructuring in Norway, although there are numerous government and private owners of generating capacity.

The new market structures in these countries share some common features that respond to the network coordination and vertical control issues that I have identified here (Hope *et al.*, 1995; Moen, 1995; Rudnick *et al.*, 1995). All of these systems have an independent system operator (typically an independent grid company) that is responsible for operating the network in a

way that maintains reliability, facilitates the economic dispatch of generators, balances loads and resources, provides a backup source of supply, and
ensures the compatibility of competition among generators with economic
dispatch and the reliability of the network. The ISO is responsible for real
time control of network facilities, including generators available and connected to the network, establishing protocols for supplying and paying for
ancillary network support services such as reactive power, spinning reserves
and standby reserves. The ISO is responsible for the physical scheduling of
generation and for economic dispatch of generators based on audited
marginal costs (or opportunity costs for reservoirs) or bid prices. There is a
wholesale market that includes a spot market organized by the ISO and a
contract market involving bilateral financial contracts written between eligi-
ble buyers (distributors or large retail customers) and sellers or with various
intermediaries linking both together. There does not appear to be any necessary incompatibility between an ISO-managed central dispatch system, an
organized spot market managed by the ISO and bilateral financial contracts
written on top of this short-term 'pooling' system. All of the systems recognize the desirability of efficient transmission prices that reflect network constraints and system losses, and that such pricing will effectively result in
spatial price differentials which will vary with network conditions. However, implementing the relevant transmission pricing principles has been far
less than perfect. Norway and Argentina appear to have made the most
progress. These countries also have substantially more structurally competitive generation sectors than do either Chile or England/Wales.

Thus, all of these systems recognize that the special physical attributes of
electricity, in particular the integrated character of the grid, the need to balance supply and demand in real time, the inability of prices reasonably to
adjust rapidly enough to do this balancing, the absence of well-defined property rights for using the grid, complex measurement requirements to match
supplies and consumption with financial obligations, etc. must be recognized efficiently to decentralize generation supply decisions and facilitate
competition in electricity. Moreover, not only is 'transmission' a natural
monopoly, but several important network functions that are integral to efficient horizontal and vertical coordination are also natural monopolies. These
include scheduling and dispatch,[12] an associated organized spot market to
deal with imbalances, around which a credible financial settlements system
can be created, and the acquisition (but not direct supply) of certain ancillary network support services from generators.

Norway is often pointed to as an example of a system that relies primarily
'on the market' rather than on 'central control'. This is a mischaracterization

[12] All generators must be scheduled and 'enough' must be under central control.

of the Norwegian system. A competitive bilateral contracts market can exist along with a network operator with substantial control over the operation of the network, central economic dispatch, and an organized spot market managed by the network operator. Those most familiar with the Norwegian system recognize this explicitly:

> The importance of effective pooling arrangements in a competitive ESI cannot be overstated. The pool provides:
>
>> a source of firm back-up and top-up power to support either generators or suppliers offering long term contracts to final consumers: without access to a Pool firm power could only be offered by generators owning a portfolio of plant, and to the extent that firm power is a necessary requirement of consumers the competitiveness of both the generation market and the final supply market would be limited;
>> a ready market for generators unable to sell their power under contract or wanting a market for spill or excess production;
>> a reference price for long or short-term contracts struck outside the Pool which provide participants with price stability not immediately available inside the pool;
>> a reference price to be used in signalling the optimal development of generation and transmission capacity on the system.
>
> In addition, of course, the Pool provides the traditional means by which generation costs can be minimized through merit order operation and the aggregation of reserve requirements. (Moen, 1995, p.5).

6. Why Bother with Competition?

It is clearly feasible to create institutions that make it possible both to support the development of a competitive generation sector and that maintain efficient horizontal and vertical relationships that are compatible with the physical attributes of synchronized AC electric power networks, least cost dispatch of generators, efficient allocation of network constraints, and maintaining supply reliability. At the heart of the problem is properly defining the role of the network operator, recognizing that a variety of network functions have natural monopoly attributes and/or are potential sources of market failure, and creating a system that yields appropriate price signals, linking generators with the network operator, and defining appropriate network operating protocols when prices cannot be expected to allocate resources efficiently. That is, it must provide a substitute governance structure for what is now accomplished with internal operating protocols in vertically and horizontally integrated firms and multilateral network coordination agreements between entities that largely do not compete with one another. Creating these new institutional arrangements is not easy in practice and those that exist all have some imperfections that lead to both operating and investment inefficiencies .

The question naturally emerges, why bother? One of the things that vertically integrated electric power systems in most developed countries do reasonably well is to dispatch generators efficiently and to take network constraints into account on their own systems when they do so. Countries like France, which are both vertically and horizontally integrated over most of the relevant network, also deal with network constraints and the interrelationships between the nodes on the synchronized networks extremely well. In the USA, with many control area operators operating pieces of the same synchronized network, a whole hierarchy of reliability councils and multilateral operating protocols have emerged to deal with the potential free rider and externality problems that would otherwise exist with so many entities exploiting a common network. These arrangements have also worked reasonably well, especially for optimizing short-run operations of generators located within power pools or on contiguous systems, and for coordinated investments in transmission capacity. However, as competition in the generation sector grows, at both the wholesale and retail levels, these network hierarchies are increasingly being stressed. The networks in all developed countries also maintain very high levels of network reliability, broadly defined.

Therefore, to answer the question 'why bother?' we must recognize that economical and reliable operation and coordination of dispersed generating facilities connected to an AC network is not a major economic problem in most systems today.[13] It is not a problem for which we need competition to fix. To the contrary, the issue is whether or not we can retain these desirable operating attributes of modern electric power networks while relying on competition in generation to improve upon other imperfections associated with vertically integrated regulated monopolies. What are these other problems that need fixing?

To the extent that there are efficiency problems with the traditional structure of privately-owned or publicly-owned vertically integrated electricity suppliers providing service on an exclusive basis in a specific geographic area, they fall into particular areas.

Generation Construction Costs and Investment Decisions: On average, roughly half of the cost of a Kwh of electricity is associated with the operating costs and carrying charges associated with generating facilities. There is substantial variation across utilities (within and between countries) in the construc-

---

[13] It was a problem in Norway prior to restructuring and, indeed, one of the goals of the reforms in Norway was to improve the integration of generators that had been developed to serve specific municipal and industrial loads.

tion costs of similar generating units (Monopolies and Mergers Commission, 1981, p.256; Joskow and Rose, 1985; Lester and McCabe, 1993) which cannot be readily explained by differences in underlying cost opportunities. Some of these variations may be explained by poor cost control incentives created by price regulation or public ownership in a monopoly environment. More generally, with vertically integrated monopolies, as in the USA before the 1980s, there was no mechanism through which companies that were particularly good at managing the construction of generating plants could expand their market and those that did not manage generation construction projects very well could be driven out of the business. Aside from joint ventures, each utility managed its own generation construction projects. Smaller utilities may have been less capable of managing more complex technologies than larger utilities and were also less innovative (Rose and Joskow, 1990). It is also often argued that the 'Averch-Johnson' effect gave utilities incentives to choose more capital intensive generating technologies (e.g. nuclear instead of coal) than was economical. There is not much empirical support for this proposition given *ex ante* projections of the construction costs of nuclear plants and future fossil fuel prices. There are good reasons to believe, however, that some utilities poorly managed the actual construction of these projects.

Operating Costs of Generating Units: The restructuring in England and Wales was driven partly by a desire to break the back of the coal miners' union and to make it possible for the electricity suppliers to turn to lower priced coal sources, both domestic and foreign. Prior to restructuring, the CEGB bought a lot of high-priced domestic coal and supported the domestic coal industry. The theory was that the combination of privatization and competition would place significant constraints on the coal industry and give the generators the flexibility to buy the cheapest fuels available. Similar high cost coal relationships involving the electricity supply sector exist in Spain, Germany, and to a much smaller extent in the USA. This is more a political economy problem than a mechanical regulatory problem since it is fairly easy to design regulatory mechanisms that provide good incentives to buy fuel as economically as possible. The costs of generating units also depend on the availability of the unit (i.e. the fraction of the year that it is not being fixed and is available to supply electricity) and their thermal efficiency. There is very substantial variation in both availability and thermal efficiency across fossil and nuclear generating units, after controlling for the underlying attributes of the technology that was chosen (Joskow and Schmalansee, 1987; Lester and McCabe, 1993). Moreover, some utilities appear to be systematically better operators than others. The regulatory process penalized and rewarded operating performance only indirectly, although a number of states began to focus on performance based incentives for performance during the 1980s (Joskow and Schmalensee, 1986). Again, the market mechanisms for driving firms to best practice maintenance and operating protocols were blunted by the institution of regulated monopoly. Finally, utilities may have incentives to keep generating units operating even when they should be closed. Under the old regime in England and Wales ancient inefficient generators were kept running to create a market for expensive coal and to maintain employment. In the USA, regulatory rules treat the remaining capital costs of 'abandoned plant' in a way that is less rewarding to shareholders than continuing operations, *as long as* the regulators do not find them operating the plant inefficiently and do not assess an even more costly penalty.

Employment Practices and Wages: The experience with restructuring, privatization, and deregulation around the world suggests that public enterprises and private firms subject to price and entry regulation employ too many workers (have low levels of labor productivity). The number of workers that have been shed by the electricity sector in England and Wales is quite impressive indeed. However, the CEGB and Area Boards had much lower levels of labor productivity than US utilities (more than 50% lower) and the sector in England and Wales may have been unusually inefficient by world standards. Nevertheless, the recent efforts by US utilities to reduce costs, in part, by reducing employment levels, suggests that there are significant opportunities for increasing labor productivity. On the compensation side, the experience with some other regulated industries is that wages fell after deregulation in the face of more competition, especially from non-unionized suppliers (Joskow and Rose, 1989). There is limited evidence that wages for production workers in the regulated sector are higher than in other sectors, controlling for various indicators of human capital (Katz and Summers, 1989). On the other hand, senior management of regulated private utilities and public enterprises are paid significantly less than managers with similar (measurable) attributes in unregulated businesses of similar size (Joskow *et al.*, 1993). The potential gains from improvements in labor productivity and wage concessions must be kept in perspective, however. In the USA, wages and benefits account for about 12% of the total cost of supplying electricity.

Pricing Inefficiencies: There are wide variations in the care that has been taken to establish electricity price structures that provide the best incentives to consumers given the relevant marginal supply costs and the budget constraints that these entities operate under. EDF offers the most sophisticated retail tariff structures in the world, especially those available to large industrial customers. The record among US utilities is less impressive. Moreover, the average cost-based regulatory system that exists in the US has a built-in predisposition to lead to prices that are poorly aligned with the relevant marginal costs. Specifically, tariffs are designed to recover the operating and fixed costs of the supplier, based on historical investment decisions and their associated costs. As a result, when there is excess capacity, prices tend to rise and when capacity is short, prices tend to fall, just the opposite of how a market would work.

Innovation: Unlike the US telephone industry, electric utilities in the USA and other countries generally are not vertically integrated into the manufacture of electric appliances or power supply equipment. This equipment is manufactured by companies like GE, Westinghouse, Toshiba, ABB etc. Customers are free to choose their own appliances and equipment for using electricity. If there are any inefficiencies in respect of innovation they are probably associated with the procurement behavior of vertically integrated utilities. There is some systematic variation in the rate at which utilities adopt new generating technologies (Rose and Joskow, 1990). Moreover, the growth of a QF/IPP market in the USA clearly stimulated innovation and speeded up diffusion of gas CCGT technology and fluidized bed boilers burning coal.

The answer to the question 'why bother?' then is that by creating a new market structure where generators can compete at wholesale and retail free from regulation at least some of these inefficiencies associated with the institution of regulated monopoly will be reduced. Certainly the inefficiencies associated with construction cost overruns in new generating projects, inefficient choices of generating technologies, excessive operating costs and poor plant maintenance, failures to close inefficient plant, excess employment at generating plants, etc. should be under substantial pressure from competition. Moreover, independent generators, brokers, and retailers are likely to have an interest in creating a regulatory environment that reduces inefficiencies in the transmission and distribution networks where regulated monopoly would continue to prevail. In a direct access regime, power supply costs will be unbundled from T&D costs and customers can choose the allocation of risks associated with changes in supply and demand conditions to match their preferences and will always have access to spot and short-term markets that will reflect changing supply and demand conditions. Thus, the generation component of a customer's electricity bill can reflect prevailing market conditions, depending upon the portfolio of supply contracts the customer chooses.

This suggests that there are potentially significant benefits from competition in the generation sector. While it would be desirable to create a governance structure that preserves (or improves upon) the efficiency properties associated with integrated network operations that take place today in vertically and horizontally integrated firms and a variety of multilateral agreements between them, our inability to replicate fully what goes on within these hierarchies in a more decentralized system does not mean that the restructuring effort is not worthwhile. The benefits associated with lower construction and operating costs overall in the supply of generation may more than offset some additional imperfections in network coordination and constraint management that may accompany horizontal and vertical restructuring. This trade-off, of course, is one of the most important lessons of the Williamson's comparative institutional choice paradigm (Williamson, 1985). What is the best that we can do in a world where market, organizational and regulatory institutions are all imperfect.

6. *Conclusions*

While the focus of this paper has been a restructuring, regulatory reform and competition in a particular network industry—electricity—similar types of issues have been, and are being, confronted in other regulated or publicly-owned network industries as well. These include telecommunications networks, natural gas pipeline networks and railroad networks. In all of these cases vertical and horizontal control relationships (hierarchical and contractual) have been, or are being, restructured to facilitate competition in the potentially competitive segments. At the same time, there remains a core set of network functions which are natural monopolies and to which access by competing suppliers of the competitive services is required. The structure, obligations, terms and conditions of service, and behavior of the network operator, have important implications for the performance of the competitive sector. It is not just a question of 'access' or the access price. Rather, it is a question of institutional re-engineering to find new governance structures that are good substitutes for the pre-reform vertical and horizontal hierarchical and contractual structures that are being broken down to promote competition at certain horizontal levels. This institutional design problem is far from trivial and has important implications for the long-term performance of these sectors.

While it would be ideal if we could identify organizational arrangements that could replicate (or improve upon) the attractive short-term vertical and horizontal coordination aspects of the prevailing industry structure *and* promote full competition at wholesale and retail in the supply of generation services, such a happy outcome is likely to be unachievable in practice. Indeed, it is likely that the rapid spread of competition in the supply of generation services, regulatory access rules that force incumbent vertically integrated firms to behave as if they are not vertically integrated, and vertical restructuring that significantly reduces the extent of vertical integration between the network operator and generators will result in some losses in short-term efficiencies associated with economic dispatch, efficient management of network constraints, the costs of reliability, and the costs of network support services. As a result, the restructuring and regulatory reform program will be desirable in the long run if these losses in short-run efficiency can be kept small, and the long-term cost reduction benefits of promoting competition in the construction and operation of generating plants more than compensate for the costs of poorer short-term horizontal and vertical coordination. Achieving a favorable trade-off should be the goal of policies aimed at promoting competition in 'natural monopoly' sectors.

Acknowledgements

Research support from the MIT Center for Energy and Environmental Policy Research is gratefully acknowledged.

References

Armstrong, M., S. Cowan and J. Vickers (1994), *Regulatory Reform: Economic Analysis and British Experience.* MIT Press: Cambridge, MA.

Bushnell, J. and S. Stoft (1995), 'Electric Grid Investment Under a Contract Network Regime,' University of California Energy Institute, mimeo, 15 August.

Chao, H. P. and S. Peck (1995), 'Market Mechanisms for Electric Power Transmission,' mimeo, 28 May.

Fehr, N-H. and D. Harbord (1992), 'Spot Market Competition in the UK Electricity Industry,' Department of Economics, University of Oslo, mimeo, May.

Gilbert, R.J. and M.J. Riordan (1995), 'Regulating Complementary Products: A Comparative Institutional Approach,' *Rand Journal of Economics,* 26(2), 243–256.

Green, R. and D. Newbery (1992), 'Competition in the British Electricity Spot Market, *Journal of Political Economy,* 100(5), 929–953.

Green, R. (1995), 'The English Electricity Industry in the 1990s', in O. J. Olsen (ed.) *Competition in the Electricity Supply Industry.* DJØF Publishing Company: Copenhagen, pp. 107–136.

Hogan, W. (1992), 'Contract Networks for Electric Power Transmission,' *Journal of Regulatory Economics,* 4(3), 211–242.

Hogan, W. (1993), 'Markets In Real Networks Require Reactive Prices,' *The Energy Journal,* 14(3), 171–200.

Hope, E., L. Rud and B. Sing (1995), 'Markets for Electricity: Economic Reform of the Norwegian Electricity Industry,' in O. J. Olsen (ed.) *Competition in the Electricity Supply Industry,* DJOF Publishing: Copenhagen, pp. 69–106.

Joskow, P. L. (1989), 'Regulatory Failure, Regulatory Reform and Structural Change in the Electric Power Industry,' *Brookings Papers on Economic Activity: Microeconomics,* 125–199.

Joskow, P. L. (1995a), 'The New Institutional Economics: Alternative Approaches,' *Journal of Theoretical and Institutional Economics,* 55(1), 248–259.

Joskow, P. L. (1995b), 'Horizontal Market Power in Wholesale Power Markets,' mimeo, August.

Joskow, P. L. and R. Noll (1994), 'Deregulation and Regulatory Reform During the 1980s,' in M. Feldstein (ed.) *American Economic Policy During the 1980s.* University of Chicago Press: Chicago, IL, pp. 367–452.

Joskow, P. L. and N. Rose (1985), 'The Effects of Technological Change, Experience and Environmental Regulation on the Construction Costs of Coal-Burning Generating Units,' *Rand Journal of Economics*, 16(1), 1–27.

Joskow, P. L. and N. Rose (1989), 'The Effects of Economic Regulation' in R. Schmalensee and R. Willig (eds) *Handbook on Industrial Organization*. North-Holland: Amsterdam, pp. 1449–1506.

Joskow, P. L., N. Rose and A. Shepard (1993), 'Regulatory Constraints on CEO Compensation,' *Brookings Papers on Economic Activity: Microeconomics*, 1–58.

Joskow, P. L. and R. Schmalensee (1983), *Markets for Power: An Analysis of Electric Utility Deregulation*. MIT Press: Cambridge, MA.

Joskow P. L. and R. Schmalensee (1986), 'Incentive Regulation for Electric Utilities,' *Yale Journal on Regulation*, 4(1), 1–49.

Joskow, P. L. and R. Schmalensee (1987), 'The Performance of Coal-Burning Electric Generating Units in the United States: 1960–1980,' *Journal of Applied Econometrics*, 2(2), 85–109.

Katz, L. and L. Summers (1989), 'Industry Rents: Evidence and Implications,' *Brookings Papers on Economic Activity: Microeconomics*, 209–275.

Lester, R. K. and M. J. McCabe (1993), 'The Effect of Industrial Structure on Learning By Doing in Nuclear Power Plant Operations,' *Rand Journal of Economics*, 24(3), 418–438.

Moen, J. (1995), 'Electric Utility Regulation, Structure and Competition. Experiences From the Norwegian Electric Supply Industry (ESI),' Norwegian Water Resources and Energy Administration, mimeo, February.

Monopolies and Mergers Commission (1981), 'The Central Electricity Generating Board,' Her Majesty's Stationary Office: London, 20 May.

Newbery, D. (1995), 'Power Markets and Market Power,' mimeo, 1 April.

Oren, S., P. Spiller, P. Vavaiya, F. Wu (1995), 'Nodal Prices and Transmission Rights: A Critical Appraisal,' *The Electricity Journal*, 8(3).

Posner, R. (1971), 'Taxation By Regulation,' *Bell Journal of Economics and Management Science*, 2(1), 22–50.

Rose, N. L. and P. L. Joskow (1990), 'The Diffusion of New Technology: Evidence From the Electric Utility Industry,' *Rand Journal of Economics*, 21(3), 354–373.

Rudnick, H., R. Varela and W. Hogan (1995), 'Evaluation of Alternatives for Power System Coordination and Pooling in a Competitive Environment,' mimeo, July.

Ruff, L. (1994), 'Stop Wheeling and Start Dealing: Resolving the Transmission Dilemma,' *The Electricity Journal*, 7(5), 24–43.

Schweppe, F. C., M. C. Caramanis, R. D. Tabovs, R. E. Bohn (1988), *Spot Pricing of Electricity*. Kluwer Academic Publishers: Boston, MA.

Williamson, O. (1975), *Markets and Hierarchies: Analysis and Antitrust Implications*. Free Press: New York.

Williamson, O. (1985), *The Economic Institutions of Capitalism*. Free Press: New York.

Williamson, O. (1993), 'Transaction Cost Economics and Organization Theory,' *Industrial and Corporate Change*, 2(2), 107–156.

Wolfram, C. (1995a), 'Measuring Duopoly Power in the British Electricity Spot Market,' November 1995.

Wolfram, C. (1995b), 'Increases in Executive Pay Following Privatization,' October 1995.

CHAPTER TWELVE

Institutions and Commitment

PABLO T. SPILLER

The thrust of this paper is that to understand the roles institutions play in society, a deep analysis of opportunism and its implications is necessary. For that purpose, a transactions costs-cum-positive political theory approach is developed, with a focus on the role of institutions and their implications for regulatory commitment. A major issue is restraining political opportunism. Countries that have succeeded in developing a healthy private sector are those that have developed institutions that restrain governmental decision-making. But such restraining is itself a political choice. Countries with electoral and legislative systems that bring about decentralized government have stronger chances of developing equilibria where government discretion is restrained.

1. Introduction

Oliver Williamson opened a new approach to institutions. In *Markets and Hierarchies* institutions are not seen simply as organigrams or chains of command whose layers are determined by the workings of communications channels. Instead, institutions are now seen as designed to deal with a basic time inconsistency inherent to most transactions, namely opportunism coupled with the inability to write fully contingent contracts. Indeed, in explaining the differences with the prior literature, Williamson writes (1975, p. 7):

> . . . (2) I expressly introduce the notion of opportunism and am interested in the ways that opportunistic behavior is influenced by economic organization. (3) I emphasize that it is not uncertainty or small numbers, individually or together that occasion market failure, but it is rather the *joining* of these factors with bounded rationality on the one hand and opportunism on the other that gives rise to exchange difficulties.

The main point of this paper is that to understand the roles institutions play in society, a deeper analysis of opportunism is necessary. Paraphrasing Williamson, (1975, p. 7), 'opportunism, in a rich variety of forms, is made to play a central role in the analysis of [institutions] herein'. This paper will focus on the role of institutions and their implications for regulatory commitment. I believe, however, that regulation is only one type of societal relation in which opportunism is particularly endemic and to which society's institutions must adapt. As discussed below, the organizational problems arising from regulation (the relation between the different components of government, the regulated firms and other interested parties) are particularly amenable to analysis using a synthesis of transaction cost economics and positive political theory. Understanding the organizational implications of opportunism is the key to understand the organization of society in its various forms, and it is particularly necessary to understand the organization of the different branches of government.[1] Looking at institutions as limiting the potential for opportunistic behavior is useful in an even more general way. But the relation between institutions and commitment is not a trivial one. Indeed, Barry Weingast's opening paragraph in his *Journal of Law, Economics and Organization* 1995 exemplifies this point: 'A government strong enough to protect property rights and enforce contracts is also strong enough to confiscate the wealth of its citizens' (Weingast, 1995, p. 1). Thus, a major problem in society is the potential for opportunistic behavior, not only by firms and economic agents, but by political agents, and in a more general way, by government. In this sense, I share Douglass North's belief that to understand the growth of the Western world a deep understanding of the evolution of its institutions is necessary (North, 1990. p. 107), to which I would add the way by which they also restrain government.

This paper, however, is not an attempt to explain the growth of Western civilization. Instead, the focus will be on a more narrow problem, namely, understanding how alternative institutions may provide regulatory commitment. It is hoped that the paper will motivate the reader to develop the theory of how Western institutions, e.g. representative democracy, independent judiciary, property rights, and so on, all interact in restraining government, and in that way, in promoting private investment, innovation and the growth of civilization.

2. *The Utilities' Problem*[2]

Three features characterize utilities: (i) their technologies are characterized by large specific, sunk investments;[3] (ii) their technologies are characterized

---

[1] In this sense, the earlier work of McCubbins *et al.* (1987, 1989) on administrative procedures in the USA can be seen as an attempt to show how the administrative process is designed so as to limit the potential for opportunistic behavior by the different parts of government. For further elaborations on the 'process provides commitment' issue, see Macey (1992) and Shepsle (1992).

[2] This section draws heavily from Spiller (1995).

[3] Specific or sunk investments are those that once undertaken their value in alternative uses is substantially below their investment cost.

by important economies of scale and scope; and (iii) their products are massively consumed. Consider, for example, an electricity distribution company. Its assets have very little value in alternative uses (it is very expensive to bring down cables and posts, to dig out trenches, etc.);[4] network externalities and economies of density imply that it may not be economical to have multiple wires deployed on the same street; and finally, its product is consumed by a large proportion of the city's population. Compare this situation to that of another industry characterized by large sunk investments: steel. While steel mills have very little value in alternative uses, the economies of scale and scope are trivial compared to the size of the market,[5] and furthermore, while everybody indirectly consumes steel products, very few individuals in society pay any attention to the price of steel. Thus, it is not simply specific investments that characterize utilities. Nor is it simply economies of scale.

Now consider newspapers. It is quite clear that there are large economies of scale and scope in the operation of city newspapers. The increase in speed of communications, and the increased use of computer design, has drastically increased the extent of economies of scale in the sector. This has translated in a reduction in the number of newspapers per city while maintaining relatively constant the readership numbers. While readers are usually a relatively large portion of the population (at least of the voting population), newspapers are not utilities. The reason being that while there may be a substantial amount of sector specific human capital (reporters' contacts with local politicians may be specific to the locality), the technology is increasingly generic. Shutting down a newspaper and moving the printing presses, their desks, computers, etc. elsewhere is becoming more and more common.

Thus, what separates the utility sector from the rest of the economy is the combination of three features: specific investments, economies of scale and widespread domestic consumption. These features are at the core of contracting problems that have traditionally raised the need for governmental regulation of utilities. See, among others, North (1990), Williamson (1988), Goldberg (1976), Barzel (1989), Levy and Spiller (1994) and Spiller (1993). In turn, they make the pricing of utilities inherently political.

The reason for the politicization of infrastructure pricing is threefold. First, the fact that a large component of infrastructure investments is sunk, implies that once the investment is undertaken the operator will be willing to continue operating as long as operating revenues exceed operating costs.

---

[4] Although the development of fiber optics has increased the value in alternative uses of their electricity poles.

[5] In some developing countries that protect the production of steel, that may not be so, as there may be just a few steel mills producing for the relatively small local market.

Since operating costs do not include a return on sunk investments (but only on the alternative value of these assets), the operating company will be willing to operate even if prices are below total average costs.[6] Second, economies of scale imply that in most utility services, there will be few suppliers in each locality. Thus, the whiff of monopoly will always surround utility operations. Finally, the fact that utility services tend to be massively consumed, implies that politicians and interest groups will care about the level of utility pricing. Thus, massive consumption, economies of scale and sunk investments provide governments (either national or local) with the opportunity to behave opportunistically *vis-à-vis* the investing company.[7] For example, after the investment is sunk, the government may try to restrict the operating company's pricing flexibility, may require the company to undertake special investments, purchasing or employment patterns or may try to restrict the movement of capital. All these are attempts to expropriate the company's sunk costs by administrative measures. Thus, expropriation may be indirect and undertaken by subtle means.

Expropriation of the firm's sunk assets, however, does not mean that the government takes over the operation of the company, but rather that it sets operating conditions that just compensate for the firm's operating costs and the return on its non-specific assets. Such returns will provide sufficient *ex post* incentives for the firm to operate, but not to invest. The company will be willing to continue operating because its return from operating will exceed its return from shutting down and deploying its assets elsewhere. On the other hand, the firm will have very little incentive to invest new capital as it will not be able to obtain a return. While it is feasible to conceive loan financing for new investments, as non-repayment would bring the company to bankruptcy, that will not however be the case. Bankruptcy does not mean that the company shuts down. Since the assets are specific, bankruptcy implies a change of ownership from stockholders to creditors. Now creditors' incentives to operate will be the same as the firm, and they would be willing to operate even if quasi-rents are expropriated. Thus, loan financing will not be feasible either. Indeed, sunk assets expropriation has been more prevalent in Latin America than direct utility takeovers or expropriation without compensation.[8] While the government may uphold and protect traditionally

---

[6] Observe that the source of financing does not change this computation. For example, if the company is completely leveraged, a price below average cost will bring the company to bankruptcy, eliminating the part of the debt associated with the sunk investments. Only the part of the debt that is associated with the value of the non-sunk investments would be able to be subsequently serviced.

[7] Note that this incentive exists *vis-à-vis* public *and* private companies.

[8] Consider, for example, the case of Montevideo's Gas Company. Throughout the 1950s and 1960s the MGC, owned and operated by a British company, was denied price increases. Eventually, during the rapid inflation of the 1960s it went bankrupt and was taken over by the government. Compare this example to the expropriation by the Perón administration of ITT's majority holdings in the Unión

conceived property rights, it may still attempt to expropriate through regulatory procedures.

The Political Profitability of Expropriation

Sunk assets' expropriation may be profitable for a government if the direct costs (reputation loss *vis-à-vis* other utilities, lack of future investments by utilities) are small compared to the (short-term) benefits of such action (achieving re-election by reducing utilities' prices, by attacking the monopoly, etc.), and if the indirect institutional costs (e.g. disregarding the judiciary, not following the proper, or traditional, administrative procedures, etc.) are not too large.

Thus, incentives for expropriation of sunk assets should be expected to be largest in countries where indirect institutional costs are low (e.g. there are no formal or informal governmental procedures, checks and balances, required for regulatory decision-making; regulatory policy is centralized in the administration; the judiciary does not have a tradition of, or the power to, reviewing administrative decisions, etc.), direct costs are also small (e.g. the utilities in general do not require massive investment programs, not is technological change an important factor in the sector), and, perhaps, more importantly, the government's horizon is relatively short (i.e. highly contested elections, need to satisfy key constituencies, etc.). Forecasting such expropriation, private utilities will not undertake investments in the first place. Thus, government direct intervention may become the default mode of operation.

The Implications of Government Opportunism

If, in the presence of such incentives a government wants to motivate private investment, then, it will have to design institutional arrangements that will limit its own ability to behave opportunistically once the private utility undertakes its investment program. Such institutional arrangements are nothing but the design of a regulatory framework, and will have to stipulate price setting procedures, conflict resolution procedures (arbitration or judicial) between the parties, investment policies, etc. In other words, regulation, if credible, solves a key contracting problem between the government and the utilities by restraining the government from opportunistically expropriating the utilities' sunk investments.[9] This, however, does not mean

---

Telefónica del Rio de la Plata (UTRP was the main provider of telephones in the Buenos Aires region). In 1946 the Argentinian government paid US$95 million for ITT's holdings, or US$623 million in 1992 prices. Given UTRP's 457,800 lines, it translates at US$1360 per line in 1992 prices (deflator: capital equipment producer prices). Given that in today's prices, the marginal cost of a line in a large metropolitan city is approximately US$650, the price paid by the Perón administration does not seem unusually low. See Hill and Abdalla (1993).

[9] See, Goldberg (1976) for one of the first treatments of this problem. See also Williamson (1976).

that the utility has to receive assurances of a rate of return nature, or that it has to receive exclusive licenses.[10] In some countries, however, such assurances may be the only way to limit the government's discretionary powers.[11]

However, unless such a regulatory framework is credible investments will not be undertaken, or if undertaken will not be efficient. Investment inefficiencies may arise in several ways.[12] A first order effect is underinvestment. Although the utility may invest, it will do so exclusively in areas whose market return is very high and where the payback period is relatively short.[13] Second, maintenance expenditures may be kept to the minimum, thus degrading quality. Third, investment may be undertaken with technologies that have a lower degree of specificity, even at the cost of, again, degrading quality.[14] Fourth, up-front rents may be achieved by very high prices which although may provide incentives for some investments, may be politically unsustainable.[15]

Therefore, by creating strong inefficiencies and poor performance, a noncredible regulatory framework will eventually create the conditions for a direct government takeover. Thus, government ownership may become the default mode of operations. Government ownership, then, reflects the inability of the polity to develop regulatory institutions that limit the potential for government opportunistic behavior.

3. *Sources of Regulatory Commitment*

Levy and Spiller (1994) argued that the credibility and effectiveness of a regulatory framework—and hence its ability to facilitate private investment—varies with a country's political and social institutions.

---

[10] Indeed, the Colombian regulation of value added networks specifically stipulate that the government cannot set their prices, nor that there is any exclusivity provisions. Thus, regulation here means total *lack* of governmental discretion.

[11] On this see more below.

[12] Williamson's basic contracting Schema applies here. See Williamson (1975).

[13] An alternative way of reducing the specificity of the investment is by customers undertaking the financing of the sunk assets to the customers. Thus, for example, in several Latin American countries, and also in Japan, the installation charge for a telephone line may range from $400 to $600. Given that the investment cost of a new line ranges from $600 to $800 in less developed countries, that initial charge essentially protects the utility from the expropriation of its sunk investments.

[14] In this sense it is not surprising that private telecommunications operations have rushed to develop cellular rather than fixed link networks in Eastern European countries. While cellular has a higher long run cost than fixed link, and on some quality dimensions is also an inferior product, the magnitude of investment in specific assets is much smaller than in fixed link networks. Furthermore, a large portion of the specific investments in cellular telephony are undertaken by the customers themselves (who purchase the handsets).

[15] The privatization of Argentina's telecommunications companies is particularly illuminating. Prior to the privatization, telephone prices were raised well beyond international levels. It is not surprising, that following the privatization the government reneged on aspects of the license, like indexation. The initial high prices, though, allowed the companies to remain profitable, even following government's deviation from the license provisions. See Spiller (1993).

Political and social institutions not only affect the ability to restrain administrative action, but also have an independent impact on the type of regulation that can be implemented, and hence affect the appropriate balance between commitment and flexibility. For example, relatively efficient regulatory rules (e.g. price caps, incentive schemes, use of competition) usually require granting substantial discretion to the regulators. Thus, unless the country's institutions allow for the separation of arbitrariness from useful regulatory discretion, systems that grant too much administrative discretion may not generate the high levels of investment and welfare expected from private sector participation. Conversely, some countries might have regulatory regimes that drastically limit the scope of regulatory flexibility. Although such regulatory regimes may look inefficient, they may in fact fit the institutional endowments of the countries in question, and may provide substantial incentives for investment.

Regulation can be thought of as a 'design' problem.[16] Regulatory design has two components: regulatory governance and regulatory incentives. The governance structure of a regulatory system comprises the mechanisms that societies use to constrain regulatory discretion, and to resolve conflicts that arise in relation to these constraints.[17] On the other hand, the regulatory incentive structure comprises the rules governing utility pricing, cross- or direct-subsidies, entry, interconnection, etc. While regulatory incentives may affect performance, a main insight from Levy and Spiller (1994) is that the impact of regulatory incentives (whether positive or negative) comes to the forefront only if regulatory governance has successfully been put into place. Commenting on the interaction among technology (institutions), governance, and price (regulatory detail) Williamson (185, p. 36) says, 'Inasmuch as price and governance are linked, parties to a contract should not expect to have their cake (low price) and eat it too (no safeguard)'. In other words, there is no 'free institutional lunch'. Now, regulatory governance is a choice, although a constrained one. The institutional endowment of the country limits the menu of regulatory governance available. Thus, regulatory commitment has two sources: the institutional endowment and regulatory governance. I discuss both seriatim.

Institutional Endowment[18]

Levy and Spiller (1994) define the institutional endowment of a nation as

---

[16] The concept of regulation as a design problem was first introduced in Levy and Spiller (1993). The terminology used here was subsequently developed in Levy and Spiller (1994).

[17] Williamson would call such constraints on regulatory decision-making 'contractual governance institutions.' See Williamson (1985, p. 35).

[18] This section draws heavily from Levy and Spiller (1994).

comprising five elements: first, a country's legislative and executive institutions. These are the formal mechanisms for appointment of legislators and decision-makers, for making laws and regulations, apart from judicial decision-making; for implementing these laws, and that determines the relation between the legislature and the executive. Second, the country's judicial institutions. These comprise its formal mechanisms for appointing judges and determining the internal structure of the judiciary; and for resolving disputes among private parties, or between private parties and the state. Third, custom and other informal but broadly accepted norms that are generally understood to constrain the action of individuals or institutions. Fourth, the character of the contending social interests within a society, and the balance between them, including the role of ideology. Finally, the administrative capabilities of the nation. Each of these elements has implications for regulatory commitment. This paper focuses on the first two.

The form of a country's legislative and executive institutions influences the nature of its regulatory problems. The crucial issue is to what extent the structure and organization of these institutions impose constraints upon governmental action. The range of formal institutional mechanisms for restraining governmental authority includes: the explicit separation of powers between legislative, executive and judicial organs of government;[19] a written constitution limiting the legislative power of the executive, and enforced by the courts; two legislative houses elected under different voting rules;[20] an electoral system calibrated to produce either a proliferation of minority parties or a set of parties whose ability to impose discipline on their legislators is weak;[21] and a federal structure of power, with strong decentralization even to the local level.[22] Utility regulation is likely to be far more credible, and the regulatory problem less severe, in countries with political systems that constrain executive discretion. Note, however, that credibility is often achieved at the expense of flexibility. The same mechanisms that make it difficult to impose arbitrary changes in the rules may also make it difficult to enact sensible rules in the first place, or to efficiently adapt the rules in

[19] For an analysis of the role of separation of powers in diminishing the discretion of the executive, see Gely and Spiller (1990) and McCubbins *et al.* (1987, 1989), and references therein.

[20] Non-simultaneous elections for the different branches of government tend to create natural political divisions and thus electoral checks and balances. See Jacobson (1990). For an in-depth analysis of the determinants of the relative powers of the executive, see Shugart and Carey (1992).

[21] Electoral rules also have important effects on the 'effective number of parties' that will tend to result from elections, and thus, the extent of governmental control over the legislative process. For example, it is widely perceived that proportional representation tends to generate a large number of parties, while first-past-the-post with relatively small district elections tends to create bipolar party configurations. This result has been coined Duverger's Law in political science. See Duverger (1954). More generally, see Taagepera and Shugart (1993). For analyses of how the structure of political parties depends on the nature of electoral rules (with applications to the UK) see Cain *et al.* (1987) and Cox (1987).

[22] On the role of Federalism in reducing the potential for administrative discretion see Weingast (1995) and references therein.

the face of changing circumstances. Thus, in countries with these types of political institutions, the introduction of reforms may have to await the occurrence of a drastic shock to the political system.

Legislative and executive institutions may also limit a country's regulatory governance options. In some parliamentary systems, for example, the executive has substantial control over both the legislative agenda and the legislative outcomes. While parliamentary systems grant such power in principle, whether they do so in practice depends upon the nature of electoral rules and the political party system. Parliamentary systems whose electoral rules bring about fragmented legislatures would not provide the executive—usually headed by a minority party with a coalition built on a very narrow set of specific common interests—with much scope for legislative initiative. By contrast, electoral rules that create strong two-party parliamentary systems, as well as some other kinds of non-parliamentary political institutions, would grant the executive large legislative powers. For an in-depth discussion of the difference between parliamentary and presidential systems, and the role of electoral rules in determining the relative power of the executive, see Shugart and Carey (1992). In such countries, if legislative and executive powers alternate between political parties with substantially different interests, specific legislation need not constitute a viable safeguard against administrative discretion, as changes in the law could follow directly from a change in government.[23] Similarly, if the executive has strong legislative powers, administrative procedures and administrative law by themselves will not be able to constrain the executive, who will tend to predominate over the judiciary in the interpretation of laws. In this case, administrative procedures require some base other than administrative law.

A strong and independent judiciary could serve as the basis for limiting administrative discretion in several ways. For example, the prior development of a body of adminstrative law opens the governance option of constraining discretion through administrative procedures. This has traditionally been the way administrative discretion is restrained in the USA, as regulatory statutes have tended to be quite vague. For an analysis of the choice of specificity of statues, see Schwartz *et al.* (1993). Note, however, that administrative law may not develop in a system where the executive has strong control over the legislative process. This issue is discussed in detail

---

[23] In the UK, regulatory frameworks have traditionally evolved through a series of Acts of Parliament. For example, major gas regulation legislation was passed in 1847, 1859, 1870, 1871, 1873, and 1875. Similarly, water regulation legislation was passed in 1847, 1863, 1870, 1873, 1875, and 1887. Systematic regulation of electricity companies started in 1882, only four years after the inauguration of the first public demonstration of lighting by a public authority. The 1882 Act was followed by major legislation in 1888, 1899, 1919, and 1922, and culminating with the Electricity (Supply) Act of 1926 creating the Central Electricity Board. See Spiller and Vogelsang (1993b) for discussions of the evolution of utility regulation in the UK, and references therein.

below. In addition, a tradition of efficiently upholding contracts and property rights opens the governance option of constraining discretion through
the use of formal regulatory contracts (licenses). This option is particularly
valuable for countries where the executive has a strong hold over the legislative process. Further, a tradition of judicial independence and efficiency
opens the governance option of using administrative tribunals to resolve
conflicts between the government and the utility within the contours of the
existing regulatory system. Finally, it provides assurances against governmental deviation from specific legislative or constitutional commitments
that underpin the regulatory system.

A Tale of Two Countries

In the remainder of the paper a theory is developed that relates the design of
regulatory governance to the nature of the country's institutional environment. Essentially, two types of institutional environments will be compared:
one in which governmental decisions are taken in a decentralized fashion,
and the other where governmental decision-making is heavily centralized.
The US is used as an example of the former, and the UK as an example of
the latter category. The widely variant evolution of regulation in these two
countries provides a useful contrast for illustrating and exploring the relation between institutions and commitment. Consider the case of telecommunications.

The main body of telecommunications legislation in the USA is still the
Federal Communications Act (FCA) of 1934.[24] This piece of legislation
specifically directs the newly created Federal Communications Commission
(FCC) to regulate interstate communications so as to provide telecommunications services at 'just, fair and reasonable prices'. Nowhere in the Act are
there specific instructions about how to obtain that general goal. Furthermore, the Act presumes the existence of a monopoly supplier of long distance services. The fostering of competition is not one of the stated goals of
the Act.

Even though the FCA is silent about competition, in the late 1950s the
FCC started a process of partially deregulating the long distance and the
customer provided equipment segments of the industry. This was a measured process. Deregulation (and entry) was allowed selectively. In long distance telecommunications, deregulation started essentially with the *Above
890* decision of 1959. In this decision, the FCC determined that any private
microwave system which met proper technical criteria would be authorized
to operate, even though common carrier facilities which could provide

[24] 47 USC 151 (1934).

service to the private system applicant already existed.[25] This decision was followed a decade later by allowing a small firm, MCI, to construct microwave facilities between Chicago and St Louis. In contrast to AT&T, MCI did not propose at that time to offer end-to-end exchange service. Instead, customers had to provide their own loop service between MCI's microsites and their own facilities. Ordinarily, this would be done through lines leased from local phone companies.[26] A year later, in the *Specialized Common Carrier Decision*,[27] the FCC granted other companies the right to provide similar specialized private line communications. In other decisions, the FCC allowed entry of some value-added carriers, providing more sophisticated services than those available.[28]

This deregulatory process has been called by industry observers the 'slippery slope' (Henck and Strassburg, 1988), as it eventually led to the break up of AT&T. While the FCC was a major force behind these deregulatory moves, the Courts were also active participants in deregulation. The first major judicial interventions concerning long distance services were the so called *Execunet* decisions.[29] In its 1976 *Execunet* decision, the FCC opened the private lines market for competition, while at the same restricted it entry to the standard interstate phone service, what is called in industry jargon, the Message Toll Service (MTS), thus prohibiting MCI from continuing to offer its *Execunet* service.[30] MCI appealed to the US Court of Appeals of the D.C. Circuit, that a year later issued its landmark *Execunet* decision which reversed the agency. This decision was followed by two decisions (*Execunet II* and *Execunet III*)[31], which required AT&T to provide whatever interconnection was needed, and imposed similar requirements to independent local telephone companies.

The *Execunet* decisions fully opened the long distance services market for competition. The major remaining problem was what price should the competitors pay for access to the network. This conflict was resolved through negotiations between AT&T and the specialized carriers. See Temin (1987) pp. 137–142. The Courts, however, rather than the agency or Congress, made public policy. The FCC was opposed to the Court's decision, in

[25] 27 FCC 359 (1959).

[26] 18 FCC 2d 953 (1970).

[27] 29 FCC 2d 871 (1971).

[28] See Knieps and Spiller (1983) for a detailed discussion of this process, and of the incentives faced by the FCC to engage in the partial deregulation process.

[29] A major previous deregulatory court decision took place in 1956 when the Court reversed an FCC decision prohibiting the use of a customer provided phone attachment. Hush-a-Phone v. United States, 238 F.2d 266 (D.C. Cir. 1956).

[30] 60 FCC 2d 25 (1976).

[31] *MCI Telecommunications Corp. v. FCC* (*Execunet I*), 561 F.2d 365 (D.C. Cir. 1977), *MCI Telecommunications Corp. v. FCC* (*Execunet II*), 580 F.2d 590 (D.C. Cir. 1978), *Lincoln Tel. and Tel. Co. v. FCC*, (*Execunet III*), 659 F.2d 1092 (D.C. Cir. 1981).

particular as it came just one year after a major FCC investigation. Finally, the main regulatory change of the 1980s, the break up of AT&T, was accomplished as a result of a settlement of the Justice Department's antitrust suit against AT&T, rather than by legislation or standard regulatory procedures.

Compare this process to the evolution of regulation in the UK. For a detailed analysis of the evolution of telecommunications in the UK see Spiller and Vogelsang (1993a). Until quite recently the British telecommunications services sector could be safely identified with British Telecom (BT) and its predecessor, the telecommunications division of the British Post Office. The Post Office controlled, maintained and developed both the telephone network and controlled the supply and maintenance of terminal equipment. The Post Office operated as a Department of State under the direct control of a Minister of the Crown until 1969, at which time it was converted into a public corporation. Prior to the separation of BT from the Post Office, the Post Office had three business centers, Posts, Giro, and Telecommunications and Data Processing, each of which had its own profit and loss accounts and balance sheet. The Telecommunications Division was separated from the Post Office in 1981 when British Telecom became a public corporation. In 1984, before its privatization, BT was converted into a public limited company (BT plc).[32]

Prior to privatization, telecommunications policy, regarding prices, investments and technology adoption, was the result of the interaction between the Post Office (later on BT), the Secretary of State, Parliament's Select Committee on Nationalised Industries and user groups as represented, for example, in the Post Office Users' National and Regional Councils. During the post-war period there were substantial changes in telecommunications policy, and in the controls over and the organization of the Post Office and its telecommunications division. See Tables 1 and 2. Although some regulatory changes involved specific legislative acts, most did not and were undertaken by Cabinet, promoted through the commissioning of White Papers and implemented via executive orders.

The fluidity of governmental policy suggests that post-war governments

---

[32] UK public enterprises have usually been organized in three ways: first, as a department of a particular ministry; second, as a public corporation; and finally, as a private company organized according to the Companies' Act, only that its majority shareholder is the government. The level of involvement of the Minister, and of Parliamentary committees (in particular the Select Committee on Nationalised Industries), falls as we move from a Department of State to a public corporation, to a private company where the government is the majority shareholder. The main difference between the first and second type of organization is that in the latter the company may borrow and can maintain its own reserves. Its board, rather than being headed by a Minister, as in a Department of State, is appointed by the Minister, who is also directly involved in the company's long-term strategic planning, while leaving the day-to-day management to the Board. In either case, however, the government has substantial discretion on the management of the enterprise, but the private company form of organization limits slightly more government discretion.

TABLE 1. Specific Telecommunications Policies from 1960 to 1980

The 1969 Post Office Act
- The Minister to make appointments to the Board
- The Minister to control investment program and borrowing
- The Post Office to provide universal service
- A Post Office Users' National Council (POUNC) and three county councils for Scotland, Wales and Northern Ireland to monitor the Post Office from the consumers' perspectives
- The Post Office had to consult with the POUNC before implementing any major initiative. The POUNC to make recommendations to the Minister
- The Post Office to become a Public Corporation

The Carter Report of July 1977
- Indicated the exerciser of market power by the Post Office
- Indicated that the 1969 Act provided few incentives to lower costs
- Criticized the accounting system and data availability
- Highlighted conflict between managers and the government
- Highlighted lack of accountability and a proper framework for decision making and project evaluation
- Post Office management was too rigid and managerial salaries were too low
- Recommending separating Posts and Telecommunications into two corporations

The 1978 White Paper on the State of the Post Office
- Did not separate telecommunications from post
- Encouraged greater decentralization of decision-making
- Instituted target cost reductions of 5% per annum over five years

TABLE 2. Main Regulatory Changes and Proposals Prior to BT's Privatization

The 1981 Beesley Report
- Recommended unrestricted resale of leased lines (private circuits)
- Recommended allowing BT to freely set prices for private circuits
- Recommended to promote network entry

The British Telecommunications Act of 1981
- Allowed some entry into VANs (to be further relaxed by 1987)
- Terminated BT's monopoly over customer premises equipment (with the exception of the first phone, to be terminated in 1985)
- Allowed licensed network entry
- Separated BT from the Post Office

The 1982 White Paper
- Proposed to sell 51% of BT
- Proposed to create Oftel (the Office of Telecommunications) with a Director General

The Duopoly Policy of November 1983
- Government announced that, for seven years, no nationwide competitor would be allowed besides BT and Mercury to supply fixed-link voice telephony

The 1984 Telecommunications Act
- Creates Oftel and the position of Director General of Telecommunications
- Requires the issuing of licenses for all PTO
- Stipulates process of license amendments
- Brings the MMC into the regulation of licensees
- Silent about price setting, except that is to be determined in the license

Source: Spiller and Vogelsang (1993a).

had substantial discretion over regulatory policy and prices, although not necessarily over the management of the telecommunications operator. As either public corporation or a department of state, the telecommunications division of the Post Office, and later on BT under public ownership, had serious management problems, arising, to a large extent from political interference and the lack of managerial incentives (Moore, 1986). Until BT's privatization, most of the regulatory changes were attempts by the incumbent government to reduce (or formalize) either the minister's or management's discretion. The fact that several White Papers, as well as the 1969 Telecommunications Act, tried to limit the scope of ministerial interference, suggests the extent of government inherent inability to commit not to interfere with the management of the public corporations.

Even though the Tory Party did not always have in its platform the privatization of state-owned enterprises, during the 1970s a movement inside the Party emerged to undo the nationalizations undertaken by previous Labour Governments. While some of the supporters of privatization in the Conservative Party saw privatization as a way to improve the fiscal situation, others supported privatization from a clear political perspective. For example, John Moore, the then Financial Secretary to the Treasury saw 'people's capitalism' as a way to change the political composition of the nation. Speaking at the Wider Share Ownership Council Forum, John Moore said: 'Our aim is to establish a people's capital market, to bring capitalism to the place of work, to the High Street and even the home' (Newman, 1986, p. 41). John Moore was also a strong supporter of employee share ownership schemes as they were applied to BT and other companies. See Newman (1986, p. 150) and Moore (1986). The privatization of BT seems to have been affected by this view, as it was done in such a way that assured widespread ownership of BT shares across the population. Whatever the reason for its privatization, the logic behind the process that started with the 1981 British Telecommunications Act called for competition and private ownership. Table 2 describes the process that led to BT's privatization.

BT's privatization, however, was not undertaken without the design of a particular regulatory governance structure. As Table 2 shows, an independent regulatory office (Oftel) was created, companies were granted licenses, a license amendment process was developed, the Monopolies and Mergers Commission was brought into the regulatory process, and price setting was instituted in the license itself rather than in the legislation. Given the nature of the UK's institutional environment, these institutional innovations provide private investors with some amount of protection against the threat of future policy changes, and thus provide the necessary commitment for private investment to take place.

There are four major differences in the evolution of the deregulatory processes in the USA and the UK. First, the role of judicial review of regulatory agencies. In the UK, the courts played no role through judicial review of regulatory decisions, while they were fundamental in the USA. Second, the role of the legislature. While telecommunications were an important issue in the US Congress during the late 1970s and early 1980s (Spiller, 1990a), Congress did not legislate the major regulatory changes in telecommunications. In the UK, however, Parliament passed several bills that were fundamental for BT's privatization (see Table 2). Third, the role of regulatory agencies. Although in the UK the Cabinet undertook major regulatory decisions (e.g. the introduction of the duopoly policy and its eventual reversal), in the USA the FCC, an independent regulatory agency subject to judicial review, was in charge of implementing the vague mandates of the Federal Communications Act. Finally, the role of licenses. Although in the USA licenses play no major role in the regulatory process, they are the key feature of regulatory governance in the UK.

I will attempt to explain the differences in the evolution of regulation in the US and the UK by developing a theory of the relation between the institutional endowment and the design of regulatory governance.

4. *Regulatory Governance: Administrative Process with Judicial Review*

Regulatory governance may take very different forms. In the USA, regulatory governance consists of a complex set of administrative procedures. A major implication of this regulatory choice is that the judiciary plays a key role in the regulatory process. Administrative law stipulates that all decisions of administrative agencies can be reviewed by Federal Courts, except for the Social Security Administration disability decisions which are heard at the Federal District Courts. The US Congress has enacted several pieces of legislation that set the standards for judicial review, the most far reaching of which is the Administrative Procedures Act. The legislation enacting an agency will usually include specific administrative procedures the agency must follow. These may simply refer to the standards introduced by the APA, or may specify alternative ones. These standards, however, are quite vague. For example, Section 706 of the Administrative Procedures Act provides that

> the reviewing court shall: (1) compel agency action unlawfully withheld or unreasonably delayed; and (2) hold unlawful and set aside agency action, findings, and conclusions found to be: (a) arbitrary, capricious, and abuse of discretion, or otherwise not in accordance with law; (b) contrary to

constitutional right, power, privilege, or immunity; (c) in excess of statutory jurisdiction, authority or limitations, or short of statutory right; (d) without observance of procedure required by law; (e) unsupported by substantial evidence in a case subject to sections 556 and 557 of this title or otherwise reviewed on the record of an agency hearing provided by statute; or (f) unwarranted by the facts to the extent that the facts are subject to trial de novo by the reviewing court.

That is, there are two issues in judicial review, substance and procedure. Both are stipulated by the APA. The Courts, however, are not restricted to interpret the APA, as they can also use the due process clauses of the Constitution. The criteria for judicial review, then, is vague. While in principle Courts decide questions of law and not of facts, providing deference to the agencies on the latter, the difference between a question of law and a question of fact is also vague.[33]

The vagueness of the criteria under which Courts can review administrative decisions is not a legislative mistake. The APA was passed precisely with the dual intention of providing the Courts with the ability to monitor the agencies, and interest groups with the ability to participate in the regulatory process. Both aspects of the APA foster participation by interested parties, and provide members of Congress with the ability to pre-empt the enaction of administrative decisions they may dislike.[34]

In a system characterized by division of powers, like in the USA, political control of judicial decisions, however, is limited. In a series of papers with Rafael Gely we developed a basic framework to understand the role of the judiciary in what is now called 'the division of powers game'.[35] The main focus of their papers is that Courts are ideologically motivated bodies with well-defined political preferences, making decisions based not on the traditional legal rules of precedent, but on the constraints imposed by the other political institutions (i.e. Congress and the Presidency).[36] In such a framework the main constraint on the Courts' power is the potential for legislative reversal. If the decision touches on a constitutional issue, reversal has to be undertaken by a constitutional amendment. See Gely and Spiller (1992) and Spiller and Spitzer (1992).

Gely and Spiller (1992) derived some useful ideal empirical hypotheses,

[33] See, e.g. *NLRB V. Hearst Publications*, 322 US 111, where the Supreme Court held that newsboys are employees under the NLRA, reversing a previous Court of Appeals decision, thus making a statement of fact, based, however, on the interpretation of the statute.

[34] See McCubbins and Schwartz (1984) for the original analysis of regulatory process as a 'fire-alarm'.

[35] See, Gely and Spiller (1990, 1992), and Spiller and Gely (1992). For other 'division of power' models see, among others, Eskridge and Ferejohn (1992a) and (1992b), Ferejohn and Weingast (1992) and Ferejohn and Shipan (1990). For a critical review of this literature see Segal (1995).

[36] Spiller and Spitzer (1992) analyze in detail the theoretical implications of assuming that Courts are not strategic players. They show that such assumption has empirical implications not consistent with current evidence.

some of which have already been subject to empirical tests. The real world, however, is more complex. Courts, agencies and legislatures have decision costs,[37] and have to make their decisions subject to binding budget constraints and substantial informational asymmetries, not the least related to the preferences of the other players.[38] In such environments, Congress can influence the Court not only through reversals, but also through impacting on their costs of making decisions. Tiller and Spiller (1995), in particular show that process requirements as well as agency and judicial budgets, appointments and judicial expansions,[39] by differentially impacting on agency and Court costs, have direct influences on regulatory outcomes, and in particular on the power of the status quo.

Judicial review in a division of powers system, however, is a double-edged sword. On the one hand judicial review may limit deviations from the status quo, but often it may be an instrument in motivating change. Gely and Spiller (1990) show how judicial review blocked the Reagan Administration's attempts to deregulate through administrative fiat. Spiller (1990) shows, however, how the judiciary was the key player in the deregulation of long distance telecommunications, with Congress being active but unable to legislate a deviation from the status quo. The difference between the two scenarios is based on the relative composition of Congress *vis-à-vis* the Courts and the Administration. The wider the disagreements among members of Congress on what the policy should be, the higher the probability that the Courts will make a drastic shift in the status quo. That was not only the case in telecommunications, but also in environmental protection (see McCubbins *et al.*, 1989) among other areas.

Why Judicial Review?

A major question is, however, why is it that the USA has such a strong tradition of judicial review of administrative agencies, while most other countries do not? The answer to this question will help our understanding of whether the US regulatory governance framework is applicable elsewhere in the world.

There are two conditions for a system of administrative procedures subject to judicial review to provide regulatory commitment. First, division of powers has to be real, that is, neither the executive nor the legislative can dominate

[37] See Spiller (1992) for the first treatment of agency discretion in a judicial hierarchy with decision costs.

[38] See, in particular, Schwartz *et al.* (1993) for an analysis of Congressional legislative action in an environment in which congressional preferences are not perfectly known by the Courts, and in which the enacting congress may not be the same as the reversing congress.

[39] For a political model of strategic judicial expansions see de Figuereido and Tiller (1995).

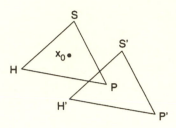

FIGURE 1.   The implications of unified systems for regulatory credibility.

the political process. Second, that the judiciary is not easily manipulable by the political parties. Under these two conditions, the Courts will naturally develop a tradition of contesting agency decisions, a legal tradition that is a basic ingredient for judicial review to provide any credibility at all. To understand why these two conditions are necessary ingredients, consider a situation where although there is a formal separation of powers, electoral rules are such that the party that wins the presidency also wins both houses of the legislature.[40] Furthermore, assume that electoral rules are such that the regional composition of the two houses are not too distinct. This is an example of false bicameralism. For a public choice perspective on bicameralism, see Levmore (1992).

Figure 1 provides such a description. It shows three players, the House (*H*), the Senate (*S*) and the President (*P*, each represented by their ideal points in a generic two dimensional policy space.[41] The triangle connecting the three ideal points consists of the bargaining set among the three players. Any policy in that set is a legislative equilibrium. The Figure also represents the initial policy decision, call it x_0. x_0 is a legislative equilibrium as a change away from x_0 will make one of the players worse off and will consequently be blocked. However, x_0 may not be a stable outcome. In particular, Figure 1 shows that a slight political change may render x_0 outside the set of legislative equilibria. If x_0 was implemented through an administrative process, then Congress may legislate procedural changes so that x_0 will change as well.

Figure 2 shows the implications for regulatory commitment of a system of division of powers that generates a large legislative bargaining set. The Figure depicts two legislative bargaining sets, one linking ideal points *H*, *S* and *P*, and another, a wider set, linking ideal points H_w, S_w, and P_w. The initial status quo, x_0, is in both sets. Now assume that there is a given

---

[40] Mexico may reflect such a system.
[41] The use of ideal points for multi-member bodies in multi-dimensional policy spaces is an oversimplification, as in general, in those conditions multi-member bodies may not be represented as having stable preferences.

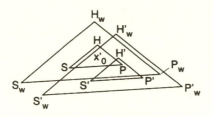

FIGURE 2.   Commitment implications of the size of the bargaining set.

change in public preferences that imply a shift of a given magnitude in all three main veto players. The relevant legislative bargaining set shifts to connect the new ideal points marked with an apostrophe. The change in political preferences was assumed to move all politicians in the same general direction so that the change did not affect the size of each of the legislative bargaining sets. With a larger bargaining set, a given preference change has a smaller probability that the initial status quo would be left outside the new legislative bargaining set, thus providing further commitment to the initial policy choice.

We have seen then that unless separation of powers generates a large legislative bargaining set, administrative procedures will not provide a credible regulatory framework as political changes will drive changes in the underlying procedures so as to modify the final regulatory outcomes. We still need to show that such type of division of powers will naturally generate a judicial tradition of challenging administrative acts.

In Spiller (1995) I have called the process that generates such judicial tradition 'Pavlovian evolution'. The point of this argument is that judicial norms will develop differently under different legislative and executive organizations. In particular, in a true division of powers system, Courts can more easily challenge administrative and regulatory decisions, both on procedures and on substance. Such interventions will, in most cases, not trigger a legislative response, leaving the Court's decision standing. That Congress pays attention to judicial decision-making and often reverses the Courts has been documented in Eskridge (1991). See also Spiller and Tiller (1994) for a model of Congressional reversals of judicial decisions arising from Courts having preferences not only over the policy space but also over judicial rules or other issues over which Congress cannot overrule the Courts. On the other hand, in very centralized systems, attempts by the Courts to reverse an administrative decision may trigger a legislative or executive response overriding the Court.

Consider, for example, Figure 3 in which the Court faces the three-veto structure characteristic of a bicameral presidential system with a fragmented

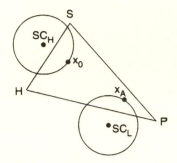

FIGURE 3. Judicial discretion in a division of powers system.

legislature, what I call a true division of powers system. Assume that the legislation is vague and as a consequence the agency attempts to implement a particular point in the legislative set, x_A, which differs from the status quo x_0. The parties may challenge the agency decision on procedural grounds. Assume, now, that the Court has preferences over the policy outcomes. Say that there are two types of Court, SC_H and SC_L. In the Figure SC_H prefers the original status quo, while SC_L prefers the agency's choice. The Court, then, may or may not reverse the agency decision. In any case, though, the Court will not be reversed as either decision is in the legislative set, and thus the Court's decision is a legislative equilibrium (Gely and Spiller, 1990).

In presidential systems that are either false-bicameral or in two-party parliamentary systems, the number of veto points is substantially reduced. In these cases the Court may not easily reverse administrative decisions without facing a challenge. Figure 4 represents the legislative set for a two-party parliamentary system, where H and S represent the two branches of the legislature and E represents the fact that the executive is drawn from the lower house.[42] In Figure 4, for example, a political move made the initial status quo untenable. An agency decision moved the policy to x_A. Attempts by the Court to reverse the agency decision (SC, in Figure prefers x_0 to $_A$) will directly trigger a legislative response, reversing the Court and bringing the policy back to x_A.[43] This, however, may not be the case in multi-party parliamentary systems, whereby governments are formed from multi-party coalitions, and where the potential for coalition break-up is substantially bigger.[44]

Here is where Pavlovian evolution may take place. A judiciary operating in a system where decision-making is substantially decentralized among the

[42] Most parliamentary systems have a bicameral legislature, but in most legislative powers are rested in the lower house, who also elects the government.

[43] See Ramseyer (1994) for a fascinating discussion of cabinet control of the judiciary in Japan, and Salzberg (1991) for a similar analysis in the UK.

[44] See, for example, Steuenberg (1995) for an analysis of judicial intervention in the euthanasia debate arising from the fragmentation of the government coalition.

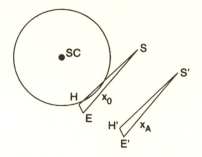

FIGURE 4. Judicial discretion in two-party-parliamentary systems

different political institutions with numerous veto points will find it possible to check the executive on its administrative decisions. Such judicial actions will usually count with some legislative support and hence would be invulnerable to a political reversal. On the other hand, a judiciary operating in a political system where the legislative and the executive process are controlled by the same political group will find that such acts of judicial independence will be punished with legislative reversals, budget cuts, lack of promotion, political demotion or even nastier political tricks.[45] In such a political environment, a judicial tradition of reviewing administrative decisions will not develop. In those systems, judicial activism will only trigger a legislative reversal and political recrimination. Thus, it is not surprising that neither in the UK nor in Japan, Courts have developed a strong tradition of judicial review of administrative actions, developing a rudimentary administrative law.[46]

To summarize, the US system of judicial review of administrative agencies' decisions is based on the nature of US legislative institutions, including electoral rules that have created a system with large number of veto points, and where there is substantial decentralization of decision-making. In such circumstances, independent judicial review can thrive. A question that needs to be asked, however, is why is it that in such an environment Congress has chosen to delegate to agencies and Courts the interpretation of their statutes, and what are the implications for regulatory commitment.

Why Delegation to Independent Agencies?

This question needs to be divided into two parts: first, is there such a thing as independent agencies, and second, why will Congress delegate to in-

[45] For example, in 1990, following clashes with the Court, the new government of President Menem, with the agreement of Congress, increased the number of Supreme Court justices from five to nine and named all new justices. See Levy and Spiller (1994).

[46] On the UK's administrative law see Baldwin and McCrudden (1987).

dependent agencies? In Spiller and Urbiztondo (1994) the first question was answered in the following way: the probability of observing independent agencies is higher in systems characterized by divided government. In systems characterized by unified government (where the preferences of the legislature and the executive are systematically aligned, as in a two-party parliamentary system) control over the bureaucracy will be stronger, with a much smaller proportion of political appointees than in systems characterized by divided government (what I call here true division of power system). The use of political appointees (including independent agencies), we claim, arises from the fact that in systems characterized by divided government the executive has much less control over the professional bureaucracy, as the latter will naturally tend to be aligned with the legislature, a political institution that tends to be longer lasting than the executive. Spiller and Urbiztondo (1994) find that such characterization of divided and unified governments holds both across countries and across cities in the USA.

In an important article, Weingast and Moran (1983) raised the Congressional Dominance Hypothesis. This hypothesis, presented in a different form by McCubbins and Schwartz' (1984) 'fire alarm' framework, suggests that independent agencies are not truly independent, as they are subject to continuous congressional oversight. Actual congressional reversal is not necessary, all that is needed is the threat of such reversal. Spiller (1992) shows that independent administrative agencies' discretion in a system of division of powers depends, among other things, on the composition of the legislature and the executive (determining the threat of congressional reversal), and also on the organization and budget of the judiciary (determining the threat of judicial reversal). In a system of division of powers, however, Congressional Dominance is a corner solution. Spiller (1990b) shows that congressional budgetary decisions of agencies reflect an internal rather than a corner solution. Thus, agencies do not respond fully to congressional desires. If this is the case, then, a basic question is why does Congress delegate to agencies who are not aligned fully with it, and what are the implications of such delegation for regulatory commitment?

Schwartz *et al.* (1993) developed a framework to understand the congressional choice between specific and vague legislation. Specific legislation is one where substantive administrative actions are specified in great detail (e.g. FCC to hold auctions for the allocation of the spectrum, EPA to organize markets for pollution rights granting utilities specific allowances), whereas vague legislation is one where congress just specifies the general principles to be interpreted by the agency and the Courts (e.g. the FCC is to implement policies in telecommunications promoting the welfare of the US citizens). They show that the choice of legislative specificity is a strategic one in a system characterized by division of powers and informational asymmetries. The rationale is that in such a system Congress cannot trust either the agencies or the Courts in implementing what the current Congress actually wants. Informational issues are important. In the absence of informational asymmetries, we have shown elsewhere that legislative intent plays no role.[47] There are several informational problems that may have implications for the choice. First, agencies and Courts may not fully know Congress' preferences on particular issues.[48] The higher the degree of uncertainty on preferences the higher the chances that agencies and Courts will err in their actions and that Congress will then have to spend resources in reversing agencies and Courts. In a separating equilibrium, then, specific legislation provides a signal about congressional preferences, in particular, that Congress cares much about this particular issue. Second, agencies and Courts may be uncertain about Congress' costs of reversing their decisions.[49] In a separating equilibrium, then, specific legislation provides a signal that the enabling congress believes it will have low reversal costs in the future. If the enabling Congress believed that its future reversal costs would be high, then there will be no point in drafting specific legislation as Courts and agencies could then deviate and the future Congress will not be able to reverse it. A major result from this analysis is that legislative vagueness and agency and judicial activism are, in equilibrium, correlated. But the correlation does not arise because of Courts of agencies wanting to follow the intent of Congress, but rather because legislative vagueness is correlated with high reversal costs and low saliency issues, environments in which agencies, and Courts, have more discretion.

Thus, delegation to independent agencies requires a system of division of powers. In this environment, legislative specificity will most probably not be the norm, as legislative costs will be high and preference homogeneity among the members of Congress will most probably be low, increasing the costs of reversing agencies and Courts. Under those circumstances, it is where agency independence can be expected, but, it is also here where judicial independence should be expected that, to some extent, counterbalances and limits the independence of agencies.

---

[47] See Gely and Spiller (1990) showing that under full information the initial legislative act has no consequence on the final equilibrium.

[48] We differentiate between uncertainty on legislators' most desired policies and on their intensity over policies. Most desired policies relate to an individual's 'ideal point'. Intensity is related to how such individual's utility falls as the policy moves away from his or hers ideal point.

[49] See Spiller (1992) where congressional reversals arise from lack of information on congressional reversal costs.

5. *Commitment in Unified Government Systems*

The previous discussion suggests that purely administrative procedures with judicial review may not provide substantial regulatory commitment in systems characterized by unified government. The main deterrent of commitment is that government controls both the administrative and the legislative processes. Thus, political changes that bring about a change in government can also bring about legislative changes. By having few institutional checks and balances, such systems have an inherent instability that raises questions about their ability to provide regulatory commitment. Nevertheless, several countries that can be characterized as having a unified form of government have developed private ownership of utilities (e.g. Japan, the UK, Jamaica, Mexico). Such countries have developed alternative institutional ways to provide regulatory commitment. Some, like the UK, Jamaica and other Caribbean countries, have based their regulatory governance structures on contract law. (See Spiller and Sampson (1995) and Spiller and Vogelsang (1995) for analyses of the regulatory structures in Jamaica and the UK respectively.) Japan, prior to the collapse of the LDP, developed internal party structures that provided for substantial regulatory commitment.[50] Other countries, e.g. Mexico, developed private ownership of utilities by providing for substantial up-front rents.[51]

A main purpose of the regulatory and institutional schemes in countries like Japan, Jamaica and the UK is to provide the regulated companies with some amount of veto power over regulatory decisions.[52] Consider the case of British utilities. British utilities are regulated by different price cap methods. The distinguishing features of these price cap methods, however, is that they are embedded in the companies' license rather than in an agency decision or piece of legislation. Indeed, the enabling laws in the UK are silent about pricing schemes. The advantage of regulatory frameworks instituted through licenses is that since the latter usually have the power of contracts between governments and the firms, any amendment to the license will usually

---

[50] See, in particular, the volume by Cowhey and McCubbins (1995) for an analysis of the organization of the LDP and its implications for policy determination.

[51] Consider, for example, the privatization of the telecommunications company, Telmex. Prior to the devaluation of 1994, Telmex residential rates were as follows: $488 for connection, $9 per month which included 100 calls, $0.15 for each 3 minutes extra of local calls, $1 for a 3 minute national long distance call, $2.4 for a 3 minute call to the USA, and $6.25 for a 3 minute international call elsewhere. Obviously, these prices are orders of magnitude of comparable US rates. This, in turn, provided Telmex with a very high rate of return during its initial few years. For example, in 1993 it had $7 billion in revenues and 43% profit margin. (Crespo, 1995).

[52] Mexico did not provide formal veto power to the company, although the fact that the company represents more than 30% of the market capitalization of the Mexican stock exchange implies that regulatory choices that will impact negatively on Telmex's profitability would not go down well with the investment community or with the government itself.

require the agreement of the company. In Britain, the law stipulates that in the event that the company does not agree to a license amendment proposed by the regulator, there is a process involving the Monopolies and Mergers Commission that the regulator may use to amend the license against the will of the company. See Spiller and Vogelsang (1993a). However, this provides credibility at the cost of inflexibility. For example, if a technological break-through eliminates any economies of scale in a segment of the market, the regulator may have to 'bribe' the company into accepting to relinquish its legal exclusive rights over that segment. In a more flexible basic engineering choice, such a decision could be taken administratively. Indeed, this was the case in Jamaica concerning the introduction of cellular telephony. See Spiller (1995). Thus, while contracts may be useful in providing assurances to the companies, they do so only by introducing rigidities in the regulatory system.

For contracts as a governance structure to provide regulatory stability, then, they must be very specific and clearly limit what the regulator can do. A license that does not specify the regulatory mechanism in any detail, but leaves the administration free to make all regulatory decisions will fail the first criteria for regulatory stability. Comparing the licenses issued in Jamaica under the Jamaican Public Utilities Act of 1966 to those issued prior to 1966 or after the privatization of 1988 shows the total failure of licenses to restrain the regulators based on the 1966 Act. See Spiller and Sampson (1993). Operating licenses in the USA, for example, do not serve as a governance structure, as they deal mostly with eminent domain and fran-chise area issues. Whether specific licences will provide regulatory credibil-ity depends on whether the Courts will see licences as binding contracts. In particular, it must be the case that Courts will be willing to uphold con-tracts against the wish of the administration. If Courts do not treat licenses as contracts, or grant the administration substantial leeway in interpreting those contracts, then, license-based regulatory contracts will fail as a source of regulatory stability. Note, then, that contracts can be implemented in nations with very strong or very weak executives, with parliamentary or presidential systems. Indeed, a basic requirement is the independence of the judiciary *and* that the judiciary sees licences as contracts.

Contract based regulations, however, are particularly appealing to polities whose legislative bargaining set is very narrow or small. In such cases, as in Figure 4, changes in political preferences would either bring about a new piece of legislation if the current regulatory regime is based on specific legis-lation, or a modification of the agency's interpretation of the statute if the current regulatory regime is based on general administrative procedures. On the other hand, if x_0 was initially hard-wired through a license, then the fact

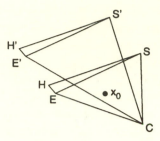

FIGURE 5.   The implications of licensing for regulatory credibility

that x_0 does not belong any more to the legislative bargaining set is irrelevant. Changes in x_0 require the acquiescence of the company. Thus, by introducing the regulatory process in the license an additional veto point is introduced, namely the company itself. Thus, the relevant set of parties required to change the status quo x_0 now also includes the company. Thus, in Figure 5, the relevant bargaining set is now the set given by the ideal points (H, S, E, C), where C represents the company's ideal point. The Figure shows how in such circumstance regulatory credibility is enhanced even in a situation where electoral changes move against the company. (For a model of regulatory decision-making in the UK, see Spiller and Vogelsang, 1994.) Thus, it is not surprising that countries like Jamaica, the UK and many of the other Caribbean countries have adopted license based regulatory systems. It would be interesting to see whether other parliamentary systems in Europe move towards such systems when and if they fully privatize their utility sectors.

Finally, informal norms may also provide some regulatory stability even if licenses can be unilaterally amended by the government. For example, the UK has been granting operating licenses since at least 1609 (see Spiller and vogelsang, 1993b). While initially licenses were granted by the King, eventually Parliament took over as the license granting institution. Licenses were granted in many different forms. Until 1919, the most common way was for a prospective utility to apply to Parliament for a particular license. A Select Committee would hear the case and either recommend it or not. The Select Committee's recommendation would then be presented to Parliament for approval. This latter step was supposed to be a simple formality. These are called Private Bills. A license could also be granted by an Order in Council, whereby the Privy Council upon recommendation of the relevant Minister and the Cabinet would grant the license. Licenses were granted also by General Acts of Parliament. Such an example is the Public Health Act of 1875 which granted the municipalities the right to establish water and gas undertakings in their districts if no one else was empowered and willing to perform such undertaking. Provisional Orders were substitutes for Private Bills. A Provisional Order would be granted by a Minister following a request for a license. The Minister's order would then be formalized by an Act of Parliament. Finally, following the 1919 Electricity (Supply) Act, the Electricity Commission, created by the Act, started issuing licenses through Special Orders, which had to be approved by the Minister of Transport. Special Orders did not have to obtain the formal approval of Parliament. Parliament, however, retained the right to reconsider those licenses (see Spiller and Vogelsang, 1993b). Since licenses were granted by Acts of Parliament, Parliament could, in principle, change the conditions under which future licenses were to be granted. Parliament, could, furthermore, go a step further and unilaterally change the operating rights of current license holders. Such parliamentary power, however, made the licenses fragile instruments. Over the years, however, Parliament has developed an informal (constitutional) norm of not revoking licenses without compensation. Indeed the only case I know of when licenses were revoked was during the massive restructuring of the electricity sector in 1926. In that case, however, the license holders that were to be shut down were given very favorable transitory rights that compensated them for whatever losses could arise from the compulsory shut down (see Spiller and Vogelsang, 1993b).

These informal norms still apply, to a large extent, in the UK, as the regulator is supposedly independent of the Secretary of State for Trade and Industry, although the latter appoints the regulator and the regulatory agency's budget is included in the Department of trade and Industry's budget. Indeed, licenses can be amended unilaterally by the government, only following a particular procedure. Spiller and Vogelsang (1995) show that this procedure provides credibility as long as the regulator, the Monopolies and Merger Commission and the Secretary of State can be thought of as politically independent of each other.[53] They show that if the three entities are politically the same, then they can manipulate the license in almost every way, eliminating any regulatory commitment that licensing as a governance structure would provide.

---

[53] Indeed, on 7 March 1995 the Director General of Electricity Supply, Prof. Stephen Littlechild, considered by most to be the architect of the UK regulatory system, reversed a price cap decision taken in August 1994 and suggested that from April 1996 distributing companies may be subject to a tighter price cap. This reversal was seen by many as showing the lack of commitment inherent in the UK. For example, the title of *The Economist* article dealing with this event is 'Incredible'. (*The Economist*, 11 March 1995, p. 74). This, however, fits the Spiller and Vogelsang (1995) model in that the regulator may make proposals at any time, but for those proposals to become policy they have to follow a particular procedure. In the case at hand, if the distributing companies would not agree to the regulator's proposal, then the regulator has the option of making a reference to the MMC. Only if a modification of the license is undertaken against the will of the companies and without reference to the MMC can it be said that a breach of the process took place.

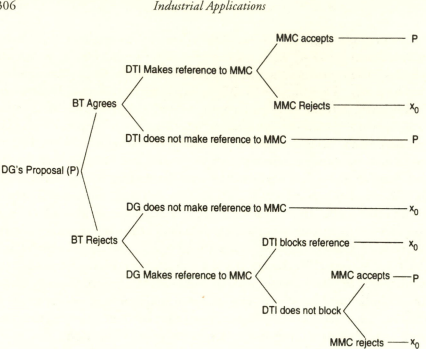

FIGURE 6.   The regulatory game in the UK. An application to telecommunications.

To see this point, consider Figure 6. The regulatory process of tele-communications in the UK can be conceived as the regulator (the Director General of Telecommunications, DG) making a proposal (P) to British Telecom (BT) to amend some of its license provisions (e.g. the price cap system, the interconnection rules, etc. with the status quo represented by x_0). If BT accepts, the Department of Trade and Industry (DTI) may object and make a reference to the Monopolies and Mergers Commission (MMC). If the MMC accepts the license amendment, then the regulator can sign the new license over the objections of the DTI. If, however, the MMC rejects the agreement between the DG and BT, then the status quo remains. If BT rejects the DG's proposal, then the DG may make a reference to the MMC. Such reference, though, can be blocked by the DTI, but only if the DTI claims that the DG's proposal breaches national security, a conceivable high standard. If the DTI does not block the reference, and if the MMC agrees with the regulator, then the DG may unilaterally amend BT's license. if, however, the MMC rejects the DG's proposal, then the status quo remains. Finally, if the DTI blocks the reference to the MMC, then again, the status quo remains. This discussion, then, shows that the license amendment procedures provides BT with some assurances against regulatory discretion insofar as the DG, the DTI and the MMC do not have similar objectives.

Informal norms come in several ways to shore up the fragility of UK institutional arrangements. First, although feasible, it would be inappropriate for the DTI to attempt to influence directly the DG. Indirect influence does, however, take place through the media and through the lower levels of the bureaucracy. Second, although the government can appoint members of the MMC at will, the MMC is the longest lasting regulatory agency with substantial public credibility, and it would not be appropriate for the DTI to replace all its members at once. Third, it would also be unheard of for the Secretary of State not to sign a license amendment that was agreed upon by BT, the regulator and the MMC. Thus, although most probably BT would not be able to block any of those actions through the Courts, the UK has developed a series of implicit understandings on how governments operate that would inflict substantial costs to a politician that drastically deviates from such norms. The emphasis on implicit norms may seem strange to those raised in the US way of government, where what is not directly illegal is proper. Issues like 'losing face' are much less important in a formalistic society as in the USA. In a society like Japan or the UK where decision-making is not public, implicit norms of conduct can be understood as an equilibrium that provides the different players in both the party in power and the private sector with incentives to invest, both in the physical sense (the private sector) as in the political sense (the politicians).[54]

Norms, however, cannot be used as analytical tools lightly, but some empirical implications can be derived from the fact that for facilitating norms to develop, political stability is a necessity. Thus, for example, countries with high political instability will not develop such supporting norms, and hence will not be able to develop regulatory structures that provide for substantial regulatory flexibility. This, indeed, is the case in Jamaica or Bolivia. These two countries have used contracts as ways to provide regulatory commitment, and have done so effectively and for long periods of time. Indeed, Jamaica regulated utilities that way from the beginning of this century until 1966 when the Jamaica Public Utilities Commission was created. Nationalization of all utilities followed in the early 1970s. In the late 1980s the telecommunications company was privatized, using again a very specific license as the basic regulatory governance instrument. Performance since privatization has been quite successful (see Spiller and Sampson, 1995). Bolivia has the longest lasting private electricity company in South America. COBEE, founded in the late 1910s, has provided electricity to La Paz and its environs. Its regulatory structure has also been based on a very specific license. Neither country's licenses, though, provide for much flexibility (see Spiller, 1995).

[54] For a similar analysis of the norms organizing the US House of Representatives, see Weingast and Marshall (1988).

6. *Final Comments*

Political opportunism has important economic implications. The focus here has been on the implications for the development of utilities, but it is clear from the discussion that similar implications can be derived for more generic economic circumstances. Restraining political opportunism, however, is not an easy task. Countries that have succeeded in developing a healthy private sector are those that in one way or another have developed institutions that restrain governmental decision-making. But such restraining is itself a political choice. Although the conditions for such choice to arise have yet to be developed, one was explored in this paper: the nature of legislative and judicial institutions. Countries with electoral and legislative systems that bring about decentralized government have stronger chances of development equilibria where government discretion is restrained. But the choice of electoral and legislative systems is itself endogenous. I will submit, though, that the same theoretical apparatus, the mixing of transaction cost economics and positive political theory, is particularly suited for this larger and most important task.

Acknowledgements

This paper was prepared for the conference celebrating the 20th anniversary of the publication of *Markets and Hierarchies*. I would like to thank Witold Henisz for very insightful comments.

References

Baldwin, R. and C. McCrudden (1987), *Regulation and Public Law*. Weidenfeld & Nicolson: London.

Barzel, Y. (1989), *Economic Analysis of Property Rights*. Cambridge University Press: Cambridge, MA.

Cain, B., J. Ferejohn and M. Fiorina (1987), *The Personal Vote*. Harvard University Press: Cambridge, MA.

Cowhey, P. and M. McCubbins (eds) (1995), *Structure and Policy in Japan and the United States*. Cambridge University Press: New York.

Cox, G. (1987), *The Efficient Secret*. Cambridge University Press: New York.

Crespo, M. (1995), 'Telmex: Slim's Pickings,' *Financial World*, 164(1), 20.

de Figueiredo, J. and E. Tiller (1995), 'Congressional Control of the Courts: A Theoretical and Empirical Analysis of the Expansion of the Judiciary,' University of California, Berkeley.

Duverger, M. (1954), *Political Parties: Their Organization and Activity in the Modern State*. Wiley: New York.

Eskridge, W.N. (1991), 'Overriding Supreme Court Statutory Interpretation Decisions,' *Yale Law Journal*, 101, No 2, 331–455.

Eskridge, W.N. and J. Ferejohn (1992), 'Making the Deal Stick—Enforcing the Original Constitutional Structure of Lawmaking in the Modern Regulatory State,' *Journal of Law, Economics and Organization*', 8, No 1, 165–189.

Eskridge, W.N. and J. Ferejohn (1992), 'The Article-I, Section-7 Game,' *Georgetown Law Journal*, **80**, No 3, 523–564.

Ferejohn, J. and C. Shipan (1990), 'Congressional Influence on Bureaucracy,' *Journal of Law, Economics and Organization*, 6, 1–20.

Ferejohn, J. and B. Weingast (1992), 'Limitation of Statutes—Strategic Statutory Interpretation,' *Georgetown Law Journal*, **80**, No 3, 565–582.

Gely, R. and P.T. Spiller (1990), 'A Rational Choice Theory of Supreme Court Statutory Decisions, with Applications to the *State Farm* and *Grove City* Cases,' *Journal of Law, Economics and Organization*, 6, 263–301.

Gely, R. and P.T. Spiller (1992), 'The Political Economy of Supreme Court Constitutional Decisions: The Case of Roosevelt's Court Packing Plan,; *International Review of Law and Economics*, 12, 45–67.

Goldberg, V. (1976), 'Regulation and Administered Contracts,' *Bell Journal of Economics*, 7, 426–452.

Henck, F.W. and B. Strassburg (1988), *A Slippery Slope: The Long Road to the Breakup of AT&T*. Greenwood Press.

Hill, A. and M. Abdala (1993), 'Regulation, institutions and Commitment: Privatization and Regulation in Argentine Telecommunications Sector.' The World Bank: Washington, DC.

Jacobson, G.C. (1990), *The Electoral Origins of Divided Government: Competition in the US House Elections, 1946–1988*. Westview Press: Boulder, CO.

Knieps, G. and P.T. Spiller (1983), 'Regulating by Partial Deregulation: The Case of Telecommunications,' *Administrative Law Review*, 35, No 4.

Levmore, S. (1992), 'Bicameralism: When are two decisions better than one?' *International Review of Law and Economics*, 12, 145–168.

Levmore, S., Frickey, P.P. and W.H. Riker (1992), 'Bicameralism: When are Two Decisions Better Than One?; Constitutional Structure, Public Choice, and Public Law; the Merits of Bicameralism,' *International Review of Law and Economics*, 12, No 2, 145–168.

Levy, B. and P.T. Spiller (1993), 'Regulations, Institutions and Commitment in Telecommunications: A Comparative Analysis of Five Countries,' *Proceedings of The World Bank Annual Conference on Development Economics*, 215–252.

Levy, B. and P.T. Spiller (1994), 'The Institutional Foundations of Regulatory Commitment: A Comparative Analysis of Telecommunciations Regulation,' *Journal of Law, Economics, and Organization*, 10, 201–246.

Macey, J. (1992), 'Organizational Design and Political Control of Administrative Agencies,' *Journal of Law, Economics, and Organization*, 8, 93–110.

McCubbins, M.D., R.G. Noll and B.R. Weingast (1987), 'Administrative Procedures as Instruments of Political Control,' *Journal of Law, Economics, and Organization*, 3, 243–277.

McCubbins, M.D., R.G. Noll and B.R. Weingast (1989), (1987) 'Structure and Process, Politics and Policy: Administrative Arrangements and the Political Control of Agencies,' *Virginia Law Review*, 75, 431–482.

McCubbins, M.D. and T. Schwartz (1984), 'Congressional Oversight Overlooked: Police Patrol vs Fire Alarms,' *American Journal of Political Sciences*, **28**.

Moore, J. (1986), 'The Success of Privatization,' in J. Kay, C. Mayer and D. Thompson, *Privatisation and Regulation: the UK Experience*. Clarendon Press: Oxford.

Newman, K. (1986), *The Selling of British Telecom*. Holt, Rinehart and Winston: London.

North, D.C. (1990), *Institutions, Institutional Change, and Economic Performance*. Cambridge University Press: Cambridge, MA.

Schwartz, E., P.T. Spiller and S. Urbiztondo (1993), 'A Positive Theory of Legislative Intent,' *Law and Contemporary Problems*, 57, 51–74.

Shepsle, K.A. (1992), 'Bureaucratic Drift, Coalitional Drift and Time Inconsistency—A Comment,' *Journal of Law, Economcis and Organization*, 8, 111–118.

Shugart, M.S. and J.M. Carey (1992), *Presidents and Assemblies*. Cambridge University Press: New York, NY.

Spiller, P.T. (1990a), 'Governmental Institutions and Regulatory Policy: A Rational Choice Analysis of Telecommunications Deregulation,' mimeo, University of Illinois.

Spiller, P.T. (1990b), 'Politicians, Interest Groups and Regulators: A Multiple Principals Agency Theory of Regulations, (or Let Them Be Bribed),' *Journal of Law and Economics*, **XXXIII**, 65–101.

Spiller, P.T. (1992), 'Agency Discretion under Judicial Review,' in *Formal Theory of Politics II: Mathematical Modelling in Political Science*, Vol. 16, No. 8/9, *Mathematical and Computer Modelling*, pp. 185–200.

Spiller, P.T. (1993), 'Institutions and Regulatory Commitment in Utilities' Privatization,' *Industrial and Corporate Change*, 2, 387–450.

Spiller, P.T. (1995), 'A Positive Political Theory of Regualtory Instruments: Contracts, Administrative Law or Regulatory Specificity,' *USC Law Review*, 69, No 2, 477–515.

Spiller, P.T. and R. Gely (1992), 'Congressional Control or Judicial Independence: The Determinants of US Supreme Court Labor Decisions: 1949/1987,' *Rand Journal of Economics*, Vol 23, No 4, 463–492.

Spiller, P.T. and C.I. Sampson (1993), 'Regulation, Institutions and Commitment: The Jamaican Telecommunications Sector,' *The World Bank*.

Spiller, P.T. and M. Spitzer (1992), 'Judicial Choice of Legal Doctrines,' *Journal of Law, Economics and Organization*, 8, 8–46.

Spiller, P.T. and E. Tiller (1994), 'Invitations to Override: Congressional Reversals of Supreme Court Decisions,' *International Review of Law and Economics*.

Spiller, P.T. and S. Urbiztondo (1994), 'Political Appointees vs. Career Civil Servants: A Multiple-Principals Theory of Political Institutions,' *European Journal of Political Economy*, 10, 465–497.

Spiller, P.T. and I. Vogelsang (1993a), 'Regulation, Institutions and Commitment: The British Telecommunications Sector.' *The World Bank*.

Spiller, P.T. and I. Vogelsang (1993b), 'Notes on Public Utility Regulation in the UK: 1850–1950,' mimeo, University of Illinois.

Spiller, P.T. and I. Vogelsang (1994), 'The Institutional Foundations of Regulatory Commitment in the UK (with applications to telecommunications),' Working Paper, University of California, Berkeley.

Spiller, P.T. and I. Vogelsang (1995), 'The Institutional Foundations of Regulatory Commitment in the UK' (with special emphasis on telecommunications), University of California, Berkeley.

Steunenberg, B. (1995), 'Courts, Cabinet and Coalition Parties: The Politics of Euthanasia in a Parliamentary Setting,' University of Twente, the Netherlands.

Taagepera, R. and M. Shugart (1993), 'Predicting the Number of Parties: A Quantitative Model of Duverger Mechanical Effect,' *American Political Science Review*, 87, 455–464.

Temin, P. with L. Galambos (1987), *The Fall of the Bell System: A Study in Prices and Politics*. Cambridge University Press: Cambridge.

Tiller, E. and P.T. Spiller (1995), 'The Choice of Administrative and Judicial Instruments: Strategy, Politics and Decision Costs in the Administrative Process,' mimeo, University of California, Berkeley.

Weingast, B.R. (1995), 'The Economic Role of Institutions: Market Preserving Federalism and Economic Development,' *Journal of Law, Economics and Organization*, 11, 1–31.

Weingast, B.R. and M. Moran (1983), 'Bureaucratic Discretion or Congressional Control: Regulatory Policy Making by the Federal Trade Commission.' *Journal of Political Economy*, 765–800.

Williamson, O.E. (1975), *Markets and Hierarchies: Analysis and Antitrust Implications*. Free Press: New York.

Williamson, O.E. (1976), 'Franchise Bidding for Natural Monopolies: In General and With Respect to CATV.' *Bell Journal of Economics*, 7, 73–104.

Williamson, O.E. (1985), *The Economic Institutions of Capitalism*. Free Press: New York.

Williamson, O.E. (1988), 'The Logic of Economic Organization.' *Journal of Law, Economics and Organization*, 88, Vol 4, 65–93.

CHAPTER THIRTEEN

Mitigating Procurement Hazards in the Context of Innovation

JOHN M. DE FIGUEIREDO AND DAVID J. TEECE

This paper extends the transaction cost economics framework to examine the contractual hazards that arise in the course of technological innovation. We identify three main strategic hazards related to future technological opportunities that may develop in business transactions: loss of technological pacing possibilities on the technological frontier, loss of technological control at or behind the frontier, and design omissions. In examining these hazards we focus on the increasingly common phenomenon of vertically integrated firms supplying downstream competitors. We then analyze how constellations of safeguards, particularly relational safeguards, can augment transaction-specific safeguards in many instances to ensure high-powered incentives are maintained. We also consider under what conditions downstream divestiture is a desirable economizing option. Supportive illustrations are drawn from the desktop laser printer and telecommunications industries.

I have spoken to many audiences about the benefits of AT&T being a vertically integrated business that had both services and equipment. ... There have been many advantages to our current structure. But the dramatic changes in our markets driven by our customers, new technologies like wireless, and public policy decisions, have opened up so many new opportunities that we need to simplify and more sharply focus our businesses to respond swiftly and effectively to those opportunities. It is not a secret that our Network Systems business has been affected by the conflicts that our Communication Services Group has been having with the RBOCs both in the public policy arena and increasingly in the marketplace as we entered the intra-LATA market. These conflicts foreshadow similar issues with some PTTs around the world. In recent months, it has become clear that the advantage of our size ... is starting to be offset by the amount of time, energy, and expense it takes to manage conflicting business strategies ... So, in this spirit, we prepare to launch three strong businesses. ...

> (Bob Allen, Chairman, AT&T.
> Message to Employees on the Restructuring of AT&T,
> 20 September 1995).

1. *Introduction*

Mitigating contractual hazards is one of the core functions of the business enterprise (Williamson, 1975, 1985, 1996a; Teece, 1980a, 1986). Vertical integration and other complex organizational arrangements often arise to safeguard transactions against the hazards of *ex post* opportunism. Nevertheless, hazards that arise in the course of business vary in gravity and magnitude. These can be severe when technological innovation is involved. Yet there have been few attempts to elucidate and enumerate innovation-driven hazards in a systematic way.

In this paper, we focus on the contractual hazards and organizational mechanisms that arise in the context of pacing, controlling and directing, current and future technological development and the products that emanate from innovation. We discuss three specific hazards that may occur in high technology transactions: poor sequencing (pacing) of developments in complementary technologies, loss of control over knowledge and intellectual property, and technological 'foreclosure'.

We limit our analysis to a class of cooperative and competitive transactions that have been largely neglected in the strategic management literature to date — vertically integrated firms supplying their downstream, non-integrated competitors. Antitrust analysis has often been suspicious of such types of transactions, viewing them as mechanisms to effectuate predatory acts, such as vertical price squeezes, by the integrated firm. However, if the integrated supplier achieves upstream efficiencies through some economies of scale or core capabilities that are difficult for independent suppliers to replicate, then it may be efficient and desirable for a non-integrated downstream competitor to source from such vertically integrated competitors. The problem that arises for the buyer is that there may be incentives for the integrated supplier, if it is dominant upstream, to disadvantage the buyer at contract renegotiation or to otherwise handicap the buyer. In many cases, the incentives of the integrated firm to act strategically may be higher than those of independent suppliers. Even if the supplier does not behave strategically, buyers may be concerned that the supplier might do so at some future date and act accordingly.

Assessing the magnitude of technological hazards for the buyer requires examination of two factors: first, whether the upstream firm possesses market power and/or the ability to appropriate quasi-rents, and second, whether there is complexity and unobservability in the transaction, in that the performance dimensions of the intermediate good being supplied is only over time revealed, thus creating monitoring problems for the customer. If these two conditions hold in a transaction involving leading edge technology, then technological hazards suggest particular organizational arrangements which provide strong safeguards.

In some contexts, transaction-particular safeguards may not suffice. Rather, individual, transaction-specific safeguards need to be augmented by a constellation of safeguards developed within the context of a broader business relationship that spans numerous transactions. Malfeasance in one transaction may then have repercussions on other transactions in the current relationship, or severe reputation effects with other exchange partners. Thus, in a number of circumstances, relational safeguards that span multiple transactions may be employed to protect against technological hazards, thereby facilitating exchange. However, if complexity, uncertainty and unobservability are sufficiently high, situations may arise when even a constellation of safeguards will not be adequate protection against contracting hazards. In these situations, vertical integration—with the associated possible loss of upstream economies—is sometimes necessary to protect against the hazards of incomplete contracting and the problematic incentives which are sometimes occasioned when a downstream firm sources from a competitor. Alternatively, integrated firms can take the 'ultimate' form of credible commitment not to behave strategically in the downstream market. The upstream integrated firm may decide to simply divest (or not integrate downstream) in order to signal that it will not behave strategically.

It should be noted at the outset that this paper does not address public policy responses. Rather, it examines how managerial solutions accomplished through contractual safeguards and organizational design can act to protect transactions against technological hazards that may arise. Its purpose is to elucidate the hazards that ensue in the context of an integrated firm supplying a non-integrated, downstream competitor, and to examine safeguards which are employed to support contractual relationships in such circumstances. The next section reviews the phenomenon of cross-competitive supply and examines the development and shortcomings of the current literature. Section 3 unravels some of the types of technological hazards that occur in the context of high technology transactions. Section 4 reviews the safeguards that firms employ to protect against these hazards in cross-competitive supply relationships. Section 5 closes with some concluding remarks.

2. *Background*

The Phenomenon: Buying From Integrated Competitors

Buying from one's competitor is not uncommon, and may be increasing in frequency. In this paper, we examine sourcing by non-integrated firms from

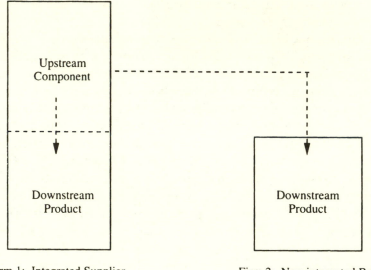

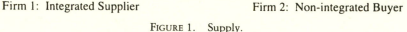

Firm 1: Integrated Supplier   Firm 2: Non-integrated Buyer

FIGURE 1. Supply.

integrated competitors in high technology markets. Figure 1 illustrates this relationship. While Firms 1 and 2 both compete in the downstream market, only Firm 1 is vertically integrated into the upstream component market. However, Firm 2 sources components, sometimes exclusively, from Firm 1. Often there may be independent component suppliers who provide feasible alternative sources of the component at the outset, yet are not awarded the supply contract by firm 2.

There are a number of reasons a firm would want to source from a competitor. The most advanced or most reliable technology may be possessed by the competitor. The cheapest component may be provided by a competitor. Mere transportation cost considerations may call for competitor supply. These and other reasons often make competitor supply a sensible strategy, provided contractual safeguards can be erected.

Examples of this abound. Consider the laser printer industry. The engines of laser printers determine, among other things, print speed and print quality; the laser printer industry contains many firms that make engines, some firms which are present only downstream, some firms which are present only upstream. It is common to see vertically integrated firms supplying engines on a contractual basis to non-integrated companies against whom they compete. Figure 2, illustrates this point. The left-hand column identifies some of the engine manufacturers. The right-hand column identifies some of the firms that are present in the desktop laser printer market. The arrows indicate

LASER ENGINE MANUFACTURERS   **LASER PRINTER MANUFACTURERS**

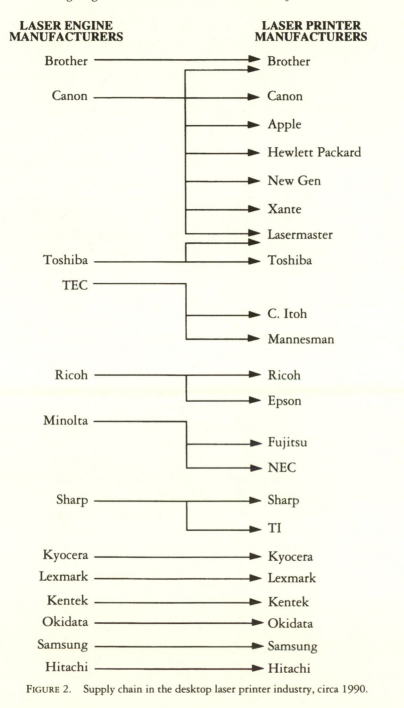

FIGURE 2.   Supply chain in the desktop laser printer industry, circa 1990.

which engine manufacturers supply which printer manufacturers. Clearly, several types of relationships exist. Perhaps the most striking example of a vertically integrated firm supplying a competitor (and one to which we will return later), is the Canon-Hewlett-Packard (HP) relationship. Canon makes both engines and printers and supplies nearly all of (non-integrated) HP's very significant volume engine of requirements. This contractual relationship has persisted between the two firms for over a decade, despite the apparent strategic hazards.

Cross-competitor supply relationships can also been seen in electronics, semiconductors, and telecommunications. One of the reasons enumerated for the recent split of AT&T into three separate, publicly traded companies was the problem of strategic conflicts between AT&T Technologies (the manufacturing arm) and the regional Bell operating companies (RBOCs), who were its traditional customers. The recent divestiture will separate the communications systems (AT&T) from the equipment manufacturing (Network Systems). As AT&T and the RBOCs evolved into competitors, the RBOCs were reluctant to buy telecommunications equipment, especially switches, from AT&T. Overseas, companies such as Deutsch Telekom in Germany and France Telecom were also wary of buying equipment from AT&T since they expected AT&T to emerge as a competitor in their national market. All this meant that competitors were passing their equipment dollars to other vendors, even when AT&T equipment might have been superior.[1]

These examples, and those that follow, serve to elucidate a common phenomenon that has been little studied—vertically integrated firms supplying competitors in the downstream market in high technology industries. We examine the conditions under which this is a stable outcome and inquire as to when contractual safeguards will be inadequate to sustain this type of relationship. Although both parties may face contractual hazards, our focus is on understanding the strategic hazards that the non-integrated firm faces.

Theoretical Antecedents

Chicago School analysts conducted the first systematic theoretical investigation into cross-competitive supply (for example, Posner, 1976, pp. 196–

---

[1] 'There's always tension when buying a majority of equipment from somebody who is also your biggest competitor', said Robert Barada, vice-president for corporate strategy and development, for Pacific Telesis Group. Spinning off the equipment arm 'will alleviate that [problem] in a big way'. Moreover, Brian Adamik, an analyst at Yankee Group in Boston, commented, 'After the break-up, Network Systems could now even sell to MCI, which wouldn't buy equipment from AT&T in the past because of the its long-distance arm.' The AT&T example has been drawn from: John Keller, 'Defying Merger Trend, AT&T Plans to Split into Three Companies,' *Wall Street Journal*, 21 September 1995, pp. A1, A16; Leslie Cauley, 'AT&T's Rivals Shrug, but Not Analysts,' *Wall Street Journal*, 21 September 1995, p. A6; Jeff Pelline, 'Giant AT&T to Break into 3 Companies,' *San Francisco Chronicle*, 21 September 1995, pp. A1, A15.

207; Bork ,1978; Posner and Easterbrook, 1981).[2] They pointed out that because monopoly rents could only be taken once in the supply chain, a firm with monopoly (or market) power had two options to retain monopoly rents. First, it could vertically integrate and charge monopoly prices in the downstream market. Equivalently, it could set the price for the intermediate good at the monopoly level and extract all the rents without forward integration. Thus, a vertically integrated firm with upstream monopoly power has little incentive to exclude downstream rivals, since forward integration is not necessary to extract upstream rents. Accordingly, vertical mergers pose no problems. If upstream Firm A and downstream Firm B merge, the merger ought not change concentration or prices. Thus monopoly power will not and cannot be extended. Vertical leveraging is simply impossible.

This view of cross-competitor supply, as it relates to business strategy, has been extended on two fronts. First, game theorists have argued that this Chicago School analysis is not a subgame perfect equilibrium (Hart and Tirole, 1990; Ordover *et al.*, 1990). Other firms in the industry may respond to a competitor's integration decision with integration and price strategies of their own. Under a variety of strategies, the subgame perfect equilibrium can result in inefficiency and a refusal to deal (Hart and Tirole, 1990, p. 212). One insight that is gleaned from this literature is that vertically disintegrated structures or parallel vertical integration may be equilibrium outcomes.

A second extension was the development of transaction cost economic analysis (Williamson, 1971, 1975, 1983, 1985). In *Markets and Hierarchies* (1975), Williamson introduced the notion of contractual hazards and contractual safeguards, primarily flowing from the possibility of *ex post* opportunism in an incomplete contracting regime. His analysis revised and enriched the Chicago approach, and added an efficiency dimension. Williamson (1975) and later Klein *et al.* (1979), showed how asset specificity could cause contractual hazards. Common ownership of such assets could ease those hazards and facilitate efficient investment. Williamson (1983) subsequently highlighted the importance of reciprocity and 'exchange of hostages' as ways to attenuate hazards which might otherwise destroy the basis for exchange. The transaction cost economics framework,

---

[2] This phenomenon is quite different from the voluminous writing on strategic alliances (for example, Parkhe 1993; Contractor and Lorange 1988; Gulati 1995). With strategic alliances, partners typically have expertise in different functional or technological areas, and the strategic alliance facilitates teaming to create new products. The success of the alliance hinges on strategic alignment and the ability of the two firms to combine their resources and capabilities to build a single product. If either firm fails, both firms lose. Our analysis differs from the strategic alliance literature in that we are primarily concerned with those transactions where the firms are competitors in the downstream market and only one firm possesses the upstream facilities which it supplies to the downstream competitor. One firm, in our analysis, possesses the resources to build and possibly to market the product before the two firms come together.

because of its focus on hazards and safeguards, is a useful point of departure for our analysis. We show that transaction cost economics can in turn be extended to embrace organizational questions when changing technology is at issue.

In much of the work of transaction cost economics, hazards are developed in a rather particular manner, often illustrated by price renegotiation, and quality degradation. These usually augment costs. We seek to expand the framework by examining contracting hazards related to the (usually partial) denial by one party of future technological and associated market opportunities.

Transaction cost economics posits that firms can protect against hazards through contractual safeguards such as penalty for premature termination, dispute resolution mechanisms, and bilateral exchange of hostages (Williamson, 1985, pp. 33–34, 1996b). While these types of safeguard do assist transactions, we go beyond the analysis of strictly discrete transactional safeguards that frequently preoccupies transaction cost economics. In cases when vertical integration is costly, a constellation of safeguards transcending the traditional, discrete transaction safeguards may be effective.[3] This constellation may include transaction specific safeguards in the traditional transaction cost sense, but also may encompass broader relational and multi-transactional structures that safeguard groups of transactions. It is the relational safeguards that may insure adequate protection of transactions, and void the need for vertical integration.

Relevance for Strategic Management

One conceptual argument we put forward is that transaction cost economics can be usefully informed by expanding the notion of hazards and safeguards. Specifically, we view contractual relationships as generating bundles of hazards, and governance structures as providing bundles of safeguards. The task of management is to identify the hazards that are attendant to a business relationship and then to create and insure that the economizing bundle of safeguards necessary for effective execution of transactions and exploitation of opportunities are in place.

We examine the contractual hazards that arise when developing and commercializing new technology, and show that discrete transactional safeguards may be usefully supplemented by multi-transactional relational safeguards. This is especially so when non-integrated firms buy from integrated competitors. Though many of our concepts are applicable to a variety of transactional arrangements, we limit our analysis to cross-competitor supply.

[3] Nickerson (1996) explores how hazards are interrelated in the trucking industry.

3. *Technological Hazards in Competitor Supply*

Several well recognized contractual hazards occur in supply situations. First, when a downstream firm must make some specific investment in order to support efficient production, it exposes its non-redeployable assets to *ex post* recontracting hazards (Williamson, 1985). If investment in specific assets is not required for efficient production, then the non-integrated downstream firm can costlessly switch suppliers and avoid all hazards. If the buyer must invest in non-redeployable assets, it could avoid the hazards associated with *ex post* recontracting through vertical integration.

Second, the characteristics of the intermediate component that is being delivered to the downstream firm might not be readily observable. This may occur because of the extreme complexity of the product or may be due to other non-observable characteristics. In short, there may be an acute monitoring problem for the downstream firm that only resolves itself over the long-run. While these two classes of problems are important, we focus instead on circumstances where new technology is at stake.

In business transactions when new technology is at stake, a less understood set of hazards may arise. This class of contracting hazards stems not so much from the extraction of quasi-rents, but from the guarding of future strategic opportunities. Integrated suppliers can, for example, exclude firms from immediate access to new knowledge, and future possibilities for technological progress. These types of situations may arise when an integrated firm has the ability to use its upstream technological prowess to exclude a downstream rival from a transaction that will open up future technological and commercial opportunities[4]. The seller's ability to pace, direct, control, and guard the development of new products and technologies are all hazards to the buyer that arise in this context. It is these technological hazards that we examine in more depth.

Out-Sourcing and Competitive Advantage: Key Components and Pacing Technology at the Frontier[5]

Technological hazards exist if a downstream firm has failed to accumulate the capabilities needed to make critical components, or has opted, for other (normally sound) business reasons, such as scale, cost, or risk, to forego production of these components. The firm may then have no choice but to pur-

[4] This notion can also be viewed as a dynamic extension of the raising rival's cost literature (Salop and Scheffman, 1983).

[5] When we speak about the frontier, we refer to a component or service being procured which enlists technology that is not ubiquitously employed in the industry. Frontier technologies are those leading edge innovations being incorporated into subsystems and components.

chase critical components from its competitors. Some components, whether commodity or customized to the producer's own downstream requirements, are simply not all that important to competitive advantage. The only strategic advantage to the integrated supplier-competitor flowing from opportunistic behavior with respect to these components is the one time benefit associated with capturing quasi-rents associated with irreversible investments already made. Loss of quasi-rents associated with employing idiosyncratic physical assets may have considerable short-run implications, but if the firm's balance sheet is strong, it need not impair long-run competitive advantage.

Contrast this to new components based on leading edge technology that convey strategic advantage. If firms wish to pace or direct the evolution of new products, then these types of components should, *ceteris paribus*, be developed internally. If such products are outsourced, the supplier gets to pace and direct the development of the technology. Transactions cost and recontracting hazards are not the core considerations; rather, it is the failure to accumulate critical competences important to the firm's overall new product development strategy which matters.

Consider Motorola as it attempts to develop battery technology for their mobile communications products.[6] Motorola can obtain nickel-cadmium (Ni-Cd) batteries from a host of suppliers. However, because the bottleneck technology for Motorola is the battery, there is benefit to accelerating/ controlling the development of more long-lasting and lighter weight batteries (e.g. fuel cells). Motorola can safely source standard Ni-Cad batteries externally, but more advanced batteries may need to be developed and sourced internally (see Figure 3). The reasons do not flow from exposure to recontracting hazards as such. Rather, control of the development process is critical to coordinate and accomplish the roll-out of new products.

Microsoft provides another illustration of how an integrated firm can pace technological development downstream. Microsoft not only retains control over the operating system (Windows) for the majority of personal computers, but also commercializes some key applications downstream. Other independent application designers rely on Windows for their applications to run. Thus, Windows acts as a constraint on some of the technological features of the downstream applications (e.g. speed and protocol of data exchange). Microsoft's ability to pace the upstream technology and its ability to exploit its operating system technology in its applications software, has helped it to become one of the dominant players in applications.

A second source of competitive advantage related to technological pacing (that may require integration) is the difficulty of accomplishing what

---

[6] See Chesbrough and Teece (1996) for a more detailed description of Motorola case.

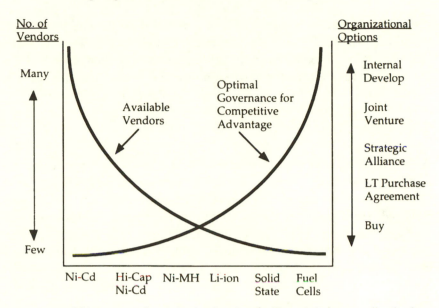

FIGURE 3. Available sources and organizational options for Motorola in battery cell technology.

Richardson (1960) and Williamson (1975) have called 'convergence of expectations'. Investment (in R&D) must be coordinated between upstream and downstream entities, and this is difficult to effectuate using contractual mechanisms. Teece (1988) has characterized innovations as either autonomous or systemic. Autonomous innovations are those that do not require coordinated activities between parties to the innovation. Each innovation can occur within its own walls and can then be 'plugged into' the bigger project. These types of innovations are pervasive when standards are present, such as the open architecture of the IBM personal computer. Systemic innovations are those developments that require coordinated action by the parties to the innovation (e.g. the development of new cameras and film which instant photography required). In order to achieve the coordinated outcomes systemic innovation requires, it is often necessary to vertically integrate (Teece, 1980b). Chesbrough and Teece (1996) have argued that coordinating the development of complementary technologies is difficult when pursued contractually. Delays are frequent and need not be strategic; they may simply flow from uncertainty and divergent goals amongst the parties. MIPS encountered this with their failed attempted to promote their Advanced Computing Environment (ACE) to compete with Sun's Scalable Processor Architecture (SPARC). MIPS set up alliances with Compaq, DEC, Silicon Graphics and other firms to pursue a RISC-based computing standard. However, as DEC and Compaq announced that they were going to reduce their commitment to ACE, the alliance soon fell apart because MIPS could not pick up the slack in some of the upstream activities. It failed to understand and develop competencies in key aspects of the technology, and was not able to create a common expectation for the alliance (Gomes-Casseres, 1994).

Technological Control at or Behind the Frontier

A second hazard that arises where new technology (at or even behind the frontier) is utilized, is the leakage of technology to competitors. Arrow (1962) first brought to light the disclosure problem in the market for know-how, and others have since elaborated on this and related technology transfer problems (Goldberg, 1977; Teece, 1981, 1985, 1986). Appropriability hazards are of concern when property rights are difficult to establish and enforce and when the knowledge is not retained entirely at the organizational level (Oxley, 1995). The leakage we have in mind can occur vertically (upstream and downstream) as well as horizontally (Silverman, 1996).

Proprietary knowledge that leaks from buyer (supplier) to supplier (buyer) in the course of fulfilling a purchase contract is especially problematic when the supplier (buyer) is integrated downstream (upstream). The argument is of course symmetric. Although an independent supplier who obtains knowledge from the buyer may choose to integrate into the downstream product, the likelihood that this will occur is small. However, a firm which is already vertically integrated downstream and supplies a downstream competitor may be able to take the know-how that has leaked to its upstream division and incorporate it into the downstream products and processes relatively quickly.[7] Downstream investments in manufacturing have already been made and small modifications may be all that is necessary to enhance competitiveness in the downstream operations. Staff engineers who understand the downstream process and product can take the know-how and improve upon the current product or process.

In the digital switching business, AT&T has had difficulty selling switches to some of the RBOCs because of fear that it will misuse commercial secrets it learns from the RBOCs. This happens because many switches are configured to the needs of each customer. In order to customize the switch, the RBOC must reveal its telephone traffic patterns, capacity utilization, infrastructure layout, and other extremely sensitive information to the switch supplier. While contractual mechanisms can be designed to protect

---

[7] When we use the term leakage, we do not mean to imply that intellectual property rights have necessarily been violated. We have in mind the quite legal imitation and emulation that takes place in the normal course of business.

this information, information flows through informal channels and internal movement of personnel, combined with the cost and difficulty of enforcement of such contractual clauses, create hazards for the buyer.[8] The ability of a competitor to use and improve upon know-how which has been inadvertently leaked may be higher for integrated suppliers than for non-integrated suppliers.

Guarding Technological Capabilities

Another disadvantage buyers may experience when market power exists upstream and intellectual property regimes are strong (Teece, 1986), is that the integrated supplier may be in a position to guard its know-how advantage and if it chooses, simply refuse to sell to its competitors. The integrated firm may have incentives to exclude its rivals from its most advanced components if this will hinder the ability of the downstream rival to participate in related or future business. By protecting its competitive advantage in this way, the integrated firm can advance its competitive position downstream. Thus, integrated suppliers may have a higher incentive to withhold (or degrade) supply than would independent firms.[9] The downstream division of the integrated firm may be able to advance its position in related and emerging markets if the upstream division does not assist downstream competitors.

For example, in digital telecommunications equipment supply, the switches hold the key to competitive advantage for many future service innovations (such as value-added network services). The purchase of switches and other equipment from AT&T has the potential for creating many hazards for the RBOCs, who may be foreclosed from the opportunity to participate in the future technological innovations if their switch supplier chooses not to add features that would enhance the RBOC's ability to compete against AT&T in telecommunication service markets. The incentives of an integrated AT&T, if it has some market power in switch manufacturing, may be to act in a manner that might disadvantage the RBOCs in domains where they currently compete or are likely in the future to compete with AT&T. The problem evaporates, however, if there are abundant actual or potential competitive supply alternatives. Vertical integration into manufacturing is just one among many possible solutions.

---

[8] We thank James Dalton of Bell South for making this point.

[9] We stress features rather than an entire product. If an independent supplier could monopolize the downstream market, then it might integrate downstream or it might charge a price for the intermediate good so that it obtains a monopoly rent. This result is less likely if only certain features of the product are not available, as in the digital switching example. For an example of this at the national level, see General Accounting Office, 'International Trade: US Business Access to Certain State-of-the-Art Technology,' *GAO Report* (GAO/NSIAD-91-278), September 1991, p. 33.

4. *Safeguarding Against Technological Hazards*

The need to safeguard incomplete contracts against *ex post* opportunistic behavior is not a new or novel concept. The need to monitor effort under technological non-separability (Alchian and Demsetz, 1972), assert control when property rights are not well-defined (Coase, 1960; Demsetz, 1967), and protect streams of quasi-rents in a competitive contracting process (Klein *et al.*, 1978) has long been recognized. Most of these analyses, however, have been concerned with vertical integration as a way to safeguard specific investments. Indeed, the paradigmatic safeguard, and the one which has received the majority of attention in the literature, is vertical integration (Williamson, 1975).

Although vertical integration is normally an effective safeguard, it is not always desirable. When poorly implemented, vertical integration can be fraught with low-powered incentives and bureaucratic costs which will impair performance and make it unattractive (Williamson, 1975, 1985, 1991; Teece, 1976, 1996). A superior alternative in many instances is to rely on contracts and develop a constellation of safeguards, enveloping many aspects of the firm's business with such protections, so that a contractual exchange that might otherwise be considered risky, can flourish.

Constellations of Safeguards

In the original concept of hostages as safeguards (Williamson, 1983), each firm places a hostage that has an *ex ante* (screening) or *ex post* (bonding) effect to support exchange. The parties' incentive to perform when bonds are held is high because exit would entail forfeiture of the hostage.[10] Thus hostages can, in many circumstances, be more cost effective than integration in supporting exchange.

However, incomplete contracting and bounded rationality make hostage exchange difficult in many circumstances where there is uncertainty as to outcomes, such as with innovation. The amount of the bond to be placed in custody is difficult to determine *ex ante* because unforeseen contingencies may render the hostage inefficiently large or, of more concern, too low in value. This is especially likely to be a problem when technological innovation and new product development is involved. In these circumstances, firms may exit the transaction—appropriating the technology, and leaving the insufficient hostage on the table for the other party. Alternatively, the

---

[10] Williamson (1983, p. 527) has noted: '...a king who is known to cherish two daughters equally [one beautiful and one ugly] and is asked, for screening purposes, to post a hostage is better advised to offer the ugly one'.

hostage may itself become the subject of the opportunistic bargaining as the ante is renegotiated.[11] While hostages may support market transactions, they do so over a limited range of situations, or in conjunction with other safeguards.

Our interest in this paper is in demonstrating the efficacy of constellations of safeguards in cross-competitive supply situations, including ones where technological hazards exist. Although contracts give guidance as to how transactions can proceed, constellations of arrangements can create a larger context in which contracts can operate. In this sense, multilateral and multi-transactional relationships are akin to relational contracts (Macneil, 1978) where contracts occur against the background of the relationship, where changes to a contract are adopted 'only in the overall context of the whole relation' (p. 890) and where often 'preservation of the relation' (p. 895) is the concern.

The Canon-HP relationship, with special reference to the laser printer industry, is illustrative. As mentioned earlier, Canon, a vertically integrated firm that makes both laser engines and laser printers, supplies all of HP's engine requirements. At first glance, it would seem there would be many contractual hazards facing HP. However, the Canon-HP transaction is embedded in a larger relationship that displays a constellation of safeguards.

Relational safeguards.   The Canon-HP relationship began long before the advent of the desktop laser engine.[12] Throughout much of the 1970s and early 1980s, Canon not only supplied laser engines for HP's midrange laser printer systems, but also engaged in some joint development with HP of floor-model printer technology. The move from midrange to desktop laser printers was only one of many steps in the printer market that the two firms took together. This historical relationship provides important context. Canon and HP had (and still have) a web of ties in numerous transactions and technologies that serve as the basis for exchange. We understand that these discrete transactions are linked through a position created in each firm referred to as the 'relationship manager'.[13] Although this manager does not have formal authority to compel divisions to cooperate, this person does have tremendous informal authority, reports to a division head, and has responsi-

---

[11] Sequential hostages often face the same problems. Some type of contractual and hybrid relationships require a number of hand-offs of a project between parties in order to achieve the goal. Both firms are better off if the project goal is reached, but incentives may exist to expropriate the other partner at each stage of development. Although the hostage is the project itself, interim knowledge gained may prove to be more valuable than the successful completion of the project. Moreover, in the last stage of the project, the last firm has the incentive to expropriate the partner because the game has come to an end. The game then unravels under most conditions.

[12] See Mowery and Beckman (1995) for a more detailed discussion of HP's strategy.

[13] We thank Lee Rhodes of Hewlett-Packard for bringing this to our attention.

bility for the smooth running of the broader strategic relationship. More-over, as overseer of the strategic relationship between the two firms, this manager also becomes a mediator should disputes develop. Through this central mechanism, transactions are 'bundled' together, albeit imperfectly, for what is a relational governance scheme. Opportunistic behavior and conflict in one transaction may change how the other contracting party views the potential for opportunism in other transactions. Bundling transactions therefore raises the cost of cheating. There is the threat that there will be loss of the entire relationship if there is substantial malfeasance in the specific transaction. Usually, loss of the entire relationship is more costly than the gains from expropriation available from a single transaction. As firms enter into larger types of relationships that involve multiple transactions, the individual transaction becomes subsumed in a web of current and future transactions. Indeed, Williamson has noted, '... interdependencies among series of related contracts may be missed or undervalued as a consequence [of examining each trading nexus separately.] Greater attention to the multilateral ramifications of contract is sometimes needed' (1985, p. 393).

Transaction-specific safeguards.   In addition to these relational safe-guards, HP possesses some discrete transactional safeguards that support exchange. One flows from the fact that HP purchases annually hundreds of millions of dollars in printer engines from Canon, representing nearly 50% of Canon's engine output. Hence, it is highly unlikely that Canon would act opportunistically with HP in laser engine supply because of the volume of business that HP represents. While this capacity is not technically transaction-specific, there is little doubt that at least some assets that support it would be stranded if HP suddenly stopped buying engines from Canon. Thus, if the non-integrated buyer represents a significant portion of the purchases of the integrated supplier, and there does not exist excess demand in the market, then it is unlikely that the supplier will opt to engage in expropriation at contract renegotiation.[14]

A second transaction-specific safeguard that protects HP from opportunism is the reputation effects that Canon would suffer if it acted opportunistically to expropriate HP or provide HP with a consistently sub-standard product. If HP effectively publicized and detailed malfeasance by Canon in laser engines, Canon might lose a large portion of its remaining customers. At best, remaining customers might update their probabilities of opportunistic behavior (Crocker and Reynolds, 1993) in their own transac-

---

[14] Williamson (1985, p. 93) addresses this in the context of 'dedicated assets' which he defines as a 'discrete investment in generalized (as contrasted with special purpose) production capacity that would not be made but for the prospect of selling a significant amount of product to a specific customer'.

tions with Canon. Given the short lifetime of a laser printer model (1–3 years), product model turnover acts to favor laser printer manufacturers. The printer manufacturer is therefore only committed to the current laser engine for the current printer (though there is the need for some continuity between models). If malfeasance occurs, the downstream buyer can obtain a new supplier for its subsequent models. The result in the extreme case, then, is that Canon could lose its entire customer base in 2–3 years. This is extreme, but illustrates how short product turns (with reasonable discount rates) enhance the need for suppliers to maintain a good reputation. Williamson discusses reputation effects and argues, 'Suffice it to observe here that reputation effect are no contracting panacea' (1985, pp. 395–396). Indeed, we argue that reputation acts in concert with other safeguards to ensure exchange.

Mixed-mode safeguards. HP's proprietary control of most aspects of its ink-jet technology provides HP's laser printer division with considerable protection against possible opportunism from Canon. The possibility that an altogether different technology can be developed, at reasonable cost, which effectively substitutes for the technology of the transaction will serve to keep the contract sustainable. Most core capabilities for the rapid roll-out of the alternative technology must exist within the boundaries of the non-integrated firm if this is to be a credible threat. The degree of protection such a safeguard provides is directly related to the degree and cost of substituting the alternative technology. The ink-jet technology that HP has developed was not created as an intentional safeguard to laser technology, but rather as an alternative technology with an independent marketing strategy. However, ink-jet technology has evolved. If Canon were to refuse to supply engines or to escalate prices, HP might credibly shift its focus from laser jet technology to the improvement of the current ink-jet technology. No doubt, HP would prefer to stay with laser printers. However, it might be able to push ink-jet technology so as to seriously challenge the laser technology. Ink-jet printers already cannibalize laser printers on the lower end of the market. The impetus given to ink-jet technology could have a substantial detrimental effect on the laser printer market and specifically on Canon, the largest supplier of laser engines in the world.

Canon has many customers for its laser engines, yet HP has (asymmetrically) exposed itself to contractual hazards with Canon if HP is looked at in isolation. However, by employing constellations of relational, transaction-specific, and mixed-mode safeguards, HP appears to have protected itself against possible opportunism by Canon and, market exchange continues between the two firms. Thus, a more global view of safeguards appears to be warranted.

Vertical Integration, Divestiture and Credible Commitments

Maintenance of high powered incentives and avoidance of bureaucratic costs are benefits retained if safeguards short of vertical integration will suffice (as described above). However, sometimes contractual and relational safeguards do not suffice. In such instances, both integration (by the purchaser) and divestiture (by the seller) serve to correct some of the hazards we have identified. They are not perfect alternatives, but they do paradoxically provide some degree of remedy to the (strategic) hazards we have identified. We consider circumstances where vertical integration may be the better solution.

Controlling the rate and direction of innovation. Where there is a need to be on the frontier of the technological possibility curve, technological pacing becomes most important. The firm that chooses (for whatever reasons) to eschew vertical integration, yet endeavors to direct the rate and direction of development using contracts, may find it difficult. As noted earlier, reliance on one's competitor for supply is problematic because of the misaligned incentives of the integrated firm. In some cases, even independent supply could be problematic. In these instances, vertical integration (internal development) may be the best way to confidently pace interrelated technological developments. This is particularly true when solutions inside an existing technological paradigm (Dosi, 1982) will suffice. This is because investment in R&D will yield a degree of predictability as to outcomes. When this is not the case (i.e. required solutions require radical advances unlikely within the paradigm), vertical integration (internal development) may be ineffective.[15]

To illustrate this point, we accumulated data on a sample of PC compatible, desktop laser printers introduced in 1992 and 1993[16]. Two characteristics often cited as determinants of the proximity of a laser printer to the technological frontier are print speed, measured by pages per minute (PPM), and print resolution, measured by the number of dots per inch (DPI) it prints. High performance is associated with greater speed and greater dot density. Figure 4, places all of these printers on a scatter plot graph. Each point is assigned an ▲, ❑ or ○, which designates who makes the engine for

[15] For a related discussion of competency-enhancing and competency-destroying innovation in centralized versus decentralized firms, see Bercovitz *et al.*, 1996.

[16] This data set is being compilied from trade magazines such as *PC World* and *PC Magazine*

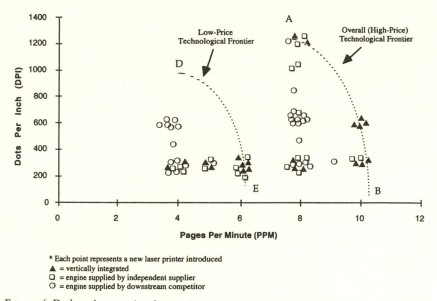

FIGURE 4. Desktop laser engine–laser printer transaction: governance decisions, 1992–1993.

the printer: the same firm that makes the printer (▲ = hierarchy), an independent upstream supplier that does not make printers (□ = independent), or a vertically integrated competitor that makes engines and printers (○ = competitor). On the outer technological frontier of desktop laser printers (represented by the AB curve), there is a high proportion of firms vertically integrated into engine and printer production.[17] This suggests that technological pacing (as well as technological control) may play a role in this industry. The second largest number of printers on the frontier source engines from independent suppliers. Only one of the 14 'frontier' printers has an engine manufactured by a competitor. This is consistent with our analysis that competitor relationships are fraught with hazards that independent supply, and certainly integrated supply, avoid.

It is also interesting to note that there is a second group of firms near 6 PPM which share the same governance characteristics as the outside frontier firms. This seems to occur because the desktop laser market has split into two segments—a high end, full feature, high-priced segment; and a low end, low feature, low-priced segment.[18] In the low-price segment, firms

---

[17] The 14 printers on the frontier represent the integration strategies of eight firms. We drew the frontiers by analyzing each printer by its list price and features. We then derived the technological frontiers by constructing a curve for each segment that approximated the leading edge technology available at each price.

[18] Beginning in 1990, the desktop laser printer market began to diverge into two segments. Preliminary analysis of the data indicates that the lower-priced printers have fewer features, less processing paper, and, in some cases, longer duty cycles.

seem to be trying to create a printer that is technologically advanced with as many features as possible, but constrained by an upper limit on list price of approximately $2,000. Hierarchical firms (and independent suppliers) show up en masse on this frontier of the low end printers (represented by the secondary 'frontier' CD), followed by a high preponderance of competitor supply. Thus, on both frontiers, firms that seem to be pacing the development of the technologies tend to be vertically integrated in the first instance, and tend not to source engines from a competitor. We must stress, however, that while suggestive, these results are highly preliminary. The data set is not complete, and controls for other independent variables have not been included.

Sustaining technological capabilities.   Maintaining technological control, even when behind the technology frontier, sometimes requires vertical integration. The two key components that technologically differentiate products in the laser printer market are the engine and the controller card. From 1984 to 1988, HP outsourced the controller cards for its laser printers to Canon. Although HP designed these cards, Canon actually manufactured the cards on its own board line in Japan. However, in 1988, HP chose to integrate this activity into their printer division in Boise. Two concerns seem to have led to this decision. First, HP felt integration would allow them to respond to changes in technological and market conditions in a real-time manner.[19] Second, we understand that HP feared that if the controller cards and engines for its laser printers were both sourced from Canon, it might lose its technology to Canon and, in effect, create a formidable competitor. The need to retain control over its own technology and ensure sustained access to key components seem to be key motivating factors in the change of HP strategy. Moreover was also the time when DRAM chips were in short supply. This may also have had an influence on HP's decision to internalize controller card production.

Design omissions.   Finally, vertical integration may be desired to guard against strategic product design manipulation. It is not surprising that in the digital telecommunications switching equipment industry with continued deregulation bringing AT&T and the RBOCs into competition, that non-integrated suppliers have emerged (e.g. DSC and Motorola). It is also not surprising to see RBOCs abandon traditional purchase relations with AT&T in favor of purchases from Northern Telecom, Ericson, NEC, and others for whom there is no strategic conflict downstream. Indeed, with the

---

[19] 'Hewlett Packard begins making component of top-selling laserjet printer,' *Business Wire*, 7 December 1988.

impending entry of the inter-exchange carriers into the local exchange, and the local exchange companies into the inter-exchange business, AT&T may have the incentive to guard its technology jealously, if by doing so it can delay the RBOCs offering new services which would require the use of AT&T product technology. Whether meritorious or not, concerns along these lines cost AT&T significant equipment sales, and appears to be a major factor behind its tripartite divestiture.

5. *Conclusion*

Thinking of contracts and governance structures as generating hazards and providing safeguards enriches our understanding of the theory of the firm. In this paper, we argued that identifying technological considerations that arise in the context of innovation gives a different perspective on the organizational problems. We have discussed a variety of safeguards. Although these may be transaction specific, many times relational or mixed-mode safeguards will be employed that span transactions and serve as a cost-effective mechanism of governance. When the parties are linked by a broad constellations of contracts, vertical integration can be avoided and high-powered incentives retained. There will be times, however, when even a rich constellation of safeguards will be insufficient. In these circumstances, we can expect to see both parallel vertical integration, or in the alternative, divestiture.

Our focus on the future opportunities and appropriability considerations that arise in technology transactions suggests a need to move to a more dynamic and evolutionary approach to organizations. Indeed, changes in governance structures over time may reflect not only the shifts in traditional economic incentives to integrate, but also exposure to strategic hazards and the need to accumulate capabilities necessary for current and future competitive advantage. An industry's structure could change over time as knowledge accumulation and diffusion change the hazards associated with sourcing from a competitor. Thus, vertical structures may be reshaped as these conflicting forces wax and wane.

Acknowledgements

We wish to acknowledge the helpful comments and assistance of Sara Beckman, Janet Bercovitz, Glenn Carroll, David Mowery, Jackson Nickerson and Oliver Williamson. A much earlier draft of this paper was presented at the 'Firms, Markets and Organizations' Conference held at Berkeley, 6–8 October 1995. We also wish to thank the Sloan Foundation and the Ameritech Foundation for their generous financial support.

References

Alchian, A. A. and Demsetz, H. (1972), 'Production Costs, Information Costs, and Economic Organization,' *American Economic Review*, 62, 777–795.

Arrow, K. J. (1962), 'Economic Welfare and the Allocation of Resources of Invention,' in National Bureau of Economic Research (ed.), *The Rate and Direction of Inventive Activity: Economic and Social Factors.* Princeton University Press: Princeton, NJ, pp. 609–625.

Bercovitz, J. E. L., de Figueiredo, J. M. and Teece, D. J. (1996), 'Firm Capabilities and Managerial Decision-Making: A Theory of Innovation Biases,' in R. Garud, P. Nayaar and Z. Shapira (eds), *Technological Learning, Foresights, and Oversights.* Cambridge University Press: New York, forthcoming.

Bork, R. H. (1978), *The Antitrust Paradox.* Basic Books: New York.

Chesbrough, H. W. and Teece, D. J. (1996), 'When is Virtual Virtuous: Organizing for Innovation,' *Harvard Business Review*, 74, 65–73.

Coase, R. H. (1960), 'The Problem of Social Cost,' *Journal of Law and Economics*, 3, 1–44.

Contractor, F. J. and Lorange, P. (eds) (1988), *Cooperative Strategies in International Business.* Lexington Books: Lexington, MA.

Crocker, K. J. and Reynolds, K. J. (1993), 'The Efficiency of Incomplete Contracts: An Empirical Analysis of Air Force Engine Procurement,' *Rand Journal of Economics*, 24, 253–264.

Demsetz, H. (1967), 'Toward a Theory of Property Rights,' *American Economic Review*, 57, 347–359.

Dosi, G. (1982), 'Technological Paradigms and Technological Trajectories,' *Research Policy*, 11, 147–162.

Goldberg, V. (1977), 'Competitive Bidding and the Production of Precontract Information,' *Bell Journal of Economics*, 8, 250–261.

Gomes-Casseres, B. (1994), 'Group Versus Group: How Alliance Networks Compete,' *Harvard Business Review*, (July), 62–74.

Gulati, R. (1995), 'Does Familiarity Breed Trust—The Implications of Repeated Ties for Contractual Choice in Alliances,' *Academy of Management Journal*, 38, 85–112.

Hart, O, and Tirole, J. (1990), 'Vertical Integration and Market Foreclosure,' *Brookings Papers: Microeconomics*, 205–276.

Klein, B., Crawford, R.A. and Alchian, A.A. (1978), 'Vertical Integration, Appropriable Rents, and the Competitive Contracting Process,' *Journal of Law and Economics*, 21 (October), 297–326.

Macneil, I. R. (1978), 'Contracts: Adjustments of Long-Term Economic Relations Under Classical, Neoclassical, and Relational Contract Law,' *Northwestern University Law Review*, 72, 854–906.

Mowery, D. C and Beckman, S. L. (1995), 'Corporate Change and Competitiveness: The Hewlett-Packard Company,' CCC Working Paper No. 95–13, University of California, Berkeley,

Nickerson, J. (1996), 'Strategy and Structure: The Role of Transactional Interdependencies on Organizational Form,' PhD dissertation, University of California, Berkeley.

Ordover, J. A., Saloner, G. and Salop, S. (1990), 'Equilibrium Vertical Foreclosure,' *American Economic Review*, 80, 127–142.

Oxley, J. E. (1995), 'International Hybrids: A Transaction Cost Treatment and Empirical Study,' PhD dissertation, University of California, Berkeley.

Parkhe, A. (1993), 'Strategic Alliance Structuring — A Game Theoretic and Transaction Cost Examination of Interfirm Cooperation,' *Academy of Management Journal*, 36, (August), 794–829.

Posner, R. A. (1976), *Antitrust Law.* University of Chicago Press: Chicago, IL.

Posner, R. A. and Easterbrook, F. H. (1981), *Antitrust: Cases, Economic Notes, and Other Materials*, 2nd edn. West Publishing: St. Paul.

Richardson, G.B.H. (1990), *Information and Investment*, Oxford University Press: Oxford.

Salop, S. and Scheffman, D. (1983), *Raising Rival's Costs*, American Economic Review, 73 (May), 267–271.

Silverman, B. S. (1996), 'Technical Assets and the Logic of Corporate Diversification,' Ph.D. Dissertation, University of California, Berkeley.

Teece, D. J. (1976). *Vertical Integration and Divestiture in the US Oil Industry*. The Stanford University Institute for Energy Studies: Stanford, CA.

Teece, D. J. (1980a), 'Economies of Scope and the Scope of the Enterprise,' *Journal of Economic Behavior and Organization*, 1, (September), 223–245.

Teece, D. J. (1980b), 'Vertical Integration and Procurement,' Unpublished Working Paper, University of California, Berkeley.

Teece, D. J. (1981), 'The Market for Know-How and the Efficient Transfer of Technology,' *The Annals of the Academy of Political and Social Science*, 81–96.

Teece, D. J. (1985), 'Multinational Enterprise, Internal Governance and Industrial Organization,' *American Economic Review*, 75, 233–238.

Teece, D. J. (1986), 'Profiting from Technological Innovation: Implications for Integration, Collaboration, Licensing, and Public Policy,' *Research Policy*, 15, 285–305.

Teece, D. J. (1988), 'Technological Change and the Nature of the Firm,' in G. Dosi (ed), *Technical Change and Economic Theory*. Pinter Publishers: London, pp. 256–281.

Teece, D. J. (1996), 'Firm Organization, Industrial Structure, and Technological Innovation,' *Journal of Economics, Behavior, and Organization*, forthcoming.

Williamson, O. E. (1971), 'The Vertical Integration of Production: Market Failure Considerations,' *American Economic Review*, 61 (May), 112–123.

Williamson, O. E. (1975). *Markets and Hierarchies: Analysis and Antitrust Implications*. The Free Press: New York.

Williamson, O. E. (1983), 'Credible Commitments: Using Hostages to Support Exchange,' *American Economic Review*, 73 (September), 519–540.

Williamson, O. E. (1985), *The Economic Institutions of Capitalism*. The Free Press: New York.

Williamson, O. E. (1991), 'Comparative Economic Organization: The Analysis of Discrete Structural Alternatives,' *Administrative Science Quarterly*, 36, 269–296.

Williamson, O. E. (1996a), *The Mechanisms of Governance*, Oxford University Press: New York.

Williamson, O. E. (1996b), 'Revisiting Legal Realism: The Law, Economics and Organization Perspective,' *Industrial and Corporate Change*, 5, 383–420.

CHAPTER FOURTEEN

The Study of Organizations and Evolving Organizational Forms through History
Reflections from the Late Medieval Family Firm

AVNER GREIF

Despite the diversity of economic environments and organizations utilized throughout history, historical studies of organizations and organizational innovations, by and large, have concentrated on the very recent past. Arguably, this reflects the perception that historical records are not rich enough, with respect to the more remote past, and organizational problems in past economies are irrelevant to contemporary organizational analysis. This paper combines historical information and game theory to demonstrate that the study of past organizations is both feasible and relevant. Specifically, it presents a game theoretical analysis of the factors that led to the emergence of the late medieval family firm in the Latin, rather than the Muslim, world. Furthermore, it explores various organizational innovations related to the family firm, evaluating their sources and the ability to combine game theory and evolutionary economics for the study of organizational evolution.

1. Introduction

Williamson, 1982, has observed that the data source most suitable for the study of organizations and organizational innovations is business history. The diversity of economic environments and organizations utilized throughout history may provide the variety required for evaluating the extent to which organizations effect economic growth and the generality of organizational theory. Furthermore, historical studies of organizations are likely to stimulate the extension of organizational theory and provide a unique perspective regarding organizational innovations. Despite this promise, however, historical studies of organizations and organizational innovations mostly concentrate on the very recent past.[1] Arguably, the factor leading to concentration on recent organizations is the perception that the historical records are not rich enough with respect to the more remote past and organizational problems in past economies are such that their study is irrelevant to contemporary organizational analysis.

This paper's main objective is to reflect on this perception and point out that the study of past organizations is feasible and relevant. For this purpose, the paper presents a preliminary historical examination of organizational innovations relating to the emergence and internal structure of the Italian family firm of the late medieval period. The study of these organizational innovations is appealing for demonstrating the possibility and potential contribution of historical analyses of past organizations for several reasons.

First, the study of the late medieval family firm demonstrates that even with respect to such an earlier period, the wealth of historical information enables a meaningful discussion. Equally informative historical records are also available with respect to various organizations for later periods. Second, this study demonstrates that organizational problems in past economies resemble those examined in contemporary organizational analysis. For example, the family firm seems to have been a response to agency problems and it was among the first organizations in Western Europe that exhibited separation between ownership and control. Hence, the study of the family firm indicates the similarity of contemporary and past organizational problems and how historical analysis of organizational development can advance the analysis of organizational innovations by shedding light on the emergence of important contemporary organizational features. Finally, the analysis of the late medieval family firm also suggests the importance of organizational analysis for the study of economic growth in general. As de Roover (1965, p. 70) has claimed, the Italians dominated the trade of Southern and Western Europe during the 13th and the 14th centuries because of their relatively more efficient business organization.

The paper, however, does not attempt to confirm de Roover's conjecture or even provide a definite study of organizational innovations relating to the family firm. It only advances tentative historical analysis indicating the feasibility and potential contribution of examining historical organizational development. The paper raises questions and indicates possibilities regarding the historical process of organizational innovations rather than rigor-

---

[1] For example, in his classical works, Chandler (e.g. 1969) pioneered the study of business organizations in the late 19th century USA. Lazonick (e.g. 1991) has conducted an historical examination of the sequential rise and fall of various economies in the recent past contributing it to their distinct business organizations. See also the essays in Temin (1991). Among the notable exceptions is Ann Carlos (e.g. Carlos and Nicholas, 1990) who has examined organizational responses to agency problems in early English stock companies.

ously confronting them with the historical evidence. Hence its historical analysis is tentative at best.

A secondary objective of the paper is to reflect on the methodology utilized to study organizational innovations. As Williamson (1985) has observed, despite the importance of organizations 'the study of organizational innovation has never been more than a poor second cousin to the study of technological innovation' (p. 404). Arguably, the study of organizational innovations has been hindered because of the limitations of the two theoretical frameworks—(classical) game theory and evolutionary economics — that have been utilized for this study. Game theoretical analysis attributes distinct organizational innovations only to differences in the underlining structures or games. At the same time, the evolutionary economics approach ignores strategic considerations that seems at the heart of organizational problems.

Game theory has been extensively used to study organizations since strategic interaction leads to organizational problems.[2] Hence, game theoretical analyses have been used to indicate the rationale beyond particular organizations and the necessary condition for organizational innovations. Holmstrom (1982) for example, utilized game theory to demonstrate the failure to cooperate in the context of team production and multi-agent moral hazard. Furthermore, he demonstrated that altering the game by introducing a particular organizational feature—the separation between ownership and control—leads to the existence of a Pareto improving equilibrium. The team thus has an incentive to implement this organizational feature implying, therefore, that the absence of such separation indicates the lack of such incentives. As this example indicates, the game theoretical approach indicates that distinct organizations would be implemented in distinct situations or games.[3]

The evolutionary economics approach to the examination of economic changes, first explored by Nelson and Winter (1982), can account for distinct trajectories of organizational innovations in the same situation or game. In contrast to classical game theory, it emphasizes dis-equilibrium and processes of change and places learning and experimentation by existing economic agents and new entrants at the center of the innovation process. This approach has been extensively used for the study of technological innovations but less so for the study of organizational innovations. This may

---

[2] Arrow (1974, p. 33) defines organizations as 'means of achieving the benefits of collective action in situations in which the price system fails'. Hence, any strategic situation presents an organizational problem.

[3] The deficiency of classical game theory to explain distinct trajectories of organizational innovations in the same game may have prompted Williamson's (1985, p. 404) to suggest to link the study of organizational innovations with Evolutionary Economics.

have been the case since the approach ignores strategic considerations that are an essence of organizational problems.

The analysis of the emergence of the family firm presented in section 2 indicates that game theoretical analysis of organizations can account for distinct trajectories of organizational innovations in the same situation. Given the same exogenous conditions, different equilibria can provide distinct incentives with respect to implementing the same organizational innovations. Furthermore, the examination of the evolution of the internal organizations of the firms conducted in section 3 indicates the need to integrate the evolutionary approach and the game theoretical approach for the study of organizational innovations. The firms' internal organization was changed in response to observed failures but the changes themselves reflect strategic considerations.

2. *The Emergence of the Italian Family Firm*

The Italians are deservedly credited for their many trade-related organizational innovations during the late medieval period. It has been claimed (de Roover, 1965) that these organizational innovations were crucial to the rise of Italian commercial dominance in the Mediterranean and European worlds during the 12th and 13th centuries. Furthermore, these innovations were of great importance to the later commercial, industrial, and financial developments in Europe. '[W]estern wealth began with the growth of European trade and commerce which started in the twelfth century in Italy ...' (Rosenberg and Birdzell, 1986, p. 35).

Important among these organizational innovations was the famous 'family firm'. The essence of the family firm, as originally developed in Italy, was that several individuals agglomerated their capital by establishing a permanent partnership with unlimited and joint liability. It was common for a family firm to dissolve and immediately reform, assuming the assets and name of the previous firm after one partner's death. Usually, several individuals in a firm were members of one family and they contributed more than half the capital of the firm. It was customary to name the firm after this dominant family. The family firm first emerged in the early 13th century in Piacenza, Siena and Lucca, and then diffused to other Italian cities.[4] In the second half of the 13th century a handful of exceptionally large family firms emerged in Florence—the Bardi, Peruzzi and the Acciaiuoli companies. These companies, as well as many other smaller family firms, had offices and branches throughout Europe and the Mediterranean from England in the

---

[4] See discussion, for example, in Sombart (1953); de Roover (1965), pp. 70–71; Rosenberg and Birdzell (1986), pp. 123–124.

west and Tunisia in the south to Rhodes in the east.[5] They traded in luxury
goods as well as staples, provided loans and other banking services, and
exchanged money. The extent of their operation is reflected in the fact that
the assets of the Bardi firm in 1335 were valued at about 1,109,081 lire (a
fiorino) (Hunt, 1994, p.181). This amount was about 4.5 times the English
king's net income as late as 1433 (Brown, 1989, p.62). The profit of the
Bardi firm between 1330 and 1332 was 92,416 lire (a fiorino) (Lopez and
Raymond, 1990, p.370–371). This was about half of the English king's net
income in 1433.

Even though the histories of various family firms were extensively examined, the sources of this organizational innovation have remained unclear.
It seems that during the 12th century traders did not agglomerate their
capital in a manner similar to that achieved by establishing family firms.
The Genoese cartulary of Giovanni Scriba, 1155–1164, the earliest Italian
source that systematically reflect contractual relationships in the post-
Roman period, contains many contracts in which a father provided his son
with the capital required to begin trading through a partnership with a non-
family member merchant. For example, in 1157, Ugo Mallonus provided his
son, Rubaldus Mallonus, with the sum of 66.66 lire that Rubaldus invested in
a partnership with Rolandus Cintracus, who invested 133.3 lire. Rubaldus
carried the capital to the Levant and was entitled to half of the net profit.[6]
Similarly, when brothers invested in trade they usually invested separately,
each of them investing his own capital, creating a short-lived partnership.[7]
Finally, the cartulary contains wills of several merchants, which specify the
allocation of the estate to the deceased's relatives and friends and which do
not reflect the existence of a family firm.[8]

Merchants from the Muslim world organized and utilized their family
capital in a similar manner during this time. The best sources for family
capital agglomeration among traders in the Muslim world during this
period are the 11th century Geniza documents. These documents reflect

[5] For a partial list of major companies and merchant dynasties, see de Roover (1965), pp. 75–77.

[6] Giovanni Scriba, No. CCXXXVI. See also No. DLXXV.

[7] The best example is of two brothers, each of whom was a prominent trader during the period from
1154 to 1164: Ingo de Volta, who invested in trade 25 times, and his brother, William Burone, who
invested in trade 13 times (see Giovanni Scriba). They always invested separately. There are contracts in
which an individual invests sums that belong to other members of his family. For example, on 27
August 1160, Ribaldus de Saraphia mentioned that he had invested 60 lire, 20 of which belonged to his
nephews, Ribaldino and Fredencione (Giovanni Scriba, No. DCCLI). It is instructive to note, however,
that these sums are explicitly referred to as owned by the nephews and not by all the family members
jointly. Furthermore, since the two nephews never appear in the 15 contracts that Ribaldus entered into,
it is reasonable to suppose that they were minors. Hence, this contract, in which an individual invests
sums that belong to other family members, very likely reflects a special situation rather than a regular
commercial practice.

[8] See, for example, the will of Ogerio Vento in Giovanni Scriba No. MXLVII. For his investment in
trade, see, for example, No. DCCCXCII; CMIV.

mainly the operation of the Maghribi traders who were Jewish trader residents in the Muslim world.[9] It is impossible to detect in these historical sources any significant difference between the Genoese and the Maghribi traders in agglomeration of capital in or outside the family.

Among the Maghribi traders, sons usually became active in long-distance commerce, but the intergenerational relationships among the Maghribi traders were not aimed at preserving the family wealth under one roof. A trader's son started to operate as an independent trader during his father's lifetime. The father would typically help the son until he was able to operate independently. After the father's death, his estate was divided among his heirs and his business dissolved.[10]

Neither the Maghribi traders of the 11th century nor the Genoese traders of the 12th century attempted to agglomerate the family capital under one roof on a permanent basis. But this similarity did not last long, as the Italian traders, including the Genoese, introduced the family firm during the 13th century. Why did the Italians, after a relatively short period of involvement in international trade, introduce the family firm? Why did the Maghribi traders not introduce a similar organization? After all, the Maghribi traders were active in long-distance commerce for several centuries, at least from the 9th to the 12th century. Why did they neither invent nor adopt a version of the 'family firm?' Were they just not innovative enough?

Although several hypotheses were advanced to explain the emergence of the Italian family firm, none of them has resolved the above questions. In his seminal work on the organization of late medieval trade, de Roover (1965) has analyzed the emergence of the family firms and advanced two interrelated hypotheses. He has argued (pp. 70–71) that it was the need of merchants and bankers from the inland cities to have representatives in port towns that motivated them to establish family firms. More generally, he has argued that better secured trade routes enabled sending goods without someone accompanying them, while merchants learned 'how to do business by correspondence rather than by personal contact' (p. 73). The possibility and ability to conduct trade through sedentary agents induced them to establish branches abroad and for that purpose they established family firms.

Yet, this argument does not withstand a comparative analysis. The Maghribis, who neither established branches nor firms, conducted their business extensively using correspondence rather than by personal contact. Furthermore, it ignores the fact that merchants from port cities such as Genoa, Pisa and Venice had employed agents in other ports and trade

---

[9] For a general introduction to the geniza documents see Goitein (1967), introduction; the value 'Geniza' in Houtsma (1978), vol. 3, pp. 987–989.

[10] Goitein (1967) pp. 180 ff; Gil (1983), vol. 1, pp. 215 ff.

centers from at least the mid-12th century. The development of banking, and the possibly greater involvement of some of the inland cities in banking activities, may have fostered the introduction of the family firm. Yet, one cannot relate distinct business activities to the development of the family firm since it was also utilized by merchants for whom trade, rather than banking, was the main activity.

Recently, Hunt (1994) has suggested that economies of scale in trade and banking have led to the emergence of the family firm. While there may have been economies of scale in such operations this explanation still leaves one wondering why family firms did not emerge in the Muslim world. Trade on a very large scale also prevailed in the Muslim world. During the 11th century, two merchants, the Jewish Tustari brothers became some of the richest people in Egypt (Gil, 1981). Similarly, the Muslim Karimi merchants operated from around 1150 to 1500 and gained, during the late 12th century, the protection of the Egyptian Sultan and domination over the spice trade between Egypt and the East. The wealth of the Karimi merchants is well reflected in the size of the loans they provided to the rulers of Egypt.[11] Hence, to substantiate that scale was the factor that led to the rise of the family firms, one has to establish that Italian trade was characterized by economies of scale while the Muslim trade was not. Given that the Muslim side of the Mediterranean was richer and more densely populated at least well into the 12th century and given that the Italian and Muslim traders traded in the same goods, in the same area, utilizing the same technology it is difficult to believe that this was the case. If the family firm simply reflects the technology of trade it is not clear why such firms emerged among the Italian traders but not among traders from the Muslim world.

The scope and purpose of this paper excludes a detailed examination of these conjectures regarding the origin of the family firm. Instead, it comes to advance another hypothesis that accounts for the emergence of the family firm in Italy and not in the Muslim world without having to assume any differences in the underlying technology of the trade. This explanation is inspired by the observation that similar to the contemporary economy, organizational problems related to agent relations were central to long-distance medieval trade.

Specifically, the efficiency of long-distance trade during the late medieval period depended, to a large extent, on the ability to mitigate an organization problem related to a specific transaction, namely, the provision of the services required for handling a merchant's goods abroad. A merchant could either provide these services himself by travelling between trade centers or hire overseas agents in trade centers abroad to handle his merchandise.

[11] For a short discussion, see Abulafia (1987), pp. 437–443.

Employing agents was efficient, since it saved the time and risk of travelling, allowed diversifying sales across trade centers, and so forth.[12] Yet, since an employed agent could embezzle the merchant's goods and would do so in the absence of supporting institutions, agency relationships couldn't be established in their absence.

The potential gains from establishing agency relations in medieval trade and the related organizational problem gave rise to the conjecture that the family firm was established since merchants could rely only on relatives to work for them abroad. Indeed, Lane (1944) noted that in the Venetian family firms each family member acted as an agent for the firm in a distinct trade center abroad. Yet, this conjecture falls short of providing an explanation for the rise of the family firm. Even before the innovation of the family firm, Italian merchants traded extensively employing overseas agents, most of whom were not family members, to work for them abroad. For example, as early as the middle of the 12th century Genoese merchants hired agents through *commenda* contracts to travel abroad to trade with the merchants' capital. The first available Genoese cartulary, that of Giovanni Scriba, 1155–1164, indicates that only 5.3% of the total trade investment did not entail agency relationships, and only 6.45% of the sum sent abroad through agents was entrusted to family members.[13]

Similarly, even a superficial examination of the internal structure of the important family firms reveals that agency relationships were usually not established among family members. For example, the Peruzzi company, probably the second-largest Italian company during the late medieval period, had 15 overseas 'branch managers', namely agents in 1335, but only three of them were members of the Peruzzi family. Similarly, in 1402, none of the overseas employees of the Medici company was a Medici.[14]

Finally, even if we suppose that agency relations within family firms were among family members, the hypothesis still cannot explain why family firms were not introduced in the Muslim world as well? After all, if Italian cities imitated each others' organizational innovations why did not merchants from the Muslim world adopt them as well? Furthermore, why was there a need for family members to cooperate through a permanent partnership?

---

[12] For the superiority of trading systems that employ agents see, for example, de Roover (1965).

[13] To examine intra- and inter-family agency relationships I have constructed the genealogy of each individual who appears in the cartulary based on Battilana (1825–1833); Belgrano (1873); Buenger (1954); Giovanni Scriba (1155–1164); Oberto Scriba de Mercato (1186, 1190); and Guglielmo Cassinese (1938). Two individuals were considered to be members of the same 'family' (i) if they were members of the same nuclear family or (ii) they were mentioned as a relative in a document or (iii) they had the same surname but were not mentioned as members of the same family. For doubts regarding the use of the 'family' as a concept in historical study, see Hughes (1974).

[14] de Roover (1965), p. 44, Table 7, p. 80 Table 19. See also the discussions in de Roover (1948, 1963, 1965, pp. 78–79); Herlihy (1985).

Why did family members not simply assist each other? Indeed, this was the case in Venice prior to the rise of the family firm. Family members established a temporary partnership that they renewed every year and each family member operated in distinct trade centers (de Roover, 1965, p. 70).

This is not to say that governance of agency relationships was necessarily not important in the innovation of the family firm. On the contrary, integrating transaction cost economics and classical game theory indicates the relationship between various governance of agency relations and the innovation of the family firm. It indicates why this innovation was introduced by the Italian traders and not by the Maghribis despite the similarity in their agency problems, technology, and environments.[15]

For an agent to be employed, he must be able to *ex ante* commit to be honest *ex post*, that is, after receiving the merchant's goods. The extent to which a legal system could have mitigated this problem was rather limited among the Maghribis and the Italians traders. As Cipolla has pointed out with respect to Italy, an agent who traded using someone else's capital 'could easily have disappeared with the capital or cheated in business conducted in far-off markets where none of his associates had any control'.[16] For agency relations to be established they had to be self enforcing.

The Folk Theorem of repeated games demonstrates that a 'reputation mechanism' can ensure such self-enforceability. Suppose an agent's per-period wage if he is employed and does not cheat is higher than his reservation utility and that a merchant conditions future employment on past conduct. If an honest agent's per-period wage is sufficiently high (relative to his reservation utility and the gains from cheating), the fear of termination makes honesty an agent's best response *ex post*, after receiving the goods. Anticipating that this would be the case the merchant can *ex ante* 'trust' the agent to be honest. The agent acquires reputation for honesty. While this intuitive discussion indicates how agency relations can become self-enforcing, it does not reveal the relations between various governance based upon such reputation mechanisms and incentive to establish a family firm. To examine these relations, a formal model is required.

Consider the following perfect and complete information One-Side Prisoner's Dilemma game (OSPD) that captures the essence of the merchant-agent organizational problem. There are M merchants and A agents in the economy, and (in accordance with the historical evidence) it is assumed that $M < A$. Players live an infinite number of periods, agents have a time discount factor β, and an unemployed agent receives a per-period reservation utility of $RU_a \geq 0$. In each period, an agent can be hired by only one

[15] For this similarity, see Greif (1994).
[16] Cipolla (1980), p. 198. With respect to the Maghribis, see Greif (1989, 1994).

merchant and a merchant can employ only one agent. Matching is random, but a merchant can restrict the matching to a subset of the unemployed agents that contains the agents who, according to the information available to the merchant, have previously taken a particular sequences of actions.[17] A merchant who does not hire an agent (that is, he trades by himself) receives a payoff of $RU_m > 0$. A merchant who hires an agent decides what wage ($W \geq 0$) to offer the agent. An employed agent can decide whether to be honest or to cheat. If he is honest, the merchant's payoff is $\gamma - W$, and the agent's payoff is W. Hence the gross gain from cooperation is γ, and it is assumed that cooperation is efficient, $\gamma > RU_m + RU_a$. The merchant's wage offer is assumed credible, since in reality the agent held the goods and could determine the *ex post* allocation of gains. For that reason, if the agent cheats, the merchant's payoff is 0 and the agent's payoff is the revenue from the business venture, that is, $\gamma > RU_a$. Finally, note that a merchant prefers receiving RU_m over being cheated or paying $W = \gamma$, since $RU_m > 0$

After the allocation of the payoffs, each merchant can decide whether to terminate his relationship with his agent or not. While the merchant can condition his decision on whether the agent has been honest or not, there is also a probability s that a 'forced separation' would occur. That is, a merchant will be forced to terminate agency relationships. This assumption captures the merchants' limited ability to commit to future employment due to the need to shift commercial operations over places and goods, and the high uncertainty of commerce and life during that period. For similar reasons, merchants are assumed to be unable to condition wages on past conduct (indeed, merchants in neither group did so). Hence, attention is restricted to equilibria in which wages are constant over time.[18] Finally, in neither group were wages a function of political or legal considerations nor were they determined by the court or a politically supported guild. Accordingly, and as is customary in similar efficiency wage models (e.g. Shapiro and Stiglitz, 1984), the analysis assumes that no subgroup is organized in a manner that affects wage determination.

Suppose for simplicity that the history of the game is common knowledge. What is the minimum (symmetric) wage offered by all merchants, for which it is an agent's best response to be honest under the threat of firing if he cheats, and the promise of being rehired if he is honest (unless forced separation occurs)? To find this wage one has to fully specify the merchants' strategies that determine the probability that an unemployed agent would

---

[17] The following assumes that the probability of re-matching with the same agent equals zero for all practical consideration.

[18] For an efficiency wage model in which this result is derived endogenously, see MacLeod and Malcomson (1989). Their approach can be utilized here as well but is omitted to preserve simplicity.

be rehired. Yet, to analyze the impact of different strategies in the same framework, the analysis initially concentrates on probabilities that are a function of the strategies. For this aim, denote as an *honest agent* an unemployed agent who was honest in the last period he was employed, and by h_h the probability that he will be hired in that period. Denote as a *cheater* an agent who cheated in the last period he was employed, and by h_c the probability that he will be hired in a given period. Proposition one specifies the minimum wage that supports cooperation.

Proposition 1. (Proof in the appendix).   Assume that $\beta \in (0, 1)$, and $h_c < 1$. The *optimal wage*, the lowest wage for which an agent's best response is to play honest, is $W^* = w(\beta, h_h, h_c, s, RU_a, \gamma) > RU_a$, and w is monotonically decreasing in β and h_h and monotonically increasing in h_c, s, RU_a, and γ.

A merchant induces honesty by the carrot of a wage which is higher than the agent's reservation utility and the stick of terminating their relationship. For a wage high enough, the difference between the present value of the lifetime expected utility of an unemployed and employed agent is higher than what an agent can gain by a one-period play of cheating, and hence the agent's best response is to be honest. The minimum wage that ensures honesty decreases in the factors that increase the lifetime expected utility of an honest agent relative to that of a cheater (that is, β, h_h) and increases in the factors that increase the relative lifetime expected utility of a cheater (that is, h_c, s, RU_a, γ).

Consider the two following strategy combinations—the *individualist* and the *collectivist* strategies. In each strategy combination a merchant hires, for a wage W^*, an unemployed agent whom he re-hires as long as cheating or forced separation does not occur. Under the individualist strategy, however, a merchant randomly hires an unemployed agent, whereas under the collectivist strategy a merchant never employs an agent who was ever a cheater and randomly hires only from among the unemployed agents who have never cheated. An agent's strategy is to play honest if, and only if, he is offered at least the lowest wage required to keep him honest which equals W^* on the path of play (but not off-the-path). Note that W^* is lower under the collectivist strategy. Each of these strategies is a sub-game perfect equilibrium as established in proposition 2.

Proposition 2. (Proof in the appendix).
Assume that under both the *individualist* and the *collectivist* strategy combinations $\gamma - RU_m \geq W^*$; then each strategy combination is a sub-game perfect equilibrium (SGPE) of the OSPD game.

The individualist strategy is SGPE because merchants are not expected to take into account the agent's past behavior when making hiring decisions. Hence each merchant perceives the probability that an unemployed agent who cheated in the past will be hired as equal to that of an unemployed honest agent since W^* will keep either agent honest. According to proposition 1, this implies that each merchant is indifferent regarding whether to hire a cheater or an honest agent. (As discussed below, when the decision to acquire information is endogenous, under individual equilibrium the merchant would not have the related information.)

Under collectivist equilibrium, because each merchant expects others not to employ a cheater, the perceived probability that a cheater will be hired is lower than that of an honest agent. According to proposition 1 this implies that a higher wage is required to keep a cheater honest (since h_b is lower for a cheater), and hence the merchant strictly prefers to hire an honest agent. The merchant's expectations are self-enforcing although cheating does not convey any information about future behavior, the agent's strategy does not call for cheating any merchant who violates the collective punishment, and merchants do not 'punish' any merchant who hires a cheater.

While the above equilibria are sub-game perfect, the situation the OSPD comes to capture was such that these equilibria may have not been 'renegotiation-proof'.[19] A central idea in the renegotiation-proof literature applied to the present game is that if it is costly to the merchant to fire an agent due, for example, to human capital specific to the relations then the threat of firing may not be credible. After cheating, there may exist another equilibrium that Pareto dominates terminating the employment relations. Among the Maghribis and the Genoese traders, however, it is likely that threat of firing was credible. It was common for a merchant to employ more than one agent at the same time and in many cases even in the same locality.[20] Furthermore, agency relations were governed by cultural rules of behavior that reduced the amount of human capital specific to the relations between a particular agent and merchant (Greif, 1993).

The self-enforceability of the individualist and collectivist strategy combinations is further enhanced if we relax the assumption that past actions are common knowledge. Indeed, acquiring and transmitting information during the late medieval period was costly, and hence the model should incorporate a merchant's decision to acquire costly information. Incorporating this element, however, implies that under the individualist strategy combination

---

[19] For a discussion of the various formulation of renegotiation proof, see Pearce (1992), Farrell and Maskin (1989).

[20] For example, the Maghribi trader Jacob ben Isma'il of Sicily had at least five partnerships at the same time (Greif, 1985, p. 133) while the average number of agents a Genoese merchant employed was four. (Based on Giovanni Scriba and refers only to the first merchant and first agent that appear in the societas or commenda contract.)

all merchants are not motivated to acquire information hence making a transition by each to collectivist strategy impossible. Under collectivist strategy, however, each merchant is motivated to acquire costly information (although cheating does not occur on the equilibrium path).

To see why this is the case, suppose that each merchant can either 'Invest' or 'Not Invest' in 'getting attached' to such network before the game begins, and his action is common knowledge. Investing requires paying a fixed amount each period, in return for which the merchant learns the private histories of all the merchants who also Invested. Otherwise, he knows only his own history. This assumption is consistent with the observation that during the late medieval period, merchants gathered information by being a part of an informal information-sharing network.

Under the individualist equilibrium, history has no value, since an agent's wage does not depend on it. Hence, no merchant will invest in information. In contrast, under the collectivist equilibrium history has value, since the optimal wage is a function of an agent's history. Merchants will Invest since an agent who cheated in the past will cheat if hired and paid the equilibrium wage. Although on the equilibrium path cheating never occurs, merchants are motivated to Invest, since this action is common knowledge and hence one who does not invest is cheated if he pays W^*. (For a formal proof, see Greif, 1994, proposition 3.)

Elsewhere (Greif 1989, 1993, 1994), I have argued that although the Maghribi and Genoese traded with similar goods in the same geographical area using the same technology, various social, political and cultural factors led to the selection of different equilibrium in each group. Specifically, among the Maghribis collectivist punishment strategy governed agency relationships while among the Genoese individualist strategy supplemented by the operation of a legal system governed agency relationships. (The legal system mainly ensured that agents would return to the city where the merchant lived.)

To substantiate this conjecture, I have examined various implications of having agency relationships governed by either equilibrium and confronted these implications with the historical records. The focus of the current analysis, however, is to examine the implication of each of the above two equilibria with respect to gains from inter-merchant capital agglomeration. Do different equilibria provide distinct motivation with respect to introducing an innovation such as the family firm?

Proposition 1 established that a reduction in the probability of forced separation, s, reduces the optimal wage. The more likely it is that there will be future relationships between a specific agent and merchant, the less that merchant has to pay his agent to induce honesty. Yet the magnitude of this reduction differs across equilibria. This is so because the decrease in wage due to the reduction in the probability of forced separation depends on the probability that a cheater will be re-hired which is a function of the merchants' strategies. The lower the probability that a cheater will be re-hired, the lower the wage reduction resulting from changing the probability of forced separation. That is, $\partial^2 W(.)/\partial h_c \partial s > 0$ (for $\beta > h_c$). Collectivist equilibrium reduces the probability that a cheater would be re-hired relative to an individualist equilibrium. Hence, the merchants' motivation to reduce the probability of forced separation is lower and may be absent. In contrast, under individualist equilibrium merchants are better motivated to establish an organization that reduces the likelihood of forced separation.

Furthermore, the higher is the probability that an honest agent will be re-hired, the lower the gain from changing the probability of forced separation. That is, $\partial^2 W(.)/\partial h_h \partial s < 0$. Furthermore, when an unemployed honest agent will be re-hired with probability one, the gain from changing the probability of forced separation is zero. The model utilized so far implies that the probability of an honest unemployed agent to be employed does not depend, on the equilibrium path, on the merchants' strategies. Yet, these strategies impact the probability that an unemployed honest agent will be re-hired, h_h, when the set of potential agents, A, increase. That is, when the economy is experiencing immigration or internal population growth as the Italian cities experienced during the period under consideration. To examine the relations between the merchants' strategies and the implication of exogenous increase in the number of agents, A, suppose that in either equilibria the pool of unemployed agents is enlarged due to the entrance of 'new' agents.[21]

Suppose that a new agent becomes available in an economy in which collectivist equilibrium prevails. It is reasonable to assume that any particular merchant is uncertain whether the new agent expects other merchants to hire him if he was hired and forced separation occurred. Such uncertainty implies that hiring a new agent would be more costly to a merchant than hiring another agent. This is so since if the new agent does not expect to be hired by other merchants if forced separation occurred, he would cheat in the wage paid to an agent who expected to be re-hired, namely, all the other (pre-entry) agents. To induce the honesty of a new agent, a wage higher than that of alternative (pre-entry) agent is required and hence merchants would prefer hiring existing agents. The collectivist punishment creates a link between the hiring process of all merchants and the wage each of them should pay his agent to induce honesty and this link is such that it reduces the merchants' profitability of hiring new agents.

[21] Formally, the analysis below relates equilibrium of one game with that of another. For elaboration, see Greif (1994).

In contrast, no such link exist under the individualist equilibrium. Each merchant is indifferent whether to hire a pre-entry agents or not even in the presence of uncertainty whether other merchants would or would not hire new agents. Therefore, if there is an entry of new agents they are as likely to be hired by merchants as pre-entry agents when an individualist equilibrium prevails. Hence, if an individualist equilibrium prevails, entry of new agents increases the merchants' motivation to reduce the probability of forced separation.

Although the underlining game among the Maghribis and Genoese traders was the same, the above game theoretical analysis suggests a source of the uneven organizational development between them. The collectivist equilibrium of the Maghribis implies that a merchant could not gain much by introducing an organization that reduced the likelihood of forced separation. Among the Italian traders—to the extent one can generalize based on the experience of the Genoese—the individualist equilibrium and the large immigration into the Italian cities implied that merchants could gain much by increasing the security of the employment they offered their agents. The family firm can be understood as a manifestation of this desire. In the Italian family firm, several traders combined their capital and formed an organization with an infinite life-span and a lower probability of bankruptcy that replaced each individual merchant in his relationship with agents.[22] The Italian social world of the period under consideration was based on the family and clan. In this social setting agglomeration of capital was, at least initially, naturally made among family members. The family firm, however, was not established to govern agency relations among family members but to govern agency relations between family and non-family members.

Combining a game theoretical and historical analysis of a basic transaction fundamental to long-distance trade during the period under consideration indicates why it was rational for Italian merchants but not Maghribis traders to agglomerate their capital through the family firm. In the same situation, distinct existing equilibria implied different incentives with respect to organizational innovation. A necessary condition for innovation to be forthcoming—for the family firm to be established—is that the merchants who could introduce it would gain from doing so. This condition was fulfilled among the Genoese—and most likely among other Italians merchants as well—but was not fulfilled among the Maghribi merchants.

The above conjecture regarding the relations between agency relations and the emergence of the family firm in Italy and not in the Muslim world

---

[22] Additional theoretical and historical work is required to establish whether and how the family firm achieved a level of commitment above that of each of its individual members. It should be noted that agency relationships in the Italian family firms were not confined to family members, as mentioned previousily in the text.

still awaits further historical research. Yet, the above discussion indicates that an issue central to the contemporary organizational theory, namely, agency relations may have been also central in the historical development of organizations since at least the 12th century. Furthermore, the analysis of the family firm indicates that similar to the situation in modern economies, agency relations and their governance influenced organizational innovations. The analysis indicates that organizational innovations can be accounted for in a game theoretical framework, reflecting not only distinct games but also different implications of distinct equilibria of the same game.

3. *Firms' Internal Structure and the Timing of Organizational Innovations*

The previous section advanced the conjecture that the rise of the family firm in Italy and not in the Muslim world relates to distinct governance of agency relations. But why did the family firm emerge when it did? If the family firm was to reduce agency costs, its introduction could have been beneficial to Italian merchants long before the 13th century when it first appeared. The above game theoretical analysis indicates the rationale behind the emergence of the family firm but not the rationale behind the timing of its emergence.[23] Furthermore, the historical records do not reflect any discrete change that could have led to the emergence of the family firm at the point in time it did.

It can therefore be concluded, in the spirit of Evolutionary Economics, that some process of learning or experimentation took place. Unfortunately the historical records do not indicate the exact nature of the process that led to the emergence of the family firm. Yet, the historical records do reflect learning processes regarding later organizational innovations that shaped the internal structure of the family firm. This section examines these processes and thereby sheds some light on the interrelations between the game theoretical and evolutionary economics approaches to the study of organizational innovations. More importantly, it indicates that the organizational problems the family firms responded to were similar to those central to modern firms, namely, the organizational problem associated with issuing debt, the organizational problem due to separation between ownership and control, and the organizational problem associated with gathering and organizing information in a meaningful manner.[24]

---

[23] Although it relates the increase in the Italian cities' population from the 12th to the 14th century to the increasing benefit of introducing the family firm.

[24] For a recent historical analysis of such development regarding the USA in the19th century, see Levenstein (1991).

The family firm during the 13th and early 14th centuries was a partnership (*compagnia*) among members of the founding family as well as non-family members. Each partner invested some capital in the company and each one's share in the profit was proportional to his investment. Each partner assumed joint and unlimited liability for the firm's debts and in this respect the family firm's internal structure substantially differed from the typical contemporary firm in which investors assume limited liability.

Yet, this difference seems to reflect distinct solutions to the same problem, namely, the organizational problem associated with issuing debt. To issue debt a firm has to commit to appropriately handle the capital entrusted to it. Such commitment is achieved in the modern economy through various means such as regulating the public disclosure of the firm's financial situation. In the late medieval period, however, the state's limited bureaucratic ability, the international scope of the Italian firms, and existing accounting procedures rendered such solutions impractical. Yet, Italian family firms solicited deposits from various sources such as the Pope, the aristocracy, merchants, and the general public throughout Europe.[25] Unlimited and joint liability may have been the mechanism that enhanced commitment to handle these funds appropriately.

That this was indeed the case and the nature of the learning process that induced retaining this feature is reflected in the economic history of Siena. Despite its relatively small size, this city had a very high share of international banking activities in the 13th century. Sapori (1938) and English (1988) have concluded that the city's decision to relax the joint and unlimited liability rule in 1310 damaged the Sienese firms' ability to issue debt and led to the city's economic decline. The Sienese had probably recognized this implication of relaxing the joint and unlimited liability role and the decision was reversed in 1342. Experimentation seems to have reinforced the original organizational feature.

This incidence also indicates that similar to the situation in modern economies, understanding economic organizations and their economic implications require examining their political foundations. For an unlimited and joint liability to enhance a firm's ability to solicit deposits, depositors have to expect that the political authority of the city where the firm's partners live would indeed enforce the unlimited liability rule if necessary. A city's authorities may indeed enforce such rule, even with respect to claims from outside depositors, if failing to do so is expected to limit the ability of the city's other firms to solicit deposits.

This implies that there are economies external to the firm—a larger number of firms in a particular city enhances each firm's ability to solicit

[25] Each year the firm credited a depositor's account with interest on his deposit.

deposits. This externality is due to the need to secure the appropriate political foundation for international borrowing and if it is important, the geographical concentration of firms engaged in international borrowing would be high. Indeed, during the 13th century Sienese firms suppressed all others in the extent to which they solicited deposits internationally, while in the early 14th century Florence took the lead. The need to secure the appropriate political foundations for the international borrowing of a family firm seem to have determined their geographical concentration.

Italian family firms retained their basic structure as unlimited and joint responsibility partnerships throughout the centuries. Yet, other features of the family firms' internal structure were altered during that time. This is particularly true with respect to the incentive scheme firms utilized to motivate their agents. Indeed, the funds invested by a firm's partners and depositors were controlled, to a large extent by the firm's agents who represented it in various trade centers abroad.

A firm's agents were recruited from the firm's city and some firms, such as the Peruzzi firm, trained their future agents both by having them serve in the firm's main office and by working under supervision in various branches. After the training period agents spent a prolonged period of time in a trade center abroad heading one of the firm's branches. In this capacity, agents had to have a great deal of discretion and authority in making business decisions. As Hunt (1994) has noted, the firms had 'centralized policy but decentralized execution' (p. 85). Agents had the power of attorney to represent the firm, and hence they could have legally committed the firm to assume a liability.

Agents could, and at times did, behave opportunistically. For example, in 1330, the Peruzzi firm accused Silimanno Bottieri, who was its agent in Bruges and England for 16 years, of defrauding the company of 5,000 florins out of the 50,000 entrusted to him. In 1336 another agent was thrown into jail in Florence for cheating the firm while operating on its behalf in Naples and Avignon. That such allegations may have had a grain of truth is well reflected in the deathbed confession of an agent, Bartolo Gherardini, who admitted that in 1340 he embezzled a sum from the Peruzzi firm.[26]

Agents could gain by acting opportunistically even without breaking the law. After all, they were in charge of making decisions, or actively participating in a decision-making process regarding various large-scale business ventures. Hence, an agent could have influenced the decision to advance his own interests rather than those of the firm employing him. As Hunt (1994) has noted, 'branch managers enjoyed personal privileges and money grants [from clients], which put considerable strain on their loyalty to the

---

[26] Hunt (1994), p. 88. Taken from Davidsohn, vol. 6, p. 390.

company interest' (p. 88). Such strain is reflected, for example, in promises made between 1338 and 1443, by the English King, Edward III whose finance depended on loans from the Italian firms. He promised substantial sums to the wives of Peruzzi agents in England and provided two employees of the Bardi firm with substantial awards (Hunt, 1994, p.88).

Therefore, the medieval firm confronted the problems of agency relations and separation between ownership and control that are also central to the modern firm. How were the family firms organized to confront these problems? How were agents induced not to embezzle from the firm and to take actions beneficial to it? Arguably, firms could mitigate this agency problem by using the partners or their family members as agents. Yet, agents were, by and large, neither partners nor related by blood to a firm's partners' families.

In 1335, for example, the Peruzzi firm had 16 branches abroad but only six of them were headed by partners. After 1337, only four branches were headed by a partner. More generally, in July 1335, the firm employed 48 individuals outside of its headquarters in Florence but only seven of them were members of the Peruzzi family. The total number of the firm's (non-partners) employees was 88 but only 18 were related to any partner. From 1331 to 1343, 136 individuals were employed by the firm abroad and only 21 were members of the Peruzzi family.[27]

How were the above organizational problems mitigated? What were, if any, the organizational innovations introduced by the family firms to mitigate them? To address these issues, the following discussion contrasts relevant aspects of firms' internal organization prior to and after the mid-14th century. Specifically, it mainly concentrates on the experience of the Florentine Peruzzi firm (1292–1343) for the earlier period and the Florentine Medici firm (1397–1494) for the latter period. Attempts are made to identify the main organizational innovations relating to agency relations and to understand their sources.

The contractual relations among firms and agents in the earlier period are consistent with the conjecture, discussed in section 2, that agency relations were governed by a bilateral reputation mechanism. Agents were usually remunerated by a yearly salary (that rose with seniority and promotion) which was credited to their personal account in the firm. The balance accrued the same interest provided to depositors. In addition, they were entitled to charge all their expenses to the firm. Salaries were high and salaries in the larger companies, like the Peruzzi and Bardi, were very high.[28]

---

[27] Hunt (1994), pp. 79, 95, 98. To simplify the presentation I consider a trade center to have a 'branch' if the firm had any permanent representation in that center.

[28] de Roover (1958), pp. 24–26. See also Hunt (1994), pp. 90–91.

That agents' high salaries were aimed at providing incentives is suggested by the observation that in the Peruzzi firm, agents who were not members of the Peruzzi family received, on average, a higher salary than employees who were family members (Hunt, 1994, p.89). To further motivate agents to labor with the firm's interest in mind, bonuses were sometimes (although rarely) provided. For example, Giovanni Bonducci, was paid the large bonus of 40 lire by the Peruzzi firm for his achievements in Puglia (Hunt, 1994, p. 91).

Agents were employed for a long period of time, sometimes for life. For example, Silimanno Bottieri, mentioned above, was an agent of the Peruzzi family for at least 16 years. Sometimes an agent's son followed in his father's footsteps and began, after reaching the appropriate age, to work for the same firm. Yet, it was very rare for an agent to achieve partnership status.[29] All agents for the Peruzzi and Medici were from Florence, perhaps to enable using the Florentine legal system to punish them if necessary.

To keep agents from becoming too involved with local interests, to reduce the motivation to give them bribes, and perhaps also to make the threat of punishing by firing, credible agents rotated among branches. In addition, partners and their relatives were often sent to monitor specific branches. For example, between December 1336 and December 1338, Giovanni Soderini, a partner in the Peruzzi firm, spent 10 months in the firm's English branch, 3 months in the Venetian branch, and visited the branch in Paris (Hunt, 1994, p. 89).

Hence, until the mid-14th century, it seems that the carrot of high salaries and long-term employment on the one hand, and the stick of firing and legal suits on the other, were used to motivate agents. Monitoring and regular reports were used to provide the firm with information regarding activities in the branches. Rotation was used to curtail the agents' involvement with local interests and discouraging bribes. Finally, the process of agents' selection and training was used to promote the agent's general and firm-specific human capital.

It is impossible to evaluate how well the above incentive scheme served the interests of the firms relative to other feasible incentive schemes. Yet, two aspects of this scheme seem, in light of modern economic theory, potentially not expected-profit maximizing.[30] First, agents were not provided with incentives by linking their per-period salary to their per-period perform-

[29] See discussion in Hunt (1994), p. 94.

[30] See discussion of agency models in Hart and Holmstrom (1985), pp. 71–106. As they emphasize on p. 105, the robust conclusion from agency models is that contracts should use all relevant information up to a sufficient statistic, and that various factors may cause contracts to exhibit simple functional forms such as linear.

ance. Second, agents' enumerations were such that they were not given incentives by sharing some of the downside risk, although some of it was endogenous in the sense that an agent could influence risk by his choice of actions and could have even gained from committing the firm to assume a high risk venture. For example, he could receive a bribe and provide a bad loan.

It is interesting to note that these two aspects of the firms' internal organization stand in sharp contrast to the practice of the Italian traders prior to the rise of the family firm. Prior to the introduction of the family firms agents' per-period salary was a function of their per-period performance. Moreover, the historical records indicate progression from an incentive system in which agents did not share some of the downside risk, to one in which they did. Specifically, in the early 12th century *commenda* contracts were the main contracts through which agency relations were established. Under the *commenda* contract the merchant provided all the capital and the agent provided only work in form of travelling abroad selling and buying merchandise. The agent's remuneration was one quarter of the net profit but he did not assume any liability if a loss occurred. Toward the end of the 12th century, however, the *commenda* was replaced by the *societas* contract in which the agent invested one-third of the capital and was entitled for one-half of the net profit. Hence, under this contract the agent's remuneration was (as before) a function of his per-period performance but in addition he assumed one-third of the capital loss. Note that under both contracts the agent's expected remuneration from his labor on the principal's capital is the same.[31]

Whether the above two organizational aspects of the early family firms, namely, that agents' per-period reward *was unrelated* to their per-period performance and that they *did not assume* any of the downside risk were expected-profit enhancing or not is impossible to evaluate directly. Contract theory suggests that if agency relations were not expected to repeat, these features were not optimal. In the historical context under consideration, however, agency relations could, and were repeated and hence, whether or not they were optimal depends on the magnitude of the relevant parameters, such as the agent's time discount factor and reservation utility. Needles to say, there is no way these parameters can be inferred from the historical records. In any case, it is clear that later family firms utilized an incentive scheme in which agents' per-period reward *was related* to their per-period performance and that they *assumed* part of the downside risk. This indicates

---

[31] That is, if an agent is to receive 100% of the gain on the capital he invested in a *societas*, and receives a half of the total gain, he is receiving a quarter of the gain on the principal's capital. Regarding the *commenda* and *societas* see Byrne (1916); Krueger (1957); and de Roover (1965), pp. 49–51.

either experimentation or learning and suggests that the early firms' incentive scheme may have not been optimal.[32]

The changes in internal organization between earlier and later family firms are well reflected in the organization of the Medici firm, considered to have had an organization typical for the later period.[33] The relations between the firm and its agents were altered by changing the internal structure of the firm itself. Unlike the early firms, each of which was a joint and unlimited liability partnership (*compagnia*), the Medici firm was made up of many such partnerships. The core of the firm, a partnership among members of the Medici family and other investors, established other partnerships with individuals who, as 'junior' partners, served as agents to the core partnership.[34] Hence, agents were not employees hired for a wage, but partners who received a share in the profit or loss of the branch they managed. Furthermore, since they were partners, they assumed unlimited and joint liability for the obligations of the branch they managed, thus making it harder for them to benefit from bribes, trade ventures, or banking transactions that were beneficial to them but unprofitable to the firm.

To demonstrate the nature of partnership contracts, how they provided incentives, and the attention paid to provide the appropriate incentives consider the following provisions of a contract signed in 1456 among the main partners of the Medici main partnership and a 'junior' partner and agent Angiolo.[35] Piero, Giovanni, and Piero de' Medici, and Gierozzo de' Pigli, and Angiolo Jacopo Tani established a partnership that was to last from 25 March 1456 to 24 March 1459 for the purpose of trade and exchange (that is, banking) in Flanders. The partnership's capital was £3,000 groat in Flemish currency, of which £500 groat were to be invested by Angiolo who was to assume the management (*governo*) of the partnership's business in Flanders. Although Angiolo invested about 17% of the capital, his share in the profit or loss was 20%.

Among the contract's other stipulations were the following: Angiolo was to live in Bruges, Flanders' commercial center, and to leave this city only for business. He agreed to manage the partnership according to 'good mercantile customs' and to follow any instruction sent from Florence. Angiolo was

---

[32] It should be noted that the historical records do not suggest significant differences in the nature of the organizational problems facing the earlier and later family firms, although the European economic environment changed drastically during the 14th century. This change was mainly due to the Black Death, the disintegration of the Mongol Empire, and the Hundred Years War. (The seminal work on the issue is Kedar, (1976). More recently, Epstein (1994) has argued that the 14th century crisis fostered economic growth due to its distributional consequences.)

[33] de Roover, 1963, p. 75; 1965, pp. 78–79.

[34] This was the case until 1445. After this year the partnerships were among the Medici as individuals and their agents.

[35] The contract was published in Lopez and Raymond (1990), pp. 206–211.

fully responsible for any loss if he deviated from instructions or stipulations in the contract, and for each offense he had to also pay a penalty. Any profit from such a deviation belonged to the partnership. A penalty was also to be paid if Angiolo got involved in gambling or brought women to his quarters. Angiolo was prohibited from lending or delivering an exchange, that is, a loan, to anyone who was not a merchant or artisan, and even with respect to them, he had to use discretion. Selling on credit to any 'lords temporal or spiritual, prelates, priests, [or] clerics' was allowed only with written permission from Florence.

Angiolo was also prohibited from conducting any business for himself in Bruges or to have such business conducted for him. Any gift given to him in money or another form which was worth more than 1 lira belonged to the partnership. He was not allowed to obligate the partnership either on his own behalf, or for that of any relative or friend, without written permission. Upon termination of the contract, the house and place of business in Bruges and the partnership's books and name would remain in the possession of the senior partners. Angiolo was to submit an annual report to Florence and had to be available for half a year after the termination of the partnership to answer any questions regarding the books. Finally, the senior partners had the right to terminate the partnership at any time.

Hence, in contrast to the internal organization of the earlier firms, later firms directly linked the per-period profit of the branch managed by an agent and that agent's income. In addition, agents assumed part of the downside risk. Finally, each partner still held a joint and unlimited liability for the deposits in the firm, thereby maintaining the firm's ability to solicit deposits.

While the above discussion reveals the rationale behind changing the agents' incentive scheme, it does not reveal the process through which this change came about. What led to this change? One possible explanation is suggested by Nelson and Winter's (1982) conceptual framework. They argued that firms have different 'routines' or organizational capabilities that they possess, and which are the conceptual equivalent of 'skills' that individuals possess. The introduction of new routines demonstrates either learning by existing firms or the entry of new firms with new routines. Thus, the differences in the organizational structure of the earlier and later firms reflects a change in routines due to the entry of new firms. Yet, the question remains, why did the entrants adopt a different routine?

The historical records do not directly indicate why later firms such as the Medici adopted an organizational structure distinct from those of earlier firms, such as the Peruzzi, that were also based in Florence. It is likely, however, that the Medici concluded that the incentive scheme used by the earlier firms was inadequate. Indeed, many of the earlier firms went bankrupt during the late 13th and first half of the 14th century. The Peruzzi firm, for example, went bankrupt in 1343 but had been unprofitable since the late 1320s if not earlier.[36] After 1330, various factors, such as the Peruzzi's bad loans to the English King, Edward III, and the increased regulation and taxation of the grain trade, contributed to the firm's decline. No explanation other than agency cost, however, has been found to account for the Peruzzi's losses during the early period.[37] Since the Medici adopted a distinct organization to govern agency relations, it suggests that they may have also perceived agency cost to have been an important factor in the collapse of the earlier firms. Therefore, they instituted a different incentive scheme to reduce further the agency cost.

The introduction of a different organization to govern agency relations seems to have been due to the observed failure of the organization used by the earlier firms. A discrete event—failure—led to organizational modification. The natural selection process entailed learning. Yet, it is important to note that the Medici's response was not of an evolutionary nature. It was a rational attempt to mitigate agency problems taking into account the strategic nature of the situation. Agents' response to their incentives scheme clearly dominated the Medici's thoughts.

The historical records indicate a different innovation process with regard to an organizational innovation complementary to that of the agents' incentive scheme. Furthermore, it also indicates awareness of the limitation of a current organizational feature. Specifically, having a multi-partnership family firm required a method of bookkeeping that enabled evaluating the profitability of each branch within the firm. It also required that each branch keep separate books, and that transactions with other branches would be recorded in a manner that reflected the relative contribution of each branch. Indeed, each of the Medici firm's branches held separate books and they dealt with each other on the same basis as with outside customers. Commissions, for example, were charged to one branch by another as if both belonged to entirely different firms. When two branches joined in a deal, it was customary to determine in advance how the profits or losses were to be divided (see de Roover, 1963, p. 78).

The accounting procedures utilized by the early firms did not seem to make such procedures possible. It is clear that the Alberti firm (1304–1332) did not use double-entry bookkeeping that enabled specification of the profit

---

[36] See discussion in Hunt (1994), pp. 156–183.
[37] See discussion in Hunt (1994), pp. 173–183. Hunt mentions the possible contribution of agency cost to the firm's decline, but considers decline in the profitability of the grain trade to be very important to its collapse.

and loss of each branch. It is doubtful whether the Peruzzi firm (1335–1343) maintained such a system, but it is clear that the Medici firm (1397–1494) utilized double-entry bookkeeping and each branch kept its own set of books. The historical records indicate there was experimentation with and learning about bookkeeping procedures throughout this period. Thirteenth century account-books are organized by business transaction, making double-entry bookkeeping impossible. In the early 14th century, debits were recorded in the front half of the ledger while credits were recorded in the rear half, but in the mid-14th century the debit was placed next to the credit either on the opposite page or in two columns on the same page. This method was referred to in Tuscany as the Venetian method, indicating an inter-city learning process.[38] It may be, therefore, the case that earlier firms, while aware of the deficiency of their incentive scheme, could not have altered it because of the limitation imposed by the knowledge of accounting. The ability to provide incentives may have been limited by knowledge regarding the organization of information.

4. *Conclusions*

The examination of the family firm demonstrates that the organizational problems that late medieval traders faced are those central to organizational theory. They had to confront agency problems, mitigate the contractual problems due to the separation between ownership and control, and devise accounting procedures appropriate for the incentive schemes they implemented. The historical records are rich enough to enable a detailed comparative examination over time and space of the organizational features utilized to mitigate these problems. Hence, the study of the family firm demonstrates that in this case, as it is with respect to many other organizations, the nature of organizational problems in past economies makes their study relevant to contemporary organizational analysis while the historical records are rich enough to make such analysis possible.

The preliminary analysis of the emergence and internal structure of the Italian family firms suggests that their emergence in Italy, rather than in the more commercially advanced Muslim world, may reflect different incentives with respect to the agglomeration of capital brought about by the distinct manner in which agency relations were mitigated. Yet, while this game theoretical analysis indicates the necessary condition for the development

---

[38] See discussion in de Roover (1965), pp. 91–92; de Roover (1963), pp. 37–38, 97–99; and Hunt (1994), pp. 101–103. The absence of appropriate accounting procedures cannot explain the failure to alter the agents' incentive scheme. After all, introducing a new accounting procedure is an organizational innovation and explaining the failure to introduce one organization feature based on the failure to introduce another is unsatisfactory.

of the family firm in Italy, it could neither account for the timing nor the location in which it emerged.

The internal structure of the family firms indicates concern with enhancing the firm's credibility to its depositors, mitigating agency problems and the problem entailed by separating ownership and control, and fostering the ability to organize and utilize information. This latter feature of the family firm was altered gradually through a process of experimentation and learning consistent with the evolutionary economics approach. Changes in agents' incentive schemes, however, were made in a discrete manner, reflecting a response to organizational failure probably profound enough to alter perceptions with respect to the usefulness of particular organizational features. While change in response to failure is consistent with the theoretical framework of evolutionary economics, the responses themselves explicitly reflect strategic considerations. It seems that the study of organizational innovations requires integrating evolutionary and strategic analyses.

The examination of evolving organizational forms in various historical episodes is likely to contribute to the development of a theoretical framework suitable for the study of organizational evolution as well as to our understanding of the nature of organizations and their economic impact.

Acknowledgements

This paper was prepared for a conference on 'Firms, Markets, and Organizations' in U.C., October 1995. Participants at this conference, and in particular Joseph Farrell, contributed valuable suggestions.

References

Abulafia, D. (1987), 'Asia, Africa and the Trade of Medieval Europe,' in M. Postan, E. Rick and M. Miltey (eds), *The Cambridge Economic History of Europe*, Vol. 2. Cambridge University Press: Cambridge.

Arrow, K. (1974), *The Limits of Organization*. Norton & Company: New York.

Battilana, N. (1825–1833), *Genealogie delle Famiglie Nobili di Genova*, 3 vols, Genoa. (published separately, 1971), Forni Editore: Bologna)

Belgrano, L. (1873), Tavole Genealogiche a Corredo Della Illustrazione del Registro Arcivescovile de Genova. Atti della Società Ligure di Storia Patria.

Brown, A.L. (1989), *The Governance of Late Medieval England, 1272–1461*, Stanford University Press: Stanford, CA.

Buenger, L. (1954), *Genoese Entrepreneurs, 1186–1211*. PhD dissertation. The University of Wisconsin, Wisconsin, MA.

Byrne, E. (1916), 'Commercial Contracts of the Genoese in the Syrian Trade of the 12th Century,' *The Quarterly Journal of Economics*, 31, 128–170.

Carlos, A. and S. Nicholas (1990), 'Agency Problems in Early Chartered Companies: The Case of the Hudson's Bay Company,' *The Journal of Economic History*, L, 853–875.

Chandler, A., Jr. (1969), *Strategy and Structure*. MIT Press: Cambridge, MA.

Cipolla, C. (1980), *Before the Industrial Revolution*, 2nd edn. Norton: New York.

de Roover, R. (1948), *The Medici Bank. Its Organization, Management, Operation, and Decline*. New York University Press: New York.

de Roover, R. (1958), 'The Story of the Alberti Company of Florence, 1302–1348, as Revealed in its Account Books,' *Harvard Business Review*, 32, 14–59.

de Roover, R. (1963), *The Rise and Decline of the Medici Bank, 1397–1494*. Harvard University Press: Cambridge, MA.

de Roover, R. (1965), *The Organization of Trade. Vol. 3. The Cambridge Economic History of Europe*, M. Postan, E. Rick and M. Miltey (eds), Cambridge University Press: Cambridge.

English, E. (1988), 'Enterprise and Liability in Sienese Banking, 1230–1350,' *Speculum Anniversary Monographs*, 12. The Medieval Academy of America.

Epstein, S. (1994), 'Regional Fairs, Institutional Innovation, and Economic Growth in Late Medieval Europe,' *Economic History Review*, XLVII, 459–482.

Farrell, J. and E. Maskin (1989), 'Renegotiation in Repeated Games,' *Games and Economic Behavior*, 1, 327–360.

Gil, M. (1981), *The Tustaris, Family and Sect* (in Hebrew). The Diaspora Research Institute: Tel Aviv.

Gil, M. (1983), *Palestine During the First Muslim Period (634–1099) 1–3* (in Hebrew and Arabic). The Ministry of Defence Press and Tel Aviv University Press: Tel Aviv.

Giovanni Scriba, (1935), *Cartolare di, 1154–1164* (in Latin and Italian), M. Chiaudano and M. Moresco (eds). S. Lattes & C. Editori: Torino.

Goitein, S. (1967), *A Mediterranean Society: Economic Foundations*. University of California Press: Los Angeles.

Greif, A. (1985), 'Sicilian Jews During the Muslim Period (827–1061),' (in Hebrew and Arabic). Master's thesis, Tel Aviv University.

Greif, A. (1989), 'Reputation and Coalitions in Medieval Trade: Evidence on the Maghribi Traders,' *Journal of Economic History*, XLIX, 857–882.

Greif, A. (1993), 'Contract Enforceability and Economic Institutions in Early Trade: The Maghribi Traders' Coalition,' *American Economic Review*, 83, 525–548.

Greif, A. (1994), 'On the Political Foundations of the Late Medieval Commercial Revolution: Genoa During the 12th and 13th Centuries,' *The Journal of Economic History*, 54, 271–287.

Guglielmo Cassinese (1938), *Notai Liguri Del Sec. XII (1190–1192)* (In Latin and Italian), M. Hall, H. Krueger and R. Reynolds (eds), Editrice Libraria Italiana: Torino.

Hart, O. and B. Holmstrom (1985), 'The Theory of Contracts,' in T. Bewley (ed.), *Advances in Economic Theory*, presented at the Fifth World Congress of the Econometric Society . Cambridge University Press: Cambridge.

Herlihy, D. (1985), *Medieval Households*. Harvard University Press: Cambridge, MA.

Holmstrom, B. (1982), 'Moral Hazard in Teams,' *Bell Journal of Economics*, 13, 324–340.

Houtsma, M. (ed.) (1978), *Encyclopedia of Islam*, 2nd edn. Leyden.

Hughes, D. (1974), 'Toward Historical Ethnography: Notarial Records and Family History in the Middle Ages,' *Historical Methods Newsletter*, 7, 61–71.

Hunt, E. (1994), *The Medieval Super-Company*. Cambridge University Press: Cambridge.

Kedar, B. (1976), *Merchants in Crisis*. Yale University Press: New Haven.

Krueger, H. (1957), 'Genoese Merchants, Their Partnerships and Investments, 1155 to 1164,' *Studi in Onore di Armando Sapori*. Institudo Editoriale Cisalpino: Milano.

Lane, F. (1944), 'Family Partnerships and Joint Ventures in the Venetian Republic,' *The Journal of Economic History*, 4, 178–196.

Lazonick, W. (1991), *Business Organization and the Myth of the Market Economy*. Cambridge University Press: Cambridge.

Levenstein, M. (1991), 'The Use of Cost Measures: The Dow Chemical Company, 1890–1914,' in P. Temin (ed.), *Inside the Business Enterprise*. Chicago University Press: Chicago, IL.

Lopez, R. and I. Raymond (1990) [1955], *Medieval Trade in the Mediterranean World*. Columbia University Press: New York.

MacLeod, W. and J. Malcomson (1989), 'Implicit Contracts, Incentive Compatibility, and Involuntary Unemployment,' *Econometrica*, 57, 447–480.

Nelson, R. and S. Winter (1982), *An Evolutionary Theory of Economic Change*. Harvard University Press: Cambridge, MA.

Oberto Scriba de Mercato, 1186, 1190, (1940) (In Latin and Italian.) M. Chiaudano and M. Della Rocca, (eds). (Documenti, XI and XVI). Turin.

Pearce, D. (1992), 'Repeated Games: Cooperation and Rationality,' in Jean-Jacques Laffont (ed.), *Advances in Economic Theory*, Sixth World Congress. Cambridge University Press: Cambridge.

Rosenberg, N. and L. Birdzell, Jr. (1986), *How the West Grew Rich*. Basic Books: New York.

Sapori, A. (1938), Le Compagnie Mercantili Toscane del Dugento e dei Primi del Trecento: La Responsabilità dei Compagni verso i Terzi. Also published (1955) as chapter 29 in Studi di Storia Economica (secolo XIII-XIV-XV). Sansoni: Florence.

Shapiro, C. and Stiglitz, J. (1984), 'Equilibrium Unemployment as a Worker Discipline Device,' *American Economic Review*, 74, 433–444.

Sombart, W. (1953), 'Medieval and Modern Commercial Enterprise,' in F. Lane and J. Riemersma (eds), *Enterprise and Secular*. Richard D. Irwin: Homewood, IL.

Temin, P. (ed.) (1991), *Inside the Business Enterprise: Historical Perspectives on the Use of Information*. Chicago University Press: Chicago, IL.

Williamson, O. (1982), 'Microanalytical Business History,' *Business and Economic History*, II, 105–115.

Williamson, O. (1985), *The Economic Institutions of Capitalism*. Free Press: New York.

Appendix:

Proposition 1. Proof: For a given h_c and h_b, to show that playing honest is optimal for the agent it is sufficient to show that he cannot gain from playing cheat one period if offered W^*. Accordingly, denote by V_b the present value of lifetime expected utility of an employed agent who, whenever hired, plays honest. Denote by V_b^u the present value of the lifetime expected utility of such unemployed honest agent. Denote by V_c^u the lifetime expected utility of an unemployed cheater (who will be playing honest in the future if hired). (The last two expressions take into account only income from the next period and on which is the first period of unemployment.) These lifetime expected utilities are:

$$V_b = W^* + \beta(1-s)V_b + sV_b^u, V_i^u = \beta h_i V_b + \beta(1 - (RU_a + V_i^u)) \, i = h, c.$$

Cheating once yields $\gamma + V_c^u$ as the agent's present value of his lifetime expected utility. Thus an agent will not cheat if $V_b \geq \gamma + V_c^u$. Substituting and rearranging yields the result that an agent's best response is playing honest if $W \geq (\Sigma - \beta s H_b)[\gamma/(1 - \beta H_c) + \beta s(P_c/(1 - \beta H_c) - sP_b)] = W^*$, where $\Sigma = 1 - \beta(1-s)$; $H_i = h_i/(1 - \beta(1 - h_i))$, $i = h, c$; $P_i = (1 - h_i)/(1 - \beta(1 - h_i))$, $i = h, c$. The properties of W can be derived from this expression using the fact that $h_c \leq h_b$.

Proposition 2. Proof:[39] Under both strategies the merchants act in accordance with the strategy assumed in proposition 1. Under the individualist strategy, $h_c = h_b > 0$ while under the collectivist strategy $h_b > 0$ and $h_c = 0$ after every history. Hence, proposition 1 holds and given W^*, an agent cannot do better by deviating. This implies that on the equilibrium path a merchant's strategy is best response. The only non-trivial part of the proof regarding off-the-path-of-play events is verifying the optimality of the merchant's hiring procedures after cheating under the collectivist strategy. Denote the probability that a cheater (honest agent) will be hired by h_c^c (h_b^c) under the collectivist strategy. Note that under this strategy h_c^c equals zero (since a cheater is not expected to re-hired), but h_b^c equals, along the equilibrium path, $sM/(A - (1 - s)M) > 0$ (since an honest agent will be hired in the future). According to proposition 1, the optimal wage for a cheater is $W_c^* = w(., h_b^c = 0, h_c^c = 0)$ and the optimal wage for an honest agent is $W_b^* = w(., h_b^c > 0, h_c^c = 0)$. Since the function w decreases in h_b, $W_c^* > W_b^*$, and a merchant strictly prefers to hire an agent who has always been honest rather than an agent who has cheated. Thus, firing a cheater and hiring only from the pool of honest agents is optimal for the merchant. Note that this implies that in another off-the-path-of-play event in which a merchant did not fire an agent who cheated him, there is no wage for which it is profitable for the merchant to employ the agent. The merchant should pay this agent at least W_c^* implying that even if this agent will be honest, the best response of the merchant is to fire him in the next period. Hence, for any $W \neq \gamma$, the agent's best response is to cheat.

---

[39] For technical reasons it is assumed that if a merchant offers $W = 0$ employment is *de facto* not taking place and the merchant receives RU_m and the agent receives RU_a; that the collectivist strategy also calls for ignoring cheating by more than one agent; and that under the individualist strategy in the off-the-path-of-play event in which a merchant did not fire an agent who cheated him, the agent's strategy specifies cheating for every wage and the merchant's strategy specifies offering $W = 0$.

PART IV

Microanalytics

CHAPTER FIFTEEN

Corporate Law and Corporate Governance

ROBERTA ROMANO

Transaction cost economics has done much to illuminate the working of corporate governance devices, and we have seen a revival of interest in corporate law and corporate governance since the 1980s, as researchers applied the tools of the new institutional economics and modern corporate finance to analyze the new transactions emerging in the 1980s takeover wave. This article focuses on three mechanisms of corporate governance, to illustrate the analytical usefulness of transaction cost economics for corporate law. It begins with the role of the board of directors, the principal governance structure for shareholders in diffusely held firms, for which Oliver Williamson provided the key conceptualization. It then extends that analysis to a form of block ownership known as relational investing, in which a large shareholder is more actively involved in firm management than is ordinarily expected of non-management shareholders. It concludes with an examination of the choice of law governing shareholder-manager relations, referred to in the literature as state competition for corporate charters, and how Williamson's framework can be fruitfully deployed for understanding the success of US corporate law. Each of the three sections sketches first the theory of the corporate governance mechanism from the perspective of transaction cost economics and then addresses the question whether corporate governance matters by discussing the empirical evidence on whether the mechanism is effective. In addition to limning Williamson's contribution, the objective is to relate theory and data, to ascertain where we are, 20 years after Williamson's fundamental contribution was first articulated in Markets and Hierarchies, and over a decade after the corporate law applications were first explicitly worked out.

1. Introduction

Corporate law and corporate governance are flip sides of the same coin. The fundamental task of corporate law is to provide a framework of governance institutions that mitigate the agency problem arising from the separation of ownership and control in the modern corporation—that the interests of the managers who control corporate decision-making may not coincide with the interests of their principals, the corporation's owners. There are a number of institutions directed at the agency problem, both internal and external control mechanisms, established or policed by corporate law: shareholder voting rights to elect the board of directors, which hires top management and sets its compensation; directors' and officers' fiduciary duties to the shareholders; federal disclosure requirements on firms and restrictions on insider trading in securities; and the market for corporate control, in which control is concentrated in a new owner and management is often replaced.

Transaction cost economics has done much to illuminate the working of corporate governance devices, and we have seen a revival of interest in corporate law and corporate governance since the 1980s, as researchers applied the tools of the new institutional economics and modern corporate finance to analyze the new transactions emerging in the 1980s takeover wave. This article focuses on three mechanisms of corporate governance, two of which have been a fertile source for the application of transaction cost economics in corporate law, and all of which are safeguards for equity interests independent of the degree of activity in the market for corporate control. It begins with the role of the board of directors, the principal governance structure for shareholders in diffusely held firms, for which Oliver Williamson provided the key conceptualization. It then extends that analysis to a form of block ownership known as relational investing, in which a large shareholder is more actively involved in firm management than is ordinarily expected of non-management shareholders. Relational investing became of interest to corporate law scholars in the early 1990s when there was no longer an active takeover market providing a backstop governance mechanism to mitigate the agency problem. The article concludes with an examination of the choice of law governing shareholder-manager relations, referred to in the literature as state competition for corporate charters, and how Williamson's framework can be usefully deployed for understanding the success of US corporate law, as the legal regime sets the parameters for all corporate governance mechanisms.

Each of the following three sections sketches first the theory of the corporate governance mechanism from the perspective of transaction cost economics, and then addresses the question whether corporate governance matters by discussing the empirical evidence on whether the mechanism is effective. Other corporate governance institutions could have been selected to illustrate the value of the transaction cost approach to corporate law scholarship. I have chosen for convenience to focus on areas with which I am most familiar, boards of directors and state competition, and one of the more topical issues today, relational investing. In addition to limning Williamson's contribution, the objective is to relate theory and data, to ascertain where we are, 20 years after Williamson's fundamental contribution was first articulated in *Markets and Hierarchies,* and over a decade after the first corporate law applications were explicitly worked out (e.g. Williamson, 1984, 1985).

2. *Boards of Directors*

The Transaction Cost Approach

Transaction cost economics offers the most compelling explanation of American corporate law's approach to the board of directors: the board represents the interests of shareholders and not other constituents.[1] As Williamson explains, this approach is appropriate because shareholders' investment in the firm is more vulnerable than that of other claimants: (i) equity is the residual claimant, the investment that stands at the end of the payout queue, and it is associated with no particular assets (in contrast to secured debt, or a worker with firm specific human capital, for example); (ii) equity alone is a claim with no periodic review or renegotiation right (i.e. there is no maturity or expiration date for stock as there is in debt or labor contracts, which enable bondholders and employees to take their resources and exit the firm if they do not like the firm's renewal offer price); and (iii) equity has no guaranteed interest payment or principal repayment (Williamson, 1984, 1985).

These characteristics make equity investment akin to a transaction-specific asset, which is difficult to protect by simple contract.[2] That is, the open-endedness of the claim makes it difficult to specify investment protection by contract at the time of investment, and as circumstances change, the lack of renegotiation opportunities that accompanies the perpetual life of the instrument prevents addressing unexpected events that adversely affect share value. Corporate charter amendments alter the equity contract midstream, but there is no requirement that management propose amendments as

---

[1] The conventional economic explanation, that allocating control to the residual claimant most efficiently allocates resources (Williamson, 1979), is a complementary explanation.

[2] Although individual shareholders in public corporations may easily sell their shares to terminate their investment in the firm, the appropriate analytical unit is the aggregate shareholders' investment, which underscores the unique characteristics of equity's relationship to the firm (Williamson, 1985, p. 304).

particular events occur or contingencies are realized,[3] and even if there were such a requirement, amendments are equally prey to the contracting problem encountered at the outset of the investment relationship, the impossible task of specifying constraints on a necessarily open-ended delegation of decision rights. Consequently, the corresponding open-endedness of board representation and fiduciary duty law, which can flexibly adapt firm decisions to particular circumstances, is better suited for protecting equity (as opposed to other types of) investments in firms.

Most non-equity investments in firms are not transaction-specific, and thus need no special protection device such as the board of directors. For most workers, with general purpose skills and knowledge, special governance structures are unnecessary because they can quit without 'productive losses to either worker or firm' (Williamson, 1985, p. 302). This is also true of much debt, which is either short term or financing readily redeployable assets that will not lose value if the creditor must repossess them (Williamson, 1985, p. 307). Where a transaction-specific component to the non-equity investment in a particular firm necessitates special protection, other governance structures besides the board of directors are more apt because of the more concrete specification of the claim on the firm.

For example, for transaction-specific debt and labor, equity collateral or contractual covenants restricting managerial actions and collective bargaining agreements requiring arbitration of grievances, respectively, are better tailored mechanisms than board representation as they can pinpoint problems and responses without diminishing the value of the class' claim. The comparison exemplifies what Williamson (1991, p. 79) terms the 'main hypothesis' of transaction cost economics, to 'align transactions which differ in their attributes, with governance structures, which differ in their costs, and competencies, in a discriminating (mainly, transaction cost economizing) way'. For safeguarding transaction-specific investments, general purpose technologies, such as the board of directors, are less effective than special purpose technologies, such as protective covenants or grievance arbitration, and thus more expensive for firms (the inputs charge a higher price for the lower level of protection of their investment). But where special purpose technologies are infeasible, the benefits of general purpose technologies are likely to exceed the costs in comparison to adopting no governance mechanism.

Williamson further notes that having non-shareholder constituencies represented on boards will adversely affect the groups' alternative governance mechanisms and correspondingly increase firms' cost of capital as other firm

[3] In many states, including the most important jurisdictions, shareholders cannot initiate charter amendments. e.g. Del. Code Ann., tit. 8, § 242(b)(1).

participants, including equity owners, adjust their relationships to the changed decision structure (Williamson, 1985, pp. 311–312). Moreover, because the various constituents' interests differ, it will raise decision-making costs (Hansmann, 1988) and, as aggregation results will be indeterminate, it may well produce in management a discretion so great that it ceases to be accountable to any constituency but itself.

Williamson's perspective on the board provides analytical support for long-standing proposals of legal commentators to enhance the role of directors independent of management, referred to as outside directors, such as those with no financial interest in the firm apart from the director retainer fee (e.g. Eisenberg, 1976). Leaving aside the question whether the board should represent the shareholders exclusively, these commentators advance their recommendations of the ideal board composition by maintaining that independent directors are less likely to be 'yes men' to management. For example, Melvin Eisenberg, as reporter to the American Law Institute's (ALI) corporate governance project, sought to implement this view by establishing majority outsider boards as the corporate standard in his draft of corporate governance principles for the ALI (American Law Institute, 1982).

In explaining why the board is a key governance mechanism for shareholders' investment in the firm, Williamson's analysis delimits the argument on representation and defines the board's principal role as a monitoring, rather than operational, function as its purpose is to safeguard the shareholders' investment in the firm (Williamson, 1985, pp. 316–317). This definition of the board's role determines the board's composition. A monitoring function is best achieved by independent (i.e. outside) directors: if inside directors (the firm's managers) could effectively monitor themselves there would be no agency problem.

Moreover, as outsiders are best-suited to monitor management, the board could not fruitfully be active in daily operational decisions, since its members will not have the requisite expertise of internal management. As Williamson notes, insiders can serve a useful role on boards by providing the outside members with 'deeper information than a formal presentation would permit', and enhancing the outsiders' ability to evaluate management's process of decision-making through direct observation in board deliberations, but these are secondary purposes to the board's central monitoring function (Williamson, 1985, p. 317).

While transaction cost economics thus provides a theoretical rationale for proposals such as Eisenberg's mandating outside directors as a mechanism for protecting shareholders' interests in the firm, Eisenberg's ALI draft produced considerable consternation from the business community and corporate law practitioners, who were opposed to an ALI document creating new standards for corporations. The ALI draft was consequently revised, eliminating the requirement of an independent board in favor of its aspirational attainment through voluntarism.[4] Notwithstanding the widespread objections to Eisenberg's mandatory independent board standard, his objective was consistent with corporate governance practice, as there has been a discernible trend of increasing to majority status the representation of outsiders on the boards of public corporations (for trend data see e.g. Hermalin and Weisbach, 1988, p. 593; Chaganti *et al.*, 1985, p. 406; Kesner and Johnson, 1990, p. 327; Klein, 1995).[5] Although Eisenberg maintained that it was necessary to mandate outside directors because shareholders do not effectively 'bargain' with managers for contract terms, the voluntary movement toward independent boards undercuts this contention and is consistent with the transaction cost view of boards as endogenously arising as a shareholder governance mechanism, and the complementary notion that insiders have incentives to provide arrangements that facilitate commitments to not exploit outside equity (Jensen and Meckling, 1976).

A less intrusive policy reform for the ALI would have been to focus on the question whether corporation codes should have default rules concerning board composition rather than Eisenberg's proposed mandates. The reason is that if, on average, shareholders perceive value in boards with all (or a certain number of) outside directors, it would reduce transaction costs if corporation codes provided that boards consist of all (or a minimum number of) outside directors (rather than as they currently require, a minimum number of directors), while permitting firms to opt out of the requirement by explicit charter provision. Such an approach is more consonant with contemporary research that views corporate law as enabling and not mandatory and emphasizes that competition generally results in contracts beneficial to shareholders without their engaging in explicit bargaining with managers (Easterbrook and Fischel, 1989). This is in contrast to Eisenberg's analysis, which does not acknowledge the impact of markets and competing investment opportunities upon managers' incentives to offer corporate structures that protect shareholders' interests.[6]

However, present practice has largely mooted the issue, as majority out-

---

[4] Critics of the ALI draft contended that because there was no evidence that independent directors increase investor returns, mandatory rules of board composition were inappropriate (e.g. MacAvoy *et al.* 1983; Scott, 1983). The research on board composition, much of it undertaken subsequent to the ALI debate, is discussed later.

[5] The encouragement of independent directors by courts, legislatures and stock exchanges (see text and accompanying notes 10–11) may have contributed to this trend.

[6] Even scholars who advocate mandatory rules recognize that in the initial equity contract managers cannot effectively exploit shareholders and emphasize instead potential problems from midstream changes in the corporate contract (Bebchuk, 1989). Although losses from midstream changes, if unanticipated, will not be capitalized in the initial stock sale, shareholders must expressly approve such changes,

sider boards are the norm. Exceptions tend to occur in firms where corporate insiders have controlling equity ownership. Inside ownership can be viewed as an alternative governance structure to outside directors, as it reduces the separation of ownership and control directly. It generates its own problems, however, potential conflicts of interest among shareholders and self-dealing by insiders. Since public shareholders invest knowingly in such firms (insiders' equity interests and board membership are fully disclosed in offering documents and ongoing filings), the cost of not placing outsiders on the board will be borne by the insiders when they issue equity, and there is no compelling need to interfere with such firms' choices.

Some commentators, extending the reasoning of advocates of outside directors, maintain that additional interests, such as workers and the public in general, need representation on the board (Stone, 1975; Nader *et al.* 1976; Weiss, 1981). This view was quite prominent in the 1970s and re-emerged in the 1990s with commentators (e.g. O'Connor, 1991) supporting the efforts of managers to avoid hostile takeovers by factoring considerations other than the offer price into the standard for fiduciary conduct during bid contests. This approach was codified in what are known as 'other constituency' statutes (statutes permitting boards to consider a variety of interests besides those of shareholders, such as employees' interests, when deciding how to respond to a takeover bid).[7] Transaction cost economics offers no analytical support for expanding board representation to non-shareholder groups, and indeed, cautions against such proposals.

In the wake of the trend toward outsider-majority boards, more recent director reform proposals have focused on making the now more numerous outside directors on boards more responsive to shareholders, such as by creating a professional independent director corps from which shareholders, rather than management, select board nominees (Gilson and Kraakman, 1991). A promising alternative to changing the nomination process is increased use of equity compensation (Elson, 1993). Both of these proposals can be rationalized from the standpoint of transaction cost economics in that they create reciprocal transaction-specific investments ('hostages') for directors—reputations and financial interests in the firm—that ensure they will

---

e.g. Del. Code Ann. tit. 8 § 242(b)(1), with the notable exception of poison pills, a takeover defensive tactic discussed below, which the board can adopt on its own if the shareholders have previously authorized issuance of blank preferred stock. While courts permit the adoption of poison pills without shareholder approval, Moran v. Household International, Inc., 500 A.2d 1346 (Del. 1985), they monitor the pills' implementation during takeover contests and overturn them where they are unreasonable (i.e. when maintaining the poison pill will defeat the bid), e.g. City Capital Associates v. Interco, Inc., 551 A.2d 787 (Del. Ch. 1988).

[7] E.g. Ohio Rev. Code. Ann. § 1701.59(E). For an assessment of these statutes, not all of which are limited to board decisions on takeovers, see Romano (1990, pp. 1163–1165, 1993c).

act in the interests of the investors who elect them (*see* Williamson, 1983). Transaction cost economics suggests that the effectiveness of outside directors is a question of fashioning the proper incentives: besides equity ownership, directors with reputational capital at stake (assuming such capital rises and falls with the value of the firm) will be more likely to act in shareholders' interest, and an independent professional director corps whose members are nominated by shareholders may facilitate investments in such reputational capital. Without proper incentives, even a majority of independent directors may not actively monitor and expeditiously replace poorly-performing managers, because of adherence to norms of consensus or other institutional constraints, such as the CEO's greater information and expertise (Lorsch and MacIver, 1989, pp. 84, 88, 93).

Empirical Studies on the Monitoring Role of Independent Directors[8]

The hypothesis of transaction cost economics that there be a monitoring role for the board is consistent with the view of most market participants and regulatory authorities that board composition makes a difference. For example, both of the major stock exchanges, the New York and American Stock Exchanges, require listed companies to have outside directors, and to have corporate audit committees populated by those directors. The market itself views outsiders favorably: there is a positive stock price effect when an outsider is appointed to a company's board, even where outside directors already constitute a board majority (Rosenstein and Wyatt, 1990).[9] In addition, courts look more favorably on defendants in shareholder suits involving defensive tactics to takeovers when outside directors make the decision, and they permit derivative suits to be dismissed by the decision of disinterested directors.[10] Corporation statutes legitimate self-interested transactions if they are approved by non-interested directors.[11] Finally, firms place a disproportionate number of outside directors on board committees that appear to have a managerial monitoring function, such as the audit and compensation committees (Klein, 1995), although the legal rules may be the motivating factor.

---

[8] For an excellent and more comprehensive review of the literature on boards of directors see Lin, 1995.

[9] The Rosenstein and Wyatt study is an example of an event study, which evaluates how stock prices react to the announcement of heretofore unexpected corporate actions or events, such as a takeover or change in a corporation's charter, as evidence of the event's impact on shareholder wealth. For a comprehensive evaluation of the technique and a recent review by one of its creators see respectively, Brown and Warner (1985); and Fama (1991, pp. 1599–1602).

[10] E.g., Grobow v. Perot, 539 A.2d 180, 186 (Del.1988); Unocal v. Mesa Petroleum, 493 A.2d 946, 955 (Del.1985).

[11] E.g. Del. Code Ann., tit, 8, § 144.

Given such practices of courts, legislatures and exchanges, an important question is how well, if at all, outside directors perform a monitoring function? While an assessment of this question is the goal of this section, there is a critical background issue that makes the assessment particularly difficult: how should we determine whether a monitoring board is successfully fulfilling its function? Should, for instance, a monitoring board be expected to enhance performance on an ordinary day-to-day basis, or over some longer horizon period, compared to non-monitoring (insider-dominated) boards, or should we expect its comparative benefit to appear only in times of exigency, acting in a crisis intervention mode, analogous to the understanding of Congress's approach to agency oversight as a fire alarm (crisis intervention in response to constituent complaints) rather than a police patrol (preventative monitoring) approach (McCubbins and Schwartz, 1984)?

One might view these polar alternatives of oversight as 'strong' and 'weak' forms of a monitoring board hypothesis, with the strength of the hypothesis of an independent board's impact on the firm associated with the information the outside directors possess about management's effort and ability. In a world with perfect information, the strong form of the hypothesis of board impact will operate: an independent board would have a continuous effect on performance, reacting immediately to management's slightest failure. This hypothesis predicts a positive correlation between board composition and performance. If we consider two of the key conditions under which the need for governance structures arises—information impactedness and bounded rationality—in conjunction with the relative expertise of outside directors versus inside management regarding firm operations, then the most effective functioning of a monitoring board will occur upon the appearance of significant difficulties in the firm's performance or other extraordinary events. This is the weak form of the monitoring board hypothesis, the crisis intervention mode. Outsiders should be able to recognize and react to gross failures of strategy and performance, as opposed to identifying nuances of differences in the performance of day-to-day operations so as to engage in the development of firm strategy. Under the weak form hypothesis of board impact, we would expect to observe a positive correlation between board composition and performance (as measured by the course of action taken), only in times of distress.

Reality is surely more complicated than this simple dichotomy suggests: in some industries, it may be easier for outsiders to identify problems at early stages of development (perhaps those with readily redeployable assets, i.e. more liquid tangible assets, whose value is easier to calculate), or certain types of outside directors might be better able to spot potential problems (e.g. CEOs, finance or accounting experts, and so forth) than others. Yet to the extent that board performance studies aggregate industries, or outsiders, such differences will not be easily identifiable and only the gross crisis intervention or weak form monitoring impact hypothesis will appear to be significant. Moreover, incremental improvements in performance from a strong form hypothesis of a monitoring board's impact on a day-to-day basis may be too small as a percentage of firm value to pick up unless measured over a very long period. However, the longer the measurement period, the more we must be concerned that any observed performance effects are due to luck or intervening exogenous causes rather than board composition.

Information conditions that vary by industry suggest an alternative to the weak form monitoring hypothesis that predicts a finding of no correlation between board composition and performance in non-exigent times: the appropriate board structure itself may well vary across industries and firms. In industries where agency costs are low (redeployable assets and robust product market competition), outside boards may not be necessary to protect equity interests. This may also be true of firms with concentrated insider stock ownership (which as already mentioned can be seen as an alternative to the governance mechanism of outside directors for diffuse share ownership). Since firms choose their governance structures, as well as their product markets, if they are organized by optimizing agents we should not find any correlation between board composition and performance because, in equilibrium, each firm will have chosen the governance arrangement that maximizes profits.

This third possibility is difficult to distinguish from the weak form of the monitoring hypothesis because the events and outcomes in which we expect to find relationships between board composition and performance under the weak form hypothesis are presumably moments of disequilibrium in which discerning a board composition effect need not refute the optimizing governance choice hypothesis. In this respect, the weak form monitoring hypothesis and optimizing governance choice hypothesis are not competing explanations. If the firms for which the optimal governance structure is an outsider board are those with a higher probability of experiencing the crisis situations in which outside directors' presence is particularly effective, then we might find a cross-sectional board effect surrounding specific events, as some unlucky firms (firms realizing a low-tail probability event) are caught with *ex post* suboptimal governance structures.

Studies of general performance effects. Several studies have examined the correlation between corporate performance (measured by a variety of accounting variables)[12] and board composition (percentage of outside directors, with varying definitions of 'outsider')[13] and the results are, at best, ambiguous. No matter what variable is used to measure performance, virtually all studies find that there is no significant relation between performance and board composition (Byrd and Hickman, 1992; Hermalin and Weisbach, 1991; MacAvoy *et al.*, 1993; Mehran, 1995; Schmidt, 1977; Stobaugh, 1993; Zahra and Stanton, 1988). One study, which used as the definition of outsider non-corporate employees only, found a significant negative relation (Agrawal and Knoeber, 1994).[14]

Two studies have found that insider boards outperform outsider boards on a number of financial ratios (Vance, 1964; Waldo, 1985). These studies are methodologically far less reliable than the other studies for several reasons: (i) many of the ratios for which inside boards had higher values do not measure performance and are of questionable benefit to shareholders without additional information (i.e. ratios measuring sales, cash flow, owners' equity, total investment, employment, plant and equipment, stock book value); (ii) statistical significance tests were not performed; (iii) most of the results are based on comparisons of a small number of firms in specific industries. Particularly given the questionable validity of the performance measures, it is difficult to interpret these data as demonstrating that outside boards are inferior to inside boards as governance devices; indeed because Waldo (1985) found outside boards outperformed inside boards in some of his ratios and in some industry sectors, he saw his evidence as supporting the theory that 'outsider dominated boards . . . perform better' (p. 53). While Vance (1964) believes his data show that inside boards are better performers, reflecting the fact that inside directors have valuable technical

---

[12] Variables used to measure performance include return on equity, return on assets, net earnings, sales growth and Tobin's Q (the ratio of a firm's market value to the replacement cost of its assets; a ratio greater than 1 is taken as an indication of high quality of the firm's management for it means that the market values the firm at an amount greater than the value of its physical assets). One study uses instead the firm's placement on *Fortune* magazine's list of admired firms (Stobaugh, 1993).

[13] While the more sophisticated studies do not include directors with material business relations with the firm in the proportion of outside directors, some count as outside directors everyone who is not an employee of the firm. The studies with the cruder classification system are not distinguished in the discussion, except for instances where the results significantly differ across classification. The literature conventionally uses the terms outsider-dominated and insider-dominated to describe a board with a majority of outside directors and inside directors, respectively, and that convention will be adopted (although sometimes 'dominated' is replaced with the term 'majority'), even though it is not, in my view, an apt expression because 'domination' of a board's decisions is likely to be a complex function of individual personalities and expertise rather than a function of the number of directors of a specific type.

[14] The Agrawal and Knoeber study is thus estimating the effect of a higher proportion of outsiders than is counted in other studies finding no effect with the same performance measure (Byrd and Hickman, 1992; Hermalin and Weisbach, 1991). Whether the statistical significance of this study would hold up with the more appropriate definition of an outsider that excludes affiliated directors is, of course, unknown; there are no other important differences in results that vary with the definition of outsider used.

expertise to aid the firm's decision-making, he concludes his ratio analysis with the more limited statement that 'there is no quantitative evidence supporting the claim that outside boards of directors are superior in performance to inside directors' (p. 45), a claim that is not at odds with the rest of the literature.

One study did find a significant positive correlation when the relation between board composition and performance was examined over time: there was a lagged, although not a contemporaneous, correlation (Baysinger and Butler, 1985a). Measuring performance as return on equity over the period 1970–1980, Baysinger and Butler found that the firms that began the 10-year interval with a higher proportion of outside directors were the better performers at the end of the period. They further found that there was no effect on performance from increasing the proportion of outsiders over the period, and that differences in performance at the start of the period were unrelated to subsequent differences in board composition. They were, however, unable to find any effect when they used a market measure for performance, changes in stock price plus dividends, and such a measure is generally preferred because accounting data are based on historical cost and do not measure what matters to investors, expected future cash flows. This is consistent with another study, by Rechner and Dalton (1986), which examined the effect of board composition on performance measured by changes in stock prices over a two-year period, 1981–1982, and found no correlation between board composition and performance. However, Schellinger *et al.* (1989) found a positive correlation between board composition and stock return adjusted for firm-risk (the standard deviation of return) for the year 1986. But because there is also a positive correlation between board composition and the firm's beta or market risk (the correlation between changes in the stock return and changes in the return on the market), their finding cannot be interpreted as clear evidence of higher performance with independent boards.

The bulk of the results of the studies, insignificant associations between board composition and firm performance, have been interpreted by the study authors in a number of ways, all of which have some threshold plausibility: (i) board composition, on average, does not affect performance; (ii) there is an optimal mix on boards of outsiders and insiders because both types of directors add value to the firm and, accordingly, we should not expect to find a cross-sectional correlation between board composition and performance in equilibrium (Hermalin and Weisbach (1991) and Baysinger and Butler (1985a) emphasize this conclusion); (iii) there is an endogeneity problem undermining the usefulness of the empirical inquiry. The third interpretation is what I termed the optimizing governance choice hypothesis and contrasted with the two monitoring hypotheses. If firms adjust their governance structures to reduce agency costs to a minimum level that is roughly the same across firms and if it is this uniform residual agency cost that affects performance, then variation in performance will be uncorrelated with actions taken to mitigate agency problems, such as board composition (Hermalin and Weisbach, 1991, p. 111). A regression of performance on board composition will therefore not uncover any effect even though an outsider-majority board reduces agency costs.

Agrawal and Knoeber (1994), whose sophisticated econometric study's result is at odds with both monitoring hypotheses and the optimizing governance choice hypothesis that they were testing, interpret their finding of a negative correlation as evidence that firms have not optimized on their choices of board structure (compared to choices of other governance mechanisms), and instead use more outsiders than are appropriate.[15] They sought to account for the endogeneity problem by estimating simultaneously the effect of choice of governance structures on performance and performance on governance structure. They found the direction of effect was one-way: only board composition had a significant effect on performance.[16]

Agrawal and Knoeber (1994) have an interesting result but I am hesitant to put great weight on their finding of sub-optimizing behavior, which is at odds with the rest of the literature. They have only one year of data compared to the five years of data in the most comparable study, by Hermalin and Weisbach (1991), that found no correlation. Both studies use the same performance measure and control for multiple governance structures, although only Agrawal and Knoeber control for simultaneity. Sample timing differences may contribute importantly to the divergent results, analogous to the tests of asset pricing models in the finance literature, in which many of the discovered pricing anomalies turn out to have strong temporal components. For example, the small firm effect was positive in

---

[15] Agrawal and Knoeber speculate that this finding may be a function of political pressures to choose outsiders without business expertise, such as environmentalists or consumer representatives, and either the directors themselves, or the underlying political pressures leading to their selection, adversely affect performance (p. 27). Consistent with this explanation is a finding by Geddes (1995) that regulated firms—utility companies—have more outsiders on their boards than non-regulated firms, which he attributes to regulators' political pressure. Another potential pressure source is the incentive to have outsider dominated boards created by the legal rules already mentioned. Such an explanation is, however, at conflict with the notion that states generally produce legal rules that benefit investors, discussed in Section 4.

[16] Agrawal and Knoeber reject, as the explanation of their finding of a negative correlation between board composition and performance, the explanation that firms increase the number of outside directors when performance is poor to enhance the board's monitoring function when most needed, because the performance variable is not significant in the regression explaining board composition (p. 24). But it should be noted that Hermalin and Weisbach (1988) find that firms do significantly increase the number of outside directors after poor performance.

the 1970s and negative in the 1980s (Malkiel, 1990, p. 194; Ibbotson Associates, 1992, pp. 109–110), the weekend effect was significant before 1973 and insignificant thereafter (French, 1980), and so forth. Under such circumstances, we must be cautious in drawing general conclusions concerning behavior.

There is a further gloss on the third interpretation that I deem most plausible: the data are not determinative of whether board composition matters, because the weak form of the monitoring hypothesis does not lead us to expect to find a general relation between board composition and performance. These data are probative only for the strong form of the hypothesis. The test of weak form monitoring is whether independent boards perform oversight functions in crisis-type situations, and it is to studies of boards and performance in the context of particular events that we must turn to determine whether board composition matters.

Studies of specific events.   Several researchers have sought to evaluate the impact of board composition in specific situations: poor performance, takeover bids and litigation. These are, in fact, tests of the weak form monitoring hypothesis. The results regarding the efficacy of outside directors are not uniform, but it is possible to discern a pattern supporting the weak form of the monitoring board thesis: outsider boards are more likely than insider boards to intervene in crisis situations, to the shareholders' benefit.

Two studies indicate that board composition matters when it comes to poor performance: majority-outsider boards are significantly more likely to fire a CEO given poor firm performance (Weisbach, 1988), and firms with majority-outsider boards are less likely to go bankrupt (Daily and Dalton, 1994). A third study found no correlation between board composition and bankruptcy filings in the retailing industry (Chaganti *et al.*, 1985). The bankruptcy studies are, however, imprecise tests of the weak form hypothesis for the accuracy of the test depends on whether a firm's decline into bankruptcy is gradual or discontinuous. In addition, there is a strategic component in the decision to file for bankruptcy which complicates direct statistical inferences regarding performance and board composition. A better test would examine what outside boards do when confronted with the prospect of bankruptcy: are they more or less likely to fire management, negotiate with creditors to avoid chapter 11, and so forth, compared to inside boards.[17]

Consistent with Weisbach's finding that after poor performance CEO

[17] We know that management turnover increases with bankruptcy, as does director turnover, although the percentage of outsiders on the board does not change significantly (Gilson, 1990), but we do not know whether the changes are affected by the board's composition at the bankruptcy filing.

resignations are more likely with an outsider board, Kini *et al.* (1995) find that CEO turnover following a takeover, when the target's pre-bid performance is poor, is concentrated in target firms that had insider-majority boards. Moreover, Morck *et al.* (1989) find that top management turnover is internally precipitated (i.e. accomplished by board action) when a company is doing poorly relative to its industry, whereas if the industry as a whole is doing poorly, management change is accomplished by hostile takeover and not by board action. While they do not control for board composition, Morck *et al.* (1989) attribute the result to outside directors' willingness to take action only when they can clearly ascribe poor performance to the incumbent management (which is revealed by poor relative performance). Warner *et al.* (1988) similarly find that there is a higher forced turnover in CEOs, not counting control changes, after poor stock performance, but they do not examine board composition, and they therefore note that their finding could as likely be due to monitoring by the board as by other managers or large shareholders. Taken together, these studies provide solid support for the weak form of the monitoring board hypothesis: outside directors will fire top management when confronted with poor performance. They also suggest that boards of directors and takeovers, as we would intuit, are alternative corporate governance devices (although Agrawal and Knoeber's simultaneous regression model failed to pick up such an effect).

Additional support for the weak form hypothesis of outside director impact can be gleaned from studies focusing on takeover activity. Examining the relation between board composition and the returns to takeover bidders, Byrd and Hickman (1992) find that bidders with outsider-dominated boards have significantly higher (less negative) abnormal stock returns on the announcement of the bid than do bidders with insider-dominated boards. Moreover, the abnormal returns associated with the second bids of the three multiple bidders that shifted from non-independent to independent boards between their two bids reversed sign compared to the first bids and became positive (p. 217). In contrast, the one multiple bidder whose board composition went from independent to non-independent, experienced negative returns on both bids (p. 218). While the numbers of firms with multiple bids are too small to be useful for statistical comparisons, these results are suggestive of a beneficial impact of outside directors on management. In addition, Lee *et al.* (1992) find higher positive abnormal returns to shareholders in management-led leveraged buyouts when outsiders are a majority on the board. The studies of acquirer behavior are consistent with the view that monitoring boards are important in the extraordinary (making a bid) as opposed to ordinary (day-to-day operations) decisions of the firm.

The impact of outside directors on the decisions of takeover targets is less clear cut. One study finds that board composition does not affect the likelihood of a takeover or the size of the premium (Shivdasani, 1993). But another finds that targets with a majority of outside directors experience significantly higher initial premiums, as well as premium revisions during the bid (Cotter *et al.*, 1996). This would appear to provide support for commentators who view managerial resistance as a mechanism for raising the premium price and thus as beneficial for shareholders (e.g. Carney,1983), but the support is limited because the study also finds that resistance and the success of the bid are not related to board composition.[18] It is, however, consistent with the weak form monitoring hypothesis: given management's decision to resist a takeover, outsider-dominated boards appear to be better able to channel the resistance into a favorable outcome for the shareholders than insider boards.

Studies of the impact of board composition on specific defensive tactics also present an ambiguous picture of the performance of outside directors of target firms in takeovers. Most commentators consider defensive tactics detrimental to shareholders because they increase bidders' costs and thus make takeovers less likely (e.g. Easterbrook and Fischel, 1981; Gilson, 1981). In this view, the presence of outside directors should reduce the probability of the board's adoption of such tactics. Defensive tactics, however, can benefit shareholders, if their result is to increase premiums rather than to defeat bids, and if shareholders are willing to trade off the possible receipt of a higher premium for the decreased likelihood of a bid occurring. This makes unclear the expected relation between board composition and defensive tactics.

Several studies have investigated the relation between board composition and the use of a poison pill strategy, which is a rights plan triggered on a hostile bid that enables target shareholders to acquire senior securities in the target or to purchase bidder shares at a discount. The board typically can redeem the rights for a nominal sum at its discretion before the hostile bidder obtains a specified block of stock, and this feature has often led to the pill's use as an auctioneering device, that management redeems, voluntarily or by court order, after the bidder raises its offering price. The studies find that there is no correlation between adoption of a poison pill and board composition (Mallette and Fowler, 1992; Davis, 1991), but the stock price effect

---

[18] The study further investigated whether the outsiders' financial incentives—equity ownership or reputational capital, proxied by the number of additional directorships held—had any effect on the process. They did not. This result cautions against putting too much faith in proposals to improve board performance by promoting equity-based directoral compensation or a professional director corps.

of a pill adoption is positive if a majority of the board is independent and negative if insiders are a majority (Brickley *et al.*, 1994). These findings can be viewed as consistent with the weak form monitoring hypothesis: the positive stock price effect of pills adopted by majority-outsider boards suggests that the market believes that outside directors effectively manage the takeover process so that pills are used to raise premiums rather than to kill deals.

Researchers have also studied the effect of board composition on the adoption of golden parachutes, lucrative management severance contracts activated by a control change, and on the payment of greenmail, repurchases of a hostile bidder's shares at a premium. Boards with a majority of outsiders are more likely to adopt golden parachutes (Cochran *et al.*, 1985), and less likely to pay greenmail (Kosnik, 1987). Whether we should interpret these findings as evidence of the efficacy of the monitoring board is not self-evident because the impact on shareholder welfare of these two defenses is disputed: some scholars contend that greenmail and golden parachutes benefit shareholders because they actually encourage bids (Shleifer and Vishny, 1986b; Macey and McChesney, 1985; Baron, 1983) while other scholars contend that these devices simply entrench management (Gordon and Kornhauser, 1986; Baron, 1983).

Event studies can arbitrate the debate over golden parachutes and greenmail, although there is considerable noise in these studies because the adoption of a defensive tactic may provide new information concerning the firm's likelihood of becoming a target. The event studies find negative price effects upon greenmail payments (Mikkelson and Ruback, 1991)[19] and positive effects upon parachute adoptions (Larckner and Lambert, 1985). These stock price effects are consistent with interpreting the board composition studies as supporting the monitoring hypothesis, for they imply that independent boards are associated with opting for value-increasing (golden parachutes), rather than value-decreasing (greenmail), defenses.[20]

Finally, researchers have also investigated the impact of board composition on the likelihood of shareholder litigation. The idea is that if outside directors are effective monitors, firms with majority-outsider boards should be less likely to be sued for misconduct (since their managers will be less likely to have engaged in misconduct) than firms with majority-insider boards. The data in these studies blur the distinction between the strong

---

[19] If returns are calculated from the time of the greenmailer's initial stock purchase through the repurchase, they are on net positive (the negative effect of the repurchase is offset by a larger positive impact of the announcement of the initial block purchase, which signals the possibility of a takeover premium).

[20] It is also possible that managers are more likely to seek golden parachutes when there is an outsider board, since a decision by an independent board is more likely to immunize a defensive tactic from court reversal, see text and accompanying note 10.

and weak forms of the monitoring hypothesis, as some lawsuits could be due to a firm gradually slipping into financial difficulty, and avoidance of such suits would require outsiders to affect performance on a continuous basis. The failure to observe a board effect under such circumstances would not contradict the weak form of the hypothesis.

Some further caveats are necessary before interpreting these studies. If, as some commentators suggest, much of shareholder litigation is frivolous (Fischel and Bradley, 1986; Romano, 1991), the presence of a lawsuit will not be an indicator of misconduct. Then we would not expect to find any correlation between board composition and lawsuit filings, unless one type of board is more likely to settle a frivolous claim than the other, hence encouraging more such filings. Such a correlation would be spurious evidence of monitoring. Moreover, since the real issue is whether outside boards prevent misconduct, we should be more concerned about the disposition, rather than the initiation, of lawsuits.

The litigation studies' findings on board oversight are inconclusive. One study finds board composition has no effect on whether a firm is sued (Romano, 1991) whereas another study finds sued firms have significantly fewer outside directors (Kesner and Johnson, 1990).[21] Neither study finds any relation between lawsuit disposition and board composition, and this makes unclear the finding of a relationship between board composition and filings. In fact, because the majority of suits in their study were dismissed and board composition had no impact on disposition, Kesner and Johnson conclude that majority-outsider boards are not more beneficial for shareholders than insider boards, despite their finding of a relation between board composition and lawsuit filing (Kesner and Johnson, 1990, p. 334).[22]

The findings of the two shareholder suit studies are not necessarily inconsistent because the samples are not comparable. Kesner and Johnson's sample excludes cases that were settled whereas Romano's does not. As is true of most civil litigation, the vast majority of shareholder suits settle (Romano, 1991). Adjudicated cases are therefore a very special sample of lawsuits; in

---

[21] Because Kesner and Johnson's sample of cases ends in 1986 (as does Romano's sample), the difference between inside and outside boards' being sued cannot be attributed to the impact of Delaware's limited liability statute, which protects outsiders from monetary liability for breach of the duty of care and was prospective legislation enacted in 1986.

[22] A third study focusing on federal securities class actions for material misstatements in initial public offerings (IPOs) filed from 1975 to 1986 found that sued firms had fewer outside directors at the time of the IPO than did firms that were not subject to a lawsuit (Bohn and Choi, 1995). The study does not, however, report whether there was a difference in board composition by lawsuit disposition. Moreover, because Bohn and Choi did not create their paired sample by matching IPO dates across the samples, the finding may be unreliable. If IPO firms are subject to similar influences on board composition as publicly-traded firms experience, then that composition has changed over time and the difference across the samples may simply reflect the time trend.

particular, plaintiffs have extremely low success rates in adjudicated share-holder suits (Romano, 1991). The difference in findings across the two stud-ies may well be due to this sample difference,[23] although there is no significant difference in board composition across settled and dismissed law-suit firms in Romano's sample.

On subdividing the sample by type of lawsuit, Romano found that firms sued for breach of the duty of loyalty (self-dealing claims) had sig-nificantly fewer outside directors at the initiation of the lawsuit, which is consistent with Kesner and Johnson's more general finding (Romano, 1990). This does not, however, unambiguously support the monitoring thesis. These firms also had significantly higher insider stock ownership. Because outsider representation on the board is negatively correlated with insider stock ownership (Romano, 1991, p. 81), which factor is driving the result cannot be ascertained. It seems more likely that the crucial variable is inside ownership, as opportunities for self-dealing increase as control increases, and inside ownership is significantly lower in the firms sued for breach of the duty of care (negligence claims), while board composition does not differ. This conjecture is consistent with the finding of Morck *et al.* (1988a) that the relation between performance and block ownership is non-monotonic, rising for blocks up to 5% and falling thereafter.

One approach to avoid the complication that lawsuit filings may not be a true measure of managerial misconduct is to study the relation of board composition to known acts of misconduct. Kesner *et al.* (1986) examined whether board composition affects the commission of illegal acts (antitrust violations). Their study is a test of the weak form monitoring thesis; the question they asked is not whether outside directors have a positive effect on firm performance but whether they prevent, or minimize the occurrence of negative events. Their idea was that outsiders may not know enough about a firm's business to be able to monitor the performance of day-to-day operations but outsiders would be able to monitor management for illegal activities (p. 792). They found no support for the proposition: there was no relation between board composition and illegal activity. Moreover, firms did not change their board composition in response to the lawsuits. They concluded that shareholders are no better served by outside directors than by insiders.

---

[23] For example, if defendants are more likely to settle than litigate nuisance suits (because the attor-neys' settlement fee demand is less than the expense of a trial), a sample that includes settled cases will not be able to detect a monitoring effect. Similarly, if plaintiffs do not pursue settlements against insider-dominated boards because such boards are less likely to obtain dismissal of a derivative suit under the arcane corporate law rules of the demand requirement, then we would expect to find a correlation between board composition and lawsuit filing in a sample excluding settlements, whether or not there is a monitoring effect.

A caveat is in order, however. Kesner *et al.* do not subdivide their sample into conduct that was clearly illegal (such as explicit price-fixing cases) and conduct that the firms might not have known was illegal until adjudicated (such as illegal merger cases). They also did not investigate whether the firms with independent boards were more likely to take action to prevent a repeat of the misconduct (i.e. whether they fired top management). It is therefore difficult to gauge whether this study is an effective test of the weak form of the monitoring hypothesis. Moreover, it is arguable that shareholders might want boards to minimize the probability of management's being detected for, rather than the probability of its committing, an antitrust violation (Posner, 1992, pp. 421–423); if this is the case, then the correlation of detected violations and board composition will not necessarily indicate a board's monitoring failure.

Although the interaction between board composition and specific events is at times ambiguous, the data are most consistent with a monitoring interpretation, that outsider boards take greater charge in extraordinary event or crisis situations and enhance share value; a positive correlation between board composition and value-increasing activities in extraordinary times persists across studies. It is appropriate, however, to close this discussion on a note of caution. It is not known if the benefits identified in the studies are due to board composition or to some other omitted correlated variable. The observed effect of board composition could be spurious because of the endogeneity of governance structures, which are a function of the quality of management itself. If high quality managers are more likely to place outsiders on boards than poor quality managers (who do not want to be monitored), a finding that shareholders are better served by outsider-dominated boards is simply proxying for the better management of those firms.

Devising an operational test of this alternative to the weak form hypothesis to explain the empirical results of specific event studies is difficult. Byrd and Hickman (1992) examined the Tobin's Q-ratios of the acquirers in their sample, contending that it is a proxy for management quality, and found no significant difference between the abnormal returns of acquisition announcements and Q-ratios (pp. 218–219). They therefore reject the managerial quality hypothesis in favor of the board monitoring hypothesis, as the better explanation of their data. It is difficult, however, to generalize from their limited exploration that the alternative management quality hypothesis has no merit. Characterizing the bulk of the data as supporting the weak form of the monitoring hypothesis is, however, in my opinion, the most compelling reading. One could, of course, object that the weak form hypothesis is not robust support for majority-outsider boards from a public policy perspective;

for instance, crisis intervention that fires the CEO only after significant underperformance of competitors may be a far more conservative strategy than shareholders would wish their boards to follow.[24] But this criticism does not undercut fully the value of independent directors. For instance, there is no evidence that investors are losing something in ordinary governance by having outsiders instead of insiders on board who will prove useful in the event of a crisis. Rather, it only further highlights the point mentioned earlier, that fashioning adequate incentives for outside directors to do their job is at the heart of corporate governance.

3. Relational Investing

If the board of directors fails to monitor management effectively and firm performance falters, a takeover bidder can offer to acquire the firm at a premium, and upon attaining control, recover its costs by replacing management and improving performance (Manne, 1965). With the collapse of the takeover market at the end of the 1980s, corporate governance commentators cast about for mechanisms to replace takeovers as managerial disciplining devices, and focused on blockholders. Block ownership of equity is considered an alternative governance mechanism to takeovers as a means of disciplining managers, as the concentration of shares, even in a less than controlling block, should produce a cost-benefit calculation that active monitoring by the investor will be worthwhile.

Commentators' interest in blockholders was fanned by the governance models of Germany and Japan, where banks or other corporations play a significant role in corporate governance, through voting proxies and cross-holdings of stock. Because there are restrictions on banks' stock ownership and the largest shareholders in US firms are institutional investors, in particular, pension funds, the German and Japanese models could not be directly adopted. The foreign blockholder structures were translated into the US context as proposals to encourage pension funds and other money managers to engage in 'relational investing', by which is meant an equity blockholder who is committed to holding its shares as a 'patient' or 'long-term' investor in the firm and thus plays a role in actively monitoring management (Dobrzynski, 1993). This translation is seen to build on the past practices of some public pension funds, which have been active in introducing shareholder proposals, and is not seen as a replacement for other solutions, such as repealing the restrictions on banks (Roe, 1994).

---

[24] I thank Henry Hansmann for raising this point. For a case study of a board firing the CEO of a poorly performing firm only after sustained pressure by shareholders see Smith (1996a).

Toward a Theory of Relational Investing

Relational investors are characterized, then, as taking on a more active, interventionist role in firm decision-making than simply electing the board of directors or intervening in crisis situations. Ayres and Cramton (1994) view relational investing as a substitute for effective independent boards (pp. 1062–1063), as well as for takeovers, and Gordon and Pound (1993) consider as essential to such investments that the holder assume a seat on the board (p. 32). The premise of many advocates of relational investing is that takeover bidders, money managers, or the market as a whole, or all three, have a 'short-term' or myopic approach to valuing equity investments, which leads to poor performance, as it forces managers to refrain from making necessary capital expenditures with long-term payoffs (Dobrzynski, 1993). In their view, a relational investor will prevent such perverse managerial behavior because, as 'patient' capital, his investment horizon differs.

This translation of relational investing into the US context is, however, questionable. As others have depicted, the multiple relationships creating the web of equity cross-holdings across Japanese firms are used to protect transaction-specific asset investments in supply relations (Kester, 1991; Gilson and Roe, 1993).[25] Such a purpose, facilitating credible commitments of interfirm business relationships, has little to do with relational investing viewed as a means to protect equity investments from expropriation by management, the US translation. Pension funds, for example, do not have additional business relations with the firms in which they invest; their equity investments come first, and are the end, not a means by which other capital investments are protected. Thus, to the extent the success of these foreign corporate governance arrangements depends on synergies derived from blockholders' multiple relationships with firms, a different rationale must be devised for the adaptation. If relational investing is to make sense in a US corporate governance context, we must ask when, if ever, would it make sense for an equity investor to assume an active role in firm management, or manager monitoring, rather than leave that role to the directors it elects?

One response is that a large holding may exhibit transaction-specificity on

---

[25] In Germany's system of universal banking, German banks have extensive credit relations with the firms over which they exercise voting control, and hence their equity relationship can similarly be understood as a means of protecting lending investments. There are, however, other explanations of these governance arrangements. Management entrenchment against takeovers and the effect of government financial regulation constraining capital markets are additional explanations of the Japanese system (Morck and Nakamura, 1995, pp. 489–491). The economic historians Tilly (1966) and Gerschenkron (1962) locate the source of the German universal bank system in the backwardness of industrial technological development as well as in avoidance of regulatory restrictions on economic development.

the individual shareholder level, either because the investor develops a special relationship with management such that it comes to value the shares as superior to other investment alternatives (Baysinger and Butler, 1985b), or because the capital market cannot absorb the sale of a large block without a price effect, given the potential signalling feature of a sale (purchasers are likely to believe that a blockholder is selling on inside information of prospective poor performance).[26] The vulnerability of equity in the aggregate to exploitation by management is therefore potentially magnified for block investors. As a result, greater protection than an independent monitoring board might be called for to induce their investment, such as the investor's direct appointment to the board or charter amendments limiting control changes and thereby guaranteeing the continuance of special relationships (Baysinger and Butler, 1985b).

Why would a firm be willing to pay to induce block ownership by relational investors? There are two possible benefits from block ownership emphasized in the literature, (i) insulating management from takeovers and other market pressures; and (ii) better monitoring of management by the blockholder (Ayres and Cramton, 1994). The first benefit is only a benefit if one believes that takeovers are detrimental to shareholders, and it is largely grounded in the view that the market is myopic. The second benefit is often introduced as necessarily related to the first: to the extent that takeovers are seen as overly excessive discipliners of management, the relational investor is viewed as engaging in a qualitatively different form of monitoring, in which management is properly insulated from takeover pressures (Ayres and Crampton, 1994). The first postulated benefit, and the second to the extent that it relies on the market myopia analysis of the first, are, in my judgment, weak reeds on which to recommend relational investing as a governance structure that benefits public investors. This is because the empirical research decisively shows that takeovers benefit shareholders (Romano, 1992) and there is scant empirical evidence that capital markets (or takeover bidders or institutional investors) are myopic.

For example, institutional investors in particular, and the market in general, positively value research and development (R&D) and other capital

---

[26] The occurrence of price pressure upon block sales is, in fact, disputed, and the data suggest any effect is small (Scholes, 1972; Holthausen *et al.*, 1987; Mikkelson and Partch, 1985; Kraus and Stoll, 1972; Dann *et al.*, 1977; Chan and Lakonishok, 1993). The best approach to the controversy may well be agnosticism until more research is undertaken (Ross *et al.*, 1993, p. 385). But if the market views a relational investor as an insider, there could be a price effect on the investor's sale even if the demand curve for stock is horizontal because of information effects. There is, however, a question whether the market will know that a relational investor is selling in time to react and depress the block's sale price, and thus render blocks illiquid to their holders *ex ante*. Reporting requirements are directed primarily at insiders, not outside investors holding less than 10%, and even these requirements do not result in disclosure simultaneous with a sale.

expenditures that have a long-term investment horizon (Chan *et al.*, 1990; McConnell and Muscarella, 1985; SEC Office of Chief Economist, 1985). In addition, firms that free themselves of takeovers with anti-takeover defenses thereafter decrease R&D expenditures (Meulbroek *et al.*, 1990). Finally, takeover targets are in industries with low levels of R&D activities, and there is no significant difference in R&D growth or intensity between acquiring and acquired firms, and between firms involved in acquisitions and those that are not (Hall, 1990, 1988; Smith, 1990). Thus, the first purported benefit, protecting management from takeovers because of market myopia, would appear to be a non-starter from the shareholders' perspective. This means that an analysis of relational investing must develop the second benefit, improved monitoring, if it is to be persuasive, and untie that benefit from the first one, management insulation from takeovers.

It is not difficult to distinguish a monitoring benefit from an entrenchment benefit. To the extent the blockholder does not invest in the firm because of altruism toward management (for instance, the manager is not a relative), or in exchange for side payments from incumbent management, it is most plausible to assume, in the absence of contractual restrictions, that the blockholder will be as willing to replace a poor manager as a hostile bidder should performance falter, and his connection to the firm should enable him to identify more quickly when management should be changed than could an outsider searching for profitable takeover targets. The blockholder may also facilitate a control change in these circumstances by mitigating the free rider problem of small shareholders in responding to a bid, since he is aware that his shares' tender is pivotal for the bid's success (Ayres and Cramton, 1994). However, although the monitoring and entrenchment benefits can be distinguished, there is no obvious reason to assume that it is cheaper for a blockholder to assume personal representation on the board than to select capable outside directors to safeguard its investment. Besides the opportunity cost of the investor's time, there are additional costs of direct board representation, such as coming under the federal insider trading rules and state fiduciary duty law, not to mention the costs of holding a large block itself, the loss of portfolio diversification (Bainbridge, 1995; Coffee, 1991; Fisch, 1994).[27]

Ayres and Cramton provide one possible justification: a relational investor may have access to information about the firm's circumstances that makes it a better monitor than any outside director whose information is obtained

---

[27] Fisch contends that to the extent money managers are evaluated by relative, as opposed to absolute, performance measures, private gains not shared by other shareholders will be necessary to induce such institutional investors to make expenditures on monitoring and engage in the other activities expected of relational investing. For specific examples of such private gains going to large shareholders who appear to fit the relational investing model, see Rock (1994).

only from its position on the board.[28] This situation is most likely to arise when the relational investor has multiple relations with the firm that provide independent information sources about the firm's business (i.e. it is a creditor or supplier in addition to equity owner), as in the Japanese corporate group or German banking context. But it does not apply to the institutional investors commentators have in mind to fulfil the relational investing role in the USA, public pension funds and other money managers.[29] Thus, to the extent Ayres and Cramton's analysis is correct, the realization of monitoring benefits from relational investing will be problematic in the US context.

It should also be noted that this justification of relational investing (information advantages from multiple relations with the firm) is a scenario in which there are serious potential conflicts of interest between the relational investor and other shareholders. This is because when a shareholder has other relationships with a firm, gains from a non-equity interest could offset stock losses from, for instance, the investor's supporting a policy entrenching incompetent managers (for examples see Rock). The benefits of relational investing to the firm of improved monitoring are likely to be integrally related to, and thus must be traded off against, the costs of increased conflict of interest opportunities.

Using the insight of transaction cost economics, the need to match transactions and governance structures, we can provide an alternative scenario for when relational investors might be more capable directors than their designees, that is less problematic than Ayres and Cramton's model in that

---

[28] Ayres and Cramton (1994) bolster their comparative advantage at monitoring explanation with the contention that relational investors are better able than takeover bidders to police moral hazard problems, but this is speculation. They develop this thesis by contending that takeovers serve to eliminate adverse selection but not moral hazard problems. This is a distinction that does not hold up well under scrutiny. Putting aside the many theories of takeovers unrelated to mismanagement rationales (see Romano, 1992), the manager disciplining theories of takeovers include both adverse selection—replacement of inefficient or incompetent managers—explanations (Manne, 1965) and moral hazard explanations—Michael Jensen's free cash flow theory of takeovers (Jensen, 1988). There is substantial empirical evidence supporting both of these explanations (Romano, 1992, pp. 129–132). Two studies have attempted to test which version, inefficient managers or free cash flow, better explains takeovers in the petroleum industry and both find the data provide greater support for the moral hazard explanation (Griffin and Wiggins, 1992; Baltagi and Griffin, 1989), a finding inconsistent with Ayres and Cramton's comparative advantage story. However, it must be acknowledged that these are tests of perhaps the best case for the free cash flow theory, since Jensen developed his explanation of takeovers with the petroleum industry in mind.

[29] There is a variant of the problem of conflicting interests from multiple relationships when the relational investor is a public pension fund: the managers of such funds are often subject to political pressure, which may lead to their endorsement of firm policies, such as fostering in-state employment, that are not in the interests of the other shareholders (Romano, 1993b). But such a conflict does not put the pension fund manager in a position to have independent knowledge about the firm's business that would facilitate its monitoring of management. This point is also valid for the potential multiple relationships between a mutual fund and a firm in which it owns stock: the fund could earn fees from managing a firm's pension fund but such a role would not provide any special insight into the firm's operations.

it mitigates the conflict of interest problem, but that is also more limited in scope, because it applies only to a specific subset of firms. The relevant firms are those with (i) the most non-redeployable assets, that is, firms with a substantial amount of intangible assets or tangible assets that are highly specialized to the business; and (ii) the most uncertain cash flows from their assets, that is, new firms whose ability to develop the value of assets is largely unknown, or firms in industries that have particularly volatile customer demand or technological needs.

For such firms, it is at least arguable that not only is equity financing preferable to debt (Williamson, 1988), but concentrated equity is preferable to diffuse ownership, because there is a greater need to ensure timely access to information and immediate ability to control management since the equity investment can be squandered without ready market detection.[30] The relational investor's own position on the board and control over a sizeable number of votes could facilitate a more timely response than would be the case with an outside board mediating the investor's access to the relevant inside information. In this regard, the outside shareholder's personal representation on the board is an even more intrusive governance structure than the independent director, of the sort reserved for the more complicated investment context (cf. Williamson, 1991, p. 84). It should be noted that the conflict of interest problem across shareholders is extremely limited in this setting: when side payments can be paid in relation to an equity holding only (because there are no multiple relations between the firm and relational investor), they can be more readily policed by the corporate law rule that prohibits payment of non pro rata dividends.

To sum up, the transaction cost gloss on relational investing suggests that if this construct has any corporate governance benefits, it will be as a governance device tailored for a small subset of firms. There are two important implications: not all firms will need blockholders, and more important, few large shareholders will need, or seek to be, relational investors. The blockholder's function depends on whether the firm's assets require a more active role—relational investing—beyond the ordinary blockholder's activities of electing directors and becoming more active in the firm's affairs in a time of crisis. In this respect, relational investing is a strong form of shareholder

---

[30] This thesis can be contrasted with Zeckhauser and Pound's contention that large shareholders can only monitor firms with low asset-specificity, where information about the firm is transparent (pp. 151–152). If information about a firm is transparent, then the market can do the monitoring work itself with no special need for large shareholders. Zeckhauser and Pound, in fact, acknowledge this critical difficulty with their thesis as they state in a footnote that 'a more refined hypothesis might suggest that some firms would be so transparent that they can be monitored even by dispersed shareholders, and that large shareholders play their most significant role with relatively, but not fully, transparent firms' (pp. 178–179).

monitoring, in contrast to the passive blockholder's crisis intervention mode of investment, which is a weak form of monitoring. Using the insight of transaction cost economics, we expect blockholders to engage in relational investing (i.e. to be strong form active monitors) only in specified instances. Namely, there should be a correlation between the non-redeployability of firm assets and the uncertainty of future cash flows and the existence of active, as opposed to passive, block investors.[31] From this perspective, relational investing—the large shareholder who is an active monitor—should be positioned on the continuum of governance structures ranging from 100% diffuse ownership with independent boards to 100% equity concentration through a takeover.[32]

Is there Empirical Support for a Transaction Cost View of Relational Investing?

Some real-world arrangements approximate the transaction cost approach to relational investing that has been advanced here. The paradigmatic example is the venture capital firm. Venture capital firms hold large equity positions in the entrepreneurial ventures they finance and are active in monitoring the business through positions on the firm's board of directors (Sahlman, 1990). The intensity of the activity, as measured by the number of board positions venture capital firms hold, increases around the time when there is CEO turnover, a time when the need for oversight is presumably greater (Lerner, 1995). As venture capital finances start-up firms, the uncertainty regarding future cash flows is quite large. More important, venture capital firms specialize their investments in particular industries, computers, electronics and communications (Barry *et al.*, 1990, pp. 456–457), which are high technology industries where assets tend to be highly firm-specific and hard to value or collateralize, particularly in the early, development stages of the business. These organizations' investments correspond precisely to the transaction cost explanation of relational investing. However, because the financing is done in stages (Sahlman, 1990), the arrangement provides the venture capital firm

---

[31] Gordon (1994) seeks to redefine relational investing by financial institutions as active choice of the board rather than active monitoring, given their unlikely relative expertise in business, as opposed to investment, decisions. While I agree with his description of the problem with proposals advocating increased relational investing by institutional investors, the better approach is not to redefine relational investing but to recognize its limited use for only a small number of firms, in which instances the relational investor, whether a financial institution or other entity, will develop the necessary expertise for engaging in continuous active monitoring of business operations. The concept of relational investing is not needed to predict that a large shareholder can and will on occasion express interest in who sits on the board of directors.

[32] For a model of block ownership that captures the continuum notion see Shleifer and Vishny (1986a).

with more control over management than the relational investor who makes a one-time capital contribution for its shares and whose role is not typically perceived as including the provision of future financing.

Venture capitalists also fulfil the 'patient' investor characteristic of commentators' definition of relational investing: the average venture capital firm lasts 8.6 years, the average holding period of a particular investment of such firms is 4.9 years (Sahlman, 1990, pp. 483–487),[33] and venture capitalists typically retain their large equity position in the business after the company goes public for at least one year after the offering.[34] Perhaps most important for the efficacy of the relational investing concept, the venture capital firm does not stand in multiple relationships with its financed entity, so it performs a monitoring role not rife with conflict of interest opportunities after the financed firm goes public.

The leveraged buyout organization (LBO firm) is another governance arrangement that, at first glance, resembles relational investing. Outside equity ownership is concentrated in the LBO firm, which sits on the board and takes an active interest in the enterprise it is financing (Jensen, 1989) and the LBO firm is a long-term investor in the enterprise. Kaplan (1991, pp. 297, 306), for instance, finds that the median time a corporation subject to an LBO remains private is between six and seven years after the LBO, and the LBO firm retains substantial equity ownership in the corporation after taking it public. However, the businesses that are best-suited for this organizational form are very different from those financed by venture capital firms, and from those which mesh with a transaction cost approach to relational investing. The difference hinges on an important distinguishing characteristic of the two organizational forms: unlike the venture capitalist, the leveraged buyout (LBO) concentrates debt as well as equity, creating a highly leveraged enterprise, which, of course, implies that the firm must have assets whose characteristics support substantial debt investments. Thus, LBO candidates are mature organizations whose assets are readily redeployable and capable of generating steady cash flows sufficient to meet substantial interest payments. For example, they are clustered in industries with low R&D intensity, such as retailing and manufacturing sectors (Lichtenberg and Siegel, 1990; Kieschnick, 1989).

The LBO firm's investments do not undercut what this article has

---

[33] Venture capital firms are organized as limited partnerships. A survey of 76 venture capital firms found that 72% had contractual lives limited to 10 years, but all had provisions to extend the partnership's life, most often for three years in one-year increments, typically upon a majority vote of the limited partners (Sahlman, 1990, p. 490).

[34] Venture capitalists average 34.3% of the equity before a company goes public, and 24.6% after the initial public offering, with the decline primarily a function of the increase in outstanding shares rather than divestiture; one year after the offering, they average 17.8% (Barry *et al.*, 1990, pp. 460, 462).

suggested to be the transaction cost rationale for relational investing. There
are two significant features that differentiate the LBO firm from a relational
investor. First, the LBO firm actually controls the firm in which it is
invested—it owns all of the outside equity and a supermajority of outstanding equity, with management typically holding the rest. The point of relational investing is quite different, to create a monitor for firms where there
is no controlling shareholder who is in an obvious position to monitor management. Second, the LBO firm's interest in an operating firm originates in a
change in control transaction, typically initiated by the LBO firm itself,
which has no previous investment in the firm, and it may unseat management when it initiates its investment. Consequently, the LBO firm is properly located in the takeover category of governance structures, rather than
relational investing, which substitutes for takeovers as a monitor of management. By contrast, venture capital investments do not have such characteristics. Venture capital firms typically do not own all of the firm's outside
equity and in most cases, the operating firm's management retains control
(Barry *et al.*, 1990, p. 460). In addition, venture capital investments are
solicited by the firm's management, are never hostile, and as partial blocks
do not work a change in the firm's control.

A third distinct possible example of relational investing, and what advocates of this governance structure may well have in mind when they recommend changing public policy in order to facilitate such investments, is
Warren Buffet and his investment vehicle, Berkshire Hathaway, Inc., an
insurance firm within a holding company structure that owns large blocks of
stock in several publicly traded companies (Dobrzynski, 1993). An analysis
of Buffett's investment strategy indicates that such a characterization is
questionable, and highlights instead that what I have identified as the weak
form of shareholder activism, analogous to the weak form of outside boards'
monitoring, crisis intervention, is the more profitable corporate governance
device for blockholders in the US context.

Buffet is a 'value' or 'growth' investor, a stock picker who makes sizeable
investments in firms that he thinks are undervalued. He is primarily interested in investing in companies, like one of his best picks, Coca-Cola, which
are stable growing firms with good management, and are not expected to
experience financial difficulties (Hagstrom, 1995). He is, in his own words,
'not a turnaround artist' (e.g. Buffett, 1990, p. 20), and he therefore seeks
investments where he will not be actively involved but will instead leave
management in place giving them his shares' proxy (Hagstrom, 1995, pp.
104, 141).

Given this description of his investment strategy, why is Buffett often
considered the paradigmatic relational investor? After making his invest-

ments, Buffett's actions appear to parallel what are considered to be the keystone of a relational investor: he often takes a seat on the board and provides management counsel on request. He also shares the 'patient' investor characterization as his expressed investment horizon: certain stocks in his portfolio are identified as 'permanent' holdings that he will never sell, although he states that he expects to hold all of his major equity investments unless they become 'overvalued' (Hagstrom, 1995, pp. 99–100, 183–184). In addition, he has taken an active management role in a time of crisis for at least one of his investments: he took command of the Salomon investment bank as interim Chairman after the disclosure of a government investigation revealing serious misconduct in Salomon's treasury-bond department.[35]

Buffett's Salomon holding is an example of a set of convertible preferred stock holdings that he has been offered on favorable terms to aid takeover-beleaguered management, another feature identified as relational investing (Rock, 1994, pp. 993–994), although this is not Buffett's principal investment activity. It should be noted that Buffett required a price higher than board representation for these investments, the additional fixed return of the preferred as well as a conversion option. In Salomon's case, he was willing to make the investment, in part, because he knew the firm's management (Hagstrom, 1995, pp. 169–170). The managements offering Buffett such blocks see him in a more favorable light than the bidders they are escaping, most likely because of his pattern of holding investments for the long haul, and not interfering with the management of his holdings. This is, no doubt, a further contributing reason for Buffett's identification as the paradigm of relational investing.

Buffet has been an extraordinarily successful investor. There is, however, no evidence that his success is a function principally of successful relational investing—active monitoring and management of the firms in which he invests—rather than a function of successful stock picking—investing in companies with good managers and good products—due to ability, luck, or both. Indeed, he characterizes his investment style as the latter, shrewd stock picking, not as the former, active monitoring and management (Hagstrom, 1995, pp. 75–80; Buffett, 1990, pp. 5–6, 16). Buffett appears to intervene in firm affairs only in situations of distress, but even then, he

---

[35] Taking an active role in times of distress is not the hallmark of relational investing. It is characterized by continuous active monitoring, as is perceived to be the role performed by Japanese and German block investors, rather than by isolated acts of crisis intervention. Analogous to the weak form of the outside director monitoring hypothesis, even a typically passive large investor will become more actively involved in firm decision-making in times of exigency, to avoid having to sell its holdings at a loss; this is not relational investing. The point of the governance model of relational investing is that there not be such crises calling for special blockholder involvement, because of the more vigilant day-to-day monitoring by the blockholder.

does not consistently become actively involved. For example, he wrote down his convertible preferred equity investment in US Air in 1994 and stepped down from the board, rather than seek more active involvement in management, when the firm's financial difficulties increased, in contrast to his taking charge of Salomon when it experienced problems.[36] It is evident that he does not envision his equity block involvement in the strong form mold of relational investing.

Moreover, Buffett's investments only vaguely resemble those for which the transaction cost explanation of relational investing is relevant. He prefers what he refers to as 'franchise' as opposed to 'commodity' firms, by which he means firms successful at product differentiation, such that they provide a good or service with quasi-monopolistic characteristics (inelastic demand) (Hagstrom, 1995, p. 78). His large investments in media companies, as well as Coca Cola, fit this category, which matches the first firm characteristic transaction cost economics identifies for relational investing, the importance of intangible assets. However, Buffett avoids firms whose earnings prospects are uncertain and whose business is thereby difficult to understand, such as the high technology sector (Hagstrom, 1995, p. 77; Buffett, 1990, p. 20), which are firms with the second characteristic transaction cost economics identifies for relational investing, uncertain cash flows.

Buffett's investments cannot be characterized as relational from a transaction cost economics perspective when their firms' asset specificity is more directly examined. The ratios of R&D expenditures to sales and of net plant, property and equipment to total assets have been used to measure asset specificity; high R&D intensity is presumed to generate highly industry- and firm-specific assets; and firms with a high fraction of fixed (tangible) assets are presumed to have high liquidation values and hence few firm-specific assets (Gompers, 1995, p. 1466). Buffett's investments do not have much asset specificity as indexed by R&D intensity, because only one of the firms reports any R&D expenditures.[37] This is consistent with Buffett's avoidance of the technology sector, where R&D spending is important.

---

[36] Of course, there are important pragmatic financial reasons for this difference. The US Air investment was a loser given the airline industry's fundamentals, which Buffett does not think will improve (Buffett, 1994, pp. 17–18), whereas Salomon's difficulties were peculiar to its management scandal and not its industry sector. Buffett's assumption of the Salomon Chairmanship would minimize the political fallout, as regulators could trust him not to cover up further misconduct, and thereby save the value of his investment.

[37] I obtained from the COMPUSTAT database the data for the year of the initial investment as well as 1993, the most recent year available, for eight of Buffett's relational investments—three of his 'permanent' common stock holdings (Coca Cola, the Washington Post, Capital Cities/ABC) and his five convertible preferred stock holdings (Salomon Inc., USAir, Champion International, American Express, and Gillette) (*see* Hagstrom, 1995). There were no data available for the remaining permanent stock investment, GEICO, on COMPUSTAT. As there were no significant differences for the two years separately or averaged, only the data for the year of purchase are reported. The one firm reporting R&D expenditures,

In addition, the average ratio of net property, plant and equipment to total assets of Buffett's investments is 0.305. This is slightly lower than the 0.34 average fixed assets ratio for New York Stock Exchange (NYSE) firms with an outside blockholder (Friend and Lang, 1988, p. 276, Table I), but the difference is not statistically significant.[38] It thus appears that Buffett's investments have about the average level of tangible assets for NYSE firms. These are, accordingly, not firms for which transaction cost economics would expect an active blockholder to be especially valuable. This finding is in keeping with Buffett's own perception: as earlier noted, he does not envision playing an active role in the management of his equity investments.

Casual empiricism, moreover, suggests that a comparative monitoring expertise explanation of Buffett's investing successes will not hold up. The Salomon investment indicates that Buffet's monitoring and control capacity cannot prevent moral hazard fiascos and that his intervention, at least on occasion, is profoundly mistaken (*Economist; Fortune*). His US Air investment is also a self-professed mistake (Hagstrom, 1995, pp. 175–176; Buffett, 1990, p. 18; Buffett, 1994, pp. 17–18). Buffet's most successful investments, such as Coca Cola, the Washington Post, and Capital Cities/ABC, are not those in which he has taken an active management role nor, of course, is active management his investment objective, although these are companies whose principal assets may be intangible,[39] the type for which relational investing should offer active monitoring benefits.

The discussion of data probative of the efficacy of a transaction cost approach to relational investing has consisted on the whole of anecdotes. This is because, while there have been several studies trying to evaluate whether large shareholders add value to firms none distinguish across firm asset or cash flow characteristics, and thus none offer evidence for or against the transaction cost explanation of when relational investing makes sense.[40]

Gillette, has a ratio of R&D to sales of 2.3%, which is higher than the average industry ratio of R&D to sales for all COMPUSTAT industries (1.3%) but lower than the median for all industries (2.66%) and lower than the average and median industry ratio of venture capital-financed firms (3.43% and 3.82% respectively) (Gompers, 1995, p. 1471).

[38] Friend and Lang divide the New York Stock Exchange (NYSE) firms in half, by insider ownership, and then subdivide these two equal-sized groups by whether there is an outside blockholder. The *t*-statistics (fixed asset ratios in parentheses) testing the difference in means for the Buffett sample against the Friend and Lang set of firms with outside blockholders for firms with insider ownership below and above the median, respectively, are 0.34 (0.343) and 0.39 (0.348). There is also no significant difference between the ratios of Buffett's investments and those of NYSE firms with no outside blockholders.

[39] The fixed asset ratios for these firms are 0.23, 0.27 and 0.17, respectively.

[40] The many studies examining the effect of large shareholders on shareholder voting outcomes do not address the efficacy of relational investing because all blockholders, passive or active, can be expected to be informed voters, although the authors of these studies typically view evidence of informed voting, such as positive wealth effects from anti-takeover charter amendments adopted by firms with concentrated equity owners, as evidence of active monitoring (e.g. Agrawal and Mandelker, 1990).

This is also true of studies of the behavior of Japanese corporate groups and German banks, the foreign governance systems offering the paradigm for relational investing.[41] One study investigating ownership and performance did control for firm characteristics of interest to transaction cost economics: Demsetz and Lehn (1985) find ownership concentration is higher for firms with greater uncertainty in their operating environment, which is consistent with the transaction cost thesis. But this study cannot be cited as an accurate test of this article's thesis concerning relational investing because the activity level of the block owners, as well as their status as insiders or outsiders, is not distinguished.

It should be noted that the evidence on whether the Japanese system of cross-holdings or German banking system increases the welfare of the public shareholders, or that of group members or German banks, respectively, is mixed. For instance, studies of Japanese and German management turnover find, similar to the US data, that boards replace management after poor stock performance, and conclude that group members and banks monitor performance consistent with the public shareholders' interest (e.g. Kaplan, 1994a, 1994b; Kaplan and Minton, 1994).[42] In addition, Japanese firms with main banks outperformed those without such relations after the US occupation forced the break-up of pre-war Japanese conglomerates (Yafeh, 1995).[43] But there is also evidence that loan repayment, rather than other indicators of financial health, is the best predictor of Japanese main bank monitoring (Morck and Nakamura, 1995, p. 490), and the data on German management turnover can be interpreted in the same light (p. 488). In addition, there is evidence that Japanese main banks extract rents from their customers, lowering profits, and favor conservative investments, hindering firm growth (Weinstein and Yafeh, 1993). Moreover, there is disagreement over whether German banks are even active in corporate governance (Shleifer and

---

[41] Although not all Japanese firms are members of groups nor are all German firms closely associated with banks, the widespread use of these arrangements, particularly for large firms, indicates that the redeployability of assets is not the motivating issue in the development of these systems and suggests that empirical research would not find much cross-sectional variation by firm assets were such a variable to be investigated.

[42] These could be seen as instances of crisis management, no different from the activities of US boards of directors, rather than successful relational investing, because under a comparative monitoring expertise explanation of relational investing, we expect to achieve better performance (i.e. faster CEO replacement) from continuous monitoring by blockholders than by outside directors.

[43] It should be noted that a concern similar to the managerial quality hypothesis discussed earlier regarding evaluation of the effect of board composition on performance can be raised concerning studies of the effect of Japanese banks on firm performance, such as Yafeh's study: if banks have enough information to select only well-run firms or firms with good prospects for long-term clients, then finding firms with main bank relationships are better performers than those without such relations may indicate not effective monitoring by banks but the high quality of the information that goes into the bank's investment decisions.

Vishny, 1995, p. 34). The mixed findings in these studies support the view that relational investing based on multiple relationships can raise troublesome issues for other shareholders.

One comparative corporate governance study is more interesting from the transaction cost perspective. Comparing US and Japanese firms' capital structures, Prowse (1990) finds that US firms exhibit a negative relation between asset specificity and leverage, but Japanese firms do not where their proportion of debt holdings is significantly correlated with their proportion of equity holdings. Prowse views this finding as evincing that the agency costs of debt (i.e. the monitoring problems to prevent risk-shifting strategies that are exacerbated by asset-specificity) are reduced by active monitoring by creditors through their equity holdings. To the extent this interpretation is correct, it suggests that equity blockholders can add value in high asset-specificity firms. But this study is, obviously, quite far from anything that could be characterized as a test of this article's relational investing hypothesis.

Another study is superficially inconsistent with the transaction cost approach to relational investing. Zeckhauser and Pound (1990) find that firms with a shareholder owning a block of at least 15% have lower earnings to price (E/P) ratios than firms with no large shareholder in low asset-specificity industries, but there is no significant difference in E/P ratio across ownership structure in high asset-specificity industry firms. There are also no significant differences in either sub-sample of firms if the block ownership variable is for 5% to 15% blocks rather than blocks of 15% or higher. They conclude that large shareholders are effective monitors, but only in 'open-information-structure' (i.e. low asset-specificity) firms. However, such a conclusion is unwarranted for several reasons besides the conventional problem with much statistical work that a simple association, without more, does not evidence causality.

First, Zeckhauser and Pound do not distinguish insider from outsider status for the 15% block owners, which renders it difficult to determine whether this is a test of outsider monitoring or insider incentive alignment as the governance device. This distinction is not trivial because studies find a nonlinear relation between performance and insider ownership that is positive for small blocks and negative for larger positions (the critical value differs across studies, some finding at above, and others below, the 15% cutoff of Zeckhauser and Pound) but no relation between performance and outsider blocks (McConnell and Servaes, 1990, 1995; Morck *et al.*, 1988).[44]

---

[44] These studies use Tobin's Q as the performance measure, which Zeckhauser and Pound reject in favor of E/P ratios, which are easier to calculate, but E/P ratios appear to be highly correlated with Tobin's Q (McConnell and Servaes, 1995, p. 139). Tobin's Q is, also, highly correlated with the variable they use to define asset-specificity, R&D expenditures. (McConnell and Servaes, 1995, p. 191).

Second, Zeckhauser and Pound do not distinguish between investors who can be characterized as active (such as those with seats on the board) and those who are passive, which is essential information for testing the relational investor monitoring hypothesis.[45]

Third, under the transaction cost view of relational investing, we would not expect to find variation in performance depending on ownership structure across industry sectors, as opposed to within sectors where relational investments are predicted to be beneficial, because the optimal governance structure differs by sector. Zeckhauser and Pound's results are aggregated across firms and industries grouped by asset-specificity in general, and thus do not provide a good test of the thesis. This point is borne out more generally by the Demsetz and Lehn (1985) result that profitability does not vary significantly with ownership concentration, including a measure of concentration predicted by industry uncertainty. Finally, the transaction-specific asset theory of relational investing advanced here does not predict that firms with high asset-specificity will have large shareholders but rather, it predicts that if large shareholders invest in such firms they will desire to be active monitors (i.e. to receive board positions). Zeckhauser and Pound's data simply do not bear upon the prediction.

It would be remiss to omit from this discussion the one empirical study of relational investments, although as with the more general studies of block ownership, its research design does not address the asset-specificity issue. Gordon and Pound (1993) collected a sample of 18 relational investments, defined as friendly blocks of equity (typically under 25%) that had board representation, which were acquired without an intent to obtain control. To evaluate whether such investments add value to the firm, they calculate the investments' 'net of market' return for multiple year holding periods.[46] They find that the investments on average mirrored the market's performance. The net-of-market returns are not statistically significantly different compared to the indices, with returns over one- two- and three-year holding periods being negative and returns over the four-year holding period positive. It should be noted that the firms' pre-relational investment returns were also not significantly different from the market.

While Gordon and Pound (1993) conclude with a highly guarded endorsement of relational investments from these data, I view the results with even greater skepticism: because the returns are not adjusted for risk,

[45] It should be noted that they do not define what they mean by monitoring and it is unclear wherher they have relational investing in mind.

[46] This return is calculated by subtracting the return on the S & P 500 Index or the Wilshire 5000 Index from the company return, over the holding period of interest. All the returns are computed for the company's common stock, although 7 of the 18 relational investments are blocks of preferred stock. Their sample includes 4 of Buffett's investments.

knowing whether they exceed or fall short of market benchmarks is not an accurate indicator of relative performance (i.e. a riskier portfolio should generate a better than market return). In any event, these data are not a test of the transaction cost monitoring perspective on relational investing.

The findings of a study by Wahal (1996) of active, albeit not relational, investors are similar, and hence perhaps instructive of what public share-holders can expect from relational investing. Wahal investigates the efficacy of pension funds' activism in corporate governance (i.e. monitoring) and finds that there is no significant improvement in the long-term stock performance (calculating multi-year holding period returns, net of market and risk-adjusted), or accounting performance, of the targeted firms. The targets also were not poor performers at the time the pension funds initiated their activities, but were in fact overperformers in poorly performing industries.

Smith (1996b) also finds no effect on operating performance from the California pension fund's (CalPERS') targeting of poorly performing port-folio firms with shareholder resolutions. But he finds a positive stock price effect for the subset of targeted firms where CalPERS' action 'succeeded'. We are unfortunately not provided with information concerning what the firms actually did in the cases that CalPERS' considered successes, which would enable us to evaluate better the connection between CalPERS' activ-ity and performance. To the extent that the successes consisted of changes in board composition (3 of 21 identifiable successful resolutions were directed at board composition), the price effect could well be indicating the market's valuation of the appointment of outside directors, which, as already noted, is positive. There is a further difference between Smith's and the other two studies that could account for the apparently divergent results. Smith's time-frame for measuring a price effect is much shorter than the period over which Wahal and Gordon and Pound calculate returns. He examines the two-day interval surrounding the announcement of CalPERS' activity or the period extending from CalPERS' initiation of a shareholder resolution to its success, an average of 21 days. He did not find any effect in the accounting data which measured performance over several years, a time frame similar to the other studies. This may indicate that none of the studies have looked at a long enough time-frame to measure the value of activism (that is, the per-year increment in improved performance from shareholder monitoring is very small), a measurement problem that may equally well apply to the board of directors' performance data.

Given the recent interest of scholars in relational investing, it is not sur-prising that there has been little systematic empirical work directly on the issue, nor any work relevant to a transaction cost approach to relational investing, investigation of the relation between asset-specificity and active block investors. Suggestive anecdotes are simply the best we can do for the present. I separately calculated asset-specificity measures for the Gordon and Pound sample of relational investments that were not held by Buffet and the results were more consistent with the transaction cost economics hypothesis concerning relational investing than those for the Buffet investments. The average fixed asset ratio of the twelve firms for which COMPUSTAT data were available is 0.25, which is statistically significantly lower than the ratio for the NYSE firms with outside blockholders (the t-statistic of -1.83 is significant at 5% for a one-tailed test). Only three firms reported any R&D expenditures but unlike the one firm held by Buffett reporting such expenses, these firms' ratios of R&D to sales were substantial: two were over 7% and the third was 17%. This suggests that a more systematic investigation of active block investors and asset specificity would be worthwhile. But my guess is that future research will not provide robust evidence of significant value from relational investing (that is, from active monitoring of management by non-manager shareholders on an ongoing basis). Rather, it is more likely to indicate that there are benefits from a weak form of shareholder activism, blockholders' efforts in crisis management, parallel to the evidence on outside boards of directors.

4. *State Competition for Corporate Charters*

Transaction cost economics provides an explanation of the dynamics of the unique federal character of corporate law in the USA which has facilitated the diffusely-owned firm for which the board of directors is a key governance structure (Romano, 1993a). The making of corporate law is crucial for understanding corporate governance, for that process impacts upon the range of potential governance structures. For example, the degree to which a legal system protects shareholder rights, the thickness of the country's capital markets, and the more likely diffusely-held public corporations are the dominant form of corporate governance, appear to be interconnected (Romano, 1993a, pp. 125, 137–138; Shleifer and Vishny, 1995).[47]

The Genius of US Corporate Law

In the USA corporations can choose their legal regime from the 50 states and the District of Columbia. There is no physical connection to the choice:

---

[47] The direction of causality (whether the protection offered by the legal system affects the liquidity of the capital market or the vigor of the capital market spurs the development of the legal system) is empirically indeterminate; most likely, there is a feedback or looping process.

a firm's statutory domicile is achieved through a paper filing in the office of the chosen state's Secretary. Firms typically incorporate locally or in Delaware; in fact, almost one-half of the largest corporations are incorporated in Delaware and the overwhelming majority of firms changing incorporation state move to Delaware (Dodd and Leftwich, 1980; Romano, 1985). Commentators have viewed this process as a competition among states for corporate charters (e.g. Cary, 1974). The motivation is financial. States benefit from incorporations as they earn revenue—incorporation fees, also referred to as franchise taxes—from the incorporation of firms, many of which would not otherwise do business in the state. Delaware's franchise tax revenue, for example, has averaged over 15% of total taxes collected over the past three decades (Romano, 1993a, pp. 7–8).

Firms move to Delaware because they anticipate undertaking transactions that will be cheaper under Delaware's law than that of the original incorporation state. The three most common transactions which reincorporating firms plan to undertake are mergers and acquisitions, public offerings and anti-takeover defenses (Romano, 1985), activities that are frequent objects of lawsuits. A comparison of a number of organizational attributes of the top 200 manufacturing firms divided into those incorporated in Delaware and those in other states found one significant difference: the Delaware firms averaged a higher number of acquisitions over their corporate lives than the non-Delaware firms (Romano, 1985, pp. 263–264). This is consistent with firms' choosing to incorporate in Delaware for transaction-based reasons. There are code provisions that directly reduce the cost of these transactions (e.g. Delaware does not require a vote by acquiring firm shareholders in stock acquisitions and has a simple majority default rule for merger votes, Del. Code Ann., tit. 8, § 251). In addition, the transactions producing reincorporation are likely to increase the prospect of shareholder litigation. When a firm expects a change in operations or activities that increases the likelihood of shareholder litigation, specific characteristics of a legal regime become important, such as the presence of a well-developed body of case law and explicit indemnification rules, for they facilitate doing business by permitting transactions to be structured with greater certainty concerning potential liability. Delaware's legal regime is pre-eminent in delivering these features for in no other state can a firm obtain a legal opinion on a proposed transaction with such ready availability and predictability. This is not fortuitous: it is part and parcel of the process by which Delaware is pre-eminent in the corporate charter market.

The transaction cost approach explains why one state, Delaware, successfully dominates the corporate charter market. A corporate charter is a relational contract: it binds together the state and firm in a multi-period relationship, in which their respective performance under the contract is not simultaneous. A corporation code must be continually revised and updated as business conditions change and new issues arise in ways that could not be foreseen to have been specified in the initial code provisions. After a firm is incorporated in a state and pays its franchise fee, it is possible that the state will fail to update its code, or alter its code in ways unfavorable to the firm, and the firm is stuck up to the point where the cost of moving falls below the cost of operating under an inferior code. In other words, the firm is in a vulnerable contracting position, which is made worse by the fact that the party with whom it is contracting, the state, is also the enforcer of the contract. Because it may have no bona fide legal recourse for breach, the firm will look for and the state will need to provide some credible means of committing itself to uphold the contract and maintain it (i.e. revise its code) in ways that do not exploit the firm. The state has an interest in doing this, its franchise revenues. For if it cannot commit to a code that eases the cost of doing business, firms will be reluctant to pay a fee for that right, or to do business with a particular state, as opposed to another provider, in the first place.

Delaware's pre-eminence in the charter market is a function of its ability to resolve credibly the commitment problem.[48] The commitment mechanism depends on its substantial investment in assets that have no alternative use at any comparable significant value than in maintaining its corporate chartering business (*see* Williamson, 1983). These assets are (i) a reputation for responsiveness to corporate concerns; (ii) a comprehensive body of corporate case law; (iii) judicial expertise in administering that law;[49] and (iv) administrative expertise in the expeditious processing of corporate filings. The intangible reputational asset is related to the substantial revenue Delaware receives from the franchise tax: because such a large proportion of its budget is financed from incorporations and it is a small state with very limited indigenous revenue sources, there is no ready substitute revenue source with which to maintain the level of services Delaware provides its citizens without a vigorous incorporation business. This makes Delaware as vulnerable to the firms as they are to it: it has too much to lose from failing to maintain a responsive corporation code. Because it is a hostage to its own success, Delaware is able to make credible its commitment to corporate law responsiveness.

Delaware's legal capital is not only a commitment device, it is a primary

---

[48] The following paragraphs are an abbreviated treatment of the thesis developed in Romano (1985) and Romano (1993a).

[49] Unlike other states, corporate law cases in Delaware are tried in only one court, the Chancery Court, facilitating the development of judicial expertise. In addition, corporate law specialists are routinely appointed to the Delaware Supreme Court.

attraction for reincorporating firms. It provides the requisite predictability for business planning for firms that will be undertaking complicated transactions such as acquisitions. The development of legal capital also feeds back into the development of its reputational capital, enhancing Delaware's credible precommitment to firms, just as the number of incorporated firms feeds back into the development of legal capital. The more firms incorporated in Delaware, the more comprehensive the case law becomes as more issues are litigated. The more comprehensive the case law, the more firms will incorporate locally. The more firms incorporated, the higher the state's reliance on franchise fees to finance its operations. And the greater the reliance on fees, the more credible the commitment to responsiveness. The large number of firms already located in Delaware not only feeds back into the development of Delaware's legal and reputational capital, but also cements its position; it gives Delaware a first-mover advantage in the charter market.

Another approach to describing Delaware's first mover advantage is in terms of network externalities, which refers to economies of scale and scope that depend on a product's adoption in large numbers (Klausner, 1995). The difference across these two economic approaches is largely in interpretative perspective, although it may also be a function of the fixity with which the two view institutions. The network externalities literature focuses on the potential for inefficiencies to arise (network users do not internalize the externalities of their product choices) and to persist. In contrast, the transaction cost approach has a propensity to view private organizations as efficient and evolving, since it emphasizes cost-reduction as a primary motivation for organizational creation and the ingenuity by which individuals devise institutions to further exchange and to adapt them to their purposes. The markets in which corporations operate greatly reduce the possibility that network externalities will lead to long-term inefficiencies in corporate charters. For example, the network externality model locates the possibility of suboptimal corporation charters from initial decisions of less than fully-informed firms, which select an inefficient provision that all other firms copy to obtain the network benefit, and permanently fixes contracts in a suboptimal state (Klausner, 1995). Such an outcome will not be sustainable in the corporate charter market over time because well-informed experts—corporate attorneys, who are repeat players advising many firms—provide the key decisional inputs into the choice of charter terms. Moreover, fixity in contract terms is not a feature of the corporate charter market. Corporation codes are continuously revised as business conditions change, as are charters, and they are enabling in approach, which permits experimentation by firms at the forefront of new business transactions.

In addition to its hostage-like assets of limited redeployability, Delaware's constitution requires changes to the corporation code to be approved by a supermajority of both state legislative houses (Del. Const., Art. IX, § 1). This provision is a useful commitment device for it makes it difficult for Delaware to reverse the direction of its code. It increases the likelihood that the legal regime can be no worse than it was at the time of incorporation, which is desirable if corporations are risk averse with respect to the legal system and adopt a strategy toward the choice of incorporation state that minimizes the worst case. It does not appear to slow corporate law reform as Delaware is one of the leading innovators, as well as imitators of corporate law reforms (Romano, 1985); this is probably due to the legislature's reliance on the corporate bar when enacting reforms (Moore 1981, p. 780). The constitutional provision also serves to preserve the value of the personal investments made by Delaware citizens in developing skills to service Delaware corporations. Only a critical election revolutionizing state politics could produce a radical reversal in the state's corporate law policy that would lead to firms' massive migration out of state.

This consideration points out that transaction cost economics explains the persistence of Delaware's success rather than its initiation, which was largely due to historical accident, Delaware being well-situated to take over the incorporation business of New Jersey, the dominant charter state, which radically revised its corporation code under the influence of the Progressive party and lameduck governor Woodrow Wilson, who was about to become President. At the time of the reform, changes in the state economy had reduced the importance of incorporation revenues in New Jersey's budget (Grandy, 1989). Delaware had previously adopted New Jersey's code and recognized its case law as binding precedent in Wilmington City Ry. Co. v. People's Ry. Co., 47 A. 245, 251 (Del. Ch. 1900). New Jersey tried to regain its preeminent position as politics changed by repealing the Progressives' corporate law reforms a few years later, but it was unable to do so.

It would be extremely difficult for any state to unseat Delaware in the chartering business, since Delaware has a first-mover advantage in offering a credible commitment in terms of reputation and case law from its starting point of a large number of incorporated firms. However, Delaware remains vigilant. It is continually updating its code (both by innovating or copying others) and seeking new business.

Despite Delaware's overwhelming lead, the other states do, in fact, appear to compete to retain as best they can the incorporations that they have, as well as to lure business away (Blackman, 1993; Harlan, 1988; Romano, 1985, pp. 233–242). This is key to the successful operation of the system. None of the essential attributes would be present in a national chartering regime: given the size of the federal budget, franchise fees can never provide the federal government with a financial incentive to be responsive to firms and not behave opportunistically. In addition, there would be no competition prodding the federal government to improve its service, unless the costs of incorporating in a foreign country, or of operating as an unincorporated entity, are considerably reduced from present levels.

A primary reason why some legal commentators propose replacing the federal system with national charters is their view that state competition produces a 'race for the bottom', whose output benefits managers not shareholders (Cary, 1974). Such commentators believe that Congress would enact more shareholder-friendly laws than the states. There is, however, scant support for the proposition that national politics would be better. The organizational advantages of managers over shareholders are just as strong at the national level as at the local level, so if the problem is a political market failure, shifting the arena will not solve it (Romano, 1988). It is also questionable whether any of the national laws affecting corporate governance benefit shareholders (see, e.g. Roe, 1994 (financial institution stock ownership regulation); Haddock and Macey, 1987 (insider trading regulation); Easterbrook and Fischel, 1983 (proxy regulation); Benston, 1973 (disclosure regulation); Schwartz, 1986 (tender offer regulation)). In fact the most severe restrictions on investors' choice of governance structures, such as the prevention of large blockholding by US financial institutions, have occurred largely in the national political arena (Roe, 1994), not in the competitive corporation codes of the states.

With the possible exception of takeovers, the rules of corporate governance do not generate externalities that would make the states the improper political unit, because they determine shareholder-manager relations and have no bearing on third parties in other states who might be harmed by corporate conduct. Limited liability toward tort claimants, where externalities are present, is the rule in all of the states and proposals for federal chartering do not recommend its abolition. Alternative statutory schemes govern firms' relations with employees which corporation codes cannot successfully trump. The takeover setting is potentially different from other issues involving shareholder-manager relations because third party bidders are affected by corporate law rules and their interests are typically not represented in the legislating state, although they are represented in Delaware and its rules tend to be more favorable to bidders than those of other states (Romano, 1993a). In addition, some commentators contend that takeovers adversely affect employees, creditors and local communities, but the bulk of the evidence does not support such externality claims (Romano, 1992, pp. 136–142). Although we can craft a theoretical argument for national regulation of takeovers, given the potential externalities, in practice, as noted and as discussed in greater detail in Romano (1988) and Romano (1993a, pp. 75–84), the national political process will not mitigate the third-party problem. It is instead likely to exacerbate the problem as there will be no safety valve for shareholders to invest in firms in a competing jurisdiction that has rules more favorable to bidders as in the current federal system, (as is true of the laws of California and Delaware).

The federal chartering system is a unique feature of American corporate law. Although there are multiple regulators of banks in the USA, because of the need to obtain federal deposit insurance and restrictions on interstate branch banking, there has been very little competition for banks among states. Besides being forced to charter in the state in which they have deposit business, to participate in the federal deposit insurance system, state-chartered banks must obtain the approval of the Federal Deposit Insurance Corporation, which applies the same criteria for its approval as does the Comptroller of the Currency in granting charters to national banks (Macey and Miller 1992, pp. 121, 109). These factors limit states' ability to compete by offering advantageous chartering terms. To the extent that there is competition, it occurs instead in a bank's choice of federal versus state regulator, and across federal regulators (the larger and sounder thrifts changed, for instance, to banks to avoid the higher insurance deposit premiums in their sector in the late 1980s). But on some important dimensions, such as the risk-based capital rules, as well as charter approval, there is no difference across federal regulator. The efficacy of competition across state and federal government banking regulation has been debated in the literature (Scott, 1977; Butler and Macey, 1988), and one commentator even views the dual system as hopelessly obsolete, contending that it should be abandoned in favor of a full-fledged system of state competition as we have for corporate charters, with the federal government's function limited to activities necessary to maintain the deposit insurance system (Miller, 1987).

Other federations—the European Union (EU) and Canada—have limited or no competition for charters (Romano, 1993a, pp. 118–140; Daniels, 1991). An important reason for the absence of competition in the EU is the choice-of-law rule: unlike the USA and other common law legal systems, European countries follow the law of a corporation's real or effective seat, which requires a significant physical presence in the state for the jurisdictional choice to be effective, rather than the statutory domicile. Reincorporation under such a rule is much more expensive than under the statutory domicile system, because physical assets must be relocated to change legal regimes. As a consequence, EU members have reduced incentives to compete for charters by offering responsive codes because the prospective benefits are minimal as the number of recruitable corporations is so small. Furthermore, there is little incentive for the EU to change the choice-of-law rule because important members, such as Germany, have corporation laws that further objectives other than shareholder-wealth maximization (Romano, 1993a, pp. 129–132). Such a regime would become unstable in a competitive system because the interests of equity investors will dominate the choice of incorporation state as their capital is the most mobile of the firms' participants.

The principal reason for the attenuated charter competition across Canadian provinces is the inability of provincial governments to control their corporation laws. Security administrators, whose jurisdiction is based on shareholder residence and not issuer domicile, are able to regulate corporate governance and can override provincial corporate law regimes. For example, the Ontario Securities Commission imposes fiduciary obligations on majority shareholders under its public interest powers (Daniels, 1991, pp. 182–184). In addition, the Supreme Court of Canada reviews all provincial appellate court decisions (Daniels). The overlapping of jurisdiction weakens a province's incentive to invest in the necessary non-redeployable assets that ensure Delaware's success because the value of such assets can be impaired without recourse by security administrators or the Canadian judiciary. It also limits the ability of a province to commit to a responsive code. Moreover, firms have less of a reason to invest in optimizing incorporation decisions, as the fate of even a code of a state acting in the utmost good faith is uncertain. This has a further feedback effect diminishing provincial incentives to compete.

An additional difference that may affect the likelihood of charter competition and is relevant to both the EU and Canada, is the preponderant corporation ownership structure. Unlike the USA, where the stock of large public corporations is typically diffusely-held, most European and Canadian corporations have controlling blockholders. Such firms may be less interested in many of the features of a legal regime on which states compete; a code offering organizational flexibility and managerial discretion, for example, is not of value to a shareholder-manager who has voting control and can run the firm essentially as he wishes. The EU national and Canadian provincial governments therefore have less to gain from competition than US states. Shareholder lawsuits are also more difficult to bring in Canada or European nations than in the USA: Canadian and European courts recognize a more limited set of fiduciary duties, and representative actions and use of contingency fees are restricted (Romano, 1993a, pp. 125–126, 134). This further lessens the benefit of charter competition since the shareholder litigation regime is an important dimension in firms' choice of domicile.

There is, however, a causality problem in this contrast of ownership structures. It is as equally possible that in the absence of charter competition, equity must be concentrated to compensate for the less responsive legal regime with more intensive monitoring of management, as it is that concentrated ownership reduces the demand for shareholder protection and thereby diminishes the benefits of state competition. There are no data of which I am aware that can identify the direction of causality, and I am uncertain whether a test could be devised that would satisfactorily answer the question of which causes which.

Does State Competition Matter?

Most commentators and market participants believe that the choice of incorporation state matters. For example, corporate law commentators perennially debate whether state competition should be replaced with national chartering legislation because they disagree over who benefits from the federal system, managers or shareholders.[50] In addition, a significant number of firms change their incorporation state and firms that do so believe that the laws of the destination state, which is usually Delaware, differ markedly from those of the state of origin (Romano, 1985, pp. 258–260). They further consider this difference to be an important factor in deciding to move (Romano, 1985, p. 258). Is there a basis for such perceptions—that is, are investors better or worse off from their firms' changing incorporation state, or more generally, from their having the option to do so under the US system of corporate charter competition?

Before turning to answer the question, it must be noted first that the transaction cost explanation of the US charter market does not stake out a claim concerning who benefits from state competition, managers or shareholders. This is because its examination of the incentives for states to respond to firms' demand for particular corporate law innovations does not need to identify who in the firm sets that demand. However, it meshes better with a system in which shareholders benefit from competition. Given the extraordinary variety in investment opportunities with which issuers of equity must compete for funds, it is questionable whether the transaction-specific assets contributing to Delaware's success would have much value, or a first-mover advantage could be sustained, if the output of the process was a legal regime adverse to shareholder interests.

In contrast to the research on the value of independent boards of directors, the vast majority of studies seeking to assess the efficacy of state competition have not investigated cross-sectional variation in performance by incorpora-

---

[50] For a review of the more recent version of the debate see Romano (1993a).

tion state. Rather they are event studies examining stock price effects. Even apart from the conventional view of stock prices as more reliable indicators of value than accounting figures, stock price studies are more efficacious than accounting studies for evaluating charter competition because the endogeneity problem raised in the evaluation of the empirical research on board composition comes up in the extreme. There is a real question whether we should expect to find cross-sectional variation in firm performance by incorporation state because the choice of domicile is an endogenous choice that depends on particular firm characteristics, the anticipated undertaking of specific transactions. As we expect firms with different governance needs to adopt different governance structures, not least of which would be the legal regime that is the baseline governance institution, performance differences should, accordingly, not relate to incorporation state differences (see Baysinger and Butler, 1985c). The impact of state competition will only be picked up in studies of stock price effects upon unanticipated domicile changes, or unanticipated corporate law regime changes, as the self-selection of the sample of affected firms eliminates the cross-sectional endogeneity problem.

Event studies of reincorporation.   There have been several event studies of reincorporations (Hyman, 1979; Dodd and Leftwich, 1980; Romano, 1985; Netter and Poulsen, 1989; Wang, 1996). Examining the price effects of a change in statutory domicile is equivalent to studying who benefits from state competition. This is because reincorporating firms are the marginal corporate charter consumers whose actions drive the market, and a price reaction will measure the market's response to the new legal regime. Measured over a variety of time periods and samples of firms, these studies find either a significant positive price effect, or no significant price effect upon firms' reincorporations. No study observes negative stock price effects.

Netter and Poulsen subdivide their sample of firms reincorporating in Delaware into firms emigrating from California, which they consider a 'shareholder rights' state because takeover defensive tactics permitted in Delaware and other states are prohibited in California, and firms reincorporating from states other than California. The California migrants experience insignificant positive returns and there is no significant difference in abnormal returns across the two samples (p. 36). Wang separates his sample between firms reincorporating in Delaware and those reincorporating in other states. He finds that only the Delaware subsample experiences significant positive abnormal returns. Taken as a whole, the five studies indicate that the market considers reincorporation to be a beneficial event for shareholders.

There is, however, an interpretative question about these results that concerns confounding events: is the positive stock price revaluation due to the change in domicile or to anticipated changes in the corporation's business following reincorporation? To investigate this possibility, Romano subdivided her sample of reincorporating firms according to anticipated transactions upon the move; the subset of firms moving to engage in mergers and acquisitions and of those moving for tax and various miscellaneous reasons experienced significant positive returns, whereas the abnormal returns of the subset moving to engage in takeover defenses are insignificant (Romano, 1985, pp. 268–272). These results are consistent with event studies of the reincorporation-precipitating transactions alone: announcements of mergers and acquisitions programs produce positive abnormal returns (Schipper and Thompson, 1983) whereas event studies of defensive tactics have mixed results of either significantly negative, positive or insignificant abnormal returns (Jarrell *et al.*, 1988). However, analysis of variance of the abnormal returns across the three groups indicated that the group differences are not statistically significant (Romano, 1985, p. 272).

The bottom line of these studies is, then, that there is no evidence that reincorporating, and hence state competition, is harmful to shareholders. There is, in fact, substantial evidence that reincorporation is a wealth-increasing event, although the positive price effects from a change in incorporation state may be a function of the market's evaluation of the transactions providing the firms' reason for moving, such as future acquisitions, rather than the value of the new domicile itself.

Other probative event studies: statute enactments and judicial decisions. While the event studies of reincorporations provide the most direct test of whether state competition makes a difference, event studies of statutory enactments and judicial decisions are also probative. Unlike the uniformity of findings in the reincorporation event studies, the studies of these phenomena have widely varying results.

The most widely studied state law phenomenon is the enactment of takeover statutes, which are intended to make hostile takeovers more difficult. Because shareholders receive substantial premiums in takeovers, legislation that reduces the likelihood of a successful takeover should adversely affect the stock prices of covered firms. The findings of studies of the stock price effects of individual takeover laws vary: many find significantly negative effects (Broner, 1987; Karpoff and Malatesta, 1989, 1995; Ryngaert and Netter, 1988; Sidak and Woodward, 1990; Schumann, 1989; Szewczyk and Tsetsekos, 1992), while others find the effect is insignificant (Jahera and Pugh, 1991; Margotta and Badrinath, 1987; Margotta *et al.*, 1990; Pugh and Jahera, 1990; Romano, 1987, 1993c). The two most comprehensive studies, aggregating between 40 and 49 statutes enacted in over 20 states, find significantly negative, albeit small, abnormal returns (Karpoff and Malatesta, 1989; Mahla, 1991).

Much, but not all, of these differences can be explained by the type of takeover statute under study.[51] The statutes less likely to constrain hostile bids (fair price and other constituency statutes) tend to produce insignificant abnormal returns while the more severely restrictive statutes (disgorgement, control share acquisition and business combination freeze statutes) have significant negative price effects. In some instances, scholars examining the price effects of the same law have disagreed over the appropriate interpretation of the data, since depending on the event window or sample of firms examined, the price effects differ (compare Margotta *et al.*, 1990 with Ryngaert and Netter, 1990). In fact, some of the studies concluding that a statute's price effects are insignificant find significant negative abnormal returns over some event windows (e.g. Margotta and Badrinath, 1987).

The takeover statute data are the strongest evidence against state competition: they suggest that competition matters, and it matters negatively, to investors. But even here the strength of such a conclusion is considerably weakened when all of the evidence is reviewed. A key result in the studies of individual state laws from the standpoint of state competition is that the adoption of Delaware's statute, which is less restrictive of takeover bids than other states' laws, had no significant stock price effect (Jahera and Pugh, 1991; Karpoff and Malatesta, 1989). It is possible that the absence of an impact was due to the market's prior anticipation of legislation after the *CTS* decision, which was decided slightly more than a month before the first public announcement that the Delaware State Bar Association was considering proposing anti-takeover legislation. But this scenario seems unlikely because two weeks later there was a newspaper report indicating that the Bar had decided not to propose any legislation, and the next public indication of the revival of the proposal occurred over five months later (see Jahera and Pugh, 1991, p. 415, for a time line of the Delaware events). Delaware lagged behind and was not a leader in adopting takeover regulation. One reason for this distinction is that many state takeover laws are enacted at the behest of a domestic firm which is the target of a hostile bid (Butler, 1988; Romano, 1987, 1988, p. 461) and in Delaware, no one firm has such influ-

---

[51] The findings of insignificance cannot readily be attributed to investor beliefs that statutes would be found unconstitutional under the Supreme Court's decision invalidating first generation statutes, Edgar v. MITE, 457 US 624 (1982), because several statutes adopted before the Supreme Court validated state takeover laws in CTS Corp. v. Dynamics Corp. of America, 481 US 69 (1987), had significant negative effects.

ence over the legislature so as to be able to obtain instant statutory protection. The state competition dynamic is therefore clearly different for takeover statutes than for other corporate law reforms,[52] and Delaware has less input in it.

Further evidence that beneficial state competition is not eviscerated in the takeover context can be gleaned from the experience of Pennsylvania's 1990 enactment of a disgorgement statute, a takeover law considered to be unusually hostile to bidders. Institutional investors pressured their firms' managers to opt-out of the statute's coverage, and a majority of firms did so (Romano, 1993a, pp. 68–69). Moreover, unlike other innovations in takeover regulation, the Pennsylvania statute was not imitated by other states. Both of these factors indicate that capital markets operate in the direction Ralph Winter (1977) conjectured in his classic defense of state chartering, to discipline managers, and thereby place a floor on deleterious state competition.

Finally, the effects of takeover statutes can be overstated. Comment and Schwert (1995) conclude that the decline in takeovers at the end of the 1980s was not a function of takeover statutes because their data provide little evidence of deterrence: takeover rates are generally not significantly lower for firms covered by statutes and statutory coverage is not a significant predictor of the likelihood of a bid. This finding renders puzzling the negative stock price effects observed from the enactment of many of the takeover statutes. Comment and Schwert's explanation is that the market overestimated the deterrent effect of the takeover statutes and underestimated their positive effect on firms' bargaining power (p. 38). They find the same result—no deterrent effect—for poison pill adoptions. Comment and Schwert do not control for anti-takeover charter amendments in their sample, and several studies find that the negative returns from takeover statutes are experienced only by firms without such charter provisions (Karpoff and Malatesta, 1989, pp. 311–312; Szewczyk and Tsetsekos, 1992, p. 15). While not all firms without defensive charter provisions are potential targets, those that are have no base of shareholder support for resistance. If there was such support, management would have proposed anti-takeover amendments; the reason why charter amendments are virtually always approved is that managements consult beforehand with proxy solicitation firms, which track institutional investors' voting records, and they only offer proposals that will succeed given their electorate. We can therefore interpret the absence of an

---

[52] A contributing factor to the different dynamics is that hostile takeovers are an endgame situation for managers—they are likely to lose their jobs after control changes. This removes the restraints on managers' opportunism with regard to the legislative lobbying process that are imposed by the prospect of repeated interaction in the capital market.

anti-takeover amendment as an indicator of shareholders' lack of confidence in their management's capacity to bargain effectively with a bidder. Consequently, without controlling for the shareholder-approved charter defenses, we cannot know for sure whether these firms' negative stock price reactions to takeover statutes were 'mistakes', as Comment and Schwert conjecture.

Overall, the takeover statute data stand as important evidence for those who would forget that state competition is not perfect. But they are not as damaging to Delaware, and thus to transaction cost economics' efficiency gloss on its first-mover advantage, as would appear on first impression.

One other statutory enactment has been extensively examined: Delaware's adoption of a limited liability statute, which enables firms to eliminate outside directors' liability for monetary damages to shareholders for violations of the duty of care. This law has been a focus of empirical research because it is one of the most recent corporate law innovations and it rapidly diffused across the states after Delaware's action: 41 states had such a statute within two years of Delaware's enactment (Romano, 1990). In addition, its anticipated welfare effects have been debated by commentators.

The limited liability statute did not have a significant price effect (Bradley and Schipani, 1989; Janjigian and Bolster, 1990; Romano, 1990). Delaware firms experienced significant negative abnormal returns on the effective date of the statute, which was two weeks after enactment, and not the other event dates occurring during the legislative process.[53] Because there was no question that the statute would become effective after it was enacted and there was significant publicity about the statute during the legislative process, no new information was released on the effective date. Consequently, the finding of negative returns on that date, which is emphasized by Bradley and Schipani in contrast to all other researchers, cannot be attributed to anything other than chance.

Because the limited liability statute's coverage was optional, it is possible that the price effect would not be apparent until investors determined whether or not their firm would be covered although if investors anticipated their firms' decisions on coverage, then we would expect any abnormal returns to be picked up at the time of the statute's enactment and not at the time of the charter amendment. The abnormal returns experienced upon firms' decisions to opt-in (which required a shareholder vote), vary depending on the event window examined. One study finds significant negative

---

[53] Romano (1990) found a significant negative return in an event interval around the Delaware Senate's action and press reports of enactment, but this result was not sustained when cumulated over all legislative event dates or event intervals. If the statute adversely affected shareholders, the negative effect should have been sustained over the cumulated legislative events, as in the studies identifying significant negative effects from takeover statutes (e.g. Sidak and Woodward, 1990).

abnormal returns over a seven-day interval (Bradley and Schipani, 1989), another finds significantly positive abnormal returns in two, three and five-day intervals and insignificant returns in the seven-day interval (Romano, 1990), and two other studies report no significant effects (Janjigian and Bolster, 1990, Netter and Poulsen, 1989). The most cogent interpretation of these data is that the limited liability statute did not affect shareholders adversely. This conclusion is more consistent with a positive than negative assessment of state competition, but it does not really shed much light on the issue.

There have been several event studies of judicial decisions. Because the courts play an important role in Delaware's maintenance of a predominant share of the corporate charter market, determining whether investors benefit from particular decisions could proxy for determining whether they benefit from state competition. Two studies investigated the effect of Delaware and other state court decisions on poison pill defensive tactics, restricting sample firms to takeover targets or the defendant corporations. These studies find significant negative price effects upon decisions upholding the pill defenses and significant positive price effects upon decisions invalidating the tactic (Kamma *et al.*, 1988; Ryngaert, 1988). As with the enactment of takeover statutes, the negative effect of decisions upholding takeover defenses evidences that state competition is an imperfect safeguard of equity interests. In another study, Weiss and White (1987) examined the stock price effect of seven Delaware Supreme Court decisions, four of which involved mergers and one which involved a hostile takeover defense, on all Delaware incorporated firms. They find no significant price reaction to any of the decisions.

Weiss and White interpret their results as demonstrating that judicial decisions are indeterminate. They conclude that investors do not consider differences in state law to be important and that states can thus not be said to compete for incorporations. Their conclusion hinges on the assumption that the decisions under study were not expected. If the market correctly anticipates how the court will rule, a not implausible assumption given the relative predictability of the Delaware court's decisions, then there should be no price effects upon the announcement of the decision. The effect would be impounded in the price earlier, such as when it became clear that the case would be decided by a court. However, identifying such an event date is a difficult, if not insoluble problem. Because most shareholder suits settle and thus produce no legal rule, but settlements occur at any time in the legal process, using systematic points in time, such as filing dates or dates of denials of motions to dismiss, will be inaccurate. We thus cannot tell whether the decisions under study were true surprises as Weiss and White maintain.

There is another explanation, independent of the issue of market anticipation, which is consonant with charter competition, besides Weiss and White's indeterminacy hypothesis, for why court decisions would not have significant stock price effects on firms other than the particular litigants. The transaction cost view of Delaware's success suggests that the benefits from judicial decisions with which investors are concerned are not particular outcomes, which event studies measure, but the declaration of a rule, which provides greater certainty for firms' planning of future transactions to avoid liability. Given the contractual nature of the firm, firm participants will be able to adjust their affairs around a particular rule's substance, if need be. This perspective reconciles the differences across the three event studies. The impact of judicial decisions, on average, is indirect, adding to the store of precedents which enable firms to assess their liability for future courses of action, and will not produce a stock price effect (other than on that of the litigant) unless the decision rule adds significantly to the costs of doing business. Judicial decisions affect share values of the litigants because the transaction's structure has already been fixed. In the takeover context, they determine the outcome of specific bids, and can have clear wealth consequences for takeover targets as well, firms for which the effect of the rule cannot be cheaply avoided.

Performance comparisons. Despite the difficulties previously mentioned with using accounting data to evaluate state competition, one study has examined whether the choice of legal regime affects performance. Comparing return on equity for a sample of firms that moved to Delaware and firms incorporated in four states identified as having strict codes (the identification was based on these states' net outflow of corporations to Delaware), Baysinger and Butler (1985c) find no difference in performance across the two groups. They interpret this result as evidence that corporate law matters, with the view that firms sort themselves across states depending upon their governance needs.[54] If different legal regimes resolve agency problems more effectively for different types of firms, then we should not expect to find performance differences across regimes in equilibrium. As long as governance arrangements are matched to organizational attributes, there should be no systematic relation between incorporation state and performance.

For this article some additional explorations were undertaken of whether the choice of law affects performance to compensate for limitations in

[54] They contend specifically that firms with concentrated ownership will prefer states with 'strict' codes because such owners want the greater control over corporate decisions that strict codes give to shareholders. They find that the firms in the non-Delaware sample have significantly higher family block holdings but there is no significant difference in the holdings of corporate insiders.

Baysinger and Butler's sample, such as their data-driven definition of strict states (which may affect the results because of misclassification, see Romano, 1993a, p. 46), and their performance measure. First, the performance of the firms in my 1985 sample of reincorporating firms was examined to determine whether these firms performed significantly better after reincorporation than all other firms in their industry (identified by 2-digit SIC codes). The investigated performance measure is changes in earnings (before extraordinary income and taxes), standardized by assets (see Weisbach, 1988). The results are no different from Baysinger and Butler's. In general, the reincorporating firms' relative performance is positive compared to their industry average. But there is no statistically significant difference in performance for the reincorporating firms as a whole or grouped by the transaction motivating the move.

The mean earnings, adjusted for industry (standard deviation in parentheses) are shown in the Table.[55]

Firms (No. obs.)	Year +1	Year +2	Year +3
Full sample (126)	0.0040 (0.1122)	−0.0003 (0.0999)	−0.0151 (0.1112)
Acquisitions (50)	0.0155 (0.0744)	0.0037 (0.1168)	−0.0129 (0.1065)
Anti-takeover (38)	0.0146 (0.0744)	0.0043 (0.0849)	0.0122 (0.0905)
Tax (14)	−0.0244 (0.1091)	−0.0022 (0.1042)	−0.0247 (0.1221)
Misc. (22)	−0.0063 (0.1221)	−0.0079 (0.0780)	−0.0580(0.1325)

It should be noted that most of the tax and miscellaneously-motivated reincorporations were to states other than Delaware, whereas most of the acquisition-motivated reincorporations were to Delaware (Romano, 1985). The reincorporating firms' performance was also compared to a paired sample of non-reincorporating firms that were not domiciled in Delaware, where the matching was by 2-digit SIC code and firm size. Because the results were no different (there were no significant differences), they are not reported.

Wang (1996) also investigated the post-reincorporation earnings performance of the firms in his study of reincorporations. He finds no statistically significant difference between the reincorporating firms and a matched sample of non-reincorporating firms. Among the reincorporating firms, the firms reincorporating in Delaware outperformed their industry, while the firms reincorporating in other states did not, but none of the differences are significant.

Second, a large number of firms that reincorporate in Delaware cannot be included in reincorporation event studies because they reincorporate just

[55] I would like to thank Jianghong Wang, doctoral student at the Yale School of Management, for compiling these data for me.

before their initial public offering (IPO) (Romano, 1985). Using post-reincorporation performance data is, in fact, the only means to examine the
impact of the choice of domicile for these firms. I constructed a paired sample of IPOs in Delaware and other states, and compared post-IPO stock
price performance of Delaware and non-Delaware issues.[56] The sample consisted of 44 pairs of IPOs issued during the 1980s; about one-third of the
IPOs were exchange-listed, with no significant difference in listing by incorporation state. The chi-square value of the crosstabulation of incorporation
state (Delaware or other) and exchange listing was 1.34. Although the data
are limited, domicile was found to have no measurable effect on performance. There is no significant difference in mean stock return across the two
groups, calculated over several periods, including from the issue's price at
open to close, where the bulk of IPO gains occurs (Brophy and Verga,
1991), and over one-day and one-year after the offer (measured from both
the closing price and the offering price).

The mean difference in returns (standard error in parentheses) across the
Delaware and non-Delaware IPO firms is shown in the Table.

Return interval	Open, Close	Open, +1	Close, +1	Open, Yr	Close, Yr
Mean ret. diff	0.0550 (0.0983)	−0.0198 (0.0531)	−0.0005 (0.0057)	0.0262 (0.1102)	−0.0278 (0.0765)

The return intervals measure from Open, the opening price on the offering
date, and Close, the closing price on the offering date, through +1, the day
after the offering date, and Yr, one year after the offering date. For a small
number of firms in the sample, Post-IPO earnings data were available. There
were no significant differences across the Delaware and non-Delaware firms,
but because this sample is so small and no longer paired, I have no confidence in the accuracy of the numbers and do not report them.

There is, then, no evidence in the performance data that state competition
is adverse to shareholders' interest. Delaware firms do not underperform
non-Delaware firms, but neither do Delaware firms outperform non-
Delaware firms. The data are most consistent with the view that the charter
market is in equilibrium: firms select the legal regime that enables them to
attain their best possible performance.

---

[56] The IPO sample was obtained from the Securities Data Company (SDC); the pairing is by offering
date, which serves as a rough control for market conditions. There were not a sufficient number of firms
in SDC's database for them to provide me with a sample paired by industry as well as offering date.
Besides the pairing by time and incorporation state, the other criterion for the offerings included in the
sample was a minimum offer size of $2 million.

5. Conclusion

As I hope this article has made clear, transaction cost economics has and can be used to illuminate key governance problems in corporate law. It identifies the benefits accruing to equity investors from independent boards of directors, relational investment (to the extent there are any benefits from such an arrangement in the US context), and state competition for corporate charters. Empirical research on how these mechanisms work to protect equity investments indicate that: (i) corporate law is best understood as providing a background organizational frame that enables parties to choose governance structures tailored to their needs: we find firms experience positive abnormal returns upon reincorporating, but no significant cross-sectional performance differences; (ii) independent directors are most effective in performing a monitoring function in extraordinary times, such as during financial distress and takeovers, than on a day-to-day basis: we find board composition matters for decisions taken in such times of stress but not for overall performance; (iii) relational investing will continue to have a limited role in safeguarding investments in the US corporate governance context, compared to crisis intervention by ordinarily passive large blockholders, as it is a governance structure that fits only a subset of firms with highly non-redeployable assets: venture capitalists provide a good example of this conjecture but systematic empirical support is missing; and (iv) the ultimate controls of performance where ownership is diffuse, as it is for most US corporations, are the markets in which these firms operate, the product, labor, capital and the backstop of all, corporate control markets, a point—the complementarity of markets and hierarchies—which was Oliver Williamson's insight of 20 years ago.

Acknowledgements

I would like to thank Ian Ayres, Stephen Bainbridge, Ron Gilson, Henry Hansmann, Alvin Klevorick, Laura Lin, Peter Schuck, Alan Schwartz, and participants at faculty workshops, at the University of Illinois at Urbana-Champagne and Yale Law Schools and the Fisher School of Accounting at the University of Florida, as well as the conference participants, for helpful comments on an earlier draft of this article.

References

Agrawal, A. and C. Knoeber (1994), 'Firm Performance and Mechanisms to Control Agency Problems between Managers and Shareholders.' Manuscript, North Carolina State University.

Agrawal, A. and G. Mandelker (1990), 'Large Shareholders and the Monitoring of Managers: The Case of Antitakeover Charter Amendments,' *Journal of Financial and Quantitative Analysis*, 25, 143–161.

American Law Institute (1982), *Principles of Corporate Governance and Structure: Restatement and Recommendations* (Tentative Draft No. 1). American Law Institute: Philadelphia, PA.

Ayres, I. and P. Cramton (1994), 'Relational Investing and Agency Theory,' *Cardozo Law Review*, 15, 1033–1066.

Bainbridge, S. (1995), 'The Politics of Corporate Governance,' *Harvard Journal of Law & Public Policy*, 18, 671--734.

Baltagi, B. and J. Griffin (1989), 'Alternative Models of Managerial Behavior: Empirical Tests for the Petroleum Industry,' *Review of Economics and Statistics*, 71, 579–585.

Baron, D. (1983), 'Tender Offers and Management Resistance,' *Journal of Finance*, 38, 331–343.

Barry, C. *et al.* (1990), 'The Role of Venture Capital in the Creation of Public Companies,' *Journal of Financial Economics*, 27, 447–471.

Baysinger, B. and H. Butler (1985a), 'Corporate Governance and the Board of Directors: Performance Effects of Changes in Board Composition,' *Journal of Law, Economics and Organization*, 1, 101–124.

Baysinger, B. and H. Butler (1985b), 'Antitakeover Amendments, Managerial Entrenchment, and the Contractual Theory of the Corporation,' *Virginia Law Review*, 71, 1257–1303.

Baysinger, B. and H. Butler (1985c), 'The Role of Corporate Law in the Theory of the Firm,' *Journal of Law and Economics*, 28, 179–191.

Bebchuk, L. (1989), 'Foreword: The Debate on Contractual Freedom in Corporate Law,' *Columbia Law Review*, 89, 1395–1415.

Benston, G. (1973), 'Required Disclosure and the Stock Market: An Evaluation of the Securities Exchange Act of 1934,' *American Economic Review*, 63, 132–155.

Blackman, P. (1993), 'Move Over Delaware!', *New York Law Journal*, pp. 5–6 (16 December).

Bohn, J. and S. Choi (1995), 'Fraud in the New Issues Markets: Empirical Evidence on Securities Class Actions.' Manuscript, Harvard University.

Bradley, M. and C. Schipani, (1989), 'The Relevance of the Duty of Care Standard in Corporate Governance,' *Iowa Law Review*, 75, 1–74.

Brickley, J., J. Coles and R. Terry (1994), 'Outside Directors and the Adoption of Poison Pills,' *Journal of Financial Economics*, 35, 371–390.

Brophy, D. and J. Verga (1991), 'The Influence of Merit Regulation on the Return Performance of Initial Public Offerings.' Working Paper 91–19, University of Michigan School of Business Administration.

Broner, A. (1987), 'New Jersey Shareholders Protection Act: An Economic Evaluation, A Report to the New Jersey Legislature.' Office of Economic Policy: State of New Jersey.

Brown, S. and J. Warner (1985), 'Using Daily Stock Returns: The Case of Event Studies,' *Journal of Financial Economics*, 14, 401–438.

Buffett, W. (1990), 'Letter to Shareholders,' Annual Report. Berkshire Hathaway, Inc.: Omaha, Neb.

Buffett, W. (1994), 'Letter to Shareholders,' Annual Report. Berkshire Hathaway, Inc.: Omaha, Neb.

Butler, H. (1988), 'Corporation-Specific Antitakeover Statutes and the Market for Corporate Charters,' *Wisconsin Law Review*, 1988, 365–383.

Butler, H. and J. Macey (1988), 'The Myth of Competition in the Dual Banking System,' *Cornell Law Review*, 73, 677–718.

Byrd, J. and K. Hickman (1992), 'Do Outside Directors Monitor Managers? Evidence from Tender Offer Bids,' *Journal of Financial Economics*, 32, 195–221.

Carney, W. (1983), 'Shareholder Coordination Costs, Shark Repellents, and Takeout Mergers: The Case Against Fiduciary Duties,' *American Bar Foundation Research Journal*, 1983, 341–392.

Cary, W. (1974), 'Federalism and Corporate Law: Reflections upon Delaware,' *Yale Law Journal*, 83, 663–707.

Chaganti, R., V. Mahajan and S. Sharma (1985), 'Corporate Board Size, Composition and Corporate Failures in Retailing Industry,' *Journal of Management Studies*, 22, 400–417.

Chan, L. and J. Lakonishok (1993), 'Institutional Trades and Intraday Stock Price Behavior,' *Journal of Financial Economics*, 33, 173–199.

Chan, S., J. Martin and J. Kensinger (1990), 'Corporate Research and Development Expenditures and Share Value,' *Journal of Financial Economics*, 26, 255–276.

Cochran, P., R. Wood and T. Jones (1985), 'The Composition of Boards of Directors and Incidence of Golden Parachutes,' *Academy of Management Journal*, 28, 664–671.

Coffee, J. (1991), 'Liquidity versus Control: The Institutional Investor as Corporate Monitor,' *Columbia Law Review*, 91, 1277–1368.

Comment, R. and G. W. Schwert (1995), 'Poison or Placebo? Evidence on the Deterrence and Wealth Effects of Modern Antitakeover Measures,' *Journal of Financial Economics*, 39, 3–43.

Cotter, J., A. Shivdasani and M. Zenner (1996), 'Do Independent Directors Enhance Target Shareholder Wealth during Tender Offers?' (forthcoming *Journal of Financial Economics*).

Daily, C. and D. Dalton (1994), 'Bankruptcy and Corporate Governance: the Impact of Board Composition and Structure,' *Academy of Management Journal*, 37, 1603–1617.

Daniels, R. (1991), 'Should Provinces Compete? The Case for a Competitive Corporate Law Market,' *McGill Law Journal*, 36, 130–190.

Dann, L., D. Mayers, and R. Raab (1977), 'Trading Rules, Large Blocks and the Speed of Price Adjustment,' *Journal of Financial Economics*, 4, 3–22.

Davis, G. (1991), 'Agents without Principles? The Spread of the Poison Pill through the Intercorporate Network,' *Administrative Science Quarterly*, 36, 583–613.

Demsetz, H. and K. Lehn (1985), 'The Structure of Corporate Ownership: Causes and Consequences,' *Journal of Political Economy*, 93, 1155–1177, reprinted in H. Demsetz (1988), *Ownership, Control and the Firm*. Basil Blackwell: New York, pp. 202–222.

Dobrzynski, J. (1993), 'Relationship Investing,' *Business Week*, p. 68 (15 March).

Dodd, P. and R. Leftwich (1980), 'The Market for Corporate Charters: 'Unhealthy Competition' versus Federal Regulation,' *Journal of Business*, 53, 259–283.

Easterbrook, F. and D. Fischel (1981), 'The Proper Role of a Target's Management in Responding to a Tender Offer,' *Harvard Law Review*, 94, 1161–1204.

Easterbrook, F. and D. Fischel, (1983), 'Voting and Corporate Law,' *Journal of Law and Economics*, 26, 395–427.

Easterbrook, F. and D. Fischel (1989), 'The Corporate Contract,' *Columbia Law Review*, 89, 1416–1448.

The Economist (1995), 'A Letter to Warren Buffett,' p. 71 (2 September).

Eisenberg, M. (1976), *The Structure of the Corporation*. Little, Brown & Co.: Boston, MA.

Elson, C. (1993), 'Executive Overcompensation—A Board-Based Solution,' *Boston College Law Review*, 34, 937–996.

Fama, E. (1991), 'Efficient Capital Markets: II', *Journal of Finance*, 46, 1575–1617.

Fisch, J. (1994), 'Relationship Investing: Will It Happen? Will It Work?', *Ohio State Law Journal*, 55, 1009–1048.

Fischel, D. and M. Bradley (1986), 'The Role of Liability Rules and the Derivative Suit in Corporate Law: A Theoretical and Empirical Analysis,' *Cornell Law Review*, 71, 261–297.

Fortune (1995), 'Is Salomon Brothers on the Block?,' pp. 70–71 (4 September).

French, K. (1980), 'Stock Returns and the Weekend Effect,' *Journal of Financial Economics*, 8, 55–69.

Friend, I. and L. Lang, (1988), 'An Empirical Test of the Impact of Managerial Self-Interest on Corporate Capital Structure,' *Journal of Finance*, 43, 271–281.

Geddes, R. (1995), 'Regulatory Constraints, Managerial Turnover and Outside Directors.' Manuscript, Fordham University.

Gerschenkron, A. (1962), *Economic Backwardness in Historical Perspective: A Book of Essays*. Belknap Press: Cambridge, MA.

Gilson, R. (1981), 'A Structural Approach to Corporations: The Case Against Defensive Tactics,' *Stanford Law Review*, 33, 819–891.

Gilson, R. and R. Kraakman (1991), 'Reinventing the Outside Director: An Agenda for Institutional Investors,' *Stanford Law Review*, 43, 863–906.

Gilson, R. and M. Roe (1993), 'Understanding the Japanese Keiretsu: Overlaps Between Corporate Governance and Industrial Organization,' *Yale Law Journal*, 102, 871–906.

Gilson, S. (1990), 'Bankruptcy, Boards, Banks, and Blockholders,' *Journal of Financial Economics*, 27, 355–387.

Gompers, P. (1995), 'Optimal Investment, Monitoring, and the Staging of Venture Capital,' *Journal of Finance*, 50, 1461–1489.

Gordon, J. (1994), 'Institutions as Relational Investors: A New Look at Cumulative Voting,' *Columbia Law Review*, 94, 124–192.

Gordon, J. and L. Kornhauser (1986), 'Takeover Defense Tactics: A Comment on Two Models,' *Yale Law Journal*, 96, 295–321.

Gordon, L. and J. Pound (1993), 'Active Investing in the US Equity Market: Past Performance and Future Prospects: A Report Prepared for the California Public Employees' Retirement System.' Gordon Group, Inc.: Newton, MA.

Grandy, C. (1989), 'New Jersey Corporate Chartermongering, 1875–1929,' *Journal of Economic History*, 49, 677–692.

Griffin, J. and S. Wiggins (1992), 'Managerial Incompetence or Managerial Shirking?' *Economic Inquiry*, 30, 355–370.

Haddock, D. and J. Macey (1987), 'Regulation on Demand: A Private Interest Model with an Application to Insider Trading Regulation,' *Journal of Law and Economics*, 30, 311–352.

Hagstrom, R. (1995), *The Warren Buffett Way: Investment Strategies of the World's Greatest Investor*. John Wiley & Sons: New York.

Hall, B. (1988), 'The Effect of Takeover Activity on Corporate Research and Development, in A. Auerbach (ed.), *Corporate Takeovers: Causes and Consequences*. University of Chicago Press: Chicago, IL, pp. 69–96.

Hall, B. (1990), 'The Impact of Corporate Restructuring on Industrial Research and Development,' in M. Bailey and C. Winston (eds), *Brookings Papers on Economic Activity: Microeconomics 1990*. Brookings Institution: Washington, DC., pp. 85–135.

Hansmann, H. (1988), 'Ownership of the Firm,' *Journal of Law, Economics, and Organization*, 4, 267–304.

Harlan, C. (1988), 'Massachusetts Bill Seeks Courts for Business,' *Wall Street Journal*, p. B6 (8 December).

Hermalin, B. and M. Weisbach (1988), 'The Determinants of Board Composition,' *RAND Journal of Economics*, 19, 589–606.

Hermalin, B. and M. Weisbach (1991), 'The Effects of Board Composition and Direct Incentives on Firm Performance,' *Financial Management*, 20, 101–112.

Holthausen, R., R. Leftwich and D. Mayers (1987), 'The Effect of Large Block Transactions on Security Prices: A Cross-Sectional Analysis,' *Journal of Financial Economics*, 19, 237–267.

Hyman, A. (1979), 'The Delaware Controversy—The Legal Debate,' *Delaware Journal of Corporate Law*, 4, 368–398.

Ibbotson Associates, Inc. (1992), *SBBI, Stocks, Bonds, Bills & Inflation 1992 Yearbook*. Ibbotson Associates: Chicago, IL.

Jahera, J. and W. Pugh (1991), 'State Takeover Legislation: The Case of Delaware,' *Journal of Law, Economics, and Organization*, 7, 410–427.

Janjigian, V. and P. Bolster (1990), 'The Elimination of Director Liability and Stockholder Returns: An Empirical Investigation,' *Journal of Financial Research*, 3, 53–60.

Jarrell, G., *et al.* (1988), 'The Market for Corporate Control: The Empirical Evidence Since 1980,' *Journal of Economic Perspectives*, 2, 49–68.

Jensen, M. (1988), 'Takeovers: Their Causes and Consequences,' *Journal of Economic Perspectives*, 2, 21–48.

Jensen, M. (1989), 'Active Investors, LBOs and the Privatization of Bankruptcy,' *The Continental Bank Journal of Applied Corporate Finance*, 27, 35–44 (Spring).

Jensen, M. and W. Meckling (1976), 'Theory of the Firm: Managerial Behavior, Agency Costs, and Capital Structure,' *Journal of Financial Economics*, 3, 305–360.

Kamma, S., J. Weintrop and P. Wier (1988), 'Investors' Perceptions of the Delaware Supreme Court Decision in Unocal v. Mesa,' *Journal of Financial Economics*, 20, 419–430.

Kaplan, S. (1991), 'The Staying Power of Leveraged Buyouts,' *Journal of Financial Economies*, 29, 287–313.

Kaplan, S. (1994a), 'Top Executives Rewards and Firm Performance: A Comparison of Japan and the United States,' *Journal of Political Economy*, 102, 510–546.

Kaplan, S. (1994b), 'Top Executives, Turnover, and Firm Performance in Germany,' *Journal of Law, Economics, and Organization*, 10, 142–159.

Kaplan, S. and B. Minton (1994), 'Appointments of Outsiders to Japanese Boards: Determinants and Implications for Managers,' *Journal of Financial Economics*, 36, 225–258.

Karpoff, J. and P. Malatesta (1989), 'The Wealth Effects of Second Generation State Takeover Legislation,' *Journal of Financial Economics*, 25, 291–322.

Karpoff, J. and P. Malatesta (1995), 'State Takeover Legislation and Share Values: The Wealth Effects of Pennsylvania's Act 36,' *Journal of Corporate Finance*, 1, 367–382.

Kesner, I. and R. Johnson (1990), 'An Investigation of the Relationship Between Board Composition and Stockholder Suits,' *Strategic Management Journal*, 11, 327–336.

Kesner, I., B. Victor and B. Lamont (1986), 'Board Composition and the Commission of Illegal Acts: An Investigation of Fortune 500 Companies,' *Academy of Management Journal*, 29, 789–799.

Kester, W. C. (1991), *Japanese Takeovers: The Global Contest for Corporate Control*. Harvard Business School Press: Boston, MA.

Kieschnick, R. (1989), 'Management Buyouts of Public Corporations: An Analysis of Prior Characteristics,' in Y. Amihud (ed.), *Leveraged Management Buyouts: Causes and Consequences*. Dow Jones-Irwin: Homewood, IL, pp. 35–67.

Kini, O., W. Kracaw and S. Mian (1995), 'Corporate Takeovers, Firm Performance, and Board Composition,' *Journal of Corporate Finance*, 1, 383–412.

Klausner, M. (1995), 'Corporations, Corporate Law and Networks of Contracts,' *Virginia Law Review*, 81, 757–852.

Klein, A. (1995), 'Firm Productivity and Board Committee Structure.' Manuscript. Leonard N. Stern School of Business, New York University.

Kosnik, R. (1987), 'Greenmail: A Study of Board Performance in Corporate Governance,' *Administrative Science Quarterly*, 32, 163–185.

Kraus, A. and H. Stoll, (1972), 'Price Impacts of Block Trading on the New York Stock Exchange,' *Journal of Finance*, 27, 569–588.

Larckner, R. and D. Lambert (1985), 'Golden Parachutes, Executive Decision-making and Shareholder Wealth,' *Journal of Accounting and Economics*, 7, 179–203.

Lee, C. *et al.* (1992), 'Board Composition and Shareholder Wealth: The Case of Management Buyouts,' *Financial Management*, 21, 58–72.

Lerner, J. (1995), 'Venture Capitalists and the Oversight of Private Firms,' *Journal of Finance*, 50, 301–318.

Lichtenberg, F. and D. Siegel (1990), 'The Effects of Leveraged Buyouts on Productivity and Related Aspects of Firm Behavior,' *Journal of Financial Economics*, 27, 165–194.

Lin, L. (1995), 'The Effectiveness of Outside Directors as a Corporate Governance Mechanism: Theories and Evidence.' Manuscript, Northwestern University.

Lorsch, J. and E. MacIver (1989), *Pawns or Potentates: The Reality of American's Corporate Boards*. Harvard Business School Press: Boston, MA.

MacAvoy, P., *et al.* (1983), 'ALI Proposals for Increased Control of the Corporation by the Board of Directors: An Economic Analysis,' in *Statement of The Business Roundtable on the American Law Institute's Proposed 'Principles of Corporate Governance and Structure: Restatement and Recommendations.'* Business Roundtable: New York.

Macey, J. and F. McChesney (1985), 'A Theoretical Analysis of Corporate Greenmail,' *Yale Law Journal*, 95, 13–61.

Macey, J. and G. Miller (1992), *Banking Law and Regulation*. Little Brown & Co.: Boston, MA.

Mahla, C. (1991), 'State Takeover Statutes and Shareholder Wealth.' PhD dissertation. University of North Carolina.

Malkiel, B. (1990), *A Random Walk Down Wall Street*. 5th edition W. W. Norton & Co: New York. (1991 Norton paperback edition).

Mallette, P. and K. Fowler (1992), 'Effects of Board Composition and Stock Ownership on the Adoption of "Poison Pills,"' *Academy of Management Journal*, 35, 1010–1035.

Manne, H. (1965), 'Mergers and the Market for Corporate Control,' *Journal of Political Economy*, 73, 110–120.

Margotta, D. and S. Badrinath (1987), 'Effects of the New Jersey Shareholder Protection Legislation on Stock Prices.' Manuscript, Northeastern University.

Margotta, D., T. McWilliams and V. McWilliams (1990), 'An Analysis of the Stock Price Effect of the 1986 Ohio Takeover Legislation,' *Journal of Law, Economics, and Organization*, 6, 235–251.

McConnell, J. and C. Muscarella (1985), 'Capital Expenditure Decisions and Market Value of the Firm,' *Journal of Financial Economics*, 14, 399–422.

McConnell, J. and H. Servaes (1990), 'Additional Evidence on Equity Ownership and Corporate Value,' *Journal of Financial Economics*, 27, 595–612.

McConnell, J. and H. Servaes (1995), 'Equity Ownership and the Two Faces of Debt,' *Journal of Financial Economics*, 39, 131–157.

McCubbins, M. and T. Schwartz (1984), 'Congressional Oversight Overlooked: Police Patrols versus Fire Alarms,' *American Journal of Political Science*, 2, 165–179.

Mehran, H. (1995), 'Executive Compensation Structure, Ownership, and Firm Performance,' *Journal of Financial Economics*, 38, 163–184.

Meulbroek, L., *et al.* (1990), 'Shark Repellents and Managerial Myopia: An Empirical Test,' *Journal of Political Economics*, 98, 1108–1117.

Mikkelson, W. and M. Partch (1985), 'Stock Price Effects and Costs of Secondary Distributions,' *Journal of Financial Economics*, 14, 165–194.

Mikkelson, W. and R. Ruback (1991), 'Targeted Repurchases and Common Stock Returns,' *RAND Journal of Economics*, 22, 544–561.

Miller, G. (1987), 'The Future of the Dual Banking System,' *Brooklyn Law Review*, 53, 1–22.

Moore, A. (1987), 'State Competition: Panel Response,' *Cardozo Law Review*, 8, 779–782.

Morck, R. and M. Nakamura (1995), 'Banks and Corporate Governance in Canada, in R. Daniels and R. Morck (eds.), *Corporate Decision-Making in Canada*. University of Calgary Press: Calgary, Canada, pp. 481–501.

Morck, R., A. Shleifer and R. Vishny (1988), 'Management Ownership and Market Valuation: An Empirical Analysis,' *Journal of Financial Economics*, 20, 293–315.

Morck, R., A. Shleifer and R. Vishny (1989), 'Alternative Mechanisms for Corporate Control,' *American Economic Review*, 79, 842–852.

Nader, R., M. Green and J. Seligman (1976), *Taming the Corporate Giant*. Norton: New York.

Netter, J. and A. Poulsen (1989), 'State Corporation Laws and Shareholders: The Recent Experience,' *Financial Management*, 18(3), 29–40.

O'Connor, M. (1991), 'Restructuring the Corporation's Nexus of Contracts: Recognizing a Fiduciary Duty to Protect Displaced Workers,' *North Carolina Law Review*, 69, 1189–1260.

Posner, R. (1992), *Economic Analysis of Law* 4th edition. Little, Brown & Co.: Boston, MA.

Prowse, S. (1990), 'Institutional Investment Patterns and Corporate Financial Behavior in the United States and Japan,' *Journal of Financial Economics*, 27, 43–66.

Pugh, W. and J. Jahera (1990), 'State Antitakeover Legislation and Shareholder Wealth,' *Journal of Financial Research*, 13, 221–231.

Rechner, P. and D. Dalton (1986), 'Board Composition and Shareholder Wealth: An Empirical Assessment,' *International Journal of Management*, 3, 86–92.

Rock, E. (1994), 'Controlling the Dark Side of Relational Investing,' *Cardozo Law Review*, 15, 987–1031.

Roe, M. (1994), *Strong Managers Weak Owners: The Political Roots of American Corporate Finance*. Princeton University: Princeton, NJ.

Romano, R. (1985), 'Law as a Product: Some Pieces of the Incorporation Puzzle,' *Journal of Law, Economics, and Organization*, 1, 225–283.

Romano, R. (1987), 'The Political Economy of Takeover Statutes,' *Virginia Law Review*, 73, 111–199.

Romano, R. (1988), 'The Future of Hostile Takeovers: Legislation and Public Opinion,' *University of Cincinnati Law Review*, 57, 457–505.

Romano, R. (1990), 'Corporate Governance in the Aftermath of the Insurance Crisis, *Emory Law Journal*, 39, 1155–1189.

Romano, R. (1991), 'The Shareholder Suit: Litigation Without Foundation?', *Journal of Law Economics, and Organization*, 7, 55–87.

Romano, R. (1992), 'A Guide to Takeovers: Theory, Evidence and Regulation,' *Yale Journal on Regulation*, 9, 119–179.

Romano, R. (1993a), *The Genius of American Corporate Law*. AEI Press: Washington, DC.

Romano, R. (1993b), 'Public Pension Fund Activism in Corporate Governance Reconsidered,' *Columbia Law Review*, 93, 795–853.

Romano, R. (1993c), 'Comment: What is the Value of Other Constituency Statutes to Shareholders?,' *University of Toronto Law Journal*, 43, 533–542.

Rosenstein, S. and J. Wyatt (1990), 'Outside Directors, Board Independence, and Shareholder Wealth,' *Journal of Financial Economics*, 26, 175–191.

Ross, S., R. Westerfield and J. Jaffe (1993), *Corporate Finance*, 3d edition. Richard D. Irwin: Homewood, IL.

Ryngaert, M. (1988), 'The Effect of Poison Pill Securities on Shareholder Wealth,' *Journal of Financial Economics*, 20, 377–417.

Ryngaert, M. and J. Netter (1988), 'Shareholder Wealth Effects of the Ohio Antitakeover Law,' *Journal of Law, Economics, and Organization*, 4, 373–383.

Ryngaert, M. and J. Netter (1990), 'Shareholder Wealth Effects of the 1986 Ohio Antitakeover Law Revisited: Its Real Effects,' *Journal of Law, Economics, and Organization*, 6, 253–262.

Sahlman, W. (1990), 'The Structure and Governance of Venture Capital Organizations,' *Journal of Financial Economics*, 27, 473–521.

Schellinger, M., D. Wood and A. Tashakori (1989), 'Board of Director Composition, Shareholder Wealth, and Dividend Policy,' *Journal of Management*, 15, 457–467.

Schipper, K. and R. Thompson (1983), 'Evidence on the Capitalized Value of Merger Activity for Acquiring Firms,' *Journal of Financial Economics*, 11, 85–119.

Schmidt, R. (1977), 'The Board of Directors and Financial Interests,' *Academy of Management Journal*, 20, 677–682.

Scholes, M. (1972), 'The Market for Securities: Substitution Versus Price Pressure and the Effects of Information on Share Prices,' *Journal of Business*, 45, 179–211.

Schumann, L. (1989), 'State Regulation of Takeovers and Shareholder Wealth: The Case of New York's 1985 Takeover Statutes,' *RAND Journal of Economics*, 19, 557–567.

Schwartz, A. (1986), 'Search Theory and the Tender Offer Auction,' *Journal of Law Economics, and Organization*, **2**, 229–253.

Scott, K. (1977), 'The Dual Banking System: A Model of Competition in Regulation,' *Stanford Law Review*, **30**, 1–50.

Scott, K. (1983), 'Corporation Law and the American Law Institute Corporate Governance Project,' *Stanford Law Review*, **35**, 927–948.

SEC Office of Chief Economist (1985), 'Institutional Ownership, Tender Offers and Long Term Investments.' Securities and Exchange Commission: Washington, DC.

Shivdasani, A. (1993), 'Board Composition, Ownership Structure, and Hostile Takeovers,' *Journal of Accounting and Economics*, **16**, 167–198.

Shleifer, A. and R. Vishny (1986a), 'Large Shareholders and Corporate Control,' *Journal of Political Economy*, **94**, 461–488.

Shleifer, A. and R. Vishny (1986b), 'Greenmail, White Knights, and Shareholders' Interest,' *RAND Journal of Economics*, **17**, 293–309.

Shleifer, A. and R. Vishny (1995), 'A Survey of Corporate Governance.' Manuscript, Harvard University.

Sidak, J. and S. Woodward (1990), 'Corporate Takeovers, the Commerce Clause, and the Efficient Anonymity of Shareholders,' *Northwestern University Law Review*, **84**, 1092–1118.

Smith, A. (1990), 'The Effects of Leveraged Buyouts,' *Business Economics*, **25**, 19–25 (April 1990).

Smith, D. (1996a), 'Corporate Governance and Managerial Incompetence: Lessons from KMART,' *North Carolina Law Review*, **74**, 1037–1139.

Smith, M. (1996b), 'Shareholder Activism by Institutional Investors: Evidence from CalPERS,' *Journal of Finance*, **51**, 227–252

Stobaugh, R. (1993), 'Director Compensation: A Lever to Improve Corporate Governance,' *Director's Monthly*, **17**,(8) (August), 1–5.

Stone, C. (1975), *Where the Law Ends: The Social Control of Corporate Behavior*. Harper & Row: New York.

Szewczyk, S. and G. Tsetsekos (1992), 'State Intervention in the Market for Corporate Control: The Case of Pennsylvania Senate Bill 1310,' *Journal of Financial Economics*, **31**, 3–23.

Tilly, R. (1966), *Financial Institutions and Industrialization in the Rhineland, 1815–1870*. University of Wisconsin Press: Madison, WIS.

Vance, S. (1964), *Boards of Directors: Structure and Performance*. University of Oregon Press: Eugene, ORE.

Wahal, S. (1996), 'Pension Fund Activism and Firm Performance, *Journal of Quantitative and Financial Analysis*, **31**, 1–23.

Waldo, C. (1985), *Boards of Directors: Their Changing Roles, Structure, and Information Needs*. Greenwood Press: Westport, CT.

Wang, J. (1996), 'Performance of Reincorporated Firms.' Manuscript, Yale School of Management.

Warner, J., R. Watts and K. Wruck (1988), 'Stock Prices and Top Management Changes,' *Journal of Financial Economics*, **20**, 461–492.

Weinstein, D. and Y. Yafeh (1993), 'On the Costs of a Bank-Centered Financial System: Evidence from the Changing Main Bank Relations in Japan.' Manuscript, Harvard University.

Weisbach, M. (1988), 'Outside Directors and CEO Turnover,' *Journal of Financial Economics*, **20**, 431–460.

Weiss, E. (1981), 'Social Regulation of Business Activity: Reforming the Corporate Governance System to Resolve an Institutional Impasse,' *UCLA Law Review*, **28**, 343–437.

Weiss, E. and L. White (1987), 'Of Econometrics and Indeterminacy.' A Study of Investors' Reactions to 'Changes' in Corporate Law,' *California Law Review*, **75**, 551–607.

Williamson, O. (1975), *Markets and Hierarchies: Analysis and Antitrust Implications*. The Free Press: New York.

Williamson, O. (1979), 'On the Governance of the Modern Corporation,' *Hofstra Law Review*, **8**, 63–78.

Williamson, O. (1983), 'Credible Commitments: Using Hostages to Support Exchange,' *American Economic Review*, **73**, 519–540.

Williamson, O. (1984), 'Corporate Governance,' *Yale Law Journal*, 93, 1197–1230.

Williamson, O. (1985), *The Economic Institutions of Capitalism*. The Free Press: New York.

Williamson, O. (1988), 'Corporate Finance and Corporate Governance,' *Journal of Finance*, 43, 567–591.

Williamson, O. (1991), 'Strategizing, Economizing, and Economic Organization,' *Strategic Management Journal*, 12, 75–94.

Winter, R. (1977), 'State Law, Shareholder Protection, and the Theory of the Corporation,' *Journal of Legal Studies*, 6, 251–292.

Yafeh, Y. (1995), 'Corporate Ownership, Profitability, and Bank-Firm Ties: Evidence from the American Occupation Reforms in Japan,' *Journal of the Japanese and International Economies* 9, 154–173.

Zahra, S. and W. Stanton (1988), 'The Implications of Board of Directors' Composition for Corporate Strategy and Performance,' *International Journal of Management*, 5, 229–236.

Zeckhauser, R. and J. Pound (1990), 'Are Large Shareholders Effective Monitors? An Investigation of Share Ownership and Corporate Performance,' in R. G. Hubbard (ed.), *Asymmetric Information, Corporate Finance and Investment*. University of Chicago Press: Chicago, IL, pp. 149–180.

CHAPTER SIXTEEN

The Road Taken
Origins and Evolution of Employment Systems in Emerging Companies

JAMES N. BARTON, M. DIANE BURTON, AND
MICHAEL T. HANNAN

Drawing on a unique archive of qualitative and quantitative data describing 100 Bay Area high technology firms within their first decade, this paper examines the models of employment relations espoused by company founders and how those models shaped the evolution of human resource management within their organizations. Information gleaned from interviews suggests that founders and others involved in designing and launching these companies had blueprints for the employment relation that varied along three key dimensions: the primary basis of employee attachment and motivation, the primary means for controlling and coordinating work, and the primary criterion emphasized in selection. Based on combinations of these three dimensions, firms in our sample cluster fall into one of four distinct types, which we label the star, factory, engineering, and commitment models. Multivariate statistical analyses document how the founder's employment model shaped the subsequent adoption and timing of various human resource policies and documents over these companies' early histories, as well as the speed with which the first full-time human resource manager was appointed. The findings are strongly suggestive of complementarities and a tendency toward internal consistency among dimensions of human resource management, and of strong path dependence in the evolution of employment systems in organizations. Some implications of these findings for transactions cost perspectives on the employment relationship are discussed.

1. Introduction

A central concern of transaction cost economics (TCE) has been to understand how employment relationships and governance structures develop around productive activities. Williamson's (1975) operating hypothesis has been that organizational forms and employment systems develop so as to minimize the transaction costs and hold-up problems facing employers and employees. These issues arise primarily from relationship-specific skills and investments (and the small numbers bargaining they induce *ex post*), task interdependencies, opportunism and informational imperfections that make spot contracting or contingent claims contracting infeasible or very costly. In more recent work, Williamson (1992) has acknowledged the prevalence of organizational inertia and path-dependent development, which have been documented in the empirical literature on organizations (Barnett and Carroll, 1995). However, he argues that inertia and path dependence likely reflect either an absence of strong competitive pressures (the scope conditions under which the hypothesis of transaction cost minimization is most intended to apply) or a situation in which the adjustment costs of getting to 'first best' exceed the anticipated incremental gains.

Williamsonian reasoning has stimulated the development of typologies of organizational employment systems. Spot contracting through markets is thought to be optimal when work is independent and easy to monitor, when the skills involved are general, and when, accordingly, employees or employers have little room for opportunism. When the parties cannot contract *ex ante* for what is to be done or circumvent problems that arise from small numbers and/or monopoly power, markets fail. Then bureaucracies are preferable, because they bind the interests of both employer and employee through long-term relationships and rely on rules and monitoring devices to discourage opportunism (Williamson, 1975, 1981). When tasks are extremely interdependent and/or difficult to monitor, team or 'clan' employment systems relying more on cultural controls (peer monitoring and internalization of values) are superior (Ouchi, 1980). Some extant empirical evidence supports the notion that the design of human resource systems and the management of employment relationships in organizations is broadly consistent with these predictions of transactions cost economics (Pfeffer and Cohen, 1984; Baron *et al.*, 1986; Cohen and Pfeffer, 1986).

However, several ambiguities complicate the process of subjecting TCE to rigorous empirical test. One applies to any approach that, like TCE, emphasizes comparative statics. It concerns the *time-frame* over which transaction cost minimization is expected to occur. Indeed, if an organization exists in a stable equilibrium or can continually adjust its employment practices in response to changes in its external environment and internal constraints, then matters are rather straightforward. However, it seems quite likely that organization employment systems are characterized by considerable path dependence. Hannan and Freeman (1977, 1984) argued that inertial tendencies in organizations are most acute in the 'core' of organizations, where the benefits of reproducibility and legitimacy are greatest and where, because of interdependencies, even a minor change has potentially enormous ramifications for other parts of the organization. For reasons that are outlined in our companion paper (Hannan *et al.*, 1996), altering the premises of employees' relationships with the organization, as well as the specific HR practices that undergird those relationships, is likely to be extraordinarily contentious, which might explain the oft-noted difficulty of achieving large-scale change in HR systems (Pfeffer, 1994). Indeed, from an economic theory standpoint, a critical objective in structuring employment relationships is establishing a reputation, *vis-à-vis* current and prospective employees (Simon, 1951; Kreps, 1996). There might be an inherent tension between developing and maintaining a strong reputation among employees in the labor market, which is predicated on continuity and stability in employment practices, and continually realigning the organization's HR activities in light of changing internal and external circumstances.

In this paper, we wish to focus on a second ambiguity that complicates efforts to test the implications of TCE reasoning for employment relationships. It concerns the *level of analysis* at which transaction-cost minimization should be expected to occur. Evidence of transaction cost economizing will be easier to discern when organizations manage a set of completely separable (i.e. non-interdependent) activities, which can each be structured and controlled through a distinctive combination of employment policies and practices, than when there are strong technological, normative, or other interdependencies among activities that necessitate common policies across disparate tasks and labor forces. Moreover, if there are inherent complementarities among sets of human resource practices, then organizational designers might have limited ability to pick and choose among specific policies in structuring employment relations and governance practices. Instead, they might have to select from among a limited number of human resource 'systems' that represent menus or clusters of human resource practices.

Similarly, there may be what (Williamson, 1975) terms 'atmospheric' benefits associated with organizing a whole menu of activities through a common set of organizational procedures and routines (e.g. a single organizational culture or set of employment practices). For instance, structuring pay, promotion and other employment practices very differently across diverse occupations or departments within an organization, even if seemingly warranted based on human capital or other considerations, might generate so much counterproductive dissent internally or illegitimacy externally as to outweigh the benefits. Accordingly, a consistent set of employment practices that might appear suboptimal for each of a set of activities might be optimal (or nearly so) for the organization as a whole.

Baron and Kreps (in press) suggest at least three reasons to expect employment practices within organizations to cluster into consistent bundles. First, as Milgrom and Roberts (1995) note in discussing the Lincoln Electric Company, there are some obvious technical complementarities among particular HR practices. For instance a start-up firm intending to invest heavily in training its workers will benefit disproportionately from carefully screening applicants and from adopting practices to reduce turnover. Conversely, companies having screened carefully and/or implemented turnover-reduction mechanisms are likely to benefit disproportionately from investments in training employees.

A second reason for expecting consistency involves the psychology of perception and cognition. Psychological theory and research indicate that messages are more salient and recalled better when the multiple stimuli being transmitted are simple and support the same message. Internal consistency, which also entails simplicity (i.e. everything follows the same basic principles), should aid employees in learning about what is expected of them and what they can expect in turn. This is also likely to offer several benefits to the employer, including: superior matching or sorting between potential employees and the job opportunities offered by the firm; reduced need for monitoring employees' activities or clarifying ambiguous or contradictory expectations; and greater ability to provide long-term incentives and career development because employees clearly understand what is expected and valued.

Baron and Kreps (in press) suggest a third category of reasons for expecting consistency in HR practices: social forces. External consistency—that is, congruence between a firm's employment system and external social norms and preconceptions—presumably facilitates learning. Both parties to the employment relation are likely to find it easier to comprehend the nature of the relationship when its employment practices consistently (and symbolically) mimic previously-internalized codes of conduct from other contexts, whether these patterns are akin to an anonymous marketplace (dog-eat-dog) or a family relationship (mutual caring). By this logic, for instance, it would be difficult for a set of founders who shared strong kinship or long-standing friendship bonds to establish a company whose personnel policies reflected either a Draconian or an arms-length posture *vis-à-vis* employees. Similarly, personnel policies that encourage employees to identify themselves as members of a corporate 'family' (long-term employment, open door policies, suggestion systems, etc.) would not seem to mesh well with other practices that convey the message that employees are interchangeable, expendable, or simply a cost that the firm must bear.

According to Baron and Kreps, the same arguments regarding consistency

among HR practices also apply to the issue of how differentiation or inconsistency in treatment among subgroups within an organization will affect
transaction costs. They note that pressures toward uniform treatment are
likely to be especially acute in organizations with: (a) high technical interdependence; (b) a labor force that is socially and demographically homogeneous; (c) a strong unified 'culture'; (d) an internal labor market and/or
extensive job rotation and lateral transferring; and (e) a broader social environment that does not legitimate differential treatment among segments of
the labor force or the society (also see Baron and Pfeffer, 1994).

These arguments regarding consistency in human resource management
posit various benefits to employers and/or employees from organizing
employment relationships around consistent HR premises and practices and
by drawing on models of social relationships from other settings. If correct,
these arguments imply that, over time, some advantages in terms of performance or survival should accrue to organizations whose employment relationships are internally consistent and/or structured to mimic other social
systems with which their employees have experience. However, another
explanation for why we might expect to observe consistency in HR systems
is less instrumental and more cognitive—namely, it may be difficult for
individuals, including those who design and manage organizations, to
espouse and enforce contradictory principles. Robert Frank (1988), among
others, has noted some important economic consequences of the psychological tendency toward cognitive consistency, both in the beliefs we hold and
in the codes of behavior we bring to different economic transactions.
According to his argument, an employer wishing to develop a reputation for
trustworthiness with suppliers and customers, for instance, will find this
harder to do unless she consistently acts in a benevolent and trustworthy
fashion (e.g. in dealing with other constituencies, such as employees). Similarly, psychological theories of consistency suggest that it creates cognitive
strain to espouse discrepant beliefs, such as the view that employees are
good, knowledgeable and trustworthy alongside the view that they require
close monitoring and powerful incentives to be motivated to comply with
the firm's objectives. This line of reasoning suggests that consistency among
HR practices—and between employment relations and other types of social
relations—may simply reflect a basic psychological tendency but not necessarily entail any implications for economic performance.

This brief overview suggests several potentially useful foci for research
on how employment relationships become established in the early years of
organizations. One concerns the degree of 'alignment' of the human resource
policies and practices of organizations with their technologies and business
strategies. Evidence on whether alignment is evident at the inception of

firms, or instead seems to be achieved gradually over time, might speak to the time-frame over which entrepreneurs are seeking to minimize transaction costs. We take up this issue in our companion paper in this issue (Hannan *et al.*, 1996). A second useful focus of research concerns the implications of 'complementarities' and the need for internal consistency—both among specific HR practices (e.g. recruitment, compensation, performance evaluation, training, job design, etc.) and in the treatment of different segments of the work-force—for the design of human resource systems. To the extent that there are complementarities among specific HR practices and interdependencies (of a technical or social character) among segments of an organization's work-force, the problem of selecting and implementing the optimal governance regime might be more complicated than a stylized TCE story would imply. It is this issue that is explored in this paper.

There has been much more writing about the prevalence and virtues of internal consistency in HR systems than careful empirical study of the matter. There are a few noteworthy exceptions to this generalization. For instance, MacDuffie's (1995) work on the worldwide automobile industry documents a tendency for firms employing so-called high commitment work systems to avail themselves of an interrelated bundle of HR practices. An interesting longitudinal study of production lines in the steel industry (Ichniowski *et al.*, 1993) shows that productivity was enhanced by adopting various HR innovations that are generally associated with high commitment work systems, but that the returns to adopting a given practice were enhanced when other elements of a high commitment work system were either adopted simultaneously or already in place within the establishment.

It should be obvious that these issues are difficult to study without knowing a great deal about how an organization evolves over time, particularly about key decisions and developments in the early years of a company that might have momentous consequences for how it evolves and performs over time. In other words, it is not clear whether meaningful theoretical inferences can be drawn from most empirical studies of employment systems in organizations, which tend to be either cross-sectional comparisons across a sample of fairly long-lived 'survivor' organizations or case studies of what has transpired in a particular setting. Most extant research on HR systems focuses on relatively mature and long-lived organizations in seeking to identify the nature and benefits of HR alignment and internal consistency. Yet if consistency among HR practices is important, and if organizational designers seek to capitalize (either intentionally or unintentionally) on models of social relationships drawn from other settings (other firms, the family, educational institutions, etc.), this should be particularly evident when organizations are assembling their employment systems in their early years.

Specifically, we should be able to find evidence not only in what the architects of nascent organizations say about what they were trying to achieve and what models they had in mind, but also in how their organizations evolved in the early years—for instance, whether the development of particular HR practices corresponds to a clear organizational blueprint and exhibits a logic of internal consistency.

The difficulty of obtaining the requisite life history data on organizations, particularly information about their formative years, might help explain why these issues have not received more attention in prior empirical research addressing employment relationships and/or transaction cost economizing. This paper reports some of the preliminary research findings from the Stanford Project on Emerging Companies (SPEC), an ongoing large-scale study designed to gather precisely this kind of information about early organization-building activities. Our goals in this paper are more descriptive than explanatory; we exploit the rich information we have obtained on the process of organization-building from interviews with founders, chief executives and senior HR officials, which describe the timing of various crucial events in the process of creating the firm's governance systems and also the imagery and intentions of the firm's architects. We use this information to identify several distinct models for organizing employment and work that recur within our sample of high technology start-ups. By examining how these models are conceptualized, constructed and articulated in the early years of start-up firms, we gain some insight into how organizational designers approach the issue of consistency and complementarities in human resource management and the extent to which they are seeking to develop employment systems that transcend particular HR practices and occupations within the firm. In our companion paper in this volume (Hannan *et al.*, 1996), we explore some of the determinants of founders' human resource models and document how those models profoundly influence subsequent organizational evolution.

2. Brief Overview of SPEC

To control for labor market and environmental conditions, we focus on firms in one region and a particular sector of economic activity: technology-oriented companies in California's Silicon Valley. The continuing flow of high tech start-ups in the Silicon Valley area provides many opportunities to collect information on the early history of interesting firms. One goal of this research is to understand how early decisions affect future outcomes, which necessitates information about the earliest days of the organization. We assumed that individuals could only reasonably recall fairly recent information; thus, we limited our study to firms that were no more than ten years of age at the time we asked them to participate in the project. A second project goal is to understand how human resource systems are established. We assumed that organizations need to be of a minimum size before facing a need for any formal systems of practices; accordingly, firms in our study needed to have at least ten employees when the study commenced (in 1994). To identify the population, we purchased extracts from two commercial databases on technology companies: *Rich's Everyday Sales Prospecting Guide* and *CorpTech*. From these sources, we drew a stratified random sample of high technology firms with headquarters in Silicon Valley, oversampling young firms and large firms (Burton, 1995). The firms we targeted for study are concentrated in computer hardware and/or software, telecommunications (including networking equipment), medical/biological technologies and semiconductors. Foreign-owned firms were excluded from the population, as were operating units of other organizations, because we were concerned that the structures and practices of such enterprises would reflect broader influences whose effects we could not adequately control.

With these restrictions, we identified 676 firms that met our selection criteria as of spring 1994. We approached 250 of these firms; 100 agreed to participate in the study.[1] Happily, there was little evidence of systematic bias in response to our request for participation (see below). Figure 1 reports the 'target' composition of firms sought through our stratified sampling plan, as well as the age and size distribution of firms in our sample.

Data Collection

Trained MBA and doctoral students conducted semi-structured interviews with the CEO and the key informants that s/he had nominated to provide information about company history and human resource practices. Informants about company history and human resource management were also asked to complete pencil and paper surveys and return them to us prior to being interviewed. (For detailed information on the data gathered in each firm, see Burton, 1995). These surveys solicited details about the firm and its history; this information was used to guide the interviews.

(i)   Founders were asked to recount the details of the founding: how the founding team was assembled, the original business plan, the planned

[1] During the summer of 1995, several hundred more firms were invited to participate in SPEC, and to date an additional 72 firms have agreed to do so, bringing the total sample up to 172 companies. The first 100 companies, which were studied during the summer of 1994, will be revisited in the summer of 1996 to update their human resource activities, organizational performance and other key information.

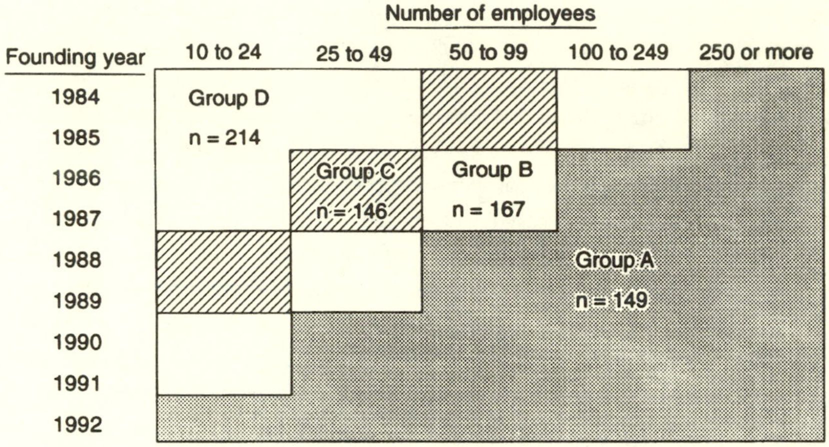

Number of employees

Founding year	10 to 24	25 to 49	50 to 99	100 to 249	250 or more
1984	Group D				
1985	n = 214				
1986		Group C	Group B		
1987		n = 146	n = 167		
1988				Group A	
1989				n = 149	
1990					
1991					
1992					

Sampling Group	Total n in Population	Desired % of Sample	Sample n Contacted	Participating Companies
A	149	60%	149	67
B	167	20%	65	19
C	146	10%	15	9
D	214	10%	21	8

FIGURE 1. SPEC sampling frame and response rate.

core competencies of the firm, sources of initial capital, initial staffing and initial employment practices. They were queried about their own professional background, external partners and stakeholders and whether there was a clear organizational 'vision' or blueprint in creating the enterprise (and, if so, where it came from). Founders were also asked to report on the firm's current structure and practices and to identify the timing and nature of major organizational changes or 'milestones'. Founder interviews typically lasted 60 minutes. Although interviewers were given a template and set of probes for these interviews, the interviews tended to follow a direction set by the founder.

(ii)   Following a similar semi-structured interview format, CEOs were asked to provide detailed information on the firm's current strategy, structure, business environment and management challenges. These face-to-face interviews typically lasted 45 minutes.

(iii) Senior managers with responsibility for human resources were asked to provide extensive information about the firm's past and current employment practices. Human resources interviews typically lasted 90 minutes.

TABLE 1.   Age and size distribution for SPEC participating companies

Founding Year	Number of employees 10 to 24	25 to 49	50 to 99	100 to 249	250 or more	Total
1984	2	2	0	3	6	13
1985	3	1	2	1	2	9
1986	0	2	0	2	4	8
1987	0	0	5	7	1	13
1988	2	2	6	12	2	24
1989	0	1	4	4	0	9
1990	4	4	1	0	1	10
1991	3	2	3	1	1	10
1992	2	1	1	0	0	4
Total	16	15	22	30	17	100

We also gathered documents from informants that record the history of the firm, its organization, and its personnel practices whenever possible (e.g. organization charts, initial business plans, personnel manuals, company forms and documents). In addition, we gathered publicly-available information about each of the firms in the study using a number of on-line database services, including Lexis/Nexis, Dialog Business Connection and ABI Inform, as well as annual reports and 10Ks for each of the public firms. For publicly-traded firms, we obtained a prospectus from the initial public stock offering.

Potential limitations of the SPEC design.   As a source of baseline data on the early organizing activities of new enterprises, we believe the SPEC project provides a unique source of data, containing richer quantitative and qualitative information on a larger, more comprehensive and representative sample of organizations than any we have encountered in the literatures on organization-building and entrepreneurship. At the same time, we are well aware of several potential limitations of the SPEC study design. First, we have gathered information about early organization-building activities by asking key individuals involved in those activities for their retrospective recollections, and such recollections are always subject to potential biases. Second, we have asked founders and senior managers to characterize their organizations and human resource practices, but there is no guarantee that their accounts correspond to the reality experienced by employees. Third, although we intentionally limited our sample to organizations that are still quite young (a median age of under six years, with 24% being four years old or younger), there is nonetheless the possibility of some sort of survivor bias characterizing our sample because we are only informed about the early histories, employment models, and organization-building activities of companies that have endured to make it into our sample. These are important concerns that deserve careful considerations accordingly, after reporting our results, we briefly assess whether and how such limitations might cloud our analysis and conclusions.

3. *Founders' Models of Employment Systems*

In this paper, we examine the actual employment practices adopted by organizations in their formative years. We also examine how those who created organizations conceived of the employment relationship. It is arguably those conceptions, as much as the specific human resource practices adopted by companies in their infancy, that should influence the subsequent evolution of organizational arrangements and employment practices within their companies. After all, when organizations are still very young and small, they might vary less in the particular HR practices they have put in place than in the *premises* that guide how they manage the work-force, which become institutionalized in organizational structures and practices at a later point in time.

Each founder in the SPEC sample was asked whether or not he or she had 'an organizational model or blueprint in mind when [you] founded the company'. (A companion question regarding the present was asked of the current CEO in each firm.) Roughly two-thirds of the founders were able to articulate some kind of HR blueprint, with almost half expressing a very clear organizational model, sometimes citing a specific organization as an illustration of what they wanted their firm to look like (or not to look like). Burton (1995) describes the wide variety of archetypes on which these founders drew in describing their organizational blueprints, ranging from the academy, to Japanese organizations, to scholarly models of management (e.g. MacGregor's [1960] Theory X and Theory Y), to a widely-shared image of 'the typical Silicon Valley start-up'. Others steadfastly disavowed the notion of having a clear organizational model *ex ante*. As one founder put it: 'Models are a source of failure for start-ups. You have to become a successful company first, then create your own model. Even the celebrated [Hewlett Packard] principles were written twenty years after the company was started.'

Upon analyzing the detailed interview transcripts obtained from each founder, we identified three recurring dimensions along which their images varied regarding how work and employment should be organized: the primary basis of organizational attachment; the primary means for controlling and coordinating work; and the primary criterion to be emphasized in selecting employees. Along each of these dimensions, in turn, we found that founders' blueprints tended to cluster into one of three distinct categories. We briefly summarize each of the three dimensions and its constituent sub-categories:[2]

Attachment

The first dimension along which founders' models vary concerns the primary basis of attachment (and retention) of employees. Three different bases of attachment were articulated by founders in recalling their organizational blueprints, which we label *love, work* and *money*.

Some founders indicated that they envisioned that creating a strong family-like feeling and an intense emotional bond with employees would inspire superior effort and increase the chances of retaining highly-sought employees over long periods of time, thereby avoiding the frequent mobility of key technical personnel that plagues Silicon Valley start-ups. One founder stated:

> I think people should be treated as human beings, as real people. And really care for them. We are still pretty much like family. We try to keep as much of that as possible even as the company is bigger. That's one thing I learned from HP [Hewlett-Packard]. Bill Hewlett still flipped hamburgers for us at the company picnic.

This quote nicely captures the familial associations underpinning this vision—the company picnic as a surrogate for the family barbecue, and the CEO (Bill Hewlett, in the anecdote) as 'Dad'. Thus, what binds the employee to the firm in this model is, simply put, *love*—an intense emotional sense of personal belonging and identification with others in the company, comparable to a family.

A large number of firms in the sample pursue cutting-edge technology, and for their employees a primary motivator is the desire to work at the technological frontier. Recognizing this, many of the founders responses reveal that they presumed that providing opportunities for interesting and challenging work would be the basis for attracting, motivating, and (perhaps) retaining employees. Here, the employees were not expected to be loyal to the firm, or the boss, or even co-workers *per se*, but instead to the project. As one founder put it:

---

[2] Note that we did not structure the interviews explicitly around these three dimensions or their sub-categories, as these emerged after we had gathered, coded and analyzed the interview transcripts. In other words, founders and CEOs were not asked to classify their models along these dimensions or into the specific subcategories but instead to provide an open-ended description of their organizational blueprint and its rationale, which we then coded after the fact.

> We wanted to assemble teams of people who are turned on by difficult
> problems. The emphasis was to build an environment of individuals who
> are performance driven, achievement oriented, customer focused, feel rela-
> tively at ease to join and disband from specific teams, skilled at interdisci-
> plinary problem solving irrespective of culture or discipline.

Finally, other founders told us that they regarded the employment relationship as a simple exchange of labor for money. One founder put this bluntly:

> [My] model is basically 'you work, you get paid.' With an assembly
> type business there is not a lot of engineering or white-collar workers
> requiring complex HR benefits or policies. We're not interested in the soft,
> warm, fuzzy stuff. Of course, we also don't want to be running a sweat
> shop.

Basis of Control

A second, related distinction in founders' models or blueprints concerns the
principal means of controlling and coordinating work. The most common
blueprint involves extensive reliance on *peer* or *cultural control*. One founder
put this as follows: 'In my mind and probably in [the co-founder's] mind
was that we would be a very open, horizontal company with an emphasis on
teamwork and all decisions made by consensus. Employees wear whatever
they want, work whenever they want.' It is taken for granted that employees
would work long hours, and peer pressure will presumably ensure that this
is done and that the hours are spent working on useful endeavors. Not surprisingly, founders who espoused this view also were likely to speak about
the importance of socializing employees to ensure that they understood the
directions in which their efforts should be aimed.

Other founders recalled that their intention was to rely on *professional control*, even if they did not explicitly use this terminology. It is clear from their
responses that these founders took it for granted that workers were committed to excellence in their work and were able to perform at high levels
because they had been professionally socialized to do so. (Not surprisingly,
this model tends to be accompanied by an emphasis on recruitment of high-
potential individuals from elite institutions.) In this model, the emphasis is
on autonomy and independence, rather than on enculturation. One founder
told us:

> Scientists like autonomy and independence. I value it myself and it's
> important to make sure that they have that. They feel the environment is
> exciting and that the leadership is there to provide the kind of place where
> their career is constantly renewing and growing. This essentially is most of
> my work—to see that they reach their maximum potential to grow.

Another founder explained:

> I give people a lot of autonomy. You perform for me, I don't care if you ever show up for work . . . So I put a lot more out there and gave more responsibility and accountability to the people and didn't monitor on a day to day basis. I truly believe that's the right style in business today.

Finally, a third group of founders espoused a more traditional view of control as being embedded in *formal procedures and systems*. The following excerpts from two founder interviews illustrate this perspective well:

> We're not hierarchical as much as we are procedures, methodologies, and systems. I really try to see that everybody in the company maintains procedures rather than just hand wave and do things any way. We don't want to be so hierarchical as to be startling, nor do we want to be so flat as to have everybody poking into everybody else's business.
>
> We run very much on a TQM philosophy. We make sure that things are documented, have job descriptions for people, project descriptions, and pretty rigorous project management techniques.

Selection

The third source of variation in founders' organizational blueprints, closely related to the preceding two, concerns the primary basis for selecting employees to join the firm. Some founders seemed to think of the firm in terms of bundles of tasks that needed to be carried out, seeking employees to carry out those tasks effectively. Time and money tend to be the paramount concerns here, so the focus was on selecting employees who could be brought on board and be up to speed as soon as possible and who would not decimate the founder's wallet or purse. As one founder put it, 'it's not who you know or what you do politically, but what you can achieve technically'. In these cases, the founders envisioned selecting employees who possessed the *skills and experience needed to accomplish some immediate task(s)*.

In other cases, founders seemed to be focused less on immediate and well-defined tasks than on a series of projects (often not yet even envisioned) through which employees would move over time. Accordingly, their focus in selection was on *long-term potential*, rather than on specific skills or relevant vocational experience. One founder articulated this point of view: 'Given the choice between a smart person and an experienced one I'll always take the smart person. You can't give someone smarts, but you can give them experience.' These founders often also spoke of the importance of reputation, network ties, and other intangible assets in evaluating potential employees.

Finally, another group of founders reported that they focused primarily on *values or cultural fit.* Like the previous group, these founders were concerned about the long-term, rather than specific short-term personnel needs, but they put heavy emphasis on how a prospective hire would connect with others in the organization: 'At the start we were seeking people with a long-term focus—no Valley job hoppers. And we were as concerned with how everyone would fit together as we were with technical ability.'

Relationships Among the Three Dimensions

Not surprisingly, these three dimensions underlying founders' conceptions of the employment system are not independent. In fact, although we have classified founders into three types on each of the three dimensions, thereby yielding 27 possible combinations, 71% of the observations for which we were able to code all three dimensions clustered in just three of the cells: a cell combining attachment to work, professional control, and selection based on potential (16 firms); another combining attachment to work, peer control, and selection based on specific tasks (17 firms); and a third combining attachment through love or emotion, peer control, and selection based on cultural fit (16 firms). The next most populous cells are those involving formal organizational controls and selection for specific skills or tasks, involving either attachment through money (6 firms) or through the nature of the work (5 firms).

Based on this clustering, we identified four pure-type employment models, reflecting combinations of the three dimensions (Table 2). We use the label 'star' to refer to the model that involves challenging work, autonomy and professional control, and selection of elite personnel based on long-term potential. We use the 'engineering' label for the blueprint combining a focus on challenging work, peer group control, and selection based on specific task abilities. We refer to the blueprint relying on emotional/familial attachments of employees to the organization, selection based on cultural fit, and peer group control as the 'commitment' model. Finally, the 'factory' model is predicated on purely monetary motivations, control and coordination through formal organization and close managerial oversight, and selection of employees to perform pre-specified tasks. That label is intended to capture the similarity between this model and the traditional factory system under early industrial capitalism, which treated employees as factor inputs, preserved discretion of the owner, and relied on a combination of pecuniary rewards, close supervisory oversight, and technical or bureaucratic controls over employees. It also conveniently captures the contemporary pejorative connotation from the employee's perspective, as in the description of a non-manufacturing workplace as a 'factory'.

TABLE 2.   Four Pure-Type Employment Models, Based on Three Dimensions[a]

	Dimensions		Employment model
Attachment	Selection	Coordination/Control	
Work	Potential	Professional	STAR
Work	Task	Peer	ENGINEERING
Love	Values	Peer	COMMITMENT
Money	Task	Managerial	FACTORY

[a]Firms that did not correspond to pure types were assigned to an employment model according to the following rules: (i) 'Love' as a basis of attachment indicates a commitment model, regardless of selection criterion or basis of control; (ii) money as a basis of attachment indicates a factory model; (iii) work as a basis of attachment combined with professional control indicates a star model, regardless of selection criterion; (iv) work as a basis of attachment without professional control indicates an engineering model.

The fact that these three conceptual dimensions—the primary basis of attachment, the primary criterion for selecting employees and the primary axis of control and coordination—are interdependent is not a surprise. Rather, the strong association among them is itself suggestive of consistency and complementarities among dimensions of human resource management. Recall that we noted three bases for consistency among HR practices: economic or technical complementarities (doing X increases the returns from doing Y and vice versa); cognitive or perceptual congruence, which facilitates learning; and congruency with broader social or cultural norms (which also helps to convey expectations and facilitate learning). Founders' HR blueprints for their start-up organizations seem to evidence all three bases of consistency.

For instance, in an organization seeking peer monitoring and in which emotional attachments to the organization itself (rather than to one's specific work assignment) are sought—perhaps to create goal congruence among differentiated subunits—there is a clear technical complementarity with selection mechanisms that screen for cultural fit and values. The very fact that many founders were able to articulate such a clear model or blueprint for how they intended to manage human resources is suggestive of the second rationale we offered for consistency—namely, the virtues of having a simple, coherent and internally consistent image of the employment relationship to communicate expectations and entitlements to employees. Although the labels 'star', 'engineering', 'commitment' and 'factory' are our own, we think they capture nicely the role expectations and treatment that typical employees in each type of organization are likely to confront.

Finally, we suggested that there may be benefits for both the firm and its employees when the organization's HR policies resonate with rules, values, and codes of conduct that employees have experienced in other social settings. Notice that each of the four pure-type employment models we identified resonates with models or behavioral scripts that prevail in other contexts. It can hardly be a coincidence, for instance, that the star employment model, which is espoused particularly by founders of firms developing medical technology,[3] corresponds so closely to the model that underlies employment relations in academia, where many of the founders and key scientific personnel sought for these start-ups are recruited. The commitment model draws instead, as we have noted, on familial images, encouraging employees to view their associations with the firm in similar terms. The engineering model, arguably the default within Silicon Valley (Saxenian, 1994), dovetails with the socialization that engineers receive in professional school and is well suited to the Valley's highly-mobile labor force, placing more value on 'cool technology' and technical contribution than on organizational loyalty or elite credentials. Finally, the austere, no-nonsense factory model communicates a very powerful and consistent message that employees are certain to have encountered elsewhere before: you work, you get paid— nothing more, nothing less.

Given the strong associations among these three dimensions, it is interesting to scrutinize the small number of cases that seem to combine discrepant or discordant foci in the founder's HR model. For instance, one founder claimed to be searching for employees based on their long-term potential, despite an emphasis on formal organizational control and financial remuneration as the basis for attachment. He stated, 'Our main goal is to stay lean and flat. I also recognize that you have to be flexible with your people'. When asked about the organization of work, this founder replied they 'don't have the resources to spend a lot of time getting everyone warm and fuzzy . . . we avoid consensus management and everyone knows who calls the shots'. Another founder emphasized values as the basis for selection and emotional or familial attachment to the firm as the primary motivator, but at the same time espoused a belief in the importance of formal controls. This firm is a family business, and it recruits employees primarily from the surrounding neighborhood and church community. The founders expected employees to be extremely flexible in their work orientation and willing to do all phases of the work, including sales, customer support and training. However, they also micro-managed the organization, insisting, for example, that a salesman who lived in Palo Alto and covered the Palo Alto geographic region drive some thirty miles each morning by 8 am to check in the office. An interesting question for subsequent research based on these data, after we have completed the intended follow-up visits to these companies, is

---

[3] Of the 15 firms in the medical sector (including biotechnology), 80% were founded with a star model, compared to 16.7% among the remaining firms (x^2 = 24.9; df = 1, p < 0.001).

whether organizational evolution and performance differ as a function of the internal consistency exhibited in firms' initial HR blueprints and practices.

4. *Organizational Consequences of Founders' HR Blueprints*

If consistency among HR practices and/or in treatment across different segments of the work-force is important, then we should detect several forms of (indirect) evidence by examining how HR systems evolve in organizations characterized by different underlying blueprints or models. First, we would expect to see systematic differences among firms, as a function of their initial HR models, in the prevalence of certain HR practices and the speed with which they were adopted. For example, we would expect that organizations embracing a commitment model are most likely (and fastest) to adopt policies and practices designed to bind employees to the organization (socialization, communication, etc.) and to undertake investments in the work-force (such as training and promotion from within) that are predicated on long-term attachments.

Second, it seems reasonable to expect that the HR models would differ in the extent to which they encourage versus discourage consistent treatment among diverse segments of the work-force. In this regard, the commitment model lies at one end of the spectrum, encouraging all employees to identify themselves as members of a single corporate family. The star and factory models seem most receptive to distinctions among individuals (based on ability and/or market forces). Accordingly, we would expect firms founded along the lines of the commitment model are less likely (and slower) than companies embracing the star or factory model to adopt compensation arrangements, job descriptions and other HR practices that differentiate among workers.

We collected data on the *timing* of the adoption of a broad set of practices and procedures related to human resource management. Of course, one possibility is that a firm has not yet adopted a given practice, in which case the record on that practice is right-censored. We use two approaches in analyzing variations in the speed of adoption as a function of the founder's employment model. One approach emphasizes early adoption, we chose to focus on the company's first two years of operation. In this analysis, we distinguish firms that adopted a given HR practice or document within the first two years from all others (combining both later adopters and non-adopters). The advantage of focusing on the early period is that founders' HR models are likely to be stable over this short period; the disadvantage is that this form of analysis does not take full advantage of the data, ignoring information on

Table 3. Effects of Founder's HR Model on Log-Odds of Implementing Various HR Policies and Documents within the First Two Years of Business: Multinomial Logit Regressions ($n = 69$)[a].

Variable	Events	Star	Engineering	Commitment
Written performance	27	1.0169	1.0135	0.9731
evaluations		(1.1144)	(1.0260)	(1.0208)
Regular company-sponsored	40	1.3599	1.3758	2.0267**
social events		(1.0629)	(0.9819)	(0.9992)
Regular company-wide	36	1.1647	1.8047*	1.2049
meetings		(1.0975)	(1.0282)	(1.0346)
Employee orientation	18	1.0909	2.0114	2.3432*
program		(1.5923)	(1.4348)	(1.4428)
In-house training	15	1.4494	0.3602	0.3267
		(1.5173)	(1.4314)	(1.5551)
Mission or values statement	13	2.8442*	1.2566	0.5934
		(1.6785)	(1.5911)	(1.6364)
Intellectual property/non-	35	2.1045*	1.5173	0.7485
competition agreements		(1.1771)	(0.9900)	(0.9775)
Standard employment	19	2.5691	2.2708	1.9067
application		(1.6238)	(1.5063)	(1.5247)
Standard evaluation form	25	1.4246	0.2223	0.4829
		(1.1768)	(1.0978)	(1.1030)
Background checks of	14	1.2064	1.6600	2.9960**
prospective employees		(1.7563)	(1.5537)	(1.5183)
Stock options	36	3.8976***	2.3204*	2.0553*
		(1.5644)	(1.2442)	(1.2613)

[a]Note: effects of size and industry are not reported; figures in parentheses are standard errors.
*$p<0.10$ **$p<0.05$ ***$p<0.01$.

timing within the first two years as well as information on the histories over the subsequent years (4.5 years, on average). We therefore supplement these analyses with a second approach, which analyzes the complete company histories and distinguishes between non-adopters and adopters. The advantages and disadvantages of this strategy are obviously the mirror image of those of the alternative.

Adoption of HR Policies and Documents within the First Two Years of Business

Table 3 reports results based on the first strategy: distinguishing firms that adopted particular HR policies and practices with their first two years of operation from the others. This Table reports estimates of the effects from a series of multinominal logit regressions. The estimated effects reported show differences in the log-odds of having adopted various human resource policies (or produced various HR documents) by the end of the firm's second year in existence.[4] These analyses control for industry (computer hardware and software, semiconductors, telecommunications, manufacturing and research were included as dummy variables, with medical-related as the omitted category) and for the number of employees each firm had by the end of its second year of operations. The columns of coefficients reported in Table 3 express the net difference in the log-odds of having adopted or implemented a given HR practice within the first two years of business between those firms founded with a particular HR model (star, engineering, commitment) and firms founded with the factory model (the omitted category).

Not surprisingly, it is clear from Table 3 that firms whose founders conceived of employment in factory terms were less likely to adopt virtually every type of HR policy and document, relative to otherwise-comparable firms that began with a star, engineering, or commitment model.[5] According to Table 3, firms whose founders espoused a star model of employment were considerably more likely to institute intellectual property or non-compete agreements and stock options within the first two years than otherwise-similar firms with a different HR blueprint, and the contrast between the star and factory categories is statistically significant in both instances. (Firms in the engineering and commitment categories are considerably less likely to grant stock options than those in the star category, but still significantly more likely to do so than firms in the factory category.) Given the dependence of star films on key technical personnel, these findings are quite sensible, suggesting that the organization acted quickly to seek to bind their key technical employees over the long-term and reduce the likelihood of their leaving.

Star firms were also significantly more likely than those with a factory model by having adopted a mission or values statement by the end of the second year. This result might suggest an effort to achieve similar ends by promoting a distinctive corporate identity very early with which key employees could identify. Alternatively, perhaps their need to recruit key

---

[4] The precise time at which an organization is 'born' is hardly straightforward. For the purpose of this analysis, a birth date was defined that corresponded to the earliest evidence of a formal organization. The main defining criteria were: (i) legal incorporation; (ii) having at least one person engaged in the enterprise full-time; or (iii) selling a product or service. This definition eliminates the possibility of human resource systems or practices being implemented before there was an existing firm. Unfortunately, it also complicates the interpretation of effects. Some firms are defined as implementing HR systems when there is a single founder working on a business plan that happens to include a mention of how future employees will be treated, whereas other firms are defined as implementing systems and practices well after employees have been hired and products have been sold.

[5] Note that a number of coefficients in Table 3 are quite large, but so are their standard errors, due to the relatively small sample size and the small number of firms having adopted certain HR practices or documents. (Table 3 only reports results for those HR policies and documents that had been adopted by ten or more firms within the first ten years.)

technical personnel from outside the labor pool of experienced Silicon Valley engineers encourages such firms to espouse their mission and values clearly to attract the best scientific and technical employees. According to Table 3, firms that began with the star model were also the most likely to have promulgated job descriptions, standard employment applications, and standard performance evaluation forms by the end of their second year. Although not statistically significant, these results are broadly consistent with the interest such firms have in attracting top-flight scientific and technical personnel and being able to evaluate who are the stars. Moreover, they might provide management with a sense of exercising some organizational control over autonomous professionals.

Table 3 also reveals that firms having embarked with a commitment model were the most likely to have implemented background checks of prospective employees, to conduct formal employee orientation programs, and to sponsor regular social events for employees. They are significantly more likely to do so than otherwise comparable organizations whose founders espoused a factory blueprint for HR. These findings suggest that, having created an organization with the intention of creating long-term relations with employees, management goes to greater lengths to screen prospective hires, is more engaged in formally orienting them to the organization, and does more to provide for employees' social welfare.

That we are able to detect differences in the existence of particular employment practices so early in the lives of these organizations, and after controlling for industry and employment size within the first two years, indicates that founders' HR blueprints were not merely rhetoric but instead exerted a significant effect on the evolution of employment relations within these companies. Moreover, our results suggest that, even within the first two years, the HR systems of these organizations are exhibiting complementarities among particular HR practices.

Time to Adoption of HR Policies and Documents

Table 4 looks at the same issue in a slightly different way, which provides us with more statistical power to detect differences among the four employment models. Most organizations in our sample (and, we suspect, in general) are not doing a great deal to formalize employment relations within their first two years. Consequently, for a number of HR policies and documents of interest, there is not much variation in adoption within the first two years to be analyzed. In Table 4, we take advantage of each firm's entire history and information obtained from surveys and interviews on the timing of arious HR practices to examine whether there are significant differences in the speed of implementing various HR practices across the four HR models.

For this purpose, we use event history techniques (Tuma and Hannan, 1984) to estimate the effects of the founder's HR model (and other covariates) on the rate of adopting the various HR practices and documents listed in Table 4.[6] We specify the underlying process in terms of organizational age (t), which we regard as continuous. That is, we regard each firm as becoming at risk of adopting each of the HR practices at birth, and we analyze the (right-censored) distribution of age at the time of adopting.[7] Let $Y_k(t)$ be a random variable that indicates whether a firm has adopted practice k at age t, $Y_k(t)=0$ if the firm has not yet adopted and $Y_k(t)=1$ if it has. We specify the effects of the founder's employment model (relative to the 'factory model', which is the omitted category) and of other covariates on the (instantaneous) transition rate or hazard as:

$$r_k(t) = \lim_{\Delta t \downarrow 0} \frac{Pr\{Y_k(t + \Delta t) = 1 \mid Y_k(t) = 0\}}{\Delta t} \qquad (1)$$

Table 4 reports estimates of Gompertz models with the following specification:

$$r_k(t) = b_k \, exp(c_k t), \, t > 0; \qquad (2)$$

$$b_k = exp\{B_k \beta_k\} \qquad (3)$$

$$c_k = exp\{\gamma_k\}. \qquad (4)$$

Here, B_k is a matrix of observations on a set of covariates that are updated annually using the standard method of 'spell splitting' (Tuma and Hannan, 1984). The covariates included are industry dummies and age-varying organizational size (employee headcount at the start of each year of observation).[8]

Before examining how founders' HR blueprints influence the adoption of specific HR policies and documents, it is interesting to consider the effects of ageing and employment growth. Considering the full set of 25 outcomes in Table 4, it is clear that growth in employment dominates organizational ageing in determining the rates at which start-up companies adopt HR policies and documents. Table 4 shows that size has significant effects on the rates of adoption for 18 of the 25 practices; each of the significant effects is positive. The effects of growth are largest and most often significant for HR

---

[6] Table 4 reports results for those HR policies and documents that had been adopted by at least twenty firms during their entire histories.

[7] One firm reported adopting, and then later abandoning written job descriptions. The models presented in this paper do not account for such reverse transitions.

[8] The models were estimated in TDA 5.7 (Rohwer, 1994).

TABLE 4. Effects of Founder's HR Model, Size, and Age on the Rates of Adopting Various HR Policies and Documents: Gompertz Models (n=69)[a]

Variable	Events	Star	Engineering	Commitment	Size	Age
Written performance evaluations	62	0.833 (0.519)	1.191*** (0.484)	1.191*** (0.467)	0.005** (0.002)	0.007 (0.005)
Organization chart	57	0.528 (0.476)	0.053 (0.439)	0.158 (0.472)	−0.0003 (0.002)	0.019*** (0.006)
Regular social events	61	1.231** (0.520)	0.630 (0.471)	1.153*** (0.445)	0.005** (0.002)	−0.013 (0.063)
Regular company-wide meetings	62	0.784* (0.469)	0.524 (0.433)	0.257 (0.442)	0.005** (0.002)	−0.014** (0.006)
Employee orientation program	49	1.376** (0.593)	0.843* (0.497)	1.201*** (0.493)	0.010*** (0.002)	−0.002 (0.005)
Company-wide electronic mail	49	1.692*** (0.567)	0.549 (0.515)	0.805 (0.498)	0.005** (0.002)	−0.003 (0.006)
In-house training	43	0.946 (0.645)	0.885* (0.530)	0.963* (0.513)	0.009*** (0.002)	0.0001 (0.006)
Mission or values statement	44	1.080* (0.590)	0.257 (0.540)	0.327 (0.533)	0.004*** (0.001)	0.004 (0.005)
Employee suggestion system	22	0.787 (0.929)	−0.722 (0.986)	1.182 (0.755)	0.001 (0.001)	0.014** (0.007)
Newsletter	26	1.246 (0.957)	1.757** (0.753)	2.214*** (0.797)	0.008*** (0.002)	0.017*** (0.006)
Intellectual property/ non-competition agreements	57	1.053** (0.489)	0.494 (0.442)	−0.069 (0.466)	0.005** (0.002)	−0.012** (0.006)
Standardized employment application	52	1.396** (0.626)	1.048** (0.529)	1.065** (0.541)	0.004* (0.002)	0.004 (0.006)
Standard performance evaluation form	63	1.089** (0.510)	0.530 (0.487)	0.636 (0.467)	0.005** (0.002)	0.008 (0.005)
Background checks of prospective employees	32	0.781 (0.760)	0.317 (0.689)	1.774*** (0.577)	0.007*** (0.002)	−0.009 (0.008)
Personnel manual or handbook	56	0.849 (0.527)	0.436 (0.443)	0.248 (0.448)	0.003** (0.001)	0.014*** (0.004)
Written job descriptions	37	0.827 (0.555)	0.021 (0.634)	0.335 (0.550)	0.0004 (0.001)	0.026*** (0.006)
Written affirmative-action plans	33	1.327* (0.696)	0.083 (0.578)	0.611 (0.581)	0.009*** (0.002)	0.017*** (0.006)
Human resources information system	35	1.279* (0.730)	0.429 (0.627)	1.452** (0.612)	0.012*** (0.002)	0.001 (0.005)
Stock options	56	1.113** (0.519)	0.740* (0.433)	0.490 (0.474)	−0.001 (0.020)	−0.006 (0.006)
Knowledge or skill-based pay	30	0.116 (0.922)	1.296* (0.753)	2.657*** (0.695)	−0.003 (0.003)	−0.002 (0.005)
Individual incentives or bonuses	50	0.837 (0.573)	0.490 (0.482)	0.659 (0.454)	0.003 (0.002)	−0.002 (0.005)
Signing bonus	21	1.202 (0.910)	0.731 (0.839)	0.397 (0.857)	0.002 (0.003)	−0.005 (0.008)
Profit sharing or gain sharing	25	1.402* (0.845)	0.349 (0.795)	1.599** (0.748)	0.002** (0.001)	0.003 (0.007)

TABLE 4.   (*cont.*)

Non-monetary awards 24	−0.399	1.149*	0.129	0.001	0.004
for performance	(0.851)	(0.698)	(0.684)	(0.001)	(0.007)
Group/team incentives 25	0.712	−0.242	0.103	0.005**	0.001
or bonuses	(0.700)	(0.748)	(0.610)	(0.002)	(0.007)

[a]Note: effects of industry categories are not reported. Figures in parentheses are standard errors.
*p<0.10** p<0.05*** p<0.01.

issues other than compensation, particularly those pertaining to formalization and standardization of employment relations and institutionalizing
means of socialization and communication (regular social events and meetings, newsletters, e-mail, orientation programs, training). Interestingly, the
effect of growth is non-significant for all of the items involving individual
rewards (stock options, skill-based pay, individual bonuses, signing bonuses,
and non-monetary rewards). However, employment growth does significantly increase the rate of adopting two forms of reward based on groups or
teams: profit or gain sharing and group- or team-based incentives and
bonuses. One obvious possible explanation for these results is that increases
in the scale (and diversity) of employment entail greater potential for free-
riding, as well as more possibility for goal conflict, necessitating group-
based reward systems. Another explanation, not inconsistent with the
previous one, is that technology firms develop their work-forces by adding
manufacturing and marketing capacity after having completed the initial
research and development phase, and the interdependencies among engineering, manufacturing and marketing created by this transition are
reflected in new compensation arrangements based on group- or company-
wide performance.

The effect of time-varying organizational age (c_k in equation 4) is statistically significant for only seven of the 25 HR practices; two of the significant
effects are negative and five are positive. The practices for which the rate of
adoption increases with age tend to involve formalization in the purest sense
of creating documents that specify employment structures and procedures
and provide organizational 'memory': organization charts, newsletters, personnel manuals, written job descriptions and written affirmative action
plans. Irrespective of size, as organizations age they appear less likely to
adopt intellectual property or non-competition agreements for 'star' employees or to implement regular company-wide meetings, which seems consistent with the above-mentioned notion of a transition from dominance by
key engineering personnel in the early years to more interdependence among
(increasingly specialized) functional areas that include manufacturing and

marketing. Overall, Table 4 suggests that employment growth dominates aging *per se* in determining adoption of the sorts of HR practices and procedures that we examined.

Table 4 reveals significant differences across the four HR models in the rate of implementing various employment policies and documents. In fact, of the 25 outcomes analyzed in Table 4, there are statistically significant differences by founder's HR blueprint for 18 (72%) of them, even after controlling for company age and time-varying employment size. The results in Table 4 generally corroborate those in Table 3. Table 4 shows that firms that began with a factory model were slower to adopt almost every type of HR policy or document listed. Bearing in mind that the statistical models in Table 4 control for industry and time-varying employment size, this is fairly strong evidence of path dependence in the evolution of employment systems. Table 4 also provides some additional evidence of differences in the evolution of HR systems as a function of the founder's blueprint. Relative to the factory model, firms whose founders embraced the three other models were somewhat faster to develop standardized employment applications, performance evaluations, newsletters, HR information systems, employee orientation programs, in-house training, social events and/or company-wide meetings, and compensation in the form of skill-based pay, profit sharing or gain sharing or stock options. (A few of these contrasts *vis à vis* the omitted category are not statistically significant.) Given the long-term attachments with employees sought through the commitment model, it is hardly surprising to find that these firms were faster than their factory-model counterparts in the same industry and with the same headcount to develop HR information systems, formalize performance evaluation, develop various policies and documents aimed at internal communication and socializing, provide in-house training, tie compensation to accumulated knowledge and skill, and share corporate profits or efficiency improvements with the workforce through profit sharing or gain sharing.[9]

Interestingly, a number of the same developmental tendencies are exhibited among firms that embraced an engineering HR model. However, the latter firms seem especially inclined to emphasize stock options and non-monetary recognition awards (both of which seem to be part of the engineering culture), and, relative to firms espousing the commitment model, they were more likely to eschew HR activities that systematize employment relations and HRM (organizational charts, job descriptions, HR information

---

[9] Commitment firms are, as we would expect, also fastest to implement employee voice and participation policies (suggestion systems, and, in supplementary analyses not reported in Table 4, quality circles and job rotation). However, too few firms have implemented these practices to enable stable and precise estimates of the statistical effects.

systems), particularly practices aimed at facilitating equity, consistency and a shared identity throughout the organization's entire work-force (profit-sharing and gain-sharing, affirmative action plans, suggestion systems, company-sponsored social events). In other words, consistent with our description of the engineering pure type, there is less evidence of a 'corporate' focus in the evolution of HR activities in firms that embarked with the engineering model; after all, engineers value 'cool technology', not cutting-edge management philosophies.

The results pertaining to the star model suggest a pre-eminent focus on adopting HR practices in order to facilitate selecting, differentiating, and rewarding the firm's stars (and justify this to external partners and investors). Consistent with Table 3, Table 4 shows that firms that began with a star model were faster than otherwise comparable enterprises founded with a factory model of employment to develop intellectual property (non-competition) agreements and stock options. They were also faster to implement standardized forms for evaluating performance, which is sensible given the focus on rewarding and retaining star performers. That focus might also explain several other results for star firms in Table 4. For instance, they implemented affirmative action plans at the highest rate; presumably, the imperative of identifying and recruiting the most talented individuals, whatever their gender or ethnicity, is nowhere stronger than in organizations embracing the star model. This might also explain their higher rate of developing human resource informations systems.

Several results in Table 4 regarding the star firms might seem less intuitive, such as their faster adoption of company-wide electronic mail, company-wide meetings, social events, mission statements and profit-sharing. We noted previously that star firms are often crafted on the model of academia, where reliance on e-mail and regular seminars and meetings ensures dissemination of the latest research results to colleagues (and where affirmative action plans are commonplace and viewed as legitimate). Furthermore, recognizing that these firms are generally in a technology race against competitors, with a fairly long lag until results of research can be commercialized and obtain regulatory approval, the reliance of these firms on such practices as mission statements and profit sharing might serve as complements to the stock grants often made to key employees in these companies, designed to keep their attention focused on the company's long-term strategic objectives and to reward them if those objectives are achieved.

We do not wish to overemphasize these statistical results, which are preliminary and certainly not unequivocal. Nonetheless, taken together, we believe the evidence we have presented on founders' conceptions of employment systems and how those conceptions shape early developments in their firms is strongly suggestive of the importance of consistency and complementarities within HR systems. Moreover, the findings suggest that the relevant unit for transaction cost economizing in designing employment relationships and governance structures may vary from organization to organization. For example, we found some evidence indicating that in enterprises embracing a star or factory model, employment practices appear to be tailored to particular work roles or even in some cases to specific key individuals. In firms embracing a commitment model, however, HR practices appear to promote stronger emphasis on consistent and equal treatment throughout the work-force; employment practices and governance regimes seem to be tailored not to the exigencies of specific work roles or subunits but instead to the needs and interests of the 'family' as a whole. The engineering model seems to be intermediate between these two extremes.

Time to First Full-time Human Resource Manager

As we have seen, firms in the SPEC sample differ considerably in the degree and speed with which they have formalized and elaborated human resource management. One event that signals a firm's commitment to elaborate and formalize HRM is appointing a full-time manager of human resources. At one extreme, some SPEC firms hired experienced human resource managers almost at the start; in one firm, it was the fourth employee hired, and in another, it was the eighth employee. The founder/CEO of another firm in the sample (with 380 employees at the time we interviewed him) reported that he has always regarded himself as the firm's HR manager because this function is too important to be delegated. At the other extreme, founders and CEOs of some other firms reported that they regard HRM as a frill at best and, at worst, an impediment to business activity. One founder and his administrative assistant handled all HR-related activities until the firm exceeded 300 employees. They were forced to employ a full-time personnel manager when a major government contract was withheld due to EEOC non-compliance. Given this extreme variation, we naturally wondered whether initial blueprints or models of the employment relation could account for some of the variation in the speed with which companies hired a full-time HR specialist.

We obtained information on the exact date when the first full-time HR manager was hired or appointed from within. Figure 2 reports the estimated cumulative hazard function for this event as a function of organizational age. The rate of hiring the first full-time HR manager increases fairly regularly

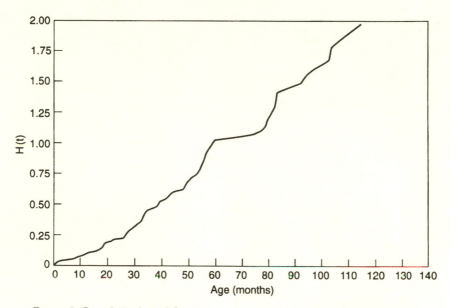

FIGURE 2. Cumulative hazard function: appointment of first full-time HR manager.

with age over the whole age range. We tried several specifications of age dependence in this analysis. A Weibull model does a reasonable job of summarizing age dependence in the hiring of a full-time HR manager, so we estimated Weibull specifications of the form:

$$r(t) = ba^b t^{b-1};$$ (5)

$$a = exp\{A\alpha\};$$ (6)

$$b = exp\{\beta\}.$$ (7)

The results appear in Table 5.

Both age and size have significant effects on the rate of hiring a full-time HR manager. The effect of size is complicated but intuitively sensible. Size has a significant age-independent effect (in the 'a-vector') and a negative age-dependent effect on the rate (in the 'b-vector'). In other words, size matters most for the youngest firms. Young firms have a high rate of making this transition only if they are large; among older firms, size does not make much of a difference. Public companies have a significantly higher rate of moving to full-time HRM, as do firms engaged in telecommunications/networking or medical technology/biotechnology.

Net of these effects, the founder's employment model has a strong and statistically significant effect on the rate of transition to full-time HRM. Compared to the omitted factory model, each of the other models has a rate

TABLE 5.   Effects on Rates of Hiring a Full-Time HR Manager: Weibull Models (n=67)

	(1)	(2)	(3)
A-vector			
Constant	−7.98	−7.90	−7.79
	(−7.33)	(−7.70)	(−7.42)
Size	0.044	0.047	0.047
	(3.77)	(3.93)	(3.87)
Public company	0.933	0.792	0.818
	(1.92)	(1.67)	(1.68)
Telecom/networking	.807	1.03	0.994
	(2.18)	(2.77)	(2.58)
Medical technology	0.643	0.136	0.112
	(1.47)	(0.315)	(0.253)
Founder HR model:			
commitment	2.08	0.877	0.711
	(2.36)	(1.27)	(0.987)
Star	2.13	1.13	0.967
	(2.50)	(1.72)	(1.41)
Engineering	2.44	0.854	0.760
	(2.73)	(1.21)	(1.05)
Founder's strategy:			
Technology race		1.31	1.20
		(2.38)	(2.10)
Technology enhancement		1.13	0.990
		(1.95)	(1.63)
Hybrid		1.54	1.45
		(2.41)	(2.19)
Cost		−3.03	−3.29
		(−1.08)	(−1.93)
Non-founder CEO			0.488
			(1.37)
B-vector			
Constant	0.165	0.190	0.144
	(1.14)	(1.33)	(0.969)
Size	−0.007	−0.006	−0.006
	(−5.51)	(−5.29)	(−5.25)
Log-likelihood	−314.2	−305.6	−304.6
Number of spells	7193	7193	7193
Number of events	67	67	67

[a]Figures in parentheses are *t*-statistics.

at least eight-times higher, according to column 1 in Table 5.[10] Column 3 in Table 5 adds an effect for having a non-founder CEO in order to determine whether departure of the founder precipitates hiring of a full-time HR manager (perhaps to implement a new model of employment relations

[10] As we document in our companion paper (Hannan *et al.*, 1996), there is a strong association between the founder's HR blueprint and the business strategy that he or she envisioned. Analyses reported in column 2 of Table 5 revealed that firms whose founders intended to compete based on technology were significantly faster in hiring a full time HR Manager than those intending to compete based on superior marketing and/or service, which in turn were faster than those intending to compete based on cost minimization. As column 2 reveals the effects of the founder's HR model are weakened substantially (and rendered statistically insignificant) after introducing controls for founder's intended business strategy.

espoused by the new chief executive). However, according to Table 5, this addition does not improve the model fit significantly.

These results suggest that even taking into account a firm's industry, early employment growth, and top executive succession, the founder's HR blueprint has a strong independent effect on the speed with which a full-time HR manager is employed. Companies whose founders espoused a more 'HR-intensive' blueprint (the star and commitment models) hire HR specialists much sooner than otherwise-comparable companies that embark with a different employment model, suggesting that their blueprints were not mere rhetoric but borne out in practice.

Methodological Concerns

We noted above several potential limitations of the SPEC design that should be borne in mind in interpreting these results, especially: (i) possible retrospective recall bias by our informants; (ii) a potential disjuncture between how top management informants characterized HR practices and the reality experienced by employees in their firms; and (iii) survivor bias and non-random response. We briefly address each of these.

Recall bias.   There is an obvious danger in asking individuals who have designed and/or managed companies to reconstruct past events. For instance, informants may unconsciously use current practice to infer a model or set of principles that guided the organization in its early years, even when none existed. Similarly, some HR models and practices may be more socially desirable than others, coloring how informants portrayed their firms and responded to our interviews.

Although we obviously cannot rule out entirely the possibility that such biases plague our results, we think their likely impact is minimal for several reasons. First, in most of the firms we studied (82%), information on the outcomes analyzed in this paper—the presence and timing of HR practices and documents and a full-time HR manager—came from a different respondent than the person who provided information on the firm's initial strategy, HR model, and early history. Second, the results reported in this paper and our companion article (Hannan *et al.*, 1996) do not differ appreciably if we subdivide firms into those in which a single respondent—versus multiple informants—provided all of the information on which our analyses were based. Third, if recall biases are at work, we would expect to see a difference in patterns of association as a function of firm age, with the oldest firms in the sample exhibiting the strongest tendency for respondents to selectively reconstruct the past. However, supplementary analyses failed to unearth such a pattern. Fourth, we reiterate that respondents were not specifically asked (or told) about the three dimensions of human resource management on which our taxonomy of models was based, or the specific categories on each dimension, or the four HR models we derived.[11] Rather, we used open-ended responses from the interviews to identify these key dimensions and categories and to develop the ideal-type HR models.

Of course, there is always a danger in using information in a sample to develop a typology that is then used to 'explain variance' among the same observations. For that reason, we have since gathered comparable data for another 72 start-up companies, which will enable us in future research to cross-validate our taxonomy and findings against this independent sample of organizations.

Management ideology versus employee reality.   Our reports of HR practice and philosophy were obtained from information provided by founders and top managers. The literature on organizational culture has documented that there is often a large discrepancy between the view of top management and the reality experienced everyday by employees (Martin, 1992), and this may be true in our study as well. However, we would make the following points. First, we are interested in understanding what organizational designers were trying to achieve when they created their enterprises and how this shaped what subsequently transpired. Therefore, information on the intentions of founders and top managers is certainly relevant for this purpose. Second, we have documented a strong correspondence between the founder's HR blueprint and the types of HR practices and documents subsequently adopted by the firm, as well as the speed with which they were adopted. This suggests that the founders' HR models were not merely fanciful rhetoric. Indeed, the mere fact that a top management respondent (e.g. the senior HR manager) reported that his or her firm has adopted some HR practice, such as knowledge-based pay or profit sharing or in-house training, does not speak to the experience that employees have within the organization. Regrettably, it was not feasible for us to sample employees within each of the 172 firms that agreed to participate in the SPEC study. However, we have gathered information on important outcomes, such as personnel turnover and employee lawsuits, which we will examine in future research to cast some light on the employee consequences and perceived legitimacy of HR practices within these organizations.

[11] Nor were respondents presented with the taxonomy of business strategies discussed in our companion paper and subsequently asked to classify themselves into one category; rather, we developed the taxonomy after the fact and assigned firms to particular categories based on information obtained from interviews, and, in many cases, from secondary sources (business plans, published articles, etc.).

Survivor bias and sample selection. Finally, some readers of earlier versions of this paper have expressed a concern that despite limiting our sample to nascent organisations, we may nonetheless have obtained a sample of 'survivor' organizations that are atypical in some respects that bear on our results or interpretations. We recognize this potential bias; indeed, it was precisely the fact of rampant survivor bias in most studies of HR policies that prompted us to undertake this study in the first place, so we find a certain irony in the criticism. We have attempted to minimize the likelihood of survivor bias in several ways.

First, as noted above in discussing recall bias, we have conducted separate analyses of organizations by age, and we do not find any noticeable differences between organizations that were founded very recently (e.g. in the last four years) versus the rest, as one would expect if the latter group reflected some survivor bias. Second, we deliberately oversampled recently-founded organizations (see Table 1) in an effort to minimize survivor bias. Third, we have augmented the sample of 100 companies analyzed in this paper by gathering data on another 72 firms, again deliberately oversampling recently-created enterprises in order to minimize the extent of survivor bias. By replicating the analyses reported in this paper and in our companion article within that independent sample, we will gain some insight into the extent of any survivor bias plaguing our analyses in these papers. Fourth, the charge of survivor bias would seem to imply that our sample consists of organizations that are relatively stable and that were somehow 'selected for'. In that context, it is interesting to note that of the 100 organizations we studied in the summer of 1994, 7 have already gone out of business or left the Bay Area by May, 1996, and another 14 have either merged with or been acquired by another company since the summer of 1994, suggesting a level of volatility within our sample that does not jibe with the notion that ours is a sample of stable 'survivors'.

Another potential source of bias is the possibility that companies consenting to participate in the first wave of our study are distinctive in ways that colored our findings. Recall that we initially invited 250 companies to participate, of whom 100 consented to do so. We conducted statistical analyses relating the decision to accept or decline our invitation to participate to employment size, age, and industry. We found little evidence of systematic differences between companies that agreed versus declined to participate. Similarly, among companies that participated, we were unable to detect any non-random pattern in the missing data pertaining to HR practice.

5. Discussion

In this paper, we have relied on a unique and rich source of data on early organization-building activities in high technology companies to explore internal consistency within HR systems. Based on information obtained from interviews with founders, we identified four distinct employment blueprints, which we termed the star, engineering, commitment and factory models. These models reflect, in turn, three interrelated dimensions of the employment relationship: the focus of employee attachment and motivation, the basis of selection, and the nature of control and coordination exercised over the labor force.

The strong interrelationships among these three dimensions and the vividness and clarity of the founder models seem consistent with the claim that strong complementarities characterize HR systems. We also found other evidence of consistency and complementarities among HR practices. For instance, we saw that the propensity of firms to adopt specific HR policies and documents and hire a full-time HR manager (and the speed with which they did so, controlling for their employment size and industry) was related systematically to the HR blueprint with which they started. Another interesting datum bearing on the consistency theme is the fact that among the firms in our sample in which family or friends of the founder(s) were listed as key partners in the creation of the company, five-sixths adopted the commitment model, whereas fewer than 30% of firms overall adopted that blueprint ($p < 0.001$) (Burton, 1995). In other words, the active involvement of family members or friends in the founding process resulted in a firm whose employment relationships were structured more along familial lines.

Of course, the most interesting question is whether consistency makes a difference for outcomes that we care about, such as organizational survival and performance, labor force turnover, and the like. Is a high degree of internal consistency at the inception of an organization necessarily a good thing, or does this limit the enterprise's ability subsequently to adapt to a changing environment? The panel aspect of SPEC, which will involve revisiting these firms over time, is intended to allow us eventually to address precisely such questions. Pending such data, one fruitful line of inquiry is to use the retrospective historical data we do have on these companies to examine whether their early evolution is influenced in discernible ways by the strategy and HR model adopted at 'birth'. We documented in this paper that the founding HR blueprint does exhibit an enduring effect on the evolution of HR practices and policies. In our companion paper (Hannan *et al.*, 1996), we show not only that the HR blueprints differ in how enduring they are, but that founders' initial strategies and HR models have more far-reaching effects, influencing such outcomes as the likelihood of the founder being replaced by a new CEO and of the firm going public. These results all suggest considerable path-dependence in organizational development. Even more interesting for this paper are Burton's (1995) findings that the founder's employment model is a stronger predictor of the firm's current HR practices (in 1994) than is the employment model espoused by the current CEO, which was measured based on 1994 information![12] This is yet another indication that organizational origins matter and that the initial premises that guided the design of employment relations exert an enduring effect on these companies, even as they grow, mature, and in some cases change strategies and top management.

Given the possibility of survivor and retrospective recall bias in our sample of organizations (which were selected in 1994 and asked retrospectively about their histories), caution is warranted in drawing strong causal inferences from the data we have analyzed. Nonetheless, we believe the SPEC sample provides richer and more detailed information on early development for a sizeable sample of organizations than any other source of organizational data with which we are familiar. As we follow these firms forward over time and observe their successes and failures, we will be in a better position to assess the implications, if any, of survivor and recall biases on the baseline data gathered from these companies in 1994–1996, which were the basis for the analyses reported in this paper.

In closing, we would note that the empirical approach adopted in this paper, as well as the particular substantive issues addressed, are very much in the spirit of *Markets and Hierarchies* (Williamson, 1975). Work organization and employment relationships have been central objects of focus in Williamson's development and elaboration of the TC framework. We have utilized the SPEC data to examine the prevailing conceptions of employment relations among the founders of 100 high tech firms, as well as how those conceptions were implemented and shaped the development of human resource management within their firms.

We believe that research along these lines has some potentially important implications for transaction cost reasoning. For instance, our analyses indicate that founders bring quite different premises and blueprints to the design of employment relations, even founders operating within the same industry. Those blueprints, in turn, shape how human resource systems and organizational structures evolve within their companies. In short, our findings strongly suggest a human resource system 'logic' that guides organiza-

---

[12] Specifically, models incorporating effects of the CEO's HR model did not fit as well as comparable specifications with effects of the founder's model.

tional designers in creating and building their firms, with organizational practices and structures evolving concurrently, as part of an interdependent system, rather than independently. Results reported in our companion paper suggest that these 'logics' change only under great pressure, implying that human resource systems may be characterized by 'punctuated equilibria' or bursts of radical change followed by small, incremental adjustments. Moreover, the apparent costliness and contentiousness of changing employment models should be reflected in increased dissent, turnover, and the like. (It is interesting in this connection to note that in SPEC firms that had changed their HR model, the current CEO was more likely to cite 'organizational and management concerns' and/or 'legal issues' when asked about the major challenges facing the company than were CEOs in firms where the HR model had remained stable). We will be exploring these issues in future research based on this sample of firms.

We also found some preliminary evidence suggesting that the HR models vary in the extent of differentiation in treatment among subgroups of workers, with the star and factory models tolerating, or even encouraging, fairly dramatic distinctions among work roles (and, in some cases, among individuals), while the more familial commitment model is at the other extreme of minimal differentiation. If borne out by future research, these speculations imply that different HR logics entail transaction cost economizing at different levels of aggregation—for instance, in 'star' or 'factory' firms, employment relations may be organized around specific individuals or roles, whereas in 'commitment' firms an overarching model of the employment relation is intended to apply to most or all employees.

We also believe our method—gathering detailed information about a sample of organizations in their formative years, as a baseline for conducting future comparative and longitudinal studies—will eventually prove highly valuable for exploring TCE's predictions regarding the determinants and consequences of how firms structure work and employment. Interestingly, in the final pages of *Markets and Hierarchies*, Williamson (1975, p. 263) makes some suggestions for future empirical research on organizational form, market structure, and corporate performance, advocating an approach very similar to what we have done in studying employment practices:

> The ambitious approach would involve a reconstruction of the history of the industry [during the period when dominance of a specific firm emerged], especially during its intermediate stage, for the purpose of assessing default and/or chance event failure. This would require that major events be reconstructed and critical decisions made by rivals and prospective entrants be evaluated.

Acknowledgements

An earlier version of this paper was presented at the Conference on 'Firms, Markets, and Hierarchies' held at the Haas School of Business, University of California at Berkeley. Authors are listed alphabetically, but authorship is shared equally. The research described in this paper has been generously supported by the Stanford Graduate School of Business, the Stanford Computer Industry Project, and the Alfred P. Sloan Foundation. We wish to thank the research team that has contributed to the SPEC project: Puneet Agarwal, Paola Bonomo, Mollie Brown, Angela Celio, Mamie Hsien, David Lam, Peter Mendel, Megan Miller, Tang-Nah Ng, Ed O'Hara, Jennifer Sellars, Eric Smith, Srija Srinivasan, Srikanth Srinivasan, and Tari Vickery.

References

Barnett, W. P. and G. R. Carroll (1995), 'Modeling Internal Organizational Change,' *Annual Review of Sociology*, 21, 217–236.

Baron, J. N., A. Davis-Blake and W. T. Bielby (1986), 'The Structure of Opportunity: How Promotion Ladders Vary Within and Among Organizations,' *Administrative Science Quarterly*, 31, 248–273.

Baron, J. N. and D. M. Kreps (In press), *Human Resources: A Framework for General Managers*. John Wiley: New York.

Baron, J. N. and J. Pfeffer (1994), 'The Social Psychology of Organizations and Inequality,' *Social Psychology Quarterly*, 57, 190–209.

Burton, M. D. (1995), 'The Evolution of Employment Systems in High Technology Firms,' unpublished PhD dissertation, Department of Sociology, Stanford University.

Cohen, Y. and J. Pfeffer (1986), 'Organizational Hiring Standards,' *Administrative Science Quarterly*, 31, 1–24.

Frank, R. H. (1988), *Passions within Reason*. Norton: New York.

Hannan, M. T., M. D. Burton and J. N. Baron (1996). 'Inertia and Change in the Early Years: Employment Relations in Young, High-Technology Firms,' *Industrial and Corporate Change*, 5

Hannan, M. T. and J. Freeman (1977), 'The Population Ecology of Organizations,' *American Journal of Sociology*, 82, 929–964.

Hannan, M. T. and J. Freeman (1984), 'Structural Inertia and Organizational Change,' *American Sociological Review*, 49, 149–164.

Ichniowski, C., K. Shaw and G. Prennushi (1993), 'The Effects of Human Resource Practices on Productivity,' unpublished manuscript, School of Business, Columbia University.

Kreps, D. M. (1996), 'Markets and Hierarchies and (Mathematical) Economic Theory,' *Industrial and Corporate Change*, 5

MacDuffie, J. P. (1995), 'Human Resource Bundles and Manufacturing Performance: Organizational Logic and Flexible Production Systems in the World Auto Industry; *Industrial and Labor Relations Review*, 48(2), 197–221.

MacGregor, D. (1960), *The Human Side of Enterprise*. McGraw-Hill: New York.

Martin, J. (1992), *Cultures in Organizations: Three Perspectives*. Oxford: New York.

Milgrom, P. and J. D. Roberts (1995), 'Complementarities and Fit: Strategy, Structure, and Organizational Change in Manufacturing,' *Journal of Accounting and Economics*, 19, 179–208.

Ouchi, W. (1980), 'Markets, Bureaucracies, and Clans,' *Administrative Science Quarterly*, 25, 129–141.

Pfeffer, J. (1994), *Competitive Advantage through People: Problems and Prospects for Change*. Harvard Business School Press: Boston, MA.

Pfeffer, J. and Y. Cohen (1984), 'Determinants of Internal Labor Markets in Organizations,' *Administrative Science Quarterly*, 29, 550–572.

Rohwer, Görtz (1994), *Transition Data Analysis (TDA)*, Version 5.7.

Saxenian, A (1994), *Regional Advantage: Culture and Competition in Silicon Valley and Route 128*. Harvard University Press: Harvard University.

Simon, H. A. (1951), 'A Formal Theory of the Employment Relationship,' *Econometrica*, 19, 293–305.

Tuma, N. B. and M. T. Hannan (1984), *Social Dynamics*. Academic: Orlando, FL.

Williamson, O. E. (1975), *Markets and Hierarchies: Analysis and Antitrust Implications*. Free Press: New York.

Williamson, O. E. (1981), 'The Economics of Organization: The Transaction Cost Approach,' *American Journal of Sociology*, 87, 548–577.

Williamson, O. E. (1992), 'Transaction Cost Economics and Organization Theory,' unpublished manuscript, Haas School of Business, University of California, Berkeley.

CHAPTER SEVENTEEN

Inertia and Change in the Early Years
Employment Relations in Young, High Technology Firms

MICHAEL T. HANNAN, M. DIANE BURTON,
AND JAMES N. BARON

This paper considers processes of organizational imprinting in a sample of 100 young, high technology companies. It examines the effects of a pair of initial conditions: the founders' models of the employment relation and their business strategies. Our analyses indicate that these two features were well aligned when the firms were founded. However, the alignment has deteriorated over time, due to changes in the distribution of employment models. In particular, the 'star' model and 'commitment' model are less stable than the 'engineering' model and the 'factory' model. Despite their instability, these two blueprints for the employment relation have strong effects in shaping the early evolution of these firms. In particular, firms that embark with these models have significantly higher rates of replacing the founder chief executive with a non-founder as well as higher rates of completing an initial public stock offering. Some implications of these findings for future studies of imprinting and inertia in organizations are discussed.

1. Imprinting, Inertia and Organizational Change

How much do origins matter for organizations? This question has pivotal importance for understanding organizational change. Despite its theoretical importance, little effort has been directed at gaining evidence that speaks directly to it. This paper takes a first step in an effort to rectify this gap in our knowledge. It reports some early results from an effort to examine processes of imprinting in a sample of young, high technology companies.

Current theory and research on organizations and industries reflect two polar views on the importance of origins. One perspective holds that organizational structures reflect mainly *current* internal and external exigencies:

465

core technology (Thompson, 1967), the structure of transaction costs (Williamson, 1975, 1981), and cultural rules about organizing (Meyer and Rowan, 1977). This view builds on the (usually tacit) assumption that structural change by organizations is unproblematic and relatively free of friction. Lack of friction causes origins (and the past, more generally) to become irrelevant as time passes and internal and external challenges change. Consequently, looking to origins should not help explain structure, once the present set of constraints has been taken into account.

The other pole in the debate holds that origins matter a great deal: origin conditions become *imprinted* on organizations, and these imprints have enduring importance (Stinchcombe, 1965; Hannan and Freeman, 1977). Although organizations might subsequently change as the challenges and opportunities change, initial conditions limit the scope of subsequent changes. This view builds on the assumption of strong hysterisis or path dependence in organizational change.

Although the possible enduring effects of origins have important substantive implications, they have been the subject of surprisingly little empirical investigation. Researchers have sought to infer answers to questions about hysterisis in organizational structure by examining organizational mortality schedules under a variety of potentially relevant conditions. For instance, Carroll and Hannan (1989) report that environmental conditions at founding have lasting effects on organizations. Specifically, the density of organizations in a population at the time of an organization's founding, which is assumed to capture the intensity of competition, affects its lifetime mortality schedule.[1] Most recent research on the inertia hypothesis has concentrated on testing Hannan and Freeman's (1984) hypothesis that change in core structures increases the hazard of mortality by reducing the advantages of accrued experience.[2] However, few researchers have had access to detailed information on the early activities of a set of organizations and on subsequent developments. Hence, we lack a clear image of the processes involved.

Historical treatments of industries and organizations document extensive change over centuries and often over much briefer spans of time. Many of today's well-recognized industries and organizational populations did not exist a century ago; indeed, many did not exist even a quarter of a century ago. Even those industries and organizational populations whose origins date to earlier centuries have undergone extensive renovations, with many organ-

---

[1] This result has turned out to be extremely robust (Hannan and Carroll, 1992), suggesting that competitive conditions at the time of an organization's inception do have long lasting effects for diverse organizational populations.

[2] Well-designed research on this issue reveals that the effects of structural change vary with organizational age. The older an organization, the greater the resulting increase in the mortality rate (Amburgey *et al.*, 1993; Barnett and Carroll, 1995; Carroll and Teo, 1996).

izational actors coming and going and industry and population structures being altered greatly. The leading organizations and organizational forms in one era seldom manage to retain their lofty positions—or even to survive—when technological, social and economic structures change sharply. In each era, upstart organizations and organizational forms rise to prominence. In the very long run (i.e. a time-scale of centuries), it seems hard to dispute that industries and other organizational worlds change by a process of *selection* in the sense of differential replacement.

What about shorter time-scales—say, decades? Here the picture becomes unclear. Much organization theory in sociology and economics has held that organizational change over such periods reflects mainly *adaptive change* by existing organizations. In this view, organizations remake themselves when the times demand it. Nelson and Winter (1982) draw the resemblance between this view and the Lamarckian position in evolutionary biology.

Beginning in the late 1970s, organizational ecologists proposed a selectionist account of organizational change (Hannan and Freeman, 1977, 1989). In this perspective, individual organizations are seen as incorporating features of the prevailing social and economic environment at their time of founding. Initial structures (especially those that are most central—see below) are thought to be subject to strong inertial forces. Therefore, individual organizations have limited capacities to reshape themselves quickly when environmental changes pose challenges to their continued growth and survival. Limits on the speed of adaptation at the organizational level create the conditions for rival to emerge and flourish. Inertia at the organizational level allows evolution at the population level.[3]

Doubtless, both adaptive change at the organizational level and selection at the organizational population level characterize many situations of interest. There is much current interest in building models that combine these processes. However, such an integration might be premature because we lack a clear understanding of some key features of the underlying processes. There continues to be value in clarifying adaptation and selection stories. Doing so focuses attention on several issues.

First, there is the issue of change versus adaptation. Discussions of these issues often focus merely on the *frequency* of change. If observations on a set of organizations reveal that structures and procedures have been altered, then it is argued that the ecological perspective does not apply. But this

---

[3] March (1991) develops an alternative scenario in which organizational learning (a central component of any purposeful adaptation story) can produce the same result. When a set of organizations specialize their learning along certain paths (an 'exploitation' strategy), they become more and more narrowly specialized and less capable of learning about other regions of the strategy space. Such specialized adaptation opens the possibility that sets of organizations using a more generalized search strategy ('exploration') can gain a foothold and thrive.

kind of reasoning misses the central point about adaptation. The fact that organizations sometimes change their structures does not, by itself, vitiate a selection argument. Successful adaptation requires that organizations be able to (i) choose the 'right' structural change; and (ii) time its implementation correctly in response to the vagaries of their shifting environments. Hannan and Freeman (1984) argued that the worst case is to incur the costs of reorganization only to find, once the new structure has been put in place, that the environment has changed to a configuration that demands further reorganization.

Any useful treatment of organizational inertia must, therefore, go beyond debates about whether organizations change. Instead, research ought frame the issues in *relative* terms, comparing the characteristic speeds of organizational transformation and environmental change. The ecological perspective holds most strongly when environments can change more quickly than organizations can remake themselves. Unfortunately, little effort has been made to calibrate these speeds for any interesting cases. This is a major gap in our understanding.

The second challenge in sorting out adaptationist and selectionist accounts of organizational change concerns the multifaceted nature of organizations. What features of structure ought to be considered? Some aspects of even the stodgiest organizations change almost continuously. Consider the contemporary US research university. The detailed profile of the organization's research activity changes by the hour, as some experiments end, others begin, and so forth. The cast of characters changes on a time-scale of months, as employees and students come and go. The organizational structure changes on a time-scale of years, as institutes and departments are created, merged, or closed. Key features of the employment relation for the professoriate, such as the institution of tenure for senior faculty, change on a time-scale of centuries. Whether such organizations are considered highly adaptive depends overwhelmingly on one's focus.

The common device for sorting out these myriad features of organizations relies on a *core-periphery* imagery. In this view, a feature forms part of the organizational 'core' if changing it requires adjustments in most other features of the enterprise. A feature lies at the periphery if it can be changed without imposing changes on other features. In this view, coreness means connectedness, elements in the core are linked in complicated webs of relations with each other and with peripheral elements.[4] Because dense webs

---

[4] It might be useful to pursue the parallels between treatments of inertia in organizational ecology with Kauffman's (1993) *NK* models. These models characterize the evolution of a system over a fitness landscape (a mapping of configurations to fitness). The evolving unit is specified as a linked set of components. N denotes the number of components and K denotes the per-component number of linkages. Kauffman's analyses and simulations reveal that the ratio of K to N determines the topography of the

of connections retard change, core features are more inert than peripheral ones (Hannan and Freeman, 1984).

Although there seems to be general agreement that some organizational features fall nearer the core than others, we see no consensus on exactly what constitutes the core. We suggest that research ought to measure connections directly and estimate the impacts of change in some features on the rate of change in others. In addition, attention to the sequence and timing of the adoption of structures and practices might help specify the composition of the core and how it varies across different types of organizations. There is a fundamental asymmetry based upon 'time's arrow'. Features adopted early in an organization's life can affect which structures and practices it adopts subsequently, but later events do not shape earlier ones. Consequently, the structures adopted in the process of initial organization-building are likely to have the broadest and longest-lived consequences — to be most core-like.

Imprinting refers to a process by which events occurring at certain key developmental stages have persisting, if not lifelong, consequences. The idea that organizations tend to imprint their founding conditions comes from Stinchcombe's (1965) elaboration of Max Weber's account of the logic of organization building. Stinchcombe argued that social and economic structures have their maximal impact on emerging organizations. Entrepreneurs must divert financial and human capital from other uses in order to build organizations. The process of mobilizing the two kinds of capital exposes their plans to intense scrutiny. Their proposals are tested against conventional wisdoms and taken-for-granted assumptions about organizations and employment. Because conventional wisdoms and taken-for-granted assumptions change over historical time (as new forms of organization flourish and others wane), the tests imposed on proto-organization also change. Consequently, the kinds of organizations that emerge in any era reflect the character of the founding period.

Imprinting requires two conditions. First, there must be an initial mapping of some external condition on the nascent organization (as suggested in the foregoing). Second, the imprinted characteristics must be fairly inert, otherwise, subsequent change will erode the association of founding conditions

---

landscape. At low *K/N*, the landscape is smooth and has few peaks. Random search has a high probability of locating the configurations of maximal fitness. Average paths of search are long, because the smoothness of the landscape means that there are few chasms that end the lifetime and thus the search. Therefore, evolution resembles ordinary hill climbing search. Search appears to be adaptive. At high *K/N*, the landscape is rugged, with many local peaks separated by regions of very low fitness. Random search tends to get caught in the local peaks. Searches that entail long-distance moves end with high likelihood in the low fitness chasms. In this scenario, inertia is the rule for long-lived systems, because those whose random search moved them some significant distance in the metric of configurations will be unlikely to have survived. Therefore, there is a connection between density of connections among components (*K/N*) and inertia.

and organizational features. It is this second condition that makes notions of imprinting central to treatments of organizational change. Evidence of imprinting provides indirect evidence of strong-form (absolute) structural inertia.

In arguing for imprinting, Stinchcombe (1965, 1979) focused on the *employment relation*. Lacking comparative data on firms, he made the argument at the level of industries. He noted that industries formed in different centuries still reflect today some of the character of their formative periods. For instance, industries formed after the 'organizational revolution' during the closing years of the 19th century and the early years of the 20th century typically employ a higher fraction of administrative workers than those with earlier origins.[5]

If Stinchcombe is right, then certain features of the employment relation are likely to be imprinted. Moreover, the character of the employment relation gets set, at least implicitly, very early in the organization's existence: when the first employees arrive and later when jobs are formalized. Arrangements made at that time might have long-lasting consequences. As Baron and Kreps (in press) argue, emerging organizations might need to commit to a stable pattern of employment relations in order to build a reputation in the labor market that will facilitate the attraction and retention of valuable employees.

In the only research that we know that bears on these issues, Baron and colleagues investigated inertia in employment systems in agencies of the California state government. Baron and Newman (1990) analyzed the interactions of age of a job category and characteristics of its incumbents on its prescribed pay rate. They found that jobs with mainly female incumbents tended to have lower prescribed pay rates and that this effect increased significantly with the age of the job. Baron and Newman (1990, p. 172) interpret this effect as indicating that 'notions of imprinting and inertia thus might fruitfully be extended to the study of work roles: cohorts of jobs founded during the same period might be expected to evince common features, such as shared selection and promotion criteria and similar degrees of ascription'.

It also turned out that organizational age affected the rate at which gender composition of jobs changed in response to changing composition of the relevant work-force. Baron *et al.* (1991) report that the youngest and oldest state agencies integrated their work-forces more quickly than agencies of intermediate age. They interpret the effect for younger jobs as agreeing with

---

[5] Carroll and Mayer (1986) used Stinchcombe's historical typology of employment systems in industrial sectors in analyzing patterns of individual careers. They found that time of origin of industry affects mobility regimes centuries and decades after founding.

the idea that inertial pressures on youthful structures are weaker than on older ones. The effect for the oldest agencies is harder to understand. Baron and colleagues suggest that this effect reflects the survivor bias in their data (the set of very old jobs is unusual in having survived for a long time and are therefore perhaps more responsive to environmental pressures). These studies make clear that age matters for the employment relationship and that the observed patterns are consistent with the hypothesis of age-dependent inertia in organizational structures and practices. However, the research design (with its survivor bias) precludes a sharp analysis of the processes by which jobs and organizations become fixed in certain configurations.

Lack of clarity about the underlying processes is a problem generally in current theories of organizational change. Consider, for instance, the timing of imprinting processes. If structures become fixed, when does this happen? Existing research focuses largely on the time of *founding*, following Stinchcombe's lead. Although imprinting plausibly reflects the conditions under which human and financial capital are mobilized, it is not obvious that lock-in occurs so early in organizational lifetimes. Close examination of the early days in organizational lifetimes suggests much learning by doing and seemingly random search for procedures and structures. Moreover, many founders eschew rules and formal structures initially and attempt to coordinate action by holding frequent meetings of the entire membership. Under such conditions, the organization might move flexibly among alternative ways of organizing. However, successful organizations inevitably outgrow this mode of coordination.[6] Perhaps lock-in processes operate strongly at the time that organizational and job structures are *first formalized*, when positions and roles get defined impersonally (without reference to the identities of incumbents) and patterns of ties among jobs are set in place. That is, an alternative view on imprinting holds that the 'clock' refers not to organizational age *per se* but instead to the intensity of formalization. A third possibility, which seems particularly germane to the case of firms begun by technologists, is that lock-in takes place after the *transition to professional management*. Discriminating among these (and perhaps other) scenarios would reveal much about the sources and likely consequences of imprinting.

We take advantage of a newly available set of data to begin to address these issues empirically. Our companion paper (Baron *et al.*, 1996) examines the origins of employment relations in a set of 100 young high technology firms in Silicon Valley. It seeks to describe how these firms varied in their initial blueprints for the employment relations, emphasizing consistency and

---

[6] In interviews, founders of the firms in our study, which is described below, often reported that a significant change in their organization's character can be traced to the period in which their work-force outgrew the company's largest meeting room.

complementarities among dimensions of human resource management and how founders' employment models shaped the early evolution of human resource policies and practices. This paper takes the second step, exploring the broader organizational implications of founders' initial blueprints. The analysis, which seeks to contribute to our understanding of how and why origins might matter, has two parts. The first addresses the extent and causes of changes in employment models over the early years. The second examines some implications of the initial blueprints for early development of these firms.

2. *Research Design*

This analysis, like that reported by Baron *et al.* (1996), uses data on the 100 firms studied in the first stage of the Stanford Project on Emerging Companies (SPEC). These firms constitute a stratified random sample of young high technology firms in Silicon Valley (defined as the part of the San Francisco peninsula from the San Francisco airport to San Jose). The sample comes from the population of firms that were reported as having been founded no earlier than 1984 and as having 10 or more employees in 1994.[7]

Our project team conducted interviews with founders, current chief executive officers (CEOs), and senior managers with responsibility for human resources. From founders we acquired information about the firm's early years. CEOs reported on current conditions and near-term prospects. Senior managers with oversight of human resources (HR) provided detailed information about changes in diverse features of the employment relation over the firm's history.

We intend to follow these firms over time. Current plans call for re-interviews in 1996 and 1999, which will enable us to relate early organizational histories to subsequent outcomes, including survival, performance, and changes in the work-force. We optimized this design for studying changes from 1994 forward. Therefore, the most dependable answers to questions about change for these firms lie several years in the future.

In the interim, we take advantage of the retrospective histories of the SPEC firms to address issues of stability and change among an unusual sample of firms. The retrospective data in hand, although not optimal, do paint a potentially interesting picture of patterns of change over the early years for 100 firms. Moreover, we have taken pains to obtain precise information on changes in the firm over its lifetime. This information allows us to examine the sequencing of changes and to estimate continuous-time stochastic models of change.

---

[7] In a few cases the sources turned out to be inaccurate. The oldest firm in our sample actually began business in 1982.

Nonetheless, we must emphasize that the cross-section of firms studied in mid-1994 comes from a 'survivor-biased' sample.[8] That is, we have sampled survivors from the birth cohorts of 1984, 1985, etc. This means that we cannot use these data to analyze the determinants of success (because we have 'sampled on this dependent variable'). Moreover, it means that effects of age on other outcomes do not have unambiguous interpretation as effects of aging. Instead, age tells both about aging and about the likelihood of having survived for a certain duration. These and other potential limitations of the research design, which are discussed in the companion paper (Baron *et al.*, 1996) should be kept in mind in considering the results we present.

The median firm in our sample was roughly 6.5 years when visited in the summer of 1994. Thus, our 100 firms provide roughly 650 firm-years in the presumably crucial formative life cycle stage. The range on age in the sample runs from 2 to 12 years (one firm turned out to be older than we thought).

This age distribution differs substantially from samples of organizations typically studied by economists and sociologists. Because the firms in SPEC are much younger than the population of comparably large firms, we expect change to be more fluid—virtually all of the well-designed research on the subject finds that rates of structural change decline with age (Barnett and Carroll, 1995). On the other hand, youth means that origins are recent. Hence, we would expect that origins would matter more in the SPEC sample than in the full population. More precisely, origins ought to be more highly correlated with current conditions for younger organizations, making it more difficult to distinguish the effects of the two sets of conditions.

The industrial environments facing these firms change rapidly. The firms in our sample are concentrated in several broad sectors of high technology: computer hardware and software, telecommunications and networking, and medical technologies and biotechnology. These high technology sectors experience rapid turnover in organizational composition. Rates of founding, acquisition, merger and bankruptcy are all high. The competitive landscape changes rapidly and nearly continuously—a firm's rivals today often differ markedly from those it faced only a year ago. Moreover, the velocity of change in product characteristics is also high. Thus, timeliness in developing and introducing new products makes an enormous difference for survival and profitability. Finally, environmental volatility is amplified by a lack of clarity of the boundaries between industries and their segments. That is, the boundaries demarcating high technology industries are faint and mutable

---

[8] It is perhaps worth noting that studies of organizations in economics and sociology routinely analyze such samples without acknowledging the threat to valid inference arising from the nature of the design.

over short time spans. Frequently, a firm's set of potential rivals cannot be bounded usefully by conventional definitions of industry.[9]

When environments are so volatile, even moderate brakes on the pace of structural change have important consequences. That is, the environments are moving so rapidly that only extremely rapid change can maintain close alignment of organizations and environments. The high level of environmental volatility also means that one can gain a great deal of information about issues of inertia and change from relatively brief spans of observation.

3. *Models of Employment and Business Strategies*

As noted above, theories of organizational change usually assume that those structural features and practices closest the organization's core face the strongest inertial force. This analysis builds on the premise that systems of employment relations and competitive strategy lie at the core. As we noted in the previous section, entrepreneurs enact an employment system, sometimes self-consciously and sometimes by default, in mobilizing financial resources to begin firms and in staffing their organizations, entrepreneurs commit to strategies, and these commitments impose binding constraints on subsequent actions. Business strategies, like employment systems, build commitments that are costly to change.

Models of the Employment Relation

As discussed in detail in the companion paper, we asked founders whether they initially planned to follow any model or blueprint in building their organizations and establishing a set of employment relations. As Burton (1995) and Baron *et al.* (1996) detail, we classified these responses according to what we regarded as the underlying images of the employment relation they reflected. We found that founders' conceptions varied along three dimensions. The first concerns the *nature of the attachment between the employee and the firm*. Three images dominate here: (i) long-term commitment (the firm as 'family'), (ii) ties based on the nature of the work—the opportunity to work on interesting and challenging work ('cool technology'), and (iii) pecuniary compensation (the employment relationship is primarily a monetary one). The second dimension refers to images of *coordination and control of work*. The dominant images of coordination include (i) managerial control with monitoring, (ii) peer and cultural control (where the employees have extensive control over the means by which work gets done but little control

---

[9] One founder of a firm in manufacturing networking products insisted that this industry lacks clear boundaries. When we asked him to name his most salient competitors, he replied 'Everyone'.

over strategic directions, projects to be pursued, etc.), and (iii) delegation to professionals of the right to influence strongly both the way in which work gets done and the larger strategic directions shaping the work. The third dimension pertains to the *firm's primary emphasis in recruiting and selecting employees*. The respondents tended to describe themselves as seeking primarily either: (i) bundles of demonstrable skills, (ii) stars and/or potential stars ('the best and the brightest'), or (iii) persons with strong fit to the organizational culture and a team orientation.

Of the 3^3 possible combinations of these categories, four predominate in the firms in which we conducted interviews. We refer to these four as the *models or blueprints of the employment relation*. They are:

- *Factory model:* pecuniary attachment, managerial control, hire for current skills;
- *Commitment model:* attachment based upon 'love', peer/cultural control, hire for cultural fit (all with a view to long-term employment);
- *Star model:* attachment to work, professional control, hire for potential;
- *Engineering model:* attachment to work (and to a project), peer control, hire for current skills (the taken-for-granted Silicon Valley model).

4. *Sources of Variation in Founders' Employment Models*

The mere existence of such diverse models among such a relatively restricted sample of organizations is itself interesting. Most sociological and economic theories of organizations suggest that organizations engaged in the same activities and utilizing the same productive resources should organize and manage their human resources similarly. Admittedly, the firms in our high technology sample are doing different things—searching for biotechnological breakthroughs, fabricating computer components, writing software, etc. but they are rather similar in their technologies, certainly relative to the economy as a whole. Moreover, we encounter startling diversity in founders' employment models even among start-up companies within the very same industry, competing directly against one another.

For example, several of the SPEC firms are working on developing computer operating systems. One of these firms exhibits a clear star model. They are extremely selective in their recruiting practices and require candidates to go through as many as 10 interviews. The culture was described as 'perfectionist', with every employee expected to make significant contributions. A competing firm, also in our sample, has a very different view of employees and the employment relationship. The CEO described his model as 'paternalistic'. He further described how he is opposed to the standard Silicon Valley mentality of 'treating people as commodities' and went on to describe all of the ways that his firm cultivates and develops employees. Yet a third firm in our sample, engaged in the same business, espouses a standard engineering model and relies exclusively on the attractiveness of their technology to recruit, motivate and retain employees.

Moreover, note that our sample, by design, controls for a number of the main sources of variation in employment systems that would be attended to by various theories from economics and sociology. For instance, all the firms in our sample have their headquarters in Silicon Valley, representing a common set of labor markets and regulatory regime. They are all new, small companies engaged in technology-related activities. Most of the founders have worked previously in other ventures within the Valley and are therefore well aware of what the prototypical Silicon Valley start-up is 'supposed' to look like. Indeed, not infrequently we encountered the same established organization—such as Hewlett Packard, DEC, IBM, Apple and Oracle— serving as a model to be emulated for some founders in our sample and as a model to be avoided for others. Also of interest is the fact that occasionally founders cited models emanating from very different industries, such as the software company that cited Ben and Jerry's (ice cream) as its positive model.

What factors, then, account for the variations we observe in founders' employment models? We are currently exploring this issue in depth, including an examination of the role that the founders, their biographies, prior relationships (if any), and ties to external partners (such as venture capitalists, lawyers, consultants and the like) play in shaping the blueprint for human resources management (for preliminary results, see Burton, 1995).

Business Strategies

One obvious factor that is especially likely to shape the blueprint for the employment relation is founders' intended business strategies. Like initial employment systems, choice of initial business strategy entails commitments both inside and outside the organization. Because both employees and external partners make investment decisions based on announced strategic directions, change in strategy imposes costs on them and they can be expected to resist such changes. In other words, basic features of business strategies ought to be difficult to change.

Moreover, there are reasons for thinking that employment models and business strategies are highly interdependent. The claim that employment practices should be closely aligned with and supportive of business strategy is the mainstay of the field of strategic human resource management (e.g.

Sonnenfeld and Peiperl, 1988; Legnick-Hall and Legnick-Hall, 1988). Certainly, business strategy bears directly on transaction cost concerns that affect the optimal organization of work and employment. For instance, within our sample, some companies are 'born' with fully-formed products, whereas founders of other companies (e.g. biotechnology start-ups) have only the vaguest notion at the firm's inception of what the end product(s) of their research and development activities will be. In the latter case, this time lag between founding the company and having developed a commercializable product that can secure regulatory approval and be marketed, coupled with the highly proprietary nature of the technology involved, presumably gives the employer a strong incentive to bind the interest of key employees to the firm over the long term.

Above it was argued that tight connectedness among a set of organizational features makes them part of the organization's core, the part of the organization that is most resistant to change. If business strategy and employment systems turn out to be highly interdependent, then we ought to expect both to be affected by initial conditions, that is, to be imprinted. Thus, we examine the relationship between employment models and business strategies over the early years for the firms in the SPEC sample in some detail.

To investigate the relationship between founders' employment models and intended business strategy, we classified firms into a series of categories describing their *dominant* strategic focus. This classification was based on content analyses of the founder interviews, supplemented (in some cases) by secondary sources (e.g. newspaper articles and industry analysts' reports) and/or other materials provided by the firm (e.g. a business plan). Coders were asked to discern from available materials what the founder(s) envisioned as their source(s) of ability to succeed in the face of competition in the product market. As in the case of the employment models, we encountered many different responses (and combinations of responses) from founders, but descriptions of their presumed distinctive competence tended to cluster into several major categories.[10]

(i) *Technological Leadership:* These firms seek to gain first-mover advantages by winning a technology race. Often, this means gaining a crucial patent or set of patents. The emphasis here is on breakthrough technology. Illustrative quotations from interviews with founders of firms classified in this category include 'Founders of [firm] had found a technical solution that worked for a problem that the world didn't even realize they had'. 'The basic core competence of the firm was the patented technology for the first complete micro-valve that used a silicon chip for fluid pressure/flow regulation.' Of

[10] For more details, see Burton (1995).

the 100 firms in our sample, 44 were classified as being in this category, which is not surprising given the industries we studied.

(ii) *Enhancement of Existing Technology:* These firms seek to produce a product similar to other companies, but they employ some general modification to the technology to gain competitive advantage. Distinctive competencies can include system integration (e.g. of software and hardware), superior quality (in terms of dependability or availability of features desired by customers), and the like. Interview transcripts from firms classified into this category included the following examples: '[T]hey knew that there was a market for optical character recognition and they wanted to outperform their existing competitors on accuracy and speed. It was a 'me-too approach'.' '[Our] competitive advantage is [in] providing *both* hardware and software expertise . . . [Our] product is the most feature-rich in the industry.' Eighteen firms were classified as being in this category.[11]

(ii) *Superior Marketing and/or Customer Service:* Firms in this category seek competitive advantage through developing or exploiting superior relations with customers, achieved through custom design of products, branding, using non-standard methods of sales or distribution, or simply by developing superior capabilities in marketing, sales, and customer service. Here are a few illustrative excerpts from interview transcripts of firms classified in this category: 'We're pretty sharp at understanding our customers' requirements before they even knew they had them. We foresee requirements, invest in them, and then deliver a product that people want.' In another company, the strategy consisted of: 'creating a second label . . . creating a strong second source to Microsoft [by offering] superior sales and marketing.' In a third, the founders '[built their] own distribution system, which almost none of [their] competitors has'. In a number of companies, the strategy consisted of creating products that respond directly to customers' idiosyncratic needs, often working interactively with customers toward that end. Twelve firms were classified as having strategies driven by marketing, sales, and/or service.

(iv) *Technology-Marketing Hybrid* [(iii) combined with either (i) or (ii)]: Another 13 firms combined a marketing-service focus with an emphasis either on enhancing an existing technology or on technological leadership. Not surprisingly, most of these hybrids (11 or the 13 firms) involved a combination of a marketing or service orientation with efforts to enhance an existing technology (by catering to specific customer needs).

(v) *Cost-Minimization:* Firms in this category seek cost advantages through superior production techniques, economies of scale, and the like. '[Firm]

[11] Two firms in which the distinctive competencies included both technological leadership and technological enhancement were categorized as being in the technological leadership category.

began as an IBM PS/2 clone maker . . . [they] knew they could build systems more cheaply than IBM.' 'The founder was frustrated at his previous company with the cost of boards and knew they could be produced more cheaply.' Three firms were classified as having a pure cost strategy. Another four combined a focus on cost minimization with some other focus (generally marketing or service) and were included in this category as well.[12]

Alignment of Strategies and Employment Models at Founding

Table 1 cross-tabulates founders' strategies and employment models. The association between the two is quite striking ($X^2 = 32.9$, $df = 12$, $p < 0.01$). Not surprisingly, founders intending to pursue a strategy of cost-minimization also were likely to champion the factory model of employment: two-thirds of firms pursuing a cost strategy espoused this employment model, compared to 7.8% of the technology leaders, 12.5% of the technology enhancers, 8.3% of those pursuing a marketing-service strategy, and 7.7% of the technology-marketing hybrid firms.

As we would expect, the star model is espoused most frequently among founders embracing a strategy of technological leadership: 39.5% of that group were classified as belonging to the star category, followed by 33% for those pursuing a marketing or service orientation and 31.3% for those planning on enhancing an existing technology. None of the firms pursuing a 'hybrid' strategy or a cost-minimization strategy was classified as being in the star model category. The comments of one founder, drawing on the scholarly contrast between 'theory X' (industrial engineering, Taylorist) and 'theory Y' (self-actualization, employee development) approaches to manage-

TABLE 1.   Relationship of Strategy and Employment Model at Founding

Founder's HR model	Founder's strategy					
	T	E	M	H	C	Total
Factory	3	2	1	1	4	11 (13%)
Commitment	6	5	6	6	2	25 (29%)
Star	15	5	4	0	0	24 (28%)
Engineering	14	4	1	6	0	25 (29%)
Total	38	16	12	13	6	85
	45%	19%	14%	15%	7%	100%

Pearsons $X^2 = 32.9$, $df = 12$, $p < 0.001$.

[12] We classified any strategy mentioning low costs as a distinctive competence into this category, even if the founder also enumerated some other competence(s), under the assumption that firms combining low costs with a marketing focus were more likely to resemble the pure cost minimizers than to resemble the marketing-driven firms that are serving idiosyncratic customer needs, engaging in concurrent engineering, and the like.

ment, provides a clear rationale for why the star model does not mesh well with a strategy centered around cost minimization:

> I set out to build a Y-type company, not an X-type. I wanted people who believed in the technology and were self-motivated. I realized after starting, however, that the reality of a bootstrap environment is that you can't afford the people who fit a Y environment. You have to settle for lower salaried people and drive them X-style. This 'settling for less' is also driven in part by greed. I simply don't want to give up the [stock] options it would take to get a high caliber person.

Technological leadership also appears to fit the engineering model of employment, which was espoused by 36.8% of founders intending to pursue that strategy. The engineering model is even more prevalent among firms that intended to combine technological and marketing-service competencies, espoused by 46.2% of founders whose firms are in the hybrid strategy category. The engineering model is also prevalent among the firms that planned to enhance an existing technology (25%). The popularity of this model within every category involving an emphasis on technology is hardly surprising, given that the engineering model of employment is the default or taken-for-granted conception within the Silicon Valley technical community.

Finally, it is interesting that the commitment model is most prevalent among firms pursuing a pure marketing-service strategy (50%), followed closely by those planning on combining technological and marketing competencies (46.2%). Presumably, companies that plan on sustaining their competitive advantage through long-term cooperative relations with customers and clients put a higher premium on long-term cooperative relations with their employees as well. These firms depend critically on the relationships that develop between their employees and the firm's long-term customers; those relationships represent valuable firm-specific investments, which are costly to replace and which the firm therefore seeks to protect by binding employees to the firm long-term. Those relationships also represent costly firm-specific investments to employees, creating an interest in long-term attachments on their part. Baron *et al.* (1996) report that firms built around the commitment model were also the fastest to adopt profit-sharing or gain-sharing, which ties employees' compensation to long-term overall company performance.

Just under a third (31.3%) of founders whose intended strategy was one of technological enhancement also championed the commitment model, compared to only 15.8% of those who intended to compete through technological leadership. Put differently, we find that founders planning on enhancing existing technologies are fairly evenly divided among the commitment, engineering and star models, with 12.5% even espousing a factory

TABLE 2. Stability and Change in Strategy

| Strategy at Founding | Strategy in 1994 | | | | | |
	T	E	M	H	C	Total
Technology race (T)	41	0	0	3	0	44 (47%)
Enhancement (E)	1	13	0	4	0	18 (19%)
Marketing/sales (M)	0	0	10	2	0	12 (13%)
Hybrid (H)	0	0	0	11	2	13 (14%)
Cost (C)	0	0	2	0	5	7 (7%)
Total	42	13	13	20	7	94
	45%	14%	13%	21%	7%	100%

Pearson's $X^2 = 325.5$, $df = 16$, $p < 0.001$.

model of employment. In contrast, each of the other strategies tended to map into only one or two of the employment models, suggesting that founders intending to compete by 'building a better mousetrap' did not agree on any particular HR recipe for doing so successfully. Another way of making the same point is to note that the two most common employment models among 'technology enhancers' account for only 62.5% of the firms pursuing that strategy; in contrast, the two most prevalent employment models capture 76.3% of the 'technological leaders', 83.3% of firms with a pure marketing-service strategy, 92.3% of firms with 'hybrid' (technology-marketing) strategies, and 100% of firms pursuing a factory model.

Changes in Strategy, Models and Alignment

Business strategies, like employment systems, build commitments that are costly to change. Accordingly, it is interesting to examine stability in these organizations' strategies, employment models, and in the alignment between the two. First, how do the strategies employed in 1994 relate to those envisioned at founding? We relied on information obtained from interviews with CEOs (supplemented in some cases by company documents and archival sources) to characterize the current strategies of these companies in terms of the same categories used to code their founding strategies. Table 2 shows the joint distribution of initial and current (1994) strategies for the 94 firms for which we had the relevant information at both points in time. It reveals that articulated strategies have been remarkably stable: only 14 of the 94 enterprises (14.9%) have changed their strategies. Close examination of the Table reveals that 7 of the 14 changers supplemented their initial focus on technological leadership or enhancements in existing technology with a marketing or service focus, hardly a major strategic shift. Not surprisingly, a few firms also moved in the opposite direction, adding a focus on technology to their initial emphasis on marketing or service. Thus, only 5 of the 94 firms (5.3%) actually abandoned their initial strategic emphasis altogether.

This degree of stability was somewhat surprising because we think of the early years as being very turbulent. As one founder told us, 'Young firms have messy lives'. Moreover, these firms face highly volatile and unpredictable environments; one expects to see firms learning about their competencies as a result of early experience and learning about the competitive landscape and reshaping their strategic directions accordingly. Indeed, the firms in this sample did change some of the detailed features of their strategies, such as which strategic partners to pursue and which of several prototype products to bring to market. But when strategies are viewed abstractly, it can be seen that radical changes in strategic direction are extremely unusual within the first few years of an organization's existence. In this sense, the way a firm positions itself at the outset matters greatly.

There is considerably greater evidence of change, however, in employment models between the time of found and 1994. We were able to code the three dimensions of employment relations (and thus the models) for both founders and 1994 CEOs for 70 firms in the sample, and Table 3 reports the joint distribution of the initial and current employment models. The fact that there is less stability in the employment models than in the business strategies is not surprising; entrepreneurs in high technology presumably know more about their products and markets *ex ante* than they know about an organization that they have not yet constructed and staffed.

Note that the four blueprints for the employment relation differ greatly in their persistence. The factory models stands at one extreme: no firm moves away from this blueprint. For the intermediate cases, about a third of the firms whose founders began with either a commitment model or an engineering model had a different blueprint espoused by the CEO in 1994. At the other extreme, the star model was replaced in about half of the cases.

TABLE 3.   Stability and Change in Models of the Employment Relation

Founder's model	CEO's model in 1994				
	Cost	Com.	Star	Eng.	Total
Cost-minimization	10	0	0	0	10 (14%)
Commitment	0	15	1	6	22 (31%)
Star	4	2	8	3	17 (24%)
Engineering	3	1	1	16	21 (30%)
Total	17	18	10	25	70
	24%	26%	14%	36%	100%

Pearson's $X^2 = 84.9$, $df = 9$, $p < 0.001$.

TABLE 4. Relationship of Strategy and Employment Model in 1994

Employment model in 1994			Strategy in 1994			
	T	E	M	H	C	Total
Cost-minimization	8	2	1	3	3	17 (24%)
Commitment	5	1	7	4	1	18 (25%)
Star	6	1	2	1	0	10 (14%)
Engineering	11	5	2	7	2	27 (37%)
Total	30	9	12	15	6	72
	42%	12%	17%	21%	8%	100%

Pearson's $X^2 = 18.2$, $df = 15$, $p > 0.10$.

Again, we see that initial configuration has a potentially important long-run effect on organizations. If these patterns turn out to hold generally, then founders who begin with the factory model have placed their firms on a trajectory that appears very difficult to abandon. At the other extreme, the star and commitment models appear 'hard to reach' from other starting configurations; firms that do not begin with these blueprints seem unlikely to evolve subsequently to them.

Given that strategies were remarkably stable and that models of employment underwent substantial change, the overall quality (or consistency) of alignment has likely changed. According to Table 4, it has indeed. The association between the dominant business strategy and the employment model is much weaker in 1994 than at time of founding. Indeed, one cannot reject the null hypothesis of no relationship between current strategy and current model in Table 4 ($X^2 = 18.2$, $df = 12$). This result suggests less apparent consistency in the match between strategy and employment model when firms have been in operation for several years than at the time of founding. We cannot rule out the possibility that the seemingly good initial alignment actually reflects the operation of a prior selection process. Suppose that alignment at inception affects survival chances strongly. Then close alignment would be more common among a sample of survivors than in the initial population of firms in these cohorts. However, this consequence of selection does not appear to explain why alignment worsens over time for a given cohort of firms. Some potential causes and implications of this apparently weakening alignment between business strategy and employment relations are discussed below.

5. *Sources of Change in the Employment Model*

We have posited that changes in an organization's basic employment model are difficult and costly to effect. What factors explain the incidence of such

TABLE 5.   Effect of Non-founder CEO on Stability and Change in Employment Models

A: Firms with a Founder as CEO in 1994

Founder's model	CEO's model in 1994				
	Cost	Com.	Star	Eng.	Total
Factory	9	0	0	0	9 (20%)
Commitment	0	12	0	1	13 (29%)
Star	1	0	6	0	7 (15%)
Engineering	3	1	0	12	16 (36%)
Total	13	13	6	13	45
	29%	29%	13%	29%	100%

B: Firms with a Non-Founder as CEO in 1994

Founder's model	CEO's model in 1994				
	Cost	Com.	Star	Eng.	Total
Factory	1	0	0	0	1 (4%)
Commitment	0	3	1	5	9 (36%)
Star	3	2	2	3	10 (40%)
Engineering	0	0	1	4	5 (20%)
Total	4	5	4	12	25
	16%	20%	16%	48%	100%

Pearson's $X^2 = 97.1$, $df = 9$, $p < 0.001$ in Panel A.
Pearson's $X^2 = 12.6$, $df = 9$, $p > 0.10$ in Panel B.

changes? It is reasonable to expect that major changes in senior management might prompt changes in blueprint for employment relations. In the case of young companies, a particularly dramatic change is the appointment of a CEO from outside the ranks of the founders. In the SPEC sample, 43% of the CEOs in 1994 were non-founders. We would expect to find more change in the employment model among firms with non-founder-CEOs for several reasons. Founder-CEOs might be expected to view their organizations as having evolved under a consistent blueprint or vision and, accordingly, tend to report that senior management's model has not changed. In contrast, CEOs who were not founders might want to stress their stamp on the organization and thus be inclined to report that the model had changed. Moreover, CEOs from outside the founding team might be brought in by investors precisely with the mandate to change some of the fundamentals of the organization and to rewrite some of the implicit contracts that might have existed previously between the firm and its employees. For these varied reasons, it is interesting to examine the joint distributions of initial and current models conditional on the status of the CEO (founder versus non-founder).

When the current CEO comes from the founding team, the CEO's model of the employment relation differs from that of the founder in only 20% of the cases. But when the CEO is a non-founder, the model differs about 60% of the time (Table 5). Should we conclude that change to a non-founder CEO is a critical event in shaping models of the employment relation in entrepreneurial firms? Perhaps. Yet, although change seems to occur more frequently for firms with non-founder CEOs, the *pattern of change* does not differ appreciably according to the status of the CEO in 1994. We see movement away from star and commitment models toward factory and engineering models in both panels of Table 5. It appears that change to non-founder CEO might speed the process of change, but it does not appear to dictate its direction.

The row marginals in Table 5 reveal an interesting fact: in 1994 the likelihood of the CEO coming from outside the founding team differs greatly by the initial employment model. In particular, more than half of the firms whose founders espoused star models had a non-founder CEO in 1994, and 41% of those that began with a commitment model had non-founder CEOs. In contrast, only 10% of those with a factory model and 24% of those with an engineering model changed. Change to a non-founder CEO does not appear to be an exogenous shock affecting a firm's employment system; rather it depends partly on the founder's initial blueprint.

Perhaps the employment models themselves generate consequences that lead directly to the appointment of a non-founder CEO. For instance, the high costs of implementing commitment and star models might create greater financial strains that undermine corporate performance or require external funding, which in turn might reduce CEO stability. On the other hand, these models might promote rapid growth or success (such as prospects for a successful IPO), making it attractive for firms to look beyond the set of founders for senior management appointments.

To investigate these possibilities further, we undertook analyses of stability and change in models of the employment relation that control for the effects of age, size, industry, founder versus non-founder CEO, and other relevant organizational conditions. In choosing the precise measure of change in the employment models, we faced the constraint that the number of possible transitions (12) is large relative to the number of firms with complete data on the relevant variables (70). Because the number of observed transitions of any type is small, analyzing the pairwise transitions does not provide much useful information. We therefore decided to aggregate over origins and destinations in measuring change; we distinguish firms that changed their employment model from those that did not. We allow the models to differ in the propensity to change by including dummy variables for founder's initial model as covariates.

TABLE 6. Effects on the Log-Odds of Changing the Employment Model (t-statistics in parentheses)

	(1)	(2)	(3)	(4)
Constant	−0.758	−1.77	−2.38	−3.25
	(−0.919)	(−1.72)	(−1.98)	(−2.25)
Age	−0.016	−0.165	−0.162	−0.198
	(−1.33)	(−1.14)	(−1.05)	(−1.14)
Size	0.0018	0.0021	0.0002	−0.0001
	(0.749)	(0.721)	(0.048)	(−0.018)
Telecom/networking	−0.280	−0.231	−0.223	0.061
	(−0.393)	(−0.277)	(−0.273)	(0.069)
Medical technology	−0.245	−1.43	−1.34	−0.716
	(−0.327)	(−1.28)	(−1.20)	(−0.606)
Founder employment model:				
Commitment	0.973	0.678	0.691	0.500
	(1.41)	(0.845)	(0.845)	(0.598)
Star	1.86	1.89	1.95	1.64
	(2.26)	(1.92)	(1.95)	(1.57)
Non-founder CEO		2.63	2.48	2.57
		(3.64)	(3.38)	(3.29)
Full-time HR			1.20	2.16
			(1.42)	(1.89)
Change in strategy				2.32
				(1.72)
Log-likelihood	−38.06	−29.86	−28.80	−27.11
Number of cases	70	70	70	70
Number of events	21	21	21	21

Table 6 reports the results of a set of four logit regressions. The dependent variable in each is the log-odds that the CEO's employment model in 1994 differs from the founder's model. Each specification controls for the effects of age in 1994, size in 1994, and industry (telecommunications and networking versus computers, semiconductor manufacturing, and others). As noted above, we also include founder's employment model on the right-hand side. Based on the results in the cross-tabulation of founder's model by CEO's model in Table 5, we estimate effects for the commitment and star models (contrasted with the other two models).

Not surprisingly given the retrospective design, age and size appear to be unrelated to change in the employment model. Similarly, industry does not predict change. Net of these other effects, however, the employment model does affect the odds of change significantly. The commitment and star models have substantially greater odds of being replaced. The estimated effect for the star model (1.86) implies that the odds of change are six times higher for firms with this model (exp[1.86] = 6.42) than for those with factory and engineering models. Therefore, the differences among employment models that can be seen in the raw cross-tabulations do not appear to be an artifact caused by differences in age, size, or industry.

In the second step (column 2), we consider the effect of change to a non-founder CEO. Adding a dummy variable that equals 1 if the CEO in 1994 is a non-founder improves the fit of the model significantly (compare the likelihoods in columns 1 and 2). Firms with non-founder CEOs have much greater odds of changing the model of employment (net of the effects of age, size, industry and founder model). Adding the strong effect of non-founder CEO actually increases the strength of the effects of the star model. Initial conditions persist in the face of the very large shock of moving outside the founding team for a CEO.

The third and fourth columns in Table 6 report the results of adding additional effects to the model. The additional covariates are two dummy variables, one which distinguishes firms that had hired a full-time human resources manager between founding and 1994, and another which indicates firms that had changed their business strategy. Both variables have large positive effects; however, neither addition improves the fit significantly over the simpler specification in the second column. Nonetheless, we find it intriguing that appointment of a full-time HR manager has a positive and significant effect on the likelihood of changing models. This result conforms to the view that HR managers come to firms with fixed agendas that might not be responsive to the firm's business context. If so, then professional HR management might be partly responsible for undermining the alignment between employment models and business strategies observed (retrospectively) at founding. In the conclusion we return to the issue of why this alignment appears to diminish over time.

6. *Founders' Models and Subsequent Developments*

Our companion paper (Baron *et al.*, 1966) presented evidence that tentatively supports the view that a founder's employment model constrains subsequent evolution of human resource policies and practices. But what about broader effects of internal business strategies and employment models on organizational evolution? This section examines the effects of initial employment models and business strategies on two important changes in the evolution of young, entrepreneurial firms: the appointment of a CEO from outside the ranks of the founders and making the transition from private to public ownership (successfully completing an IPO).

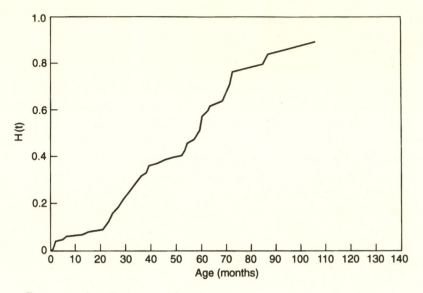

FIGURE 1. Cumulative hazard function: appointment of first non-founder CEO.

Change to a Non-founder CEO

We noted above that the appointment of a non-founder CEO is an occasion for major restructuring. We found that this event increases substantially the likelihood of change in senior management's espoused blueprint for the employment relation. Yet there was also evidence in Table 5 of an association between he founder's employment model and the likelihood that a non-founder serves as CEO in 1994. In this section, we investigate the possibility that the founder's model affects this transition directly. We do this in analyses that control for some of the other observable causal influences, including aging, growth, and industry.

We make use of the fact that we obtained the exact timing of the appointment of the first non-founder CEO. The methods of event-history analysis (Tuma and Hannan, 1984) are used to estimate effects of covariates on the rate of first transition (from founder to non-founder CEO). We specify the underlying process in terms of *organizational age* (t). That is, we regard each firm as becoming at risk of the appointment of a non-founder CEO at birth; and we analyze the (right-censored) distribution of age at the time of such appointment.

Let $Y_k(t)$ denote the state of one of the qualitative processes of interest, with state space: $Y(t) = 0, 1$. In the case at hand, let $Y(t) = 0$ indicate that only founders have served as CEO by age t and $Y(t) = 1$ indicate that a non-founder serves as CEO at age t. Then, the hazard of shifting to a non-CEO founder is defined as:

$$r(t) = \lim_{\Delta t \downarrow 0} \frac{Pr\{Y(t + \Delta t) = 1 | Y(t) = 0\}}{\Delta t}, t > 0.$$

We summarize the (unconditional) age-variation in the rate with the (transition-specific) cumulative hazard function:

$$H(t) = \int_0^t r(u) \, du$$

Figure 1 plots the estimated cumulative hazard function for this event. The slope of the function tangent to this estimated function over any reasonably small interval approximates the underlying rate. It appears from this plot that the rate is low for young organizations and becomes higher, but variably so, at older ages.

In building models that incorporate heterogeneity among firms, we tried several specifications of age dependence, using both piecewise constant and parametric specifications. The best fits come from a Weibull model. The parameterization of the Weibull model that we estimate has the form.[13]

$$r(t) = ba^b t^{b-1}, \quad t > 0, \tag{1}$$
$$a = \exp(x'_{,}\alpha), \tag{2}$$
$$b = \exp(x'_{,}\beta), \tag{3}$$

where $r(t)$ denotes the rate of moving to non-founder CEO for firm i at age t, in months and x_t is a vector of covariates. (The log-linear relationships in (2) and (3) are useful because the transition rate must be non-negative.) In general, the covariates vary with age for each organization. Time variation in covariates are accommodated by the standard method of 'spell splitting', which breaks each firm's history into monthly subspells and updates the values of the covariates at the beginning of each subspell (Tuma and Hannan, 1984; Blossfeld and Rohwer, 1995). The number of spells in this analysis are the number of observed firm-months throughout the lifetime of each company.

Table 7 reports maximum likelihood estimates of the effects of various covariates on the rate of first transition to non-founder CEO.[14] As was the case for change in the model of employment, size and age have negligible effects. Both effects (the effect of size in the 'a-vector' and the constant representing the effect of pure aging in the 'b-vector') are statistically non-significant. The effects of the two industrial categories and ownership status (public versus private) are also non-significant.

---

[13] Henceforth, we suppress the subscripts indexing the origin and destination states. These should be clear in the context of each analysis.

[14] We used TDA (Rohwer, 1994) to estimate this and subsequent event-history models.

TABLE 7.   Effects on Rates of Transition to a Non-
founder CEO (*t*-statistics in parentheses)

A-vector	
Constant	−6.19
	(−8.56)
Size	0.010
	(0.569)
Telecom/Networking	0.406
	(1.24)
Medical Technology	−0.382
	(−1.07)
Founder employment model:	
Commitment	1.24
	(1.84)
Star	2.15
	(3.06)
Engineering	0.748
	(1.07)
Founder strategy:	
Technology race	0.504
	(1.70)
Marketing/Service	−0.981
	(−1.96)
Public company	0.016
	(0.039)
B-Vector	
Constant	0.176
	(1.27)
Log-liklihood	−265.30
Number of spells	7193
Number of events	39

See text for explanation of the 'a-vector' and 'b-vector'.

Table 7 documents that the founders' models of employment relations significantly affect rates of appointment of a non-founder CEO. The commitment, engineering, and star models of employment have higher transition rates than the (excluded) factory model. If the factory model stands at one extreme, the star model stands at the other. The estimates in Table 7 imply that the transition rate for firms with star model founders is approximately 8.5 (exp[2.15] = 8.58) higher than for firms with factory model founders (conditional on the covariates). This difference in rates for star and factory models is highly significant. The difference between he commitment and factory models is also large (the ratio of the rates is approximately 3) and this difference is significant at the 0.10 level.

Initial business strategies also have substantial and statistically significant effects on the rate. Firms whose initial strategy placed primary emphasis on competing by superior marketing and service, where continuity presumably matters for maintaining partnerships with customers, were much less likely to see the appointment of a non-founder CEO. In contrast, firms engaged at the start in a technology race were more likely to experience this event.

These effects of employment model on founder-CEO persistence shed a different light on the instability of the star and commitment models. The high likelihood that these models will be changed appears to reflect at least partly the effect of these models on the persistence of a founder as CEO. In other words, the star and commitment models tend not to persist because founders with these models are likely to be replaced with non-founders. We suspect that the impermanence of founder leadership in firms begun with star and commitment models has something to do with implicit contracts. Neither the factory model nor the engineering model implies any implicit long-term contract between the firm and its employees. However, a star system typically involves implicit contracts that give very strong control over strategic directions in technology development to the technical stars. And a commitment system involves extensive implicit contracts with all classes of workers that they be treated as 'family'. We think that these contracts are typically thought to bind the founders. If the founders come to symbolize the cultures reflected in these implicit contracts, then it is difficult to change features of the employment relation as long as founders remain at the helm. Change might then require that an outside be brought in as chief executive.

Completion of an Initial Public Offering

Many founders report that their initial business plans called for their firms to become public companies at some point. Succeeding in going public is an important concern in many—if not most—young, high technology firms. Such firms frequently offer inexpensive 'founders' stock' and/or options to purchase the firm's stock on favorable terms at a future date to some—if not all—early hires. Both types of compensation are largely illiquid unless a firm becomes a public company. Not surprisingly, completion of an initial public offering (IPO) is widely regarded as an early sign of success in the Silicon Valley business community. Nearly a third of the firms in the SPEC sample had completed an initial public offering by mid-1994. In this section, we explore whether the rate of IPO depends upon the firm's initial conditions, specifically on the founder's strategy and model of the employment relation.

Because we know the exact timing of IPOs, we again use the method of event-history analysis. Figure 2 summarizes the age variation in the rate of

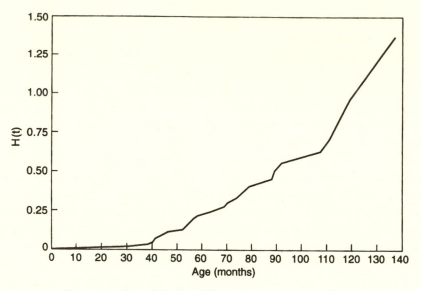

FIGURE 2.   Cumulative hazard function: initial public offering.

IPO. The pattern differs considerably from that found for appointment of a non-founder CEO. Very few firms experienced an IPO within their first three years.

Again, we tried several specifications of age dependence in this analysis, using both piecewise constant and parametric specifications. In this case, the best fits come from a specification that breaks age into pieces and estimates a constant for each age segment. Let τ_p indicate the time (age) of the start of the pth segment, with $\tau_0 = 0$. The models we estimate have the form:

$$r(t) = \exp(x_t'\alpha)\exp(\phi_p), \qquad t \in (\tau_p, \tau_{p+1}), \, t > 0.$$

We use three age segments: (0–35 months, 36–71 months, and 72 or more months). Again, we use the method of 'spell splitting' (by month of age) to update the values of time-varying covariates.

The empirical specifications used resemble those already discussed in the previous analyses. Table 8 reports the relevant results. As expected from examining Figure 2, the rate of going public is very low for the first three years. The rate is substantially higher over the rest of the age range, and the rates differ little for the second and third segments. These results suggest that these firms have little chance of undergoing an IPO for the first three years or so. The transition rate jumps and remains nearly constant over age from that point.

Again, we find that employment size does not affect the rate. However, industry does: firms in telecommunications, networking, medical technology and biotechnology have substantially higher rates of going public than those in the excluded set (computer industry, semiconductor industry and other industries). The difference is statistically significant for the telecommunications/networking industry in both specifications in Table 8 and for medical technology/biotechnology in one of them.

The founder's model of employment has a surprisingly strong impact on the rate of IPO. The rates for the three included models are much higher than for the excluded factory model. The difference is large and statistically significant for the star and commitment models. Holding constant age, size, and industry, firms whose founders had star or commitment models go public at roughly 10 times the rate of firms whose founders had a factory model.

Further research is needed to clarify the mechanism(s) that produce a relationship between employment models and rates of IPO. Several possible mechanisms seem plausible. The relationship might stem from the logic of initial organization. For instance, our companion paper (Baron *et al.*, 1996) shows that firms founded on star models are more likely than others to grant stock options to employees, which creates a strong internal demand for an early IPO. Alternatively, employment models might directly affect chances of early success. That is, firms built on star and commitment models might develop differently in ways that make the firms especially attractive to outside investors, thereby enhancing opportunities for an IPO. An additional possibility is that the star and commitment models are costly models. Firm adoption of one of these models is actually a proxy for slack resources commanded by the founder which may be related to later ability to go public. We intend to pursue these different alternative explanations in future research.

Initial business strategy also affects the rate of going public. Exploration of various specifications revealed that two strategies—the technology race and marketing/service strategies—differ most strongly from the rest. We include dummy variables that distinguish these two strategies from he combined set of other strategies (technology enhancement, hybrid and cost). With this set of contrasts, firms that began by entering a technology race had significantly higher rates of going public and those with a marketing/service strategy had lower rates (but not significantly so).

The second column of Table 8 adds an effect of status of the CEO (non-founder versus founder). The results show that the rate of IPO for firms whose current CEO is not a founder was nearly triple that of firms that stayed with founder top management. This difference in transition rates is highly significant. We also see that controlling for the status of the CEO weakens the effects of the star and commitment models. This is to be expected, given that we have already seen that CEO/founder status is power-

TABLE 8.　Effects on Rates of Initial Public
Offering (*t*-statistics in parentheses)

	(1)	(2)
Age segment (ϕ_p):		
0–35 months	−10.7	−10.4
	(−8.82)	(−8.58)
36–71 months	−8.31	−8.20
	(−8.22)	(−8.18)
72 months or more	−7.80	−7.72
	(−7.76)	(−7.75)
Size	0.010	0.010
	(4.35)	(4.47)
Telecom/Networking	1.05	0.902
	(2.19)	(1.81)
Medical technology	0.696	1.05
	(1.31)	(1.97)
Founder employment model:		
Commitment	2.35	1.68
	(2.56)	(1.77)
Star	2.52	1.69
	(2.73)	(1.74)
Engineering	1.04	0.545
	(1.18)	(0.610)
Founder strategy:		
Technology race	1.22	1.21
	(2.61)	(2.56)
Marketing/Service	−1.23	−0.702
	(−1.61)	(−0.911)
Non-founder CEO		1.09
		(2.65)
Log-likelihood	−210.52	−207.0
Number of spells	7193	7193
Number of events	31	31

fully affected by these models of employment. That is, controlling for status of the CEO is tantamount to controlling for one of the consequences of the initial models. This pair of results suggests a tendency for firms whose founders had star or commitment models to acquire non-founder CEOs in the process of becoming public companies. Very often this means bringing in seasoned managers to take the helm of firms that were founded and managed initially by engineers or scientists. It might also mean renegotiating implicit contracts about employment, as we discussed above.

7. Conclusions

Before assessing progress toward unraveling the causes of 'lock-in' in organizations, we repeat the cautions raised at the outset. Although the data gathered in the first phase of SPEC provide unusual detail on the early histories of organizing and of crafting employment relations, they are less than ideal. The main limitation is that we are analyzing a sample of survivors, albeit survivors over a reasonably short time span. Moreover, we base our conclusions on a relatively small number of events. The panel study, once completed (in five years or so), will provide much more dependable information about the main questions addressed here.

Having stated these cautions, we think that this first glimpse at the histories of many young, high technology firms suggests that initial conditions matter a great deal, even within the turbulent early years. We find the pervasive impart of the founder's blueprint for the employment relation both surprising and impressive. We did not expect to find that the founder's employment model would affect rates of change in top management, success in going public, and establishment and elaboration of formal human resources management. This range of effects, along with their strength, makes us want to delve more deeply into these matters.

An especially intriguing finding reported in this paper is that the close alignment between business strategies and HR models at the time of founding had completely vanished by 1994, when these firms were studied. There are a number of explanations for this provocative result. One obvious possibility is that close alignment is easier to achieve in the early years because start-ups are more homogeneous than older, larger firms with respect to their tasks and labor forces, thereby enabling start-ups to construct a single employment system or governance regime that envelops most or all of the employees. To put it differently, with growth in the scale, complexity, and heterogeneity of their tasks and employees, transaction cost economizing in a firm's employment system may occur at ever-lower levels of aggregation, rather than at the level of the organization as a whole or major subunits with it.

If this is true, a worthwhile question for future research is whether specific business strategies and/or employment models are more or less flexible in coping with this transition. One might expect, for instance, that firms in which the employment relationship is initially conceptualized and structured in terms of the star or factory models might be able to cope with these pressures toward internal differentiation more easily than firms that adopt the commitment model at their inception. Similarly, one might imagine that firms pursuing a strategy of technology leadership view key technical personnel as their major competitive asset, adopting particular HR policies and practices designed to attract, nurture, and retain those individuals, but displaying less regard for individuals engaged in other domains of activity (e.g. manufacturing, marketing) by virtue of the firms anticipated technical monopoly. In contrast, firms seeking to enhance an existing technology are likely to need to coordinate their technical core more closely with other functional areas of the firm, which may push them in the direction of adopting employment policies that are more consistent throughout the organization.

In addition, there may be particular types of firms and strategies for which the evolutionary trend is in the opposite direction—that is, toward more consistent treatment among different segments of the organization over time. For instance, companies founded around a strategy of technology leadership may find, once their initial success attracts the attention of competitors, that they need closer integration between technical personnel and those engaged in manufacturing and/or marketing their products, and that this is impeded by an organizational culture and HR system that has traditionally treated the latter as second-class citizens.

We are excited by the long-term prospects for examining these issues in more depth once we have gathered panel data on the SPEC firms. We conclude by outlining some of the next steps in this program of research. The second phase of the study, currently nearing completion, adds information on another 75 firms with the same profile. We have managed to find many younger firms in the second stage (as we have improved our ability to identify possible target firms). Using data from the second phase, we can validate our coding of employment models and business strategies and also check on the robustness of the patterns described in this (and the companion) paper. Then, combining the data from the two phases, we will gain enough statistical power to conduct more refined analyses of imprinting. For instance, we can compare patterns of relationships over the first few years of age for the older and younger firms in the sample. Such comparisons will allow us to assess the importance of survivor bias in affecting our results.

The most interesting possibilities lie in analyses of the planned panel data. Once we have made repeated observations on the firms in the sample, we will be in a position to test more interesting specifications of various imprinting stories. This is because we will be able to estimate the effect of origins on outcomes at time 2 (and subsequent times) controlling for the observed structures and practices in mid-1994. If imprinting has relevance to employment relations in these high technology firms, we ought not to be able to eliminate the effects of origins on outcomes by controlling in a very detailed manner for the history of the firm to the time of our first waves of observations. Such analyses promise to shed the clearest light yet on processes of organizational imprinting.

Acknowledgments

An earlier version of this paper was presented at the conference 'Firms, Markets and Hierarchies' held at the Haas School of Business, University of California at Berkeley. The research reported here was supported by the Stanford Graduate School of Business and the Alfred P. Sloan Foundation. Paola Bonomo, Ed O'Hara, and Eric Smith conducted most of the interviews on which this research is based. David Lam and Jennifer Sellars did most of the work of coding business strategies, and Puneet Agarwal, Mollie Brown, Angela Celio, Mamie Hsien, Peter Mendel, Tang-Nah Ng, Sri Srinivasan, Srija Srinivasan and Tari Vickery provided excellent research assistance. Glenn Carroll, John Freeman and Susan Olzak offered useful suggestions on an earlier draft. We appreciate the help of all of them.

References

Amburgey, T. L., D. Kelly and W. P. Barnett (1993), 'Resetting the Clock: The Dynamics of Organizational Change and Failure,' *Administrative Science Quarterly*, 38, 51–73.

Barnett, W. P. and G. R. Carroll (1995), 'Organizational Change,' *Annual Review of Sociology*, 21, 217–236.

Baron, J. N., M. D. Burton and M. T. Hannan (1996), 'The Road Taken: Origins and Early Evolution of Employment Systems in Emerging Companies,' *Industrial and Corporate Change*, 5, 239–275.

Baron, J. N. and D. M. Kreps. In press. *Human Resources: A Framework for General Managers.* John Wiley: New York.

Baron, J. N., B. S. Mittman and A. E. Newman (1991), 'Targets of Opportunity: Organizational and Environmental Determinants of Gender Integration Within the California Civil Service, 1979–1985,' *American Journal of Sociology*, 96, 1362–1401.

Baron, J. N. and A. E. Newman (1990), 'For What It's Worth: Organizations, Occupations, and the Value of Work Done by Women and Nonwhites,' *American Sociological Review*, 55, 155–175.

Blossfeld, H-P. and G. Rohwer (1995), *Techniques of Event-History Modelling.* Erlbaum: Hillsdale, NJ.

Burton, M. D. (1995), *The Evolution of Employment Systems in High Technology Firms,* unpublished PhD dissertation, Stanford University.

Carroll, G. R. and M. T. Hannan (1989), 'Density Delay in the Evolution of Organizational Populations: A Model and Five Empirical Tests,' *Administrative Science Quarterly*, 34, 411–430.

Carroll, G. R. and A. C. Teo (1996), 'Creative Self-Destruction among Organizations: An Empirical Study of Technical Innovation and Organizational Failure in the American Automobile Industry, 1885–1982,' *Industrial and Corporate Change*, 5, 2.

Carroll, G. R. and K. U. Mayer (1986), 'Job Shift Patterns in the Federal Republic of Germany: The Effects of Social Class, Industrial Sector, and Organizational Size,' *American Sociological Review*, 51, 33–341.

Hannan, M. T. and G. R. Carroll (1992), *Dynamics of Organizational Populations.* Oxford University Press: New York.

Hannan, M. T. and J. Freeman (1977), 'The Population Ecology of Organizations,' *American Journal of Sociology*, 32, 929–964.

Hannan, M. T. and J. Freeman (1984), 'Structural Inertia and Organizational Change,' *American Sociological Review*, 49, 149–164.

Hannan, M. T. and J. Freeman (1989), *Organizational Ecology.* Harvard University Press: Cambridge, MA.

Kauffman, S. A. (1993), *The Origins of Order: Self-Organization and Selection in Evolution*. Oxford University Press: New York.

Legnick-Hall, C. A. and M. L. Legnick-Hall (1988), 'Strategic Human Resources Management: A Review of the Literature and a Proposed Typology,' *Academy of Management Review*, 13, 454–470.

March, J. G. (1991), 'Exploration and Exploitation in Organizational Learning,' *Organization Science*, 2, 71–87.

Meyer, J. W. and B. Rowan (197), 'Institutionalized Organizations: Formal Structure as Myth and Ceremony.' *American Journal of Sociology*, 83, 340–363.

Nelson, R. and S. Winter (1982), *An Evolutionary Theory of Economic Change*. Belknap: Cambridge, MA.

Rohwer, G. (1994), *TDA (Transition Data Analysis) Version 5.7*. University of Bremen.

Sonnenfeld, J. A. and M. A. Peiperl (1988), 'Staffing Policy as a Strategic Response: A Typology of Career Systems.' *Academy of Management Review*, 13, 588–600.

Stinchcombe, A. L. (1965), 'Social Structure and Organizations,' in J. G. March (ed.) *Handbook of Organizations*. Rand McNally: Chicago, pp. 142–193.

Stinchcombe, A. L. (1979), 'Social Mobility and the Industrial Labor Process,' *Acta Sociologica*, 22, 217–245.

Thompson, J. D. (1967), *Organizations in Action*. McGraw-Hill: New York.

Tuma, N. B. and M. T. Hannan (1984), *Social Dynamics: Models and Methods*. Academic Press: Orlando, FL.

Williamson, O. E. (1975), *Markets and Hierarchies: Analysis and Antitrust Implications*. Free Press: New York.

Williamson, O. E. (1981), 'The Economics of Organization: The Transaction-Costs Approach.' *American Journal of Sociology*, 87, 548–577.

CHAPTER EIGHTEEN

Creative Self-Destruction among Organizations

An Empirical Study of Technical Innovation and Organizational Failure in the American Automobile Industry, 1885–1981

GLENN R. CARROLL AND ALBERT C. Y. TEO

A hotly debated question of organizational theory—especially evolutionary theories of organization—asks how inert are organizational structures. Answering the question requires analysis of not only organizational change but also of the consequences of change for organizational survival. This study examines one such organizational change—technical innovation—and its effects on the failure rates of American automobile producers from 1885 to 1981. Technical innovations are shown to generate primarily beneficial effects for the firms spawning them and primarily detrimental effects for competitor firms. However, analysis of certain organizational contexts— large organizations in particular—suggests that the risks of innovation may on occasion outweigh benefits. The findings imply that some theories of strategic management need rethinking.

1. Introduction

A major difference among evolutionary theories of organization concerns the degree to which individual organizations are viewed as inertial. At one end of the continuum lies the economic-evolutionary theories of Nelson and Winter (1982). They view organizations as somewhat adaptable, capable of transformations undertaken in response to environmental change. At the other end of the continuum are the ecological-evolutionary theories of Hannan and Freeman (1977, 1984). In these theories, organizations typically are stymied by their structures, which represent the culmination of previous decisions, political deals and normative orientations.

The theoretical implications of the inertia issue reach far beyond evolutionary formulations. Most theories of organization concern optimal design in equilibrium and implicitly assume that organizational change is frictionless, relatively cost-free and without major risk. To the extent this assumption does not hold, these theories need to be re-evaluated and perhaps revised. So too may public policies designed to improve industrial performance since they usually target existing organizations and rely on their successful transformation.

Although debated frequently, the inertia issue is not investigated as thoroughly as it should be. The ratio of rhetoric to research is high. And, as with much rhetoric, misrepresentations abound. Many organizational researchers avoid directly confronting the issue, preferring instead to make (often implicit) assumptions about inertia and then getting on with the primary theoretical or substantive focus of their work.

We report here a study designed to introduce evidence on organizational inertia. Our efforts are synthetic. Following recent research (Haveman, 1992; Amburgey *et al.*, 1993; Barnett and Carroll, 1995), we argue that progress on the inertia issue can be made by specifying conditions where organizational change will be beneficial and where it will be detrimental. Adopting such an approach requires consideration of: (i) the content of organizational change; (ii) the process of change *per se*; and (iii) the organizational and technological context of change.

We investigate American automobile manufacturing firms and the effects of technical innovations on organizational failure across much of the history of the industry. Intuition would suggest that innovations convey a beneficial effect on the longevity of firms introducing them.[1] So too would Nelson and Winter (1984), who put technical innovation at the center of their theoretical efforts and envision it as the main way firms overcome or alter their selection environments. Thus, an observed detrimental effect of innovation (an important organizational change more directly related to performance than others studied to date) would provide compelling evidence that organizational change can be costly, disruptive and inherently risky. It would also add the possibility of 'self-destruction' to Schumpeter's (1942) famous view of technical change as creative destruction. A similar idea can be found in March's (1982, p. 567) discussion of how firms in difficult times often pur-

---

[1] This would be especially likely given the bias probable in defining innovations retrospectively. Consider, for instance, the view of Vicenti (1994, p. 32): 'A pitfall for all historians, of course, is that we know the outcome of the events we study. This knowledge cannot help but color our selection and interpretation of those events. Historians of technology need to be especially alert to this pitfall since technological problems, to a greater degree than social ones, often find solutions that a majority of people regard as in some sense 'correct''.

sue risky strategies, thus leading to a situation where, 'for those that do not survive, efforts to survive will have speeded up the process of failure'. Although the paradoxical outcome may be the same in both scenarios, in creative self-destruction initial change is not driven by decline or crisis but by an attempt to advance technology and improve the position of the firm, whatever its current state.

Such effects of organizational change need not be universal. Indeed, for innovation, a universal detrimental effect would likely not be credible. However, the relevant literatures suggest that effects generated by technologically oriented organizational change depend on (i) the extensiveness of a technical innovation and (ii) the age of the organization; and (iii) the size of the organization. These effects need not correspond with predictions about the contexts spawning innovations in the first place—in other words, we decouple arguments about the sources of innovation from those about the beneficial firm-level impact of innovation. In our view, empirical findings of contingent effects of technical innovation would go a long way towards reconciling the different views of evolution in organizational populations.

This study follows in the spirit of remarks about studying organizational failure made by Williamson (1985): 'Focusing attention on failures ... would help to avoid the mistaken conclusion the modern business enterprise is an uninterrupted sequence of successful refinements' (1985, p. 404). Although little transaction cost research adopts this approach, a recent study of American paper mills from 1900–1940 by Ohanian (1994) suggests its value.[2] She finds that given industry conditions, most mills regularly showed the levels of vertical integration expected by transaction cost theory. But she also finds that as industry conditions changed over time, this alignment or isomorphism obtained overwhelmingly as a result of selection, not the adaptation of individual mills.

2. *Theoretical Considerations*

Although all evolutionary theories posit some organizational inertia, specific theories differ in degree. It is convenient to frame the issue around the works of leading and highly influential theorists. On one side sit Nelson and Winter (1982), who advance an economic evolutionary theory of business firms. They understand clearly that some retention process is necessary for evolutionary theory. Nelson (1995, p. 54) writes: 'It is presumed that there are strong inertial tendencies preserving what has survived the selection process'. However, these theorists also insist that inertia in organizations can be overcome. Consider, for instance, Nelson's (1995, p. 69) statement that

[2] We are indebted to John de Figueiredo for directing this study to our attention.

unlike phenotypes (living organisms) that are stuck with their genes, firms are not stuck with their routines. Indeed they have built in mechanisms for changing them'. This theme plays itself out most clearly in Nelson and Winter's writing on technical innovation, where they depict firms as capable of intentionally developing new processes and products that transform industries and their corresponding selection environments.

On the other side of the issue are Hannan and Freeman (1977, 1989), who advocate an ecological evolutionary theory of organizations. They assert that most fundamental organizational variation arises from the appearance of new types of organizations rather than from transformation of existing organizations. In their view, 'inertial pressures prevent most organizations from radically changing strategies and structures' (Hannan and Freeman, 1989, p. 22). They take care to note that their definition of inertia is relative, thus denying that their argument implies organizations never change: 'Rather, it means that organizations respond relatively slowly to the occurrence of threats and opportunities in the environment' (Hannan and Freeman, 1989, p. 70). They also specify a hierarchy of inertial forces (1984, 1989), labeling those characteristics most difficult to change (such as stated goals, forms of authority, basic technology, and marketing strategy) as core features. By definition, changing a core feature of an organization requires extensive other changes in peripheral structures.

Hannan and Freeman's arguments frequently are interpreted to mean that organizational change is extremely rare or even impossible, a claim that many regard as implausible (Nelson, 1995; Dosi *et al.*, 1993). Yet this is clearly a misinterpretation, even as it applies to core features. The confusion likely arises because many fail to realize that Hannan and Freeman's arguments often are not so much about change itself as about successful change, change that improves or enhances an organization's life chances and around which key evolutionary questions revolve. We understand their views to be something like the following. Any core change is difficult to enact, but looking across the entire world of organizations, change in core structures can and does occur all the time. However, core change that actually improves organizational life chances is more the exception than the rule. The reason this is so stems from not only the uncertainty of how to change the organization to enhance effectiveness but also from costs and risks associated with the change process itself.[3]

[3] The differences between Nelson and Winter (1982) and Hannan and Freeman (1989) and their respective followers is sometimes characterized as analogous to the distinction in bioecology between Lamarckians (who hold that acquired or learned traits can be inherited) and Darwinists (who deny that such traits can be inherited) respectively. While not inappropriate, this distinction takes the debate into a realm that we believe is misleading because it revolves primarily around a biological mechanism (generational inheritance) that has no unambiguous or straightforward parallel in organizational evolution. We think the debate is more usefully framed within purely organizational issues.

Recent work on organizational change suggests a way to reconcile these apparently disparate views with each other. A growing body of careful empirical research reveals that organizational change can generate either substantial content or process effects on performance, including mortality (for a review, see Barnett and Carroll, 1995). Content effects consist of consequences arising from the substance of what is changed in the organization at two points in time. So, for instance, reorganization of a shop-floor yielding production efficiencies would constitute a positive content effect based on the differences between the new and the old floor designs. Process effects comprise those consequences emanating from change *per se*. An example of a negative process effect would be a labor action that occurs when a shop-floor reorganization is attempted and ends up dividing the company and leading to failure. Obviously, a complete assessment of the effects of organizational change on organizational performance and survival must weigh both content and process effects.

Interpreting the differences between Nelson-Winter and Hannan-Freeman on inertia within this framework is revealing. In our view, Nelson and Winter focus primarily on content changes in organizations, the capabilities associated with particular social and technical arrangements. (They use the logic of comparative statics to make assessments.) They clearly recognize that uncertainty and experimentation probably lead to failure because of wrong decisions (negative content effects) but they hold out the promise a successfully directed search for, say, technical innovation (massive positive content effect). Oddly enough, despite sensitivity to many social and process issues, Nelson and Winter do not usually even consider the possibility of negative process effects associated with organizational change. They implicitly assume them to be trivial or not significant and thus their calculus depends primarily on content. By contrast, Hannan and Freeman seem to ignore or discount content effects and focus primarily on process.[4] They theorize about the difficulty and precariousness of the change period but usually do not take into account the potential performance consequences of exactly what is being changed. Indeed, it sometimes appears that Hannan and Freeman view content changes resulting in large positive effects as arising primarily from luck, especially of timing.[5]

By this interpretation, the debate in evolutionary organizational theory depends on whether content or process effects dominate in actual instances of organizational change. The empirical research to date suggests a con-

[4] There is irony here in that sociologists Hannan and Freeman appear more attentive to the costs and risks of change than economists Nelson and Winter, who seem more attuned to social structure and its consequences.

[5] Indeed, underlying the debate is another, often unstated, point of contention about the rationality of managerial action. We regret that our analysis here cannot address this issue.

tingent answer: it depends on the organizational form and organizational characteristics. However, Nelson and Winter might rightfully complain that the acid test for their position has not been conducted because the organizational changes that have been studied tend to be rather mundane or commonplace, for example, changes in newspaper publication frequencies (Amburgey *et al.*, 1993) and changes in the service areas of voluntary social service agencies (Singh *et al.*, 1986) and diversification by savings and loan associations (Haveman, 1992). They also may not have clear or direct performance implications. None of these studies has tracked systematically the firm-specific consequences of industrywide innovations, ideas, products and techniques that no competitor has introduced previously, although technical change has been studied (see Barnett, 1990, 1994). For that reason we undertook such tests and report them here. The disadvantage of using innovation is that it introduces modeling constraints precluding the full separation of content and process effects. This is because each innovation event is unique and occurs to only one firm, thus presenting no possibility of controlling for existence in the content state (see Barnett and Carroll, 1995). In other words, content and process effects are combined in the effects of the innovation variables. We overcome this unavoidable limitation by hypothesizing about overall expected effects based on assessment of whether content or process effects will dominate in a particular context.

We study the effects of technical innovation in the American auto industry across much of its history. In departing from common practice, we consider the effects of innovations on firms as potentially distinct from the sources of innovation. This leads to predictions suggesting that those contexts where innovations are most likely to appear (e.g. large firms) are not necessarily those where the effects of innovation will be most beneficial for the firm's viability. Such a focus not only makes the test more critical for evolutionary concerns, it also brings into play theories about technological change and innovation (e.g., Dosi, 1982, 1988; Tushman and Anderson, 1986; Malerba and Orsenigo, 1993; Utterback, 1994).

3. Hypotheses

Innovation is typically defined as the novel combination of input materials or activities for potential economic gain. Although the first step in such an effort almost always involves some sort of idea, invention or discovery, even broad conceptions of innovation define it by the implementation or commercial introduction of the idea.[6] For instance, Kamien and Schwartz (1982,

---

[6] This general type of definition follows in the tradition of Schumpeter (1934, 1942), who drew a sharp distinction between invention and innovation, stressing the economic implications of the latter.

p. 2) define innovation as 'all those activities, from basic research to invention to invention to development and commercialization that give rise to a new product or means of production'. The definition excludes research and development activities that are not implemented in one form or another. It includes new types of products as well as new processes for making those products.

A difficult question involves whether innovations should be defined on the basis of their success or impact. The typical study of innovation regards innovation as the dependent variable and stops observation with the innovation event. Innovation is assumed to have positive or beneficial effects for the firm in which it occurs. Virtually everyone agrees that new products which replace old ones with the same function constitute innovations (e.g. digital watches). Changes in process that dramatically improve quality or productivity (e.g. the moving assembly line) are also universally labeled innovations. More controversial are new products and processes that are intended to yield economic gains but which fail to do so (e.g. IBM's OS/2 operating system). By most views, these would not be innovations—the definition is tied up with at least short-run success or improvement, what we might call positive content effects. The problems here are exacerbated by questions regarding the definition of short run. Products and processes that show immediate improvement over existing options would generally be regarded as innovations. But what about those which initially fail to improve but do so later? How long should be the window for potential delayed effects? Innovation is frequently used synonymously with technical advance or progress (e.g. Kamien and Schwartz, 1982). Even if this is not the case, selective attentiveness to success likely biases our classification of products and activities, especially retrospectively. That is, new combinations that fail are unlikely to come to our attention or to get recorded in the same way as those that succeed.

One of the great contributions of Nelson and Winter's (1982) evolutionary theory has been to demonstrate how misguided it is to build theory about technical change based primarily on this kind of outcome-defined information. Indeed, their view of how positive technical change comes about stresses decision-making under uncertainty, expects many failures in the process and allows for the operation of chance as well as apparently unrelated social events (see also Dosi, 1982, 1988). However, they also envisage a competitive selection environment which assesses fitness based heavily on a firm's technological capabilities. So when confronted with technical innovations defined on the basis of their impact, this framework leaves little doubt about its expectation: the firm's fitness should increase momentarily and its chances of failure will be diminished, at least initially. Despite the lack of firms in the industry with successful prior experience in implementing the innovation, the potential costs and risks of necessary subsequent organizational changes (negative process effects) are presumed to be nil or minor, certainly smaller in consequence than the innovation itself. With elapsed time, the beneficial effects may attenuate as other firms adopt similar or alternative innovations.

It is somewhat unfair to say that Nelson and Winter completely ignore the possibility of organizational problems associated with implementing an innovation. For instance, they write about the difficulty of adjusting complementary routines in response to a new routine or innovation (see Winter, 1982; Nelson, 1995). However, it seems to us that they see such difficulties as blocking or limiting the introduction of the innovation in the first place. So, if there are many routines to be adjusted, the firm is unlikely to develop or introduce the innovation. This outcome might be regarded as arising from the anticipated future costs and risks of the innovation. However, we are making a different point. Although future costs and risks might be anticipated and lead to behavior with respect to the innovation, we also believe that technical innovations are often undertaken and implemented without full regard for, or understanding of the costs and risks involved for the whole firm. For example, the manager of a division may direct resources to the development of a particular innovation that favors his interests and those of his division even though the subsequent adjustment costs and risks for the rest of the firm are huge. It is these post-introduction innovation costs and risks of organizational change that we believe Nelson and Winter and many other analysts fail to attend to fully. Our first hypothesis is therefore:

1. *Technical innovation by a firm momentarily enhances its life chances.*

What about other firms' innovations? Presumably, in any competitive market a firm stands to lose—at least in the short term—if its competitors introduce technical innovations (especially if those innovations are proprietary or inimitable). This is one of the basic insights of Schumpeter's (1942) notion of creative destruction. The appeal of new products or product features or the lowered costs associated with an innovation represent positive content effects and give other firms a potential competitive advantage. Whether this potential is realized depends on at least two considerations: (i) the magnitude of the advantage and (ii) the ease with which competitors might adopt or imitate the innovation. Both factors, in turn, are often seen as depending on how much a departure from previous practice an innovation represents. Innovations that are radical, frame-breaking or competence-destroying are commonly viewed as potentially greater in impact and more difficult for existing competitors in the industry to incorporate than are those which are incremental, continuous or competence-enhancing (Tushman and Romanelli, 1985).

Nonetheless, empirical research shows that technological change with only a small contemporaneously perceived effect on performance can wreak havoc within an organizational population (Henderson and Clark, 1990; Iansiti, 1995). From the point of view of a firm adjusting to developments in its environment, the issue is not only what innovations are appearing in competitors' products but how many are appearing simultaneously. The problem of adjustment likely gets magnified non-linearly as multiple innovations emerge because attention and other resources are limited, coordination problems are exacerbated, and there is greater likelihood that an important or difficult-to-imitate innovation will need to be confronted. These short-term effects of innovation by competitor firms should be evident even if some innovations eventually benefit the entire industry by, say, expanding the market. So from arguments about both content and process effects we expect the following hypothesis:

2. *Technical innovations by competitor firms momentarily diminish a firm's life chances.*

Radical innovations are generally regarded as more likely to come from new entrants and once they appear, new firms are thought to be more likely to incorporate them than older firms. By this view, innovations introduced by existing firms tend to be incremental or continuous in nature (Tushman and Anderson, 1986; Henderson and Clark, 1990; Utterback, 1994). However, even if accurate, this observation does not necessarily imply that innovations brought forth by existing firms will be implementable with equal ease—under certain conditions the risks and costs involved may generate dominant negative process effects. Numerous analyses suggest that the degree to which an innovation is embedded in a larger technical production system is critical. In Teece's (1988) terms, an autonomous innovation is one that requires little additional adjustment in a firm's production and marketing arrangements. A systemic innovation is one that requires substantial re-engineering of other technical dimensions as well as the possible reconfiguration of organizational structure. In large and complex products—such as automobiles—it is possible to assess the extensiveness of other technical changes implied by the introduction of an innovation. For example, introducing the first all-steel open car body required considerably more adjustment elsewhere than did introducing the first motor-driven electric horn. Because extensive changes are difficult to complete and likely to be disruptive, we expect that they entail higher costs and risks. If they get high enough, then the overall innovation effort may be life-threatening, possibly generating dominant negative process effects or what we call 'creative self-destruction'. When coupled with the previous hypothesis, this observation leads us to argue that innovation effects may be non-linear, depending on the extensiveness of the innovation:

3. *The more extensive a firm's technical innovation, the more likely it will momentarily diminish the firm's life chances.*[7]

It may be that the costs and risks entailed by introducing an innovation depend heavily on the characteristics of the organization where it resides. Theory and research suggest that both older and larger organizations may be more inertial, thus presenting greater difficulties for implementing a technical innovation and more likely to foster negative process effects.

Organizational age may correspond with inertia because of what Barron *et al.* (1994) call the liability of senescence. According to this view, as organizations age they accumulate rules, routines and structures. They also become embedded in networks of exchange partners that generate normative expectations about their identities. Accumulated rules, routines, and structures impose constraints on organizational action, as do normative expectations. So if an old organization succeeds in developing a technical innovation, then it probably finds it difficult to make the subsequent changes necessary for full integration and coordination. Moreover, the costs and risks incurred in the implementation effort may increase the risks of failure. Amburgey *et al.* (1993) found exactly such an effect of age for newspapers moving from one publication frequency to another and for those changing the character of their content. For such relatively commonplace changes, it is usually possible to learn from other firms who have successfully made a similar transformation, thus reducing costs and risks. For industrywide innovations, we would expect at least some type of creative self-destructive effect. This leads to the next hypothesis:

4. *The older a firm, the more likely a technical innovation will momentarily diminish its life chances.*

Theory and research on technology frequently investigate the role that organizational size plays in stimulating or inhibiting innovation (Kamien and Schwartz, 1982). A popular theme holds that larger organizations are more likely to generate incremental innovations while small organizations are the likely sources of radical innovations. For instance, Winter (1984) argues that small, entrepreneurial firms are at a disadvantage in developing incremental innovations because they lack the necessary complementary assets. Similarly, he contends that large established firms find that existing

---

[7] The literature also advances a number of other arguments predicting the effects of extensive innovation by other firms on a firm's life chances. For example, Tushman and Rosenkopf (1992) argue that technological discontinuities of a competence-destroying kind generate an era of ferment and selection. Utterback (1994) makes similar arguments. Most of the research on the topics examined here looks for these types of effects rather than those hypothesized here. To avoid blurring the focus of this paper, we do not present formal hypotheses for these effects. However, we do estimate and report models that decompose innovation by other firms according to level of extensiveness.

products and assets constrain their ability to develop radical innovations. Even if generally accurate, this pattern does not preclude the possibility of some non-conforming cases in either direction (see Henderson and Cockburn, 1995).

More importantly, the organizational context spawning an innovation may not necessarily be the best context for its commercial exploitation (see March, 1989). Why? First, the resources required to generate an innovation often differ from those needed to successfully implement it and any given organizational context is more likely to have either set of resources rather than a balanced set of both. Second, the interests and incentives of those persons responsible, on the one hand, for potentially spawning innovations and those, on the other hand, responsible for implementing innovations frequently diverge in organizational settings. Third, there is the inherent difficulty of accurately predicting the future impact of an anticipated innovation, especially in a complex organizational setting. So, rather than assume (as do most theories) that organizational size plays a similar role in both processes, we decouple questions about effects of innovation from those about sources. More specifically, we take the innovation as given and ask whether it is more likely to achieve its potential in small or large organizations.

Large organizations tend to be more complex. Both size and complexity magnify the usual problems of control and coordination within an organization. An innovation introduced into such a context thus entails lots of adjustments, many minor, some perhaps major, by other persons and in other routines. Because so many actors are potentially affected, the chances of encountering opposing interests are high. Even if this is not the case, many actors who need to make adjustments will fail to understand the rationale or will misunderstand what they need to do (in perhaps a process not unlike that discussed by Kreps, 1996). Indeed, the complementary assets that give large organizations their advantage in many arenas, including perhaps spawning innovation, may create liabilities in innovation because each asset needs to be integrated and coordination is costly and risky. For instance, in studying technological changes in the manufacture of mainframe computers, Iansiti and Khanna (1995, p. 354) conclude that: 'the organizational challenge is not simply in the development of specific competences on their own individual merits, but also on the management of the complex web of interrelationships between them and the existing product and production system'. For these reasons, we predict that creative self-destruction will depend on organizational size:

5. *The larger a firm, the more likely a technical innovation will momentarily diminish its life chances.*

4. *Research Design, Data and Methods*

The research design guiding our analysis constitutes what is typically referred to as a population study. Rather than use a sample, we examine data on all automobile producers known to operate in the USA. We investigate the period from 1885 to 1981, the beginning of the industry to the latest date covered by our major sources. By tracing the fates of many individual producers, we can estimate the effects of organizational characteristics and conditions on firm mortality, an important performance variable. Complete coverage over the extended period allows us to investigate clearly how change unfolds over the lives of firms and the history of the industry. It also permits testing of theories without assuming temporal equilibrium.

The long-term population design is particularly useful in evaluating claims about innovation and organizational mortality since we observe most of the industry's innovations and we follow individual firms long enough to observe consequences. In a first set of analyses (pertinent to the first three hypotheses), we examine the life chances of producers following the emergence of innovations inside the firm and by competitors. We also investigate the consequences of variations in the extensiveness of innovations for automobile design and manufacture. In a second set (pertinent to the fourth and fifth hypotheses), we look for possible effects of the organizational context of innovation. In particular, we test for interaction effects between technical innovation and measures of organizational size and age. To our knowledge, such an analysis has not been conducted for any industry. Informative as they are, comparable studies of the consequences of organizational change have not previously examined true industrywide innovations (see Barnett and Carroll, 1995).

The organizational data we analyze come from our attempt to code information on all producers of automobiles from 1885 to 1981. The cornerstones of our coding are the three volumes of the *Standard Catalog of American Cars* (Kimes and Clark, 1989; Gunnell *et al.*, 1987; Flammang, 1989). Two important sources of supplementary information are the *New Encyclopedia of Motor Cars* (Georgano, 1982) and the *World Guide to Automobile Manufacturers* (Baldwin *et al.*, 1987). For contemporary periods, we also used Kutner (1979) and Automotive News (1993).

Each of the main sourcebooks represents the culmination of years of work by groups of historians, journalists, collectors and others. The *Standard Catalog* builds carefully on previous lists and compilations from a wide variety of sources including industry directories, newspapers, trade journals, city directories and magazines. It contains entries for every car known to have been built in the USA, as well as all incorporated automobile manufacturers and those manufacturers listed in industry directories. The entries contain capsule histories of each car or manufacturing concern, along with detailed technical information when available. The *Standard Catalog* strives to provide comprehensive coverage of the American industry. The supplemental sources provide additional historical and technical information and, on rare occasions, contain some cars not found in the *Standard Catalog*.

Entries in the sources are usually organized by car 'marque' (or 'make'). Our interest in organizations required a time-consuming process of aggregating this information to the firm level.[8] Some firms consist of more than one marque. For example, General Motors currently produces cars under the following separate marques: Buick, Cadillac, Chevrolet, Oldsmobile, Pontiac and Saturn. In years past GM manufactured cars under the following discontinued marques: Cartercar, Elmore, Ewing, LaSalle, Marquette, Milburn, Oakland, Rainier, Scripps-Booth and Welch. Some marques shifted successfully across firms over time. For instance, Cadillac started out as the product of Cadillac Automobile Company in 1903; the firm changed its name to Cadillac Motor Car Company before it was eventually acquired by General Motors in 1909.

The aggregated firm-level data file contains information on all known producers as well as many unsuccessful attempts at production for commercial sale. We distinguish among them by defining as a producer an automobile manufacturer that reached a level of production sufficient to generate any revenue, however small. This definition includes many small producers.

For each producer firm, we determine a beginning date at which operations commence and an ending date at which mortality occurs or observation ends (technically referred to as 'censored' cases). When exact dates appear in the sources, we use those. In many instances, however, the main source gives detailed 'seasonal dates' such as late spring, midsummer, early autumn, etc. We coded these season references and converted them to precise numerical dates within the year. In other instances, we know only the year in which an event ended.

We developed procedures to deal with imprecise dates known only to the year and to make dates of differing levels of precision comparable to each other.[9] Basically, our procedures use the midpoint of the period over which an imprecise date creates uncertainty. So, for example, a firm that is known only to start and stop production in 1910 could possibly have a lifetime of

---

[8] This is actually a 'within industry' definition of the firm since we do not consider activities outside of automobile manufacturing.

[9] Imprecise dating creates what is known as time-aggregation bias. Our procedures are consistent with Petersen's (1991) recommendations for dealing with this problem.

anywhere from one day to a full year. Our procedures set the lifetime at 0.5 year, the midpoint of the uncertain range.

Our analysis revolves around rate or hazard function models of the mortality process. As is conventional, we define the rate of mortality at the organizational level as the probability of mortality in an infinitesimally small interval (see Blossfeld *et al.*, 1989). We estimate regression-like effects of covariates on the rate using the TDA statistical package (Rohwer, 1993; Blossfeld and Rohwer, 1995). Preliminary analysis showed that a good-fitting model for this purpose is the commonly used Gompertz model. In this model the rate is specified as

$$r(t) = \exp[\beta_0 + \beta_1 X_1(t) + \ldots + \beta_k X_k(t)] \exp([\Upsilon_0 + \Upsilon_1 Z_1(t) + \ldots + \Upsilon_m Z_m(t)]t)$$

where t represents age and $X(t)$ and $Z(t)$ are covariates. A negative coefficient Υ_0 indicates negative or declining age dependence in mortality. Covariates can be included in either the age-independent vector (signified by the $X(t)$ variables above) or the age-dependent vector (shown as $Z(t)$ above). Most of our analysis uses a loglinear specification of covariates with inclusion in the age-independent vector. As is conventional, we split spells every year in order to update values of the covariates (see Rohwer, 1993).

The analysis uses the following variables, either constructed from the automobile data files or compiled from other sources:

Density—N(t). This variable measures contemporaneous organizational population density (divided by 100). It indicates the total number of producer organizations in the population in a year. As suggested by prior theory, we also use the square of this variable, divided by 10,000 for ease of reporting (see Hannan and Carroll, 1992). Density variables are lagged one year to ensure exogeneity.

Density at Founding—N(0). This variable gives the organizational population density at the time of an organization's founding. This covariate is fixed for each organization. In reporting, we divide its value by 100.

Size(t). A variable recording the realized production capacity of a firm in terms of number of cars. This variable is updated annually and relies on numerous sources, which often differ by firm. We report effects of this variable divided by 1000. For firms for which some but not all information on capacity could be found, we interpolated missing years. For firms for which no information could be found, we assumed they were small producers and assigned a random value below the lowest quartile for that period. Sensitivity analysis shows that these procedures do not have great effects on findings.

Age. Years the firm has spent in automobile production.

Industry Production. Indicates the total number of cars produced in the USA in a year. Taken from various annual issues of the Motor Vehicle Manufacturing Association's *World Motor Vehicle Data* . Measured in millions of cars.

GNP. Records annual estimates of Gross National Product (in hundreds of billions of dollars) at 1958 prices. Coded from *Historical Statistics of the United States* (US Department of Commerce, 1975) and *Statistical Abstract of the United States* (US Department of Commerce, Various years).

Periods. Relies on the assessment of Altshuler *et al.* (1984) to define periods of technological/organizational regimes in the world automobile manufacturing industry. Codes a set of three dummy 'effect' variables corresponding to the dates associated with these regimes: (I) Mass Production, which takes the value of one from 1902–1981; (ii) Product Differentiation, which takes the value of one from 1950–1981; and (iii) the Japanese Just-In-Time/Total Quality Control (JIT/TQC), which takes the value of one from 1968–1981. We use these variables as control variables; we do not use them here to look for the contingent effects of innovation suggested by some life cycle theories of industry evolution (see Dosi, 1988; Nelson, 1995).

World War II. A dummy variable which takes the value of one for the years 1942–1945, the period when World War II disrupted normal domestic production.

Innovation (t). Our measures of technical innovation come from the extensive collection effort by Abernathy *et al.* (1983). Using a wide variety of industry sources and relying on their expert knowledge of the industry, these investigators generated a firm-specific chronological list of product and process innovation in American automobile manufacture (see Abernathy *et al.*, 1983, p. 150–151 for discussion of sources). Their effort defines an innovation event as the earliest significant commercial introduction in the USA of a new product or process. The list attempts to be comprehensive. It contains 641 innovations for the period 1893 to 1981 that we could use in our analysis. It includes many innovations by small firms (such as Autocar and Monarch). While the list links most innovations to specific car makers, it also attributes ten innovations to 'all producers' or 'most producers' (these tend to be regulation-induced innovations such as the safety front shoulder harness). Another 26 innovations are attributed to component suppliers. Because our interest lies with the competitive effects of innovation, we excluded these 36 innovations from the analysis. The remaining innovations were matched to the appropriate firm spell and used to construct a time-varying integer variable, *Innovation (t)*, which measures the number of innovations a firm introduces in a given year. As a modeling convenience, we treat this variable as exogenous and estimate its association with the rate of firm failure. To test for possible delayed consequences of innovation, we also use various lagged versions of this variable. The various lags allow us to separate short-term and long-term effects of innovation. Coefficients associated with these variables represent tests of hypothesis 1. They measure the jump or drop in the mortality rate in the periods immediately following development of an innovation in a firm (see Barnett and Carroll, 1995 for further discussion of the modeling approach).

Others' Innovations (t). This variable uses the innovation data to construct annual time-varying measures of the total number of innovations by all other firms in the industry. We use again various lagged versions to look for longer-term effects on competitors' innovations. Models with these variables constitute tests of hypothesis 2.

Extensiveness of innovation. Abernathy *et al.* (1983) rated each innovation according to its overall impact on the production process. We collapse their seven-point rating scale into two categories, which we label Low (values 1 to 3) and High Extensiveness (4 to 7) of innovations. We subdivide innovations by the focal firm and by competitors according to this rating in order to conduct tests of hypothesis 3.

Age × Innovation (t). This interaction variable is constructed by multiplying organizational age by the innovation variable. It provides the basic tests for hypothesis 4.

Size (t) × Innovation (t). This interaction variable is constructed by multiplying organizational size by the innovation variable. It provides the basic tests for hypothesis 5.

The modeling approach to organizational change used here is dictated in part by the innovation variable. Because each innovation is by definition a unique event, it is not possible to introduce controls for the content of change (see discussion of models in Barnett and Carroll, 1995). To do so in even a rudimentary way would require complete diffusion data on the dates of adoption of each innovation for each automobile producer. The coefficients associated with innovation in this modeling framework thus combine content and process effects and pertain to the overall effects predicted by the hypotheses.[10]

5. *Findings*

Table 1 gives a descriptive overview of the data. Obviously, many firms entered automobile production (see Carroll and Hannan 1995 and Carroll *et al.* 1994 and 1995 for more detail). Most of these firms started small and remained small. In addition, most did not advance a technical innovation

---

[10] For analysis of a single innovation, the V-8 engine, and its spread through the organizational population, see Teo (1994).

TABLE 1. Technical Innovation in the American Automobile Manufacturing Industry, 1885–1981

Number of firms observed in production	2149
Number of technical innovations	641
Number of firm-year spells	8625
Number of technical innovations with:	
low extensiveness score	515
high extensiveness score	126

during their period of operation. A few firms, however, put forward more than one innovation. A look behind these numbers reveals familiar companies, and for the most part these multiple innovation firms experienced commercial success, at least temporarily.

Table 2 presents estimates of Gompertz models of organizational mortality. These models include a baseline model (equation 2.1) of organizational evolution with the conventional variables of density, age and size dependence (see Hannan and Carroll, 1992). They also include models with specifications designed to represent basic tests of hypotheses 1, 2 and 3, those arguments about the overall effects of technical innovation (2.2) and its extensiveness (2.3).

The estimated baseline model shown in equation (2.1) compares favorably to most previous research. Density variables display their usual pattern: nonmonotonic U-shape effects of contemporaneous density and positive effect of density at founding (see Hannan and Carroll, 1992). Organizational age and size both show negative effects. These estimates are all statistically significant and increase our confidence in the quality of the data.

Equation (2.2) contains variables indicating whether the focal firm put forth a technical innovation in any of the last four years. It also includes similar variables measuring the number of technical innovations advanced by other firms, presumably competitors. The innovation variables for the focal firm show negative or beneficial effects on mortality, as predicted by hypothesis 1. Moreover, these effects are strongest immediately following the innovation and then attenuate with time elapsed from the innovation: each of the successive lagged variables shows a weaker effect than its predecessor (although the effects of the two longest lags are not significant). By contrast, innovation by other firms increases the death rate, at least initially, as expected by hypothesis 2. Lagged effects of this variable are not significant until the third year, when it shows a negative effect on mortality (an effect that could reflect survivorship). Overall, these estimates provide strong support for hypotheses 1 and 2. These findings also provide face validity to the innovation measures.

TABLE 2.   Maximum Likelihood Estimates of Effects of Technical Innovation on Organizational Mortality of Automobile Producers 1885–1981. (Standard errors shown in parentheses)

Equation No.	(2.1)	(2.2)	(2.3)
Constant	−0.330*	−0.448*	−0.585*
	(0.121)	(0.130)	(0.135)
$N(t)/100$	−0.705*	−0.776*	−0.838*
	(0.124)	(0.128)	(0.134)
$N(t)^2/10000$	0.084*	0.098*	0.102*
	(0.028)	(0.029)	(0.032)
$N(0)/100$	0.323*	0.330*	0.317*
	(0.038)	(0.039)	(0.039)
$Size(t)/100$	−0.153*	−0.129*	−0.128*
	(0.024)	(0.023)	(0.023)
Industry Production	0.055	0.033	−0.018
	(0.040)	(0.041)	(0.044)
GNP	−0.324*	−0.249*	−0.206*
	(0.080)	(0.082)	(0.084)
Periods			
Mass Production	0.447*	0.368*	0.516*
	(0.119)	(0.126)	(0.135)
Product Differentiation	0.442*	0.185	0.318
	(0.224)	(0.245)	(0.244)
JIT/TQC	−0.381	−0.564	−0.528
	(0.347)	(0.347)	(0.359)
World War II	−0.632	−0.641	−0.680
	(0.723)	(0.723)	(0.724)
Age	−0.092*	−0.089*	−0.089*
	(0.007)	(0.007)	(0.007)
Innovation(t)		−1.06*	
		(0.354)	
Innovation($t-1$)		−1.01*	
		(0.383)	
Innovation($t-2$)		−0.315	
		(0.253)	
Innovation($t-3$)		−0.161	
		(0.234)	
Others' Innovation(t)		0.035*	
		(0.007)	
Others' Innovation($t-1$)		0.003*	
		(0.007)	
Others' Innovation($t-2$)		0.004	
		(0.007)	
Others' Innovation($t-3$)		−0.017*	
		(0.007)	
Low Ext. Innovation(t)			−1.50*
			(0.492)
Low Ext. Innovation($t-1$)			−1.04*
			(0.435)
Low Ext. Innovation($t-2$)			−0.196
			(0.295)

TABLE 2. Continued

Equation No.	(2.1)	(2.2)	(2.3)
Low Ext. Innovation($t-3$)			-0.270
			(0.317)
High Ext. Innovation(t)			-0.039
			(0.575)
High Ext. Innovation($t-1$)			-0.915
			(0.998)
High Ext. Innovation($t-2$)			-0.921
			(0.935)
High Ext. Innovation($t-3$)			0.048
			(0.474)
Others' Low Ext. Innovation(t)			0.028*
			(0.008)
Others' Low Ext. Innovation($t-1$)			-0.020*
			(0.008)
Others' Low Ext. Innovation($t-2$)			-0.000
			(0.008)
Others' Low Ext. Innovation($t-3$)			-0.010
			(0.008)
Others' High Ext. Innovation(t)			0.061*
			(0.018)
Others' High Ext. Innovation($t-1$)			0.074*
			(0.016)
Others' High Ext. Innovation($t-2$)			0.021
			(0.016)
Others' High Ext. Innovation($t-3$)			0.013
			(0.007)
Log L	-3865.0	-3825.8	-3809.9
N	8625	8625	8625

* $p \leq .05$

Equation (2.3) presents a model very similar to (2.2) in that variables for innovation by the focal firm and others are included. However, here the innovation variables are broken down into subcategories based on extensivenss of the innovation. High extensiveness implies that substantial re-engineering of other parts of the automobile or the manufacturing process is required for implementation of the innovation. Low extensiveness implies the reverse. For focal firm innovations, the most interesting aspect of the estimates is that while innovations with low extensiveness show significant negative or beneficial effects on mortality, highly extensive innovations show no significant effects. The absolute values of the highly extensive innovation variables are also smaller than the low extensiveness innovation variables. Both patterns might arise if the highly extensive innovations are riskier and more difficult to implement—the overall beneficial effect of innovation is diminished in these instances. Nonetheless, because of the lack of significant effects for the highly extensive innovations, we regard these findings as, at best, weakly supportive of hypothesis 3.

Effects of other firms' innovations show a very different pattern. For these variables, the greatest effects arise from the highly extensive innovations, which in all cases raise the focal firm's mortality (the longest two lags are not significant). Less extensive innovations by other firms show a similar competitive effect in the first year, but it switches to a negative effect in the first lag and then becomes non-significant in later lags. Overall, however, the pattern would seem to support somewhat predictions by those who theorize about technological discontinuities and selection (Tushman and Romanelli, 1985).

Table 3 presents estimates of models specified as tests of hypotheses 4 and 5, the arguments about organizational age and size. By these arguments, the organizational context of technical innovation matters. So, in addition to the main effects of innovation, age and size, these models also contain variables interacting the innovation variable and organizational variables.

Equation (3.1) shows that when included in the model of innovation effects, the interaction of age and innovation is positive but not statistically significant. Evidently, older and younger organizations experience similar effects of technical innovation on mortality, thus casting doubt on hypothesis 4. By contrast, equation (3.2) suggests strongly that organizational size matters greatly for technical innovations. Although large organizations show lower death rates and technical innovation lowers death rates, the significant positive effect of the size-innovation interaction variable shows that innovation in large organizations is initially much less beneficial for mortality than it is in small organizations. That is, the larger the organization within which technical innovation occurs, the greater the associated risks. This finding is consistent with hypothesis 5.

Equation (3.3) provides a check against the findings from (3.1) and (3.2). It reports estimates of a model including both interaction terms, innovation with both organizational age and size. These estimates agree with those discussed above. The age-related interaction variable is positive but not significant while the size-related variable is positive and significant. The evidence therefore supports hypothesis 5 but fails to do so for hypothesis 4.

Finally, equation (3.4) in Table 3 reports estimates of a more complex interaction between organizational size and innovation. This equation specifies an additional interaction between a second-order size variable (size squared) and innovation. The polynomial interaction allows the detrimental effects of size to decrease for the largest firms, a pattern consistent with the long-lived nature of the industry's largest firms. The estimate of the second-order interaction is negative and significant; its inclusion improves the fit of

TABLE 3. Maximum Likelihood Estimates of Effects of Organizational Context of Technical Innovation on Mortality of Automobile Producers 1885–1981. (Standard errors shown in parentheses)

Equation No.	(3.1)	(3.2)	(3.3)	(3.4)
Constant	−0.447*	−0.448*	−0.447*	−0.448*
	(0.130)	(0.130)	(0.130)	(0.130)
$N(t)/100$	−0.773*	−0.775*	−0.773*	−0.769*
	(0.127)	(0.127)	(0.127)	(0.127)
$N(t)^2/1000$	0.097*	0.098*	0.097*	0.096*
	(0.029)	(0.029)	(0.029)	(0.029)
$N(0)/100$	0.330*	0.330*	0.330*	0.328*
	(0.039)	(0.039)	(0.039)	(0.039)
$Size(t)/100$	−0.130*	−0.132*	−0.131*	−0.144*
	(0.023)	(0.023)	(0.023)	(0.024)
Industry Production	0.035	0.034	0.035	0.035
	(0.041)	(0.041)	(0.041)	(0.041)
GNP	−0.250*	−0.249*	−0.250*	−0.250*
	(0.082)	(0.082)	(0.082)	(0.082)
Periods				
Mass Production	0.366*	0.369*	0.367*	0.365*
	(0.126)	(0.126)	(0.126)	(0.126)
Product Differentiation	0.183	0.184	0.182	0.178
	(0.245)	(0.245)	(0.245)	(0.245)
JIT/TQC	−0.565	−0.565	−0.565	−0.566
	(0.346)	(0.346)	(0.346)	(0.346)
World War II	−0.634	−0.642	−0.636	−0.640
	(0.723)	(0.723)	(0.723)	(0.723)
Age	−0.090*	−0.089*	−0.089*	−0.088*
	(0.007)	(0.007)	(0.007)	(0.007)
Innovation(t)	−1.35*	−1.07*	−1.34*	−2.10*
	(0.457)	(0.355)	(0.455)	(0.6307)
Innovation($t-1$)	−1.02*	−1.01*	−1.02*	−1.07*
	(0.384)	(0.384)	(0.385)	(0.401)
Innovation($t-2$)	−0.320	−0.314	−0.317	−0.288
	(0.254)	(0.253)	(0.253)	(0.250)
Innovation($t-3$)	−0.164	−0.160	−0.163	−0.183
	(0.236)	(0.234)	(0.236)	(0.250)
Others' Innovation(t)	0.035*	0.035*	0.035*	0.035*
	(0.007)	(0.007)	(0.007)	(0.007)
Others' Innovation($t-1$)	0.003	0.003	0.003	0.003
	(0.007)	(0.007)	(0.007)	(0.007)
Others' Innovation($t-2$)	0.004	0.004	0.004	0.004
	(0.007)	(0.007)	(0.007)	(0.007)
Others' Innovation($t-3$)	−0.017*	−0.017*	−0.017*	−0.017*
	(0.007)	(0.007)	(0.007)	(0.007)
Age × Innovation(t)	0.072		0.067	
	(0.049)		(0.049)	
[Size(t)/100] × Innovation(t)		0.012*	0.011*	0.277*
		(0.002)	(0.002)	(0.077)
[Size(t)^2/1000] × Innovation(t)				−0.048*
				(0.022)
Log L	−3825.0	−3825.1	−3824.5	−3818.4
N	8625	8625	8625	8625

* p ≤ .05

the model. Thus, we conclude that innovation is precarious for large firms in the industry but not for the very largest.

6. *Discussion*

Social scientists in many different areas increasingly recognize both the importance and difficulty of appropriate organizational design. This theme is perhaps nowhere so pronounced as in the current literature on strategic management. Advocates of the so-called resource-based view of the firm stress the notion that organizational structure and capabilities account for much variation in firm performance. In assessing the sources of contemporary competitive advantage, for instance, Teece and Pisano (1994, p. 538) pinpoint 'capabilities', which they describe as 'strategic management in appropriately adapting, integrating, and re-configuring internal and external organizational skills, resources, and functional competences toward changing environment'. This school also emphasizes the difficulty of identifying and replicating appropriate organizational designs. Again, consider Teece and Pisano (1994, p. 540): 'entrepreneurial activity cannot lead to the immediate replication of unique organization skills through simply entering a market and piecing the parts together overnight. Replication takes time and the best of practice may be illusive'.

We have no serious arguments with these claims and we generally applaud these efforts to highlight the strategic importance of organizational factors. However, we also believe that they do not go far enough. Typically, analyses of this kind focus on equilibrium designs and fail to consider the potential risks of failure associated with actually changing the organization. (So too do many other kinds of analyses, including the game theory models of industrial organization economics.) As a consequence, the advice that comes from such analyses usually tells organizations to engage in re-engineering or redesign, to make it radical or comprehensive and to do it quickly (Tushman and Romanelli, 1985). A more general prescription involves development of inherent capabilities to undertake transformation and reconfiguration on a regular basis (Teece and Pisano, 1994).

The frictionless world implied by this view would be a nice one for managers if it existed. But the research reported here, and the many prior studies in organizational sociology that it builds on, suggest this world is mainly fantasy (see Barnett and Carroll, 1995). Using data on technical innovations, organizational changes that are undoubtedly positively biased in their effects on organizational outcomes, the findings show that in some contexts—large organizations, in particular—the momentary risks of the change process itself diminish and potentially overwhelm any possible benefits from the content of the change. With great deference to Schumpeter (1942), we call this phenomenon 'creative self-destruction'. We note that it appears to occur in the automobile industry for all types of innovations.

The basic message we take from this finding and the research program behind it is simple: when the aim is to improve existing firms, alternative organizational designs must be evaluated not only against each other but with the costs and risks of transformation from the existing design factored in. Weighing the transitional costs and risks of transformations against the likely gains of new designs may very well lead to different prescriptions than when those costs and risks are ignored.

We also think that the findings presented here suggest a reconciliation of the differing positions on organizational inertia found in evolutionary theories of organization. By our assessment, neither the position of Nelson and Winter nor that of Hannan and Freeman is fully tenable as it is typically characterized. Our data suggest that as an organizational population evolves, firms regularly develop technical innovations and these innovations potentially alter firms' life chances in a positive way. This occurrence runs counter to a strong inertia interpretation often attributed to Hannan and Freeman. At the same, we find in certain contexts suggested by Hannan and Freeman (1984), namely, within large organizations (but not the very largest), the potential benefits of innovation may be outweighed by the major risks associated with the change it induces. That large organizations contain many complementary assets and routines that likely need to be recalibrated in response to the innovation agrees with some of Nelson and Winter's notions about organizations (see Winter, 1982; Nelson, 1995). But, in our view, their typical story conflates type of innovation (radical or incremental) and size of firm (small and entrepreneurial or large and established) in a way that assumes ease of implementation and little risk. In other words, innovations that may be costly and highly risky will likely not appear in the first place. Obviously, we think the issues should be unpacked, that the organizational contexts thought to spawn innovations should be analyzed separately from those thought to produce beneficial impact. We further believe that doing so will lead to a stronger evolutionary theory of organizations.

Acknowledgements

This paper was prepared for the conference, 'Firms, Markets and Hierarchies,' held in Berkeley, 6–8 October 1995. The research reported here was supported by assistance from the Alfred P. Sloan Foundation and the Institute of Industrial Relations, U.C. Berkeley. This report comes from a larger collaborative research project with Michael T. Hannan of Stanford University on the worldwide automobile industry. We appreciate the helpful suggestions of Lyda Bigelow, Giovanni Dosi, John de Figueiredo, Bronwyn Hall, Michael T. Hannan, Marc-David Seidel, Lucia Tsai, and Michael Tushman.

References

Abernathy, W. J., K. Clark and A. Kantrow (1983), *Industrial Renaissance*. Basic: New York.

Altshuler, A., M. Anderson, D. Jones, D. Roos and J. Womack (1984), *The Future of the Automobile*. MIT Press: Cambridge, MA.

Amburgey, T. L., D. Kelly and W. P. Barnett (1993), 'Resetting the Clock: The Dynamics of Organizational Change and Failure,' *Administrative Science Quarterly*, 38, 51–73.

Automotive News (1993), 'America at the Wheel: 100 Years of the Automobile in America,' 4 September, special issue.

Baldwin, N., G.N. Georgano, M. Sedgwick and B. Laban (1987), *The World Guide to Automobile Manufacturers*. Facts on File: New York.

Barnett, W. P. (1990), 'The Organizational Ecology of a Technological System,' *Administrative Science Quarterly*, 35, 31–60.

Barnett, W. P. (1994), 'The Liability of Collective Action: Growth and Change Among Early Telephone Companies.' in J.A.C. Baum and J. Singh (eds), *Evolutionary Dynamics of Organizations*, pp. 337–354, Oxford University Press: New York.

Barnett, W. P. and G. R. Carroll (1995), 'Modeling Internal Organizational Change,' *Annual Review of Sociology*, 21: 217–236.

Barron, D. N., E. West and M. T. Hannan (1994), 'A Time to Grow and a Time to Die: Growth and Mortality of Credit Unions in New York, 1914–1990,' *American Journal of Sociology*, 100, 381–421.

Blossfeld, P., A. Hammerle and K. U. Mayer (1989), *Event-History Analysis*. Lawrence Erlbaum: Hillsdale, NJ.

Blossfeld, H-P. and G. Rohwer (1995), *Techniques of Event-History Modeling*. Lawrence Erlbaum: Hillsdale, NJ.

Carroll, G. R. and M. T. Hannan (1995), 'Automobile Manufacturers,' in G.R. Carroll and M.T. Hannan (eds), *Organizations in Industry: Strategy, Structure and Selection*, pp. 195–214. Oxford University Press: New York.

Carroll, G. R., M. T. Hannan, L. Bigelow, M-D. Seidel, A. Teo and L. Tsai (1994), 'Before Production: Organizing Activities and Founding Events in the American Automobile Industry from 1886–1982.' Working Paper 94–14, Center for Research in Management, U.C. Berkeley.

Carroll, G. R., L. Bigelow, M-D. Seidel and L. Tsai (1995), 'The Fates of De Novo and De Alio Producers in the American Automobile Industry, 1885–1981,' *Strategic Management Journal*, forthcoming.

Chandler, A. D. (1962), *Strategy and Structure*. MIT Press: Cambridge, MA.

Dosi, G. (1982), 'Technological Paradigms and Technological Trajectories: A Suggested Interpretation of the Determinants and Directions of Technical Change,' *Research Policy*, 11, 147–162.

Dosi, G. (1988), 'Sources, Procedures and Microeconomic Effects of Innovation,' *Journal of Economic Literature*, 26, 1120–1171.

Dosi, G., O. Marsili, L. Orsenigo and R. Salvatore (1993), 'Learning, Market Selection and the Evolution of Industrial Structures.' CCC Working Paper 93–9, Haas School of Business, U. C. Berkeley.

Flammang, J. M. (1989), *Standard Catalog of American Cars 1976–1986*, 2nd edn. Krause: Iola, WI.

Flink, J. J. (1988), *The Automobile Age*. MIT Press: Cambridge, MA.

Georgano, G.N. (Ed.) (1982), *The New Encyclopedia of Motorcars: 1885 to Present*, 3rd edn. E.P. Dutton: New York.

Gunnell, J. A., D. Schrimpf and K. Buttolph (1987), *Standard Catalog of American Cars 1946–1975*, 2nd edn. Krause: Iola, WI.

Hannan, M. T. and G. R. Carroll (1992), *Dynamics of Organizational Populations*. Oxford University Press: New York.

Hannan, M. T. and J. Freeman (1977), 'The Population Ecology of Organizations,' *American Journal of Sociology*, 82, 929–964.

Hannan, M. T. and J. Freeman (1984), 'Structural Inertia and Organizational Change,' *American Sociological Review*, 49, 149–164.

Hannan, M. T. and J. Freeman (1989), *Organizational Ecology*. Harvard University Press: Cambridge, MA.

Haveman, H. A. (1992), 'Between a Rock and a Hard Place: Organizational Change and Performance under Conditions of Fundamental Environmental Transformation,' *Administrative Science Quarterly*, 37, 48–75.

Henderson, R. (1993), 'Underinvestment and Incompetence as Responses to Radical Innovation: Evidence from the Photolithographic Alignment Equipment Industry,' *Rand Journal of Economics*, 24, 248–270.

Henderson, R. and K. Clark (1990), 'Architectural Innovation: The Reconfiguration of Existing Product Technologies and the Failure of Established Firms,' *Administrative Science Quarterly*, 35, 9–30.

Henderson, R. and I. Cockburn (1995), 'Managing Product Development Across Organizational Boundaries: Exploring the Diffusion of 'Rational' Drug Discovery.' Paper presented at the Academy of Management Meetings, Vancouver.

Iansiti, M. (1995), 'Technology Integration in the Product Development Process.' Paper presented at the Academy of Management Meetings, Vancouver.

Iansiti, M. and T. Khanna (1995), ' Technological Evolution, System Architecture and the Obsolescence of Firm Capabilities,' *Industrial and Corporate Change*, 4, 333–361.

Kamien, M. and N. Schwartz (1982), *Market Structure and Innovation*. Cambridge University Press: Cambridge.

Kimes, B. R. and H. A. Clark (1989), *Standard Catalog of American Cars 1805–1942*, 2nd edn. Krause: Iola, WI.

Kreps, D. M. (1996), 'Markets and Hierarchies vs (Mathematical) Economic Theory,' *Industrial and Corporate Change*, this issue.

Kutner, R. M. (1979), *The Complete Guide to Kit Cars, Auto Parts and Accessories*. Auto Logic: Wilmington, DE.

Lawrence, P. and D. Dyer (1983), *Renewing American Industry*. Free Press: New York.

Malerba, F. and L. Orsenigo (1993), 'Technological Regimes and Firm Behavior,' *Industrial and Corporate Change*, 2, 45–72.

March, J. G. (1982), 'Footnotes on Organizational Change,' *Administrative Science Quarterly*, 26, 563–597.

March, J. G. (1989), 'Exploration and Exploitation in Organizational Learning,' *Organization Science*, 2, 71–87.

Nelson, R. R. (1995), 'Recent Evolutionary Theorizing about Economic Change,' *Journal of Economic Literature*, 33, 48–90.

Nelson, R. R. and S. G. Winter (1982), *An Evolutionary Theory of Economic Change*. Harvard University Press: Cambridge, MA.

Ohanian, N. Kane (1994), 'Vertical Integration in the US Pulp and Paper Industry, 1900–1940,' *Review of Economics and Statistics*, 76, 202–207.

Petersen, T. (1991), 'Time-Aggregation Bias in Continuous-Time Hazard Rate Models,' in P.V. Marsden (ed.), *Sociological Methodology 1991*, Vol. 21, pp. 263–290. Basil Blackwell: Oxford.

Rae, J. B. (1984), *The American Automobile Industry*. Twayne: Boston, MA.

Rohwer, G. (1993), *TDA (Transitional Data Analysis) 5.2*. European University Institute: Florence.

Rosenbloom, R. S. and C. M. Christensen (1994), 'Technological Discontinuities, Organizational Capabilities, and Strategic Commitments,' *Industrial and Corporate Change*, 3, 655–685.

Schumpeter, J. A. (1942), *Capitalism, Socialism and Democracy*. Harper and Row: New York.

Singh, J. R. House and D. Tucker (1986), 'Organizational Change and Organizational Mortality,' *Administrative Science Quarterly*, 31, 587–611.

Teece, D. J. and G. Pisano (1994), 'The Dynamic Capabilities of Firms: An Introduction,' *Industrial and Corporate Change*, 3, 537–556.

Teece, D. J. (1988), 'Technological Change and the Nature of the Firms,' in G.Dosi, C. Freeman, R. Nelson, G. Silverberg and L. Soete (eds), *Technical Change and Economic Theory*. Pinter: London.

Teo, A. C. (1994), *Innovation and Firm Longevity: The Experience of American Automakers, 1880 to 1981*. Unpublished Doctoral thesis.University of California at Berkeley.

Tushman, M. L. and P. Anderson (1986), 'Technological Discontinuities and Organizational Environments,' *Administrative Science Quarterly*, 31, 439–465.

Tushman, M. L. and E. Romanelli (1985) 'Organizational Evolution: A Metamorphosis Model of Convergence and Reorientation,' in L.L. Cummings and B.Staw (eds), *Research in Organizational Behavior*, Vol. 7, pp. 171–222. JAI: Greenwich, CT.

Tushman, M. L. and L. Rosenkopf (1992), 'Organizational Determinants of Technological Change,' in L.L. Cummings and B. Staw (eds), *Research in Organizational Behavior*, Vol. 14, pp. 311–347. JAI: Greenwich, CT.

US Department of Commerce (Bureau of the Census) (1975) *Historical Statistics of the United States, Colonial Times to 1970*. US Government Printing Office: Washington DC.

US Department of Commerce (Bureau of the Census) Various Years. *Statistical Abstract of the United States*. US Government Printing Office: Washington DC.

Utterback, J. (1994), *Mastering the Dynamics of Innovation*. Harvard Business School Press: Boston, MA.

Vicenti, W. G. (1994) 'The Retractable Airplane Landing Gear and the Northrup 'Anomaly': Variation-Selection and the Shaping of Technology,' *Technology and Culture*, 35, 1–33.

Williamson, O. (1975) *Markets and Hierarchies*. Free Press: New York.

Williamson, O. (1985) *The Economic Institutions of Capitalism*. Free Press: New York.

Winter, S. G. (1984) 'Schumpeterian Competition in Alternative Technological Regimes,' *Journal of Economic Behavior and Organization*, 5, 287–320.

Author Index

Subject Index